Patients,
Physicians,
and
Illness

Patients, Physicians, and Illness

A Sourcebook in Behavioral Science and Health

Third Edition

Edited by
E. Gartly Jaco

THE FREE PRESS
A Division of Macmillan Publishing Co., Inc.
NEW YORK

Collier Macmillan Publishers
LONDON

The Free Press
A Division of Macmillan Publishing Co., Inc.
866 Third Avenue, New York, N. Y. 10022

Collier Macmillan Canada, Ltd.

Library of Congress Catalog Card Number: 78-63407

Printed in the United States of America

printing number

1 2 3 4 5 6 7 8 9 10

Library of Congress Cataloging in Publication Data

Jaco, E. Gartly, ed.
  Patients, physicians, and illness.

  Includes bibliographical references and index.
  1. Social medicine--Addresses, essays, lectures.
2. Sick--Psychology--Addresses, essays, lectures.
3. Medical care--United States--Addresses, essays,
lectures. I. Title.
RA418.J32 1979   362.1'0973   78-63407
ISBN 0-02-915850-8

To Adele, my wife,
whose healing powers far surpass
those of the greatest physician

Contents

Preface to the Third Edition

The task of compiling this anthology, which tries to embrace the entire scope of behavioral science and health in a single volume, becomes increasingly difficult with each edition. Not only has the amount of research and scholarly activity accelerated during the past few years but their focus and scope have shifted and expanded, particularly into the large-scale social, political, and economic fields. We hope that this new edition reasonably reflects these developments and changes of the past half decade.

Although much of the basic structure of the previous edition has been retained in this edition, the reader may note expansion in the areas of public policy and the organization of health-delivery systems. These areas have received particularly increasing attention by social and behavioral scientists in recent years and show promise of even greater concern and study in the forthcoming period.

The first section of this volume presents concerns about present health and medical care in American society and raises important issues as a prologue to the chapters to follow.

The second part deals with the existence of disease in society and the patterns of utilization of health services, combining the epidemiology of illness with measures of the usage of health-care facilities and services, which are uniquely intertwined health phenomena.

The third section, again the largest part of the book as in the previous editions, is concerned with societal efforts to cope with disease and injury at the microlevel, presenting the major components of health and illness behavior—the sick role and the patient role and healers and healing behavior—also complex and interrelated sets of behaviors.

Society and the organization of health-service systems comprise the fourth part, including articles on both the micro- and macrolevels of analysis. This section has been the most expanded and updated from the previous editions, reflecting an arena of increasing interest by social and behavioral scientists.

An epilogue on some ethical considerations of the future of health care in the United States concludes this anthology.

Only eight chapters are retained from the previous edition, further indicating the rapid change and expansion in scope of interest and scholarly activity of behavioral scientists in the health field. Many excellent articles have regrettably been omitted because of space limitations; indeed, the agony of making a final selection from among so many good studies is undoubtedly the most difficult aspect of the editor's role.

We give our special thanks and appreciation to all the contributors and to the publishers of reprinted articles, who are acknowledged separately, and whose cooperation has made this new edition possible.

E. GARTLY JACO

The Contributors

W. Timothy Anderson
Department of Sociology, Boston University

Dan E. Beauchamp, Ph.D.
Department of Epidemiology, School of Public Health, University of North Carolina

John C. Cassel, M.D.
Department of Epidemiology, School of Public Health, University of North Carolina (deceased)

Philip Cole, Ph.D.
Department of Epidemiology, School of Public Health, Harvard University

Jesús M. De Miguel, Dr., M. Phil.
Department of Sociology, Universidad Autonoma de Madrid

Daniel Charles Feldman
Graduate School of Management, Northwestern University

Renée C. Fox, Ph.D.
Department of Sociology, University of Pennsylvania

Eugene B. Gallagher, Ph.D.
Department of Behavioral Science, University of Kentucky Medical Center

Basil S. Georgopoulos, Ph.D.
Institute for Social Research, University of Michigan

Barney G. Glaser, Ph.D.
Graduate Program in Sociology, University of California Medical Center at San Francisco

Susan Gore, Ph.D.
Department of Sociology, University of Massachusetts—Boston

David T. Helm
Department of Sociology, Boston University

E. Gartly Jaco, Ph.D.
Division of Health Behavior, Department of Preventive Medicine and Community Health, University of Texas Medical Branch, Galveston

Berton H. Kaplan, Ph.D.
Department of Epidemiology, School of Public Health, University of North Carolina

John H. Knowles, M.D.
President, The Rockefeller Foundation

Theodor J. Litman, Ph.D.
School of Public Health, University of Minnesota Medical Center

Judith Lorber, Ph.D.
Department of Sociology, Brooklyn College, The City University of New York

John B. McKinlay, Ph.D.
Department of Sociology, Boston University

Floyd C. Mann, Ph.D.
Institute for Social Research, University of Michigan

Hans O. Mauksch, Ph.D.
Department of Community Medicine & Family Practice, University of Missouri—Columbia Medical Center

David Mechanic, Ph.D.
Center for Medical Sociology and Health Services Research, University of Wisconsin at Madison

Alfred E. Miller, M.D., Ph.D.
Special Assistant to the Deputy Assistant Secretary for Legislation (Health), Office of the Secretary, Department of Health, Education, and Welfare

Talcott Parsons, Ph.D.
Professor Emeritus, Department of Social Relations, Harvard University

Henry B. Perry, III, M.D., Ph.D.
Department of Surgery, Maine Medical Center, Portland, Maine

Elianne Riska, Ph.D.
Department of Sociology, Michigan State University

Sam Schulman, Ph.D.
Department of Sociology, University of Houston (deceased)

Herbert Shore, Ed.D.
Executive Director, Dallas Home for the Jewish Aged

Stephen M. Shortell, Ph.D.
School of Public Health & Community Medicine, University of Washington

Richard T. Smith, Ph.D.
University of Maryland, Baltimore County, and School of Hygiene & Public Health, Johns Hopkins University

Daisy L. Tagliacozzo, Ph.D.
Department of Sociology, University of Massachusetts—Boston

James A. Taylor
Department of Speech, Temple University

Andrew C. Twaddle, Ph.D.
Department of Sociology, University of Missouri—Columbia

Carol A. Whitehurst, Ph.D.
Department of Sociology, University of Iowa

Prologue.   Some Issues in American Health Care

Despite technological and other advances in American medicine during the past decades, rising concerns about and criticisms of the delivery of medical care to the American people spring from more and more sources—from the government, the consumer, and other private and public groups in American society. Such criticisms have ranged from accelerating costs of such care without apparent improvements in its quality, depersonalization and fragmentation, lack of access to good care by the poor, elderly, minorities, and rural communities, to excessive emphasis upon curative at the expense of preventive care, to mention some current commentary. Many providers of health care have denied such allegations or have attempted to minimize the thrust of such charges, further exacerbating the debate. Others are puzzled: How can there be "health care problems" with a system of such apparent high quality? Occasional surveys of the American public report ambivalent findings: Most people praise their own, personal physicians and the care they provide, yet are increasingly critical of the medical profession, hospitals, and other providers when viewed as a totality. These responses suggest that public concern is directed more to the mode and manner by which health services are *offered* or made available to the American people than to the quality of such care itself. In sum, the health-care delivery *system* or lack of a system is the major target of current criticisms rather than the *individual providers* of health care.

A developing public policy toward health/medical care in American society will probably evolve from the continuing debates and discussions over national and universal health insurance programs now contemplated for this nation. Many of these issues are involved in the emerging policies and programs increasingly emanating from the federal government and are thus important considerations that will probably have an impact on the ultimate role government may or may not play in the delivery of health and medical care to the American people.

The first two chapters of this volume present two "diagnoses" of the maladies afflicting our national health-care "system." Dr. John Knowles presents a cogent analysis of the key problems and issues confronting health care in the United States. Although he is optimistic about the eventual resolution of these problems, Dr. Knowles is well aware of the need to correct many shortcomings.

From the perspective of political economy, Professor John McKinlay offers a stimulating and provocative analysis of what he regards as the major problem confronting the American health delivery system—the misdirected efforts to cope

1

with the "downstream" medical care problems while ignoring the "real manufacturers of illness" in American society and economy.

These articles offer a challenging prologue to the chapters that follow, by pointing out the many causes and problems afflicting the current American health care "system."

But how did we get that way?

The articles to follow provide data and analyses that will illuminate our understanding of the forces and processes that have contributed to the present status of health care in American society.

1 Doing Better and Feeling Worse: Health in the United States

In the mid-nineteen-fifties, the United States became the first country in the world to shift from a predominantly blue-collar society of industrial workers to a predominantly white-collar society of service workers. By 1970, over 62 per cent of the labor force was employed in services such as communications, transportation, public utilities, trade, finance, education, health, police, public administration, and research. Scientific and technological advances resulted in the transition from a rural-agricultural to an urban-industrial society, a society committed to improving the quality of life through the development of services to meet human needs. In every discussion of human services, issues of cost, quality, and accessibility immediately become paramount.

These problems are particularly pressing in the field of health. The economic and emotional devastation visited upon individuals and families as a result of unexpected and unanticipated disease, disability, or death appears to be, at least in our culture, more important than crises that recur in other aspects of American life. Consequently, there exists a profound national concern that, despite a massive increase in health expenditures together with a marked expansion in health workers over the past decade, the nation's health has improved less than was promised or expected. The benefits have not appeared to justify the costs. To make matters worse, broad indicators of social pathology, including drug abuse, illegitimate births, divorce rates, crime and violent behavior, learning difficulties, and psychological problems—the last most frequently found in the uncertainty of adolescence or the loneliness of old age—tell us that the nation is not as healthy as it should be. While some of these problems result from ignorance, poverty, suppression of civil rights, and unequal opportunities for employment and education—all major societal maladies—it is thought that medicine can, and should, assume at least part of the responsibility for preventing, curbing, or curing these conditions.

Although it is often claimed that the United States has no national health policy and that a crisis exists in the American health system, neither statement is quite true. A "health policy" *has* evolved, and though it cannot be called a "system" in any sense, it has very specific characteristics. Thus, for example, public responsibility has been assumed for financing services—and, in specific instances, facilities—for the care of certain groups; these include the indigent sick (through Medicaid, which is left to individual states for implementation), the elderly (through Medicare, which is part of the federal Social Security System), the mentally ill, members of the armed forces and veterans, and indigent Amer-

Reprinted from *Daedalus*, 106:1-7, Winter, 1977, by permission of the author and Publisher.

ican Indians and migrant workers. Health care, however, remains largely a private, pluralistic system: 60 per cent of the total expenditure comes from private sources. Because of inflation, improvement in the quality and quantity of services, and of accessibility to them, not to speak of wholly new services, health expenditures have markedly increased. They have risen threefold from $39 billion (5.9 per cent of the gross national product) in 1965 to $119 billion (8.3 per cent of the gross national product) in 1975. It is estimated that $134 billion will be spent in 1976. Much of this will go to cover hospital bills, physicians' fees, and drug costs.

We have developed an acute, curative, hospital-based system which favors older people, particularly those over 65 who represent 10 per cent of the population and consume about a quarter of all health expenditures. In 1975, hospitals took in $47 billion, physicians' services came to $22 billion, and drugs costs, $11 billion. There is evidence of gross over-use of all three—they consumed 67 per cent of the total national health expenditure—but no one knows quite how to deal with the problem. The situation is made all the more serious by the lack of emphasis on the detection and prevention of disease. Health education (including school health services and counseling on nutrition), rehabilitation services, and lower-cost chronic-hospital extended care, including nursing home facilities, are all slighted. There is a serious deficiency in the numbers of accessible community health centers. We have emphasized high-cost, hospital-based technologies to the neglect of other services where the benefits are much greater relative to costs incurred, such as those involved in rehabilitation. It is significant that legislation for renal dialysis was passed long before legislation was enacted to stimulate the detection and treatment of hypertension.

Health insurance has generally emphasized hospital and surgical expenses. Coverage has been less extensive, in order of decreasing magnitude, for regular medical expenses, ambulatory care, dental care, drugs, psychiatric care, home health services, preventive care, and family-planning services. As of 1975, about 90 per cent of all hospital-care expenditures was paid by third-party payers (37 per cent was covered by private health insurance; 53 per cent was paid for by the government); 60 per cent of payments for physicians' services came from third parties, leaving 40 per cent to direct payment by consumers; only 14 per cent of drug and dental expenses were covered by insurance of any kind.

There has been increasing specialization in medical (and postgraduate) education; over 70 per cent of all American physicians are specialists. While there is one medical doctor for every 645 people, there is only one general or primary-care physician for every 4,771 people. Unfortunately, we depend on the "free market" and on foreign medical graduates for the rational distribution of manpower. This has resulted in serious imbalances, both within specific geographic areas and among the various specialties. Between 1963 and 1973, the number of foreign-trained physicians practicing in the United States increased from 11.2 to 19.5 per cent of the total. Between 1962 and 1971, 75,639 foreign medical graduates entered the United States and 77,867 physicians were graduated from American medical schools. Because of problems of access, discontinuity, and high cost of specialized care, not to speak of depersonalization, a renewed interest in general or family practice ("primary care") has recently developed.

The prevailing American medical system is based on solo, fee-for-service practice—sometimes in the form of self-incorporated groups of physicians. Salaried physicians, pledged to deliver comprehensive service under contract with specific consumer groups on a prepaid, per capita basis, are rare. The delivery systems are sometimes well planned, as, for example, is the Kaiser-Permanente Foundation in California, but they are more often haphazard. Over 90 per cent of all active physicians are directly involved in patient care, with some 62 per cent of them committed to office-based practice.

The labor market in the health-care industry is changing rapidly. Between 1950 and 1970, the numbers employed in health services rose from 1.7 million (2.96 per cent of those totally employed) to 4.3 million (5.6 per cent); the number of women rose from 65 to 75 per cent of the total; of the 4.3 million employed, 2.7 worked in hospitals (this is 65 per cent of all health workers and 3.5 per cent of the total labor force). While less than 3 per cent of physicians and surgeons are black, over 20 per cent of dieticians and practical nurses are black. There is considerable evidence to suggest that the work ethic among health workers, doctors included, has also changed: collective bargaining among all health workers, including hospital interns, residents, and even practicing physicians, is increasingly common.

Public health interests have been, and continue to be, isolated from American medical education and practice. Issues that influence health, such as nutrition, family size, population density, environmental mobility, poverty, racism, sexual practices, unemployment, housing, transportation, and the like, are rarely taken into account in any overall calculation of the health needs of the nation. At the same time, there is a trend toward what one critic has described as "medicalizing everything." Thus, certain conditions, such as criminal behavior and juvenile delinquency, alcoholism, and heroin addiction, once thought to be examples of personal irresponsibility requiring punishment (including imprisonment) are now thought to be socially induced conditions, for which society as well as the individual is held responsible. Very substantial efforts are being made to determine where medical and psychiatric treatment, rather than incarceration, may better serve both the individual and the community interest.

Governmental support for medical research has increased markedly, although it is now leveling off. Between 1950 and 1975, expenditures for health research and development in this country increased from $160 million to over $4.7 billion; the federal government provided over two-thirds of this amount. More recently, expenditures have not grown so markedly, and most of them have involved categorical and contractual arrangements. Government sources provide 34 per cent of the funds for the construction of research and medical facilities; private sources provide the rest. Biological research and technological development are heavily favored over proposals for improved health services and social-science research.

The ethics of medicine is also receiving new emphasis, exemplified in "right-to-die" and "patient bill-of-rights" manifestoes and in the development of specific requirements for ethical guidelines in human experimentation. The courts have also been actively involved: increased litigation, larger awards to plaintiffs, and the consequential rise in the cost of malpractice insurance make the issue of the rights and responsibilities of patients—as well as of physicians—a very compelling one. Complex ethical problems attendant upon organ transplant, sickle-cell detection, renal dialysis, and amniocentesis to detect mongolism are also being discussed, along with the more emotionally charged issues—the "right to die," abortion, and the like.

Many argue that greater attention must be given to the training of health professionals (including physician's assistants and nurse practitioners) and to a change in the locus of training (e.g., baccalaureate programs for nurses) and problems of licensing and re-licensing physicians.

The interest in national health insurance remains high. Twenty-five million Americans have no medical insurance whatsoever; fewer than half of those under 65 (90 million people) and virtually none over 65 (21 million people) are covered against the ruinous cost of "catastrophic" illness. Partly because of this, there is increasing consumer unrest, although the majority of Americans today still place crime, drugs, and the high cost of living, inflation, housing, schools, unemployment, and corruption in government above health care when they list their major grievances. Those that express dissatisfaction with the health-care system cite high costs, particularly those attendant upon catastrophic illness, as their principal complaint. They also worry about the quality of health care, the accessibility of services, and the impersonality and frequent lack of continuity often associated with the "medical encounter." . . .

The American people have clearly come to expect much from medicine, especially in recent years, but they have matched these rapidly rising expectations with rising anxieties over the cost, quality, and accessibility of health services. Many within the profession believe that both the expectations and the anxieties are the result of a definition of health that has become much too broad and that certain limits on the responsibility to society of the medical profession need to be established. At a time when the relations between health, illness, and medicine are being viewed in wholly new ways and are acquiring new meanings in our culture, some talk of too much "medicalization," and argue for "demedicalization"—a return to a simpler set of health practices—even as others call for greater efforts toward realizing the advantages that only an improved science and technology can provide. They say that we are only at the beginning of a "scientific revolution" in the health field, although, if that is so, it becomes all the more incumbent upon us to develop effective ways of assessing the economic, social, ethical, and medical impact of new technologies before they are generally introduced into practice. Medicine ought not to be berated for the high cost of "halfway" technologies when definitive technologies are not available. And unless more support for fundamental research is forthcoming, definitive (i.e., curative or preventive) technologies will not be developed that can markedly reduce the cost of disease.

The evolution of and support for the American biomedical-research effort and the present subdivision of responsibility—whether in the National Institutes of Health or in other agencies—were developed at a time when sustained growth and stability of funding were taken for granted. New approaches are needed, if only because these assumptions are now in jeopardy. Medical knowledge and scientific technologies have raised profound moral and ethical questions that must be addressed. The assessment of the quality of care rendered by physicians involves not only a delineation of the "samaritan" function, but also an understanding of all that derives from technological advances, for the physician is required to choose from among the technologies available to him. The complexities of assessing "quality" in an era when chronic and degenerative diseases have replaced acute infectious ones as the primary health problem demand long-term study. They call for an understanding of the interaction between the multiple variables in both the causation and the course of a disease, if therapy is to be evaluated effectively (this is, incidentally, an area where computers have much to offer).

The pressing need for more primary-care practitioners, recognized by the profession and the public alike, and the need to delineate more clearly the functions and responsibilities of the university and the teaching hospital are already producing substantial changes in medical education and in health-care delivery. The evolution of the various professional, governmental, and consumer groups interested in, and responsible for, health—now viewed by most American citizens as a fundamental "right"—represents a typical American response. The health industry is pluralistic, competitive, and essentially comitted to the tenets of a laissez-faire ethos. It involves sharing by public and private interests with diverse power centers; it is based upon multiple decision-making mechanisms; it tolerates multiple conflicts (although they are increasingly frustrating to all concerned). Any discussion of financing mechanisms and national health insurance brings with it certain hopes for cost controls, for improvements in the quality of health care, and for accessibility to services for all. It presumes a more rational utilization of services (requiring definitive changes in the behavior of both providers and consumers) and an improved organization of delivery systems. Sober reflection reveals the complexity of the subject—what may and may not be expected— and the unknowns that indicate the need for further research. The current debate is taking place in an intellectual vacuum of ideological bias and self-fulfilling prophecies. The individual's responsibility for his own health is supposed to be self-evident; how the rights of the individual relate to the social good of the community and of the nation that are required to bear the costs of his irresponsibility and poor health habits is less obvious. Changes in behavior are notoriously difficult to achieve; add to this the problems resulting from the steadily expanding array of drugs, unnatural food additives, and environmental contaminants that also influence health and the full dimensions of the problem become apparent. They call for a more rigorous legislative effort which in turn presumes a citizenry sufficiently enlightened to know its interests and civic-minded enough to participate actively in the democratic process.

The health of children determines the future strength of the nation, so statistics on this score are particularly dispiriting. To improve the situation, comprehensive efforts in integrated local service systems directly related to the schools must be introduced. These will stress the application of what is known, while seeking to lessen those recalcitrant social forces—ignorance and poverty—that condition the health of children. Mental illness is another of the country's major health problems. A scientific revolution has taken place with the advent of modern psychopharmacologic research; these advances, together with others that stem from recent research in human behavior, offer new hope in the care and cure of those afflicted with mental illness, but much remains to be done, particularly on the social and cultural level. Physicians have always performed a vital social function in responding to distress; the relief of apprehension has profoundly beneficial psychic as well as somatic effects on the patient and on his level of ease or dis-ease. The understanding physician is able to influence the patient's behavior, whether in his compliance with therapeutic regimens, his willingness to improve his health habits, or in his capacity to cope with death and dying. . . .

There is reason for optimism. We know that the infant-mortality rate is once again declining after a period of stability; deaths from heart disease have dropped below one million for the first time since 1967, and deaths from heart attack are 7 per cent below the level of 1970; over the past 25 years, death rates for practically all major diseases have decreased in the age group 45 to 64 (notable exceptions are cancer, cirrhosis of the liver, bronchitis, and emphysema); overall death rates have declined and the life expectancy has increased; and the gap between rich and poor, black and white has continued to narrow. We have developed the finest biomedical research effort in the world, and our medical technology is second to none. The poor have both gained greater access to health services and are using the services gained. Medicare has benefited the elderly. Medical education is improving, and increasing numbers of women and blacks are gaining entry into medical schools. Delivery systems are also improving and primary-care physicians are once again being trained. National programs to reduce smoking and to detect and treat hypertension have been remarkably successful. New knowledge is being generated about the hazards of drugs, faulty diets, and environmental contaminants, and the nation has shown its willingness to ban the production and use of certain toxic substances.

And yet we feel dis-eased. We find intolerable the levels of deprivation and ill health suffered by significant numbers of the American people, and not only among the elderly. While trying to balance public and private interests, maintaining the ideal of individual freedom even as we assert the imperatives of social responsibility and justice, we know that we are confronted with complexities that call for ways of thinking that are not bound to the old and exhausted ideologies of an earlier day. It is a new kind of pragmatism that is needed, one that admits that truth is plural and contingent, but that takes into account the strengths and weaknesses that exist without being overwhelmed by either the exaggerated hopes of science and technology or the despair of poverty and ignorance. The challenge to the United States is to estimate correctly what reason, confronted by irrefutable facts, can accomplish, particularly at a time when something more than a reputation for humanity is called for.

JOHN B. McKINLAY

2 A Case for Refocussing Upstream: The Political Economy of Illness

My friend, Irving Zola, relates the story of a physician trying to explain the dilemmas of the modern practice of medicine:

"You know", he said, "sometimes it feels like this. There I am standing by the shore of a swiftly flowing river and I hear the cry of a drowning man. So I jump into the river, put my arms around him, pull him to shore and apply artificial respiration. Just when he begins to breathe, there is another cry for help. So I jump into the river, reach him, pull him to shore, apply artificial respiration, and then just as he begins to breathe, another cry for help. So back in the river again, reaching, pulling, applying, breathing and then another yell. Again and again, without end, goes the sequence. You know, I am so busy jumping in, pulling them to shore, applying artificial respiration, that I have *no* time to see who the hell is upstream pushing them all in".[1]

I believe this simple story illustrates two important points. *First*, it highlights the fact that a clear majority of our resources and activities in the health field are devoted to what I term "downstream endeavors"—in the form of superficial, categorical tinkering in response to almost perennial shifts from one health issue to the next, without really solving anything. I am, of course, not suggesting that such efforts are entirely futile, or that a considerable amount of short-term good is not being accomplished. Clearly, people and groups have important immediate needs which must be recognized and attended to. Nevertheless, one must be wary of the *short-term nature* and *ultimate futility* of such downstream endeavors.

Second, the story indicates that we should somehow cease our preoccupation with this short-term, problem-specific tinkering and begin focussing our attention upstream, where the real problems lie. Such a reorientation would minimally involve an analysis of the means by which various individuals, interest groups, and large-scale, profit-oriented corporations are "pushing people in", and how they subsequently erect, at some point downstream, a health care structure to service the needs which they have had a hand in creating, and for which moral responsibility ought to be assumed.

In this paper two related themes will be developed. *First*, I wish to highlight the activities of the "manufacturers of illness"—those individuals, interest groups, and organizations which, in addition to producing material goods and

---

[1] I. K. Zola, "Helping—Does It Matter: The Problems and Prospects of Mutual Aid Groups." Addressed to the United Ostomy Association, 1970.

From *Applying Behavioral Science to Cardiovascular Risk*, Proceedings of American Heart Association Conference, Seattle, Wash., June 17–19, 1974, pp. 7-17. © 1974 American Heart Association. Reprinted by permission of the author and Publisher.

services, also produce, as an inevitable byproduct, widespread morbidity and mortality. Arising out of this, and *second,* I will develop a case for refocussing our attention away from those individuals and groups who are mistakenly held to be responsible for their condition, toward a range of broader upstream political and economic forces.

The task assigned to me for this conference was to review some of the broad social structural factors influencing the onset of heart disease and/or at-risk behavior. Since the issues covered by this request are so varied, I have, of necessity, had to make some decisions concerning both emphasis and scope. These decisions and the reasoning behind them should perhaps be explained at this point. With regard to what can be covered by the term "social structure", it is possible to isolate at least three separate levels of abstraction. One could, for example, focus on such subsystems as the family, and its associated social networks, and how these may be importantly linked to different levels of health status and the utilization of services.[2] On a second level, one could consider how particular organizations and broader social institutions, such as neighborhood and community structures, also affect the social distribution of pathology and at-risk behavior.[3] Third, attention could center on the broader political-economic spectrum, and how these admittedly more remote forces may be etiologically involved in the onset of disease. . . .

A political-economic analysis of health care suggests that the entire structure of institutions in the United States is such as to preclude the adequate provision of services.[4] Increasingly, it seems, the provision of care is being tied to the priorities of profit-making institutions. For a long time, criticism of U.S. health care focussed on the activities of the American Medical Association and the fee

[2]See, for example, M. W. Susser and W. Watson, *Sociology in Medicine*, New York: Oxford University Press, 1971. Edith Chen, et al., "Family Structure in Relation to Health and Disease," *Journal of Chronic Diseases*, Vol. 12 (1960), pp. 544–567; and R. Keelner, *Family Ill Health: An Investigation in General Practice*, Charles C. Thomas, 1963. There is, of course, voluminous literature which relates family structure to mental illnesses. Few studies move to the level of considering the broader social forces which promote the family structures which are conducive to the onset of particular illnesses. With regard to utilization behavior, see J. B. McKinlay, "Social Networks, Lay Consultation and Help-Seeking Behavior," *Social Forces*, Vol. 51, No. 3 (March, 1973), pp. 275–292.

[3]A rich source for a variety of materials included in this second level is H. E. Freeman, S. Levine, and L. G. Reeder (Eds.), *Handbook of Medical Sociology*, New Jersey: Prentice Hall, 1972. I would also include here studies of the health implications of different housing patterns. Recent evidence in this area suggests that housing—even when highly dense—may not be directly related to illness.

[4]Some useful introductory readings appear in D. M. Gordon (Ed.), *Problems in Political Economy: An Urban Perspective*, Lexington: D. C. Heath & Co., 1971, and R. C. Edwards, M. Reich and T. E. Weisskopf (Eds.), *The Capitalist System*, New Jersey: Prentice Hall, 1972. Also, T. Christoffel, D. Finkelhor and D. Gilbarg (Eds.), *Up Against the American Myth*, New York: Holt, Rinehart and Winston, 1970. M. Mankoff (Ed.), *The Poverty of Progress: The Political Economy of American Social Problems*, New York: Holt, Rinehart and Winston, 1972. For a more sophisticated treatment, see the collection edited by D. Mermelstein, *Economics: Mainstream Readings and Radical Critiques*, New York: Random House, 1970. Additionally useful papers appear in J. B. McKinlay (Ed.), *Politics and Law in Health Care Policy*, New York: Prodist, 1973, and J. B. McKinlay (Ed.), *Economic Aspects of Health Care*, New York: Prodist, 1973. For a highly readable and influential treatment of what is termed "the medical-industrial complex," see B. and J. Ehrenreich, *The American Health Empire: Power, Profits and Politics*, New York: Vintage Books, 1971. Also relevant are T. R. Marmor, *The Politics of Medicare*, Chicago: Aldine Publishing Co., 1973, and R. Alford, "The Political Economy of Health Care: Dynamics Without Change," *Politics and Society*, 2 (1972), pp. 127–164.

for service system of physician payment.[5] Lately, however, attention appears to be refocussing on the relationship between health care arrangements and the structure of big business.[6] It has, for example, been suggested that:

> ... with the new and apparently permanent involvement of major corporations in health, it is becoming increasingly improbable that the United States can redirect its health priorities without, at the same time, changing the ways in which American industry is organized and the ways in which monopoly capitalism works.[7]

It is my impression that many of the political-economic arguments concerning developments in the organization of health care also have considerable relevance for a holistic understanding of the etiology and distribution of morbidity, mortality, and at-risk behavior. In the following sections I will present some important aspects of these arguments in the hope of contributing to a better understanding of aspects of the political economy of illness.

An Unequal Battle

The downstream efforts of health researchers and practitioners against the upstream efforts of the manufacturers of illness have the appearance of an unequal war, *with a resounding victory assured for those on the side of illness* and the creation of disease-inducing behaviors. The battle between health workers and the manufacturers of illness is unequal on at least two grounds. In the *first* place, we always seem to arrive on the scene and begin to work after the real damage has already been done. By the time health workers intervene, people have already filled the artificial needs created for them by the manufacturers of illness and are habituated to various at-risk behaviors. In the area of smoking behavior, for example, we have an illustration not only of the lateness of health workers' arrival on the scene, and the enormity of the task confronting them, but also, judging by recent evidence, of the resounding defeat being sustained in this area.[8] To push the river analogy even further, the task becomes one of furiously swimming against the flow and finally being swept away when exhausted by the effort or through disillusionment with a lack of progress. So long as we continue to fight the battle downstream, and in such an ineffective manner, we are doomed to frustration, repeated failure, and perhaps ultimately to a sicker society.

[5]E. Cray, *In Failing Health: The Medical Crisis and the AMA*, Indianapolis: Bobbs-Merrill, 1970. J. S. Burrow, *AMA—Voice of American Medicine*, Baltimore: Johns Hopkins Press, 1963. R. Harris, *A Sacred Trust*, New York: New American Library, 1966. R. Carter, *The Doctor Business*, Garden City, New York: Dolphin Books, 1961. "The American Medical Association: Power, Purpose and Politics in Organized Medicine," *Yale Law Journal*, Vol. 63, No. 7 (May, 1954), pp. 938–1021.

[6]See references under footnote 4, especially B. and J. Ehrenreich's *The American Health Empire*, Chapter VII, pp. 95–123.

[7]D. M. Gordon (Ed.), *Problems in Political Economy: An Urban Perspective*, Lexington: D. C. Heath & Co., 1971, p. 318.

[8]See, for example, D. A. Bernstein, "The Modification of Smoking Behavior: An Evaluative Review," *Psychological Bulletin*, Vol. 71 (June 1969), pp. 418–440; S. Ford and F. Ederer, "Breaking the Cigarette Habit," *Journal of American Medical Association*, 194 (October, 1965), pp. 139–142; C. S. Keutzer, et al., "Modification of Smoking Behavior: A Review," *Psychological Bulletin*, Vol. 70 (December, 1968), pp. 520–533. Mettlin considers evidence concerning the following techniques for modifying smoking behavior: (1) behavioral conditioning, (2) group discussion, (3) counselling, (4)

Secondly, the promoters of disease-inducing behavior are manifestly more effective in their use of behavioral science knowledge than are those of us who are concerned with the eradication of such behavior. Indeed, it is somewhat paradoxical that we should be meeting here to consider how behavioral science knowledge and techniques can be effectively employed to reduce or prevent at-risk behavior, when that same body of knowledge *has already* been used to create the at-risk behavior we seek to eliminate. How embarrassingly ineffective are our mass media efforts in the health field (e.g., alcoholism, obesity, drug abuse, safe driving, pollution, etc.) when compared with many of the tax exempt promotional efforts on behalf of the illness generating activities of large-scale corporations.[9] It is a fact that we are demonstrably more effective in persuading people to purchase items they never dreamt they would need, or to pursue at-risk courses of action, than we are in preventing or halting such behavior.[10] Many advertisements are so ingenious in their appeal that they have entertainment value in their own right and become embodied in our national folk humor. By way of contrast, many health advertisements lack any comparable widespread appeal, often appear boring, avuncular, and largely misdirected.

I would argue that one major problem lies in the fact that we are overly concerned with the war itself, and with how we can more effectively participate in it. In the health field we have unquestioningly accepted the assumptions presented by the manufacturers of illness and, as a consequence, have confined our efforts to only downstream offensives. A little reflection would, I believe, convince anyone that those on the side of health are in fact losing. . . . But rather than merely trying to win the war, we need to step back and question the premises, legitimacy and utility of the war itself.

The Binding of At-Riskness to Culture

It seems that the appeals to at-risk behavior that are engineered by the manufacturers of illness are particularly successful because they are constructed in such a way as to be inextricably bound with essential elements of our existing dominant culture. This is accomplished in a number of ways: a) Exhortations to at-risk behavior are often piggybacked on those legitimized values, beliefs, and norms which are widely recognized and adhered to in the dominant culture. The idea here is that if a person *would only do X*, then they would also be doing Y and

---

hypnosis, (5) interpersonal communication, (6) self-analysis. He concludes that:

> Each of these approaches suggests that smoking behavior is the result of some finite set of social and psychological variables, yet none has either demonstrated any significant powers in predicting the smoking behaviors of an individual or led to techniques of smoking control that, considered alone, have significant long-term effects.

In C. Mettlin, "Smoking as Behavior: Applying a Social Psychological Theory," *Journal of Health and Social Behavior*, 14 (June, 1973), p. 144.

[9]It appears that a considerable proportion of advertising by large corporations is tax exempt through being granted the status of "public education." In particular, the enormous media campaign, which was recently waged by major oil companies in an attempt to preserve the public myths they had so carefully constructed concerning their activities, was almost entirely non-taxable.

[10]The mind boggles at the remarkable success the promoters of Listerine have had in persuading large numbers of people to use twice a day what they publicly admit to hating.

Z. b) Appeals are also advanced which claim or imply that certain courses of at-risk action are subscribed to or endorsed by most of the culture heroes in society (e.g., people in the entertainment industry), or by those with technical competence in that particular field (e.g., "doctors" recommend it). The idea here is that if a person *would only do X,* then he/she would be doing pretty much the same as is done or recommended by such prestigious people as A and B. c) Artificial needs are manufactured, the fulfilling of which becomes absolutely essential if one is to be a meaningful and useful member of society. The idea here is that if a person *does not do X, or will not do X,* then they are either deficient in some important respect, or they are some kind of liability for the social system.

Variations on these and other kinds of appeal strategies have, of course, been employed for a long time now by the promoters of at-risk behavior. The manufacturers of illness are, for example, fostering the belief that if you want to be an attractive, masculine man, or a "cool", "natural" woman, you will smoke cigarettes; that you can only be a "good parent" if you habituate your children to candy, cookies, etc.; and that if you are a truly loving wife, you will feed your husband foods that are high in cholesterol. All of these appeals have isolated some basic goals to which most people subscribe (e.g., people want to be masculine or feminine, good parents, loving spouses, etc.) and make the claim, or imply, that their realization is only possible through the exclusive use of their product or the regular display of a specific type of at-risk behavior. Indeed, one can argue that certain at-risk behaviors have become so inextricably intertwined with our dominant cultural system (perhaps even symbolic of it) that the routine public display of such behavior almost signifies membership in this society.

Such tactics for the habituation of people to at-risk behavior are, perhaps paradoxically, also employed to elicit what I term *"quasi-health behavior."* Here again, an artificially constructed conception of a person in some fanciful state of physiological and emotional equilibrium is presented as the ideal state to strive for, if one is to meaningfully participate in the wider social system. To assist in the attainment of such a state, we are advised to consume a range of quite worthless vitamin pills, mineral supplements, mouthwashes, hair shampoos, laxatives, pain killers, etc. Clearly, one cannot exude radiance and success if one is not taking this vitamin, or that mineral. The achievement of daily regularity is a prerequisite for an effective social existence. One can only compete and win after a good night's sleep, and this can only be ensured by taking such and such. An entrepreneurial pharmaceutical industry appears devoted to the task of making people overly conscious of these quasi-health concerns, and to engendering a dependency on products which have been repeatedly found to be ineffective, and even potentially harmful.[11]

There are no clear signs that such activity is being or will be regulated in any effective way, and the promoters of this quasi-health behavior appear free to

[11] Reports of the harmfulness and ineffectiveness of certain products appear almost weekly in the press. As I have been writing this paper, I have come across reports of the low quality of milk, the uselessness of cold remedies, the health dangers in frankfurters, the linking of the use of the aerosol propellant, Vinyl Chloride, to liver cancer. That the Food and Drug Administration (F.D.A.) is unable to effectively regulate the manufacturers of illness is evident and illustrated in their inept handling of the withdrawal of the drug, betahistine hydrochloride, which supposedly offered symptomatic relief of Meriere's Syndrome (an affliction of the inner ear). There is every reason to think that this case is not

range over the entire body in their never-ending search for new areas and issues to be linked to the fanciful equilibrium that they have already engineered in the mind of the consumer. By binding the display of at-risk and quasi-health behavior so inextricably to elements of our dominant culture, a situation is even created whereby to request people to change or alter these behaviors is more or less to request abandonment of dominant culture.

The term "culture" is employed here to denote that integrated system of values, norms, beliefs and patterns of behavior which, for groups and social categories in specific situations, facilitate the solution of social structural problems.[12] This definition lays stress on two features commonly associated with the concept of culture. The *first* is the interrelatedness and interdependence of the various elements (values, norms, beliefs, overt life styles) that apparently comprise culture. The *second* is the view that a cultural system is, in some part, a response to social structural problems, and that it can be regarded as some kind of resolution of them. Of course, these social structural problems, in partial response to which a cultural pattern emerges, may themselves have been engineered in the interests of creating certain beliefs, norms, life styles, etc. If one assumes that culture can be regarded as some kind of reaction formation, then one must be mindful of the unanticipated social consequences of inviting some alteration in behavior which is a part of a dominant cultural pattern. The request from health workers for alterations in certain at-risk behaviors may result in either awkward dislocations of the interrelated elements of the cultural pattern, or the destruction of a system of values and norms, etc., which have emerged over time in response to situational problems. From this perspective, and with regard to the utilization of medical care, I have already argued elsewhere that, for certain groups of the population, underutilization may be 'healthy' behavior, and the advocacy of increased utilization an 'unhealthy' request for the abandonment of essential features of culture.[13]

The Case of Food

Perhaps it would be useful at this point to illustrate in some detail, from one pertinent area, the style and magnitude of operation engaged in by the manufacturers of illness. Illustrations are, of course, readily available from a variety of

atypical. For additionally disquieting evidence of how the Cigarette Labeling and Advertising Act of 1965 actually curtailed the power of the F.T.C. and other federal agencies from regulating cigarette advertising and nullified all such state and local regulatory efforts, see L. Fritschler, *Smoking and Politics: Policymaking and the Federal Bureaucracy*, New York: Meredith, 1969, and T. Whiteside, *Selling Death: Cigarette Advertising and Public Health*, New York: Liveright, 1970. Also relevant are *Congressional Quarterly*, 27 (1969) 666, 1026; and U.S. Department of Agriculture, Economic Research Service, *Tobacco Situation*, Washington: Government Printing Office, 1969.

[12]The term "culture" is used to refer to a number of other characteristics as well. However, these two appear to be commonly associated with the concept. See J. B. McKinlay, "Some Observations on the Concept of a Subculture" (1970).

[13]This has been argued in J. B. McKinlay, "Some Approaches and Problems in the Study of the Use of Services," *Journal of Health and Social Behavior*, Vol. 13 (July, 1972), pp. 115–152; and J. B. McKinlay and D. Dutton, "Social-Psychological Factors Affecting Health-Service Utilization," chapter in *Consumer Incentives for Health Care*, New York: Prodist Press, 1974.

different areas, such as: the requirements of our existing occupational structure, emerging leisure patterns, smoking and drinking behavior, and automobile usage.[14] Because of current interest, I have decided to consider only one area which is importantly related to a range of largely chronic diseases—namely, the 161 billion dollar industry involved in the production and distribution of food and beverages.[15] The present situation, with regard to food, was recently described as follows:

> The sad history of our food supply resembles the energy crisis, and not just because food nourishes our bodies while petroleum fuels the society. We long ago surrendered control of food, a vital resource, to private corporations, just as we surrendered control of energy. The food corporations have shaped the kinds of food we eat for their greater profits, just as the energy companies have dictated the kinds of fuel we use.[16]

From all the independent evidence available, and despite claims to the contrary by the food industry, a widespread decline has occurred during the past three decades in American dietary standards. Some forty percent of U.S. adults are overweight or downright fat.[17] The prevalence of excess weight in the American population as a whole is high—so high, in fact, that in some segments it has reached epidemic proportions.[18] There is evidence that the food industry is manipulating our image of "food" away from basic staples toward synthetic and highly processed items. It has been estimated that we eat between 21 and 25 percent fewer dairy products, vegetables, and fruits than we did twenty years ago, and from 70 to 80 percent more sugary snacks and soft drinks. Apparently, most people now eat more processed and synthetic foods than the real thing. There are even suggestions that a federal, nationwide survey would have revealed how serious our dietary situation really is, if the Nixon Administration had not cancelled it after reviewing some embarrassing preliminary results.[19] The survey apparently confirmed the trend toward deteriorating diets first detected in an earlier household food consumption survey in the years 1955–1965, undertaken by the Department of Agriculture.[20]

[14]Reliable sources covering these areas are available in many professional journals in the fields of epidemiology, medical sociology, preventive medicine, industrial and occupational medicine and public health. Useful references covering these and related areas appear in J. N. Morris, *Uses of Epidemiology*, London: E. and S. Livingstone Ltd., 1967; and M. W. Susser and W. Watson, *Sociology in Medicine*, New York: Oxford University Press, 1971.

[15]D. Zwerling, "Death for Dinner," *The New York Review of Books*, Vol. 21, No. 2 (February 21, 1974), p. 22.

[16]D. Zwerling, "Death for Dinner." See footnote 15 above.

[17]This figure was quoted by several witnesses at the *Hearings Before the Select Committee on Nutrition and Human Needs*, U.S. Government Printing Office, 1973.

[18]The magnitude of this problem is discussed in P. Wyden, *The Overweight Society*, New York: Morrow, 1965; J. Mayer, *Overweight: Causes, Costs and Control*, Englewood Cliffs: Prentice Hall, 1968; National Center for Health Statistics, *Weight by Age and Height of Adults*: 1960–62. Washington: *Vital and Health Statistics*, Public Health Service Publication #1000, Series 11, #14, Government Printing Office, 1966; U.S. Public Health Service, Center for Chronic Disease Control, *Obesity and Health*, Washington: Government Printing Office, 1966.

[19]This aborted study is discussed in M. Jacobson, *Nutrition Scoreboard: Your Guide to Better Eating*, Center for Science in the Public Interest.

[20]M. S. Hathaway and E. D. Foard, *Heights and Weights for Adults in the United States*, Washington: Home Economics Research Report 10, Agricultural Research Service, U.S. Department of Agriculture, Government Printing Office, 1960.

Of course, for the food industry, this trend toward deficient synthetics and highly processed items makes good economic sense. Generally speaking, it is much cheaper to make things look and taste like the real thing, than to actually provide the real thing. But the kind of foods that result from the predominance of economic interests clearly do not contain adequate nutrition. It is common knowledge that food manufacturers destroy important nutrients which foods naturally contain, when they transform them into "convenience" high profit items. To give one simple example: a wheat grain's outer layers are apparently very nutritious, but they are also an obstacle to making tasteless, bleached, white flour. Consequently, baking corporations "refine" fourteen nutrients out of the natural flour and then, when it is financially convenient, replace some of them with a synthetic substitute. In the jargon of the food industry, this flour is now "enriched". Clearly, the food industry employs this term in much the same way that coal corporations ravage mountainsides into mud flats, replant them with some soil and seedlings, and then proclaim their moral accomplishment in "rehabilitating" the land. While certain types of food processing may make good economic sense, it may also result in a deficient end product, and perhaps even promote certain diseases. The bleaching and refining of wheat products, for example, largely eliminates fiber or roughage from our diets, and some authorities have suggested that fiber-poor diets can be blamed for some of our major intestinal diseases.[21]

A vast chemical additive technology has enabled manufacturers to acquire enormous control over the food and beverage market and to foster phenomenal profitability. It is estimated that drug companies alone make something like $500 million a year through chemical additives for food. I have already suggested that what is done to food, in the way of processing and artificial additives, may actually be injurious to health. Yet, it is clear that, despite such well-known risks, profitability makes such activity well worthwhile. For example, additives, like preservatives, enable food that might perish in a short period of time to endure unchanged for months or even years. Food manufacturers and distributors can saturate supermarket shelves across the country with their products because there is little chance that they will spoil. Moreover, manufacturers can purchase vast quantities of raw ingredients when they are cheap, produce and stockpile the processed result, and then withhold the product from the market for long periods, hoping for the inevitable rise in prices and the consequent windfall.

The most widely used food additive (although it is seldom described as an additive) is "refined" sugar. Food manufacturers saturate our diets with the substance from the day we are born until the day we die. Children are fed breakfast cereals which consist of 50 percent sugar.[22] The average American adult consumes 126 pounds of sugar each year—and children, of course, eat much more. For the candy industry alone, this amounts to around $3 billion each year. The American sugar mania, which appears to have been deliberately engineered, is a major contributor to such "diseases of civilization" as diabetes, coronary heart disease, gall bladder illness, and cancer—all the insidious, degenerative conditions which most often afflict people in advanced capitalist societies, but which

[21]This is discussed by D. Zwerling. See footnote 16.

[22]See *Hearings Before the Select Committee on Nutrition and Human Needs*, Parts 3 and 4, "T.V. Advertising of Food to Children," March 5, 1973 and March 6, 1973.

"underdeveloped," non-sugar eaters never get. One witness, at a recent meeting of a U.S. Senate Committee, said that if the food industry were proposing sugar today as a new food additive, its "metabolic behavior would undoubtedly lead to its being banned."[23]

In sum, therefore, it seems that the American food industry is mobilizing phenomenal resources to advance and bind us to its own conception of food. We are bombarded from childhood with $2 billion worth of deliberately manipulative advertisements each year, most of them urging us to consume, among other things, as much sugar as possible. To highlight the magnitude of the resources involved, one can point to the activity of one well-known beverage company, Coca-Cola, which alone spent $71 million in 1971 to advertise its artificially flavored, sugar-saturated product. Fully recognizing the enormity of the problem regarding food in the United States, Zwerdling offers the following advice:

> Breaking through the food industry will require government action-banning or sharply limiting use of dangerous additives like artificial colors and flavors, and sugar, and requiring wheat products to contain fiber-rich wheat germ, to give just two examples. Food, if it is to become safe, will have to become part of politics.[24]

The Ascription of Responsibility and Moral Entrepreneurship

So far, I have considered, in some detail, the ways in which industry, through its manufacture and distribution of a variety of products, generates at-risk behavior and disease. Let us now focus on the activities of health workers further down the river and consider their efforts in a social context, which has already been largely shaped by the manufacturers upstream.

Not only should we be mindful of the culturally disruptive and largely unanticipated consequences of health intervention efforts mentioned earlier, but also of the underlying ideology on which so much of this activity rests. Such intervention appears based on an assumption of the *culpability of individuals* or groups who either manifest illness, or display various at-risk behaviors.

From the assumption that individuals and groups with certain illnesses or displaying at-risk behavior are responsible for their state, it is a relatively easy step to advocating some changes in behavior on the part of those involved. By ascribing culpability to some group or social category (usually ethnic minorities and those in lower socio-economic categories) and having this ascription legitimated by health professionals and accepted by other segments of society, it is possible to mobilize resources to change the offending behavior. Certain people are responsible for not approximating, through their activities, some conception of what *ought* to be appropriate behavior on their part. When measured against the artificial conception of what ought to be, certain individuals and groups are found to be deficient in several important respects. They are *either* doing something that they ought not to be doing, *or* they are not doing something that they ought to be

[23]Dr. John Yudkin, Department of Nutrition, Queen Elizabeth College, London University. See p. 225, *Senate Hearings*, footnote 22 above.

[24]D. Zwerling, "Death for Dinner." See footnote 16 above, page 15.

doing. If only they would recognize their individual culpability and alter their behavior in some appropriate fashion, they would improve their health status or the likelihood of not developing certain pathologies. On the basis of this line of reasoning, resources are being mobilized to bring those who depart from the desired conception into conformity with what is thought to be appropriate behavior. To use the upstream-downstream analogy, one could argue that people are blamed (and, in a sense, even punished) for not being able to swim after they, perhaps even against their own volition, have been pushed into the river by the manufacturers of illness.

Clearly, this ascription of culpability is not limited only to the area of health. According to popular conception, people in poverty are largely to blame for their social situation, although recent evidence suggest that a social welfare system which prevents them from avoiding this state is at least partly responsible.[25] Again, in the field of education, we often hold "dropouts" responsible for their behavior, when evidence suggests that the school system itself is rigged for failure.[26] Similar examples are readily available from the fields of penology, psychiatry, and race relations.[27]

Perhaps it would be useful to briefly outline, at this point, what I regard as a bizarre relationship between the activities of the manufacturers of illness, the ascription of culpability, and health intervention endeavors. *Firstly,* important segments of our social system appear to be controlled and operated in such a way that people must inevitably fail. The fact is that there is often no choice over whether one can find employment, whether or not to drop out of college, involve oneself in untoward behavior, or become sick. *Secondly,* even though individuals and groups lack such choice, they are still blamed for not approximating the artificially contrived norm and are treated as if responsibility for their state lay entirely with them. For example, some illness conditions may be the result of particular behavior and/or involvement in certain occupational role relationships over which those affected have little or no control.[28] *Thirdly,* after recognizing that certain individuals and groups have "failed," we establish, at a point downstream, a substructure of services which are regarded as evidence of progressive beneficence on the part of the system. Yet, it is this very system which had a primary role in manufacturing the problems and need for these services in the first place.

[25]This is well argued in F. Piven and R. A. Cloward, *Regulating the Poor: The Functions of Social Welfare*, New York: Vintage, 1971; L. Goodwin, *Do the Poor Want to Work?*, Washington: Brookings, 1972; H. J. Gans, "The Positive Functions of Poverty," *American Journal of Sociology*, Vol. 78, No. 2 (September, 1972), pp. 275-289; R. P. Roby (Ed.), *The Poverty Establishment*, New Jersey: Prentice Hall, 1974.

[26]See, for example, Jules Henry, "American Schoolrooms: Learning the Nightmare," *Columbia University Forum* (Spring, 1963), pp. 24-30. See also the paper by F. Howe and P. Lanter, "How the School System is rigged for failure," *New York Review of Books*, (June 18, 1970).

[27]With regard to penology, for example, see the critical work of R. Quinney in *Criminal Justice in America*, Boston: Little Brown, 1974, and *Critique of Legal Order*, Boston: Little Brown, 1974.

[28]See, for example, S. M. Sales, "Organizational Role as a Risk Factor in Coronary Disease," *Administrative Science Quarterly*, Vol. 14, No. 3 (September, 1969), pp. 325-336. The literature in this particular area is enormous. For several good reviews, see L. E. Hinkle, "Some Social and Biological Correlates of Coronary Heart Disease," *Social Science and Medicine*, Vol. 1 (1967), pp. 129-139; F. H. Epstein, "The Epidemiology of Coronary Heart Disease: A Review," *Journal of Chronic Diseases*, 18 (August, 1965), pp. 735-774.

It is around certain aspects of life style that most health intervention endeavors appear to revolve and this probably results from the observability of most at-risk behavior. The modification of at-risk behavior can take several different forms, and the intervention appeals that are employed probably vary as a function of which type of change is desired. People can *either* be encouraged to stop doing what they are doing which appears to be endangering their survival (e.g., smoking, drinking, eating certain types of food, working in particular ways); *or* they can be encouraged to adopt certain new patterns of behavior which seemingly enhance their health status (e.g., diet, exercise, rest, eat certain foods, etc.). I have already discussed how the presence or absence of certain life styles in some groups may be a part of some wider cultural pattern which emerges as a response to social structural problems. I have also noted the potentially disruptive consequences to these cultural patterns of intervention programs. Underlying all these aspects is the issue of behavior control and the attempt to enforce a particular type of behavioral conformity. It is more than coincidental that the at-risk life styles, which we are all admonished to avoid, are frequently the type of behaviors which depart from and, in a sense, jeopardize the prevailing puritanical, middle class ethic of what ought to be. According to this ethic, activities as pleasurable as drinking, smoking, overeating, and sexual intercourse must be harmful and ought to be eradicated.

The important point here is which segments of society and whose interests are health workers serving, and what are the ideological consequences of their actions?[29] Are we advocating the modification of behavior for the *exclusive* purpose of improving health status, or are we using the question of health as a means of obtaining some kind of moral uniformity through the abolition of disapproved behaviors? To what extent, if at all, are health workers actively involved in some wider pattern of social regulation?[30]

Such questions also arise in relation to the burgeoning literature that links more covert personality characteristics to certain illnesses and at-risk behaviors. Capturing a great deal of attention in this regard are the recent studies which associate heart disease with what is termed a Type A personality.[31] The Type A personality consists of a complex of traits which produces:

[29]Some interesting ideas in this regard are in E. Nuehring and G. E. Markle, "Nicotine and Norms: The Reemergence of a Deviant Behavior," *Social Problems*, Vol. 21, No. 4 (April, 1974), pp. 513–526. Also, J. R. Gusfield, *Symbolic Crusade: Status Politics and the American Temperance Movement*, Urbana, Illinois: University of Illinois Press, 1963.

[30]For a study of the ways in which physicians, clergymen, the police, welfare officers, psychiatrists and social workers act as agents of social control, see E. Cumming, *Systems of Social Regulation*, New York: Atherton Press, 1968.

[31]R. H. Rosenman and M. Friedman, "The Role of a Specific Overt Behavior Pattern in the Occurrence of Ischemic Heart Disease," *Cardiologia Pratica*, 13 (1962), pp. 42–53; M. Friedman and R. H. Rosenman, *Type A Behavior and Your Heart*, Knopf, 1973. Also, S. J. Zyzanski and C. D. Jenkins, "Basic Dimensions Within the Coronary-Prone Behavior Pattern," *Journal of Chronic Diseases*, 22 (1970), pp. 781–795. There are, of course, many other illnesses which have also been related in one way or another to certain personality characteristics. Having found this new turf, behavioral scientists will most likely continue to play it for everything it is worth and then, in the interests of their own survival, will "discover" that something else indeed accounts for what they were trying to explain and will eventually move off there to find renewed fame and fortune. Furthermore, serious methodological doubts have been raised concerning the studies of the relationship between personality and at-risk behavior. See, in this regard, G. M. Hochbaum, "A Critique of Psychological Research

. . . excessive competitive drive, aggressiveness, impatience, and a harrying sense of time urgency. Individuals displaying this pattern seem to be engaged in a chronic, ceaseless, and often fruitless struggle with themselves, with others, with circumstances, with time, sometimes with life itself. They also frequently exhibit a free-floating, but well-rationalized form of hostility, and almost always a deep-seated insecurity.[32]

Efforts to change Type A traits appear to be based on some ideal conception of a relaxed, non-competitive, phlegmatic individual to which people are encouraged to conform. Again, one can question how realistic such a conception is in a system which daily rewards behavior resulting from Type A traits. One can clearly question the ascription of near exclusive culpability to those displaying Type A behavior when the context within which such behavior is manifest is structured in such a way as to guarantee its production. From a cursory reading of job advertisements in any newspaper, we can see that employers actively seek to recruit individuals manifesting Type A characteristics, extolling them as positive virtues.[33]

My earlier point concerning the potentially disruptive consequences of requiring alterations in life style applies equally well in this area of personality and disease. If health workers manage to effect some changes away from Type A behavior in a system which requires and rewards it, then we must be aware of the possible consequences of such change in terms of future failure. Even though the evidence linking Type A traits to heart disease appears quite conclusive, how can health workers ever hope to combat and alter it when such characteristics are so positively and regularly reinforced in this society?

The various points raised in this section have some important moral and practical implications for those involved in health related endeavors. *First*, I have argued that our prevailing ideology involves the ascription of culpability to particular individuals and groups for the manifestation of either disease or at-risk behavior. *Second*, it can be argued that so-called "health professionals" have acquired a mandate to determine the morality of different types of behavior and have access to a body of knowledge and resources which they can "legitimately" deploy for its removal or alteration. (A detailed discussion of the means by which this mandate has been acquired is expanded in a separate paper.)[34] *Third*, [it] is possible to argue that a great deal of health intervention is, perhaps unwittingly, part of a wide pattern of social regulation. We must be clear both as to whose interests we are serving, and the wider implications and consequences of the activities we support through the application of our expertise. *Finally*, it is evident

on Smoking," paper presented to the American Psychological Association, Los Angeles, 1964. Also, B. Lebovits and A. Ostfeld, "Smoking and Personality: A Methodologic Analysis," *Journal of Chronic Diseases* (1971).

[32]M. Friedman and R. H. Rosenman. See footnote 31.

[33]In the *New York Times* of Sunday, May 26, 1974, there were job advertisements seeking "aggressive self-starters," "people who stand real challenges," "those who like to compete," "career oriented specialists," "those with a spark of determination to someday run their own show," "people with the success drive," and "take charge individuals."

[34]Aspects of this process are discussed in J. B. McKinlay, "On the Professional Regulation of Change," in *The Professions and Social Change*, P. Halmos (Ed.), Keele: Sociological Review Monograph, No. 20, 1973, and in "Clients and Organizations," chapter in J. B. McKinlay (Ed.), *Processing People—Studies in Organizational Behavior*, London: Holt, Rinehart and Winston, 1974.

from the arguments I have presented that much of our health intervention fails to take adequate account of the social contexts which foster and reinforce the behaviors we seek to alter. The literature of preventive medicine is replete with illustrations of the failure of contextless health intervention programs.

The Notion of a Need Hierarchy

At this point in the discussion I shall digress slightly to consider the relationship between the utilization of preventive health services and the concept of need as manifest in this society. We know from available evidence that upper socioeconomic groups are generally more responsive to health intervention activities than are those of lower socio-economic status. To partially account for this phenomenon, I have found it useful to introduce the notion of a *need hierarchy*. By this I refer to the fact that some needs (e.g., food, clothing, shelter) are probably universally recognized as related to sheer survival and take precedence, while other needs, for particular social groups, may be perceived as less immediately important (e.g., dental care, exercise, balanced diet). In other words, I conceive of a *hierarchy of needs*, ranging from what could be termed "primary needs" (which relate more or less to the universally recognized immediate needs for survival) through to "secondary needs" (which are not always recognized as important and which may be artificially engineered by the manufacturers of illness). Somewhere between the high priority, primary needs and the less important, secondary needs are likely to fall the kinds of need invoked by preventive health workers. Where one is located at any point in time on the need hierarchy (i.e., which particular needs are engaging one's attention and resources) is largely a function of the shape of the existing social structure and aspects of socioeconomic status.

This notion of a hierarchy of needs enables us to distinguish between the health and illness behavior of the affluent and the poor. Much of the social life of the wealthy clearly concerns secondary needs, which are generally perceived as lower than most health related needs on the need hierarchy. If some pathology presents itself, or some at-risk behavior is recognized, then they naturally assume a priority position, which eclipses most other needs for action. In contrast, much of the social life of the poor centers on needs which are understandably regarded as being of greater priority than most health concerns on the need hierarchy (e.g., homelessness, unemployment). Should some illness event present itself, or should health workers alert people and groups in poverty to possible future health needs, then these needs inevitably assume a position of relative low priority and are eclipsed, perhaps indefinitely, by more pressing primary needs for sheer existence.

From such a perspective, I think it is possible to understand why so much of our health intervention fails in those very groups, at highest risk to morbidity, whom we hope to reach and influence. The appeals that we make in alerting them to possible future needs simply miss the mark by giving inadequate recognition to those primary needs which daily preoccupy their attention. Not only does the notion of a need hierarchy emphasize the difficulty of contextless intervention programs, but it also enables us to view the rejection as a non-compliance with health programs, as, in a sense, rational behavior.

How Preventive Is Prevention?

With regard to some of the arguments I have presented, concerning the ultimate futility of downstream endeavors, one may respond that effective preventive medicine does, in fact, take account of this problem. Indeed, many preventive health workers are openly skeptical of a predominantly curative perspective in health care. I have argued, however, that even our best preventive endeavors are misplaced in their almost total ascription of responsibility for illness to the afflicted individuals and groups, and through the types of programs which result. While useful in a limited way, the preventive orientation is itself largely a downstream endeavor through its preoccupation with the avoidance of at-risk behavior in the individual and with its general neglect of the activities of the manufacturers of illness which foster such behavior.

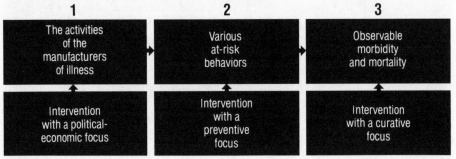

Figure 2-1.

Figure 2-1 is a crude diagrammatic representation of an overall process starting with (1) the activities of the manufacturers of illness, which (2) foster and habituate people to certain at-risk behaviors, which (3) ultimately result in the onset of certain types of morbidity and mortality. The predominant curative orientation in modern medicine deals almost exclusively with the observable patterns of morbidity and mortality, which are the *end points* in the process. The much heralded preventive orientation focuses on those behaviors which are known to be associated with particular illnesses and which can be viewed as the *midpoint* in the overall process. Still left largely untouched are the entrepreneurial activities of the manufacturers of illness, who, through largely unregulated activities, foster the at-risk behavior we aim to prevent. This *beginning point* in the process remains unaffected by most preventive endeavors, even though it is at this point that the greatest potential for change, and perhaps even ultimate victory, lies.

It is clear that this paper raises many questions and issues at a general level—more in fact than it is possible to resolve. Since most of the discussion has been at such an abstract level and concerned with broad political and economic forces, any ensuing recommendations for change must be broad enough to cover the various topics discussed. Hopefully, the preceding argument will also stimulate discussion toward additional recommendations and possible solutions. Given the scope and direction of this paper and the analogy I have employed to convey its content, the task becomes of the order of constructing fences upstream *and* restraining those who, in the interest of corporate profitability, continue to push people in. In this concluding section I will confine my remarks to three selected areas of recommendations.

Recommended Action

a. Legislative Intervention. It is probably true that one stroke of effective health legislation is equal to many separate health intervention endeavors and the cumulative efforts of innumerable health workers over long periods of time. In terms of winning the war which was described earlier, greater changes will result from the continued politicization of illness, than from the modification of specific individual behaviors. There are many opportunities for a legislative reduction of at-riskness, and we ought to seize them. Let me give one suggestion which relates to earlier points in this paper. Widespread public advertising is importantly related to the growth and survival of large corporations. If it were not so demonstrably effective, then such vast sums of money and resources would not be devoted to this activity. Moreover, as things stand at present, a great deal of advertising is encouraged through granting it tax exempt status on some vague grounds of public education.[35] To place more stringent, enforceable restrictions on advertising would be to severely curtail the morally abhorrent pushing in activities of the manufacturers of illness. It is true that large corporations are ingenious in their efforts to avoid the consequences of most of the current legislative restrictions on advertising which only prohibit certain kinds of appeals.

As a possible solution to this and in recognition of the moral culpability of those who are actively manufacturing disease, I conceive of a ratio of advertising to health tax or a ratio of risk to benefit tax (RRBT). The idea here is to, in some way, match advertising expenditures to health expenditures. The precise weighting of the ratio could be determined by independently ascertaining the severity of the health effects produced by the manufacture and distribution of the product by the corporation. For example, it is clear that smoking is injurious to health and has no redeeming benefit. Therefore, for this product, the ratio could be determined as say, 3 to 1, where, for example, a company which spends a non-tax deductible $1 million to advertise its cigarettes would be required to devote a non-tax deductible $3 million to the area of health. In the area of quasi-health activities, where the product, although largely useless, may not be so injurious (e.g.,

---

[35]There have been a number of reports recently concerning this activity. Questions have arisen about the conduct of major oil corporations during the so-called "energy crisis." See footnote 9. Equally questionable may be the public spirited advertisements sponsored by various professional organizations which, while claiming to be solely in the interests of the public, actually serve to enhance business in various ways. Furthermore, by granting special status to activities of professional groups, government agencies and large corporations may effectively gag them through some expectation of reciprocity. For example, most health groups, notably the American Cancer Society, did not support the F.C.C.'s action against smoking commercials because they were fearful of alienating the networks from whom they receive free announcements for their fund drives. Both the American Cancer Society and the American Heart Association have been criticized for their reluctance to engage in direct organizational conflict with pro-cigarette forces, particularly before the alliance between the television broadcasters and the tobacco industry broke down. Rather, they have directed their efforts to the downstream reform of the smoker. See E. Nuehring and G. E. Markle, footnote 29, page 19.

nasal sprays, pain killers, mineral supplements, etc.), the ratio could be on, say, a 1 to 1 basis.

Of course, the manufacturers of illness, at the present time, do "donate" large sums of money for the purpose of research, with an obvious understanding that their gift should be reciprocated. In a recent article, Nuehring and Markle touch on the nature of this reciprocity:

> One of the most ironic pro-cigarette forces has been the American Medical Association. This powerful health organization took a position in 1965 clearly favorable to the tobacco interests. . . . In addition, the A.M.A. was, until 1971, conspicuously absent from the membership of the National Interagency Council on Smoking and Health, a coalition of government agencies and virtually all the national health organizations, formed in 1964. The A.M.A.'s largely pro-tobacco behavior has been linked with the acceptance of large research subsidies from the tobacco industry—amounting, according to the industry, to some 18 million dollars.[36]

Given such reciprocity, it would be necessary for this health money from the RRBT to be handled by a supposedly independent government agency, like the FDA or the FTC, for distribution to regular research institutions as well as to consumer organizations in the health field, which are currently so unequally pitted against the upstream manufacturers of illness. Such legislation would, I believe, severely curtail corporate "pushing in" activity and publicly demonstrate our commitment to effectively regulating the source of many health problems.

b. The Question of Lobbying. Unfortunately, due to present arrangements, it is difficult to discern the nature and scope of health lobbying activities. If only we could locate a) who is lobbying for what, b) who they are lobbying with, c) what tactics are being employed, and d) with what consequences for health legislation. Because these activities are likely to jeopardize the myths that have been so carefully engineered and fed to a gullible public by both the manufacturers of illness *and* various health organizations, they are clothed in secrecy.[37] Judging from recent newspaper reports, concerning multimillion dollar gift-giving by the pharmaceutical industry to physicians, the occasional revelation of lobbying and political exchange remains largely unknown and highly newsworthy. It is frequently argued that lobbying on behalf of specific legislation is an essential avenue for public input in the process of enacting laws. Nevertheless, the evidence suggests that it is often, by being closely linked to the distribution of wealth, a very one-sided process. As it presently occurs, many legitimate interests on a range of health related issues do not have lobbying input in proportion to their numerical strength and may actually be structurally precluded from effective participation. While recognizing the importance of lobbying activity and yet feeling that for certain interests its scope ought to be severely curtailed (perhaps in the same way as the proposed regulation and publication of political campaign contributions), I am, to be honest, at a loss as to what should be specifically recommended. . . . The question is: quite apart from the specific issue of changing indi-

---

[36]E. Nuehring and G. E. Markle, footnote 29 above, page 19.

[37]The ways in which large-scale organizations engineer and disseminate these myths concerning their manifest activities, while avoiding any mention of their underlying latent activities, are discussed in more detail in the two references cited in footnote 34 above.

vidual behavior, *in what ways could we possibly regulate the disproportionately influential lobbying activities of certain interest groups in the health field?*

c. Public Education. In the past, it has been common to advocate the education of the public as a means of achieving an alteration in the behavior of groups at risk to illness. Such downstream educational efforts rest on "blaming the victim" assumptions and seek to *either* stop people doing what we feel they "ought not" to be doing, *or* encourage them to do things they "ought" to be doing, but are not. Seldom do we educate people (especially schoolchildren) about the activities of the manufacturers of illness and about how they are involved in many activities unrelated to their professed area of concern. How many of us know, for example, that for any 'average' Thanksgiving dinner, the turkey may be produced by the Greyhound Corporation, the Smithfield Ham by ITT, the lettuce by Dow Chemical, the potatoes by Boeing, the fruits and vegetables by Tenneco or the Bank of America?[38] I would reiterate that I am not opposed to the education of people who are at risk to illness, with a view to altering their behavior to enhance life chances (if this can be done successfully). However, I would add the proviso that if we remain committed to the education of people, we must ensure that they are being told the whole story. And, in my view, immediate priority ought to be given to the sensitization of vast numbers of people to the upstream activities of the manufacturers of illness, some of which have been outlined in this paper. Such a program, actively supported by the federal government (perhaps through revenue derived from the RRBT), may foster a groundswell of consumer interest which, in turn, may go some way toward checking the disproportionately influential lobbying of the large corporations and interest groups.

[38]For a popularly written and effective treatment of the relationship between giant corporations and food production and consumption, see W. Robbins, *The American Food Scandal*, New York: William Morrow and Co., 1974.

I

Society,
Illness,
and the
Use of
Health Services

The existence of disease, injury, and death is a universal fact of life in every human society; no society or its members are totally free from these morbid conditions. What is perhaps not so well known or recognized is the accumulating evidence that these events do not necessarily occur randomly nor by mere chance within human populations, groups, communities, and societies.

Social epidemiology is concerned with determining the patterns and uniformities of rates of illness (morbidity) and death (mortality) in specific segments of society and social structures that will lead to "causal" factors of such conditions. Rates of specific illnesses have been found to vary by certain social characteristics such as social class and socioeconomic status, ethnic and racial groups, types of families, social and cultural mobility, ecological factors like urban and rural residence, and so on.

Closely associated with epidemiologic variations in disease patterns are similar social variations in rates of utilization of health-care facilities and services. Indeed, too often these rates have been used to "measure" the former epidemiologic conditions, since rates of hospitalization, for example, are often the only quantitative data available. This use has occasionally led to false assumptions about "true" rates of incidence and prevalence of disease for many segments of society, since the amount of *treatment* or *care* for an illness may not truly measure the *actual* amount of *illness* or *morbidity* for the same social group or population.

Nevertheless, the epidemiology of morbidity and mortality is related to and involved with the epidemiology of health-care facilities and services treating and coping with such morbidity and are bound together in a complex of health-related behaviors. Both epidemiologies are important and legitimate concerns of behavioral science research and analysis, and they both provide an empirical basis upon which health-care programs, services, and systems are developed. To the extent the health-care delivery system meets and copes with the fundamental epidemiologic conditions of a society, that particular system is or is not functioning effectively in that society. That is, unless the health system of a society has an impact on the incidence and prevalence of morbidity of its members, that system is inadequately coping with disease and injury for that society, and is courting criticism and related discontent from the consumers and their representatives.

The articles in this section present the complex epidemiologic picture of morbidity in the United States and the differential societal meanings of illness that contribute to the differential frequency of illness among different sectors of society. A comprehensive survey of the broad spectrum of morbidity, including utilization of health facilities, is provided by the extensive report by Philip Cole, the first chapter in this section. These data offer an epidemiologic base for the studies that follow.

The results of an extensive survey of hospital use in a large American metropolitan area before the advent of Medicare and Medicaid is reported by Carol

Whitehurst and E. Gartly Jaco. Although the initial data suggest differential hospitalization rates were related to such variables as socioeconomic status, ethnicity, race, insurance coverage, and the like, most of these variances were accounted for by two other major variables—age and seriousness of the illness. This study also provides a baseline for comparative studies of the utilization of health services after the introduction of major American governmental health-care programs.

A very comprehensive analysis of the family as a basic health-care unit is provided in the next chapter by Theodor Litman. Dr. Litman documents the significance of the family in a wide array of health-related behaviors that affect the health of individuals, community, and society.

The final article of this section by Berton Kaplan, the late John Cassel, and Susan Gore analyzes social factors that promote health and prevent illness, supplementing the foregoing studies. Social support networks are presented in various ways which could prevent the onset of illness and also be integrated into health related programs.

3 Morbidity in the United States

Through the first third of the present century a population's mortality rate was accepted as a measure of its ill-health. Although this was appropriate then, since most serious illnesses resulted from fatal diseases of relatively short duration, mortality data alone do not provide a complete picture of disease. They do not, for example, reflect the ill-health resulting from many significant nonfatal conditions such as arthritis, mental illness, and impairment of limbs and sensory organs. Nor do they reflect fully a population's experience even with some fatal diseases of long average duration, such as the more indolent malignancies. Now, with increasing numbers of older persons in our population and the decrease in acute disease mortality, the limitations of mortality data are such that they must be supplemented with other measures of health.

The problems associated with efforts to gain a more inclusive picture of illness are apparent. Unlike death, the onset of illness usually is not obvious; also, while cause of death usually is ascertainable, the specific nature of illness often is not. A particular insufficiency is that whereas deaths must be reported to a central agency, most illnesses need not. Efforts to overcome these problems have included both ongoing and ad hoc morbidity studies. A review of the development of morbidity measurements is presented in MacMahon and Pugh's *Epidemiology: Principles and Methods*.[1] This chapter is concerned only with the more general aspects of morbidity in the United States. Many of the data presented are derived from reports of the National Center for Health Statistics and are subject to their limitations.[2, 3, 4] It is emphasized that these data refer to the civilian noninstitutional population only. . . .

Problems in Definition

"Morbidity" as a general term is applied to measures of both incidence and prevalence of disease. A major difficulty is encountered in attempting to define morbidity precisely, however, because the range of illness is so great. One extreme of this range is represented by clearly recognizable conditions that limit activity or lead to death. The other extreme is nebulous and is represented only by vague symptoms. Some persons may disregard such symptoms and not consider themselves ill; others, similarly or even less affected, may for a variety of motives

Reprinted from C. L. Erhardt and J. E. Berlin, eds., *Mortality and Morbidity in the United States*, Cambridge: Harvard University Press, 1974, Chap. 4, by permission of the author and Publisher.

exaggerate symptoms.[5] Nonetheless, some operable definition of morbidity, however arbitrary, must be adopted before any attempt at measurement can be made.

The National Health Interview Survey (NHIS), a continuous weekly series of interviews with members of households representative of the United States, has used the following concept:

> Morbidity is basically a departure from a state of physical or mental well-being, resulting from disease or injury, of which the individual affected is aware. Awareness connotes a degree of measurable impact on the individual or his family in terms of the restrictions and disabilities caused by the morbidity. Morbidity includes not only active or progressive disease but also impairments, that is, chronic or permanent defects that are static in nature, resulting from disease, injury, or congenital malformations.[6]

There are major difficulties in trying to measure morbidity with the above as the underlying concept. For example, morbid conditions are not necessarily permanent, or of constant severity. During remission, some conditions may not be regarded as illness by the person affected and therefore are not reported to the interviewer unless probing questions are asked. Even the most probing interviews, however, yield an underestimate of morbidity, since examination often reveals conditions of which the individual is unaware. Although the NHIS definition would exclude these discovered conditions, there are several arguments in favor of including them: the conditions do exist after all; and whether the affected person is aware of it or not, there may be an associated disability.

Difficulties in defining and assessing morbidity notwithstanding, the division of morbid conditions into chronic and acute categories has been especially useful. The value of this distinction derives from focusing attention on measures of prevalence with respect to chronic conditions, and measures of incidence with respect to acute conditions. Checklists of conditions and impairments were prepared especially for use in the health interviews. As employed in the Health Interview Survey,

> A condition is considered to be chronic if (1) it is described by the respondent in terms of one of the chronic diseases on the "Check List of Chronic Conditions" or in terms of one of the types of impairments on the "Check List of Impairments" . . . or (2) the condition is described by the respondent as having been first noticed more than 3 months before the week of the interview.

On the other hand, "An acute condition is defined as a condition which has lasted less than 3 months and which has involved either medical attention or restricted activity." Obstetric deliveries and diseases associated with pregnancy are included with the acute conditions.[6]

Important in assessing the impact of both chronic and acute conditions is the concept of disability. This has been defined in many different ways. In 1966, for a national study of disability in the noninstitutionalized civilian adult population, the Social Security Administration defined disability "as a limitation in the kind or amount of work (or housework) resulting from a chronic health condition or impairment lasting 3 or more months."[7] Although the definition was commensurate with the objectives of that particular study, the criteria of work limitation and extended duration to define disability are more specific and restrictive than those used by the National Health Interview Survey. Categories of disability used in the NHIS include and specify work-loss days, restricted-activity days, and bed-disability days as well as major activity limitation. The relatively unrestricted definition of the NHIS is, "Disability is a general term used to describe any temporary or long-term reduction of a person's activity as a result of illness or injury."[6]

Deficiencies of Data

No concept or definition of morbidity is completely satisfactory and it is necessary therefore to have some appreciation of the limitations of morbidity data. These deficiencies vary with the uses the data are to serve, the severity of the illnesses studied, the ease and precision of diagnosis, and the efforts made to collect data systematically.

The use to which the data are put determines the type and quality of data required. Morbidity data are usually gathered for etiologic research, surveillance for alterations in disease frequency, and administrative decision-making with respect to needs, costs, and quality of health care.

For etiologic investigations, incidence data are almost always required. Prevalence data are less acceptable for this purpose, since prevalence necessarily reflects those factors related to duration of illness and survival as well as to onset of illness. An etiologic study usually will require incidence data that are, furthermore, nearly complete for a designated period and a designated population. Finally, in such studies it is usually important to assess the amount of unavailable or missing information and the extent to which the data are unrepresentative.

Information collected for surveillance usually will relate also to incidence, especially for acute conditions. For chronic conditions, prevalence data are generally acceptable. More important than the type of data or its completeness, for purposes of surveillance, is the emphasis that must be placed on comparability and uniformity of ascertainment.

For administrative purposes, both prevalence and incidence data may be useful, although only crude estimates of needs result unless severity of impairment and average duration of illness can be estimated.

In general, the data from the National Center for Health Statistics are ascertained with a high degree of uniformity and completeness and thus are well suited for surveillance. When supplemented with information from ad hoc studies, the data probably also serve the needs of planners very well.

Acute Conditions

Variation by Age and Sex

The incidence rates of many acute conditions vary considerably from year to year because short-term epidemics are common. To provide a representative picture, therefore, Table 3-1 shows the average annual experience during the four years ending June 1968.

Table 3-1   Average annual incidence of acute conditions and associated disability reported in interviews per 100 persons by age and sex according to specified condition groups: United States, June 1965–June 1968
(civilian noninstitutional population)

Condition group	Male					Female				
	All ages	Under 6	6-16	17-44	45 & over	All ages	Under 6	6-16	17-44	45 & over
	Annual incidence per 100 persons									
All acute	194	359	244	158	118	208	341	244	204	136
Infective and parasitic	24	60	39	14	7	25	54	39	20	10
Respiratory	107	208	132	84	69	119	208	146	110	76
Upper respiratory	68	153	85	48	40	75	156	97	62	45
Influenza	35	43	43	32	26	39	42	46	44	27
Other	4	12	4	3	3	4	11	3	4	3
Digestive system	9	15	10	8	8	10	13	11	11	8
Injuries	34	39	40	38	21	23	29	23	22	21
Other acute	19	38	23	14	14	31	37	25	41	21
	Days of restricted activity per 100 persons per year									
All acute	722	970	814	597	682	851	910	802	827	892
Infective and parasitic	96	224	169	47	37	102	192	179	70	53
Respiratory	331	558	389	226	306	384	542	417	320	377
Upper respiratory	171	367	226	104	117	195	353	244	146	159
Influenza	125	128	140	101	140	154	134	151	146	175
Other	35	63	22	21	49	34	56	21	28	44
Digestive system	34	37	26	26	49	41	30	25	47	51
Injuries	189	53	162	251	198	153	54	98	139	245
Other	72	97	70	48	91	171	91	84	252	166
	Days of bed disability per 100 persons per year									
All acute	296	413	349	245	259	377	392	393	381	353
Infective and parasitic	47	93	83	28	17	52	84	91	40	27
Respiratory	160	245	201	122	132	189	229	232	165	171
Upper respiratory	71	134	103	53	39	82	122	120	65	60
Influenza	69	67	86	59	68	87	70	100	84	87
Other	19	44	11	10	25	20	36	12	15	24
Digestive system	17	17	14	13	24	19	9	12	23	24
Injuries	46	17	30	66	49	44	21	26	41	70
Other	27	40	21	16	38	72	49	33	112	62

Source: National Center for Health Statistics, Series 10, Tables 5, 6, and 7 of nos. 26, 38, 44, and 54, Washington, December 1965 to June 1969.
Note: Incidence excludes conditions involving neither restricted activity nor medical attention.

As age increases, the incidence rates of acute conditions decrease for both sexes and for all conditions. The phenomenon is very striking for some conditions, such as upper respiratory, and much less so for others, such as injuries. It is also of interest that the incidence rates for males and females are similar in the youngest age groups, but above age 16 rates are higher for women. The excess for women aged 17–44 persists even when the residual category of "other acute" conditions—which includes deliveries and diseases associated with pregnancy—is subtracted from the total. The higher incidence rates of acute diseases among women, like their higher prevalence rates of chronic conditions, are in contrast with their lower mortality from the same conditions.

Disability

Several concepts are used by the Health Interview Survey to estimate disability among persons with acute conditions. A day of "restricted activity" is one in which a person substantially reduces the amount of normal activity for that day because of a specific illness or injury. In addition to work, usual activity applies to school attendance or to any other activity usual for that day, such as recreation on a holiday. Further, any day in which more than half the daylight hours are spent in bed because of a specific illness or injury is considered a "bed-disability" day as well as a restricted-activity day. Finally, an "activity-restricting condition" is one that had caused at least one day of restricted activity during the two calendar weeks before the interview week.[6]

For the specified acute conditions, the pattern of restricted activity differs from the incidence pattern in that the low point is established earlier in life: at 17–44 years among males and at 6–16 years among females (Table 3-1). However, as with incidence, the rate of restricted activity is lower for females than for males at ages under 17, but is appreciably higher at older ages. Much of the excess restricted activity in the residual category among women aged 17–44 results from deliveries and diseases associated with pregnancy. However, substantial excess is evident for each acute condition with the exception of injuries. At age 45 and over, the average annual number of days of restricted activity per 100 women, 892, was about one-third higher than that per 100 men.

Females have a higher average annual number of bed-disability days beginning at age 6: below that age, the sexes are nearly equal. Even after the residual category is subtracted, the rate of bed-disability days for women aged 17–44 exceeds that of men by nearly 18 percent. The average annual rate of bed-disability days at ages 45 and over is more than one-third higher for women than for men.

Specific Conditions

Respiratory conditions, principally the common cold, accounted for somewhat more than one-half of all acute conditions reported during the four years ending June 1968 (Table 3-1). Incidence rates for this category decline sharply with advance in age and generally are higher for females than for males: in the 17–44 age group, the rate for women exceeds that for men by nearly one-third. The age-associated decline in the incidence rate of respiratory conditions results largely from the declining rates for upper respiratory conditions. The rates for influenza do not decline until later in life, and the rates for other respiratory conditions are low and stable beyond childhood. During the four-year period encompassed by the data, males were restricted in usual activity because of respiratory conditions at an average annual rate of 3.3 days per man, half of which were bed-disability days. The rate varied from a high of 5.6 days for boys under age 6, to a low of 2.3 days for men at ages 17–44; the range for females was from 5.4 days to 3.2 days for the same age groups.

The second most frequent category of acute conditions among men is injuries, accounting for about 18 percent of the total. The rate is high for the broad age range up to 45, then drops by about 50 percent to a rate of 21 per 100 at older ages. For females, the incidence rate for injuries is about 30 percent lower than the rate for males, with a high of 29 per 100 at ages under 6 and a gradual decline with advance in age. For men, an average of 1.9 days was lost annually from usual activity because of an injury, but the range among age groups was wide: the low of 0.5 day was at ages under 6, and the high of 2.5 days was at ages 17–44. Among females, an annual average of 1.5 days of restricted activity resulted from injuries; at ages under 6, the rate was the same as that for boys, then rose steadily to a peak of 2.5 days at ages 45 and over.

The incidence rate for infective and parasitic conditions is about the same for the two sexes, but this category ranks second for females and third for males. The rates for this cause decline sharply but uniformly for both sexes with advance in age. The associated days of restricted activity also decline sharply with advance in age from about two days annually at ages under 17, to an average of about one-half day at higher ages. Overall, about one-half of the restricted-activity days were bed-disability days.

Only 5 percent of acute conditions were attributed to conditions of the digestive system, among which dental conditions have a prominent role. The incidence rate is nearly identical for men and women, and both sexes show a similar trend of declining rates with advancing age. The pattern of days of restricted activity differed from that of the incidence rates in showing a sharp rise in both sexes for older men and for women in the 17–44, as well as in the 45 and over, age group. For most age-sex groups, bed-disability days accounted for about half the restricted-activity days.

Among the category of "other acute conditions" for females, about one-fifth were reported as genitourinary disorders and one-eighth as deliveries and disorders of pregnancy and the puerperium. Among males, over one-fourth of this residual category was reported as diseases of the ear, one-sixth as diseases of the skin, and about one-tenth as headaches. These conditions were also prominent among females.

Secular Trends

As is true for chronic conditions, trends for acute conditions as a whole for the United States are available only since July 1957 (Table 3–2). During fiscal year 1958, the first full year of record, the highest incidence rates for the period of the survey were observed in every age-sex group. Lowest rates were recorded in 1967 and 1968; this finding too is relatively constant over the age-sex groups. Although highest rates were seen in the earliest years for which data are available, there is no evidence of systematic trend in the incidence of acute conditions during the decade ending June 1969.

It is apparent from Table 3–3 that most fluctuation in the incidence rates of acute conditions is caused by outbreaks of respiratory disease, principally influenza. For most of the years, the rates for the other broad condition groups and even the residual category are quite stable.

This lack of trend in the incidence rate of acute conditions over a short term is quite different from that which would be seen if data were available for a substantially longer period. The high death rates early in this century from condi-

Table 3-2   Annual incidence of acute conditions reported in interviews per 100 persons by age and sex: United States, each fiscal year ending June 1958 to June 1969 (civilian noninstitutional population)

Sex; fiscal year ending June	Age						
	All ages	Under 5	5-14	15-24	25-44	45-64	65 & over
Male							
1969	202	333	274	206	173	137	94
1968	183	348	249	175	146	114	85
1967	185	350	251	172	146	121	93
1966	203	362	271	189	172	124	123
1965	203	394	274	179	146	134	124
1964	200	368	274	191	152	128	103
1963	204	371	269	183	163	135	117
1962	208	383	286	183	159	133	119
1961	194	374	259	169	146	124	112
1960	190	364	238	168	152	129	115
1959	205	372	295	164	159	136	105
1958	248	406	347	251	194	157	155
Female							
1969	211	320	273	239	206	142	106
1968	196	319	240	224	183	136	106
1967	195	330	237	217	183	128	111
1966	220	361	273	229	208	152	131
1965	222	370	275	230	200	157	139
1964	216	366	270	222	197	151	124
1963	233	366	267	236	222	182	151
1962	236	350	302	238	226	169	135
1961	210	372	252	207	195	143	124
1960	216	357	272	207	197	151	143
1959	224	333	296	230	207	149	158
1958	272	402	355	291	247	194	169

Source: National Center for Health Statistics, Series 10, Table 17 of nos. 15, 26, 38, 44, 54, and 69; no. 10, Table 20; no. 1, Table 25; Series B, no. 34, Table 1; no. 24, Table 3, and no. 29, Table 19; no. 18, Table 3; and no. 6, Table 8, Washington, December 1958 to June 1969.

Note: Excluded are conditions involving neither restricted activity nor medical attention.

tions such as typhoid fever, diphtheria, poliomyelitis, and others, attest that these now rare conditions once were common.

Relation to Family Income

Incidence rates of acute conditions have a complex relation to family income, one that changes with age. Incidence rates among the young are related directly to family income, but among the elderly the relationship is inverse (Fig. 3-1). However, for several condition groups the association with family income differs from the overall pattern. The most striking of these are conditions of the digestive system—age-adjusted incidence rates among persons with an annual family income of under $2,000 being twice as high as those among persons with a

Table 3-3 Annual incidence of acute conditions and associated disability reported in interviews per 100 persons according to specified condition groups: United States, each fiscal year ending June 1958 to June 1969
(civilian noninstitutional population)

Measure; fiscal year ending June	Condition group					
	Total	Infective and parasitic	Respiratory	Digestive	Injuries	All other
Incidence per 100 persons per year						
1969	207	23	122	10	24	28
1968	189	22	106	9	29	24
1967	190	24	104	9	28	25
1966	212	25	126	10	25	25
1965	213	28	116	11	30	28
1964	209	30	110	11	30	28
1963	219	24	127	11	28	28
1962	222	27	128	12	29	26
1961	202	28	110	13	28	23
1960	203	24	119	11	26	23
1959	215	26	126	12	29	22
1958	260	23	169	14	28	26
Days of bed-disability per 100 persons per year						
1969	419	47	250	21	47	55
1968	337	44	185	18	44	47
1967	297	45	147	16	45	44
1966	366	54	196	20	47	48
1965	349	55	170	18	45	61
1964	346	60	157	20	52	57
1963	380	54	206	20	43	57
1962	381	57	202	19	44	59
1961	332	61	150	19	47	55
1960	369	56	197	20	41	55
1959	360	53	190	17	49	51
1958	519	53	352	20	43	50

Source: National Center for Health Statistics, Series 10, Tables 5 and 7 of nos. 10, 15, 26, 38, 44, and 54; no. 1, Tables 9 and 11; no. 69, Tables 1 and 3; Series B, no. 34, Tables 4 and 6; no. 24, Tables 1 and 9, and no. 29, Table 19; no. 18, Tables 3 and 15; and no. 6, Tables 8 and 20, Washington, December 1958 to June 1969.
Note: Excluded are conditions involving neither restricted activity nor medical attention.

family income of over $7,000. Influenza also shows an inverse association with family income, while the category of "other respiratory conditions" shows no variation among family income groups.

It is quite difficult to separate the effects of the two major factors that contribute to the data: the real differences in disease experience, and the availability of and willingness to use medical services. The latter cannot be discounted. But it is true that the overall association of incidence rates with family income applies to acute conditions of varying degrees of severity. This suggests that real differences in disease experience are well reflected by Figure 3-1.[8]

Chronic Conditions

Variations by Age and Sex

In recent years, about 50 percent of the civilian noninstitutional population of the United States has been reported in the Health Interview Survey as having one or more chronic conditions (Table 3-4). Even at ages under 17, one or more chronic conditions were reported for nearly 25 percent of males and more than 20 percent of females. This is the only age group in which the prevalence rate for males exceeds that for females. The increased prevalence rate of chronic conditions with advance in age is striking. More than 50 percent of persons of both sexes in the 17–44 age group are afflicted, as are about 70 percent of persons aged 45–64, and about 85 percent of persons aged 65 and over.

Along with increasing prevalence rates of persons affected with a chronic condition, advancing age is accompanied by an increasing frequency of multiple

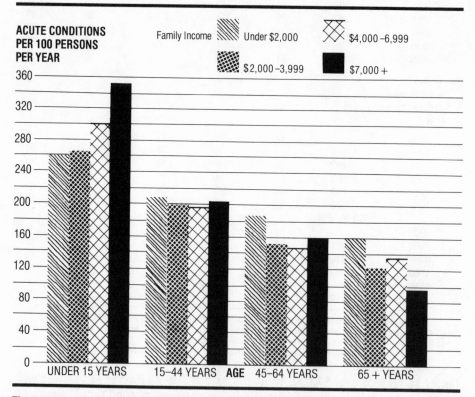

Figure 3-1. Incidence of acute conditions per 100 persons per year, by family income and age: United States, July 1962–June 1963 (excludes all conditions involving neither restricted activity nor medical attention) (Source: National Center for Health Statistics, Pub. Health Service Publ. 1000, Series 10, No. 9, Part VII, Fig. 1, May 1964).

Table 3-4 Percent of persons with one or more chronic conditions by activity limitation status and mobility limitation status reported in interviews, according to sex and age: United States, July 1965–June 1966 (civilian noninstitutional population)

Limitation	Male					Female				
	All ages	Under 17	17-44	45-64	65 & over	All ages	Under 17	17-44	45-64	65 & over
One or more chronic conditions	47.7	23.8	52.4	68.6	83.5	50.4	20.9	55.2	72.4	86.5
With limitation of activity[a]	11.7	1.9	7.8	20.1	51.2	10.8	1.8	6.9	17.7	40.3
Not in major activity	2.4	1.0	2.4	4.3	4.0	3.3	1.0	2.7	5.7	7.9
In amount or kind of major activity	6.3	0.7	4.5	11.4	26.4	6.3	0.7	3.8	10.8	24.6
Unable to carry on major activity	3.0	0.2	0.9	4.4	20.8	1.2	b	0.4	1.2	7.8
With limitation of mobility	3.0	0.4	1.3	5.1	17.2	3.3	0.3	1.1	4.3	19.3
Has trouble getting around alone	1.5	b	0.8	3.0	6.7	1.5	b	0.7	2.4	7.5
Needs help in getting around										
Special aid	0.7	b	0.3	1.0	5.1	0.6	b	0.2	0.5	4.1
Another person	0.2	b	b	b	1.3	0.4	b		0.4	2.5
Confined to the house										
Not confined to bed	0.4	b	0.2	0.6	2.7	0.6	b	0.2	0.7	4.0
Confined to bed	0.2	b		0.3	1.4	0.2	b	b	b	1.2

Source: National Center for Health Statistics, Series 10, no. 45, Tables 1 and 2, Washington, May 1968.
[a]Major activity refers to ability to work, keep house, or engage in school or preschool activities.
[b]Figure does not meet standards of reliability or precision.

chronic conditions. In the Health Interview Survey for July 1957 to June 1958, the prevalence rate of persons reporting three or more chronic conditions was less than 1 percent at ages under 15 years but was about 30 percent among persons 65 and older.[9]

Disability

Disability is assessed in terms of limitation of activity or of mobility. Although a larger proportion of females than males generally reported having one or more chronic conditions, a smaller proportion reported some limitation of activity. During the interval July 1965 to June 1966, 1.2 percent of females and 3.0 percent of males were reported to be disabled to the extent that they could not carry on their major activity; that is, gainfully employed persons were unable to work, housewives could not do housework, school-age children could not attend school, and preschool children were unable to play with others (Table 3–4). Overall, 6.3 percent of persons of both sexes were limited in some way with respect to the amount or kind of their major activity. The prevalence rate of persons limited in some way with respect to their major activity rises steadily with age, but the differences between the sexes are slight. However, the prevalence rate of persons unable to carry on their major activity is higher for men than for women in every age group. Of course, this may reflect the heavier work usually done by men rather than any real difference in the health of the two sexes.

Measures of mobility limitation are more amenable to valid interpretation than are measures of activity limitation. Differences in prevalence rates of mobility limitation are slight between the sexes, while differences among age groups are great. Indeed, the apparent slight excess mobility limitation of women over men may simply reflect the fact that within the oldest age group the average age of women, because of their longevity, is higher than that of men. The prevalence of mobility limitation to some extent parallels the prevalence patterns of activity limitation. During the year ending June 1966, almost 15 percent of persons with some limitation of activity, other than in their major activity, were also limited in mobility. This figure was 22 percent among persons with some limitation of their major activity, and 61 percent among persons unable to carry on their major activity.[10]

Specific Conditions

Turning from general measures of the impact of chronic diseases, such as activity limitation, to estimates of relatively specific conditions, some striking differences exist between the illness experiences of the two sexes as well as among the different age groups.

For persons under age 45, by far the most prevalent specific condition is orthopedic impairment, excluding paralysis and absence of parts (Table 3–5). However, the rate for males, nearly 80 per 1,000, is greater than that for females, 57 per 1,000. For both sexes, about 17 percent of those afflicted have some limitation of activity. In the under-45 age group, both sexes have the same second-ranking condition, digestive conditions, which limited activity of about 10 percent of afflicted persons. The third-ranking condition for females in this age group is arthritis and rheumatism with a prevalence rate of 21 percent, about double the rate for males. However, the proportion of afflicted women with activity limitation is less than the comparable figure for men. It is unknown whether this disparity is a result of (a) women actually having a higher prevalence of milder disease, (b) the fact that most interviews are conducted with women, who generally act as proxies for their spouses, (c) the reluctance of men to report less severe conditions, or (d) some combination of these factors.

Among men under age 45, the third-ranking condition is hearing impairments; however, this condition apparently limited the activity of only about 6 percent of afflicted persons. About 10 percent of persons in this age group reported visual impairments—conditions that limited the activity of 17 percent of afflicted men, but only 10 percent of afflicted women. Finally, among men in this youngest age group, diseases of the cardiovascular system have a prevalence rate of 16 percent, as compared with a figure of about 22 percent for women. In both sexes, about 40 percent of those reporting a heart condition and 10 percent of those reporting high blood pressure also reported some associated activity limitation.

During the middle years, 45–64, orthopedic impairments and digestive conditions continue to rank first and second among men, while third rank is taken by arthritis and rheumatism. For women, the picture is markedly different: the arthritis and rheumatism category assumes first rank, orthopedic impairments are second, while high blood pressure and digestive conditions rank third and fourth. In moving from the younger to these middle years, particularly striking increases in prevalence rates (about ten-fold) are seen among both sexes for arthritis and rheumatism and for cardiovascular conditions. For other conditions, increases were only two- to five-fold. Not only do the prevalence rates of the chronic conditions increase markedly with age, but the proportion of afflicted persons who suffer activity limitation is also increased. This is true for all conditions with the exception of hearing impairments.

At ages 65 and over, as at younger ages, the prevalence rates of high blood pressure and arthritis and rheumatism are far greater among women than among men. Orthopedic and visual impairments are also more frequent among elderly women than among elderly men. In this age group, 25 percent of men and nearly 40 percent of women are afflicted with arthritis and rheumatism. The prevalence rate of high blood pressure is more than twice as high among women (22 percent) as among men (9 percent). However, heart conditions have nearly equal prevalence rates, about 17 percent, in both sexes.

A review of the prevalence rates of chronic conditions does not adequately convey the impact of these diseases among the elderly, especially elderly men. Compared with younger persons afflicted with a chronic condition, the proportion of elderly persons with some activity limitation was increased for every condition in both sexes, except for heart conditions among women. In general, the prevalence rates of persons having some activity limitation as a result of one of the specified conditions are three to four times as high among the elderly as among those in the middle age range. For example, among men the prevalence rate for limitation of activity resulting from vascular lesions of the central nervous system soared from 5 per 1,000 (66.0 percent of a rate of 8.0 per 1,000) at ages 45–64 to 30 per 1,000 (71.3 percent of a rate of 40.0 per 1,000) at ages 65 and over.

Table 3-5 Prevalence rates per 1,000 population for selected chronic conditions reported in interviews and percent causing activity limitation by age and sex: United States, July 1963–June 1965 (civilian noninstitutional population)

Sex; condition	Rate per 1,000 population			Percent causing activity limitation		
	Under 45 years	45-64 years	65 years and over	Under 45 years	45-64 years	65 years and over
Male						
Heart conditions	6.9	67.3	168.7	40.6	62.4	70.1
High blood pressure	9.1	57.2	94.4	9.0	13.0	29.9
Arthritis and rheumatism	10.2	113.4	251.6	20.2	23.0	33.7
Digestive conditions	38.5	136.0	223.3	9.3	18.9	22.7
Vascular lesions of central nervous system	a	8.0	40.0	a	66.0	71.3
Visual impairments	11.1	38.9	127.1	16.9	24.6	32.7
Hearing impairments	19.0	87.1	259.0	5.2	4.3	6.2
Orthopedic impairments (excluding paralysis or absence)	79.6	163.4	173.7	16.8	26.8	35.3
Female						
Heart conditions	7.8	53.5	171.1	38.7	58.5	58.5
High blood pressure	13.9	118.8	219.2	10.5	16.3	23.2
Arthritis and rheumatism	21.0	205.8	388.5	15.6	21.2	31.0
Digestive conditions	29.7	115.1	198.1	11.1	17.4	19.1
Vascular lesions of central nervous system	.5	6.8	33.0	a	63.9	69.6
Visual impairments	10.0	40.2	160.3	10.2	16.0	31.2
Hearing impairments	13.9	55.1	182.7	6.8	4.3	5.6
Orthopedic impairments (excluding paralysis or absence)	57.0	130.7	196.5	17.6	25.2	32.7

Source: National Center for Health Statistics, Series 10, no. 32, Tables 21 and 26, Washington, June 1966.
aFigure does not meet standards of reliability or precision.

Secular Trends

Information on trends in the prevalence rates of chronic conditions in the United States is available for the period since the start of the Health Interview Survey in July 1957 (Table 3–6). The most notable feature of the data is the consistent rise, after the first year of the survey, in the prevalence rate of persons of both sexes reporting one or more chronic conditions. Indeed, this consistent rise is seen within each age group. Overall, during the decade spanned by the data, the rate increased among men from 39 to 49 percent, among women more slowly from 44 to 51 percent.

The trends shown in Table 3–6 may have several explanations apart from a genuine rise in the prevalence rates of chronic conditions. As experience with the survey was gained, it is likely that the quality of reporting improved. Apparent increase may have resulted from changes in interviewing technique, in the checklists used to ascertain chronic conditions, and in the rules for coding medical terms. Notable increases resulted from a change in the method of data elicitation in 1966 and 1967. Since 1957, diagnostic techniques have advanced and screening procedures have become widespread so that the average duration of some conditions, and hence their prevalence rates, have increased. Increased survival as a result of improved treatment methods may also have increased the prevalence rate of persons afflicted with chronic conditions. Finally, it must be remembered that the age groups used to display the data are broad, and during the ten-year period there have been changes in the age structure of the population within these groups. For example, in 1960, among men aged 65 and over, only 31.8 percent were 75 or older. However, by 1970, the proportion had risen to 35.4 percent.

Available data do not permit evaluation of the relative importance of the factors that could explain the apparent rise in the prevalence rates of chronic conditions. It may be, however, that most of the rise after 1965 is artifactual. Much of it may have resulted from increased reporting of less serious conditions. Thus, while the proportion of the population with some activity limitation did rise gradually, the proportion of the population unable to carry on major activity because of a chronic condition increased only from 2.1 to 2.3 percent during the ten-year period from July 1957 to June 1966.[10]

The effects of procedural changes in data elicitation on the reported prevalence rates of chronic conditions are shown in Table 3–7. The rates for three successive two-year periods show substantial increases in reported frequencies of high blood pressure and arthritis and rheumatism. Most of the increases resulted from the use of more searching probe-questions to uncover the presence of these conditions. Other conditions show slight and inconsistent changes.

Finally, since these data relate to noninstitutional persons, the rates for most conditions, especially among the aged, underestimate the prevalence of ill-health in our population. . . .

Relation to Family Income

As with acute conditions, the frequency of chronic conditions has a complex relation to family income. Table 3–8 shows the overall inverse relation of the prevalence rate of chronic conditions to family income. The pattern for chronic

Table 3-6   Percent of persons with one or more chronic conditions reported in interviews: United States, each fiscal year ending June 1958 to June 1967

(civilian noninstitutional population)

Fiscal year ending June	Male						Female					
	All ages	Under 17	17-24	25-44	45-64	65 & over	All ages	Under 17	17-24	25-44	45-64	65 & over
1967	48.7	24.6	44.4	57.1	70.4	85.2	51.0	21.8	44.8	61.1	72.6	86.6
1966	47.7	23.8	42.3	57.3	68.6	83.5	50.4	20.9	43.9	60.9	72.4	86.5
1965	44.6	22.7	37.6	52.2	64.0	81.9	48.0	20.0	41.1	58.0	68.2	84.6
1964	43.5	22.0	37.0	50.0	63.2	80.2	46.9	19.2	40.3	56.0	67.5	83.9
1963	43.2	21.6	35.9	50.1	62.6	79.9	45.7	18.6	39.2	54.6	65.9	82.2
1962	41.9	21.1	43.9		61.9	79.0	45.4	18.2	49.7		65.7	82.4
1961	41.2	—	—	—	—	—	44.0	—	—	—	—	—
1960	39.9	—	—	—	—	—	42.3	—	—	—	—	—
1959	38.9	—	—	—	—	—	42.0	—	—	—	—	—
1958	39.1	18.8a	39.0b		57.6	75.2	43.5	16.0a	45.3b		63.3	80.6

Source: National Center for Health Statistics, Series B, no. 11 (Table 10); Series B, no. 36 (Table 10); Series 10, no. 5 (Table 8), no. 13 (Table 8), no. 25 (Table 9), no. 37 (Table 9), no. 43 (Table 9); and unpublished data. Data for July 1961–June 1962 estimated from Series 10, no. 17 (Table 1) and no. 5 (Table 8), using population from no. 4 (Tables 18 and 22).
a Ages under 15.
b Ages 15-44.

Table 3-7   Prevalence rates per 1,000 population for selected chronic conditions reported in interviews by age: United States, fiscal years ending June 1962 to June 1967

(civilian noninstitutional population)

	Fiscal year ending June					
Condition	All ages			Ages under 45		
	1962-63	1964-65	1966-67	1962-63	1964-65	1966-67
Heart conditions	32.3	33.0	39.8	8.6	7.4	11.2
High blood pressure	35.9	41.2	60.6b	9.8	11.5	21.0b
Arthritis and rheumatism	69.6	73.8	86.2b	15.2	15.7	19.2b
Digestive conditions	65.7	68.5	67.6	34.0	34.0	34.1
Vascular lesions of central nervous system	4.7	5.1	7.6	a	0.4	0.6
Visual impairments	26.1	28.8	29.7	9.3	10.5	11.3
Hearing impairments	42.2	45.7	45.3	15.4	16.4	17.0
Orthopedic impairments (excluding paralysis or absence)	84.7	94.8	100.6	59.6	68.1	72.8
	Ages 45-64			Ages 65 and over		
	1962-63	1964-65	1966-67	1962-63	1964-65	1966-67
Heart conditions	58.9	60.1	71.8	158.6	170.0	186.9
High blood pressure	77.3	89.1	128.5b	147.8	164.1	213.2b
Arthritis and rheumatism	154.7	161.2	192.2b	304.4	328.1	362.8b
Digestive conditions	120.0	125.2	121.8	191.2	209.3	203.4
Vasuclar lesions of central nervous system	7.1	7.4	11.7	33.5	36.1	51.5
Visual impairments	35.3	39.6	39.3	136.6	145.6	148.6
Hearing impairments	63.8	70.5	69.4	203.4	216.3	208.0
Orthopedic impairments (excluding paralysis or absence)	133.9	146.4	158.6	170.5	186.4	185.2

Source: National Center for Health Statistics, unpublished data.
[a] Figure does not meet standards of reliability or precision.
[b] Increase in prevalence primarily due to revised probe questions.

Table 3-8 Percent of the population with one or more chronic conditions, by family income and age: United States, July 1962–June 1963

Age	All incomes[a]	Under $2,000	$2,000-3,999	$4,000-6,999	$7,000 and over
			Family income		
All ages	44.5	57.6	46.5	40.6	42.9
Under 15	19.5	19.2	19.4	18.8	20.8
15-44	46.0	48.3	45.3	46.2	46.6
45-64	64.3	76.8	68.3	62.3	61.1
65 and over	81.2	86.4	81.4	77.2	76.2

Source: National Center for Health Statistics, Series 10, Table 1 in Part VI of no. 9, Washington, May 1964.
[a]Includes persons with unknown incomes.

conditions differs from acute conditions in that it changes relatively little with age. There is only one suggestion of a direct relation between prevalence rates and family income—in the under-15 age group—but it is neither strong nor consistent. Figure 3–2 gives considerable insight into the cause of the inverse association that generally prevails. Whereas the association is strong and consistent for severe conditions (with activity limitation), it is weak and actually reversed for milder conditions. This provides some evidence that the chronic illnesses are themselves responsible for the inverse relation of prevalence rates to family income. Presumably, activity-limiting conditions also limit the affected individual's income-earning capacity.

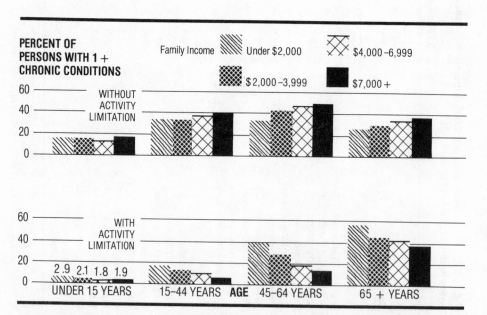

Figure 3-2. Percentage of persons with one or more chronic conditions, with and without activity limitation, by age and family income: United States, July 1962–June 1963 (Source: National Center for Health Statistics, Pub. Health Service Publ. 1000, Series 10, No. 9, Part VI, Fig. 2, May 1964).

Utilization of Medical Care

The data presented thus far are drawn primarily from a continuous survey of the population with the major disadvantages that responses are dependent on memory and that interpretations of interview questions are subjective. To some extent these deficiencies may be overcome by employing other indexes of morbidity, such as rates of physician visits and of utilization of hospitals. Rates of hospital utilitzation have the advantage of objectively documenting an episode of ill-health, with the duration of hospitalization as an indicator of its severity. However, major difficulties with such data include the changing indications for hospitalization with time, and the different use of hospitals by various subgroups of the population.

Available data on hospital utilization come from the Hospital Discharge Survey, a continuing nationwide survey conducted by the National Center for Health Statistics. Estimates are based on information transcribed from the medical records of a sample of noninstitutional, short-stay general and special hospitals in the United States. Excluded from these are military and Veterans Administration hospitals and discharges of well newborn infants.

Hospital Discharge Rate

Table 3-9 shows the annual rate of hospital discharges according to age and sex for the United States in 1967. The rate for females, 171.0 per 1,000, is about 40 percent higher than that for males at 120.1. However, if discharges following obstetric deliveries are excluded, the rate for females becomes 135.5, or only about 13 percent higher than the male rate. It is apparent, however, that even excluding deliveries, women are more frequently hospitalized than men during the ages 15-44. The rates for females during this middle period are generally about 18 percent higher than those for men. Yet both from the time of birth through age 14 and from age 65 on, women exhibit lower hospitalization rates than men. Since men have higher mortality rates than women (and higher incidence rates as well, for those conditions on which such data are available), it is unclear why hospitalization rates for men would be lower than those for women at any age.

It is apparent that hospitalization rates, in addition to varying with sex, rise sharply with advancing age: the *rate of rise* also increases with advance in age. An exception to this is women aged 55-64 who show a rate no higher than women aged 45-54. Although not evident from the table, about 45 percent of discharges under age 1 for both sexes are ill newborn.[11]

Length of Stay

For both sexes, as with the discharge rate, there is a steady increase in length of hospital stay with advancing age (Table 3-10). In comparison of the sexes the only discrepancy appears for the age group 15-44 in which the average length of stay for men, 7.3 days, is about 12 percent higher than the average for women. This is of interest in that, within the same age group, the hospital discharge rate for women was appreciably higher than that for men. In fact, the annual rate of days of care in this age group reflects the combined effects of these two measures; for women aged 15-44 the annual rate of days of care was 879.1 per 1,000 (excluding deliveries) compared to 675.8 for men, an excess of 30 percent.[11]

Table 3-9   Number and annual rate of discharges from short-stay hospitals per 1,000 population by age and sex: United States, 1967

Age	Both sexes			Male		Female		
	Numbers	Rates		Numbers	Rates	Numbers	Rates	
		Including deliveries	Excluding deliveries				Including deliveries	Excluding deliveries
All ages	28,417	146.9	128.5	11,202	120.1	17,140	171.0	135.5
Under 15	4,474	74.8	74.6	2,497	82.1	1,960	66.7	66.4
Under 1	1,015	287.4		571	316.7	439	254.0	66.4
1-4	1,185	75.9		670	84.0	512	66.9	
5-14	2,274	56.0		1,257	60.9	1,009	50.5	
15-44	12,279	161.6	114.9	3,323	92.2	8,934	223.6	134.8
15-24	4,846	158.9		1,157	81.1	3,681	227.0	
25-34	4,011	181.3		953	90.2	3,052	263.8	
35-44	3,423	146.3		1,213	108.2	2,202	180.9	
45-64	6,386	161.1	160.9	2,998	158.1	3,370	163.0	162.7
45-54	3,328	149.2		1,452	135.3	1,869	161.5	
55-64	3,057	176.3		1,546	187.8	1,501	164.8	
65 and over	5,215	289.1	289.1	2,352	300.7	2,846	278.5	278.5
65-74	2,818	246.6		1,332	262.1	1,478	232.9	
75 and over	2,397	362.4		1,020	372.0	1,368	353.4	
Not stated	62	—		31	—	30	—	

Source: National Center for Health Statistics, Series 13, Tables 1, 3 and 4 of no. 9, Washington, May 1962.
Note: Figures for both sexes include those for whom sex was not stated. Detailed figures do not always add to totals and sub-totals in original publication.

Physician Visits

The number of physician visits per person per year, according to age and sex, is shown in Table 3-11. Overall, there is a steady rise in physician visits with advancing age. This trend is less spectacular but more consistent among males. As compared to females of the same age, males under 17 have a higher frequency of physician visits, but this is completely and strikingly reversed in the next age group. In all age groups over 17, women have a higher frequency of visits than men. The pattern for adult women is somewhat unexpected in showing no trend from the 17-44 to the 45-64 age groups. Since women in the 17-44 age group have about one visit per woman per year for antepartum and postpartum care, the figure given in Table 3-11 for this age group should be reduced to 4.1 for purposes of comparison with the figure for men.[8] Even so, women in this age group would have about 30 percent more visits than men. This discrepancy between the sexes declines steadily with advancing age. Thus, in the 65 and over age group, although women do have a higher frequency of physician visits than men, the number is only about 20 percent higher. The higher figure for women is in compliance with their higher reported frequency of both chronic and acute conditions. However, the possibility that these visits are for relatively minor conditions is suggested by the facts that hospital discharge rates for men and women are more similar and, as is well known, mortality rates for women are lower (at given ages) than those for men.

Relation to Family Income

As was apparent from interview data, family income is related to both the incidence rate of acute conditions and the prevalence rate of chronic conditions. It would thus seem likely to be associated with utilization of medical care. Table 3-12 shows the association of family income with several measures of use of medical care. As might be anticipated, the relationships are complex, especially in the variation among age groups.

Overall, there is an inverse association of discharge rate with family income, rates for the lowest income group being about 75 percent greater than for the highest. However, while the same general pattern is seen in all age groups up to

Table 3-10   Average length of hospital stay in days by age and sex: United States, 1967

Age	Both sexes	Male	Female Including deliveries	Female Excluding deliveries
All ages	8.4	9.0	8.1	9.0
Under 15	5.5	5.5	5.5	5.5
15-44	6.2	7.3	5.8	6.5
45-64	10.1	10.2	10.1	10.1
65 and over	14.1	13.5	14.7	14.7

Source: National Center for Health Statistics, Series 13, Table 10 of no. 9, Washington, May 1972.

Table 3-11   Number of physician visits per person per year by age and sex: United States, 1969

Sex	All ages	Under 17	17-44	45-64	65 & over
Both sexes	4.3	3.6	4.2	4.7	6.1
Male	3.7	3.7	3.1	4.1	5.5
Female	4.7	3.4	5.1	5.2	6.6

Source: National Center for Health Statistics, Series 10, Table 9 of no. 70, Washington, April 1972.

age 75, the trend is strongest for an intermediate group aged 17–44. The trend is moderately strong in the under-17 age group and the 45–64 group, but barely perceptible at ages 65–74, and is reversed for persons aged 75 and over. Data on length of stay tend to be similar to those on discharges and thus to reinforce the overall trend of less hospital use with increasing family income. However, among persons aged 65 and over—the major consumers of hospital services—no strong associations of length of stay with income are apparent.

The data on physician visits show relatively consistent associations with family income over age groups. In the youngest age group, under 17, there is a consistent positive association. For young adults, 17–44, the association is positive but weak. For persons aged 45–64, the association is once again distinct and in the oldest age group, 65 and over, the association with family income is yet stronger.[12] . . . .

Discussion

Most of the information on morbidity currently available in the United States is provided by continuous health interview surveys of the population and is expressed in terms of the incidence rates of acute conditions and the prevalence rates of chronic conditions. The most notable feature of acute conditions, in addition to appreciable fluctuations in incidence rates over time, is the inverse association of incidence rate with age. In general, women have higher incidence rates than men and sustain more resultant disability. Major differences in incidence rates appear between persons with different family incomes; these are especially marked for the digestive conditions, which are nearly twice as frequent among persons with low family income (under $2,000) as among those with higher income (over $7,000).

The chronic conditions also show a striking association with age, but unlike acute conditions the association here is direct. Again, chronic conditions are more frequent among women than among men, but the associated disability is similar for both sexes. There is a strong inverse association of the prevalence of chronic conditions and family income. However, the data suggest that low income levels are themselves an effect, rather than a cause, of chronic conditions.

In addition to these interview data, morbidity can be assessed through information on utilization of medical care. Data on hospital discharge rates, length of hospital stay, and physician visits have been presented, and the patterns that emerge largely corroborate those based on interview data. . . .

Table 3-12 Discharges from short-stay hospitals per 1,000 population, average length of hospital stay for discharges, and percent of population with one or more physician visits within a year, by age and family income: United States, 1968-69

Age and family income	Discharges per 1,000 population	Average length of stay	Physician visits per 100 population
All ages			
All incomes[a]	125.6	9.1	69.4
Under $3,000	174.4	12.3	66.2
$3,000-$3,999	151.1	11.1	65.9
$4,000-$6,999	133.5	8.7	68.0
$7,000-$9,999	116.5	7.7	69.5
$10,000-$14,999	106.9	7.3	71.8
$15,000 and over	101.2	8.0	74.5
Under 17 years			
All incomes	62.6	5.6	68.5
Under $3,000	79.8	7.5	56.8
$3,000-$3,999	74.3	6.6	59.4
$4,000-$6,999	64.7	5.6	65.2
$7,000-$9,999	61.3	5.1	69.3
$10,000-$14,999	58.9	4.8	72.7
$15,000 and over	49.7	6.1	77.2
17-44 years			
All incomes	147.4	6.8	70.9
Under $3,000	175.5	7.5	71.3
$3,000-$3,999	194.3	8.5	70.0
$4,000-$6,999	173.1	6.7	70.3
$7,000-$9,999	146.3	6.5	70.5
$10,000-$14,999	127.4	6.2	72.1
$15,000 and over	108.8	5.9	73.7
45-64 years			
All incomes	143.1	11.3	67.4
Under $3,000	189.6	14.4	65.7
$3,000-$3,999	133.6	14.2	64.8
$4,000-$6,999	149.7	11.1	66.3
$7,000-$9,999	140.5	10.1	67.2
$10,000-$14,999	137.2	9.8	69.0
$15,000 and over	127.0	9.5	71.9
65-74 years[b]			
All incomes	209.2	14.5	71.3
Under $3,000	225.4	14.0	69.1
$3,000-$3,999	205.9	13.8	70.9
$4,000-$6,999	195.4	15.1	73.6
$7,000-$9,999	222.9	16.3	72.7
$10,000-$14,999	214.0	11.0	75.4
$15,000 and over	209.6	13.3	78.7
75 years and over			
All incomes	271.7	16.4	
Under $3,000	247.5	17.2	
$3,000-$3,999	282.5	16.2	
$4,000-$6,999	262.7	16.0	
$7,000-$9,999	337.3	14.1	
$10,000-$14,999	242.1	17.4	
$15,000 and over	406.6	15.3	

Source: National Center for Health Statistics, Series 10, Tables 3 and 15 of no. 70, Washington, April 1972.

[a]Includes unknown income.

[b]Data for "physician visits" apply to ages 65 and over.

. . . [The] general impression of lower disease frequencies among persons with higher levels of education and income suggests that the health inequities that exist in the United States can be diminished further by increases in the over-all standard of living, especially through education.

References

1. B. MacMahon and T. F. Pugh, *Epidemiology: Principles and Methods* (Boston: Little, Brown and Co., 1970), p. 66.

2. E. Balamuth, *Health Interview Responses Compared with Medical Records*, Pub. Health Service Publ. No. 1000, Series 2, No. 7 (National Center for Health Statistics: July 1965).

3. W. G. Madow, *Interview Data on Chronic Conditions Compared with Information Derived from Medical Records*, Pub. Health Service Publ. No. 1000, Series 2, No. 23 (National Center for Health Statistics: May 1967).

4. C. F. Cannell, F. J. Fowler and K. H. Marquis, *The Influence of Interviewer and Respondent: Psychological and Behavioral Variables on the Reporting in Household Interviews*, Pub. Health Service Publ. No. 1000, Series 2, No. 26 (National Center for Health Statistics: March 1968).

5. T. Parsons, "Definitions of Health and Illness in the Light of American Values and Social Structure," in E. G. Jaco, ed., *Patients, Physicians, and Illness* (Glencoe, Ill.: The Free Press, 1958), pp. 165–187. [See Chapter 7 in this edition.]

6. National Center for Health Statistics, *Health Survey Procedure: Concepts, Questionnaire Development, and Definitions in the Health Interview Survey*, Pub. Health Service Publ. No. 1000, Series 1, No. 2 (May 1964), pp. 4, 42, and 45.

7. L. D. Haber, "Identifying the Disabled: Concepts and Methods in the Measurement of Disability," *Soc. Sec. Bull.* 30:17–34 (Dec. 1967), p. 22.

8. P. S. Lawrence et al., *Medical Care, Health Status, and Family Income*, Pub. Health Service Publ. No. 1000, Series 10, No. 9 (May 1964), Sec. IV, Table 4.

9. G. A. Gleeson, *Limitation of Activity and Mobility Due to Chronic Conditions, United States, July 1957-June 1958*, Pub. Health Service Publ. No. 584, Series B., No. 11 (Public Health Service: July 1959), Table A.

10. C. S. Wilder, *Limitation of Activity and Mobility Due to Chronic Conditions, United States, July 1965-June 1966*, Pub. Health Service Publ. No. 1000, Series 10, No. 45 (National Center for Health Statistics: May 1968), Tables A and B.

11. A. L. Ranofsky, *Utilization of Short-Stay Hospitals, Summary of Nonmedical Statistics, United States-1967*, Vital and Health Statistics, Series 13, No. 9 (National Center for Health Statistics: May 1972), Tables 7, 9, and Appendix Table II.

12. C. Namey and R. W. Wilson, *Age Patterns in Medical Care, Illness, and Disability, United States, 1968-1969*, Vital and Health Statistics, Series 10, No. 70 (National Center for Health Statistics: April 1972).

CAROL A. WHITEHURST and E. GARTLY JACO

4 Hospital Utilization Before Medicare-Medicaid: A Baseline Study

The conventional view is that people go to hospitals because they are diseased or otherwise are objectively in need of hospital services; it is suggested here, however, that other factors may also help explain hospital use. One way to view it is as a coping process or response to one's environment and life situation, in which people perceive, evaluate, and act upon signs and symptoms as a way of dealing with the social environment (Mechanic, 1968). The response is not necessarily "rational" (in the sense of being objectively the most efficient way of combatting the physical disease) but may involve a-rationalities such as the weighing of other, nonmedical factors (economic, social, and psychological). Illness behavior refers to the activities undertaken to discover a remedy or define the state of health when a person feels ill, and its stages are dependent on factors in the social environment as well as on those of the disease. It may be a coping response to situational difficulties, a culturally and socially learned response, an attempt to seek secondary advantages, or some combination of these (Mechanic, 1966). Hospital use represents one sort of illness behavior, although perhaps a type in which the patient has less discretion over it. Thus, perceptions of disease, evaluations of it as a problem, and subsequent health- or illness-related actions are differentially distributed in the population, and these responses will have some influence on the individual's decision to use or not to use hospital services.

The approach taken here is that the decision of the potential user of hospital services is influenced by his position in the social structure, and it is seen as a process of dealing with a complex array of nonmedical factors, or "contingencies" (Goffman, 1968). For present purposes, these contingencies involve five categories: (1) recognition of need for care (influenced by past experience, impact of symptoms on one's life, ability to tolerate illness, sensitivity to pain or other signs and symptoms); (2) competing needs and motives (economic cost, loss of work); (3) health values, attitudes, and knowledge (meaning of illness and dependency, receptivity to modern medical care, psychological resistance to hospitalization, degree of sophistication about health care); (4) obstacles and alternatives (lack of resources, including insurance; psychological obstacles because of fear of discrimination or poor treatment; alternatives to hospitalization such as family care); and (5) availability of help (beds, personnel, and facilities available). This "contingency model" represents one possible approach among several to the study of hospitalization—the sociodemographic approach (McKinlay, 1972).

This study was made possible by DHEW grant HM 00296-01 and several intramural grants from the University of California at Riverside.

Design, Method, and Sample

The term "hospital utilization" is used here to designate the use of acute, short-term hospitals for in-patient curative care, and the analysis is confined to urban hospitals. Extensive data were collected at admission and discharge from a systematic sample of 30,000 patients admitted to the fourteen short-stay hospitals in Minneapolis, Minnesota, for the two-year period of 1963–1964. The sample used, after elimination of normal birth deliveries and cases incorrectly coded, was 24,327. Although other data were collected, the author's analysis was confined to diagnosis, age, sex, occupation, education, insurance coverage, color, nativity, religion, marital status, living arrangement, and family size. (For a complete description of this study, see Whitehurst, 1974.)

The major dependent variable, rate of hospital utilization, had two components: actual length of stay in number of days, and rates of admission in terms of the ratio of patients per thousand population. Because these are interdependent factors, they are handled separately. The independent variables considered in this analysis are age, sex, socioeconomic status, and family. The major intervening variable is seriousness of diagnosis, which could influence the effects of the independent variables on the dependent one. The method used was "control by elimination" (Schnore and Cowhig, 1959–60), in which the aggregate of patients being analyzed at each stage controls for the factors previously analyzed. Thus, the "standard group" at each stage consists of persons of a certain age, after age has been considered and analyzed as an independent variable.

The standard group for the analysis as a whole consists of patients 30 to 49 years old and in the "low serious" range, in order to control for the effects of extremely serious diagnoses and of either very young or very old age. The analysis also excluded all cases of normal birth delivery because of the extreme bias such cases introduce in terms of their short stays, high admission rates, and distortion of the significance of sex differences in utilization.

Seriousness of Diagnosis

Seriousness of the medical diagnosis was considered relevant to discretion in use of the hospital. Seriousness has two components: the problem is more serious if it needs immediate attention and if it is more life-threatening. When the medical problem is compelling to the extent that it could not be ignored regardless of values, economic constraints, barriers, alternatives, and so on, it is considered a "serious" problem. Seriousness of illness is important because the more serious the diagnosis the more likely an individual is to take some health-oriented action. Perceived seriousness is usually considered in a number of studies to be one of the major reasons, if not the foremost reason, for seeking medical care (Rosenstock, 1966; Freidson, 1970; Kasl and Cobb, 1966; Suchman, 1965; Apple, 1960; Wilson, 1963; Antonovsky, 1972; Leveson, 1972; Field, 1953). There is evidence of a reasonably close relationship between perception of disease and actual disease, so that it can be concluded that it is at least partly the objective condition that will influence the illness behavior and action taken. Andersen has found empirically that the "need component" is more closely related to the use of medical services than the predisposing or enabling conditions, particularly in the case of the least discretionary form of care, such as hospitalization. Thus, hospital use may be better predicted by the nature of the patient's illness than by environmental factors (Andersen, 1968).

For present purposes seriousness was measured by a number of components that were intercorrelated, including the major diagnosis (classified by a panel of three judges as most likely to be serious, least likely to be serious and other), presence or absence of secondary diagnoses, total bill, time of day admitted, and day of week admitted (because of the urgency implied by the nature of nonroutine admissions). The resulting "index of seriousness" had values ranging from 2 to 18 because of the weighting of the components, but the actual mean seriousness score for all patients was 4.45. In order to control for the effects of extremes in seriousness or urgency on utilization, subjects used for analysis were those with scores of 5 or less.

Age

Severity or seriousness of diagnosis is generally found to increase with age (Cartwright, 1967; Mechanic, 1968; Suchman, 1965), as does limitation of activity through chronic disease and disability (USDHEW, NCHS, Series 10, 1973; Mechanic, 1968). Studies consistently find that the aged have the longest average lengths of stay and the highest admission rates, whereas the young have the lowest admission rates and the shortest lengths of stay (Anderson, 1973; Andersen and Anderson, 1967; Anderson and Sheatsley, 1967; Passman, 1966; Wirick, 1962; USDHEW NCHS, Series 10, 1966, 1969, 1971; Series 13, 1967). Clearly, increasing age is related to higher rates of morbidity and mortality, chronic disease and disability, and seriousness of illness. Age is also related to higher rates of utilization of medical services, presumably because of higher levels of morbidity for older people.

In the present study the correlation between age and seriousness was found to be .22, significant beyond .0001. Thus, age and seriousness were not only closely related but also had to be controlled in order to analyze the relationship of age to the dependent variables. Table 4-1 shows that rate of admission increased from a low of 7.2 per 1,000 population for males under 10 years of age to a high of 48.7 per 1,000 for males 80 and over. Although the pattern was less clear for women, because of the tendency for women's admissions to reach a relatively high point early in life and level off, the lowest rate was found for the youngest age category and the highest rate for the oldest.

Length of stay was clearly longest for the oldest age category (11.6 days), shortest for the youngest (5.0 days), and in between for those 30 to 64 years of age

Table 4-1: Rate of admission by age-sex categories (all patients excluding normal deliveries: N = 24,327) per thousand population

Sex	Age groups								
	-10	-19	-29	-39	-49	-59	-69	-79	80+
Male	7.2	7.9	10.7	12.1	17.3	23.3	27.5	34.2	48.7
Female	5.7	8.0	24.4	22.3	27.8	26.9	26.8	35.5	40.9

(8.4 days). Seriousness of diagnosis also significantly distinguished between the youngest age category and the oldest (see Table 4–2). Chi-square analysis of a 20 percent random subsample was significant beyond .0001 for the three age categories and the two seriousness categories. Thus, because of the high correlation between age and seriousness, age was subsequently controlled, and a "standard group" of people aged 30 to 49 was used for analysis to eliminate its biasing effect.

Sex

Sex of the patient seems ambiguously related to morbidity although clearly related to mortality. Women outlive men by at least five to seven years (see, for instance, Twaddle and Hessler, 1977), but this fact has not been clearly shown to be related to greater overall morbidity in men. Women are generally felt to be more health-seeking and more protective of their own health than are men (Coe, 1970; Mechanic, 1968) as well as being more protected from environmental risks (Benjamin, 1965; Coe, 1970; Hunter, 1962; Mechanic, 1968; Susser and Watson, 1971; Wrong, 1966). Females may have higher morbidity rates for acute conditions, except injuries and childhood diseases, but the picture is unclear for the chronic conditions (Anderson, 1963; Coe, 1970; Susser and Watson; but see Twaddle and Hessler, 1977, for a different view on chronic conditions). Morbidity figures are confounded by methods of reporting, lack of controls for age, and inability to determine objective rates of conditions because of women's greater tendency to report illness and disabilities; but longer average length of life for females should increase their susceptibility to chronic diseases.

Women have been found to have greater inclinations than men to use medical facilities (Anderson, 1963; Cartwright, 1967; Mechanic, 1968; Susser and Watson, 1971) and are less skeptical about medical care (Suchman, 1965). Thus, we would expect women to have higher rates of admission than men of the same age and seriousness categories, but possibly to have shorter average stays because of the tendency to begin care earlier at a less complicated stage. (By controlling for seriousness in the present analysis, we attenuated this factor. In fact, however, there was no difference in seriousness scores for men and women for the entire sample.)

Utilization of health services in general has been found to be greater for women, including physician visits, preventive care, and hospital admissions (Anderson, 1967; Andersen and Anderson, 1967; Anderson and Andersen, 1972; USDHEW NCHS, Series 10, 1964, 1965, 1966, No. 30, 1970, 1971; Series 13, 1967 No. 2, 1967 No. 3, 1970, 1973). Even excluding admissions for birth-deliv-

Table 4-2:   **Mean length of stay and seriousness (excluding deliveries) by age (N = 24,327)**

Age	Stay (days)	Seriousness
0 to 29	5.01	4.06*
30 to 64	8.39	4.42
65 to 99	11.56	5.08*

*p < .01

ery, women are admitted to hospitals at somewhat higher rates than are men. However, men are generally found to have longer lengths of stay (Andersen and Anderson, 1972; USDHEW NCHS, Series 10, 1965, 1966, 1967, 1969, 1970; Series 13, 1967 No. 2, 1967 No. 3, 1973; Wirick, 1962), even when admissions for deliveries are excluded.

If the earlier argument is valid, men should be less likely to recognize a need for care because of less attendance to bodily signs and symptoms or because of greater denial of them, among many possible reasons. Men might be expected to have greater competing needs and motives in terms of a dependent family, the fear of losing a job or income if hospitalized, or the fear of "giving in" to illness and becoming dependent. Men may have a less health-oriented attitude and less knowledge about health and health facilities, and they may also be more likely to have the alternative of family care at home. (Women are significantly more likely to be living alone or with others who are not relatives.) Thus, men would be expected to have somewhat lower rates of admission, which might also suggest higher rates of seriousness of diagnosis and longer lengths of hospital stay.

Table 4-3 shows that in the present analysis women clearly have higher rates of admission for all age categories but the elderly. When using the standard group of patients aged 30–49, the difference in admission rates is significant beyond .01. Controlling for seriousness, the difference in rates remains significant beyond .01. Men and women of age 30–49 are found to have virtually identical scores on seriousness (4.2). However, the average length of stay for men aged 30–49 is significantly ($p < .01$) longer at 7.5 days than that of women at 7.0 days. Controlling for seriousness, the difference, though small, remains significant (Table 4-4).

Thus, men seem to be no more seriously ill than women when admitted to the hospital, but they are admitted at lower rates and stay longer once admitted. Significant differences are found in the diagnoses for which men and women are admitted, but none of any great importance for social characteristics, including occupational level, education, marital or family status, and insurance coverage. Although sex of the patient cannot be said to determine utilization, this factor obviously is related to predictable patterns of hospital use. The contingency model

Table 4-3:   Rate of admission by sex of patient (excluding deliveries) and age (patients aged 30 to 49, N = 7,126)

Age	Men	Women
0 to 29	8.5*	11.1*
30 to 64	17.3*	25.9**
65 to 99	33.6	33.3
patients 30–49	14.4*	24.0**
30–49 and low serious	12.0*	20.0**

*p < .05
**p < .01

Table 4-4:   Mean stay for patients aged 30–49 (N = 7,126, excluding deliveries) and seriousness of diagnosis

Total	Men	Women	
All patients	7.53	6.98	p < .01
Low serious	6.04	5.76	p < .05

seems to be relatively compatible with the findings of this section, at least insofar as the five contingencies can all help to predict men's lower rates of admission. However, the longer average stay of men is not adequately dealt with by this model.

Socioeconomic Status (Occupational Level, Years of Education, Insurance Coverage)

Socioeconomic status has generally been considered to be inversely related to morbidity, chronic disease, mortality, and infant mortality, although the relationship to the entire range and types of morbidity is far from clear (Bice, 1971; Bloom, 1963; Graham, 1963; Kadushin, 1964; Koos, 1954; Lawrence, 1948; McBroom, 1970; McKinlay, 1972; Richardson, 1969). However, at least before Medicare and Medicaid, the lower socioeconomic statuses utilized health-care facilities less often than higher statuses, despite greater need (for example, see Andersen, 1968; Andersen and Anderson, 1967; Graham, 1957; McKinlay & McKinlay, 1972; Muller, 1965; Rosenblatt & Suchman, 1964; Ross, 1962; Stoeckle & Zola, 1964; USDHEW NCHS 1963 No. 2; White, 1968). Hospital-utilization patterns for the lower social statuses are ambiguous, and seem to be highly influenced by the possession (or lack) of health insurance. Length of stay is generally found to be inversely related to socioeconomic status, presumably because the poor are more seriously ill (Donabedian, 1976; Herman, 1972; Muller, 1965; USDHEW NCHS 1963 No. 2 and No. 3; Wirick, 1962).

Persons of the lowest socioeconomic levels are felt to underutilize primarily because of financial barriers, including not only inability to pay for expensive medical care but also less access to care, greater difficulty in taking time off from work, lack of transportation, lack of child care, and so on. One factor that helped eliminate this economic barrier before Medicaid and Medicare was health insurance, as possession of health insurance tends to increase utilization (see Donabedian, 1976). However, the lowest income levels are the least likely to have health insurance. Although this fact is still true today, it was, of course, a much more important factor in pre-Medicare days when the Department of Health, Education, and Welfare (HEW) indicated that insurance paid for only about 40 percent of health care per year (USDHEW NCHS, 1963, p. 151). In general, those who possess health insurance have higher rates of hospital utilization than do those who do not. Health insurance helps reduce the financial barrier to utilization, although other factors in the lives of the poor may also lead to underutilization, including values, group expectations, knowledge, information, and orientation toward treatment.

In the present analysis, socioeconomic status was indicated by three factors: Occupational level, as measured by Edwards' Occupational Rating Scale and put into four categories;[1] education, put into three categories designated "elementary" (eight years or less), "high school" (9-12 years), and "college" (one or more years); and health insurance, put into three categories designated "none"

[1]Category I: unemployed and not in work force; II: unskilled and semiskilled; III: skilled, clerks, and kindred; IV: proprietors, managers, and professionals.

(no hospital insurance of any kind), "welfare" (coded as receiving state categorical aids or social security benefits), and "regular" (any other form of insurance coverage). Occupational level and education are presented here separately because of the differences in the patterns, although their intercorrelation was .46.

The lower socioeconomic statuses would be expected to be higher on seriousness of diagnosis than the higher statuses, based on the review of the literature. The present analysis found that, controlling for age, the lowest occupational category clearly had the highest seriousness score (p < .001) and the two highest had the lowest scores. The lowest educational category had the highest seriousness score. Those with regular insurance had the lowest seriousness scores, and those with none or welfare had the highest (p < .001). Seriousness of illness therefore was associated with lower occupational levels, lower education, and less health insurance.

Rates of admission for patients aged 30–49, uncontrolled for seriousness, tended to show the lowest rates for the lowest socioeconomic categories (Table 4–5). However, the highest socioeconomic categories did not necessarily show the highest rates of admission. Length of stay tended to be inversely related to education, occupation, and insurance in that stays were somewhat longer for the lower two occupational categories, for the least educated, and for those with no health insurance coverage or welfare only. Most of these differences, however, were small and not significant. Controlling for seriousness of diagnosis, only education showed a significant inverse relationship with length of stay.

Thus, controlling for seriousness, it can be concluded that socioeconomic factors are only slightly related to length of hospitalization, and even controlling for seriousness (as has been done here), it is possible that the range of seriousness allowed could still account for socioeconomic differences in length of stay. On the other hand, lower-class patients may have more difficulty in obtaining release from hospitals for reasons not necessarily related to the seriousness of their conditions (Sussman, 1969). The data indicate that most of the socioeconomic difference in length of stay seems to be explained by seriousness, although not all of it.

Length of stay varies not only with insurance coverage but also with the interaction of health insurance and socioeconomic factors. Table 4–6 shows that there is a tendency for those with insurance to have longer average stays than those without, with the exception of those in the highest occupational and educational categories. The differences are not significant for education, but the interaction of insurance and occupational level seems to indicate that insurance coverage is most associated with increased length of stay for a middle-level category

Table 4-5: Rates of admission by socioeconomic factors, patients aged 30–49 (N = 7,126, excluding deliveries) by sex

Occupational Category	Men	Women		Education	Men	Women	Health Insurance	Men	Women
I	9.0	*	elementary		6.6	10.9	none or welfare	6.6	17.8
II	16.3	*	high school		12.2	17.9	regular	15.7	21.0
III	20.3	*	college		11.9	23.0			
IV	10.3	*							

* Not available.

(Category III), whereas it is actually associated with shorter stays for the highest level. That is, insurance seems to have the greatest influence on behavior at the middle levels. The data also indicate that rates of admission are strongly related to possession of health insurance, particularly at the lower occupational levels.

Socioeconomic factors and health insurance status for the entire sample tend to be related to seriousness of diagnosis and age but not to sex. When age and seriousness are controlled, occupational level, education, and insurance status continue to be somewhat related to length of stay, but in less direct ways. The patterns found are compatible with predictions from the model in that rates of admission generally increase with increasing status, and length of stay decreases. The explanation usually offered for this pattern suggests that the lower social statuses tend to delay care, worsen their conditions, and have to stay longer as a result.

However, even when controlling for seriousness, differences in length of stay remain (Table 4-7). Lower socioeconomic levels were suggested to have lower recognition of need, greater competing needs (health values less conducive to obtaining early care), greater obstacles to obtaining adequate care, and fewer alternative resources. However, this analysis does not answer the question of which aspects of lower socioeconomic status account for differential patterns of utilization. Cultural and family factors may provide the key.

Marital and Family Factors

Variables in family and living situations have been found to be related to morbidity, mortality, and utilization of medical services. A number of researchers have concluded that both morbidity and mortality are lower for the married than for the unmarried, and tend to be highest for those living alone or socially isolated (Mechanic, 1968; Schnore & Cowhig, 1959-60; Susser & Watson, 1971; Sussman, 1969). The selection for marriage of healthier individuals, the care and help and mutual watchfulness of marital partners in preserving health, and the regularity of diet and life-style are among the reasons suggested. Sussman

Table 4-6:   Mean lengths of stay by socioeconomic factors (patients aged 30-49, excluding deliveries) and seriousness of diagnosis

Occupational category	all 30–49 (N = 7,126)	low serious (N = 5,645)
I (low)	7.29	6.04
II	7.23	6.01
III	6.74	5.70
IV (high)	7.23	5.72
Education		
elementary	*8.22	6.56**
high school	*7.24*	*5.91**
college	6.62*	*5.59
Health Insurance		
regular	*7.01	5.85
welfare	*8.47	5.98
none	8.35	6.46

*p < .05
**p < .01

Table 4-7:   Length of stay by insurance status and socioeconomic factors (patients aged 30–49, excluding deliveries, low serious, N = 5,645)

Occupational category	No insurance	Regular
I (low)	5.6	5.9
II	5.3	6.1
III	4.8	5.8
IV (high)	6.5	5.6
$X^2 = 74.82, 3\,df, p < .001$		
Education		
elementary	7.4	6.5
high school .	5.0	5.9
college	6.2	5.6
$X^2 = 4.76, 2\,df, p < .10$		

attributes differences in morbidity to psychological well-being resulting from security, affection, and attention, as opposed to the loss or lack of emotional support which can lead to lower resistance to illness.

In line with these findings, it is also found that the unmarried and those living alone have longer stays, but there is some disagreement over whether the unmarried have lower or higher rates of admission. Much of the confusion is explained by the lack of controls on age and admissions for birth delivery. One theory suggests that the family helps to keep the patient healthier and out of the hospital, resulting in lower rates for the married (and members of families) (Kosa and Robertson, 1969). Another theory holds that the urban middle-class family provides pressure on the sick person to get professional care earlier, thus resulting in higher rates of admission for the married (Parsons and Fox, 1952). This theory would also predict that persons living alone would have lower rates of admission, more serious illness, and longer average length of stay. Undoubtedly this relationship is also complicated by the seriousness of the medical problem, since, for example, the family would be expected to provide home care for the less seriously ill member but probably would not hesitate to hospitalize one who was seriously ill. This theory would suggest that family members should be more, rather than less, seriously ill than persons living alone at the time of hospitalization.

In the present study, marital status, living arrangement, and family size were examined for their relationship to rates of admission and length of stay. Rates of admission, based on estimates from census data, showed that on the whole the married and the unmarried did not differ significantly, although the divorced and separated had high rates within the unmarried category and the never married had rates comparable to those of the married. Those living alone had much higher rates than those living with family or with others, and those living in a household of one had much higher rates than those living in any other sized household. These rates of admission were uncontrolled for age and seriousness, which could account for most of these relationships.

When controlled for age, seriousness of diagnosis was slightly lower for the married than for the unmarried, but this was accounted for by the divorced and separated, and to a lesser extent, the widowed. The differences were much more pronounced for men. The same general pattern was found for living arrangement and family size, in that those living alone and in the smallest households had high seriousness scores (Table 4–8). As a single measure, "family status" referred to

Table 4-8: Mean seriousness score by family and marital status (patients aged 30–49, excluding deliveries, N = 7,126)

Marital status		Family status	
Married	*4.21	With family	4.20**
Unmarried	*4.37	Without family	4.42**
single	4.19		
div. or sep.	4.59		
widowed	4.30		

*p < .01
**p < .001

those who were married or living with their immediate families, and all others. Those "without families" had significantly higher seriousness scores. Controlling for age and seriousness, the married continued to have significantly shorter stays, and those living alone or with others had longer stays than those living with immediate families. Persons living in households of one had the longest mean stay, and those in households of four or more had the shortest stays, although these differences were not significant (Table 4–9). Thus, controlling for age and seriousness, marital and family factors continue to influence average length of stay. The married and those living with immediate families had significantly shorter stays than their counterparts. Family size seemed to make little difference as long as the family consisted of at least two members.

Family status was found to be closely associated with age (corrected contingency coefficient .40) and significantly to seriousness of diagnosis (.10), as well as to sex and health insurance. Thus, those living without families are more likely to be old, high in seriousness, female, and without health insurance. Consequently, rates of hospital admission based on the entire population when these factors are not controlled would be misleading, and the present data do not indicate that admissions rates are either higher or lower for those without families. However, although the differences are very small and often not significant, there is some indication that the unmarried and those living alone are more seriously ill and have longer average stays, even when controlling for age and seriousness. Thus, the family does seem to provide an environment to which the hospitalized patient can return sooner than the person living alone.

Patients without families were also found to have consistently longer average length of hospital stay regardless of socioeconomic status or health insurance. Family status makes a difference in length of stay primarily because of its relationship to the factors of age and seriousness of diagnosis; but the family may also influence length of stay by inducing the patient to obtain earlier hospital care

Table 4-9: Mean length of stay by marital and family status (patients aged 30–49, low seriousness of diagnosis, excluding deliveries, N = 5,645)

Marital status		Family status	
Married	*5.74	With family	**5.74
Unmarried	*6.47	Without family	**6.55
single	6.32		
div. or sep.	6.48		
widowed	6.96		

*p < .01
**p < .001

or making it easier for the physician to consider earlier discharge to the home than otherwise. The findings fit the contingency model insofar as those who are likely to recognize their need for medical care, who have health values conducive to seeking such care, and who have the fewest obstacles as well as alternatives to hospital care will be the most likely to become hospital patients.

The presence of a family seems to contribute to this "patient pattern" in that members of families may be somewhat more likely to recognize their need because other members of the family tend to note signs of illness and point them out. Competing needs in the form of family responsibilities might discourage early admission, but the possibility that other family members may assume burdens lessens these competing needs. Health values vary by family status, as people with families may be more concerned with the long-term health of their children, spouses, and selves. Families also have better alternatives to hospitalization, which should reduce average length of stay rather than keep the family member out of the the hospital altogether, because of the relatively nondiscretionary nature of hospitalization.

Summary and Conclusions

The data for this study were collected before the passage of Titles 18 and 19 of the Social Security Amendments of 1965 establishing the Medicare and Medicaid health-care assistance programs by the federal government of the United States. Today the possession of these forms of governmental health insurance may diminish the patterns of utilization, especially those related to age and socioeconomic status. For this reason, it is considered important to establish baseline pre-Medicare-Medicaid data in order to be able to interpret the later effects of these programs on health-care utilization. Changes in utilization patterns have been shown to have occurred since these programs (Ament, 1967; Newman, 1972; Monteiro, 1973).

One major purpose of this study was to explore the importance of seriousness of diagnosis in the use of hospital care. The hypothesis that higher levels of seriousness would be associated both with higher rates of admission and longer average stays received strong support. Seriousness of diagnosis was also found to be closely related to age, and to some extent to indicators of social deprivation and social isolation. Thus, the objective condition stood out clearly as the most important influence on hospital use, but the seriousness of the condition was not randomly distributed in the population.

Therefore, outside of establishing that people go to the hospital because they are objectively in need of care, we have also established that there are subtle and complex processes occurring which influence the use patterns. Independently, each of the social factors considered contributes relatively little to what could be predicted from a knowledge of age and seriousness alone, but patterns found in the data suggest that people may either go to or refrain from going to the hospital in ambiguous situations because of conditions in the social environment.

Sex of patient, socioeconomic status, and family factors are related to patterns of hospital utilization, but when controlled for seriousness of diagnosis and age, the patterns become less clear and many of the relationships become nonsignificant. However, the data indicate that the social aggregates who have longer stays and lower rates of admission (low socioeconomic status, those unmarried and living alone) may represent isolated or "alienated" people who postpone health care. The interesting research question for a comparison with post-Medicare-Medicaid patients is whether these same people increase rates of use and decrease their length of stay along with their levels of seriousness. The elderly clearly seem to increase their use of medical facilities with medical insurance (Ament, 1967), but is this equally true of cultural groups that may have reasons other than economic for avoiding the health-care system?

The findings from this study are generally consistent with the notion of illness behavior and the idea of contingencies that influence the illness-behavior process. The components of the contingency model receive some support, particularly "competing needs and motives" (indicated by socioeconomic factors including health insurance coverage) and "obstacles and alternatives" (indicated primarily by family and status). "Recognition of need," although not refuted, received no direct support, and the factor of "health values and attitudes" was not directly measured by these data. In combination, the influence of social factors on hospital utilization could be viewed as quite significant, but independently each variable has little influence on the outcome, and age and seriousness of illness account for most of the explained variation in this study.

References

Ament, R. P.
    1967   "Medicare boosts bed usage by elderly." Modern Hospital 108 (February): 81–82.

Andersen, Ronald
    1968   A Behavioral Model of Families' Use of Health Services. Research Series No. 25. Center for Health Administration Studies. Chicago: University of Chicago Press.

Andersen, Ronald, and Odin W. Anderson
    1967   A Decade of Health Services. Chicago: University of Chicago Press.

Anderson, James G.
    1973   "Demographic factors affecting health services utilization: a causal model." Medical Care 2 (March-April): 104–120.

Anderson, Odin W.
    1963   "The utilization of health services." Pp. 349–367 in Howard E. Freeman et al. (eds.), Handbook of Medical Sociology. Englewood Cliffs: Prentice-Hall.

Anderson, Odin W., and Ronald Andersen
    1972   "Patterns of use of health services." Pp. 386–406 in Howard E. Freeman, et al. (eds.), Handbook of Medical Sociology. Englewood Cliffs, New Jersey: Prentice-Hall.

Anderson, Odin W., and Paul B. Sheatsley
    1967   Hospital Use—A Survey of Patient and Physician Decisions. Research Series No. 24, Center for Health Administration Studies. Chicago: University of Chicago Press.

Antonovsky, Aaron
    1972   "A model to explain visits to the doctor: with specific reference to the case of Israel." Journal of Health and Social Behavior 13 (December): 446–454.

Apple, Dorrian
    1960   "How laymen define illness." Journal of Health and Human Behavior 1 (Fall): 219–225.

Benjamin, B.
    1965   Social and Economic Factors Affecting Mortality. The
           Hague: Mouton.

Bice, T. W.
    1971   "Medical care for the disadvantaged: report on a survey of
           use of medical services in the Baltimore Standard Met-
           ropolitan Statistical Area, 1968–1969." Final report of re-
           search conducted under contract number HSM 110 69 203,
           NCH SRD.

Bloom, Samuel W.
    1963   The Doctor and His Patient. New York: The Free Press.

Cartwright, Ann
    1967   Patients and Their Doctors. New York: Atherton Press.

Coe, Rodney M.
    1970   Sociology of Medicine. New York: McGraw-Hill Book
           Company.

Donabedian, Avedis
    1976   Benefits in Medical Care Programs. Cambridge: Harvard
           University Press.

Field, Minna
    1953   Patients Are People. New York: Columbia University Press.

Friedson, Eliot
    1970   Profession of Medicine. New York: Dodd, Mead and Com-
           pany.

Goffman, Erving.
    1968   "The moral career of the mental patient." In Earl Rub-
           ington and Martin S. Weinberg (eds.), Deviance: The In-
           teractionist Perspective. New York: The Macmillan Com-
           pany.

Graham, Saxon
    1957   "Socioeconomic status, illness, and the use of medical ser-
           vices." The Milbank Memorial Fund Quarterly 35 (Janu-
           ary): 58–66.
    1963   "Social factors in relation to the chronic illnesses." Pp.
           65–98 in Howard H. Freeman et al., Handbook of Medical
           Sociology. Englewood Cliffs: Prentice-Hall.

Herman, Mary W.
    1972   "The poor: their medical needs and the health services avail-
           able to them." The Annals of the American Academy of
           Political and Social Science 399 (January), The Nation's
           Health: Some Issues, 12–21.

Hunter, Donald
    1962   The Diseases of Occupations. Boston: Little, Brown and
           Company.

Kadushin, Charles
    1964   "Social class and the experience of ill health." Sociological
           Inquiry 34: 67–80.

Kasl, S., and S. Cobb
    1966   "Health behavior, illness behavior and sick-role behavior."
           Archives of Environmental Health 12 (February): 246–266.

Koos, Earl L.
    1954   The Health of Regionville. New York: Columbia University
           Press.

Kosa, John, and Leon S. Robertson
    1969   "The social aspects of health and illness." In John Kosa et
           al. (eds), Poverty and Health. Cambridge: Harvard Univer-
           sity Press.

Leveson, Irving
    1972   "The challenge of health services for the poor." The Annals
           of the American Academy of Political and Social Science 399
           (January), The Nation's Health: Some Issues: 22–29.

McBroom, W. H.
1970   "Illness, illness behavior, and socioeconomic status." Journal of Health and Social Behavior 11 (December): 319–326.

McKinlay, J. B.
1972   "Some approaches and problems in the study of the use of services—an overview." Journal of Health and Social Behavior 13 (June): 115–152.

McKinlay, J. B., and S. M. McKinlay
1972   "Some social characteristics of lower working class utilizers and underutilizers of maternity care services." Journal of Health and Social Behavior 13 (December): 369–382.

Mechanic, David
1966   "Response factors in illness: the study of illness behavior." Social Psychiatry 1: 11–20.

1968   Medical Sociology—a Selective View: New York: The Free Press.

Monteiro, Lois A.
1973   "Expense is no object . . . : income and physician visits reconsidered." Journal of Health and Social Behavior 14 (June): 99–115.

Muller, C.
1965   "Income and the receipt of medical care." American Journal of Public Health 55 (April): 510–521.

Newman, Howard N.
1972   "Medicare and Medicaid." Pp. 114–124 in The Annals of the American Academy of Political and Social Science 399 (January), The Nation's Health: Some Issues.

Parsons, Talcott, and Renee Fox
1952   "Illness, therapy, and the modern urban American family." The Journal of Social Issues 8: 31–44.

Passman, M. J.
1966   "Hospital utilization by Blue Cross members in 1964 according to selected demographic and enrollment characteristics." Inquiry 3 (May): 82–89.

Richardson, William C.
1969   "Poverty, illness and the use of health services in the United States." Hospitals 43 (July): 34–40.

Rosenblatt, D., and E. A. Suchman
1964   "Blue-collar attitudes and information toward health and illness." Pp. 324–338 in A. B. Shostak and W. Gomberg (eds.), Blue-Collar World. Englewood Cliffs: Prentice-Hall.

Rosenstock, I. M.
1966   "Why people use health services." Milbank Memorial Fund Quarterly 44 (July): 94–127.

Ross, John A.
1962   "Social class and medical care." Journal of Health and Human Behavior 3 (Fall): 35–40.

Schnore, Leo F., and James D. Cowhig
1959–   "Some correlates of reported health in metropolitan
60   centers." Social Problems 7 (Winter): 218–226.

Steele, James L., and William H. McBroom
1972   "Conceptual and empirical dimensions of health behavior." Journal of Health and Social Behavior 13 (December): 382–392.

Stoeckle, John D., and Irving K. Zola
1964   "After everyone can pay for medical care: some perspectives on future treatment and practice." Medical Care 2: 36–41.

Suchman, Edward A
1965   "Social patterns of illness and medical care." Journal of Health and Human Behavior 6 (Fall): 114–128.

Susser, M. W., and W. Watson
1971   Sociology in Medicine. London: Oxford University Press.

Sussman, Marvin B.
1969   "Readjustment and rehabilitation of patients." In John Kosa et al. (eds.), Poverty and Health. Cambridge: Harvard University Press.

Twaddle, Andrew C., and Richard Hessler
1977   A Sociology of Health. St. Louis, Mo.: C. V. Mosby.

US Department of Health, Education, and Welfare. National Center for Health Statistics.

Series 10
1963   Family Income in Relation to Selected Health Characteristics. Washington, D.C.: No. 2.

1964   Medical Care, Health Status, and Family Income: United States—1963. Washington, D.C.: No. 9.

1965   Persons Hospitalized by Number of Hospital Episodes and Days in a Year: United States—July 1960–June 1962. Washington, D.C.: No. 20.

1966   Hospital Discharges and Length of Stay: Short-Stay Hospitals: United States—July 1963–June 1965. Washington, D.C.: No. 30.

1966   Age Patterns in Medical Care, Illness, and Disability: United States—July 1963–June 1965. Washington, D.C.: No. 32.

1967   Current Estimates from the Health Interview Survey: United States—July 1965–June 1966. Washington, D.C.: No. 37.

1969   Persons Hospitalized by Number of Hospital Illness Episodes and Days in a Year: United States—July 1965–June 1966. Washington, D.C.: No. 50.

1970   Current Estimates from the Health Interview Study: United States—1968. Washington, D.C.: No. 60.

1971   Current Estimates from the Health Interview Survey: United States—1969. Washington, D.C.: No. 63.

1973   Limitation of Activity Due to Chronic Conditions: United States—1969 and 1970. Washington, D.C.: No. 80.

Series 13
1966   Patients Discharged from Short-Stay Hospitals: United States—October-December, 1964. Washington, D.C.: No. 1.

1967   Utilization of Short-Stay Hospitals—Summary of Nonmedical Statistics: United States—1965. Washington, D.C.: No. 2.

1967   Utilization of Short-Stay Hospitals by Characteristics of Discharged Patients: United States—1965. Washington, D.C.: No. 3.

1970   Inpatient Utilization of Short-Stay Hospitals by Diagnosis: United States—1965. Washington, D.C.: No. 6.

1973   Average Length of Stay in Short-Stay Hospitals: Demographic Factors—United States—1968. Washington, D.C.: No. 13.

White, E. L.
1968   "A graphic presentation on age and income differentials in selected aspects of morbidity, disability, and utilization of health services." Inquiry 5 (March): 18–30.

Whitehurst, Carol A.
1974   Some Social Factors in the Use of Short-Stay Urban Hospitals: A Medical-Sociological Analysis. Unpublished doctoral dissertation, University of California at Riverside.

Wilson, Robert N.
1963 "Patient-practitioner relationships." Pp. 273–295 in Howard Freeman et al. (eds.), Handbook of Medical Sociology. Englewood Cliffs: Prentice-Hall.

Wirick, G. C.
1962 "Population survey: health care and its financing." Pp. 61–361 in W. J. McNerny et al., Hospital and Medical Economics. Chicago: Hospital Research and Education Trust.

Wrong, Dennis
1966 Population and Society. New York: Random House.

5 The Family in Health and Health Care: A Social-Behavioral Overview

Since the seminal efforts of Richardson in the mid-nineteen forties, increasing interest has been evidenced on the part of both medical and social scientists alike in the role of the family in health and illness.[1] The work of Lawrence, Haggerty, Cartwright, as well as Alpert, Kosa and associates, for instance, has lent support to the notion that a family does indeed constitute a basic unit in health and medical care, exhibiting characteristic patterns of morbidity, response to symptoms and utilization of medical services and facilities.[2]

Yet as Vincent noted over a decade ago, it has only been within the past few years or so that a significant number of investigators have given sustained and systematic attention to either the role of the total family in individual illness, or the impact of illness upon family life, or the way the family contributes to illness and health care.[3] As a matter of fact, it really has only been within the past twenty years or so that behavioral scientists have effectively penetrated the methodological and socio-moral constituents to family research per se.[4]

Thus, while a considerable amount of knowledge has been gleaned concerning familial interaction, power relations, kinship structure, socialization patterns and the like, with the notable exception of the efforts of the work of Sussman and associates at Case Western Reserve,[5] such major issues as familial response, ad-

[1]Richardson H. *Patients Have Families.* Commonwealth Fund, New York, 1945.

[2]Lawrence P. S. Chronic illness and socio-economic status. *Publ. Hlth Rep.* **63**, 1507, 1948; Haggerty, R. J. Family diagnosis: Research methods and their reliability for studies of the medical social unit, the family. *Am. J. publ. Hlth* **55**, 1521, 1965; Cartwright A. Some Methodological Problems Encountered in a Family Morbidity Survey. Unpublished Doctoral Dissertation, London University, 1961; Kosa J., Alpert J. J., Pickering M. R. and Haggerty R. J. Crises and stress in family life: A reexamination of concepts. *Wisconsin Sociol.* **4**, 11, 1965; Kosa, J., Alpert J. J. and Haggerty R. J. On the reliability of family health information—A comparative study of mothers: Reports on illness and related behavior. *Soc. Sci. & Med.* **1**, 165, 1967.

[3]Vincent C. The family in health and illness: Some neglected areas. *Ann. Am. Acad. Political Soc. Sci.* **346**, 109, 1963.

[4]Hill R. Sociology of marriage and family behavior: A trend report, 1945–56. *Current Sociol.* **7** (1), 5, 1958; For an excellent exploration of some of the major constraints to the sociological study of the family, see Hobbs, D. F., Jr. and Sussman M. B. Impediments to family research: A symposium. *J. Marriage Fam.* **27**, 410, 1965.

[5]In a study of mutual aid and support among middle and working class families in Cleveland, Ohio, Sussman found that help during illness appeared to comprise the major form of assistance provided by members of kin-related families and was provided in approximately 92 per cent of the ill-

Revision of a position paper prepared for the Fourth International Conference on Social Science and Medicine, Elsinore, Denmark–August 12 to 16, 1974. Condensed from the author's "The Family as a Basic Unit in Health and Medical Care: A Social Behavioral Overview," *Social Science & Medicine*, 8:495–519, September, 1974. Reprinted by permission of the author and Publisher.

justment and behavior in health and illness have generally escaped the empirical involvement and theoretical interest of the family sociologist.

Although still relatively limited, a cursory review of the published literature reveals a rather broad spectrum of empirical and theoretical concern ranging from Parsons and Fox's classic indictment of the contemporary-modern American family in health and illness to the explorations of Sussman and Slater, Davis, Farber, Litman, and Deutsch and Goldston among others in the area of chronic illness and rehabilitation; and Simmons and Freeman, Meyers and Roberts, etc. in mental health and mental illness; to the economic analyses of family budget planning of Weeks and the innovative empirical work of Haggerty, Roghmann and Pless at Rochester; Kosa, Alpert and associates at Harvard; and Anderson at Chicago.[6]

Over the course of the last two decades, the family has variously been treated not only as an independent, dependent and intervening variable, but a precipitating, predisposing and contributory factor in the etiology, care and treatment of both physical and mental illness, and as a basic unit of interaction and transaction in health care as well.

In view of the recent interest that has developed in the role of the family in health and illness, as witness the focus of the World Health Organization on the

nesses reported to have occurred among kin-related families living within the area studied. While respondent-parents and respondent-siblings reciprocal relations did not differ significantly, illness assistance between families living some distance apart generally was given only where a family member either was, or was believed to be, critically ill or suffering from a long-term illness. In contrast to kin-related families living in the same neighborhood, there were no such expectations for help in routine illnesses. Moreover, there did not appear to be any evidence of significant class differences in the amount of help given or received during an illness of a family member. On the other hand, 76 per cent of the low-income and 84 per cent of the high-income subjects studied by Bell and Boat reportedly could count on extended family aid in cases of illnesses lasting a month or longer. See Sussman, M. B. The isolated nuclear family: Fact or fiction. *Soc. Problems* **6**, 333, 1959; Bell, W. and Boat, M. D. Urban neighborhoods and informal social relations. *Am. J. Sociol.* **62**, 391, 1957.

[6]Parsons T. and Fox R. Illness, therapy and the modern American family. *J. Soc. Issues* **8** (4), 31, 1952; Sussman M. B. Working Draft, Part I—Family Unit, Critique of Selected Scales and Indexes Available for Measuring the Relationship of Family Behavior to the Etiology and Cause of Chronic Illness and Disability, Project 94 U44, Association for the Aid of Crippled Children; Sussman M. B. *et al. Rehabilitation and Tuberculosis: Predicting the Vocational and Economic State of Tuberculosis Patients*, Case Western Reserve University, Cleveland, 1964; Slater, S. B. The Functions of the Urban Kinship Network Under Normal and Crisis Conditions. Unpublished Paper presented before the Annual Meetings of the American Sociological Association, San Francisco, Calif., August 1967; Davis F. Polio in the Family—A Study of Crisis and Family Process. Unpublished Doctoral Dissertation, University of Chicago, June 1958; Davis F. *Passage Through Crisis: Polio Victims and Their Families*. Bobbs-Merrill, Indianapolis, 1963; Farber B. Family Organization and Crisis: Maintenance of Integration in Families with a Severely Mentally Retarded Child. *Monographs Soc. Res. Child Development, Series No. 75* **25** (1), 1960; Litman T. J. The family and physical rehabilitation. *J. Chron. Dis.* **19**, 211, 1966; Kronick J. The Rehabilitation of Stroke Patients: An Experimental Analysis of the Effects of Physical and Social Factors in Determining Recovery. Unpublished Report, Department of Social Work and Social Research, Bryn Mawr, 1962; Dager E. Z. Family Integration and Response to Heart Disease. Paper presented at the Purdue Farm Cardiac Seminar, No. 15, September 1958; Jacobson M. M. and Eichhorn R. L. How farm families cope with heart disease: A study of problems and resources. *J. Marriage Fam.* **26**, 166, 1964; Johnson W. Longitudinal study of family adjustment to myocardial infarction. *Nursing Res.* **12**, 1963; Deutsch C. P. and Goldston J. A. Patient and Family Attitudes and Their Relationship to Home Placement of the Severely Disabled. Paper prepared for the Annual Meetings of the American Psychological Association, Cincinnati, Sep-

statistical aspects of the family as a unit in health studies in 1971 and 1975,[7] the publication of Crawford's *Health and the Family: A Medical Sociological Analysis*,[8] and the special issue of the *Journal of Comparative Family Studies* (1973) devoted to the family, health and illness,[9] it would seem appropriate at this time to review the present state of the art concerning the family as a basic unit of health and medical care and suggest some potential areas for further inquiry. In so doing, however, our attention will be confined primarily to an examination of the role of the family in physical rather than in mental health and illness.

Theory and Methods

As indicated earlier, with the exception of the efforts of Sussman and associates, empirical and theoretical interest on the part of family sociologists in the role of the family in health and illness has been extremely limited. As a result, like much of medical sociology, empirical inquiry in this area has tended to be theoretically eclectic, representing the contributions of a variety of fields and disciplines. In a comparison of the relative adequacy of two different theoretical

tember 4, 1959; Hoffer C. R. and Schuler E. A. Measurement of health needs and health care. *Am. Sociol. Rev.* **13**, 719, 1948; Hassinger, E. W. and McNamara R. L. Family Health Practices Among Open-Country People in a South Missouri County. University of Missouri Agricultural Experiment Station, Research Bulletin No. 699, 1959; Hay D. G. and Larson O. F. Use of Health Resources by Rural People in Two Western New York Counties. Department of Rural Sociology, Mimeo, Bulletin No. 31, New York State College of Agriculture, 1952; Weeks H. A. *Family Spending Patterns and Health Care.* Harvard University Press, Cambridge, 1961; Weeks, H. A., Davis M. and Freeman H. Apathy of families toward medical care. In *Patients, Physicians and Illness* (edited by Jaco E. G.), pp 148–158. The Free Press, New York, 1958; Kosa J., Alpert, J. J. and Haggerty R. J. On the reliability of family health information: A comparative study of mothers' reports on illness and related behavior. *Soc. Sci. & Med.* **1**, 165, 1967; Alpert J. J., Kosa J. and Haggerty, R. J. A month of illness and health care among low-income families. *Publ. Hlth Rep.* **82** (8), 705, 1967; Haggerty, R. J. and Alpert J. J. The child, his family and illness. *Post-Grad. Med.* **34**, 228, 1963; Andersen R. A Behavioral Model of Families. Use of Health Services. Center for Health Administration Studies, Research Series No. 25, 1968; Freeman H. E. Attitudes toward mental illness among relatives of former patients. *Am. sociol. Rev.* **26**, 59, 1961; Freeman H. E. and Simmons O. G. Mental patients in the community: Family settings and performance levels. *Am. sociol. Rev.* **23**, 147, 1958; Freeman H. E. and Simmons O. G. Wives, mothers and the post-hospital performance of mental patients. *Soc. Forces*, **37**, 153, 1958; Freeman H. E., Simmons O. G. and Bergen B. J. Possessiveness as a characteristic of mothers of schizophrenics. *J. abnorm. soc. Psychol.* **58**, 271, 1959; Freeman H. E. Attitudes toward mental illness among relatives of former patients. *Am. sociol. Rev.* **26**, 59, 1961; Freeman H. E. and Simmons O. G. Feelings of stigma among relatives of former mental patients. *Soc. Prob.* **8**, 312, 1961; Freeman H. E. and Simmons O. G. Treatment experiences of mental patients and their families. *Am. J. publ. Hlth* **51**, 1266, 1961; Freeman H. E. and Simmons O. G. *The Mental Patient Comes Home* Wiley, New York, 1963; Meyers J. and Roberts B. *Family and Class Dynamics in Mental Illness.* Wiley, New York, 1959.

    [7] Report on Consultation on the Statistical Aspects of the Family as a Unit in Health Studies, December 14–20, 1971, WHO, Geneva, DSI/72-6, 1971; Litman, T. J. ed: *Statistical Indices of Family Health.* Report of a WHO study group. Technical Report Series. 587. Geneva, World Health Organization, 1, 1976.

    [8] Crawford C. O. (editor) *Health and the Family: A Medical Sociological Analysis.* Macmillan, New York, 1971.

    [9] Larsen D. E. and Larson L. E. Family health and illness. *J. Compar. Fam. Studies* **4**, Special issue, 1973.

approaches within one discipline—sociology—to explain the way families react to illness, for instance, Adams has concluded that the structural-functionalist conceptualization of illness in the family appears to be more applicable to the attitudes of well people while that of the social behaviorists tends to better explain the social meaning of illness for those who are ill.[10]

On the whole, much of our early knowledge of the role of the family in health care has been the product of either fairly broad-based national or regional surveys, such as that conducted by the United States National Health Survey, or panel studies of subscribers to select prepaid insurance programs.[11] For the most part, attempts at either longitudinal or intergenerational analyses of family health patterns and practices have been relatively limited, if not nonexistent.

Noting the relative paucity of available data and the need for more sophisticated statistical information concerning the family and health care, the final report of the special World Health Organization Consultation on the Statistical Aspects of the Family as a Unit of Health Studies observed:

> In spite of its central position in society, the family has been infrequently studied from the public health point of view. The complex interrelationships between health and the family virtually constitute *terra incognita*. In the form presented or available, statistics too often tell very little about the family setting although this is undoubtedly a major factor in, for example, the rearing of children and the development and stabilization of adult personality. Many of the strains and maladjustments which place an increasing burden on paediatric, general medical and psychiatric services can be understood and efficiently tackled only after due attention has been given to the family setting. The fact that the family is a unit of illness because it is the unit of "living" has been grossly neglected in the development of statistical tools suitable for coping with this set of problems, and in the provision of statistical data essential for an investigation of the individual as part of the family in illness as well as health.[12]

Methodologically, research in the area of health care and the family has embraced a variety of designs and techniques ranging from the use of demographic and census data[13] and household interview surveys[14] on one hand to model building and the exploration of innovative data collection procedures on the other.

---

[10]Adams M. Functionalism Versus Social Behaviorism in the Current Sociology of Illness: A Test of the Empirical Adequacy of Theory. Unpublished Doctoral Dissertation, University of Minnesota, 1962.

[11]Anderson O. W. and Feldman J. J. *Family Medical Costs and Voluntary Health Insurance: A Nationwide Survey*. McGraw-Hill, New York, 1956; Anderson O. W. and the staff of NORC. *Voluntary Health Insurance in Two Cities: A Survey of Subscriber Households*. Harvard University Press, Cambridge, 1957; Anderson O. W., Colette P. and Feldman, J. J. Family Expenditure Patterns for Personal Health Services, 1953 and 1958, Research Series No. 14, Health Information Foundation, 1960; Woolsey T. D. The concept of illness in the household-interview for the United States national health survey. *Am. J. publ. Hlth* **48**, 703, 1958; Freidson E. *Patients' Views of Medical Practice—A Study of Subscribers to a Pre-Pay Medical Plan in the Bronx*. Russell Sage Foundation, 1961; Densen P. M., Jones A. W., Balamuth E. and Shapiro S. Pre-paid medical care and hospital utilization in a dual choice situation. *Hospitals* **36**, 63, 1962.

[12]Report, World Health Organization Consultation, *op. cit.*, p. 2.

[13]For an extensive examination of the use of demographic analysis in the study of family health, see Herberger L. The Demographic Approach to the Study of Family Health. Report, World Health Organization, *op. cit.*, Annex III, pp. 61–76.

[14]For example, see Miller F. J. W. *Principles Underlying the Design of a Family Health Study*, WHO/PA/241-59, WHO, Geneva, 1959.

Models and Designs

Haggerty, for instance, has sought to examine the relationship of family functioning and disease or dysfunction in the family or its members through what has been termed "family diagnosis." Based on the general theory of family functioning, the model encompasses three major functional categories: (1) past medical experiences and attitudes toward health; (2) internal functions including relations to the family of origin, internal role relations, family dominance, child-rearing practices, etc. as well as the physical environment; and (3) external functions, e.g. social mobility, social isolation, and recreational activities. Since ratings are obtained for several family functions without reference to known disorders, the technique differs conceptually from the diagnostic labels of malfunction (deficiency, depending and deprivation) used in the Newcastle Study.[15,16]

Andersen, on the other hand, in one of the most ambitious efforts to date, has attempted to explain familial utilization of health services through the development of a multifaceted behavioral model involving the relationship between predisposing, enabling and need factors and health service use. According to Andersen, the propensity for some families to use more health services than others may be attributed to such predisposing factors as family composition, health beliefs and social structure. But regardless of the predisposition to do so, some means must be available to permit such action to be taken. These enabling conditions, if you will, may include both family as well as community resources. Yet even assuming the presence of predisposing and enabling conditions, he notes, the family must still perceive illness or its possibility among its members before taking any action. Thus, the amount of illness perceived by the family as well as the way the family responds to its perception comprise the third element in the model—need. The final component is, of course, the actual utilization of health services, which may be either discretionary or nondiscretionary in nature. While the use of health services generally involves less discretion than the purchase of most consumer goods and services, Andersen reports that family discretion appears to be lowest in the case of hospitalization, intermediate for physician services and highest for dental care.[17]

In addition to the above, Roghmann and Haggerty have suggested a "Flow Model" for use in the study of how families and their members, especially mothers and their children, transcend over a sequence of days through various states of stress, illness and utilization.[18] Finally, Crawford has proposed a fairly complicated four-dimensional paradigm which seeks to take into consideration

[15]Haggerty R. J. Family diagnosis: Research methods and their reliability for studies of the medical social unit, the family. *Am. J. publ. Hlth* **55**, 1521, 1965.

[16]Miller F. J. W. *et. al. Growing-up in Newcastle-upon-Tyne.* Oxford University Press, London, 1960; Spence J. C. *et. al. A Thousand Families in Newcastle-upon-Tyne: An Approach to the Study of Health and Illness in Children.* Oxford University Press, London, 1954.

[17]Andersen R. A Behavioral Model of Families' Use of Health Services. Research Series No. 25, Center for Health Administration Studies. University of Chicago, Chicago, 1968.

[18]Roghmann K. and Haggerty R. J. Family stress and the use of health services. *Int. J. Epidemiol.* **1** (3), 279, 1972.

the relationship of disease, state of illness and the context of care for the analysis of health and the family.[19] Unfortunately, as with most efforts of this type, both the Haggerty and Andersen models as well as those of Roghmann and Crawford require more extensive exploration and refinement.

In a somewhat different vein, the applicability and value of intergenerational family analyses to health-care research has recently been demonstrated by Litman in an extensive study of the health and health care of a sample of families living within a large midwestern American metropolitan area.[20] Following the pioneering work of Reuben Hill and associates at the University of Minnesota Family Study Center, an intensive, multifaceted exploratory study of the health attitudes, values, beliefs, experiences and practices of a sample of 201 nuclear families, approximately 69 three-generational lineages living within the Minneapolis-St. Paul metropolitan area, was undertaken between 1966–1967. Each family was interviewed five times over the course of the fifteen-month study period. Data of both a cross-sectional as well as longitudinal nature were obtained.[21]

A number of facets of the relationship between the family and health care were explored, including the socialization of health attitudes, values, knowledge and beliefs, family decision making in health and health care, and the role of the family in health and illness behavior. Interestingly enough, not only did generational differences tend to persist regardless of social class, but, in most cases, social-class differences as far as health and health care were concerned appeared to be largely a function of generation.

Intergenerational analysis, as will be indicated later, especially lends itself to an examination of not only the interaction of family members but the totality of intrafamilial transactions within the context of historical time as well. Moreover, in terms of health care, such a design facilitates assessment of both the socialization of health attitudes, values and beliefs, as well as the dynamic aspects of the health behavior of families and family members within and throughout the three phases of the life cycle.

Finally, in a somewhat different vein, Klein has recently sought to explore the applicability of Hill's ABCX model of family crises to family adaptation and response to chronic kidney disease.[22]

The Current State of the Art

Although plagued by methodological imprecision, limited empirical inquiry and minimal involvement or integration with family theory, much has neverthe-

[19]Crawford C. O. (editor) *Health and the Family: A Medical-Sociological Analysis*, pp. 121–122. Macmillan, New York, 1971.

[20]Litman T. J. Health Care and the Family: A Three Generational Study. An Exploratory Study Conducted Under a Grant No. CH00167-02 from the Division of Community Health Services, United States Public Service; Health care and the family: A three-generational analysis. *Med. Care* **9**, 67, 1971; also in *Sourcebook in Marriage and the Family* (edited by Sussman M. B.) pp. 268–279. Houghton Mifflin, Boston, 1974.

[21]Hill R. *et al. Family Development in Three Generations*. Schenkman, Cambridge, 1970.

[22]Klein S. Familial Coping with the Crisis of Chronic Illness. Unpublished Doctoral Dissertation, University of Minnesota, 1975.

less been gleaned concerning the role of the family in health and medical care. A review of the current state of the art reveals a rather rich and insightful literature representing the contributions of a diversity of fields and disciplines.

The Socioepidemiology of Family Health

The role of the family as a hereditary link, causal agent or source of communication in the disease process has been the subject of a number of socioepidemiological investigations.[23] Downes, for example, has noted an association in the occurrence of chronic illness in both spouses, while the concentration or clustering of illness episodes within families has been reported by others.[24]

As one might suspect, family units tend to experience illness at a higher rate than any given individual.[25] For instance, in a study of low-income families, Alpert et al. calculated that while, on the average, individual family members reported a symptom every thirteen days, their families did so every three days.[26] As a matter of fact, not only were an overwhelming number of illness-related events reported to take place within the family circle, but the daily routine of family life was frequently interrupted by the occurrence of symptoms and the actions taken for their relief as well. Moreover, it has been estimated that the ratio of medical nonattended symptoms to medically attended symptoms may be in the magnitude of seven to one.

Disease, Illness and the Family

As Haggerty and Alpert have observed, in addition to genetic factors, the common infectious diseases afford the clearest evidence of the important part the family may play as a source of illness. The direct spread of infectious agents, for example, may occur more easily within the family group than any other social context. Moreover, they note, not only may the family be a source of a child's illness and a factor affecting its outcome, but the child's illness may have a signifi-

[23]See Litman T. J. The family and health care. Chap. 6: Social epidemiologic and demographic aspects. In *The Sociology of Medicine and Health Care: The First Fifty Years—A Bibliography*. Glendessary Press, San Francisco, 1974; and Cobb S. *et al.*, The intra-familial transmission of rheumatic arthritis. *J. Chron. Dis.* **22**, complete issue for September, 1969.

[24]Downes J. Chronic illness among spouses. *Milbank Meml. Fund q. Bull.* **25**, 334, 1947; For example see: Dingle J. H. *An Epidemiological Study of Illness in Families*. Academic Press, New York, 1959; Dingle J., Badger G. and Jordan W. S. Jr., *Illness in the Home*. Case Western Reserve University Press, Cleveland, 1964; Dingle, J. H. *et al.* A study of illness in a group of Cleveland families—I. Plan of study and certain general observations. *Am. J. Hygiene* **58**, 16, 1953; Badger G. F. *et al.* A study of illness in a group of Cleveland families—V. Introduction and secondary attack rates on indices of exposure to common respiratory diseases in the community. *Am J. Hygiene* **58**, 179, 1953; Kellner R. *Family Ill Health: An Investigation in General Practice*. Charles C. Thomas, Springfield, 1963; Fox, J. P. and Hall L. E. Continuing surveillance of families for studying the epidemiology of viral infection. *Int. J. Epidemiol.* **17**, (1), 31, 1972; Bortner R. W., Rosenman R. H. and Friedman M. *J. Chron. Dis.* **23**, 39, 1970.

[25]Pratt L. The significance of the family in medication. *J. Compar. Fam. Studies* **10**, 14, 1973.

[26]Alpert J. *et al.* A month of illness and health care among low income families. *Publ. Hlth Rep.* **82**, 705, 1967.

cant effect on the family and represent the "presenting symptoms" of illness in other family members as well.[27]

The relationship between the health of children and the outcome of disease and family environment, for example, was dramatically demonstrated in the famous Newcastle studies of Miller et al.[28] Similarly, in a series of studies conducted at the University of Rochester in New York, Haggerty and associates found that such common crises as the death of grandparents, change of residence, loss of father's job, etc. occurred significantly more often in a two-week period prior to the appearance of a streptococcal infection than in the two weeks afterward, apparently serving to lower the patient's resistance to infection. There was also an indication that age, intimacy of contact and family organization tend to influence susceptibility to streptococcal infection.[29]

Family Influence on Illness

The relationship between such familial sociocultural factors as ethnicity, social status, community of origin and residential mobility and the behavioral retardation of children has been demonstrated by the work of Lei, Butler and Sabogh among a stratified random sample of Anglo and Mexican-American households in a southern Californian city of about 100,000 population. Moreover, for both Mexican-American and Anglos, the single most important variable explaining the presence or absence of a behaviorally retarded child in the family was the mother's education:

> For Mexican-Americans, families with a retarded child are more "culturally deprived" than their counterparts. They tend to be more immersed in their own "ethnic subcultures" and less integrated into the "dominant culture". . . . For those Mexican-Americans not yet assimilated, their culturally-isolated environment, their high degree of mobility and the low educational level of parents all are important factors in producing behaviorally retarded children.

As a matter of fact, while the father's status is usually considered more influential in determining the social status of the family, among both the Anglo and Mexican-American children studied, the mother's educational status was found to play a more important role in the children's behavioral performance than the father's status. Moreover, families who were culturally and/or socioeconomically disadvantaged were more likely than those who were not so disadvantaged to have behaviorally retarded children.[30]

[27]Haggerty R. J. and Alpert J. J. The child, his family and illness, Postgrad. Med. 34, 228, 1963.

[28]Miller F. W. et al. Growing Up in Newcastle-upon-Tyne, Oxford University Press, London, 1960.

[29]Haggerty R. J. Family crises: The role of the family in health and illness. In Ambulatory Pediatrics (edited by Haggerty R. J. and Green M.) pp. 774–776. Saunders, Philadelphia, 1968; Meyer R. J. and Haggerty R. J. Streptococcal infections in families: Factors altering individual susceptibility. Pediatrics 29, 539, 1969.

[30]Lei T.-J., Butler E. W. and Sabogh G. Family socio-cultural background and the behavioral retardation of children. J. Hlth & soc. Behav. 13, 318, 1972.

Family Health and Illness Behavior

As indicated earlier, the family unit may play a pivotal role in determining not only whether a family member will receive care but, if so, whether it should be provided by the family at home.[31]

Efforts to treat illness and promote good health, for instance, may often conflict with behavior patterns and attitudes in the home. Not infrequently, Mabry has observed, difficulties may be encountered in coordinating the goals of medicine with those of the family. As a result, some families may appear to be either indifferent or uncooperative because the therapeutic regimen prescribed has not taken an effective place among interlocking family functions, values and habit patterns.[32]

The family, then, as we shall see, in one way or another tends to be involved in the decision-making and therapeutic process at every stage of a member's illness, from diagnosis to treatment and recuperation.

The process of "becoming a patient" and availing oneself of the use of various health services encompasses a series of decisions and events involving the interaction of a number of persons including family, friends and professional providers of care.[33] On the whole, the role the family may play in the process varies over time depending upon the nature of the condition—i.e. whether acute, chronic or terminal, its perceived severity, the degree of familial concern as well as the member affected and the other members of the family involved—and transcends every stage of a member's illness, from diagnosis through treatment and recuperation.

Roghmann and Haggerty, for instance, have reported marked variation in the type and nature of complaints or symptoms experienced by different family members.[34] Robinson, on the other hand, found that the signs the wife-mother used to interpret as "illness" on the part of other family members varied with the family status of the individual member being evaluated.[35]

The Family and the Lay Referral Network

The decision as to whether a member's illness should be treated at home or with the assistance of a professional source of care tends largely to be negotiated within the family setting. Richardson, for example, in a study of low-income urban households, found that approximately half of the persons with illness episodes reportedly consulted another person in the family, specifically concerning

[31]Andersen R. A Behavioral Model of Families' Use of Health Services, Research Series No. 25, Center for Health Administration Studies. University of Chicago, Chicago, 1968.

[32]Mabry J. H. Medicine and the family. *J. Marriage Fam.* **26**, 161, 1964.

[33]See: Suchman E. Stages of illness and medical care. In *Patients, Physicians and Illness* (edited by Jaco E. G.) pp. 155–171. The Free Press, New York, 1972; Zola I. K., Shostak S. and Gomberg W. (Eds) Illness behavior of the working class, in *Studies of the American Worker*. Prentice-Hall, Englewood Cliffs, New Jersey, 1964.

[34]Roghmann K. and Haggerty R. J. The diary as a research instrument in the study of health and illness behavior experiences with a random sample of young families. *Med. Care* **10**, 143, 1972.

[35]Robinson D. *The Process of Becoming Ill*. Routledge & Kegan Paul, London, 1971.

what they should do about a particular condition.[36] Similarly, Knapp and associates at Ohio State found that family members and friends were the most frequently mentioned interpersonal source of information concerning home remedies and self-medication, exceeding both the physician and pharmacist in this regard.[37]

The reliance on a rather extensive network of nonprofessional sources of medical advice and consultation has been described by Freidson in terms of his classic formulation of the lay referral system.[38] Such a system, Booth and Babchuk have suggested, may not be as extensive as originally conceived, however, consisting primarily of autonomous dyads rather than an array of kin and acquaintances. In addition, they note, there may be a repatterning of one's source of counsel over the course of the family life cycle, i.e. from spouse to adult child (usually the daughter), and from coworkers, upon retirement to family members.[39]

Our own findings, on the other hand, indicated that the decision to seek out some form of professional assistance for an ill family member generally rested with the wife–mother (64.7%), followed by the husband (15.7%) and the two spouses together (13.1%), with the husband somewhat less likely to have acted in this capacity in the married-child generation. Interestingly enough, the prime role played by the wife–mother in the decision to seek medical care for her children and herself did not appear to extend to that of her spouse, who was almost twice as likely to assume such responsibility over his own medical problems. While such findings tend to contrast with those reported by Twaddle, they seem to be consistent with what was found by Booth and Babchuk.[40]

Finally, while 88 per cent of the patients seeking care for head and neck cancer studied by Miller reportedly discussed their symptoms with at least one person, most often their spouse (45.7%), prior to an examination by a professional practitioner, there appeared to be significant social-class differences as well. Upper- and middle-class respondents, for instance, regardless of sex, were significantly more likely to consult with their spouse before seeking professional care than were their lower-class counterparts.[41]

Source of Medical Care

On the whole, there seems to be fairly consistent evidence that most families tend to rely on at least one physician as their primary source of care or regular

[36]Richardson W. Measuring the urban poor's use of physicians' services in response to illness episodes. *Med. Care* **8**, 132, 1970.

[37]Knapp D. A., Knapp D. E. and Engle J. The public, the pharmacist and self medication. *J. Am. Pharmacol. Ass.* **56**, 460, 1966.

[38]Freidson E. Client control and medical behavior. *Am. J. Sociol.* **65**, 377, 1960; *Patients' Views of Medical Practice—A Study of Subscribers to a Prepaid Medical Plan in the Bronx.* Russell Sage Foundation, New York, 1961; Also see Kadushin C. *et al. Why People Go to Psychiatrists*, pp. 296–297. Atherton, New York, 1969.

[39]Booth A. and Babchuk N. Seeking health care from new resources. *J. Hlth & soc. Behav.* **13**, 90, 1972.

[40]Litman T. J. *Health Care and the Family: A Three Generational Study, op. cit.*; Booth A. and Babchuk N. *op. cit.*; Twaddle A. Health decisions and sick role variations. *J. Hlth & soc. Behav.* **10**, 105, 1969.

[41]Miller M. H. Seeking advice for cancer symptoms. *Am. J. publ. Hlth* **63**, 956, 1973.

family doctor. As Koos noted long ago, while families may consult a different physician in special circumstances, the family doctor remains the one to whom they turn for all their family's ordinary medical needs.[42] Although in most cases this role has tended to be assumed by the solo general practitioner, there is some indication that group-practice arrangements and medical clinics have recently begun to be conceived as serving in this capacity as well.[43]

Whether or not family units have a regular doctor, however, would appear to be related to such factors as family composition, age of the head of household, length of residence and family income. Hassinger and McNamara, for instance, reported that families with children, younger heads and higher income were more likely than those without children, with older heads and lower incomes to have such a source of care.[44] Similarly, in their study of Aluminum City, Sheps, Sloss and Cahill found that a larger proportion of families with children had received care from their regular family practitioner during the two-year period of study than did single-member units or married couples without children. In addition, both the age of the head of the household unit as well as length of residence in the area appeared to affect the extent to which families reportedly relied on the services of a regular family doctor. Newer families in the community, for instance, were less likely to have such a regular source of medical care than their more established counterparts, a finding quite similar to that reported recently by Wolfe and Badgley who found such ties to a single source of care associated with increased use and residential stability.[45] Family income, on the other hand, only appeared to have an effect on whether or not family members had a regular source of medical care among married couples without children.[46]

Selection

As Andersen has noted elsewhere, the use of health services tends to involve less discretion than the purchase of most consumer services, ranging from a great deal in the case of dental and physician services to very little vis-à-vis hospitalization.[47] On the whole, like Freidson and others, our own findings suggest that the families' choice of physician tends to be governed more by their perception of the practitioner's interpersonal relations, professional competence and proximity than the size and decor of the office, medical school graduated from or diplomas on the wall.[48]

[42]Koos E. *The Health of Regionville*. Columbia University Press, New York, 1954.

[43]Litman T. J. *Health Care and the Family: A Three Generational Study, op. cit.*

[44]Hassinger E. and McNamara R. L. *Relationship of the Public to Physicians in Rural Settings*. Agricultural Experiment Station, Research Bulletin No. 653. University of Missouri, Columbia, 1958.

[45]Wolfe S. and Badgley R. F. Patients and their families. Part 2 of The family doctor. *Milbank Meml. Fund q. Bull.* **50**, 73, 1972.

[46]Sheps C. G., Sloss J. H. and Cahill E. Medical care in Aluminum City—I. Families and their "regular" doctors. *J. Chron. Dis.* **17**, 815, 1964; also in Kerr L. White (editor) *Medical Care Research*, pp. 91–102. Pergamon Press, Oxford, 1965.

[47]Andersen R. A. Behavioral Model of Families' Use of Health Services. Research Series No. 25, Center for Health Administration Studies, University of Chicago, Chicago, 1968.

[48]Freidson E. *Patients' Views of Medical Practice—A Study of Subscribers to a Prepaid Medical Plan in the Bronx*. Russell Sage Foundation, New York, 1961; Litman T. J. *Health Care and the Family: A Three Generational Study, op. cit.;* Jenny, Frazier, Bagramian and Proshek, on the other

But while the patient and family may use considerable discretion in their selection of a primary source of health care, once the decision has been reached, their control over either the process and/or site of hospitalization tends to be virtually foreclosed. Once the patient has sought physician services, Andersen and Sheatsley observed, his, and we might add the family's, judgement and discretion are greatly reduced in lieu of the physician's recommendations regarding hospital-related services.[49]

On the whole, the control the phsyician holds over the hospitalization process, at least in the United States, tends to be virtually complete. As a matter of fact, if one had any doubts as to the pervasive nature of his gatekeeper functions over the institution, they tend to be readily dispelled by the experiences reported by our own study families. Thus, not only was there evidence that the phsyician maintained a virtual monopoly over the decision of *if* and *when* to hospitalize (88%), but with few exceptions, the physician's preference proved to be the primary factor governing selection of the site of care (77.6%). Moreover, there appeared to be little evidence that the patients and their families either were knowledgeable or aware of the limited options to hospital care afforded them by their choice of practitioner. Only a quarter of our respondents were able to correctly identify their physician's hospital affiliations. Half made at least some error in their identification, usually listing fewer hospitals than were available to them, while another quarter were completely in error. Nor was there any indication that knowledge of the practitioner's hospital ties had any bearing on the patients' choice of physician. Such delegation of responsibility and control over the hospitalization process, then, appears to be made within a vacuum of ignorance and condescension, sustained by the patients' and families' ill-informed and disinterested acquiescence.[50]

Utilization

Although most utilization studies have traditionally focused primarily on individual decision making, tending to ignore the important influence of kin and friendship networks, there is increasing evidence that the family does play a significant role as well.[51] Weeks, for example, has explored the problem of familial apathy toward medical care, while an attempt by Salloway and Dillon to attribute

hand, found that parents with high SES scores were significantly more likely to cite professional competence as the reason for their satisfaction with their child's dentist, while the relationship of the dentist to the child was the reason most often given by low SES patients: see Jenny J., Frazier P. J., Bagramian R. A., Proshek J. M. and Vincent J. An ecological study of family dental behavior and children's caries experiences—Summary, final report. Resident Grant No. DH00183, Division of Dental Health, United States Public Health Service, Division of Health Ecology, University of Minnesota, School of Dentistry, Mimeo, 1973.

[49]Anderson O. and Sheatsley P. Patients, Physicians and the General Hospital. A Social Survey of Decisions and Use in Massachusetts. 1960–1961. Research Series No. 24, p. 84. University of Chicago Center for Health Administration Studies, Chicago, 1967.

[50]Litman T. J. *Health Care and the Family: A Three Generational Study. op. cit.*

[51]McKinlay J. B. Some approaches and problems in the study of the use of services: An overview. *J. Hlth & soc. Behav.* **13,** 115, 1972; Salloway J. C. and Dillon P. B. A comparison of family networks and friend networks in health care utilization. *J. Compar. Fam. Studies* **4,** 131, 1973.

delay in the use of health services to the size of one's friendship and family networks produced rather mixed results, with the former tending to facilitate utilization and the latter associated with diminished rates of use.[52] On the other hand, while Abernathy and Schrems found that proximity to a primary care facility had a direct bearing on the families' selection of a source of care (i.e. the further the distance, the less likely the choice of facility), distance alone did not seem to adversely affect the families' overall utilization of services.[53] Apparently, other variables such as the accessibility, acceptability, appropriateness and adequacy of the service, and the perceived susceptibility and seriousness of the condition, etc. may come into play and must be taken into consideration as well.

The Influence of Family Size, Composition and Life Cycle

The propensity for some families to use more health services than others has been attributed by Andersen to such predisposing factors as family composition, health beliefs and social structure.[54] Similarly, an intensive review of the literature by Eichhorn and Aday suggests that the effects of family size and composition on the use of health services may be linked to differences in income, age and sex.[55] The absence of any significant difference in the utilization of pediatric services for children from broken, lower SES families than those which were more intact, on the other hand, led Wingert *et al.* to conclude that familial stability and intactness, as far as health care is concerned, may not necessarily be synonymous. Broken families, they contend, may be just as stable with regard to child health as their more intact counterparts, due to hidden family arrangements, the influence of outside agencies, or the assumption of the medical and nursing function by the mother.[56]

Family Size

In a recent review of the literature on family health-care patterns, Andersen and Kasper observed that family size has proven to be a fairly useful indicator of utilization.[57] In addition to serving as a relatively strong predictor of how families

[52]Weeks H. A. Apathy of families toward medical care: An exploratory study. In *Patients, Physicians and Illness* (edited by Jaco E. G.) The Free Press, New York, pp. 159–164, 1958; Salloway J. C. and Dillon P. B. *op. cit.*

[53]Abernathy W. J. and Schrems E. L. Distance and Health Services: Issues of Utilization and Facility Choice for Demographic Strata. Research Paper No. 19. Stanford University Graduate School of Business, Palo Alto, 1971.

[54]Andersen R. A Behavioral Model of Families' Use of Health Services. Research Series No. 25. University of Chicago Center for Health Administration Studies, Chicago, 1968.

[55]Aday L. and Eichhorn R. C. *The Utilization of Health Services: Indices and Correlates—A Research Bibliography*, 1972. DHEW Publication No. (HSM) 73-3003. United States Government Printing Office, Washington, 1972.

[56]Wingert W. A. *et al.* The influence of familial organization on the utilization of pediatric emergency services. *Pediatrics* **42**, 743, 1968.

[57]Andersen R. and Kasper J. D. The structural influence of family size on children's use of physician services. *J. Compar. Fam. Studies* **4**, 116, 1973.

utilize general medical-care services,[58] family size has been found to have a significant influence on whether a child receives well-baby care or other health services,[59] as well as the amount spent on health care per family member. On the whole, the relationship between family size and the use of health services appears to be an inverse one—the larger the family, the fewer the services used per person.[60] Nevertheless, it should be noted that Picken and Ireland found no significant relationship between social class or family size and the level of physician consultation for fathers and mothers in their study of medical care-seeking behavior in Edinburgh, Scotland.[61]

Finally, while the basic relationship between family size and utilization has been reasonably well documented, with the exception of the recent work of Andersen and Kasper, little attempt has been made to provide a theoretical framework or a more detailed empirical analysis to better understand this relationship and its implications for health care.[62]

Life Cycle

In addition to the influence of family size, McEwan as well as Bruce have suggested the important role the life cycle may play in determining variations in the social and economic behavior and health experiences of the family and its members.[63] On the whole, families tend to exhibit considerable variation in their needs and use of health services over the course of the life cycle. Thus, prechild families, characterized by small size and young, healthy adult members, tend to use relatively few health services, while those in the reproductive years are likely to consume large quantities of hospital and physician services, largely those associated with maternal and child care. As the size of the family begins to decline as the children leave home, there is a concomitant reduction in the total amount of medical care consumed, offset in part by an increase in use per family member associated with the susceptibility of the aged to the onset of chronic illness.[64]

[58]Andersen R. *A Behavioral Model of Families' Use of Health Services, op. cit.*; Andersen R., Smedby B. and Anderson O. W. Medical Care Use in Sweden and the United States. Research Series No. 27. University of Chicago Center for Health Administration Studies, Chicago, 1970.

[59]Morris W., Hatch M. H. and Chipman S. Deterrents to well-child supervision. *Am. J. publ. Hlth* **56,** 1232, 1966; Aday L. A demonstration of families' social status and their relationship to children's utilization of health services (Unpublished manuscript). Johns Hopkins University Department of Medical Care and Hospitals, Baltimore, 1971; Hare E. S. and Shaw G. K. A study of family health—I. Health in relation to family size. *Br. J. Psychiat.* **111,** 461, 1965.

[60]Andersen R. and Kasper J. D. *op. cit.*

[61]Picken B. and Ireland G. Family patterns of medical care utilization: Possible influence of family size, role and social class in illness behavior. *J. Chron. Dis.* **22,** 181, 1969.

[62]Andersen R. and Kasper J. D. *op. cit.*, 116.

[63]McEwan P. J. M. The Social Approach. Working Paper, Consultation on Statistical Aspects of the Family as a Unit in Health Studies, World Health Organization, December 14–20. (DSI/SAE/71.4) 1971; Bruce J. A. Family practice and the family: A sociological view. *J. Compar. Fam. Studies* **4,** 10, 1973.

[64]Andersen R. *A Behavioral Model of Families' Use of Health Services. op. cit.* 6; Andersen R. and Anderson O. Family Life Cycle and Use of Health Services. Unpublished Paper, Presented at Annual Meeting of the American Sociological Association, 1965.

Moreover, the time in life that a member may be incapacitated by a serious illness may have a lot to do with the kind of problems created for the family and their financial, social and psychological resources for resolving it.[65] Yet despite such variations in the volume and type of services used by families throughout the life cycle, research in this area is still quite limited.

Health Maintenance and Medication Behavior

Among the essential tasks performed by the family, health maintenance and home care involve the use of a considerable quantity of health services. Families tend to rely not only on a rather wide range of methods for health maintenance, but each generation appears to have adopted their own particular prescription for good health, depending on their previous training and experience, stage of life and sociocultural background. In our own study, for example, we found that while the senior generation seemed to place considerable reliance on the Protestant Ethic "work hard and keep busy," as well as fresh-air and exercise, their married grandchildren opted for either doing nothing special at all to keep well or relying on the wonders of vitamins.

Interestingly enough, only one per cent of the total sample included regular or annual medical checkups in their prescription for good health. The rather low saliency with which such periodic examinations were held was further reflected in the failure of the adult members, ostensibly the husband, in almost half of the study families to avail themselves of regular routine medical checkups. As a matter of fact, despite an apparently greater preoccupation with their relatively poorer state of health, the senior generation generally trailed their other two lineages in this regard.

The comparatively poor routine medical surveillance practiced by the grandparent and, to a lesser degree, parent generation, tends to be matched by their failure to avail themselves of other preventive measures such as routine immunizations, periodic Pap smears, proctoscopic examination, chest X-rays, etc. Such findings, we would suggest, not only raise some serious questions concerning the efficacy of such health-maintenance measures to these two generational groups, but also further underscore the failure of those who potentially stand to gain the most by taking advantage of them.[66]

Despite the claims of Adams[67] as well as Parsons and Fox[68] to the contrary the family has long carried out an extensive medication role in our society which, as Pratt[69] has recently noted, has been sustained and even extended by certain forces of industrialization. In addition to health maintenance and preventive medi-

[65]Jacobson M. M. and Eichhorn R. L. How farm families cope with heart disease: A study of problems and resources. *J. Marriage Fam.* **26**, 166, 1964.

[66]Litman T. J. Health care and the family: A three-generational analysis. *op. cit.*

[67]Adams B. N. *The American Family, A Sociological Interpretation,* p. 84. Markham, Chicago, 1971.

[68]Parsons T. and Fox R. Illness, therapy and the modern urban American family. *J. Soc. Issues* **8** (4), 31, 1952.

[69]Pratt L. The significance of the family—Medical. *J. Compar. Fam. Studies* **4**, 13, 1973.

cine, home medication may include the care and treatment of minor illnesses and injury. A nationwide survey of the Federal Drug Administration in the United States, for instance, revealed considerable reliance on self-medication for sore throats, coughs, head colds, upset stomachs, etc.[70] Such self- and home-medication practices, Pratt suggests, may serve as an acceptable alternative or supplement to professional care.[71]

On the whole, American families, at least, appear to maintain a fairly extensive inventory of drugs and medications on hand for the provision of home treatment.[72] Generationally, on an absolute, unadjusted basis, the married-child generation tends to exceed each of their other lineages in the use of most pharmaceutical products, i.e., allergy medications, cold pills, salves and ointments, pain relievers, tranquilizers and sleeping pills. Only in the case of the use of cardiovascular drugs and medications were they exceeded by their grandparents and parents. When adjusted for family size, however, a quite different pattern emerged, with the senior generation recording the greatest number of items per person.

Like Roney and associates, our own study revealed considerable reliance on self-selection in the purchase and use of pharmaceutical products and a disturbing tendency toward retention and use of prescribed medications far beyond their useful or recommended life. Generationally, the senior generation, followed by the parent generation, were the most likely to have kept such medication beyond their prescribed life, with the married grandchildren least likely to have engaged in such practices.

Finally, despite some rather stange and potentially dangerous medication practices, the overall level of misuse or inappropriate use of such products was considerably less than expected. Of the more than 3,000 items listed, only fifteen per cent were adjudged to have been inappropriatedly used.[73]

Although it has long been recognized that females tend to consumer more drugs and medications than their male counterparts,[74] there is some evidence, at least, to suggest that much of this disproportionate usage may be attributed to a very specific woman—the wife–mother. For instance, in a study of the medication practices of a sample of midwestern American families, we found the wife–mother to be by far the major source of medication use within the family setting, considerably outdistancing all other family members in this regard. In view of her apparent inability and reluctance to assume the sick role when ill, due to the severe strain her prolonged incapacitation might have on the functioning of the family, it is hardly surprising that she should rely on such preventive and curative measures to sustain her and permit her to carry on her normal family role.[75]

[70]Federal Food and Drug Administration. *A Study of Health Practices and Opinions,* United States Department of Health, Education and Welfare, Washington, June 1972.

[71]Pratt L. *op. cit.*

[72]Roney J. G. and Nall M. L. *Medication Practices in a Community: An Exploratory Study.* Stanford Research Institute, California, 1966.

[73]Litman T. J. *Health Care and the Family: A Three Generational Study. op. cit.*

[74]Aday L. and Eichhorn R. The Utilization of Health Services: Indices and Correlates—A Research Bibliography, 1972. DHEW Publication No. (HSM) 73-3003, National Center for Health Services Research and Development, p. 19, 1973.

[75]Litman T. J. *op. cit.*

The Parental Role in Health and Medical Care

Although there have been few studies which have dealt directly with health learning, it would appear that a good share of health and illness behavior, i.e., definition of signs and symptoms, patterns of utilization, health practices, etc., is acquired within the family setting.[76] In the case of our own study, the respondent's parents, irrespective of generation, were by far the most frequently mentioned source of health attitudes and opinions (41.7%), followed by the spouse (15%), health personnel (15%) and the mass media (8.3%).[77]

There also appears to be some evidence to suggest that families' use of medical care services may be related to such factors as the parents' level of education, their concern about their own health[78] and feelings of powerlessness and alienation,[79] as well as the existence of a close-knit, nonscientific ethic tradition.[80]

In addition, parental attitudes toward the child and their relationship to him have been found to have a direct effect on the family's ability to manage and treat medical problems. Davis, for instance, observed that ambivalent identification of the child's role and uncertainty about how to treat him resulted in management problems for the parents.[81] Similarly, Khurana and White reported that indifferent parents were more likely than other types of parents, including the overanxious and overindulgent, to have children whose diseases were poorly controlled.[82] Lewis and Feichner, on the other hand, found that families who dealt with the mental illness of a member in a more "sympathetic, understanding manner" were less likely to place the patient in a role of complete dependency.[83]

The Role of the Mother in Health and Illness

The significant role played by the wife–mother as a primary agent of health behavior in the family is becoming increasingly clear. For instance, in a survey of the food habits and attitudes of a sample of Minnesota school children, the mother was found to serve as a prominent influence in matters of health and nutrition.[84] As a matter of fact, perhaps the most persistent theme running through our three generation study was the rather pervasive role played by the wife–mother in the health and health care of the family. For, whatever the mea-

[76]Mechanic D. Religion, religiosity and illness behavior—The special case of the Jews. *Hum. Org.* **22**, 202, 1963.

[77]Litman T. J. *op. cit.*

[78]Mechanic D. The influence of mothers on their childrens' health attitudes and behavior. *op. cit.*

[79]Morris N., Hatch M. H. and Chipmant S. S. Deterrents to well-child supervision. *Am. J. publ. Hlth* **56**, 1232, 1966.

[80]Suchman E. A. Social patterns of illness and medical care. *J. Hlth hum. Behav.* **6**, 2, 1965.

[81]Davis F. *Passage Through Crisis: Polio Victims and Their Families,* pp. 124–125. Bobbs-Merrill, Indianapolis, 1963.

[82]Khurana R. C. and White P. Attitudes of the diabetic child and his parents toward illness. *Postgrad. Med.* **48**, 72, 1970.

[83]Lewis V. and Feichner A. Impact of admission to a mental hospital on the patient's family. *Ment. Hyg.* **44**, 503, 1960.

[84]Litman T. J. *et al.* Foods and food habits as viewed by a sample of Minnesota school children. *J. Am. Dietet. Assoc.* **50**, 1964.

sure used, illnesses incurred, medical and health services used, anticipated difficulty in assuming the sick role, potential impact of illness on the family, or primary source of familial assistance in times of illness (the parental mother), the wife–mother remained the central agent of cure and care within the family complex.[85]

In addition to playing a primary function in the family for defining and organizing responses to the child's symptoms, Alpert *et al.* noted that the mother is also the family member most likely to take action in response to such symptoms as well.[86] Similarly, Aday found mothers' attitudes and behavior to be especially relevant for explaining their children's different utilization of health services.[87]

However, since there may be considerable variation in the mother's ability to recognize discomfort or illness in a family member or make judgements concerning the behavioral signs of distress, her definitions and expectations of the illness and means of seeking out relief may conflict with those of the health professional and lead to either over- or underutilization of his services.[88]

Immunization Behavior

In addition to the influence of her own health habits on that of her children,[89] the mother tends to exert considerable control over the child's immunization behavior as well. Such factors as the mother's education, socioeconomic status, previous experience relating to the condition, and amount of information given, for instance, have been found to be closely associated with a willingness to participate in a polio vaccination program.[90] Moreover, Elling has noted the important role the mother's own reflective self concept, i.e., her estimation of how she is regarded by the physician, may play in determining her willingness to participate in a prophylactic program.[91] Merrill and associates, on the other hand, have emphasized the importance placed on mothers' perceptiveness of how their

[85]Litman T. J. *Health Care and the Family: A Three Generational Study, op. cit.* The impact of her influence need not be confined solely to within the family setting *per se*. Skipper and Leonard, for instance, have demonstrated the significant role the mother may play in deterring the child's response to hospitalization: see Skipper J. K. Jr. and Leonard R. C. Children, stress and hospitalization: A field experiment. *J. Hlth & soc. Behav.* **9**, 275, 1968.

[86]Alpert J. J. *et al.* Medical help and maternal nursing care in the life of low income families. *Pediatrics* **39**, 749, 1967.

[87]Aday L. A. Dimensions of family's social status and their relationship to children's utilization of health services (Unpublished manuscript). Johns Hopkins University. Department of Medical Care and Hospitals, 1971. Also see Aday L. A. and Eichhorn R. *op. cit.,* pp. 29–30.

[88]Mechanic D. *Human Organization, op. cit.;* Stine O. C. and Chuaqui C. Mothers' intended actions for childhood symptoms. *Am. J. publ. Hlth* **59**, 2035, 1969.

[89]Pratt L. Child-rearing methods and children's health behavior. *J. Hlth & soc. Behav.* **14**, 61, 1973.

[90]Clausen J. A. *et al.* Parent attitudes toward participation of their children in polio vaccine trials. *Am. J. publ. Hlth* **44**, 1526, 1954; Deasy L. L. Socioeconomic status and participation in the poliomyelitis vaccine trial. *Am. sociol. Rev.* **21**, 185, 1956.

[91]Elling R., Shittmore R. and Quem M. Patient participation in a pediatric program. *J. Hlth hum. Behav.* **1**, 183, 1960; Family Culture and Participation in a Rheumatic Fever Clinic, Unpublished Doctoral Dissertation, Yale University, 1957.

peers will act.[92] Similarly, the failure of a group of lower-class mothers to have their children immunized was attributed by Gray and Moody to a perceived lack of reinforcement from their friends and neighbors.[93] But while maternal decision making was found by Tyroler *et al.* to be a determinant of the family's immunization practices, the direction of the effect appeared to vary by social class, with the attitude of the father toward acceptance a major factor in lower-status families.[94]

Dental Behavior

The pre-eminent role the mother plays in the health and medical care of her family extends to the area of dental behavior as well. As Rayner has noted, while a number of studies have demonstrated an association between the children's dental-health practices and those of their mothers, few have identified the factors which have shaped the latter's behavior.[95] Metz and Richards, for instance, examined the effect of income and parents' education on children's practices, both individually, jointly and in combination,[96] whereas Kriesberg and Treiman, among others, found a direct relationship between frequency of dental visits and socioeconomic status. In addition, education and income, both separately and together, appeared to be highly correlated with preventive dental care.[97] Moreover, while Lambert and Freeman found a statistically significant correlation between family income and the mother's preventive dental practices, there was no demonstrably significant relationship between adult preventive behavior and education.[98]

Nevertheless, like Rayner,[99] the latter found a strong, positive relationship between the mother's own dental practices and those of her children.[100] Finally, parental beliefs and practices about regular and early dental visits were reported by Kriesberg and Treiman to be particularly important predictors of the use of preventive dental services by teenagers.[101]

[92]Merrill M. H., Hollister A. C., Gibbens S. and Haynes A. W. Attitudes of Californians toward poliomyelitis vaccination. *Am. J. publ. Hlth* **48**, 146, 1958.

[93]Gray R. M. and Moody P. M. The effect of social class and friends' expectations on oral polio vaccination participation. *Am. J. publ. Hlth* **56**, 2028, 1966.

[94]Tyroler H. A. *et al.* Patterns of preventive health behavior in populations. *J. Hlth hum. Behav.* **6**, 128, 1965.

[95]Rayner J. F. Socioeconomic status and factors influencing the dental health practices of mothers. *Am. J. publ. Hlth* **60**, 1250, 1970.

[96]Metz A. S. and Richards L. G. Children's preventive visits to the dentist: The relative importance of socioeconomic factors and parents' preventive visits. *J. Am. College Dent.* **34**, 204, 1967.

[97]Kriesberg L. and Treiman B. R. Preventive utilization of dentists services among teenagers. *J. Am. College Dent.* **29**, 28, 1962.

[98]Freeman H. E. and Lambert C. Jr. Preventive dental behavior of urban mothers. *J. Hlth hum. Behav.* **6**, 141, 1965.

[99]Rayner J. F. *op. cit.*

[100]Freeman H. E. and Lambert C. Jr. *op. cit.*

[101]Kriesberg L. and Treiman B. R. *op. cit.*

The Impact of the Mother's
Illness on the Family

In view of both her rather pervasive and pivotal role as an agent of cure and care within the family setting, the mother may find it not only extremely difficult to fulfill her obligations to all the members of the household when one or more is ill,[102] but she may experience considerable difficulty in maintaining her own normal role and responsibility when she herself is the one who is ill. As a matter of fact, as we indicated earlier, she may exhibit a great deal of reluctance to accept the sick role. Mechanic, for instance, observed that mothers were more likely to seek medical care and advice for their children than for themselves and appeared much more willing to accord their children the right to the sick role than themselves.[103] Mothers apparently are considered to be less vulnerable and their activities too important to be disrupted by illness.

In contrast to her husband, her own illness or prolonged incapacitation may be viewed as a serious threat to family functioning. Koos, for example, found that when the mother became sick, family life became disorganized,[104] whereas when the father was sick, the family's standard of living decreased. Similarly, Hollingshead and Rogers found that while chaos tended to accompany the mental illness of the wife, this was not the case for mentally ill husbands.[105] The same was true in our own study, where unlike her husband, the illness or prolonged incapacitation of the wife was regarded as a potentially serious blow to family functioning.[106]

Moreover, while both her husband's and children's illness were generally reported to have meant more work and concern for the wife–mother, her own illness precipitated the need for others to do more work around the house and assume new duties and responsibilities. Furthermore, there was also evidence that she may be missed and wanted by the children (5.8%), a nurturance function, we might add, hardly matched by her spouse (1.4%).

Sick Role

As far as the sick-role behavior is concerned, not only does the wife tend to be the least able and willing to give into the sick role when sick[107] but, according to a study by Bell and Phillips, she may play a significant role in defining and legitimizing her husband's "right to assume the sick role" as well.[108]

[102]McNamara M. Psycho-social problems in a renal unit. *Br. J. Psychiat.* **131**, 1231, 1967.

[103]Mechanic D. Influence of mothers on their children's health attitudes and behavior. *Pediatrics* **33**, 445, 1964.

[104]Koos, E. *Families in Trouble*. King's Crown Press, New York, 1946.

[105]Rogers L. and Hollingshead A. *Trapped: Families and Schizophrenia*. Wiley, New York, 1965.

[106]Litman T. J. *Health Care and the Family: A Three Generational Study. op. cit.*

[107]Litman T. J. *op. cit.*

[108]Bell G. D. and Phillips D. L. Playing the sick role and avoiding responsibility. Unpublished Paper Presented Before the Sixth World Congress on Sociology; Petroni F. A. Significant others and illness behavior: A much neglected role contingency. *Sociol. Quart.* **10**, 32, 1964

Influence of Family Size

Since Parsons' seminal conceptualization of the sick role, there has been speculation that sick-role performance is not only a function of the physical fact of illness itself, but is also sensitive to the support or lack of support received from one's significant others. In a study of the sick-role perceptions of a sample of husbands and wives in a large midwestern community, Petroni found that neither family size nor social class alone tends to influence sick-role performance, but rather the joint effects of the two together are a factor. Thus, lower-class persons from large families were less apt to report themselves ill or seeking medical care than lower-class respondents from small families—while sick-role behavior in middle-class families did not appear to be contingent upon family size.[109] Moreover, of all the attributes of the sick role, the "right to cut down on one's usual role activities" was considered to be the least legitimate by the spouse, conditioned in large part by the perceived severity of the illness.[110]

Health Care and the Family: Some Familial Aspects of Health and Medical Care

Over the course of the past several years, the generally widely accepted view of the modern American family as a predominantly small, isolated, nuclear, conjugal unit, with few children, and physically and functionally isolated from kin, has come under increasing challenge.[111] While industrial society has limited the family's formal social and economic functions, the notion of the existence of a contemporary, neo-local nuclear family structure, closely linked within a matrix of reciprocal relations among bilateral kinship lines, encompassing several generations, has gained increasing empirical and theoretical support.[112] Although by no means a replica of its 1890 predecessor, its modern urban analogue remains a viable, optional system based upon reciprocation and exchange among bilateral kinship lines transcending several generations. As each member unit develops a set of roles in terms of its expectations of aid and assistance under varying condi-

[109]Petroni F. A. Social class, family size and the sick role. *J. Marriage Fam.* **31**, 728, 1969.

[110]Petroni F. The implications of age, sex and chronicity in perceived legitimacy to the sick role. *Sociol. Soc. Relat.* **53**, 180, 1969.

[111]Litwak E. Geographical mobility and extended family cohesion. *Am. Sociol. Rev.* **25**, 355, 1960; Occupational mobility and extended family cohesion. *Am. Sociol. Rev.* **25**, 10, 1960; The use of extended family groups in achievement of social goals: Some policy implications. *Soc. Problems* **7**, 177, 1959-1960.

[112]Also in Sussman M. B. (editor) *Sourcebook in Marriage and the Family,* pp. 82–89. Houghton Mifflin, Boston, 1968; Sussman M. B. The help pattern in the middle-class family. *Am. sociol. Rev.* **18**, 22, 1953; Family continuity: Selective factors which affect relationships between families at generational levels. *Marriage Fam. Living* **16**, 112, 1954; Activity patterns of post-parental couples and their relationship to family continuity. *Marriage Fam. Living* **27**, 338, 1955; The isolated nuclear family: Fact or fiction. *Soc. Problems* **6**, 333, 1959; Intergenerational family relationships and social role changes in middle age. *J. Gerontol.,* **15**, 71, 1960; Parental aid and married children: Implications for family functioning. *Marriage Fam. Living* **24**, 320, 1962; Sussman M. B. and Burchinal L. Kin family network: Unheralded structure in current conceptualizations of family functioning. *Marriage Fam. Living* **24**, 231, 1962; Farber B. Family and kinship. In *Sourcebook for Marriage and the*

tions mutual expectations of reciprocity evolve over time which subsequently encompass the total system. The actual structuring of the relationships, moreover, generally tends to be a function of ecological residence, degree of kinship, and intergenerational ties, especially those between mothers and daughters.[113]

Familial Patterns of Assistance

In a study of mutual aid and support among middle- and working-class families in Cleveland, Ohio, for instance, Sussman found that help during illness comprised the major form of assistance provided by members of kin-related families, occurring in some 92 per cent of the illnesses reported. But while reciprocal relations between respondent-parents and respondent-siblings did not appear to differ significantly, illness assistance between families living some distance apart generally was given only when a family member either was, or was believed to be, critically ill or suffering from a long-term illness. There were, furthermore, no significant class differences in the amount of help given or received during an illness of a family member.[114] On the other hand, 76 per cent of the low income and 84 per cent of the high income subjects studied by Bell and Boat reportedly could count on extended family aid in cases of illnesses lasting a month or longer.[115]

Like Sussman and associates, we found there to be considerable family reliance on the parental mother as the main source of comfort and assistance in times of illness. Over twice as many respondents (85), for instance, mentioned her in this regard as mentioned her husband (41). Almost a third (27.4%) indicated that they would likely look to both parents for assistance.

In addition, there also appeared to be some interesting generational differences in the family's perceived patterns of support. Thus, while the respondent's mother (29.2%), father (20%), both parents (29.2%) or mother-in-law (10.8%) were considered by the married-child generation as its main source of potential support in time of crisis, their parents and grandparents reportedly were more likely to turn to their daughter, either within (16.4%, 30.9%) or outside our study (13.4%, 21.8%), their son (11.9%, 25.5%) or someone outside the family net-

---

Family (edited by Sussman M. B.) pp. 4–14. Houghton Mifflin; Boston, 1968; Sussman M. B. The urban kin network in the formulation of family theory. In *Families in East and West* (edited by Konig R. and Hill R.) Mouton, Paris, 1970; Sussman M. B. Family systems in the 1970's: Analyses, policies and programs. *The Annals* **396**, 40, 1971; Sussman M. B. and Slater S. B. Reappraisal of urban kin networks: Empirical evidence. Paper presented at the Annual Meetings of the American Sociological Association, Los Angeles, August 28, 1963.

[113]Sussman M. B. Urban kin network in the formulation of family theory. Paper presented at the Ninth International Seminar in Family Research, Tokyo, Japan, September, 1965; also see: Sweetser D. A. Mother–daughter ties between generations in industrial societies. *Fam. Process* **3**, 332, 1964; Asymmetry in intergenerational family relationships. *Soc. Forces* **41**, 346, 1963; The effect of industrialization on intergenerational solidarity. *Rural Sociol.* **31**, 156, 1966; Urbanization and the patrilineal transmission of farms in Finland. *Acta Sociologica* **70**, 215, 1964; Intergenerational ties in Finnish urban families. Paper presented at the 62nd Annual Meeting of the American Sociological Association, San Francisco, August 29, 1967.

[114]Sussman M. B. The isolated nuclear family: Fact or fiction. *Soc. Problems* **6**, 333, 1959.

[115]Bell W. and Boat M.D. Urban neighborhoods and informal relations. *Am. J. Sociol.* **62**, 391, 1957.

work (23.9%, 10.2%) for assistance ($x^2 = 152.377$, df—28, $N = 187$, $c = 0.670$, $P < 0.001$). Similarly, while the impact of a member's illness was generally confined to the nuclear family itself, extending to few outside the immediate household, when reliance on outside assistance was sought (6%), primarily in illnesses involving the wife–mother (70%), the parental mother again proved to be the major source cited in both the married-child and grandparent generations. The central role played by the parental mother in times of illness, then, as a major focus of the demands of both her own married offspring and her progenitors, appears to be clear indeed. How well she performs this task and at what price to her own family unit, however, warrants further investigation.[116]

Parsons and Fox Revisited

In their classic lament several years ago concerning the role of the family in health and medical care, Parsons and Fox proposed that the modern urban American family possessed certain structural and organizational weaknesses that mitigated against the performance of its traditional sick-care function and gave rise to its reliance on the services of extrafamilial institutions of health care.[117] Although largely intuitive and highly pessimistic, their position would appear to have received at least partial empirical support from the findings of our study of the health practices and behavior of a sample of midwestern American families. Almost half (43.2%) of the families studied, for instance, regardless of generation, indicated that they would find it fairly, if not very, difficult to care for a sick member at home for any prolonged period of time. Moreover, a majority of the sample families (58.6%) indicated complete and ready willingness to relinquish responsibility for the care of the sick to the hospital, ostensibly in the belief that the ill member would receive better care there. But while there was fairly general agreement (80.2%) that convalescence might better be provided at home, almost a third (31.8%) of the families indicated that they would be unable to care for a sick person at home under any circumstances, with the elderly somewhat more likely to express this feeling than the other two generations, primarily due to the physical inability to do so. Finally, although almost 75 per cent of the younger generation families endorsed the notion that an ill family member has a right to expect care from his or her family, their grandparents, those most likely to be the recipient of such care, appeared to have the most misgivings about them doing so.[118]

On the other hand, as Peterson has noted, while apparently entirely willing to delegate responsibility for the cure and care of a sick member to the hospital, the contemporary modern American family has not discarded completely its traditional function of taking care of those who are ill but not sick enough to be hospitalized. As a matter of fact, in sheer quantitative terms, such care accounts for

[116]Litman T. J. *Health Care and the Family: A Three Generational Study. op. cit.*

[117]Parsons T. and Fox R. Illness, therapy and the modern urban American family. *J. Soc. Issues* **8**, 31, 1952.

[118]Litman T. J. *Health Care and the Family: A Three Generational Study. op. cit.;* also see: Health care and the family—A three generation analysis. *Med. Care* **9**, 67, 1971.

the major proportion of all illness episodes.[119] How well it is performed and how well equipped the family may be to do so, however, remains an open question.

Compliance Behavior

Of central importance in home treatment is that the physician's instructions be followed as directed. Once treatment is prescribed, it is assumed that both the patient and the family will follow through. The outcome of a patient's illness, then, may in part be a function of the way the family carries out the physician's instructions regarding treatment. Unfortunately, as Davis has pointed out, this may be somewhat less than desired. Approximately one out of every three patients, for example, may be expected to default on their doctor's orders.[120] In addition to broken appointments,[121] there may be a breakdown in the maintenance of a medication regimen as well. Approximately 35 per cent of the children undergoing a ten-day course of oral penicillin therapy were reported by Mohler *et al.* to have failed to do so because the parents failed to give them the drug for the prescribed period.[122] Similarly, the incidence of serious error in home treatment and management of patients with diabetes and tuberculosis is also well documented.[123] Oakes *et al.*, on the other hand, found that compliance to a hand-resting splint regimen increased when the patients perceived that their family members expected them to wear it as prescribed.[124]

The ultimate success of the family's involvement in home treatment may in large part revolve around its ability and preparation to do so. Unfortunately, in many cases this may be far less than desired. As a matter of fact, not only did our own study families tend to exhibit a rather low level of knowledge and information concerning matters of health (almost 80% [78.6%] failed a modified version of the 1966 CBS National Health Test), but the ill-preparedness and lack of so-

[119]Peterson E. T. The impact of adolescent illness on parental relationships. *J. Hlth & soc. Behav.* 13, 429, 1972.

[120]Davis M. S. Variations in patients' compliance with doctors' orders: Analysis of congruence between survey responses and results of empirical investigations. *J. Med. Educat.* 41, 1037, 1966.

[121]Haggerty R. C. *et al.* The Child, his family and illness. *Post Grad. Med.* 34, 228, 1963.

[122]Mohler D., Wallen D. G. and Dreyfus E. G. Studies in the home treatment of streptococcal disease, failure of patients to take penicillin by mouth as prescribed. *New Engl. J. Med.* 252, 116, 1955.

[123]For an extensive examination of the problem of patient compliance to a prescribed regimen, see: Davis M. S. Predicting non-compliance behavior. *J. Hlth & soc. Behav.* 8, 265, 1967; Davis M. S. and Eichhorn R. Compliance with medical regimens: A panel study. *J. Hlth hum. Behav.* 4, 240, 1963; Davis M. S. Variations in patients' compliance with doctors' advice: An empirical analysis of patterns of communication. *Am. J. publ. Hlth* 58, 274, 1968; Davis M. S. Variations in patients' compliance with doctors' orders: An analysis of congruence between survey responses and results of empirical investigations. *J. Med. Educ.* 41, 1037, 1966; Watkins J. D. *et al.* A study of diabetic patients at home. *Am. J. publ. Hlth* 57, 1967; Litman T. J. Illness behavior and the pharmacist: The need for greater professional involvement. *Wisconsin Pharmacy Extension Bulletin,* January 1969; Brands A. J. The quality of medical care and home treatment. Mimeographed Report, Division of Indian Health, U.S. Public Health Service, 1967.

[124]Oakes T. *et al.* Family expectations and arthritis patient compliance to a hand resting splint regimen. *J. Chron. Dis.* 22, 757, 1970.

phistication exhibited on the part of our senior generation families were particularly disconcerting as well.

In addition to being more inner-directed and likely to view health as a private matter than their married children or grandchildren, more passive and less inquisitive in their doctor–patient relationships, and more reliant on folk fatalism than scientific medicine in their approach to matters of health, our senior generation families exhibited an appalling lack of knowledge and ability to perform such rudimentary home-care techniques as taking a temperature either orally (39% did not know how vs. 12.4% overall) or rectally (70% vs. 30%), take a pulse (74% vs. 48%), stop bleeding (64.8% vs. 34%), provide artificial respiration (85% vs. 52%), give an enema (37% vs. 26%), or use a rectal suppository (43% vs. 28%) (where in the case of the latter two they were nearly matched by their married grandchildren).

In view of the above, it is not surprising that patient compliance to medical regimes tends to be less than expected. Moreover, the common medical assumption of universal family understanding and preparation for home care would seem in need of considerable reassessment. Finally, it would appear that Parsons and Fox's classic indictment of the modern American family may have far wider applicability than originally intended, extending across more than one generation.[125]

Illness, Family Structure and Family Functioning

Despite considerable evidence from pediatric and psychiatric literature concerning the relationship between family structure and family function on one side and behavioral and emotional problems of children on the other, Pless and Roghmann have noted, the relationship of the effects of illness and other disruptions on the stability, happiness and functioning of the family appears to be less well researched.[126]

In an excellent review of the relation of family structure to health and disease, Chen and Cobb noted a striking relationship between parent deprivation and a number of medical and psychosomatic disease, notably suicide, tuberculosis and accidents. In addition, the possible existence of a chain of events progressing from parental loss through certain emotional states to altered physiologic function which may contribute to disease was postulated. In contrast, while there appeared to be little association between sibship size and health and disease, the ratio of the number of eldest to youngest children in the family appeared to be a fairly useful predictive tool. Finally, despite a marked relationship between marital status and overall mortality, the relationship to specific conditions, i.e., tuberculosis, suicide, influenza and pneumonia, etc. tended to be far less striking, although why this is the case is not clear.[127]

[125]Litman T. J. Health care and the family: A three generation analysis. *Med. Care* **9**, 67, 1971.

[126]Pless J. B. and Roghmann K. J. Chronic illness and its consequences. *J. Pediatrics* **79** (3), 351, 1971.

[127]Chen E. and Cobb S. Family structure in relation to health and disease: A review of the literature. *J. Chron. Dis.* **12**, 544, 1960.

On the other hand, there also appears to be some evidence that illness and its familial consequences may be inversely related to family size. In the case of our own study, for example, not only did patients in larger families, i.e., five members or more, tend to be laid up for shorter periods of time, but their illnesses appeared less likely to have posed any serious problems for their families or to have had any dramatic effect on their families' role relations. Moreover, whereas small to average size families (two to four members) were reportedly more likely to have experienced role revisal and inconvenience as a result of a member's illness, those of moderate to average size demonstrated much greater resilience and adaptability through an accentuation of their normal roles. There appeared to be no significant relationship, however, between family size and whether or not a member's illness had an adverse effect on family relations, nor was there any evidence that smaller families were any more likely to be brought closer together than pushed further apart as a result of such an experience.[128]

The Impact of Illness on Family Functioning

Hill has suggested that in a period of crisis such as that caused by the illness of a family member, the family's structure may be modified as the member's capacity to perform his usual roles is reduced. The family may thus enter a state of disequilibrium in which a readjustment of power and role relationships takes place until a new equilibrium is established. The length of time needed to reestablish equilibrium tends to be dependent upon the type of crisis, the member's definition of the crisis and the resources available to meet it:

> Families experience significant strains when members become diabetics, rheumatic fever patients, or experience congestive heart failure and demand special considerations. . . . Such illnesses require a reallocation of the patient's roles to others within the family. . . . Expectations shift, and the family finds it necessary to work out different patterns. . . .[129]

Thus, just as the family may affect the member's illness, so too may the member's illness affect the family. An increase in role tension and somatic symptoms on the part of both patient and spouse as a result of the partner's illness has been reported by Klein, Dean and Bodgonoff.[130] Farber, on the other hand, has noted the arrest in the cyclical nature of the family's organization, the disruption of familial integration and the reduction in the family's prestige within the community as a result of mental retardation.[131] Furthermore, while less than half

---

[128]Litman T. J. *Health Care and the Family: A Three Generational Study, op. cit.*

[129]Hill R. R. Social stresses on the family. *Soc. Casework* **39**, 42, 1958.

[130]Klein R., Dean A. and Bogdonoff M. The impact of illness upon the spouse. *J. Chron. Dis.* **20**, 241, 1968.

[131]Farber B. Effects of a severely mentally retarded child on family integration (Monograph). *Soc. Res. Child Develop.* **24** (2), Serial No. 71, 1959; Farber B. Family organization and crisis: Maintenance of integration in families with severely retarded child (Monograph). *Soc. Res. Child Develop.* **25** (1), Serial No. 75, 1960; Farber B. Perception of crisis and related variables in the impact of a retarded child on the mother. *J. Hlth hum. Behav.* **1**, 108, 1960; Farber B. Marital integration as a factor in parent–child relations. *Child Develop.* **33**, 1, 1962; Farber B., Jenne W. C. and Toigo R. Family crisis and the decision to institutionalize the retarded child. *Research Monograph of the NEA Council on Exceptional Children,* Series A. No. 1, 1960; Farber B. and Ryckman D. B. Effects of severely mentally retarded children on family relationships. *Mental Retard. Abst.* **2**, 1, 1965.

(43%) of the families studied by Salk *et al.* felt that they had been socially restricted as a result of their child's hemophilia, over three-fourths reported an adverse effect on family mobility, i.e., ability to change jobs, place of residence, or to travel.[132]

According to Cohen, the family's adjustment to their child's illness may be related to its customary pattern of dealing with stress.[133] The reaction of parents, for instance, to a fatal long-term illness in their children has been the subject of an extensive review by Gordon and Kutner.[134] The "coping process" has been explored by a number of investigators including Birenbaum (mental retardation), Meadows (congenital deafness), Davis (polio), Roghmann, Hecht and Haggerty (acute illness), and, most recently, Klein (kidney disease).[135]

On the whole, the extent to which the member's illness may affect his or her family's role relations appears to be a function of the nature of the illness itself. That is, the more prolonged and complicated the illness, the greater the likelihood it will have an effect on the member's role relations. Thus, while almost 60 percent of the acute cases studied by Litman had reportedly had either no appreciable impact on the family's role relations or had precipitated role accentuation (22%) or inconvenience (8%), the reverse was true for those cases which were of a more chronic or complex nature. Not only were the latter more apt to have had any appreciable effect on other family members (33%) but they were much more likely to have led to role accentuation (30%) and alterations (12%) as well! Although in most cases (61%) the patient's illness did not tend to create any serious difficulty for other family members, the major problems encountered seemed to involve the inconvenience and restricted mobility imposed on others by the patient's illness.[136]

Within the family, the wife–mother (33%), especially in the married-child generation, followed by her husband (10.6%) and children, proved to be the family member most affected by the patient's illness, regardless of the condition involved. While the husband tended to be the person most affected by the illness of the spouse and vice versa, the impact of their children's illnesses primarily centered on the wife–mother (55% vs. 3% for her spouse).

The Impact of Illness on Family Solidarity

Although most of the illnesses (75.5%) reportedly had had little effect on family solidarity, an equal number appeared to have either brought the family

[132]Salk L., Hilgartner M. and Granich B. The psychosocial impact of hemophilia on the patient and his family. *Soc. Sci. & Med.* **6**, 481, 1972.

[133]Cohen P. C. The impact of the handicapped child on its family. *Soc. Casework* **43**, 137, 1962.

[134]Gordon N. B. and Kutner B. Long term and fatal illness and the family. *J. Hlth hum. Behav.* **6**, 190, 1965.

[135]Birenbaum A. The mentally retarded child in the home and the family cycle. *J. Hlth & soc. Behav.* **12**, 55, 1971; Non-institutionalized roles and role formation: A study of mothers and emotionally retarded children. Unpublished Doctoral Dissertation, Columbia University, 1968; Davis F. *Passage Through Crisis.* Bobbs Merrill, Indianapolis, 1963; Meadows K. P. Parental response to the medical ambiguities of congenital deafness. *J. Hlth & soc. Behav.* **9**, 299, 1968.

[136]Litman T. J. *Health Care and the Family: A Three Generational Analysis, op cit.* Similar findings have been reported by Peterson E. *op cit.* and Downey K. J. Parents' reasons for institutionalizing severely mentally retarded children. *J. Hlth hum. Behav.* **6**, 147, 1965.

closer together or made their relationship more difficult. Interestingly enough, there were fairly marked generational differences in the response of the parent families and that of their married offspring. Thus, whereas a member's illness in the parent generation tended to have a more integrating effect on the family, the opposite was true for their married children, with increased tension, worry, anxiety and concern being the major problems encountered. On the whole, acute conditions were less likely to have affected family relations than the more serious, chronic ones.

On the other hand, there appeared to be a direct relationship between the perceived severity of the member's illness and its impact on the family's relations ($x^2 = 154.35$, d$f = 4$, N—707, $P < 0.001$).

But while there was some indication that the more serious the member's condition, the greater the likelihood that it would bring the family closer together, such salutary effects may be quite limited. Families whose members were considered to be seriously ill, for instance, were about equally as likely to have been brought closer together as driven further apart as a result of the member's condition. Apparently, in the face of such strain, familial cohesion is subject to the severest test, with the outcome left very much in doubt. What it is that allows some families to be drawn closer together under such circumstances and others to fall apart warrants further investigation.

On the whole, however, there appeared to be little, if any, evidence that perceived family solidarity, marital happiness or close family ties provides any particular hedge against the disruptive impact of a member's illness on the family relations. As a matter of fact, if anything, the opposite appeared to be true. Whereas the cohesion of an extremely close, well integrated and maritally happy family may be severely strained as a result of a member's illness, such an event may serve to bring those with more disparate family ties closer together. Why this should be so remains unclear and in need of further study.

Finally, it should be noted that we were unable to discern any evidence to support the notion that egalitarian families, i.e., those in which the family decision-making process tended to be shared or mixed, were any less likely to be adversely affected by a member's illness than their more maternally dominated counterparts.

The Impact of a Member's Hospitalization on the Family

The sudden and/or prolonged incapacitation of a family member due to hospitalization may have a rather variable effect on the family and its members. While almost a third (31.4%) of the cases reported in our own study did not appear to create any major problems for the family, most did, ranging from just "missing" the patient (19.6%) to disruption of home activities (15.2%), inconvenience (9.8%), restricted mobility (8.7%), to role alteration or reversal (12.5%). On the whole, upper- and working-class families tended to experience somewhat more difficulty in this regard than those in Class III and V, although the differences were not statistically significant.

Surprisingly, there appeared to be little, if any, relationship between either whether or not the member's hospitalization posed any major problems for the family or the nature of the problems incurred, and such variables as degree of family solidarity, closeness of family ties or perceived marital happiness. Nor were there any discernible differences in the familial impact of the member's hospitalization and the estimated difficulty the family would have in providing care at home.

Within the family, as expected, the patient's hospitalization seemed to have had the most disruptive effect on the activities of the wife–mother, especially in the married-child generation. This proved to be true regardless of who was hospitalized, the nature of the family's role orientation, or degree of perceived family solidarity.

But while the patient's hospitalization generally had little, if any, impact on his or her family's relations (59%), when it did, the effect was nearly four times as likely to be cohesive (33%), as disruptive (8.4%). Moreover, there were no discernible generational differences, nor did there appear to be any significant relationship between the impact of the member's hospitalization on his or her family ties and the latter's estimated family solidarity, closeness or marital happiness. Our study families, then, not only displayed considerable resiliency in the face of the hospitalization of one of their members, but the effect of such an event, if any, on family life proved to be more ameliorative than disruptive in nature, a function of the family's definition of the situation and its reaction to it .[173]

The Family and Physical Rehabilitation

The occurrence of a serious, chronic illness may have a profound impact on family function and role allocation which, in turn, may threaten the chances for successful rehabilitation. The ability of the patient to re-assume his or her pre-illness role responsibilities or to establish a new role in the family, Sussman and Slater have suggested, may be a function of not only the nature of the patient's physical condition but his or her "centrality" to the family unit as well. Of central importance are:

1. the degree of perception of the disruption and need for a re-allocation of roles;
2. the availability and capacity of someone to assume the patient's role responsibilities;
3. the impact of the member's illness on the clarity and consistency of the family's roles during the time he or she is incapacitated;
4. the extra burdens, if any, that may be placed on other family members due to the patient's illness, either assuming responsibilities left by the patient or picking up the slack by providing additional services for his or her care.[138]

Thus, Deutsch and Goldston found that re-establishment of the home situation for the disabled person seemed to rest upon the degree of role reversal in-

[137]Litman T. J. *op cit.*
[138]Sussman M. B. and Slater S. B. *op. cit.*

volved[139] while Mueller reported that the patient's attitude toward his family may be instrumental in overcoming dependency induced by extensive, long-term hospitalization.[140] Similarly, Sussman and Slater found a significant relationship between post-discharge success and the ratio of responsibility for household tasks performed by the patient to all tasks performed in the household (Patients, Rehabilitation, Responsibility Ratio—PRRR).[141] Dow, on the other hand, on the basis of an analysis of family reaction to the crisis of a disabled child, concluded that such a reaction is a function of both the nature of the family structure and the nature of the crisis itself.[142] Our own investigations of the rehabilitation performance of the orthopedically disabled person undergoing treatment at two midwestern therapeutic centers, however, revealed that the family may play an important albeit indirect role in the rehabilitation process. While there appeared to be little significant relationship between rehabilitation response and degree of family integration per se, there was considerable evidence that the family, as an interacting unit, may play an important supportive role during the course of the patient's convalescence. For the most part, the patients studied tended to look to, and receive, comfort and encouragement for their immediate families. On the other hand, therapeutic performance declined in the absence of such familial reinforcement. In addition, patient response seemed to be enhanced when therapy could be conceived to take place in terms of eventual re-entry into an established family constellation, rather than as an individual or personal matter.[143]

Finally, the important role the family may play in legitimizing the disabled patient's conception of himself as "sick-dependent," "well-dependent," "independent," etc. has been explored in the works of both New and Kronick.[144] Nevertheless, the total family impact on the patient's illness–career patterns, from onset to post-discharge success, still remains unclear and in need of further empirical inquiry.

Some Questions and Suggested Areas for Further Research

It would appear, then, that the family does indeed constitute a basic unit in health and medical care. Yet, as rich and insightful as the literature to date has

[139]Deutsch C. P. and Goldston J. A. Family factors in home adjustment of the severely disabled. *Marriage Fam. Living* 122, 312, 1960.

[140]Mueller A. D. Psychologic factors in rehabilitation of paraplegic patients. *Arch. Physical Med. Rehabilit.* 43, 151, 1962.

[141]Sussman M. B. and Slater S. B. *op. cit.*, p. 117.

[142]Dow T. Family reaction to crisis. *J. Marriage Fam.* 27, 363, 1965.

[143]Litman T. J. The family and physical rehabilitation. *J. Chron. Dis.* 19, 211, 1966; The influence of concept of self and life orientation factors upon the rehabilitation of orthopedic patients. Unpublished Doctoral Dissertation, Microfilm No. 61-3677, University of Minnesota, 1961; The influence of self conception and life orientation factors in the rehabilitation of the orthopedically disabled. *J. Hlth hum. Behav.* 3, 252, 1962; An analysis of the sociologic factors affecting the rehabilitation of physically handicapped patients. *Arch. Physical Med. Rehabilit.* 45, 12, 1964; Kelman H. R., Muller J. N. and Lowenthal M. Post-hospital adaptation of a chonically ill and disabled rehabilitation population. *J. Hlth hum. Behav.* 5, 4, 1964.

[144]New, P.K. *et al.* The support structure of heart and stroke patients: A study of the role of significant others in patient rehabilitation. *Soc'l Sci. Med.,* 2, 1968, 185; Kronick, J. The rehabilita-

been, much remains to be learned. Among some of the more intriguing questions and potential areas for further inquiry, we would suggest, are the following.

A. Some General Considerations

1. First and foremost, there is a need for greater application and integration of family theory in health care research. With but few notable exceptions, the problems of health and health care have largely been ignored in family sociology and the research that has been done is devoid of family theory. Thus, our knowledge about family health behavior needs to be tied to more general theory and vice versa. How, for instance, does illness compare with other family crises in terms of its effect on family organization and function?

2. As Bruce and McEwan have suggested, further attention should be directed at the applicability of the family life cycle to health and medical care and its relationship to variations in the medical concerns and behavior of family members.[145]

3. Following the work of Petroni, additional exploration of the importance of family size and SES as a sick-role contingency would seem warranted as well. Moreover, in view of the apparent inverse relationship that exists between perceived support if the sick role is taken and the family's experience with illness, further attention should be directed at determining the nature and implications of the desensitizing effect of high illness incidence and experience on family members.[146]

B. The Impact of Illness on the Family

1. Much more also needs to be learned concerning the family dynamics of health and illness. For instance, what is it that allows some families to be drawn closer together and others to disintegrate as a result of a member's illness, and how and in what ways are families able to cope with the onset and subsequent demands of a member's illness?

2. Additional research is needed on the impact of illness on specific role relationships among family members and on their relationships to each other.[147]

3. To what extent, if any, does illness, especially an illness of a long-term, chronic and debilitating nature, alter the relationships between the patient and kin and among the kin themselves?

a. More, for instance, needs to be learned about the role played by the family support system in times of illness, especially as concerns members outside the immediate household, i.e., extended-family members. Which

---

tion of stroke patients: An experimental analysis of the effects of physical and social factors in determination of recovery. Unpublished report, Bryn Mawr College, Dept. of Social Work and Social Research, 1969.

[145]Bruce J. Family practice and the family: A sociological view. *J. Compar. Fam. Studies* **4** (Special Issue), 4, 1973.

[146]Petroni F. Variations in perceived legitimacy to the sick role: The influence of significant others, chronicity, sex and generational factors. Unpublished Doctoral Dissertation, University of Minnesota, 1967; also see Litman T. J. *Health Care and the Family: A Three Generational Study. op. cit.*

[147]Peterson E. *op. cit.*

line, maternal or paternal, tends to serve as the main source of family assistance and why?

b. Under what circumstances and in what kinds of families is the extended-family network brought into play?

c. At what point, under what conditions and at what price—social as well as economic—do kin become involved in the care and treatment of ill member(s)?[148]

d. More needs to be learned about the nature and extent of the family's support system in times of illness and the reciprocal effects that the provision of such assistance has on the latter's familial relations.

e. In addition, particular attention should be directed at the role played by the parental mother as the central source of assistance and support for each of the other two lineages, her preparation and capacity to play such a role, and its impact on both her own and her family's life. Moreover the role played by the husband–father during the course of a member's illness remains largely unexplored.

C. Family Adaptation, Adjustment and Response to Illness

1.   In addition to the above, more needs to be learned about what goes on within families of varying life styles and structures when a member is stricken by illness (acute as well as chronic).

a. How are various family decisions relative to the care and treatment of the ill member reached?

b. Do different types of illnesses have different impacts on different types of families, and why?

c. What impact does a member's illness have on individual family members and their relationships to each other? To what extent is their reaction a function of their perception of the illness, its severity, etc.?

2.   How permanent is the impact of a member's illness on the family's cohesion—are such effects merely transitory, tied strictly to the period of crisis, or are they of a more permanent, long-lasting nature?

3.   In the case of the hospitalized, chronically ill or disabled patient, further attention should be focused on the acceptance of the disabled member within the family constellation, the nature and extent of the attendant familial role reversal and disruption, as well as the reaction of the family to the stress and strain caused by curtailed family income and reliance on outside support. What effects, if any, do different types of family settings, e.g. intact, nonintact, nuclear, extended, pseudo, etc., have on the care and treatment of the disabled?[149] What roles are available to the disabled within various family types and what consequences do they pose for postdischarge adjustment and success?

[148]Sussman M. B. and Slater S. B. *op. cit.*, pp. 146–147.

[149]Gibson G. and Ludwig E. G. Family structure in a disabled population. *J. Marriage Fam.* **30**, 63, 1968.

4. Further exploration of the coping mechanisms used by families to adapt to the impact of a serious or chronic illness of one of its members as well as the family's influence on the coping style of the ill member also needs to be undertaken.[150]

5. In addition, as Farber and Ryckman have suggested, more needs to be learned concerning the effectiveness of the strategies developed by families to cope with the illness of its member, particularly illnesses of a long-term, stigmatized nature. For instance, what are the conditions that affect the willingness of the family to either forestall institutionalization or readmit one of its ill members into the home after a period of institutionalization?[151] What price does the family and its members pay for retaining the afflicted member at home?

D. Home Treatment

1. In view of the extensive use and misuse of both prescription and nonprescription drugs and medications within the family, their nature and extent, patterns of socialization and familial variation deserve further exploration.

2. More also needs to be learned concerning the role played by the family and its members, particularly the mother, in the administration of home care and treatment.

   a. What effect, if any, does variation in the family's knowledge and experience in health matters play in the delivery of medical care at home?

   b. What pressures are placed on the family and its members in serving as a noninstitutional source of care?

   c. How and in what way is family life altered and what "price" is paid by the family and its members in assuming responsibility for the home care of the chronically ill?

   d. What factors seem to be associated with successful home care?

   e. Finally, additional research is needed on the nature and extent of home treatment performed within the family setting, how it is organized and dispensed within the context of family life, and its interface with other systems, familial as well as professional.[152] What kind of families, for instance, are most likely to assume and retain responsibility for the care and treatment of an ill member? How closely does the family's perception of the illness, its nature, consequences, etc. mesh with that of the physician and what effect does this have on the delivery of medical care?

---

[150]Klein S. D. Familial coping with the crisis of chronic illness: Conceptual classification and preliminary stages in theory building. Unpublished Paper, University of Minnesota Family Study Center, 1972.

[151]Farber B. and Ryckman D. B. *op. cit.,* p. 9; also see: Meyer H. Problems relative to the acceptance and reacceptance of the institutionalized child. *Arch. Pediat.* **73,** 271, 1956; Simmons O. and Freeman H. E. *The Mental Patient Comes Home.* Wiley, New York, 1963; Birenbaum A. The mentally retarded child in the home and the family cycle. *J. Hlth & soc. Behav.* **12,** 55, 1971.

[152]Pratt L. The significance of the family in medication. *J. Compar. Fam. Studies* (Special Issue), **4,** 13, 1973.

BERTON H. KAPLAN
JOHN C. CASSEL
and
SUSAN GORE

6 Social Support and Health

In human communication systems, what is the function of social support in the etiology, precipitation, course and recovery from disease? In what way does social support ameliorate stress? In what ways does social support act to promote health? While many researchers[30] have speculated on the importance of social support and a few have proclaimed it to be significant in myocardial infarction [8, 49] there is little strong empirical evidence to confirm the role it may play in health and illness. This is not surprising: attempts at conceptualization and measurement have been inadequate, discipline-bound (or study-bound), and usually formulated for post-hoc interpretation of unexpected, but striking findings.

Basic Purposes

The purpose of this paper is to unravel some important dimensions of the social support concept and to help clarify the place of the study of social support in biomedical research.

There are really four basic questions that concern us:

1. What is the place of the social support hypothesis in understanding biomedical events? What is the evidence concerning the effects of social support on the individual's health and well-being? What kinds of diseases have been attributed to the absence (or lessening) of support? This involves focusing on social support as an independent or conditioning variable.*

2. What does social support alter in the person? What are the mechanisms in the social environment (the institutions, social roles, self-perceptions, relationships, etc.) that maintain, produce, or remove the supply of supports available to an individual?

*This question raises the old problem of the conceptualization of social integration in the Durkheimian[14] sense. Durkheim was interested in social support as an independent variable and how it affected mental health, namely suicide. He was, however, also interested in support as a dependent variable, that is: what types of conditions affect or predict the level of social integration? In the first case, the emphasis is on the health of the individual. In the latter, the question focuses on the health of society. In a classic sociological sense, what is the link between "social integration" and support?

This paper is dedicated to John Cassel, M.D., a remarkable epidemiologist, a creative and vital force in modern medicine, and a great friend and colleague. Ellen Friedman provided excellent research assistance.

Presented at American Public Health Association Meetings, November 9, 1973, San Francisco, Calif. Reprinted from *Medical Care*, XV:47–58, Supplement, May, 1977, by permission of the authors and Publisher.

3. Experimentally, is there a more useful way of ordering the multidimensional properties of social support for further work? The multidimensionality of social support requires a clarification of the relevance of varying types of social support for the individual, and the mechanisms that permit affiliative needs to be met by socially supportive networks need to be better understood.
4. What are the medical care policy implications of existing data on social support?

Clearly, this paper cannot do full justice to each of these areas, accordingly, we only provide selective documentation.

Psychosocial Factors in Disease Etiology

In previous papers,[11, 41] we have indicated that there may be two types of psychosocial processes of importance in disease etiology. The first are those deleterious or stressor factors which enhance disease susceptibility; the second would be protective factors which buffer or cushion the organism from the effects of noxious stimuli (including psychological stressor factors).

We have suggested further that a characteristic common to most stressor situations is the inability of the individual to obtain meaningful information that his actions are leading to desired consequences. For example, such circumstances would pertain in most situations of role conflict, role ambiguity, blocked aspirations and cultural discontinuity. The protective factors we believe are largely a function of the nature, strength and availability of social supports. It is our contention that the joint effects of these two sets of factors determine to a considerable extent the susceptibility of the organism to physicochemical disease agents (including microorganisms, toxins, chemicals, nutritional deficiencies, et cetera). In this instance, we do not conceptualize those psychosocial factors as being directly pathogenic, but as conditioning variables determining susceptibility to a wide variety of disease outcomes. The specific manifestations of those disease outcomes we are suggesting will be a function of the genetic constitution of the individuals and the nature of the psysicochemical insults they encounter.

If such a formulation is correct, it would indicate that actions designed to prevent disease should be focused on attempts to change these psychosocial factors, rather than on efforts at early case findings and detection of disease. Modification of these factors should lead to the prevention of a wide variety of manifestations of ill health. Of the two sets of postulated factors it would appear further that strengthening social supports is more immediately practical than attempting to reduce the occurrence of the stressor situations. Therefore, this paper is concerned with attempts at further definition and clarification of the nature of social supports. It is hoped that improved conceptualization will lead to the development of more adequate instruments for their measurements and direction for attempts at modification. Before presenting these ideas, we will briefly summarize some of the evidence for the notion that the absence of adequate social supports increases the susceptibility of the organism to various forms of disease. We also present some of the theories to explain the possible biological and psychological processes which might operate.

Both animal and human studies have provided evidence of the protective effect that the presence of important other members of the same species confers on the individual under some form of stress. Conger *et al.*,[12] for example, have shown that the efficacy with which an unanticipated series of electric shocks (given to animals previously conditioned to avoid them) can produce peptic ulcers is determined, to a large extent, by whether the animals are shocked in isolation (high ulcer rates) or in the presence of litter mates (low ulcer rates). Henry *et al.*,[23] have been able to produce persistent hypertension in mice by placing the animals in intercommunicating boxes all linked to a common feeding place, thus developing a state of constant territorial conflict. Hypertension occurred, however, only when the mice were "strangers." Populating the system with litter mates did not produce these effects. Liddel[32] found that a young goat isolated in an experimental chamber and subjected to a monotonous conditioning stimulus will develop traumatic signs of experimental neurosis, while its twin in an adjoining chamber, and subjected to the same stimulus, but with the mother goat present, will not.

The evidence from human studies is somewhat more conflicting. To a large extent we believe this to be due to lack of recognition by many investigators that social supports are likely to be protective only *in the presence* of stressful circumstances. Thus, the majority of studies have contented themselves with attempts at relating the absence of some form of social support to disease or with the effect of some postulated stressful situation to disease, but have rarely examined the joint properties of the stressful situation together with the availability and nature of the social supports as they related to disease. Despite this, a number of studies have produced reasonably convincing, if somewhat indirect, evidence implicating the absence of social supports in disease genesis. Holmes,[24] for example, has shown that the highest rates of tuberculosis in Seattle occurred in those people who, because of their ethnic group, were distinct unaccepted minorities in the neighborhoods in which they lived (even when they lived in affluent upper socio-economic class neighborhoods); and in those people of whatever ethnic group who were living alone in one room, who had had multiple occupational and residential moves and who were often single or divorced. In short, the disease was occurring more frequently in "marginal" people who, for one of various reasons, had no friends, family or intimate social group to which they could relate. Similar findings have been reported for schizophrenia,[13,36] multiple accidents,[47] suicide,[25] and respiratory diseases other than tuberculosis.[25] Separation from the family and evacuation from London during World War II appeared more deleterious for London children than enduring the blitz with their families.[48] Combat studies have suggested the effectiveness of the small group (platoon, bomber crew) in sustaining members under severe battle stress.[34] As will be recognized, these latter studies have indeed examined the effect of social supports under some form of presumed stressful situation, the blitz in one instance and combat in the other. The degree to which the subjects were in fact exposed to such stressors was, however, not measured; the existence of stressors being implicit rather than explicit. In one recent study, however, both the stressors and the supports were more directly measured.

Nuckolls *et al.*,[41] studied the joint effects of these two processes on the out-come of pregnancy. The data were obtained on 170 primipara between the ages of 18 and 29 of similar social class, all being delivered by the same obstetrical services. The stressors were measured by a life-change score calculated from the schedule of recent experience as developed by Holmes and Rahe[26] which was administered at 32 weeks of pregnancy. Social supports (or as they were termed "psycho-social assets") were measured by an instrument designed to assess the subject's feeling toward herself and her pregnancy and her relationship with her husband, her parents and his parents, and friends and neighbors in the community. This instrument was administered prior to the 24th week of pregnancy. Following delivery, all medical records were reviewed "blind" and any complications of pregnancy or delivery (using the criteria developed by the Collaborative Study on Cerebral Palsy, Mental Retardation and Other Neurological and Sensory Disorders of Infancy and Childhood) were recorded. Using these criteria, the Collaborative Study found some 50 per cent of primapara had one or more complications. The rate for the present sample was 47 per cent. Taken alone, neither the life-change score nor the psychosocial asset score were significantly related to complications. However, when considered jointly it was found that 91 per cent of the women with a high life-change score but low asset score had one or more complications, whereas only 33 per cent of women with an equally high life-change score but with a high asset score had any complications.

Taken together, these studies would suggest that at both the human and animal levels the presence of another animal of the same species may, under certain circumstances, protect the individual from a variety of stressful stimuli. The mechanisms or processes through which such interpersonal relationships may function had so far been largely a matter of speculation. Theories have been advanced, however, at both the biological and the psychosocial level. Perhaps one of the more attractive theories at the biological level is that propounded by Bovard.[5,6] He suggests that stressful psychological stimuli are mediated through the posterior and medial hypothalamus leading via the release of a chemotransmitter to the anterior pituitary to a general protein catabolic effect. He further suggests that a second center located in the anterior and lateral hypothalamus when stimulated by an appropriate social stimulus (namely the availability of a supportive relationship) calls forth in the organism a "competing response" which inhibits, masks or screens the stress stimulus such that the latter has a minimal effect. While these mechanisms have been reasonably well documented in animal research and do indeed afford a plausible explanation for many of the findings reported above, there is as yet no unanimity that such processes function in this manner in humans. However, there is a diverse literature on the role of social support and health.*

---

*It is important to point out that there are a number of traditions in the literature which lend important justification to examining the function of social support as a preventor of disease, or as an ameliorating factor. The major traditions are those stemming from the classical sociological tradition of Durkheim, Tonnies, Simmel, and others as well as the present interest in social participation and the like; the social psychological tradition, for example, the Lewinian tradition and its contemporary; the religious and philosophical traditions as exemplified in the work of Schracter, Brewster Smith and others; the psychoanalytical tradition, with reference to problems of intimacy as found in Freud,

Some Assessment of the Mechanisms of
Social Support

Most of the studies which we have all seen and which utilize the concept of social support either implicitly or explicitly tend to define (or assume) support as one of the following:

1.   Support is the "metness" or gratification of a person's basic social needs (approval, esteem, succorance, etc.) through environmental supplies of social support. (The best attempt at classification and discussion of metness is found in Henry Murray's *Exploration of Personality*.[39] Basically, all humans and all primates have needs which can be satisfied only through social interaction with others).*

2.   Support is defined by the relative presence or absence of psychosocial support resources from significant others. Work in social psychiatry has focused on the deleterious effects of support *loss* through death, separation or any change in the environment which disrupts existing social relationships. Presumably, loss of social support leads to unmet needs of the individual, which are suggested by the following:

a.   Studies which establish the high death rate for spouses (particularly husbands) following bereavement for their partner.[42]

b.   In-depth psychological interviews with families moved from Boston's West End through urban renewal efforts. These findings suggest these individuals, especially the women, experience a grief syndrome similar to that evidenced in bereavement. Both depression and physical symptoms are manifest up to and beyond a two-year period after the move. Fried and Gleicher argue that these outcomes are explained more by lost gratifications from the old neighborhood than deficits in the new. Residents, especially non-working mothers, benefited from the structural crowding through increased communication, sharing and exchanges of tangible support, *i.e.*, what is often called "mutual aid." Relocation in a new neighborhood meant that these needs were met only with difficulty.[17]

c.   In explaining the similarities in disruptive and inappropriate social behavior among institutionalized population, Gruenberg[19] has argued that the "Social Breakdown Syndrome" evolves from the initial withdrawal of support by friends, family and community from the individual who is having difficulty meeting social obligations. Their lack of support further discourages the individual in his faith that he can perform, resulting in his inability to take care of himself or in his institutionalization.

d.   The work of Alexander Leighton[30] and colleagues gives support to the hypothesis that changes in social relationships result in psychiatric disability if basic human needs can no longer be met. Leighton refers to these needs as "striving sentiments" and argues that changes in the physical and social environment which interfere with patterns of social interaction will result in poor health.

Erickson, Lowenthal, Weiss and others; the comparative biological tradition as exemplified in the work of Harry Harlow and in the popular work of Desmond Morris; and in somewhat overlapping fashion, the social psychiatric tradition which has its continuities especially in Durkheim and is expressed in the work of Alexander H. Leighton, Tom Langner, Morley Beisner, Jerome Myers and others.[3, 4, 13, 15, 21, 22, 31, 38, 40]

*See the appendix (to this chapter) compiled from work by Gore[18] and Pinneau.[43]

e.   Finally, in a study of psychiatric utilization among affiliated and unaffiliated college students, Segal *et al.*[46] found that for adjusted and maladjusted (according to MMPI criteria) psychiatric utilization was significantly higher for the non-affiliated. He interpreted these findings to suggest that affiliated students more easily met needs for esteem in their daily interactions, while the unaffiliated experience more insecurity about self worth. This interpretation seems quite plausible if we view therapy visits as a kind of secondary (*i.e.*, professional) social support.

These studies (with the exception of Segal's) establish a loss or alteration in the presence of supportive others, which is assumed to result in unmet needs and ultimately psychiatric and physical disability. This interpretation is in line with French's[16] elaboration of P-E Fit (person-environment fit) theory. Persons who do not receive enough support from their social environments to meet their needs will, with time, experience psychologic and physiologic strain. This P-E fit framework will be utilized through the remainder of the paper.

Other research has focused on the presence or absence of environmental supplies or resources or the fit between the person and his social environment. This approach focuses on social integration and embraces such dimensions as: 1) The negative end of the support supply continuum: social isolation;[1] 2) The use of "objectively" measured behaviors such as amount of social affiliation;[45] and 3) Those socially facilitative or inhibitive aspects of the environment (*i.e.*, the social structure, institutions, relationship, norms) that set constraints on supportive behavior.[9]

Durkheim[14] was interested in the phenomenon of social support, and how its absence affects mental health, namely suicide. He was perhaps most concerned with support as a dependent variable, *i.e.*, in the types of social structures needed for the adequate integration of the individual.

The work of Langner and Michael[29] on mental health risk again deals with the lack of support supplies, *i.e.*, isolation. Their work does not demonstrate whether isolation leads to mental illness, or mental illness to isolation. However, their work does establish that the crucial distinction is that between having no friends and having one or more.

Focusing on the positive dimensions of mental health, Bradburn, Caplovitz[7] and colleagues have established that high affiliators have greater avowed happiness than low affiliators. This, they argue, can be explained by the voluntary nature of affiliation. Since people are free to terminate unsatisfying relationships, continued interaction contributes to positive satisfactions, which balanced against dissatisfactions, affects mental health.

Caplovitz indirectly takes up the issues of metness of needs in considering satisfaction with social relationships. He found high affiliators who are dissatisfied with the extent of their affiliation have higher avowed happiness than satisfied low affiliators. This finding might be interpreted to suggest that need-meeting through affiliation further increased the need for affiliation. High affiliators who are less satisfied want more interactions and therefore have strong needs for affiliation. Questions of this kind suggest that a comprehensive model of social support mechanisms should include the dimension of personal need and a determination of the level at which the need is satisfied.

The above findings and interpretations represent a sample of the relevant work which tends to focus on the pathological consequences of environmental change which reduces support, or on the state of social isolation which results in unmet needs. Much less attention, however, has been devoted to the healthful consequences of adequate support and the processes by which support becomes effective.

Earlier in this paper we referred to the conditioning effect of social support on the relationship between environmental stress and disease. Findings from some studies indicate social support serves to ameliorate or buffer the effects of stress for the individual.[43]

In his study of NASA administrators, scientists and engineers, Caplan[10] found that stress arises from ambiguities within work-related roles and that it can be ameliorated by supportive interpersonal relations on the job, particularly those with one's subordinates. Since peers and supervisors may be perceived as the sources of the inconsistencies, they are not likely candidates to be called upon for support. Caplan suggests that relations with subordinates are effective because the person expects that they will help him to remedy the situation. This might involve either *tangible support* (help to get the job done), or *appraisal support* (help in redefining the role expectations). In either case, the fit between the individual and his work environment is improved.

With regard to this appraisal function of social support, the laboratory work of Schacter[45] provides a useful point of departure. He studied the effects of experimentally induced states of anxiety on the desire to be with people, *i.e.*, "the affiliative tendency." His results seem to suggest that affiliative tendencies are the manifestations of "needs for anxiety reduction and needs for self-evaluation." Ambiguous situations or feelings lead to a desire to be with others as a means of socially evaluating and determining the "appropriate and proper reaction."

An illustration of what might be considered the conditioning effect of *emotional support* comes from a study of the mental and physical health consequences of unemployment due to factory shutdown.[18] It was found that those men who had the emotional support of their wives while unemployed for several weeks had few illness symptoms, low cholesterol levels, and did not blame themselves for the loss of the job. Those who were *both* unemployed and unsupported had the most disturbing health outcomes. In this study, the support of wife and friends did not result in finding new employment sooner, but the men who had support fared better in other respects during the period of unemployment and made a more rapid return to normal, as indicated by measures taken at later visits. Thus, while support did not alter the objective stress, *i.e.*, time unemployed, it evidently buffered the men's perception of its severity, and enabled them better to cope with the experience.

The available literature provides us with evidence of the importance of social support, but with few clues about the dynamics of support processes. Given both the weakness in conceptualization and the inadequacy of measurement, it seems crucial that systematic theoretical and empirical attention be addressed to exploring the following types of variables:

1. Psycho-emotional needs of the person, *i.e.*, needs which can be met socially and have a social basis

2. Relationships as sources of support; both types of relationships and characteristics of these relationships such as complementarity, obligation, *i.e.*, the normative structure within which interaction takes place.

3. Characteristics of the environment, including types of stresses or deleterious social processes and the structural characteristics which may inhibit or facilitate supportive behaviors and relationships.

4. The interaction of the above three classes of variables. How does Person-Environment Fit occur?

The following section of this paper will be devoted to the second and third classes of variables. We will attempt to interpret them as social support supplies in the language of social networks theory.

Social Networks as Support Availability

The work of Leighton on integration and mental health,[30] studies of group ethnic cohesiveness among the Rosetans,[9] and Matsumoto's[35] observations on the Japanese society show how important the support of dependency needs is to health. All this leads us to the Arsenian and Arsenian[2] concern with "tough" and "easy" culture and Leighton's facilitating or integrating[30] social systems as supportive of needs. The previous section of this paper has detailed and documented this point. (See the Appendix for a tentative summary list of mechanisms.)

As indicated in the previous section, while there are various approaches to social support, much of the past work is scattered and nonaccumulative. What are the properties of social support? How are they measured? What are the characteristics of communities that facilitate support? What kind of social conditions are necessary to maximize the fit between personal needs and the objective social environment?

The social network theory of Mitchell[37] appears to be most pertinent and useful, since it cuts through much of the literature and integrates the various mechanisms into a measurable framework. We suggest that this framework helps to clarify the interplay of variables that constitute the opportunity for social support. We are exclusively concerned with the *dimensions* of social support.

A social network included the people one communicates with, and the links within these relationships. The properties of social networks are first *morpholog* and refer to the links in the network. The dimensions of morphology are anchorage, density, reachability and range.[37] The second property is *interactional* or communicated criteria. These properties refer to the nature of the links. that is their content, directedness, durability, intensity, and frequency. All these dimensions are defined as follows:

Morphology (Necessary Conditions) or Accessibility Criteria

Anchorage. The person or group networks. Anchorage has two properties— length and complexity: a) What is the shortest path(s) to others from a specific individual or group? b) Is it simple or multiplex (this refers to the number of alternatives or substitutes available)?[37] The more the better; the shorter, the better.

Reachability. The extent the person can use and contact people *important* to him. Reachability involves importance in a range with any number of steps from any starting point. The larger the number of contacts you can reach in the fewest number of steps is considered compact versus the opposite continuum of small numbers who can be reached in a greater number of steps. The optimum conditions allow a large number of valent, meaningful contacts within a short period of time.

Density. This implies connectedness. These are the lines of communications of those in the network who *know* one another and the extent to which links do exist between members of your "set." The focus is on denseness, the proportion of people in the set who know one another.

Range. Number of *direct* contacts—few to many. These may be homogeneous to heterogeneous types of contacts, that is, the contacts may or may not share common values. For example, the sameness of social background of the members in each network yields an ease of supportive facilitation, but the emphasis is on directness or how immediate are the range of contacts.

The above refers to the *shape* of the individual's network[28] and presents the necessary conditions for creating an opportunity structure for meeting whatever supportive needs exist.

Interactional Properties of Support

Content (Support). Concerns the *meanings* that persons in the network give their relationships. Support provides nourishment to self-esteem, normative affirmation, dependency relatedness, clarification of expectations if needed, and the discharge of disturbing effects, etc.

It seems that if supportive tasks and strategies are to be better conceptualized and measured, we need a better and new classification approach, which we cannot comment on in this paper. What does need to be done is to examine the question of supportive tasks and strategies around at least ten categories:

1. Rituals, such as religious and other social rituals, which are supportive.
2. Values and beliefs of a religious and ethical sort, particularly by which individuals are supported.
3. Normative consensus, the supportive function of shared norms.
4. Interpersonal exchanges, the way in which social networks supply supportive needs.
5. The fit between role(s) and dependency needs.
6. The intimacy-nurturant mechanisms or support. The opportunities for actual closeness.
7. The way support is given to the self in interaction with others.
8. The self-supports in terms of the self's interaction with itself as an aspect of identity. This context would be the classification of self mechanisms of support—the "I'm OK strategies."
9. Social support as the discharge of negative effects and the strategies for emotional discharges in social context.
10. Social support from a sociodemographic view with regard to one's status, such as married, divorced, and the like.

Directedness. Refers to amount of reciprocity; the direction of the interaction, *e.g.*, subordinate or superordinate; the direction of the flow; the ability to mobilize others.

Intensity. Degree individuals are prepared to honor obligations and exercise rights of support, the strength of commitment.

Frequency. The number of times interaction is actually counted.

In summary, Mitchell's categories refer to 1) morphology—the available structure for support and indicated dimensions, and 2) actual interactional dimensions. These are thus properties of structure and properties of function, together the opportunity structure for support. The hypothesized relationships are: 1) The greater the structural availability, the greater the health protectiveness; and 2) The greater the support functions, the more health protective the network.

Just how these network properties actually work will also be affected by the preexisting level of stress, personality factors, and habitual modes of social network skills. Kaplan[27] has suggested an Intimacy Scale be developed out of these categories, buildings on the work of Lowenthal[33] and Erickson.[15] It is also apparent that links to the literature on coping behavior[20] is crucial in the developing of a more adequate theory of affiliate need meeting and level of adaptation.

An illustration of the above support opportunities and strategies is drawn from Kaplan's[28] observations of Re-Evaluation Counselling. Briefly, Re-Evaluation Counselling is a peer group system of self-help to manage and reduce personal distress through a series of supportive efforts. Kaplan's observations are that these supportive efforts involve at least the following social mechanisms: 1) an immediate community network of others on whom to call to express distress in time of crisis; 2) an ongoing co-counselling system to express chronic distress (each member takes the role of counselor and/or counselee); 3) an ideology and set of practices that enhance self-esteem through self-validating comments and games; 4) a group in which high morale and getting better is encouraged; 5) a series of meetings and relating styles which encourage love of self and others; 6) a theory that by discharging (talking, shaking, hitting pillows, role playing, crying, etc.), a person can overcome rigid ways of behavior and hurts which create current distress; 7) a set of practices that loosen repression, *e.g.*, safety in allowing self disclosure, allowing rage to be felt and expressed; and 8) a modeling opportunity in which to learn how to disclose real feelings, solicit love from others, and develop a more correct and positive self-image.

Policy Implications for Medical Care

What are the policy implications of the point of view that asserts that social supports ameliorate stress? Those holding this perspective would argue that:

1. Early childhood education (before and in school) should pay close attention to encourage need-affiliation tasks and strategies. How do you socialize to avoid anomie?
2. Modern family medical practice should include a work-up of one's "personal networks" and life stresses (*e.g.*, life changes, work, family) and consider the possibility of providing or helping to provide more

functional social networks as an integral responsibility of the health care system. The use of lay counselors as developed by Pless[44] and the development of outreach personnel represent a beginning in this direction.

3. Modern work settings (a large part of one's life and locus of self-esteem) should take special note of the need to facilitate the building of high-morale work relationships as being protective.

4. Special attention should be given to a medical-religion dialogue that builds personal networks that are the locus of personal and community support. There is a medical-epidemiological basis for Buber's "I-Thou" philosophy!

5. The medical system of the future must consider becoming "human development centers." Development problems and diseases would be treated along the life cycle arc. Prevention would be a primary goal, along with treatment and rehabilitation. But health and disease would embrace the social, the psychological as well as the biological arenas of human life. Treatment would likewise embrace these three areas. Support "therapy" is but one type of need input that such centers would include as part of their development-adaptation efforts.

6. Using life cycle and institutional settings, it is now important to classify the presumptive stressor situations and the probably supportive actions *and* mechanisms which could buffer, reduce or eliminate the consequences of noxious life situations. For example, the Holmes-Rahe list of stressors (*e.g.*, death, move) each suggest appropriate supportive strategies.

7. Perhaps, like assertiveness training, we can create better group techniques to improve affiliative and coping skills to manage or modify like stresses, to be called Affiliative/Coping Assertiveness Training. (See forthcoming paper on this by the first author.)

Summary

We have thus emphasized the importance of social support as protective of health. We have also begun to ascertain the key questions that should be addressed; initiated a new synthesis of the great variety of types of support; suggested some synthesizing criteria of social support, and finally, have commented on the policy implications of the social support hypothesis.

Appendix

Some Social Support Mechanisms (A Tentative Formulation)

It is clear that the concept of social support is in need of clarification about the types of personal support needs, the characteristics of the objective social support supplies, and the types of actual support mechanisms. The following appendix is offered so that others may wish to examine our efforts in this direction.

List 1. Characteristics of the person: psychoemotional needs which must be socially gratified:

- security
- affection
- trust
- intimacy
- nurturance-succorance
- belongingness
- affiliation
- approval

List 2. Characteristics of or changes in the *objective* environment that alter the state or quantity of social support supplies:

Studies of loss of loved ones and the effect on survivors:

- work on bereavement and the subsequent death of widowers (the quicker readjustment of the spouse if children are present)
- children separated from families during wartime
- Jerome Myers' life change inventory classifies events as "loss events" versus "gain events," removing versus providing social support

Changes in the physical environment: the effects of poverty, disasters, crises, urbanization, physical and social mobility:

- includes Leighton's work
- sociocultural change
- forced relocation due to urban renewal and resulting grief reactions

Types of social structures:

- Arsenian and Arsenian's paths—tough—easy paths to meeting needs
- Matsumoto's study of Japan—dependency serving and valued
- Roseto, Pennsylvania
  (Both of these focus on the primariness of the social organization)

List 3. A *tentative* summary of support mechanisms:

- Appraisal opportunities—the chance to evaluate "what's going on," reality reassurances.
- Persuasion—the chance to tell the "other" that his dissonant cognitions can be made consistent and rewarding.
- Normative fit—the comfort, the consensus, the complementarity one feels in shared supportive norms, *e.g.*, your reference group versus "others."
- Group solidarity—the feeling of "we-ness," oneness, that comes out of social binding encounters; familiarity needs.
- Intimacy opportunities—the opportunity to share the most personal thoughts.
- Role-self rewards/approval—the self-esteem that comes from approved feedback for roles well performed, *e.g.*, as friend.

- Dependable social networks—the set of dependable others, for social support, crises, community, reliable norms.
- Tangible support—concrete events that help, *e.g.*, a raise, a praise.
- Love of significant others—especially spouse and friends, God, etc.

References

1. Adams, B. M.: Interaction theory and the social network. Sociometry **30**:64, 1967.

2. Arsenian, J., and Arsenian, J. M.: Tough and easy cultures. Psychiatry **11**:377.

3. Beiser, M.: Psychiatric followup study of normal adults. Am. J. Psychiatry **27**:1464, 1971.

4. ———: A study of personality assets in the community. Arch. Psychiatry **24**:244, 1971.

5. Bovard, E. W.: The balance between negative and positive brain system activity. Perspect. Biol. Med. **6**:116, 1962.

6. ———: The effects of social stimuli or the response to stress. Psychol. Rev. **66**:267, 1959.

7. Bradburn, N., and Caplovitz: Reports on Happiness. Chicago, Aldine Press, 1965.

8. Bruhn, H. G., *et al.*: Evidence of "emotional drain" preceding death from myocardial infarction. Psychiatr. Digest **29**:34, 1968.

9. Bruhn, J. G., Wolf, S., Lynn, T. N., *et al.*: Social aspects of CHD in a Pennsylvania German community. Soc. Sci. Med. **2**:201, 1968.

10. Caplan, R. D. : Organizational Stress and Individual Strain: A Social Psychological Study of Risk Factors in Coronary Heart Disease among Administrators, Engineers, and Scientists. Research Center for Group Dynamics, JSR, University of Michigan, 1971.

11. Cassel, J. C.: The relation of the urban environment to health: implication for prevention. Mt. Sinai J. Med. NY, in press.

12. Conger, J. C., Sawrey, W., and Turrel, E. S.: The role of social experience in the production of gastric ulcers in hooded rats placed in a conflict situation. J. Abnorm. Psychol. **57**:216, 1958.

13. Dunham, J. H. : Social structures and mental disorders: Competing hypotheses of explanation. Milbank Mem. Fund Q. **39**:259, 1961.

14. Durkheim, E.: Suicide. Glencoe, Ill., The Free Press, 1957.

15. Erickson, E. H.: Identity and the Life Cycle. Psychological Issues Monograph No. 1, New York, International University Press, 1959.

16. French, J. R. P., Rodgers, W., and Cobb, S.: Adjustment as person environment fit. *In* Coping. G. Coelho, Ed. New York, Basic Books, 1974.

17. Fried, N.: Grieving for a lost home. *In* The Urban Condition. New York, Basic Books, 1963.

18. Gore, S.: The influence of Social Support in Ameliorating the Consequences of Job Loss. Unpublished dissertation, Ann Arbor, University of Michigan, 1973.

19. Gruenberg, C.: The social breakdown syndrome, some observations. A. J. Psychiatr. **123**:12, 1967.

20. Hamburg, D. A., Coelho, G. V., and Adams, J. E.: Coping and adaptation. *In* Coping and Adaptation. G. V. Coelho, D. A. Hamburg, and J. Adams, Eds. New York, Basic Books, 1974.

21. Harlow, H., Harlow, M. D., and Suomo, S. J.: From thought to therapy. Am. Sci. **59**:538, 1971.

22. Henry, J.: The variant properties of a personal community. An Anthropologist **60**:827, 1958.

23. Henry, J. P., Meehan, J. P., and Stephens, P. M.: The use of psychosocial stimuli to induce prolonged hypertension in mice. Psychosom. Med. **29**:408, 1967.

24. Holmes, T.: Multidiscipline study of Tuberculosis. *In* Personality Stress and Tuberculosis. P. J. Sparer, Ed.

25. ———: Personal communication.

26. ———, and Rahe, R.: The social readjustment rating scale. J. Psychosom. Res. **11**:213, 1967.

27. Kaplan, B. H.: Duke Stroke Study in process.

28. ———: An observational study of reevaluation counselling, in process. See also, Thomas J. Scheff: Reevaluation Counselling: Social Implications. Seattle, Rational Press, 1972.

29. Langner, T., and Michael, S.: Life Stress and Mental Health. New York, Free Press, 1960.

30. Leighton, A.: My Name Is Legion. New York, Basic Books, 1959.

31. ———: Psychiatric disorders and the social environment: An outline for a frame of reference. *In* Psychiatric Disorder in The Urban Environment. B. H. Kaplan, Ed. New York, Behavioral Publication, 1971.

32. Liddell, H.: Some specific factors that modify tolerance for environmental stress. *In* Life Stress and Bodily Disease. H. C. Wolff, S. G. Wolff, Jr., and C. C. Hare, Eds. Baltimore, Williams and Wilkins, 1950.

33. Lowenthal, M. F., and Haven, C.: Interaction and adaption, intimacy: A critical variable. Am. Sociol. Rev. **33**:20, 1968.

34. Mandelbaum, D. G.: Soldier Groups and Negro Soldiers. Berkeley, University of California, 1952.

35. Matsumoto, Y. S.: Social stress and coronary heart disease in Japan: A Hypothesis. Milbank Mem. Fund Q. **48**, 1970.

36. Mishler, E. G., and Scotch, N. A.: Sociocultural factors in the epidemiology of schizophrenia: A review. Psychiatry **26**:315, 1963.

37. Mitchell, J. C., Ed.: Social Networks and Urban Situations. Manchester, Manchester University Press, 1969.

38. Morris, D.: Intimate Behavior. New York, Random House, 1971.

39. Murray, H.: Explorations in Personality. New York, Oxford University Press, 1938.

40. Myers, J. K., Lindenthal, J., and Peper, M.: Life events and psychiatric impairment. J. Nerv. Ment. Dis. **152**:149, 1971.

41. Nuckolls, K. B., Cassel, J. C., and Kaplan, B. H.: Psychosocial assets, life crisis and the prognosis of pregnancy. Am. J. Epidemiol. **95**:431, 1972.

42. Parkes, N., Benjamin, B., and Fitzgerald, R. E.: Broken Heart: A study of increased mortality among widowers. Br. Med. J. **1**:740, 1969.

43. Pinneau, R.: A working paper, complementarity and social support. Unpublished memorandum, Ann Arbor, University of Michigan, September 8, 1972.

44. Pless, I. B.: Chronic illness in childhood: The role of lay family counsellors. Paper delivered at Health Services Research Conference, Chicago, December 8-10, 1971.

45. Schachter, S.: Psychology of Affiliation. Palo Alto, Stanford University Press, 1959.

46. Segal, B., Weiss, E., and Sokol, R.: Emotional adjustments, social organization, and psychiatric treatment. Am. Sociol. Rev. **30**:584, 1965.

47. Tillman, W. A., and Hobbs, C. E.: Social background of accident free and accident repeaters. Am. J. Psychiatry **106**:321, 1949.

48. Titmuss, R. M.: Problems of Social Policy. H. M. Stationery Office, London, 1950. Quoted by Everett W. Bovard. *In* The effects of social stimuli or the response to stress. Psychol. Rev. **66**:269, 1959.

49. Wolf, S.: Psychosocial forces in myocardial infarction and sudden death. *In* Society, Stress and Disease. L. Levi, Ed. London, Oxford Press, 1971.

Health and Illness Behavior: Societal Coping with Disease and Injury

Aware of the hazards of illness and death and their differential effect on various segments and populations of a society, that society will evolve ways and means of coping with such assaults. Disease itself is not perceived or responded to in the same manner by individuals and groups but in terms of the value systems, norms, and attitudes prevailing in the society and culture. Medicine and its definitions of illness make up only one aspect of the value systems and orientations toward disease.

Once perceived as a threatening condition with negative evaluation and meaning, illness may become institutionalized into a set of behavioral norms within a network of social relationships and behavior which Parsons has termed the *sick role*. Thus, when behavior related to illness is normatively organized into a pattern, a social role, the sick role becomes a meaningful mode of reacting to and coping with the existence and potential hazards of sickness by a society, and may or may not differ from the criteria and norms of the physician and other healers in the same society. In this manner human societies and their sub-components do not leave to chance the existence and consequent threats of disease but respond by establishing norms of behavior, expectations, and organized relationships that define illness and health behavior for their members. Consequently, as society's criteria for health and illness vary and change, the definitions and nature of the sick role correspondingly change. *Health* then becomes essentially a social value, with attached normative components, as defined in meaningful terms by society for its members, and thereby accounts for the tremendous variety of definitions of health among human societies around the world and among the various components of the same pluralistic society, such as in the United States and other Western countries.

That is, *health* then becomes *behavior* performed by actors socialized to its *positive* normative aspects, and illness also becomes a form of behavior in response to conditions and forces *negatively* viewed by society.

Correspondingly, as a society or some of its components try to determine the "causes" of illness, the notion arises that if such causes can be controlled, then disease can be "prevented." Intervening into the causal processes, breaking a link in the causal chain of events, can reduce if not eradicate the effects of illness on that population or part of society affected. When large-scale epidemics plagued much of Europe centuries ago, efforts to control the spread of such contagious, infectious diseases were given special support and impetus. The value of "public health" and "preventive medicine" arose as the gradual successes of public-health practices—in purifying the water supply, removing wastes, and making other efforts to clean up the environment along with asepsis and other measures to restrict the dangers of disease and immunize populations against its effects—began to effectively reduce the ravages of contagious diseases after the germ theory of such diseases became accepted.

Despite the demonstrated fact that public-health practices were far more instrumental in lengthening life expectancy and reducing the misery of infectious diseases than curative medicine, the latter has continued to form the major thrust and value system of scientific medicine in the United States probably more than in any other society. Efforts to attend the sick and injured, to alleviate pain and misery, and to succor the victims of disease and disability still receive far more public and professional support than do efforts to prevent such illness and injury. With society focusing on curative medicine and the alleviation of the consequences of disease and injury, behavioral scientists also have concentrated more on the sick role and illness behavior than on behaviors related to health and the prevention of disease. Thus more research has studied sociobehavioral factors that may be potentially involved in the causal onset of illness than factors that may *prevent* the onset of such diseases. Perhaps the idea prevails, borrowing from medical science perspectives, that if we can determine what behavioral factors "cause" disease, we can then be able to prevent such conditions from causing such disease in the future. This, however, may be a too simplistic notion of behavioral etiology of illness, firstly; and also it may be probable that an entirely different, albeit related, set of behavioral conditions may be needed to *prevent* diseases or to intervene against their effects, irrespective of those behaviors having pathologic or illness-inducing consequences. Until this question is thoroughly researched, we can only speculate with minimum precision about specific behavioral aspects related to effective prevention of disease.

This section presents articles dealing with health and illness behavior—the sick role, the patient role, and healers and healing behavior—all of which make up an institutionalized sub-set of interrelated behaviors, norms, values, and attitudes of persons interacting in complex sets of organized relationships whose key objective is to comprehend and cope with illness and its consequences.

A.   The Sick Role

The first part of this section presents a series of studies dealing with social, psychological, and cultural responses to illness in terms of one of the most frequently used terms in medical sociology, that of the sick role. Talcott Parsons has pioneered this concept with his classic description of the sick role, particularly in American society, in the first chapter of this section.

An insightful extension of the concept of sickness as role behavior with a corresponding social status is offered by Andrew Twaddle, whose analysis has many potential insights into health as a social status.

A thorough critique of the Parsonian conception of the sick role and related formulations is presented by Eugene Gallagher, with conceptual developments that may enrich such pioneering contributions to the sociology of illness.

7 Definitions of Health and Illness in the Light of American Values and Social Structure

The aim of the present paper is to try to consider the socio-cultural definition of health and illness in the United States in the light, in the first instance, of American values, but also in terms of the ways in which the relevant aspects of the value system have come to be institutionalized in the social structure. I shall give primary attention to mental health, but will also attempt to define its relation to somatic health and illness as carefully as possible. I shall also try to place the American case in comparative perspective.

First, it is important to try to define the respects in which health and illness can be considered to be universal categories applying to all human beings in all societies and to distinguish them from the respects in which they may be treated as socially and culturally relative. It will be possible here to say only a few rather general things, but the development of social science does, I think, permit us to be somewhat more definite than it has been possible to be until rather recently.

There is clearly a set of common human features of health and illness; indeed more broadly there is probably a set of components which apply perhaps to all mammalian species. There is no general reason to believe that these common components are confined to somatic illness; my view would be that there are also such components for mental illness. It does, however, seem to be a tenable view that there is a range, roughly, from the "purely somatic" to the "purely mental"—both of course, being limiting concepts—and that as one progresses along that range the prominence of the factors of relativity as a function of culture and social structure increases. The importance of the "interpenetration" between somatic and mental aspects is so great, however, that it would be a mistake to draw a rigid line, in any empirical term, between them.

One point is relatively clear. This is that the primary criteria for mental illness must be defined with reference to the social *role-performance* of the individual.[1] Since it is at the level of role-structure that the principal direct interpenetration of social systems and personalities come to focus, it is as an incapacity to meet the expectations of social roles that mental illness becomes a problem in social relationships and that criteria of its presence or absence should be formulated. This is of course not at all to say that the state which we refer to as mental, as of somatic, illness is not a state of the individual; of course it is. But that

---

[1]Both health and illness, in general, I would like to treat as states of the individual person; the "pathology" of social systems, real and important as it is, should not be called "illness" nor the absence of it, "health." Cf. Talcott Parsons, "The Mental Hospital as a Type of Organization," in *The Patient and the Mental Hospital*, edited by Milton Greenblatt, Daniel J. Levinson, and Richard H. Williams, New York: Free Press, 1957.

state is manifest to and presents problems for both the sick person and others with whom he associates in the context of social relationships, and it is with reference to this problem that I am making the point about role-performance.

At the same time I would not like to treat mental health as involving a state of commitment to the performance of *particular* roles. Such a commitment would involve specific memberships in specific relational systems, i.e., collectivities. Mental health is rather concerned with *capacity* to enter into such relationships and to fulfill the expectations of such memberships. In terms of the organization of the motivational system of the individual, it therefore stands at a more "general level" than do the more specific social commitments.

There is a set of mechanisms in the operation of which social system and personality aspects are interwoven, which make possible the many complex adjustments to changing situations which always occur continually in the course of social processes. It is when the mechanisms involved in these adjustive processes break down ("adjustive" as between personalities involved in social interaction with each other) that mental illness becomes a possibility, that is, it constitutes one way in which the individual can react to the "strains" imposed upon him in the course of social process. This can, of course, occur at any point in his own life cycle from the earliest infancy on. Also, I take for granted that mental illness is only one of several alternative forms which "deviance" can take, again at every stage. Mental illness, then, including its therapies, is a kind of "second line of defense" of the social system vis-à-vis the problems of the "control" of the behavior of its members. It involves a set of mechanisms which take over when the primary ones prove inadequate. In this connection it can also be readily seen that there are two main aspects of the operation of the mechanisms involved. First, the individual who is incapacitated from performing his role-functions would be a disturbing element in the system if he still attempted to perform them. Hence we may say that it is important to have some way of preventing him from attempting to do so, both in his own interest and in that of the system itself. Secondly, however, there is the therapeutic problem, namely of how it is possible to restore him to full capacity and return him to role-performance after an interval.

So far, I have been speaking of mental health with special reference to its place in the articulation between social system and personality. Mental health—and illness—are states of the personality defined in terms of their relevance to the capacity of the personality to perform institutionalized roles. For analytical purposes, however, I have found it necessary to make a distinction, which a good many psychologists do not make, between the personality and the organism. They are, of course, not concretely separable entities, but they are analytically distinguishable systems. There would be various ways of making the distinction, but for present purposes I think it is best to put it that the personality is that part of the mechanisms involved in the control of concrete behavior which genetically goes back to the internalization of social objects and cultural patterns in the course of the process of socialization. The organism, as distinguished from this, consists of that part of the concrete living individual which is attributable to hereditary constitution and to the conditioning processes of the physical environment. Hence, from the point of view of its relation to the personality, it is that aspect of the mechanisms controlling behavior which is not attributable to the experience of socialization in and through processes of social interaction.[2]

It will be noted that I have been careful not to say that the mechanisms through which the personality component of the concrete individual functions are not "physiological." In my opinion, it is not the distinction between physiological and in some sense "mental" processes which is the significant one here. Indeed, I think that *all* processes of behavior on whatever level are mediated through physiological mechanisms. The physiological mechanisms which are most significant in relation to the more complex forms of behavior are, however, mainly of the nature of systems of "communication" where the physiological mechanisms are similar to the physical media and channels of communication. Hence, in both cases the content of "messages" cannot be deduced from the physical properties of the media. In the higher organisms, including man, it seems clear that the focus of these mechanisms rests in the central nervous system, particularly the brain, and that the next level down in the order of systems of control has to do with the hormones which circulate through the blood stream.

It is important to stress this "interpenetration" of personality and organism, because, without it, the complex phenomena usually referred to as "psychosomatic" are not understandable. Correspondingly, I do not think that the way in which *both* somatic and mental health and illness can fit into a common sociological framework is understandable without both the distinction between personality and organism and the extreme intimacy of their interpenetrating relationship.

Coming back to the relation of both to the social system, I should like to introduce a distinction which has not been consistently made by sociologists either in this or in other connections, but which I think is very important for present purposes. This is the distinction between *role* and *task*. There are many different definitions of the concept role in the sociological literature. For my present purpose, however, I think one very simple one is adequate, namely a role is the organized system of participation of an individual in a social system, with special reference to the organization of that social system as a collectivity.[3] Roles, looked at in this way, constitute the primary focus of the articulation and hence interpenetration between personalities and social systems. Tasks, on the other hand, are both more differentiated and more highly specified than roles; one role is capable of being analyzed into a plurality of different tasks.

Seen in these terms I think it is legitimate to consider the task to define the level at which the action of the individual articulates with the *physical* world, i.e., the level at which the organism in the above analytical sense is involved in interaction with its environment in the usual sense of biological theory. A task, then, may be regarded as that subsystem of a role which is defined by a definite set of

[2]I have put forward this general type of view on two previous occasions. For the general conception of the relation of personality to the internationalization of social and cultural objects, see Parsons and Bales, *Family, Socialization and Interaction Process*, New York: Free Press, 1955. A more extended discussion of the relation of personality and organism will be found in Parsons, "An Approach to Psychological Theory in Terms of the Theory of Action," American Psychological Association, *Studies in General Theory*, ed. Sigmund Koch, New York: McGraw-Hill, 1958.

[3]This definition clearly matches that put forward by Merton as the "role-set." See R. K. Merton, "The Role-Set," *British Journal of Sociology*, June, 1957.

physical operations which perform some function or functions in relation to a role and/or the personality of the individual performing it. It is very important that processes of communication, the *meanings* of which are by no means adequately defined by the physical processes involved at the task level, are not only included in the concept of task, but constitute at least one of the most important, if not *the* most important, categories of tasks, or of components of them.[4]

Coming back to the problem of health and illness, I should now like to suggest that somatic illness may be defined in terms of incapacity for relevant task-performance in a sense parallel to that in which mental illness was thought of as incapacity for role-performance. In the somatic case the reference is not to any particular task, but rather to categories of tasks, though of course, sudden illness may force abandonment of level rather than any particular task.[5] Put the other way around, *somatic health is, sociologically defined, the state of optimum capacity for the effective performance of valued tasks.*

The relation between somatic and mental health, and correspondingly, illness, seen in this way, bears directly on the problem of levels of organization of the control of behavior. It implies that the "mind" is not a separate "substance" but essentially a level of organization, the components of which are "non-mental," in the same basic sense in which, for example, the hypothetical isolated individual is "non-social." It further implies that the mental level "controls" the somatic, or in this sense, physical, aspect of the individual, the "organism." Somatic states are therefore necessary, but in general *not* sufficient conditions of effective mental functioning.[6]

The Problem of "Cultural Relativity" in Health and Illness

Our present concern is with the relation of personality and organism on the the one hand, the social system and its culture on the other. It is now possible to say something on the question of the relations between the universal human

[4]Thus I am at present engaged in the task of writing a paper on the institutionalization of the patterns of health and illness in American society. The "technique" I have chosen for this task is manipulating the keyboard and other parts of the typewriter. This process clearly engages the hands and fingers, eyes, and other parts of the physical organism; internally above all, the brain. The physical result is the arrangement on a number of sheets of paper, previously blank, of a very large number of what we call linguistic symbols; letters arranged in words, sentences and paragraphs. I could have chosen alternative techniques, such as writing longhand with a pen, or possibly dictating to a machine. In these cases the physical result might well have been different. But in any case the "significance" of the task is only partly "physical"; it lies more in the "meanings" of what has been physically "written." Finally, the task of writing this paper is only one rather clearly defined subsystem of my *role* as sociologist.

[5]Referring to the writing task, a paralysis of both arms would obviously incapacitate me for writing this and other papers on the typewriter, and for all other manual tasks, but not necessarily for dictating them to a secretary.

[6]This view of the relation of mind and body and in turn, their relations to the two great categories of health and disease with which we are here concerned, does not imply that all "somatic"

elements and the socio-culturally variable ones in health and illness on both levels. Clearly, by the above definition, *all* human groups have highly organized personalities which must be built up by complex processes of the sort we call socialization and which are subject to various sorts of malfunctioning at the level of social adjustment which has been referred to. All human societies have language, a relatively complex social organization, complex systems of cultural symbols and the like. The individual in such a society, however "primitive," is always involved in a plurality of different roles which are the organizing matrix of the various tasks he performs.

Clearly this personality element of the structure of the individual person is closely interpenetrating and interdependent with the organic–somatic aspect. Hence, there are clearly "problems" of both somatic and mental illness and health for all human groups. Furthermore, all of them are deeply involved with the structures of the social system and the culture.

That there are uniformities in the constitutions of all human groups at the organic level goes without saying, and hence that many of the problems of somatic medicine are independent of social and cultural variability. Thus such things as the consequences and possibilities of control of infection by specific bacterial agents, the consequences of and liability to cancerous growths and many other things are clearly general across the board. This is not, however, to say that the *incidence* and probably degrees of severity of many somatic diseases are not functions of social and cultural conditions, through many different channels. But within considerable ranges, independent of the part played by such factors etiologically, the medical problems presented are essentially the same, though of course, how to implement medical techniques effectively is again partly a socio-cultural problem.

It follows from the conception of personality put forward here that constancies in the field of mental health are intimately related to uniformities in the character of culture and social structure. Here it is particularly important that, after a period in which a rather undiscriminating version of the doctrine of "cultural relativity" was in the ascendant, much greater attention has recently come to be paid to the universals which are identifiable on these levels. It is not possible here to enter into any sort of detail in this field, but a few highlights may be mentioned.

Most fundamental, I think, is the fact that every known human society possesses a culture which reaches quite high levels of generalization in terms of symbolic systems, including particularly values and cognitive patterns, and that its social structure is sufficiently complex so that it comprises collectivities at several different levels of scope and differentiation. Even though, as is the case with most of the more "primitive" societies known, there is scarcely any important social structure which is not, on a concrete level, a kinship structure, such kinship

---

phenomena can be analyzed as standing on one level. For various reasons it seems to me that at least one comparably basic distinction needs to be made within the organism, as defined above, namely, between the "behavioral" system and what might be called the "homeostatic" system (what Franz Alexander call the "vegetative" system—cf. his *Psychosomatic Medicine: Its Principles and Applications,* New York: W. W. Norton and Co., Inc., 1950). For present purposes, however, it is not necessary to go into these further refinements.

systems are clearly highly differentiated into a variety of subsystems which are functionally different from each other.

With minimal exceptions, the nuclear family of parents and still dependent children is a constant unit in all kinship systems, though structural emphases within it vary.[7] It is clearly the focal starting point for the process of socialization and the source of the primary bases of human personality organization. But the nuclear family *never* stands alone as a social structure, it is always articulated in complex ways with other structures which are both outside it and stand on a higher level of organization than it does. This involvement of the nuclear family with the wider social structure is, from the structural point of view, the primary basis of the importance of the incest taboo, which, as applying to the nuclear family, is known to be a near universal.[8] Put in psychological terms, this means that the internalization of the object systems and the values of the nuclear family and its subsystems, starting with the mother–child relation, constitutes the *foundation* of personality structure in all human societies. There are, of course, very important variations, but they are all variations on a single set of themes. Because the internalization of the nuclear family is the foundation of personality structure, I suggest that *all mental* pathology roots in disturbances of the relationship structure of the nuclear family as impinging on the child. This is not in the least to say that there are not somatic factors in mental pathology; some children may well be constitutionally impossible to socialize adequately. But the *structure* of pathological syndromes which can legitimately be called mental will always involve responses to family relationships.

It is, however, equally true and important that in no society is the socialization of an adult exhausted by his experience in the nuclear family, and hence is his personality *only* a function of the familial object systems he has internalized. Correspondingly, mental pathology will always involve elements in addition to disturbances of the nuclear family relations, especially perhaps those centering about peer-group relations in the latency period of adolescence. These other factors involve his relations to social groups other than the nuclear family and to higher levels of cultural generalization and social responsibility than any of those involved in the family.

It is thus, I think, fully justified to think of both mental and somatic pathology as involving common elements for all human groups. But at the same time both of them would be expected to vary as a function of social and cultural conditions, in important ways, and probably the more so as one progresses from the more "vegetative" aspects of organic function and its disturbances to the more behavioral aspects and then from the "deeper" layers of personality structure to the "higher" more "ego-structured" layers. It is also probable that the lower in this range, the more the variation is one of incidence rather than character of pathology, the higher the more it penetrates into the "constitution" of the illness itself.

[7] Cf. M. Zelditch, Jr., "Role Differentiation in the Nuclear Family," Chapter VI of Parsons and Bales, *Family, Socialization and Interaction Process,* New York: Free Press, 1955.

[8] For a general discussion of the significance of the incest taboo, cf. Talcott Parsons, "The Incest Taboo in Relation to Social Structure and the Socialization of the Child," *British Journal of Sociology*, Vol. V:101–117, June, 1954.

Health among the Problems of Social Control

Health and illness, however, are not only "conditions" or "states" of the human individual viewed on both personality and organic levels. They are also states evaluated and institutionally recognized in the culture and social structure of societies. Can anything be said about the ways in which the constancy–variability problem works out at these levels?

Clearly the institutionalization of expectations with respect both to role and to task performance is fundamental in all human societies. There must, therefore, always be standards of "adequacy" of such performance and of the "capacities" underlying it which must be taken into account, and hence, a corresponding set of distinctions between states of individuals which are and are not "satisfactory" from the point of view of these standards. But by no means all types of "conformity" with performance-standards can be called "health" nor all types or modes of deviation from such conformity "illness." Are the categories health and illness, as we conceive them, altogether "culture-bound" or is there something about them which can be generalized on the social role-definition level? To answer this question, it will be necessary to enter a little more fully into the sociological problems presented by these definitions.

Since I am attempting to deal with illness in the context of "social control," I should like to approach the problem in terms of an attempt to classify ways in which individuals can deviate from the expectations for statuses and roles which have been institutionalized in the structure of their societies. In spite of the fact that it will complicate matters, it seems unavoidable to deal with the problem on two different levels.

The first of these two levels concerns the relation of the problem of health and illness to the whole range of categories of deviant behavior. In this connection, I shall attempt to assess the relative importance given to the health complex in different types of society and to show that it is particularly important in the American case. The second level will take up the problem of selectivity and variation *within* the health–illness complex itself. Here, I shall discuss how this relates to selective emphasis on the different components of the role of illness and of the therapeutic process, and will attempt to show that, not only does American society put greater stress on the problem of illness than do other societies, but that its emphasis in defining the role and in therapy are also characteristically different.

I shall outline the classification I have in mind on the first level in terms of the way it looks in our own society and then raise the question of how universally it may be assumed that the relevant categories are, in fact, differentiated from each other in different societies. The first category is that of the control of the capacities of units in the social structure in the sense in which this conception has been discussed above in connection with the definition of health and illness. Every society must have important concern for the level of these capacities. The present context, however, is that of social control, not socialization, so it is not a question of how these capacities come to be developed in the first place, but rather of how tendencies to their disturbance can be forestalled, or, once having occurred, can be rectified.

Though comparable considerations apply to collectivities as units, in the present context the relevant unit is the human individual, and with reference to him we must consider both of the two aspects which have been distinguished, namely, somatic and mental health. Capacity, it will be remembered, is thought of as standing on a more "general" level than commitment to any particular role or task obligations. It does, however, include the motivation to accept such obligations given suitable situation and opportunity.

There is a second category of problem of social control in relation to the individual which in another sense also stands on a more general level than any particular action-commitments. This may be called the problem of *morality*. This concerns the state of the individual person, but not with respect to his capacities in the same sense as these are involved in the problem of health, but with respect to his commitment to the *values* of the society. This is the area of social control which has traditionally been most closely associated with religion, especially when the reference is to the person, rather than to any collective unit of the society. When I associate the problem with religion, I do not wish to imply that every attachment to a religion or religious movement automatically implies reinforcement of commitment to the values of a *society*. This is by no means necessarily the case. The point is, rather, that it is in the sphere of religious orientation, or its "functional equivalents" at the level of what Tillich calls "ultimate concern," that the individual must work out the problem of how far he is or is not committed to the values of his society.

There is, of course, a great deal of historical and cross-cultural variation in the ways in which individuals may be treated as standing in religious states which need to be remedied or rectified. It seems, however, to be sound to distinguish two very broad types, namely, those involving "ritual impurity" of some sort, and those involving the problem of "salvation" or "state of grace" in a sense comparable to the meanings of these terms within the Christian tradition. In speaking of religion in this connection, I also do not wish to rule out cases which do not include an explicitly "supernatural" reference in the meaning we would tend to give that term. Thus from a "humanistic" point of view the problem still exists of ensuring commitment to the humanistic values. Perhaps the best single example of this reference is the ritualistic aspect of classical Chinese culture with its "secular" ideal of the "superior man."

Both the above two contexts of the problem of social control of individuals refer to rather generalized states of individuals which may be conceived to "lie behind" their commitments to more differentiated and particularized role-obligations and norms. If both of these latter categories be interpreted in the context of social system involvement, then it is a problem in every society how far different elements in its population maintain operative commitments on both these levels which are compatible with the social interest.

The reference to norms, which I have in mind in the first instance in a society as a whole, focuses on the legal system. Any going society must cultivate a rather generalized "respect for law," and this must be specified in several directions to come down to the level of particular legal obligations.

It is important to note that commitment to law-observance stands on a level more general than that involved in any particular role. Such principles as honesty in the sense of respect for the property rights of others, "responsibility" in the sense of obligation to fulfill contractual obligations once entered into, or recognition of the general legitimacy of political authority; none of these is specific to any particular role in a particular collectivity. In a highly differentiated society like our own, the practicing legal profession may be said to carry out functions of social control in this field which are in some ways parallel to those of the medical profession in the field of health.[9]

Of course, commitment to norms is by no means confined to the norms which in a modern type of society are given the "force of law." But the law first may serve as a prototype, and second is, in a well-integrated society, necessarily the paramount system of norms with respect to the society as a system, though norms of "morality" may, as noted above, take precedence on a religious or purely "ethical" level. "Below" the legal level, however, every collectivity in the society has some set of rules, more or less formalized, to which it is essential to secure some order of commitment on the part of its members.

The last of the four contexts in which the problem of social control in the present sense arises is that of commitment to role-obligations in particular collectivities. This also is a broad category running all the way from obligations of marriage to a particular spouse, and of occupational commitment in a particular "job" to the obligations of the citizen of loyalty to his national government. One would expect mechanisms of social control to cluster about this area. In our own society, this is the least differentiated of the four, but certain relatively specialized agencies have begun to emerge. On the "lower" levels, social work is one of the more prominent. "Industrial sociology," so far as it is oriented to the problem of the individual worker as a member of a formal organization, is another. This is the area of which Chester Barnard spoke[10] as that of "efficiency" in the technical meaning he gave to that term.

I have taken the space to review these four different contexts of the problem of social control, because I think it is essential to have such a classification as a basis for placing the treatment of any of these problems in a comparative setting. In a highly differentiated society like our own, these four functions have become relatively clearly differentiated from each other, and the operative processes of social control are, with certain indefinite borderlines, of course, to be found in the hands of different organizational agencies. The last of the four I outlined is by a good deal the least firmly institutionalized as a distinct function and it is probably significant that, in our society, it is most fully worked out, through social work, for the lower status-levels of the society.

The present situation with respect to differentiation cannot, however, be said to be typical of all societies; indeed, I doubt whether any case can be found where a comparatively close approach to completeness in this differentiation can be found.

Two major "axes" of differentiation were implicit in the classification I have just presented. Both need to be taken into account in placing the problem of health and illness relative to the others. The first of these may be called the differentiation in terms of orientation, on the one hand, to the exigencies of the *situation* in which the person must act; on the other hand, orientation to or through *normative patterns*. The second axis concerns not this problem, but that of

[9]Cf. Talcott Parsons, "A Sociologist Looks at the Legal Profession," in *Essays in Sociological Theory,* Revised Edition, New York: Free Press, 1954.

[10]C. I. Barnard, *The Functions of the Executive*, Cambridge:Harvard University Press, 1938.

whether the "problem" lies in the state of the person as a whole, at a level deeper than the problem of his acceptance of particular obligations, or whether it lies in the question of his "willingness" to accept certain more specific obligations, to particular norms and classes of norms—and to particular roles in particular collectivities.

The first of these two axes differentiates the types of deviance involved in illness and disturbance of commitments to collectivities on the one hand from those involved in disturbance of commitments to norms and to values on the other. The second axis differentiates the problems of illness and of disturbance of commitment to values on the one hand from the problems of commitment to collectivities and to normative patterns (rules and law) on the other. The tabular arrangement [on p. 130] may be helpful to the reader.

It is in terms of the first axis that one fundamental type of differentiation involving health can be made, that which treats health as a "naturalistic" state which is not to be explained by or treated through religio–magical media. It is of course a commonplace that in all nonliterate societies, with relatively minor exceptions such as fractures, this differentiation has not yet taken place, and much the same can be said about the high civilizations of the Orient such as India and China until touched by Western medicine. This of course is in no way to say that "therapies" which are couched in magico–religious terms are necessarily ineffective. On the contrary, there is much evidence that they have been very effective in certain cases. It would, however, hardly be denied that with the clear differentiation of roles in this area which has taken place in the modern world, much greater effectiveness has been made possible over at least a very large part of the range.

Though differentiation on the first axis discriminates the problem of health from that of the "ritual" state of the individual, or his state of grace or, more generally, commitment to values, it fails to discriminate between the more general level of his state "as a person" and his commitment to the more specific obligations of societal membership and activity. Here a problem which has been very central in the modern world in drawing the line between problems of mental health and of law seems to be a major one. This is the question of whether and how far the "deviance" of the individual from conformity with social expectations can be considered to be "intentional," i.e., the question of how far he may legitimately be held *responsible* for his actions. In one area, at least, this has in fact come to be accepted as a main differentiating criterion and, I think, rightly so.

Let me try to elucidate a little some of its implications in the present context. It has long been one of the principal criteria of illness that the sick person "couldn't help it." Even though he may have become ill or disabled through some sort of carelessness or negligence, he cannot legitimately be expected to get well simply by deciding to be well, or by "pulling himself together." Some kind of underlying reorganizing process has to take place, biological or "mental," which can be guided or controlled in various ways, but cannot simply be eliminated by an "act of will." In this sense the state of illness is involuntary. On the other hand, both obedience to norms and fulfillment of obligations to collectivities in roles are ordinarily treated as involving "voluntary" decisions; the normal individual can legitimately be "held responsible."

	Disturbance of Total Person	Disturbance of Particular Expectations
"Situational" Focus	Problem of "capacities" for task and role performance	Problem of commitments to collectivities (Barnard's "efficiency")
	Illness as deviance Health as "conformity"	Disloyalty as deviance Loyalty as conformity
"Normative" Focus	Problem of commitments to values, or of "morality" "Sin" and "immorality" as deviance	Problem of commitments to norms, or of "legality" "Crime" and "illegality" as deviance
	State of grace or "good character" as conformity	Law-observance as conformity

Certainly both in fields such as law and in that of collectivity obligations, there are many cases where failure to live up fully to "formal" obligations is not "blamed on" the individual. But the distinction is, on the whole, clear; if he is not "ill" (or in a state of ritual impurity, or "sin"), or willfully recalcitrant, it must be the fault of somebody else or of "the system." The essential basis of this possibility of "holding responsible" is the particularity of specific norms and role-obligations. A normal person has the capacity to accept or reject particular obligations without involving a reorganization of the major structures of his personality or of his body. It is only when there is a "disturbance" which goes beyond these particularities that we can speak of illness, or of disturbed commitment to values.[11]

This same problem occurs in the relation to the commitment to values as operating through religion and cognate mechanisms. It is very clear that among many nonliterate peoples, states of ritual impurity are treated as outside the control of the individual victim. They are states for which he may not legitimately be held responsible, except, and this is a most important exception which applies to illness as well, for subjecting himself to the proper treatment institutionally prescribed for those in such a state. In general, some ritual performance is called for, which may even sometimes be self-administered, to "rectify" his state.

Without attempting to discuss the situation in other major religions, it is a very important fact that the conception of original sin in the Christian tradition defines the situation in a cognate way. Though retroactively and mythologically Adam is held to have sinned "voluntarily," the burden of original sin on mankind is held not to be the responsibility of the individual, but something which is inherent in the human condition. Conversely, it cannot be escaped from without outside help.

Here it is important to distinguish original sin from the infraction of the norms and role-obligations of a religious collectivity. I think it can fairly be said that that aspect of "sin" which is treated by religious authorities as *within* the

[11]An interesting case of difficulty with respect to the line of discrimination discussed above is presented by Mark Field in his study of Soviet medical practice, where pressure has been put on physicians, more than in our own system, to provide excuses for avoiding extremely onerous and rigorously enforced role-obligations. Cf. his *Doctor and Patient in Soviet Russia*, Cambridge: Harvard University Press, 1957.

responsibility of the individual is strictly analogous to the civil responsibility for law-observance and/or the responsibility for living up to the obligations of a particular role, in this case of church-membership. Christianity thus has institutionalized the differentiation of these two aspects of the problem of social control. Original sin belongs, with respect to *this* axis of differentiation, on the same side as does illness.

With respect to the major categories I have been discussing for the last few pages, societies may be expected to differ in two major respects. The first I have already been stressing, namely with respect to the *degree* to which these major types of deviance are *differentiated from each other* and the functions of social control with respect to them institutionalized in differentiated agencies. In an evolutionary sense (with societal, not organic reference) they may be said all to have originated in religion.[12] Priests and magicians have thus been the "original" agents of social control everywhere. The roles of physician, of lawyer and, if you will, of "administrator" and social worker have only gradually and unevenly differentiated off from the religious roles.

The second range of variation concerns the relative stress put on conformity with social expectations in each of these categories and hence the seriousness with which deviance in each is viewed, and the importance given to building up effective mechanisms of social control in the area in question as distinguished from others. Thus in a society like that of Hindu caste in India, the overwhelming emphasis seems to have been religious, with ritual purity on one level, the problem of control of and emancipation from the Hindu counterpart of Christian original sin on another as the primary preoccupations. The neglect of health as Westerners understand it in India (until very recently) is too well-known to need emphasizing. Soviet society may be said to be a type which puts primary emphasis on effective role-performance in the socialist state and hence to bend its primary efforts to controlling the commitments of the population (above all through "propaganda" and "agitation")[13] to exerting the utmost effort, especially in production. Finally, with differences, of course, it may be suggested that both classical Rome and modern England have laid more stress on law and integration through the legal system than any other of the major features with which this discussion has been concerned.

Seen in this perspective, contemporary American Society is, with respect to the institutionalization of mechanisms of social control, probably as highly differentiated as any known, certainly as any outside the modern Western world. But among those which are highly differentiated, it is also one which places a very heavy emphasis on the field and problems of health and illness relative to the others, probably as high as any. It is also clear that our concern with problems of health has increased greatly since about the turn of the present century, and furthermore, that the emergence of the problem of mental health into a position of salience, on anything like the scale which has actually developed, is a new phenomenon.

[12]This is a major thesis of Durkheim in *The Elementary Forms of the Religious Life*, New York: Free Press, 1947.

[13]Cf. Alex Inkeles, *Public Opinion in Soviet Russia*, Cambridge: Harvard University Press, 1950.

A Restatement of the Criteria of Health
and Illness

Before attempting to relate this emphasis systematically to American values and social structure, it would be well to attempt to state somewhat more precisely what seem to be the principal general characteristics of health and illness seen in the context of social role structure and social control.

Health may be defined as the state of optimum *capacity* of an individual for the effective performance of the roles and tasks for which he has been socialized. It is thus defined with reference to the individual's participation in the social system. It is also defined as *relative* to his "status" in the society, i.e., to differentiated type of role and corresponding task structure, e.g., by sex or age, and by level of education which he has attained and the like. Naturally, also there are qualitative ranges in the differentiation of capacities, within sex groups and at given levels of education. Finally, let me repeat that I am defining health as concerned with capacity, not with commitment to *particular* roles, tasks, norms or even values as such. The question of whether a man wants to remain with his wife or likes his particular job or even feels committed to refrain from highway robbery is not *as such* a health problem, though a health problem may underlie and be interwoven with problems of this sort.

Illness, then, is also a socially institutionalized role-type. It is most generally characterized by some imputed generalized disturbance of the capacity of the individual for normally expected task or role-performance, which is not specific to his commitments to any particular task, role, collectivity, norm or value. Under this general heading of the recognition of a state of disturbance of capacity, there are then the following four more specific features of the *role* of the sick person: 1) This incapacity is interpreted as beyond his powers to overcome by the process of decision-making alone; in this sense he cannot be "held responsible" for the incapacity. Some kind of "therapeutic" process, spontaneous or aided, is conceived to be necessary to recovery. 2) Incapacity defined as illness is interpreted as a legitimate basis for the *exemption* of the sick individual, to varying degrees, in varying ways and for varying periods according to the nature of the illness, from his normal role and task obligations. 3) To be ill is thus to be in a partially and conditionally *legitimated* state. The essential condition of its legitimation, however, is the recognition by the sick person that to be ill is inherently *undesirable*, that he therefore has an obligation to try to "get well" and to cooperate with others to this end. 4) So far as spontaneous forces, the *vis medicatrix naturae*, cannot be expected to operate adequately and quickly, the sick person and those with responsibility for his welfare, above all, members of his family, have an obligation to *seek competent help* and to cooperate with competent agencies in their attempts to help him get well; in our society, of course, principally medical agencies. The valuation of health, of course, also implies that it is an obligation to try to *prevent* threatened illness where this is possible.

These criteria seem very nearly obvious on a common sense level in our society, but some aspects of their subtler significance become evident when we consider the way in which, through the channels of mental and psychosomatic illness, the balance of health and illness comes to be bound up with the balance of control of the motivation of individuals in their relation to the society as a system. This is what I had in mind in discussing illness in the context of the problems of deviance and social control in the first place. I shall not take space to go into this set of problems here, since they have been dealt with elsewhere, but will only call attention to them, and draw a few inferences.[14]

The most important inferences for present purposes concern the importance of *two* related but distinct functions for the society of the health–illness role structure. The first of these is the *insulation* of the sick person from certain types of mutual influence with those who are not sick, and from association with each other. The essential reason for this insulation being important in the present context is not the need of the sick person for special "care" so much as it is that, motivationally as well as bacteriologically, illness may well be "contagious." The motives which enter into illness as deviant behavior are partially identical with those entering into other types of deviance, such as crime and the breakdown of commitment to the values of the society, partly they are dynamically interrelated with these so that stimulation of one set of motives may tend to stimulate others as well.

In the light of the motivational problem the important feature of insulation is the deprivation, for the sick person, of any claim to a more general legitimacy for his pattern of deviance. As noted above, the conditional legitimation which he enjoys is bought at a "price," namely, the recognition that illness itself is an undesirable state, to be recovered from as expeditiously as possible. It is at this price that he is permitted to enjoy the often very powerful gratifications of secondary gain. But the importance of the institutionalization of the role of illness is not confined to its bearing on the motivational balance of the sick person. As Durkheim pointed out for the case of crime, the designation of illness as illegitimate is of the greatest importance to the healthy, in that it reinforces their own motivation *not* to fall ill, thus to avoid falling into a pattern of deviant behavior. The stigmatizing of illness as undesirable, and the mobilization of considerable resources of the community to combat illness is a reaffirmation of the valuation of health and a countervailing influence against the temptation for illness, and hence the various components which go into its motivation, to grow and spread. Thus, the sick person is prevented from setting an example which others might be tempted to follow.

The second important implication of institutionalization of the roles is that being categorized as ill puts the individual in the position of being defined as "needing help" and as obligated to accept help and to cooperate actively with the agency which proffers it. The role of illness, that is to say, channels those categorized as belonging in it into contact with therapeutic agencies. It is therefore involved in both negative and positive mechanisms of social control, negative in that the spread of certain types of deviance is inhibited, positive in that remedial processes are facilitated.

[14]I have dealt with them primarily in the following places: *The Social System*, Chapter X, New York: Free Press, 1951; the paper "Illness and the Role of the Physician," *American Journal of Orthopsychiatry*, July 1951, pp. 452-460, also printed in Kluckhohn, Murray and Schneider, *Personality, in Nature, Society and Culture*, 2nd Edition, New York: Alfred A. Knopf, 1953, and in somewhat more specialized context in T. Parsons and R. Fox, "Illness, Therapy, and the Modern Urban American Family,"*Journal of Social Issues*, Vol. 8, pp. 31-44.

An interesting and important intermediate aspect may also be noted. By defining the sick person as in need of help and tending to bring him into relation to therapeutic agencies, the role of illness tends to place him in a position of *dependency on* persons who are *not* sick. The structural alignment, hence, is of each sick person with certain categories of nonsick, not of groups of sick persons with each other.[15]

American Values and the Health Problem

Now let us turn to the question of the way in which American values and social structure may be said to operate selectively with reference both to the place of the health–illness complex among other mechanisms of social control and with respect to emphases within the health–illness complex itself. To start with it will be necessary to sketch the main outline of the American value system in the relevant respects.

I would like to suggest that even so complex and highly differentiated a society as our own can be said to have a relatively well-integrated system of institutionalized common values at the societal level. Ours I shall characterize as a pattern emphasizing "activism" in a certain particular sense, "worldliness" and "instrumentalism." Let me try, briefly, to explain these terms.

In the first place, a societal value system concerns the orientations of members to conceptions of what is desirable for the society itself and as a whole as a system or object of evaluation. Only derivatively does it provide patterns of evaluation of the individual. When I refer to activism, I mean that in relation to *its* situation or environment, the society should be oriented to mastery over that environment in the name of ideals and goals which are transcendental with reference to it. The relevant environment may be either physical or social, but because of our relative isolation from other societies until the last generation or so, the physical environment has been particularly prominent in our case. The reference point for exerting "leverage" on the environment has been, historically, in the first instance religious. It will not be possible here to go into the question of the sense in which or degree to which this is still the case; nevertheless, the main orientation clearly is one of maintaining the pattern of mastery, not of "adjustment" to the inevitable. In no field has this been more conspicuous than that of health where illness has presented a challenge to be met by mobilizing the resources of research, science, etc., to the full.

When I speak of the "worldliness" of the American value system, I mean that, in spite of its religious roots, the *field* of primarily valued activity is in practical secular pursuits, not in contemplation or devotions, or aesthetic gratifications. In its societal application this means a conception of an ideal *society*, originally the Kingdom of God *on Earth*, in a secularized version a good society

[15]The latter does of course happen in hospital situations. It has been clearly shown (Cf. Ivan Belknap, *Human Problems of a State Mental Hospital*, New York: McGraw-Hill Book Co., 1956, and Barbara Burt Arnason, unpublished Ph.D. Dissertation, Radcliffe College, 1958) that in mental hospital settings the social group of chronic patients, particularly in a kind of symbiosis with attendants, can, under certain circumstances, come to constitute a seriously *anti*-therapeutic social community.

in which such ideals as liberty, justice, welfare and equality of opportunity prevail.

Finally, when I speak of "instrumentalism," I refer to the fact that, in the first instance for the society as a system, there is no definitive "consummatory" state which is idealized, no definitive societal goal state which is either attained or not—as in the case of "communism." There is rather an indefinite perspective of possible improvement, of "progress" which fulfills by degrees the ideal by moving in the right *direction*.

The absence of a definitive goal for the system as a whole places the primary active achievement emphasis on the level of the goals of *units* and measures their achievements in appropriate terms. There is a kind of "liberal" pluralism in that any unit in the society, individual or collective, has liberty to pursue goals which to it may seem worthwhile, but more importantly, there are standards of *contribution* to the progress of the society. Perhaps the most obvious (though not the only) field of such contribution is that of economic productivity, for it is the productivity of the economy which is the basis of the availability of facilities for attaining *whatever* goals may seem most worthwhile, since income as generalized purchasing power is non-specific with respect to particular uses. This is the most generalized basis of opportunity to do "good things." But equally important is the provision of the society with units which have the *capacity* for valued achievement.

I may note that collective units and their achievements are of the utmost importance in the American system, for example, the business firm. But their achievements are fundamentally dependent on the capacities and commitments of the human individuals who perform roles and tasks within them. It is in this connection that the relevance of the valuation of health appears. For the individual, the primary focus of evaluation is universalistically judged *achievement*. The possibility of achievement is, of course, a function of opportunity at any given point in his life cycle, which in turn is a function of the economic level of the community, because openings both for self-employment, e.g., in independent business, and for employment by others, are a function of markets and of funds available through whatever channels. But on a "deeper" and in a sense more generalized level, this achievement is dependent on two basic sets of prior conditions which underlie his capacities, namely, on education in the broadest sense, and on health. It is in the first instance as an essential condition of valued achievement that the health of the individual is itself valued.

There is another very central strand in the pattern of our evaluation in both respects. This is the relation of both education and health to the valuation of *equality* of opportunity. For reasons which cannot be gone into here, but which bear above all on the high level of structural differentiation of our society, it is one which shows a great deal of mobility of resources. Ascribed status is relatively minimized. The "pluralism of goals" which has to do with the instrumental emphasis in our value system raises the problem of "justice" with great acuteness. One aspect of this is distributive justice with references to the allocation of rewards. But with the emphasis on active achievement, even more crucial than justice of reward distribution is that of *opportunity* for value achievement. But education and health are clearly more fundamental conditions of achievement than is access to investment funds or to employment, since they condition capacity to exploit opportunity in this narrower sense. Hence, *access* to education and to health services becomes, in a society like our own, a peculiarly central focus of the problem of justice in the society.

On technical grounds I do not classify education as a function of social control in a society.[16] Within the field of problems of social control, as discussed above, the problem of health clearly constitutes the "rock bottom" of the series.There seem, when the problem is seen in this light, to be a number of reasons which I may review briefly, why it has emerged into a position of special prominence in contemporary America.

First, and of course a very important point, the development of medicine and of the health sciences underlying and associated with it has made possible an entirely new level of control of illness, both preventive and therapeutic, far higher than has ever existed before in history. There is, of course, interdependence. American medicine did not just take over a medical science ready-made, but has developed the European beginnings with an energy and resourcefulness probably matched only in the field of industrial technology. There is, hence, interdependence between the development, on the one hand, of medical science and technology, and on the other, of interest in, and concern for, effective handling of health problems.

Secondly, the order of significance of the problems of social control, starting with commitment to paramount values themselves, running through commitment to norms, then to roles and tasks, is probably, in a very broad sense, of evolutionary significance. This is to say that there is a tendency for a problem area to emerge into salience only when, to a degree, the ones ahead of it in the priority list have in some sense been "solved." This is not to say that any of them ever are definitively solved, but in a relative sense one can speak of solution.

It is not possible to discuss this question here in detail. But it may be suggested that by the mid-nineteenth century, with the very important exception of the problem of the South, a certain national unity had been achieved in terms of values and norms.[17] It can then be further suggested that in the latter half of the nineteenth century there was concentration on the problems of setting up the new industrial system with the institutionalization of the principal role-categories which have to go into that, notably, of course, an occupational role system which was structurally quite different from that of the earlier society of "farmers and mechanics." Not least important in this connection was the institutionalization of the repercussions of these changes on the family, because of the drastic nature of the differentiation of occupational from familial roles. From the point of view of the individual, it may be said that the development of the industrial economy provided, in terms of a structural type congruent with American values, a new level of solution of the problem of opportunity.

From this point of view, one might say that after the turn of the century the stage was set for a new level of concern with the problems of education and health, which have indeed figured very prominently in this period, though not by any means to the exclusion of the others. Their importance is, I think, further ac-

[16]In my own technical terms, it is a "pattern-maintenance" function.
[17]Dr. R. N. Bellah, in an unpublished paper, has suggested the great importance of revivalist religion in the former of these contexts.

centuated by another feature of the development of the society. This is the fact that, with the development of industrialization, urbanism, high technology, mass communications and many other features of our society, there has been a general *upgrading* to higher levels of responsibility. Life has necessarily become more complex and has made greater demands on the typical individual, though different ones at different levels. The sheer problem of capacity to meet these demands has, therefore, become more urgent. The motivation to retreat into ill-health through mental or psychosomatic channels has become accentuated and with it the importance of effective mechanisms for coping with those who do so retreat.

Seen in terms of this kind of historical perspective, it makes sense, I think, that *the first major wave of development of the health institutions was in the field of somatic illness and the techniques of dealing with it, and that this has been followed by a wave of interest in problems of mental health.* This is partly, but by no means wholly, because the scientific basis for handling somatic illness has developed earlier and farther. In addition to this, it is well known that the resistances to recognizing the existence of health problems are stronger in the field of mental than of somatic health. Furthermore, a larger component of the phenomena of mental illness presumably operates through motivation and is hence related to the problems and mechanisms of social control. Social changes, however, have not only increased the strain on individuals, thus accentuating the need for mechanisms in this area, but some of the older mechanisms have been destroyed or weakened and a restructuring has been necessary.

For one thing, levels of mental pathology which could be tolerated under pre-industrial conditions have become intolerable under the more stringent pressures of modern life; this probably includes the pushing of many types of personality over the borderline into overt psychosis, who otherwise would have been able to "get along." Furthermore, the family, for example, has undertaken a greatly increased burden in the socialization and personality-management fields, and new institutional arrangements for dealing with the health problems of its members are required. This seems, for example, to be one major factor in the rapid spread of hospitalization.[18]

I may sum up this aspect of the discussion by saying that both by virtue of its value system, and by virtue of the high level of differentiation of its social structure, American society has been one in which it could be expected that the problem of health, and within this more particularly of mental health, would become particularly salient. Its "liberal" cast which militates against highly stringent integration with reference to a system goal tends to emphasize the problem of getting units to "come along." The human individual is the end of the series of units on which the functioning of the society depends, and is hence the "last resort" in this connection. At the same time, the activistic orientation of the society militates against any orientation which would be inclined to let individuals "rest on their oars," but puts very much of a premium on the protection and development of capacity in the sense in which I have discussed it here.

The same factors, particularly seen in the context of the stage of development of the society, tend to prevent too strong an emphasis on any of the other

---

[18]Cf. Parsons and Fox, *op. cit.* for a further analysis of this problem.

primary problems and modes of social control. Generally, I think, contrary to much opinion, it can be said that the American society is very firmly attached to its primary values, so much so that they tend to be placed outside the field of serious concern. There is, to be sure, much controversy about what are alleged to be changes in values. But a careful analysis, which cannot be entered into here, will reveal that very much, at least, of this does not lie at this level, but rather at ideological levels.

A very good example of this is the amount of concern displayed over the developing salience of problems of mental health, and the scope given to the permissive and supportive elements in the orientation to the mentally ill. But people who show this concern often forget to emphasize the other side of the coin, namely, the equally prominent concern with therapy, with bringing the mentally ill back into full social participation, which above all means into full capacity for achievement. Particularly revealing, I think, is the conception that the therapeutic process involves active *work* on the part of the patient, his seriously *trying* to get well. He is conceived of as anything but a passive object of the manipulations of the therapeutic personnel.

American Selectivity within the Patterns of Health and Illness

I have argued above that among the problems and mechanisms of social control, both the values and the social structure of American society will tend to place emphasis on the problems of health and illness which concern commitment to roles, as compared with those of commitment to collectivities, to normative rules, or to the values themselves. This essentially is to say that it is *capacity* which is the primary focus of the problem of social control for us. With the increasing complexity and "maturity" of the society in turn, the problem of motivation to adequate role-performance and hence to mental health becomes a salient one.

The problem now arises of what kind of selectivity we may expect, on the basis of the above analysis, *within* the complex of illness, and the corresponding attitudes toward therapy, relative to other ways of treating the problem of illness as such. In order to approach this question, I would like to use the formulation of the main components of the definition of illness, as stated previously herein, as my main point of reference. The first point, namely, a disturbance of capacity, is general, and is the link with the foregoing discussion of selectivity among the problems of social control. This is to say that in the United States we are more likely to interpret a difficulty in an individual's fulfilling social role-expectations as a disturbance in capacity, i.e., as illness, than is true in other types of society with other types of value systems.

The other four criteria, it will be remembered, were exemption from role-obligations, holding the patient not responsible for his state, conditional legitimation of the state, and acceptance of the need for help and of the obligation to cooperate with the source of the help.

My suggestion is that, compared with other societies in which other value systems have been institutionalized, in the American case the heaviest emphasis among these tends to go to the last. Essentially, this derives from the element in the American value system which I have called "activism" above. The implication of that element, in the context of the others to which it relates, is for the personality of the individual, the valuation of *achievement*. This in turn, as was developed above, implies a strong valuation of the capacities which underlie achievement, capacities which are primarily developed through education or socialization and protected and restored through health services. But in the American case, this does not imply that the primary stress is on the dependency aspect of the "need for help"—I shall return to the question of the role of dependency presently. It is rather, from the point of view of the society, the attitude which asserts the desirability of *mastery* of the problems of health, and from that for the individual sick person, the obligation to cooperate fully with the therapeutic agency, that is to *work* to achieve his own recovery. The rationale of this is plainly that, if he is not motivated to work to attain the conditions of effective achievement, he cannot very well be considered to be motivated to the achievements which require good health as a condition.

It might then be said that the other three components of the role of illness are institutionalized as subsidiary to, and instrumental to, this one. With respect to legitimation there is a particularly strong emphasis on its *conditional* aspect, that illness is only legitimized so long as it is clearly recognized that it is intrinsically an undesirable state, to be recovered from as expeditiously as possible. Similarly, with the factor of exemption from role-performance and the "admission" that the patient cannot be held responsible in the sense discussed above. In this connection, there is a very important relation to the scientific aspect of our cultural tradition. That the patient "can't help it" is simply one of the facts of life, demonstrated by medical science. Where scientific evidence is not available, the tendency is to give the benefit of the doubt to the possibility that he can help it. Thus, we tend to be relatively suspicious of plans for "free" health care because of the readiness to impute malingering wherever objective possibility for it exists.

I shall wish to suggest very tentatively how this American emphasis on active therapy differs from emphases in other societies, but before taking this up, I would like to try broadly to answer two other sets of questions about the American case. The first of these is how the patterning of illness in our society relates to the problem of the *directions* of deviant behavior, the second to selective emphases among the social components involved in the therapeutic process.

In a previous publication, I attempted to classify the directions which deviant orientations might take in terms of three major dimensions, two of which were very close to, if not identical with, those set forth by Merton.[19] These were first the variation between *alienation* from social expectations and *compulsive conformity* with them, second between *activity* and *passivity*, and third between *object*-primacy and *pattern*-primacy. The first two of these are the ones selected by Merton.

In terms of these first two dimensions, illness clearly belongs in the general category of a type of deviance categorized by alienation and by passivity. This general type I have designated as withdrawal whereas Merton calls it "retreatism." This tendency to withdrawal as the most prominent type of deviance is

[19]Cf. *The Social System*, New York: Free Press, 1951, Chapter VII, and R. K. Merton, *Social Theory and Social Structure*, New York: Free Press, 1957, rev. ed., Chapter IV.

typical of American society generally. But some of the dynamics of it are relevant to the questions of selectivity within the components of the pattern of illness.

Before entering into these, however, it may be noted that with respect to the American pattern of illness, I think it can be said that the primary focus is object-oriented rather than pattern-oriented. This is above all because illness focuses at the level of capacity for role and task performance, not at the level of norms or values and conformity with them. This would also be true of illness generally but for reasons which will be discussed presently. I think it likely that it is more accentuated in the American case than others.[20]

What, then, can be said to be some of the main patterns of motivational dynamics relevant to the problem of illness in American society and their relation in turn to these features of the role of illness as an institutionalized role? I may start by suggesting that all patterns of deviant behavior, as distinguished from creative alteration of the cultural or normative tradition, involves the primacy of elements of *regressive* motivational structure in the psychological sense.[21] But for different types of deviance and within the category of illness as a type of deviance there will be selective emphases on different phases of psychological regression.

It is not possible to enter into all the complications here, but I suggest that in the American case, the primary focus lies in the residues of the pre-oedipal mother–child relationship, that phase of which Freud spoke as involving the "first true object-attachment." The basis on which this develops goes back to the very great and increasing prominence in socialization of the relatively *isolated* nuclear family. The "American dilemma" in this case is that the child is, typically, encouraged to form an extremely intense attachment to the mother at this time, while at the same time he is required later to break more radically with this early dependency because the process of emancipation from the family of orientation is pushed farther and faster than in other systems. Independence training, that is to say, forms a particularly prominent part of our socialization process and the strength of the mother attachment is an essential condition of its successful carrying out.

The alienation involved in the motivation to illness may then be interpreted to involve alienation from a set of expectations which put particular stress on independent achievement. Because of this complex, the importance of the passivity component of the deviance expressed in illness is particularly great, because the ambivalent motivational structure about the dependency–independence problem is particularly prominent. Therapy then focuses on the strengthening of the motivation to independence relative to dependency and on overcoming the alienation, focussing on the expectations of independence and, through it, achievement.[22]

I suggest, then, that the American pattern of illness is focussed on the problem of capacity for achievement for the individual person. Therapeutically, re-

[20]By the three criteria, then, of alienation, passivity, and object-orientation, the pattern of illness should be considered a case of "compulsive independence" (*Social System, op. cit.,* p. 259). Compulsive independence in this case may be interpreted to involve reaction-formation against underlying needs, as I shall note.

[21]A fuller discussion of the nature of the "regression scale" will be found in *Family, Socialization and Interaction Process, op. cit.,* especially Chapter II.

[22]In this light the motivation to illness may, with only apparent paradox, be characterized as a case of "compulsive independence from the requirement to be independent." It is a kind of "to hell with it all" pattern of withdrawal.

covery is defined for him as a *job* to be done in cooperation with those who are technically qualified to help him. This focus then operates to polarize the components of the "problem" in such a way that *the primary threat to his achievement capacity which must be overcome is dependency.* The element of exemption from ordinary role-obligations may then be interpreted as permissiveness for temporary relief from the strains of trying hard to achieve. The patient is permitted to indulge his dependency needs under strictly regulated conditions, notably his recognition of the conditional nature of the legitimacy of his state, and exposure to the therapeutic task.[23]

These elements of the situation relate in turn to the components of the therapeutic process. I have elsewhere[24] designated these, in terms of role-pattern, as permissiveness, support, selective rewarding and reinforcement. An essential point is that the dependency component of the deviance of illness is used constructively in the therapeutic pattern, essentially through what is in certain respects a recapitulation of the socializing experience. This is to say that through permissiveness to express dependency, both in exemption from role-obligations and in supportive relations to others, the patient is encouraged to form a dependent attachment to others. The permissive and supportive treatment of the sick person, by giving him what he wants, undercuts the alienative component of the motivational structure of his illness. He finds it much more difficult to feel alienated toward social objects who treat him with kindness and consideration than he would otherwise be disposed to feel—though, of course, there may be a problem, particularly with some types of mental illness, of getting him to accept such kindness and consideration, even to accept his need for the exemptions permitted by virtue of illness.

At the same time the element of dependency, through "transference," is the basis of a strong attachment to therapeutic personnel, which can then be used as a basis of leverage to motivate the therapeutic "work" which eventually should result in overcoming the dependency itself, or mitigating it sufficiently so that it no longer interferes so seriously with his capacities. Building on this, then, the active work of therapy, adapting to the fundamental conditions of the biological and psychological states of the patient, can take hold and operate to propel toward recovery.[25]

[23]Unfortunately, there will be no opportunity here to take up the empirical problem of how far the available data on illness bear out this interpretation of the central importance of the dependency-independency axis. Not only do I suggest that this is more important in the American case than in others but also that it applies to somatic as well as mental illness. The ulcer complex is widely believed to relate especially to this problem. It may also be suggested that the special concern with polio in America related to our horror of the dependency which the permanent cripple must bear. Almost better death than not to be able to do one's part, but remain dependent on others.

[24]Cf. *The Social System, op. cit.*, Chapter VII and Parsons, Bales and Shils, *Working Papers in the Theory of Action,* Chapter V. In earlier versions, what I am now calling selective rewarding was called "denial of reciprocity" (this term emphasized only the negative aspect) and what I now call reinforcement was called "manipulation of rewards." The new term for the latter emphasizes the continuity of a *pattern* of rewards over time.

[25]In Parsons and Fox, *op.cit.*, it was suggested that the trend toward hospitalization, again in cases of both mental and somatic illness, was related to these factors. On the one hand, it is related to technological exigencies of modern medicine. Also it is a way of relieving the family of burdens of "care." But at the same time it is both a way of protecting the family from the patient, that is above all the impact of his dependency needs on other members, and the point of primary present impor-

I should finally like to turn to a brief and very tentative suggestion of the main differences between the orientations to illness in the United States and in two other modern societies, namely Soviet Russia and Great Britain. Let us take the Soviet case first.[26]

Whereas in the American case I suggested that our concern with capacity for role-achievement put the primary emphasis on the restoration of that capacity through therapeutic work, the general orientation of Soviet society is different; it is to the attainment of a collective goal for the society as a whole, the "building of socialism." With reference to the problem of illness this tends to shift the emphasis from the obligation to cooperate in therapy to the problem of responsibility and non-responsibility. This is most conspicuous in the field of mental illness where the Soviet attitude is an extreme antithesis of our own precisely on this point.[27] One very telling expression of it is the complete prohibition of psychoanalysis, whereas psychoanalysis has had greater success in the United States than in any other country. My interpretation of this would be that psychoanalysis is a threat from the Soviet point of view, because through the theory of the unconscious, it so strongly emphasizes the elements in the personality of the individual which are outside this voluntary control. It would give too plausible excuses for too many for the evasion of responsibility. In the American case, on the other hand, psychoanalysis is defined more as offering *opportunity* for constructive therapeutic work, to the patient as well as the therapist.[28]

The same general strain seems to be conspicuous, from Field's account, in the field of somatic medicine. The attitude seems to be one of reluctant concession to human frailties. Of course, it is part of socialism to have a national medical service, but at the same time party and administrative personnel keep strict watch on the medical people to be sure that they do not connive to malingering which—because of the great severity of labor discipline—they have been under strong pressure to do. To American eyes the Soviet treatment of illness seems to be marked by a certain perfunctoriness, as if it were up to the patient to prove that he is "really" sick rather than it being the physician's role to investigate the possibilities on his own. I suggest that this may be more than a matter of scarcity of personnel and resources; it is probably at least in part an authentic expression of Soviet values.

Reinforcing this conclusion is the probability that illness is not the primary type of deviance for Soviet society in the sense that I have argued it is in the American case. I think it probable that what I have called "compulsive acquiescence in status-expectations" is the most prominent type. This, of course,

---

tance, of protecting the patient from his family. The family, that is to say, is very likely to be "overprotective" and over supportive. Because of the temptations of "seduction" of the patient into more or less permanent dependency, it lacks the basis of effective leverage which a more "impersonal" agency may be in a position to exert. Also, it was noted above, there is reason to believe that the acuteness of the dependency problem has been increasing with recent developments in family structure.

[26]My most important sources on Soviet medicine are Field, *op. cit.*, and R. A. Bauer, *The New Man in Soviet Psychology.* I am also indebted to Dr. Field for suggestions made in personal discussion which go beyond his book.

[27]Cf. Bauer, *op.cit.*

[28]The extent to which the ego as distinct from the id has come to be emphasized in American versions of psychoanalysis seems to fit with this interpretation.

very generally does not appear overtly as deviance at all and hence is difficult to detect.[29]

There is, however, another side of the Soviet picture, just as there is in the American case of polarity between the emphasis on active mastery and the problem of dependency. This is that in medical care, especially in the hospital, there seems to be a particularly strong supportive emphasis. This is to say that, once the status of being sick is granted, there is not nearly so strong an emphasis on the conditional character of its legitimacy as in the American case, and patients are encouraged to relax and to enjoy being taken care of.[30]

This suggests a permissiveness for regression, but one which is differently structured from the American. It is less the need to express dependency on particular social objects which does not threaten essential acceptance or belongingness. Psychologically it suggests primacy of oral components rather than of the mother–child love-attachment.

Thus, on the one hand, the role of illness is not given nearly so wide a scope in Soviet Russia as in the United States, particularly in the direction of mental illness. At the same time, it is also differently structured in that the primary focus is the problem of the responsibility of the individual rather than his capacity in our sense to achieve and to cooperate in recovery. The permissive element is more for "rest," for relaxation from responsibility, than it is for the direct expression of object-oriented dependency.

The British case does not seem to be quite so clear, but I think it is different in important ways from either the American or the Soviet. By contrast, with the other two, British society has a particularly strong integrative emphasis. From this point of view, illness is not so much a threat to the achievement of the individual or to his responsibility as it is a threat to his *status* as an acceptable member of the society and its various relevant subgroupings. The main emphasis in treatment then would be on reintegration, an element which is always present, but is more strongly stressed in the British case than in others.

One important type of evidence is the particularly strong British feeling that the sick individual has a *right* to care in case of illness. The whole welfare state is related to the integrative emphasis in the society, but the particularly full coverage provided by the National Health Service for the whole population is one very salient aspect of this general orientation. On the part of the nation and its health agencies then, it is strongly declared that illness, far from jeopardizing the individual's status, gives him special claims on the collectivity. The burden of proof is not nearly so much on him that he is "really" sick as in either the American or the Soviet cases. One might speak of a scale of decreasing "tolerance of the possibility of malingering" in the order, British, American, Soviet.

Another interesting point is that, with respect to the scope given to the recognition of mental illness, the British case is intermediate between the American and the Soviet; this includes the position of psychoanalysis. I suggest that this has to do with the very strong British emphasis on the importance of self-control in social relations. Somatic illness is generally clearly beyond the respon-

[29]Cf. *Social System, op. cit.* This is Merton's "ritualism."
[30]On this point I am directly indebted to Dr. Field (personal discussion).

sibility of the individual, and generally the legitimacy of illness is not made so highly conditional as in the American case. But capacity is not so highly valued and mental disturbance is not to the same extent seen as an opportunity for therapeutic achievement. The deliberately encouraged regression which, with all the differences, is shared by the Soviet and American cases is substantially less conspicuous in the British.

The above are, as I have emphasized, extremely tentative and sketchy impressions of relatively systematic differences between American, Soviet, and British selectivities in the definition of health and illness, and in the roles of patient and of therapeutic agencies. I have introduced them and carried the analysis as far as I have, only to try to give some empirical substance to the general view of the nature of variability from one society to another in those respects that have been presented herein.

8 The Concept of Health Status

Biological Parameters of Health Status*

In order to deal adequately with the concept of health as a *social status*, it is necessary to adequately define the bio-physical parameters of health status. That is, health must be understood first as a *bio-physical status*.

One of the attributes of man is that he is an organism. As an organism he has certain basic needs which must be met before he can function in any supra-organic sense (e.g. as a psychological, social or cultural being). As an organism he is composed of cells, tissues, and organs, which must function adequately and in reasonable harmony to ensure biological continuity. Like any organism, man can play host to other organisms in ways that may enhance or jeopardize the continuity of his biological functioning. Inter- or intra-organic relationships, to the extent that they jeopardize this functioning, can result in reduced capacities or death, which prejudice functioning in higher level systems. The central point for sociology is that failure to meet biological needs on a large enough scale will result in the failure of higher system levels [1].

To the extent that the organic nature of man is objectively known and that changes in inter- and intra-organic relationships predict capacity reduction or death, health and illness may be considered objective phenomena which pose a problem of reality orientation relative to the ways in which they are conceived by different groups in the population.

Biological and Medical Theories

The major disciplines concerned with man as a biological being are biology and medicine. Biology is concerned with the organic and intra-organic relationships of living things, and medicine is concerned with intervention into these relationships toward the goal of increasing capacities or forestalling death. Biology, therefore, can be seen as a science, upon which the profession of medicine is based.

Even within biological parameters, however, the issue of health status is far from settled. Kosa and Robertson [2] have identified at least four "main ideas

---

*In this paper, *status* refers to major categories for differentiating members of society. This sociologically meaningful labels are those which alter behavioral expectations. *Role* refers to the behavioral expectations held by others for the individual in question, as determined by general cultural norms relative to proper behavior and particular social identities held by the individuals in question. *Behavior* refers to the kinds of actions engaged in, which vary with general cultural expectations, expectations held by others in the form of roles, and situational contexts which define possibilities and alternatives and impose problems with which the individual must cope.

This is a revised version of a paper presented at the 1970 American Sociological Association meeting and at the Second International Conference on Social Science and Medicine, Aberdeen, Scotland. Reprinted from *Social Science & Medicine*, 8:29–38, January, 1974, by permission of the author and Publisher.

that have developed modern medicine since the time of Louis Pasteur". These include the germ theory of disease, epidemiological theory, the cellular concept of disease, and the mechanistic concept. The first of these provided the impetus for traditional medicine in the conquest of infectious illness; the second is associated with public health; the last with surgery; and the third has been influential in the search for causes of chronic and degenerative diseases.

Moreover, there is little consensus within medicine regarding the extent to which the focus of physicians and other health workers should be limited to the biological parameters of illness. The preamble to the World Health Organization Constitution states: "Health is a state of complete physical, mental and social well being, and not merely the absence of disease or infirmity". Attention in the medical literature is increasingly being given to the psychological, social and even cultural dimensions of illness.

Operationally, however, the philosophical tradition of positivism has dominated thinking about physical illness. Hence, there is wide consensus among medical people that illness is any state that has been diagnosed as such by a competent professional. This assumes objective standards against which the functioning of an organism can be measured, the significance of deviation assessed, and health status accordingly assigned. Assigning health status, or making diagnosis, consists of placing the proper label on the individual. With the individual thus categorized, notions of cause and proper treatment automatically follow. Alternatively, there is a view that whoever feels ill should be regarded as sick. This orientation, which reflects the philosophical tradition of idealism, is more prominent in the field of psychological disorders. While an attempt is still made at a diagnosis, there is less consensus in the field around specific categories, and less information is presumed to follow relative to etiology and treatment.

Signs and Symptoms

While the medical criteria for defining illness tend to be bio-physical or behavioral, the recognized evidence in support of health status designation is not unitary. Two types of evidence are generally recognized by physicians. The first of these, labelled "signs", consists of directly observable events such as fevers, palpable masses, measurements of blood pressure, and the results of laboratory analysis. These signs are seen as objective evidence of illness which fit the positivistic criteria of being independent of human thought or will. They are, therefore, seen as more definitive of health status than are symptoms. Symptoms differ from signs in that they are not always directly observable by the physician, but rather become known through the reporting of the patient. Symptoms can include changes in feeling states, or capacities, or other changes noted by the patient, and causing him concern. Symptoms are seen as "softer" forms of evidence by most physicians than are signs. In the absence of corroborating signs, symptoms are generally not held as in themselves defining health status. The relative emphasis placed on signs and symptoms by different physicians corresponds to the differences between illness as an event defined by the diagnosis of a physician, and illness defined by the reported self-designation of patients noted by Kosa and Robertson above.

The Life Cycle

While they are seen as objective, signs of illness are not necessarily unambiguous. Not only are there many parameters of measurable biological functioning which may or may not be consistent with one another, but also standards of normality are not necessarily fixed for any one of these measures. One of the major sources of variation in this regard is the cycle of growth, development, and deterioration which can be seen as the biological aspect of the life cycle. Starting with infancy, and into the young adult years, biological capacities tend to be augmented. That is, that as a biological organism the individual is capable of undertaking more complex tasks. The monitoring of this process of increasing capacities is a major aspect of the practice of pediatrics, subsumed under the concepts of growth and development. After the young adult years, the process of cellular deterioration proceeds at an increasingly more rapid rate than cellular regeneration and the biological capacity of the organism deteriorates, culminating ultimately in death.

Corresponding with this cycle of growth, development and deterioration are changes in the measurable parameters of biological functioning. To take only one example, blood pressure tends to increase with increasing age, not only statistically, but also relative to standards of acceptability. In standard medical practice, therefore, the normality or abnormality of any given sign is assessed relative to individuals of the age under consideration.

Illness As Deviance

From a sociological perspective, health and illness are related to problems of deviance, conformity and social control. Illness is explicitly designated as a form of deviant behavior, while health is viewed as conforming behavior [3]. From this perspective the medical care system is seen as a social control system. An understanding of the deviance perspective requires that we explicate health as a norm, the functional importance of health and illness to the social system, and the processes by which deviance becomes labelled and thereby subject to control. Furthermore, some understanding is needed of the relevant sanctioning processes.

Health As a Norm: Normality and Illness

Many frames of reference can be employed in the assessment of health status. From a biological frame of reference we have already noted that health can be defined with reference to cells, to organs, or their inter-relationship. These biological perspectives, however, do not exhaust the range of phenomena which serve to define health status. While they underlie many of the other perspectives, it seems likely that social and psychological frames of reference may be even more important in this regard. Different groups of "sick" or potentially "sick" people may define illness in terms of changes in feeling states (a psychological orientation), changes in capacities (a social orientation), or in terms of other changes which involve neither capacity nor feeling state orientations (presumably a more specifically biological frame of reference). We will return to this point below. For the present it is sufficient to note that a wide variety of frames of reference can be employed in the designation of health status.

Given the fact of social variability in the definition of health and illness, as well as variability in the degree to which different individuals meet these definitions, it is evident that universal consensus on the question of who is healthy and who is ill must be difficult to achieve. Nonetheless, almost everyone would agree that some people are "well" and others are "ill", and that there are differences in the degree to which those defined as ill are sick.

Keeping this variety in mind, we may conceptualize a state of *perfect health*, as an ideal toward which people are oriented rather than a state they expect to attain. From a biological standpoint, perfect health might be seen as a state in which every cell of the body is functioning at optimum capacity and in perfect harmony with each other cell; or a state in which each organ functions at optimum capacity and in harmony with each other organ. From a psychological standpoint, perfect health may be defined as a state in which the individual feels that he is in perfect harmony with his environment and capable of meeting any contingencies. From a social standpoint, perfect health may be a state in which an individual's capacities for task and role performance are optimized. It is axiomatic that by any accepted standards, individuals never attain perfect health. As one physician is fond of saying, "A healthy person is someone who has been inadequately studied" *

Illness, on the other hand, can be defined in terms of signs, symptoms, capacities for role performance, and feeling states which fall within the experience of most individuals. While the criteria used to define illness may vary in the degree to which any given criteria must be present for an individual to be called "ill", individuals are relatively certain that illness can be defined with clarity. The point at which an individual is said to be "sick" and how sick he is said to be are variables which crucially involve problems of social definition.

As virtually no one attains perfect health, and not everyone is defined as ill, there must be a range of less than perfect health which is defined as normal. What is considered normal for one individual may be considered abnormal for another. An individual whose job requires a high degree of physical proficiency, for example an athlete, might be defined as ill with a relatively small deviation from perfect health; while an individual who is without an occupation, for example a retired old person, might be considered normal with a relatively large deviation from perfect health. Thus, there may be considerable overlap between behavior, symptoms, or other clues which are defined as normal, and those considered "ill" (Fig. 8–1).

The extent of overlap might be relatively small if the criteria defining illness are specified to only one frame of reference, or if reference is made to only one group of people, and relatively large if all possible definitions and all cultures are considered. It is likely that the number of conflicts over definition are substantially smaller as we move from the center of the shaded area in Fig. 8–1 toward either end of the continuum. Two points seem crucial: first, to the extent that we must talk about normal health within the context of group and cultural definition, rather than perfect health or any other fixed definition, health becomes a social

---

*Dr. Alexander Burgess of Brown University has asked that this statement not be attributed to him. Accordingly, his wishes will be respected and no attribution will be made.

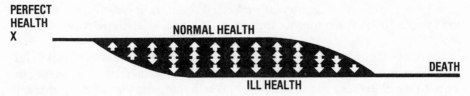

Figure 8-1.

norm. Second, there is a substantial area in which the definition of health and illness is subject to variability both within and among societies as compared with a smaller range at either extreme in which non-social clues are sufficiently strong to preclude the need for social definition.

Capacities and Functional Requisites

The major sociological studies devoted to the problem of defining health and illness are explicitly oriented toward the concept of health as a norm [4]. Talcott Parsons [3] takes as his starting point the cultural value system of the society, and from this derives the concept of health and illness as a problem in deviant behavior.

Parsons argued that the major value of modern, urban western industrialized societies can be described as "instrumental activism". That is, the environment is seen as capable of manipulation and the culture is not only supportive of, but dependent upon, activities oriented toward environmental manipulation. The core problem of defining health and illness, however, is common to societies with widely differing value systems, and the activist orientation of modern societies provides for differences in emphasis rather than in the more fundamental criteria for defining illness. Basically all societies face problems of continuity, or system maintenance. That is, certain tasks are essential to the survival of the society, and these must be accomplished. Health is thus a functional requisite of social systems, and every society has a vested interest in maintaining levels of capacities in its population sufficient to ensure that these fundamental tasks are performed.

The problem of defining health and illness, therefore, relates to the problem of status and role, insofar as role and task performance are fundamental in all human societies. In Parsons' words, "There must, therefore, always be standards of 'adequacy' of such performance and the 'capacities' underlying it which must be taken into account, and hence a corresponding set of distinctions between states of individuals which are and are not 'satisfactory' from the point of view of these standards". In other words, capacities are always assessed relative to a normative standard. Those failures to meet normative standards which are assessed as being the result of deficiencies in capacity tend to be defined as illness while other labels such as sin, disloyalty and crime tend to be attached to those failures defined as within the motivational control of the individual.

Health may therefore be defined as "the state of optimum capacity of an individual for the effective performance of the roles and tasks for which he has been socialized. It is thus defined with reference to the individual's participation in the social system" [3]. Illness is also "a socially institutionalized role type. It is most generally characterized by some imputed generalized disturbance of the capacity of the individual in normally expected role or task performance which is not specific to his commitments to any specific task role, collectivity norm or value'' [3].*

It is the relationship between capacities and the general problem of tasks and roles in the society that provides the specifically sociological frame of reference to the problem of defining health and illness. It is in this sense that capacity changes were identified above as being more socially oriented than were other changes which might be seen as defining illness in a larger context.

Labelling "Theory"

To say that the focus on capacities provides the specifically sociological orientation toward illness does not mean that social processes are not involved when other system referents, such as biological or psychological, serve to define health status. As in the case with any other social status, the designation of individuals as "well" or "ill" is at some levels a matter of social definition involving some minimal degree of consensus between the individual concerned and the significant others who serve as his status definers. Inconsistencies or conflicts in these definitions raise problems similar to those found in other spheres of life.

When the terms "healthy", "ill" and "normal" are used to refer to statuses, we use the term "status" in a general sense as a social designation. That is, a status is a kind of social label which can be attached to an individual, and which defines to some extent how he is expected to behave and how others should behave toward him.

In understanding any social designation, we should know not only *what* is defined, but *who* does the defining. For any general designation, broad criteria are likely to be provided by virtue of membership in the total population of the society. These criteria may be specified in different ways in different sub-populations, where different values may be operative, and further specified in different interaction contexts in which the specific other people who are involved in the problem of defining a status may apply different criteria. These people may be thought of as *status definers* to the extent that they provide definitions for an individual whose status is in question, and thus create "pressures" on him to re-evaluate who he is.

With reference to health problems, the society provides certain broad criteria for deciding who is to be called "ill". Different sub-populations select certain of these criteria and play down others, providing cultural variation in the criteria used. Further, different individuals, varyingly reflecting values of the total population and the sub-populations of which they are members, may be quite diverse in the criteria used to assign the status "sick" to people with whom they

---

*It should be noted with respect to Parsons' original article that a distinction is made between mental and physical illness. This is done by first distinguishing between the concepts of role and task. A role is defined as "the organized system of participation of an individual in a social system with special reference to the organization of that social system as a collectivity". A task is regarded as "that subsystem of a role which is defined by a definite set of *physical* operations which perform some function or functions in relation to a role, and/or the personality of the individual performing it". Somatic illness is defined in terms of incapacity for task performance, while mental illness is defined as incapacity for role performance. In neither case is the reference to specific roles or tasks but to the more generalized capacities underlying them.

are concerned. How much of a deviation from "perfect health" is required for various individuals to be defined as having "ill health", then, differs from one individual to another, depending upon, in part, who is involved in making the definition. Hence, within any given society, there is likely to be considerable overlap between normal health and ill health, as shown above.

Figure 8-2 shows some of the alternative ways in which the definition of a person may change from "well" to "sick".* The likely starting point is a state in which neither the individual nor his status definers think of him as sick (Cell A). The end result of the process of re-definition is a state (Cell D) in which both the individual and his status definers designate him as "sick". Cells B and C represent disagreement between the individual and his status definers.

In some situations, the definitions may coincide throughout the process of re-definition. In this case, the movement is directly from Cell A to Cell D. In other situations, the movement may be from Cell A to Cell B in which the individual defines his health as normal, while his status definers designate him as sick. In this instance, the individual may be thought of as "resisting the fact that he is sick". If, on the other hand, the movement is from Cell A to Cell C wherein the individual defines himself as sick, while the other status definers think of his health as normal, the individual may be thought of as malingering or hypochondrial. In either case, there is a conflict between the individual's self-definition, and the definition given by those around him. To the extent that there is a pressure for uniformity of definitions, there may be a process of bargaining which can result in either a "retreat" to Cell A, or an "advance" to Cell D.

Health As a Stratification Variable

Health and illness are social statuses not only in the sense of being meaningful labels applied to individuals, but also parameters of social stratification. That is, health is a social status in a hierarchical as well as a labelling sense. Health is both a social value and one of the criteria employed in the evaluation of one person or group by another. It has been argued elsewhere that evaluation is central to the process of social stratification [6].

In general, all other things being equal (a state of affairs that can be empirically demonstrated only in a relative sense), it is regarded as preferable to be healthy rather than sick. Since health and illness are seen as relative states of the organism or personality, it is often discussed comparatively, as a matter of the degree to which one individual is seen as healthier than another, even while both are regarded as being in a state of normal health. On the other side, people are regarded as being slightly, moderately, or severely ill. The hierarchical arrangement of degrees of health and illness is consistent with the model proposed in Fig. 8-1.

To the extent that the health of the individual is (1) taken into account in placing a value on his worth, and hence becomes a factor in determining his life chances, or (2) seen as a life chance in itself, it becomes a part of the process of social stratification.

The commitment of effort to an individual or group generally takes into account capacities for defined normal role and task performance. To the extent that

*A similar point is made by Williams [5] in a table relating role definers to extent of impairment.

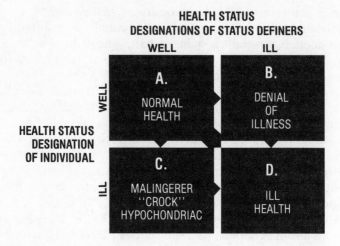

HEALTH STATUS
DESIGNATIONS OF STATUS DEFINERS

Figure 8-2.

these capacities are diminished or lacking, the individual or group will be assigned a lower value and the loss of the social unit in question will be seen as less consequential. Closely related, life values tend to associate with the amount of life expected to be remaining, and hence to another dimension of imputed capacities.

Variations in Health Status Designation

Insofar as changes in biological or psychological functioning are presumed to lead to predictable outcomes, generally defined as undesirable, health can be defined as an objective phenomenon. Because of the observability of alternative outcomes associated with objective symptoms and because of broad consensus on the ultimate criteria for defining illness as falling within the pervue of technical medical competence. there are likely to be social norms for defining health and illness on which broad consensus can be obtained. It appears likely that consensus could also be obtained relative to the desirability of good health. *Health can thus be seen as a social goal felt in common by all groups.* As is the case with any goal, however, *the salience of health must be assessed relative to other goals.* Thus, while there may be broad consensus that health is desirable, it does not necessarily follow that health has the same priority in all contexts.

Both the priority assigned to health, therefore, and the specific criteria employed to assess health status can be expected to vary within societies. Not all groups relate to the central value system of society in the same ways and significant variations in emphasis are found from group to group. In addition, in societies as complex as that in the United States, many groups must relate simultaneously to the core value system of the society and to the values imported from outside the society. Furthermore, different groups of people may have different objective experience with specific symptoms, and the same symptom may be seen as leading to different outcomes in different groups. The designation of health status also may reflect the differential possibilities for intervention in biological and psychological processes available to different groups within the society, a factor which would affect the salience of any given health status designation.

A first step in identifying variations in health status designation therefore would require a close look at sub-societal population variations. In addition, account must be taken of the differing situations with which individuals must cope, leading to a focus on situational factors as they influence variations in health status designation.

Sub-societal Population Variations

One way of approaching variations in the criteria for defining health status is to conceptualize, as suggested above, a body of norms seen as most applicable in the society as a whole. Different groups in the population, reflecting in part different value systems, and in part the different situations with which they must cope, can be seen as specifying these norms and modifying them in different ways. Hence, as we move from the total population of a society to various sub-societal populations the criteria employed for the designation of health and illness can be expected to vary. Two such types can be described in American society, both of which relate to the problem of social stratification. Hence, we will briefly note some of the variations in health status designation associated with socio-economic status and ethnicity.

Socio-economic status. While much has been written on socio-economic status differentials in the incidence and prevalence of disease, the utilization of medical care facilities, and health maintenance practices, scant attention has been given to variations in the criteria used to assess health and illness. With reference to somatic illness, only two major studies have been found which focus on the problem of status designation with reference to socio-economic status.

Koos [7] studied the health and illness behavior patterns of a small town in upstate New York. As part of his study he presented a household sample with a list of 17 medically important symptoms. The respondents were asked to report whether each symptom warranted the attention of a physician. For each symptom listed, the highest status respondents were uniformly more likely to report a need for medical attention than were the lowest status respondents. For all but two symptoms, loss of appetite and persistent backache, at least 75 per cent of the Class One respondents reported a need for medical attention. In only three instances did more than half the Class Three respondents report such a need. Each of these involved bleeding. Class differentials were related to age, the role of the individual in the family, past experience, group experience and culture content.

Drawing on earlier studies [8, 9], Gordon [10] identified four criteria which could be used to validate the occupancy of the status sick. These were: prognosis, symptoms, being under the care of a physician, and functional incapacity. He presented a list of 12 descriptions of illness states to a sample of 808 residents of New York City, and found that prognosis was the most important factor in designating someone as sick. The poorer or more uncertain the prognosis, the greater the tendency to define someone as sick. This held across class lines with no significant difference between low status and high status respondents. With functional incapacity controlled, the presence of symptoms and being under the care of a physician were more likely to validate the status "sick" among high status respondents than among low status respondents. Functional incapacity, on the other hand, was relatively more important in low status groups as compared with high status respondents with education being a more important dimension than income.*

  Ethnicity. Much more has been written about the relationship between ethnicity and illness behavior than on socio-economic status and illness behavior. Furthermore, where both have been treated simultaneously, ethnicity seems to be the more important predictor of illness behavior (Mechanic [13]). Further support for this contention is being developed in yet unpublished findings from the Brown Health Study [14].

  Few of the studies on the relationships between ethnicity and illness behavior, however, focus on the problem of health status designation. Of the four that have been found, two limit their focus to a single symptom, pain. Zborowski [15, 16] studied the cultural factors in responses to pain among "old American", Italian, Irish and Jewish subcultures. He found that Italians and Jews were characterized by emotionally "open" responses to pain and were likely to vocalize their discomfort. The reasons for their "emotional" responses were found to differ. The pain itself was significant to the Italians while the implications of pain were the most significant factor to the Jews. By contrast, the "old Americans" and Irish did not vocalize or complain of their discomfort and took a more stoical attitude. Details of their responses differed, in that the Irish seemed to deny the pain while the "old Americans" would report the pain experience in some detail while maintaining a detached attitude. Wolff [17] noted that while different cultural groups had the same threshold at which pain was perceived, their responses to pain were highly variable. He related this variability to differences in traditions of stoicism or emotionalism and on the meaning assigned to the painful experience.

  Zola [18] studied the complaints presented by patients in the out-patient clinic of a large urban, university affiliated teaching hospital. Focusing on a limited set of medical diagnoses, he found that Italians presented a significantly more elaborate description of their symptoms than did the Irish. Furthermore, while the Irish denied that their symptoms had any effect on their relations with other people, the Italians characteristically reported the disruption of interpersonal relations as a major part of their complaint.

  Drawing on a classification of symptoms proposed by Bauman [19], Twaddle [14] studied the first symptoms of illness reported by a sample of older married males in Providence, Rhode Island. In that study it was found that feeling state changes, predominately pain and weakness, were the most important for all ethnic groups studied. Italian Catholics, Protestants and Jews, however, did show characteristic differences. Feeling state changes were the only sign of illness reported by the Italians. When the first sign of illness was not a feeling state change, however, the Protestants reported changes in capacities, while the Jews

---

*The relative emphasis on functional incapacity in most of the status groups seems to have a "carry-over" to the field of mental health. Hollingshead and Redlich [11] and Langner, *et al.* [12] have suggested that feeling state changes, such as depression, are relatively more important as signs of mental illness among higher status populations while behavior problems are relatively more important among lower status populations. An important qualification must be noted, however; among low status groups, behavioral problems, while seen as indicators of some difficulty, do not necessarily get referred directly to psychiatrists. It is more likely that such problems will be referred to the police or courts and it is from there that the referral to the psychiatrist is made.

reported changes which involved neither capacity changes nor feeling state changes.

Ethnic differentials in the criteria employed for the designation of health status can be seen as related to core concerns of the various sub-cultures. These concerns lead to ethnic differentials in the rewards and costs attached to illness, and differences in illness behavior as well as differences in the status designation.

Protestants, for example, can be seen as having an instrumental orientation relative to other cultures. This leads to a focus on work (Weber [20]; Lenski [21]) and other role obligations. This in turn leads to a focus on capacities as definitive of illness which, because of their direct link to social roles, means a focus on disruptions in social systems as the defining characteristic of illness. The major cost of illness can be seen as an impairment relative to the performance of normal role and task obligations, and recovery of these capacities is the major reward offered by medical care.

Italians are relatively more concerned with the expressive aspects of interpersonal relationships which leads to an emphasis on feeling states as the defining characteristic of illness. Hence, for the Italians, disruptions of the personality system are more definitive than for Protestants. In this instance, isolation from others is the major cost of illness, and increased attention may be seen as a reward of medical care.

For Jews, the cultural emphasis seems to be on survival, producing, as a major characteristic, anxiety and perception of threat. This leads to a focus on relatively subtle signs and symptoms which involve neither capacity nor feeling state changes, and disruptions in the biological system are seen as more definitive of illness. In this case, uncertainty is the major cost of illness, and diagnosis is the major reward of medical care.

With these cultural emphases, assuming that the typical illness first disrupts biological systems before disrupting personality and social systems in that order, Jews might be expected to have a relatively short period of delay between the onset of symptoms and the seeking of medical care, while relatively long delay would be characteristic of the Protestants, and the Italians would be expected to be in the middle. Unpublished data from the Brown Health Study confirm this prediction. Moreover, it would be expected that Jews would co-operate most fully with their treatment agents as a way of coping with anxiety in reducing the biological threat. Because of the "impersonal" detached attitude of most physicians co-operation might be expected to be poorest among the Italians while the Protestants would be intermediate. While no systematic data on this point are known, it is consistent with the author's observations in several field settings.*

Situational Variations

As important as cultural and sub-cultural factors are in providing criteria for the definition of health and illness, and in ordering the priority of health relative

*Sub-population variations in the criteria used to designate health status tend to be persistent, not only because of their transmission within families, but also because they tend to be reinforced in interpersonal contacts outside of the family. People with similar life chances and life styles tend to live in the same neighborhoods (Hawley [22]). There is thus not only a high density of interaction among people with similar values and goals, but also there is a residential segregation from people with alternative values and goals.

to other values, these considerations do not exhaust the factors that must be taken into account. Behavior, including health status designation, is also influenced by "certain conditions which comprise the situation including the state of the organism, the objective environment, and the subjective manner in which these are perceived, evaluated, and made conscious" (Volkart [23]). Relative to the designation of health status, at least three major elements of the situation seem crucial: the nature of the "well roles" of the individual whose status is in question; the nature and severity of his symptoms, and inter-personal influence.

Well roles. If illness is conceived as a deviation from a state defined as normal, the empirical assessment of health status must proceed from a base line of presumptions relative to the activities and related capacities regarded as normal for the individual in question. As the question of health status is logically prior to the question of sick roles, so also is the question of normal roles logically prior to the question of health status. Different roles and tasks require different capacities. The consequences of any given impairment therefore cannot be assessed except relative to the specific roles and tasks affected. For example, the inability to run the mile in less than 6 min may be seen as inconsequential to most males. To an athlete specialized in long distance running, however, this limitation may be seen as a serious disability. While in the former case, this given capacity level may be seen as well within the normal range, in the latter it may well be a sign of illness. Relative to occupational roles, the same level of disability relative to the biological system may have different consequences for people in different jobs. A strained back, for instance, may be incapacitating to someone whose job consists of loading trucks, while it can be relatively trivial to somebody who is an executive. By the same token, a headache may be trivial to the truck loader, while it can be incapacitating to the intellectual.

Specific incapacities, therefore, must be evaluated relative to the tasks and roles they affect. If a specific biological capacity is not required for the performance of normal roles it is less likely to be regarded as significant than would be the case if it impairs normal activities. Furthermore, the greater the importance attached to the activity affected, the more likely it is that a specific biological change will be noticed and seen as important.

The Nature and Severity of Symptoms

The nature and severity of symptoms are closely linked to the question of well roles. The extent to which symptoms are noticed and the degree of importance attached to them are likely to be related to the question of their present or future expected impact on normal activities. In addition, several other factors are likely to be important, including the physical manifestations of the "disease" (how clear the symptoms are to the individual and his status definers), the individual's "impression management" (his compliance, grimaces, etc., or their absence), the familiarity of the condition to the status definers (including their conceptions of the disease, the medical risks involved, the symptoms and the disabilities), the assumptions of causability (involving the notion of how "voluntary" the disease is, the extent to which its cause is "natural" or the result of "sin" etc.), the amenability of the disease to treatment and recovery, and the prognosis over time for duration and impairment relative to the above factors.

If a symptom affects a valued activity or characteristic [24] or is defined as posing a threat to others relative to their health statuses, the symptom is more likely to be regarded as significant, and the individual concerned more likely to be defined as ill. The more obvious the symptom to the individual and others around him, the more likely the status of sick is to be assigned.

Status definers. The third element of the situation, the patterns of influence brought to bear on the individual whose status is in question, is of critical importance. It is through the influence of other people in interaction with the individual that societal and sub-population norms are implemented with reference to the symptoms and normal activities of a specific individual. The influence of various status definers will vary depending on the expertise they are presumed to possess, and on the nature of their relationship with the individual in question (Fig. 8–3). A key element of these relationships can be conceptualized as the extent to which each status definer is seen as having a "stake" in the outcome of an illness for the individual in question. Impairment of expressive functions, for example, may be of critical importance to family members, while having little or no importance for an employer, who may be more interested in instrumental functioning (cf. Mechanic [9]).

The influence of other people on the process of status designation and on illness behavior is increasingly being documented. Knutson [25] has observed that the actual performed role differs according to which status definer is considered,

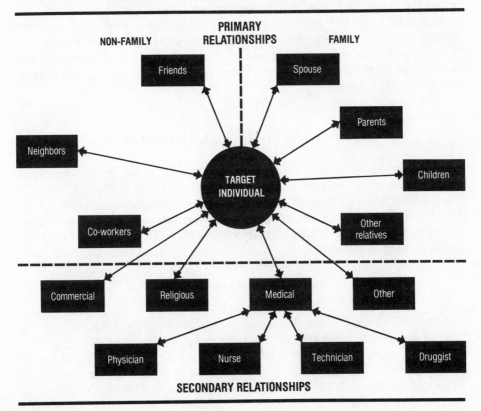

Figure 8-3.

hence the individual in the status of a "sick Person" can be expected to behave differently in relation to his wife, his children, his physician, his boss, a nurse, a co-worker, etc. Each of these role definers may have expectations derived from a different framework of interaction, and consequently their expectations might be expected to vary.

Mechanic [26] has shown that college students tend to define themselves as sick and to seek medical care in ways which were oriented toward parental expectations. While they did not conform exactly to the expectations of their parents relative to health care, they did approximate these expectations. Variation was in part explained by the fact that the expectations of each parent were not seen as identical, and the student was closer to one than the other in his behavior.

Relative to the recovery process, Roth [27] has shown that hospitalized tuberculosis patients develop a system of norms for assessing health status, as a method of structuring the passage of time in the course of recovery. Freidson [28] in the formulation of his "lay referral system" has demonstrated the importance of interpersonal influence and culture in the designation of health status and the selection of a treatment agent.

In a study of older married males in Providence, Rhode Island, Twaddle [17] found that with the first appearance of a symptom the individual usually consulted with his spouse. If there was agreement that an important deviation from normal health had occurred, a physician was usually contacted immediately. If, on the other hand, there was disagreement between the individual and his spouse, or the spouse's opinion was not valued, consultation was initiated with other family members, neighbors, friends, and co-workers. When someone who was regarded as authoritative, either because of a similar prior illness experience or because of special training, suggested seeing a physician, a physician was usually consulted with little delay.

The Process of Health Status Designation

As indicated by the above discussion, little attention has been given to the problem of assessing health status in the sociological literature. Enough has been done, however, to warrant an attempt at a more systematic statement. This should serve the dual function of codifying the current state of our knowledge, and highlighting areas in need of further investigation. The following, therefore, should be taken as tentative.

Ambiguity, Reality Orientation, and Bounded Rationalities

At one level, health and illness can be seen as objective phenomena which relate to measurable parameters of biological and psychological functioning, and which predict outcomes relative to the continuity of the organism. The ability to make such predictions, however, is mostly limited to physicians and others with specialized medical training. Relative to others, medically trained persons are expert in knowing the relevant parameters, the procedures for measuring them, and in making the necessary predictions. Such people are therefore assumed to have a relatively reality oriented set of criteria for assessing health status. Laymen, on the other hand, often find changes in biological and psychological functioning *inherently ambiguous.* Changes in capacities, feeling states, and physiological processes, therefore, are, except in their extreme manifestations, not necessarily definitive of health status changes. Rather, they are the "signals" that raise questions as to their meaning, specifically with reference to expectations for continued functioning and consequently health status.

It has been suggested (Mechanic [29]) that people typically respond to symptoms by first attempting to interpret them as normal. It is only when they are unable to cope with the symptoms within the framework of normality that the question of illness is seriously entertained. Health and illness are assessed, therefore, within a normative framework in which cultural and group norms and past experience combine to frame a "bounded rationality" (Simon [30]) for assessing health status.

Influence Patterns and Situational Constraints

The "sick status" may be approached from the standpoint of a starting time before there is any question to the individual, or anyone else, of a condition having implications of present or future role disability or both. In his well status, the individual can be perceived as having a set of rights and obligations which may be placed in jeopardy if he is defined as sick or becoming sick. In other words, the imposition of any change in the definition of his capabilities by a person's status definers may differentially affect various rights and/or demands in the eyes of various others.

If a more or less ambiguous biological or psychological change has been produced, questions may be raised relative to the state of his health. If the signs of illness are relatively unambiguous and severe, the individual may have little say about his health status designation. If, for example, he becomes paralyzed, unconscious, or unable to communicate, a change in health status may be defined and acted upon by others. In the more general case, however, signs of illness are characterized by their ambiguity. In this case, the designation of health status changes is negotiated between the individual and the other people around him. Depending on presumptions of expertise, power and good will, the influence of any particular other person varies in strength. If there is agreement between the individual and these others that a significant change in health status has taken place, and that the change is presumed to be serious, a physician or other treatment agent may be sought.

Physicians are often the ultimate status definers relative to health. Because of their training and expertise, the status definitions of physicians are generally more influential than those of others.

Discussion

The failure to give more explicit attention to the study of health status is an important oversight in the field of medical sociology. Given that social roles are expectations attached to statuses, it is difficult to provide sociologically meaningful discussions of roles in the absence of clarity relative to the statuses involved.

It is possible that much of the variation in illness behavior which has been attributed to differences in ways of coping with illness can be attributed to differences in the ways in which illness is defined. This is especially true insofar as such studies are taken as evidence limiting the applicability of the sick role formulation. If there is little variability in the kinds of expectations brought to bear on persons defined as sick, and great variability in the conditions under which such definitions are made, the types of illness behavior observed will be diverse.

To summarize, the following points seem important in the case of somatic illness: (1) health and illness are normatively defined. They constitute standards of adequacy relative to capacities, feeling states, and biological functioning needed for the performance of those activities expected of members of the society. These normal expectations vary by age and sex. (2) Health and illness have biological parameters. That is, they are status designations made with reference to the norms of biological functioning. This is the case whether medical or nonmedical criteria are employed in assessing health status. Medical criteria are the more powerful relative to the specificity of health status designations, and to the making of reality oriented predictions relative to causes and consequences, within a biological frame of reference. (3) Except in extreme cases, deviations from normality are inherently ambiguous. Health status changes do not follow automatically from biological changes, but rather, the latter are events requiring interpretation. Depending on the extent to which a deviation is assessed, and the significance attached to it, health status changes may or may not follow biological changes. The skillful use of medical criteria serves to reduce but not eliminate this ambiguity. (4) While there may be some broadly held norms general to any given society, these tend to be specified and elaborated by different groups within the society. Hence, the normative standards against which health and illness are judged vary with medical training, social class, and ethnicity. (5) The situations in which these norms for assessing health and illness are applied are also variable. Different situations require different capacities, and alter the rewards and costs of alternative health status designations. (6) Health status consists of a number of labels applied to an individual by himself and by others with whom he interacts. As with other social labelling processes, health status consists of those labels agreed upon between an individual and various status definers.

The process of health status designation can, therefore, be seen as consisting of interaction between an individual and his status definers, in which normative standards of adequacy are applied to the individual in the context of a specific situation, to assess his capacities for present or future role and task performance. Critical issues in the study of health status must include the criteria employed for assessing health and illness, the situations to which these criteria are applied, the characteristics of the people who do the defining, and the consequences of alternative definitions relative to behavioral expectations.

References

1. Buckley, W. *Sociology and Modern Systems Theory,* Prentice-Hall, Englewood Cliffs, N.J., 1967.

2. Kosa, J. and Robertson, L. The social aspects of health and illness. In *Poverty and Health* (edited by Kosa, J., Antonovsky, A. and Zola, I.), Harvard University Press, Cambridge, 1969.

3. Parsons, T. Definitions of health and illness in the light of American values and social structure, in Jaco, E. (Ed.) *Patients, Physicians and Illness,* Free Press, Glencoe, 1958; *Social Structure and Personality*, Free Press, New York, 1965.

4. Lewis, A. Health as a social concept, *Bri. J. Sociol.*, **4**, 109, 1953.

5. Williams, J. Disease and deviance, *Soc. Sci and Med.*, **5**, 219, 1971.

6. Parsons, T. A revised analytical approach to the theory of social stratification, in Bendix, R. and Lipset, S. (Eds) *Class Status and Power*, Free Press, Glencoe, 1953.

7. Koos, E. *The Health of Regionville,* Columbia University Press, New York, 1954.

8. Apple, D. How laymen define illness. *J. Hlth Hum. Behav.*, 219, 1960.

9. Mechanic, D. The concept of illness behavior. *J. Chron. Dis.*, 15, 189, 1962.

10. Gordon, G. *Role Theory and Illness,* College and University Press, New Haven, 1966.

11. Hollingshead, A. and Redlich, F. *Social Class and Mental Illness,* Wiley, New York, 1958.

12. Langner, T. and Michael, S. *Life Stress and Mental Health: The Midtown Manhattan Study,* Free Press, New York, 1963.

13. Mechanic, D. Illness and cure, in Kosa *et al., op. cit.,* 1969.

14. Twaddle, A. Health decisions and sick role variations, *J. Hlth & Soc. Behav.,* **10**, 105, 1969. "Life Values. Life Chances and Life Styles: A Stratification Model" (unpublished).

15. Zborowski, M. Culture components in response to pain. *J. Soc. Iss.,* **8**, 16, 1952.

16. Zborowski, M. *People in Pain,* Jossey-Bass, San Francisco, 1969.

17. Wolff, H. Disease and the patterns of behavior, in *The Hour of Insight*, pp. 29–41 (Edited by MacIver, R.), Institute for Religious and Social Studies, New York, 1954.

18. Zola, I. Culture and symptoms, *A. Sociol, Rev.,* **31**, 615, 1966.

19. Baumann, B. Diversities in conceptions of health and physical fitness, *J. Hlth Hum. Behav.,* **2**, 39, 1961.

20. Weber, M. *The Protestant Ethnic and the Spirit of Capitalism,* Scribners, New York, 1958.

21. Lenski, G. *The Religious Factor,* Doubleday-Anchor, Garden City, 1961.

22. Hawley, A. *Human Ecology,* Ronald, New York, 1950.

23. Volkart, E. W. I. Thomas, *International Encyclopedia of the Social Sciences,* Macmillan and Free Press, New York, 1968.

24. Barker, R. *et al. Adjustment to Physical Handicap and Illness,* New York, Social Science Research Council, Bulletin 55, 1953.

25. Knutson, A. *The Individual, Society and Health Behavior,* Russell Sage Foundation, New York, 1965.

26. Mechanic, D. Perception of parental response to illness: a research note, *J. Hlth Hum. Behav.,* **6**, 253, 1965.

27. Roth, J. *Timetables,* Bobbs-Merrill, Indianapolis, 1963.

28. Freidson, E. *Patients' Views of Medical Practice,* Russell Sage Foundation, New York, 1961.

29. Mechanic, D. *Medical Sociology,* Free Press, New York, 1968.

30. Simon, H. *Models of Man,* Wiley, New York, 1957.

EUGENE B. GALLAGHER

9 Lines of Reconstruction and Extension in the Parsonian Sociology of Illness

Introduction

Whoever sets out to acquire a sociologically-informed understanding of health and illness processes in contemporary society soon becomes aware of the profound contributions which Talcott Parsons has made. His published work in this area commenced with the seminal analysis of the doctor–patient relationship which appeared as Chapter Ten of *The Social System* [1] and has continued with attention to the sociological implications of psychosomatic theory; the status of health as a societal value; sociocultural aspects of medical research and medical education; the social structure of the mental hospital; death in its medical and cultural meanings; and other topics. Parsons has brought his theoretical acumen, searching insight, and breadth of empirical knowledge to bear upon an imposing range of health–illness phenomena.

A great deal of Parsonian theory on health and illness has developed within the framework of a systematic development of sociological theory, rather than in an attempt to bring a bounded range of health phenomena within theoretical purview. In his strenuous efforts toward theoretical closure and systematization, Parsons has perhaps practiced a selectivity of his own in relation to empirical fact. If a chain of theory is to span significant phenomena within the health–illness realm more adequately, it may be that more concepts must be formed and linked.

An example of the fruitful way in which Parsons has developed theory which pertains to illness and yet which has significance for the analysis of social systems is to be found in his analysis of the role of the physician. Taking medicine as a prototypical profession, he elucidated the important position of the professions in contemporary society. This in turn led to a more penetrating sociological analysis of many other structural features of modern society, such as certain convergent trends of capitalist and socialist socio-economic systems, the institutionalization and application of science, and the omnipresent growth of large-scale organization. When one considers how greatly sociological analysis has benefitted from the original Parsonian formulations concerning the roles of physician and patient, my criticism of that formulation here will perhaps seem petty and

This paper was presented in a session on The Sick Role at a meeting of the International Sociological Association in Toronto, Canada, in August 1974. Professor Andrew Twaddle of the University of Missouri served as organizer and chairman of the session. Professor Talcott Parsons of Harvard University, whose sociology of illness furnishes the critical base for this article, was discussant at the Toronto session. Professor Parsons subsequently elaborated and published his remarks. The interested reader is referred to his article: The sick role and the role of the physician reconsidered. *Health and Society* (The Milbank Memorial Fund Quarterly), Summer 1975, pp. 257–278.

Reprinted from *Social Science & Medicine*, 10:207–218, May, 1976, by permission of the author and Publisher.

carping. My hope in offering it is that it will lead not only to increased sociological acuity on doctor and patient but importantly to a significant gain for systematic sociological theory. It will also become clear that I am not taking pot-shots at early formulations, so much as attempting to bring more recent Parsonian concepts within a common critical perspective. Finally, although I do not believe it is the office of sociological theory to account for every detail of social reality, I have developed this critical perspective with a certain attentiveness to what seem to me to be important current facts and trends in the realm of health and illness.

Illness—Maladaptation or Deviance?

There are, in my opinion, two Parsonian conceptions of illness. The earlier and better-known conception views illness as a form of deviance. The second conception views illness as maladaptation. I view these two conceptions as relatively distinct and the relation between them as theoretically problematic. Each conception has a distinct set of implications concerning the nature of the challenge which illness poses for the actor who bears it and for the social system. The major portion of my critique will deal with the deviance conception. It seems to me that the lines of theoretical extension necessitated by shortcomings in the deviance conception can be supplied from a full analysis of illness as a problem in adaptation, that is, from the second approach.

This anticipation provides a convenient sequence for the following critique. I will first discuss the conception of illness as maladaptation, thereby generating a set of theoretical implications which are relevant to the subsequent examination of limitations in the deviance conception.

Parsons regards somatic health as the *adaptive* capacity of the human organism which underlies and sustains behavior directed toward the accomplishment of goals. Mental health is the capacity of the personality to commit its resources and to mobilize the behavioral repertoire of the organism toward valued goals. It appears that both orders of health are, in the Parsonian four-functional system scheme, analogous to *capital* in an economic system [2, 3].

It is instructive to consider this in economic terms and then to look at its implications for the conceptualization of health as adaptive capacity. An economy without capital would, in the limiting extreme, have its productive capacity totally committed to particular lines of production with no room for maneuver in response to changes in natural resources and changes in market demand. It also has nothing set aside to replace tools and other capital equipment which are used up in the process of production. Such an economy would be extremely brittle and vulnerable. The hypothetical primitive-paradise type of economy in which human wants are gratified through the bounty of nature immediately and effortlessly is a zero-capital economy. Such an economy would be captive to changing external circumstances and completely dependent upon a physical environment which never depletes itself. The counterpart to a zero-capital economy in terms of health is more difficult to conceive, though it is perhaps not straining the analogy too far if we recall the sense in which a person, following an extreme effort or stress, may be said to have "spent" his health. The implication is that though he exists as an organism, he lacks adaptive capacity for the pursuit of goals. The case of the very ill person whose life is sustained by biomedical technology, while he himself is disabled from productive social participation, is another example.

Both common sense and medical science tend to see health as a bounded, self-sufficient state of internal integrityof the organism. The adaptation concept as found in Parsons is somewhat different in that it has a very significant external or situational reference. It refers to the fitness of the organism to engage in productive behavior in an environment consisting of natural and socio-cultural objects. The state of health presumes nothing about the range or selection of goals which may be pursued through the behavior of the organism. Health is uncommitted capacity. The terms in which adults appreciate the playful exuberance and raw energy of children—their "animal spirits"—remind us of the relatively unsocialized, precommitted aspect of organic health.

The earlier Parsonian framework viewed ill health as a category of *deviance* within a social system and, correspondingly, health as a category of conformity. This view of illness ignores, but does not deny, the position of the organism in a physical and sociocultural environment. It is also essentially silent on questions about the etiology and distribution of disease, and about environmental hazards or supports for health, all of which refer to the relation of the human actor to situational contingencies affecting biological processes. On the other hand, the deviance framework immensely facilitates sociological analysis of many health–illness phenomena because it views illness as *motivated* behavior with a structured consistent tendency toward deviance. Parsons' theoretical analysis of the sick role and of the role of physician as an agent of social control is a well known development within the deviance framework.

The Sick Role and Therapy Paradigms

I would like to summarize the essentials of the sick-role and the "therapeutic" role, which stand as discrete paradigms within the larger deviance framework. The purpose of this summary is not to review what many readers already know well, but rather to establish a basis for subsequent analysis of problematic features and limitations.

The sick role paradigm consists of these features: (1) Illness is viewed as involuntary. The occupant of the sick role is held not to be responsible for his condition. (2) The occupant is exempted from his usual work, family, civic and other obligations. The extent of exemption depends upon the nature of his illness condition. (3) The sick role is conditionally legitimate. The occupant is expected to do what he can to restore his health. (4) He is expected to seek competent help in his efforts to restore his health.

The "therapeutic" role or therapy paradigm consists of these features: (1) The therapist maintains a stance of permissiveness toward the patient. He suspends usual normative expectations in regard to the performances which would otherwise be expected of the patient and in regard to normatively disruptive features of the patient's conduct or attitudes. (2) The therapist supports the sick person, affirming his worth and maintaining an even-handed, considerate attitude toward him. (3) The therapist maintains a detachment or reserve within the relationship, abrogating the reciprocity found in most social relationships. This "denial of reciprocity," in Parsons' terminology, is an essential platform for therapeutic leverage. (4) The therapist reinforces, through approval, normative components of the patient's motivation. He negatively influences deviant components through disapproval or ignoring.

Limitations of the Parsonian View

During the two decades since it was first set forth, the deviance conception of illness has come under close scrutiny and criticism. Much of the criticism has run to the empirical comprehensiveness of the foregoing role paradigms: can they explain the diverse behavior associated with illness and treatment? Some of the empirical shortfall has led to the generation of verbal categories to cover pseudo- and quasi-illness conditions such as pregnancy and hypochondriasis [4].

Other critiques would discard the deviance framework in favor of theories which view illness as a sociologically unproblematic biological process and treatment as the straightforward application of scientifically valid knowledge.

In the critique which I develop here, I shall focus upon three problematic areas in the deviance conception, as follows:

First, the deviance conception fails to account for the situation of the patient with a chronic somatic illness or disability [5, 6].

The therapy paradigm focuses especially on mental illness, which tends to have long-term or chronic manifestations. The sick-role paradigm, in contrast, has aptness for understanding acute somatic illness. Neither formulation is well-adapted to the special features of chronic somatic illness.

Second, it fails to account for *preventive* health care, or health maintenance, as an element of normative lay conduct and of the professional responsibility of the physician. There is a significant zone of overlap between preventive and chronic care which is correspondingly not well conceptualized. Preventive care refers not only to the maintenance of good health among healthy persons but also the prevention or forestalling of adverse consequences of recognized disease. A related category of preventive care concerns persons who, though in current good health, are at high risk from genetic, environmental, or behavioral factors.

Third, it presents a relatively undifferentiated picture of the *social structure of health care.* In its insightful focus upon the dynamics of the doctor–patient relationship, it pays little attention to the possibility that the varied types of physician role, coupled with variations in the setting of medical practice, may induce systematic differences in patient performance and expectations. Neither does it consider the sphere of "medical" responsibility within the total realm of "health" care. In part this is related to the second point above, namely, the problematic status of preventive health care within the doctor's role.

These problem areas will be attended to separately and also in their significant interrelationships. They will be analyzed in the light of the contrast proposed above, namely, whether *deviance* or *adaptation* provides the better sociological framework for understanding illness [7].

Another analytical contrast stemming from Parsonian theory concerns the balance of *technical* and *moral* components in the doctor's role. This issue is also related to limitations in the deviance model of illness and therapy.

These problem areas are to some extent addressed in several of Parsons' papers. Even if there is occasional illumination upon these topics, I believe that in relation to the main thrust of the deviance framework they have been substantially neglected.

Chronic Illness

The deviance framework and, more particularly, the sick-role paradigm does not easily accommodate chronic illness because of its indefinitely long or life-long duration. In acute illness, the individual can look forward to the restoration of health. He is ill and cannot directly wish or will himself healthy. He may simply wait, treat himself, or seek medical attention, but in any event he assumes a patient role with some exemption from ordinary obligations until his health returns.

In chronic illness, exemption from normal social obligations cannot be justified by the prospect of a return to productive function and social participation. Neither can the obligation to seek treatment or to cooperate with treatment orders be so justified. It is well comprehended within the deviance framework that treatment involves professional attention which can gratify and reinforce regressive wishes of a dependent character. At the same time, treatment may subject the patient to various rigors such as induced pain, untoward drug effects, surgical mutilation, and curtailment of personal freedom in matters of diet and style of life. Where such stresses are chronically prolonged, the patient's tendency may be to "give up".

An adequate conceptualization of the position of the patient with a chronic illness and of the position of the professional treater requires additional elements lying outside the deviance framework. The view of illness as a problem in adaptation is useful if viewed as supplementary rather than alternative to deviance. Adaptation suggests the idea of best fit between an impaired organism and an environment which to some degree reciprocally accommodates itself to the special needs and limitations of the patient. It is important to note that adaptation in this sense implies optimization of function but it does not require completely disposable, uncommitted resources which can be freely directed toward goals external to the situation. It should not be supposed that the allocation of energies and skills within the social system toward coping with problems of chronic illness requires justification entirely in terms of the absolute increment of adaptive capacity which it sustains or salvages. Value-conceptions concerning human dignity and quality of life play an important part. To some extent, the question of justification is diffused because chronic illness and impairment are coped with not only by professionals, but also by lay persons in the social system outside of professional contexts. This tends to relativize the criteria of adequate adaptation to a unit level rather than to impose a more uniform, universalistic standard throughout the social system, such as would be characteristic of professionals where they have exclusive responsibility.

Another theoretical problem which is accentuated in the case of chronic illness is the nature of the patient's obligation to *cooperate* with competent professional help. The patient, as the saying goes, "places himself in the hands" of the doctor. Yet this formula is not entirely adequate because unchecked reliance upon the doctor or helper intensifies the trend toward dependency, always present in any case. The therapy paradigm recognizes this tendency and specifies that the professional, as an agent of social control, regulates dependency—sometimes inducing it and at other times curbing it, in the interests of cure or return to health. The professional is an authentic exponent and a trustworthy enforcer of health norms. This formulation seems satisfactory up to a point but it fails to allow for the very important sense in which the patient *autonomously* relates to the professional. That is, while the patient defers to the greater technical expertise of the professional and follows doctor's orders, he does not delegate moral authority. He may well cooperate, but if he does, it is not because his independent control is already pre-empted by the professional's conduct as a legitimate representative of a moral order but rather because it "makes sense" for him to do so— in the sense of an autonomous ego. He is not simply compliant. The problem of how to conceptualize the working relationship between patient and doctor is also a call for clarification of the Parsonian idea of collectivity-orientation. The degree of loyalty generated within the relationship means that, whatever their other social memberships, doctor and patient constitute a solidarity group and moral community. But insofar as values of the social system permeate this community, it seems that the patient as well as the doctor must embody the relevant values. This is of particular importance in the case of chronic somatic illness. The question of what constitutes an adequate level of rehabilitation following a paralyzing automobile accident depends not only upon the objective parameters of nerve and muscle damage, but also upon the patient's values and upon the level of social support he can command from his family and others. The patient's command of facilities in his physical environment also bears upon rehabilitation prospects. These are important elements which lie largely outside the control of the physician and other treatment professionals.

The treatment of chronic illness draws upon elements of family and lay social support which require more theoretical recognition than they have received in the Parsonian framework. Many chronic diseases and disabling conditions are characterized by an indefinitely long plateau rather than rapidly progressive deterioration. Diabetes, cardiac incapacity, blindness, stroke, paraplegia, renal disease and major accidental injury are a few common examples. The professional response to such conditions is usually described as management rather than treatment. Under professional tutelage, the patient learns to accept the limitations of his condition, neither overestimating his liabilities on the side of exaggerated dependency, nor underestimating them on the opposite side of denying his condition or rebelling against it. The professional here plays the familiar stabilizing and balancing role, negotiating a course between permissive over-indulgence of the patient and a harsh overexpecting stance. Professional conduct toward the acute patient requires a therapeutic balance between permissiveness and discipline according to the Parsonian model. The same formula applies to the chronic patient but there are additional noteworthy considerations.

The patient must come to accept his condition and to manage his own treatment and rehabilitation within the limits of what the physician can delegate to lay implementation. It seems appropriate to conceive of this as a learning process, in that cognitive content must be mastered, and in that the patient acquires specific behavioral skills for self-medicating and diet, using prostheses, performing tests of body function, caring for therapeutic equipment, as the case may be.

A Chronic Illness Example:
The Patient on Home Dialysis

An example which well illustrates how extensive the chronic patient's sphere of self-management may be is that of the renal failure patient on home dialysis. Two or three times weekly he must attach his blood circulation to a dialyser, with varying amount of assistance from other lay helpers. The portion of his body where the connection is made is a surgically-induced aperture or fistula which once established is serviceable for a long time if it is asceptically maintained. The dialysis equipment must likewise be kept sterile. As part of the dialysis process, the patient must also prepare the chemical solution, according to a medical prescription which applies biochemical and physiological knowledge to his individual functioning. He must monitor his blood pressure and other parameters during the process. At the end of the dialysis session, he must be unhooked from the dialyser. The requirement of periodic attachment to the dialyser restricts his geographic mobility. Above and beyond the dialysis process. the patient must maintain a rigid dietary regime. There are still other constraints, such as the economic burden, associated with the total home dialysis maintenance program.

Patient Autonomy, Medical Control,
and Family Support

Home dialysis affords a clear but by no means unique example of the large measure of active responsibility assumed by the patient with a chronic illness. The dialysis patient might be said to operate from a delegated authority from the doctor; instead of being cared for by the doctor directly, or by a nurse of doctor's orders, he cares for himself under medical supervision. Is the patient's activity the same, in the Parsonian paradigm, as his making the effort expected of him in his conditionally legitimate role to minimize the scope and effects of his illness?

A full theoretical handling of this question leads to a formulation which would accord a substantial *autonomous* component to the role of the patient in the patient-doctor collectivity. That is the patient in a chronic illness situation is not simply a paramedical person, with delegated authority from the doctor, who happens to be focusing his efforts upon himself; neither is he engaging in "cooperation" with the doctor in the ordinary sense in which the patient is expected, as part of the patient role, to comply with medical orders.

The greater scope recommended here for patient autonomy, in the situation of chronic illness, goes beyond the patient's contractual freedom to maintain or to terminate his relationship to a particular doctor, or with medical care altogether. *That* freedom on the patient's part exhaustively describes the measure of autonomy recognized in the Paronsian sick-role paradigm. It suffices for the acute patient but not for the chronic patient. The increment in patient autonomy which is recommended here for theoretical analysis of the chronic patient role suggests two other extensions.

First, there is greater scope for the patient's values and resources to have a regulative effect within the doctor-patient collectivity, in affecting goals and the selection of medical techniques. In the acute model of the patient role, the only important question turns on the technical capacity of the doctor as a practitioner of scientific medicine to cure the illness. Is the patient's condition one which can be properly diagnosed, given the state of medical knowledge? If diagnosible, does an effective remedy exist? In the sense of Max Weber's category of substantive rationality, the doctor uses all available resources toward the accomplishment of the absolute goal of restoration of the patient's health. Other goals may figure in the total context of responsibility and decision-making in chronic illness.

Second, extending the chronic patient role to include value-autonomy permits more scope for consideration of adaptation as a relevant perspective for assessing health problems and conditions. Adaptation has an environmental and situational reference so that given two patients with the same chronic condition in terms of medical assessment, one may be better adapted in and to his physical and social setting than the other. The question of what constitutes good adaptation depends upon value-patterns at the broadest societal level and the articulation of these values in communities and social groups. Age and sex norms are important. For young adults, adaptation includes capacity for marriage, reproduction, and satisfactory parenting. American society places great emphasis, as Parsons and others have noted, upon an individual's economic and occupational performance in the context of a value system which emphasizes active instrumental achievement. Thus, the state of good adaptation also includes, prominently, capacity for occupational function and achievement.

A cross-national comparison will suggest the way in which societal values—not always highly integrated within a given society—can affect standards of adaptation. It is significant in relation to chronic illness in the United States that substantial public monies and voluntary funds are spent to rehabilitate disabled individuals. The primary goal is to enable the individual to resume a work role. This may be variously accomplished by vocational re-training, provision of prosthetic or sensory devices, psychological counseling, or other measures suited to the capabilities and needs of the individual. However, employers feel little legal obligation or moral pressure to hire patients who have been rehabilitated. These contradictory forces bearing upon employment prospects can be explained by the fact that the same societal value which seeks to equip the disabled person to achieve occupationally also seeks to maximize the profit opportunities of the firm or producing unit—its own distinctive measure of corporate achievement—by granting it broad discretion in personnel policies. By contrast, English society, with a strong integrative focus, places a legal obligation upon employers to hire a minimum quota of workers with certified disabilities and chronic conditions.

While occupational performance is a paramount consideration in defining levels of adaptation for the chronic patient, other kinds of performance count as well. For the older male, and for adult females of a wide age range, social participation in kinship and community contexts is important, as is the capacity to engage in economic consumption processes such as purchase of goods. A more minimal level of adaptation occurs when the maximum expectation of the patient may be simply that of direct self-care in meeting biological needs and in the preservation of communicative function and physical mobility. At these various levels of adaptation, the value-autonomy of the patient is a continuous pressure within the context of the doctor-patient relationship.

Closer attention to the special properties of the chronic patient role reveals another point at which the Parsonian model needs elaboration. The Parsonian conception of the doctor's role is "technological" in that the doctor is expected to exercise his skill and judgment in the light of available scientific knowledge. It is not only that medical intervention must be consistent with scientific knowledge but, more significantly, that the bioscientific basis is the distinctive quality of modern medical practice. The doctor is most thoroughly seated in his medical role when he can diagnose and treat his patient's problem in scientific terms.

The emergence of modern medicine as a distinct profession and as the dominant vehicle in society for the professional handling of illness owes much to the establishment of an empirically valid biological science. As Eliot Freidson notes, it was only with this development that medicine achieved a following among the public amounting to a majority of assent, and that competing, non-scientific doctrines concerning human ills and their remedy became substantially outmoded [8].

Under the technological approach to medical problems, the doctor's attention and energy are focused upon overcoming the problem with available knowledge and technique. Nothing is required from the patient, indeed no contribution is possible beyond voluntary entry into the relationship—the placing of one's self under care. The patient can always refuse to follow the doctor's orders, discharge himself prematurely from the hospital or otherwise fail to comply with medical regimens. But so long as he does comply, the initiative and decision-making in the relationship is on the doctor's side.

Such is the case in the Parsonian model of the relationship, which best fits acute illness. The desired end to be sought is restoration of the patient's health. This end is not weighed against other ends nor is it balanced against available effective means. The unilateral dedication of the doctor to this end gives it an absolute character. In the Parsonian model, the patient's ambivalence, tending toward deviant resistance to getting well, excludes any autonomous patient impact upon the determination of ends or the weighing of means. The doctor's discernment and strategic pressures in selectively reinforcing the "healthy" parts of the patient's motivational system mark him as the only responsible party in the collectivity. The doctor also has moral authority in the relationship. The doctor's moral authority is secondary to his functionally specific technical expertise in matters of health. Nevertheless, the moral authority component of any role which contains it cannot be a purely incidental element. In the Parsonian conception of the physician as agent of social control, moral authority is an essential ingredient of the role.

In coping with the problems of chronic illness, neither the doctor's technical skill nor his moral authority are sufficient to insure the optimum feasible result. It was suggested earlier that questions of the relationship of the patient to his physical and social environment are of critical importance in promoting the patient's adaptive capacity. Employment policies must bend somewhat, households as physical and temporal environments must accommodate the special requirements and needs of the chronic patient, and motivational resources of families must be adjusted to sustain the patient.

The Parsonian literature at various points intimates that the medical role and medical institutions cannot deal with problems of the patient's social and physical environment. As a basis for discussion, we may focus upon the idea that patients are readily hospitalized by doctors because the hospital as a physical site and social organization affords maximum impact for the doctor's technical expertise and for his moral influence against the deviant, withdrawal tendencies associated with illness. Hospitalization isolates the patient from his family, which cannot provide an adequate emotional posture in the face of an ill member. Parsons and Fox state, "—the optimal balance between permissive–supportive and disciplinary facets of treating illness is peculiarly difficult to maintain in the kind of situation presented by the American family. Medicotechnical advances notwithstanding, therefore, therapy is more easily effected in a professional milieu, where there is not the same order of intensive emotional involvement so characteristic of family relationships" [9].

Certainly there are hazards associated with permitting the patient to be dealt with as a sick person within the family context. However, there are equal hazards in isolating the patient, particularly the chronically ill patient, from family and community. The Parsonian deviance model of illness (acute illness handled by the technological doctor) casts a blind eye upon these latter tendencies.

The deviant potential in illness motivation is presumably less pronounced in the case of the acute patient than the chronic patient. Isolation from the family through hospitalization is less necessary for motivational reasons, though hospitalization may be more essential for the doctor to render competent diagnosis and effective intervention. With the chronic patient, the problem of deviant motivation is presumably greater. Isolation of the chronic patient from the family through hospitalization has the advantage of exposing the patient to the balance of support and discipline which doctors, nurses and others can provide from their position of professional objectivity. However, the strangeness and impersonality of hospital and other institutional environments can also adversely affect the rehabilitation prospects of chronically ill patients, particularly over an extended period. An analogy can be drawn between the "failure-to-thrive" syndrome which afflicts infants deprived of normal maternal succour [10], and the adaptation failures which occur with some regularity among chronically-ill adults who undergo long-term institutional care. "Adaptation failures" include not only failure to achieve a maximum level of function consistent with the health problems but, in the extreme, a decline of functions such as physical mobility, mental alertness, and communicative capacity. Such negative results are exacerbated when, as frequently happens, the organizational and physical facilities in the institutional care of chronic illness are grossly inadequate. The essential question here, however, is whether professional care away from the family, even with abundant facilities, can indeed provide the requisite balance of support and discipline to counter withdrawal tendencies in chronic illness. Questions of incentive and stimulation for patient performance must also be considered within the category of support and discipline.

We suggest that professional care has certain inherent liabilities, not contemplated within the Parsonian model, for coping with chronic illness. Removing the patient from his family and household may also have undesirable effects. This has certainly been demonstrated in regard to mental illness, and we suggest that similar tendencies apply to chronic somatic illness as well. Students of "labelling" phenomena have identified a range of negative effects when a person is professionally diagnosed as mentally ill [11].

172 Patients, Physicians, and Illness

These effects ramify within the circle of family and peers of the patients, serving to stabilize stigma. The same lay contexts which earlier maintained a posture of denial and toleration in the face of troublesome behavior on the part of the patient tend subsequently to adopt a new posture of rejection once a diagnosis is established and especially if the patient is hospitalized [12].

The characteristic attitude of early denial and toleration is consistent with the Parsonian notion that the family, in its lack of objectivity, supports deviant behavior. The rapid shift from inclusion to exclusion of the patient-member is a social process which occurs readily in the absence of a balanced, objective professional perspective. However, the Parsonian model of illness, in focusing upon acute illness dealt with by the technology-oriented doctor, does not give sufficient weight to the negative effects which can result from too ready a resort to medical processes.

Medico-Centrism

Part of the difficulty with the Parsonian framework is that it is "medicocentric." It places the figure of the doctor at the center of health care processes. Insofar as the sick person cannot himself cope with his illness, he turns to the doctor. The individual doctor can directly handle many problems of many patients from his own skill, judgment, time and energy. Insofar as he cannot personally deliver complete care to all his patients, he in turn relies upon a hospital which brings a complex of staff and equipment into play for the patient's benefit, upon medical specialists to whom patients are referred, and upon other non-medical specialists and facilities in a community context. These varied resources, medical and non-medical, hospital-based and community-based, expand and supplement the services which the doctor directly provides. They are for the most part called into action at the request of the patient's doctor and function on his delegated authority. Even the hospital operates as the instrumental agent and moral representative of the doctor. Parsons notes the moral aspect particularly in regard to mental hospitals, where he suggests that the hospital as a whole and not only the psychiatrist must be an adequate object of transference for the patient [13]. The hospital through its organizational structure, multiple grades and types of personnel, and informal atmosphere must inspire the trust and confidence of the patient and present him with the same salutary balance of support and discipline which the individual physician does. This is the logic of the Parsonian framework, in its medico-centrism.

Beyond a certain point, it seems inevitable that the vigor and authority of the physician, as the principal and legitimizer of the entire health care system, becomes attenuated, losing its moral force against the deviance potential in illness. However much influence the doctor has in the individual doctor–patient relationship, it cannot be delegated or transferred very far in a chain of medical referral or a hospital hierarchy. A large-scale business enterprise can, with the assistance of rational accounting techniques and in reliance upon mechanisms of contract and property, maintain a profit orientation which systematically affects every role and process in the entire organization. Health care organizations operate from medical charisma and initiative, as an equivalent to the profit orientation of private enterprise. The Parsonian framework makes an admirable case for the centrality and potency of the medical role. One may doubt, however, that health care organizations function in a consistent therapeutic and rehabilitative fashion when a great deal of patient care is done in the name of the doctor and not by the doctor himself. The dilution of medical charisma seems especially likely when the doctor is recognized as a technical scientific expert rather than a moral authority. His agents and representatives do not occupy positions of ritual or official significance with commensurate derived charisma. Contra-therapeutic effects occur not only because the force of orders is spent through a chain of referral, in the sense in which the voltage in a power transmission line drops over distance, but also because the patient as a personality system has strong needs for direct relationship with an identifiable individual helper. The stress of illness and its regressive forces generate additional need for a continuity and concentration of support which duplicates the parent role in the family of orientation.

Whatever the lack of conceptual resources in Parsonian theory to account for this problem in health care, it can be said that the lack exists not only in the theoretical framework but also as a major problem in the operation of the health care system itself. Likewise, if the Parsonian technological doctor turns tail in the face of the patient's family and carries out his own quasi-deviant withdrawal by hospitalizing the patient, again it may be said that the flaw in the theory corresponds to a defect in the contemporary system of medical care.

The flaw in the theory is that it overestimates the therapeutic impact of the physician and medical institutions. It correspondingly underestimates the potential therapeutic impact of the family and other lay supportive systems. Separation of the patient from his family may lead to rejection of the patient. Additionally, the environment of the hospital or other health organizations may fail to provide adequate incentive toward recovery or adaptation.

The defect in the system is that physicians are deficient in recognizing and coping with the impact of the patient's social relationships and customary physical environment upon his disease and his treatment. This blind spot in professional practice stems directly from the nature of medical practice and the social structure of medical care, both of which place heavy emphasis upon the cognitive understanding of disease process. The patient is, so to speak, placed under a microscope. With high magnification, the field of observation narrows. The complaint of the patient that the doctor thinks of him only as a specimen of pathology is not new. Our reason for repeating this criticism here is to place contemporary concern with defects in medical care into a theoretical context.

Technical and Moral Differentiation in the Social Structure of Medical Care

Parsons' model of the doctor–patient relationship gives strategic recognition to the implications of the fact that the doctor attempts to ground his treatment in rational scientific knowledge. The knowledge base upon which the doctor draws is the corpus of biomedical science, which is cumulatively progressive in the light of new discoveries and more effective modes of incorporating basic knowledge into clinical practice. Nevertheless, the clinician copes constantly with problems of uncertainty in regard to diagnosis and treatment. Are his inferences from clinical data to the underlying pathology correct? Assuming correct diagnosis, will the currently accepted mode of treatment produce the same beneficial result in *this* particular patient? In addition to uncertainties stemming from limitations in scientific knowledge, many doctors feel burdened by their personal limitations as practitioners in attempting to apply knowledge for the benefit of their patients. "Keeping up" in practice can be almost as stressful as "surviving" in medical school.

The accumulation of knowledge and technique is the major factor behind the growth of medical specialization and the highly differentiated social structure of contemporary medical care. The Parsonian scheme penetrates the core of the doctor–patient relationship, but it does not give sufficient scope to the social structure of medical care. The diverse roles, organizations, financial mechanisms, legal–ethical norms, and other elements by which contemporary health care is provided are of intrinsic sociological interest, even from the standpoint of their taxonomic variegation. Beyond that, the question may be raised as to whether the role of the patient is indeed the same throughout the health care system. While one is free to study or to ignore the health care system as a significant object in itself, the study of the doctor–patient relationship beyond a certain point may require attention to the broader structures which support it.

The problem proposed here is: at a level of theoretical generalization which is not merely descriptive of empirical detail, how to account for the variations in the doctor–patient relationship?

An obvious point of attack is to compare the patient under specialist care with the patient who is under the care of a general practitioner or so-called primary care physician. Are the norms which pattern patient–specialist relationships the same as those which pattern the relation of a patient to a general practitioner? This question is largely unresolved within Parsonian theory.

It seems that the medical specialist has more firmly in mind than does the general practitioner a notion of cognitive rationality as an operative goal influencing his conduct with the patient. As a specialist he has mastered a particular body of knowlege and technique; there is a significant sense in which the skillful and conscientious exercise of specialized knowledge is the principal focus of his professional responsibility, with less regard for the outward effectiveness of the effort. Such is the point behind the wry humor, "The operation was a success but the patient died."

At the functional level of role-analysis in terms of which the doctor counters the deviance potential in illness, it is to be expected in Parsonian terms that the general practitioner plays a stronger social control role than the specialist. Empirical evidence suggests that general or primary practice is most likely to be rendered in a "local" context in which there is a similarity between patient and doctor not only in terms of geographic propinquity but also in terms of ethnic, religious or racial characteristics. In such circumstances the patient and doctor are likely to form a moral dyad crystallized around common values in addition to health [14].

Such is the case in underdoctored rural regions and urban ghettos of the United States, where the few physicians present tend to be general practitioners. It seems a reasonable inference from the Parsonian theory of deviance to suppose that the general practitioner is better able than the specialist to represent values to the patient. The paracitioner's anti-deviance influence is largely implicit rather than "official" in the relationship. In remote or ghetto areas, the value system tends to be traditionalist and possibly variant from the dominant value system of the society. But the anti-deviance potential of a health professional role such as that of the "barefoot doctor" in contemporary China may be mobilized equally on behalf of the dominant values of the total society, particularly in a highly politicized society. In the United States, primary-care physicians trained in family medicine as well as physicians' assistants, nurse-clinicians and other "front line" health professionals may reinforce not only the value-complex of health but also the dominant American value of "instrumental activism," as Parsons has characterized it.

The general practice physician is apt to be geographically insulated, professionally isolated and restricted in his capacity to represent dominant social values. In rural areas, the town doctor may enjoy high civic status in the community but he is nonetheless culturally and professionally isolated. In urban areas, the general practitioner is less shielded by civic status and he is more likely than the urban specialist to engage in solo community practice with little professional peer contact and no hospital connections. Moreover, unlike the specialties, general practice has lacked a core area of technical focus—there is no particular standard of bioscientific knowledge and innovative technique by which the practitioner measures his professional responsibility. It is not strongly argued here that the general practitioner, more than other professionals, requires constant peer support and cognitive stiumulus as an identity prop; like Parsons, I believe that the process of professional training and legitimation can develop a durable sense of responsibility and competence which sustains the practitioner in a variety of concrete practice environments. Nevertheless, the foregoing consideration calls into question whether the integration of the practitioner with other components of the health care system at the primary level of medical care and with the dominant values of society is strong enough to serve as sufficient basis for him to counter the deviance potential which he encounters in his patients. Freidson has analyzed the effect of medical practice which is independent of social controls emanating from the medical profession and highly dependent upon the goodwill of patients through the "lay referral" system. He has built a convincing case that such practitioners tend to adapt and compromise their professional judgment in favor of patient expectations [15].

In this practice context, the doctor may support the patient's favorite self-diagnosis, prescribe drugs uncritically and engage in other expediencies. The category of practitioners who are substantially independent of other professionals and correspondingly dependent on patients includes several kinds of specialists which, in addition to general practitioners, tend to engage in solo community practice in the American health care system. It extends to pediatricians, obstetricians, psychiatrists, general surgeons and specialists in internal medicine.

An urgent problem of international dimensions is the world-wide emigration of physicians from poor nations to rich nations, which offer not only the prospect of a higher living standard but also the opportunity to practice medicine under better-resourced conditions. This pattern of emigration obviously generates a severe dislocation in medical care. It also needs to be understood in terms of the theoretical issues under consideration here. Once they have permission to practice in the host country, many emigrating physicians practice a "front-line" brand of medicine, even if they have received specialty training previously. In sharp contrast to the previously-noted tendency of patient and primary-care physician to constitute a moral dyad within a commuity and societal context, the emigrant physician may be relatively disadvantaged in his capacity to project or represent critical social values to the patient. This aspect of the general problem has of course received much less attention than the "brain drain" and medical care manpower aspects.

In health care systems which are under central control, such as England's National Health Service, patients gain access to specialists mainly through referral by a general practitioner. In such systems, the specialist frames his contribution to the patient's welfare in terms of his expertise as consultant, leaving to the general practitioner the tasks of coping with the patient's deviance potential and effecting adjustments between his medical regime and the resources of his household and family. Specialists who receive patients only through referral tend to view the referring physician, rather than the patient himself, as their client. Thus the specialist has less sense of moral responsibility toward the patient, though of course his professional dedication may be strong and his skill level high.

My argument here has been that the burden of value-representation falls less upon referral specialists, and more upon community-based doctors, especially general practitioners. The latter group, however, is frequently enmeshed in variant values of the patient or community and thus not well situated to exert a major thrust on behalf of the dominant values of the larger society. This deficiency would be akin to the weakness of the nuclear family in maintaining a firm value stance with their patient-member. This contention in Parsonian theory was discussed above. In our analysis, we accepted that contention but doubted that it was more than one factor among others affecting the decision of doctors to hospitalize patients, or to treat them on an ambulatory basis. In suggesting here that the community-based doctor, like the family, may be an inadequate "enforcer" of social system values, I avoid as incorrect the principle that these primary care agents are ineffective value transmitters simply because they are numerous in society or because they have no recognized value-defining status or responsibility. Parsonian concepts of deviance, conformity, and value orientation do not presume that, in order to represent and enact common values, the actor must possess an official status in the social system or a high order of commitment to its political framework.

The relation of political values to the general value-framework is in itself a vital nexus in the social system, and it varies between different kinds of society. In a highly politicized, totalitarian type of society, the medical profession has little independent capacity to generate significant social values. In a liberal individualistic society, such as the United States, where individuals and groups have the opportunity and indeed responsibility to develop value-conceptions which are compatible with broad system goals, the medical profession plays a stronger and more independent role. Health can become such a value in its own right. Somatic and mental health assume special significance as adaptive resources for the individual achievement of valued goals. To accept this formulation is to go beyond the general functionalist postulate that possession of sufficient health by members of a society is essential for goal attainment. It is precisely the difference between these two formulations which, I believe, Parsons has in mind in saying that American society places a heavy emphasis, within the whole domain of social control, upon problems of health and illness.

Preventable Ill Health

Despite the acknowledged emphasis upon health, there are many widely prevalent conditions of ill health in the American population which are due to voluntary neglect and abuse. I have in mind widespread practices such as cigarette smoking, overeating, lack of exercise, excessive alcohol consumption, overuse of proprietary and even prescription medicines, and unsafe use of motor vehicles. These well-known behaviors are responsible for much obesity, high blood pressure, cardiac and respiratory disease, alcohol and drug dependence, and for many accidental injuries. The prevalence of preventable chronic illness and disability does not invalidate the concepts of illness as a form of deviance or of health as a value of particular importance in American society, but it does invite scrutiny and explanation. We may consider the implications of the preventable illness phenomenon both for the medical profession and for the public whose health is jeopardized.

It is a fact of sociological significance that the medical profession collectively and physicians individually have adopted a predominantly passive stance in the face of much patient conduct which is detrimental to good health. A small segment of physicians, primarily those based in academic preventive medicine, are exercised about this but the great majority are indifferent. In what sense can it be said then that the physician functions as an agent of social control, particularly in view of the American value emphasis upon health?

The answer seems to lie in several interrelated circumstances. If doctors are not preventively-oriented, many patients are still less so. They want medical care after the damage is done, not before. Commonly, they seek medical immunity from the consequences of unhealthful behavior rather than medical advice about the potential harm of such behavior. For example a patient may seek medication which will insure weight loss without regard to diet.

This preference for a "technological" solution is not always a vain hope. Often enough, medical success with established pathology rests upon medicines which have no behavioral equivalent: insulin for diabetes, digitalis for cardiac arrhythmias, antibiotics for bacterial infections are well-known examples. Pregnancy is scarcely a disease but it is relevant here to note that contraceptive steroids are a popular and effective technological means of controlling reproduction.

Much modern health progress—increased longevity, decreased infant and maternal mortality, higher health levels into advanced old age—has depended upon control of the physical environment rather than upon clinical medicine and events within the doctor–patient relationship. Pure water and food, improved nutrition and sanitary waste disposal have probably contributed more to length of life than has the clinical use of antibiotics. In turn, antibiotics have contributed more than surgery; and surgery may well have contributed more than the efforts of doctors to have their patients alter dietary, smoking and drinking habits.

On the doctor's side, his training and orientation are attuned to illness rather than toward the maintenance of health. This is particularly true of specialists but also of primary-care physicians, to a great extent in view of their common pathology-oriented medical education. It is indisputable that the health of many people could be maintained at a higher level for a greater portion of a longer life-span if they could be persuaded to adopt more healthful modes of living. Many doctors would agree with this proposition and nevertheless assert that health promotion is not their job. Also, from the standpoint of cognitive validity, the adverse consequences of excessive smoking, eating and drinking do not fall even-handedly upon all those who indulge; aetiology and pathogenesis in the individual case are multi-determined. Some people break the rules and get away with it. A person can smoke heavily for decades and die of renal failure from an intractable kidney infection; be grossly overweight and develop multiple sclerosis; drive recklessly and succumb to a heart attack in his sleep. Doctors are well aware of these paradoxes. Many are not particularly in favor of mass screening for early disease, believing it a more valid and efficient use of their time and skill to deal with definite pathology.

The doctor's social control function does not seem to occur at the level of prevention through moral exhortation. The doctor has a full exposure to the existential vicissitudes of disease which remain despite advances in scientific control and understanding. He is no stranger to uncertainty. Perhaps such exposure reinforces the active determination to do whatever can be done in the fact of established disease, along with a more passive non-judgmental acceptance of the patient's accustomed mode of living.

The social control function is lodged, rather, in the heart of the doctor-patient relationship and consists of the suasion which the doctor exerts upon the patient for cooperation with treatment where the patient's behavior makes a difference. Frequently enough, all the patient need do is to make his body available, and the doctor does the rest, as in surgery. The Parsonian social control paradigm was developed at the other extreme, with impaired mental health and psychotherapy most centrally in mind. I believe that it has substantial applicability in the somatic realm also, especially in regard to chronic disease. But a need then arises to specify the scope and relevance of the social control concepts.

Is it, for example necessary that the patient has exhausted his personal opportunities and resources for prevention of disease and for self treatment before he "turns to" the doctor, as a professional court of higher or ultimate recourse? Such is the strong implication of the Parsonian paradigm; the patient seeks out the doctor for his medical competence, but the lurking element of the doctor's moral authority seems to depend, according to the paradigm, upon his not being sought out too readily. It seems a questionable theoretical tactic to vest his role, distinct from other sources of social control, with too exclusive or unilateral an influence in matters of health. It would be a mistake also to suppose that the doctor, despite his own commitment to rational scientific medicine, imposes a similar belief system upon the patient or offers a repudiative challenge to alternative theories of disease or treatment which the patient may entertain. While scientific medicine has achieved substantial cultural hegemony in relation to traditional folk medicine and various pseudo-scientific doctrines, the latter still commands considerable popular interest [16]. So long as the patient's reliance upon alternative theories does not directly interfere with the medical treatment, the doctor tends not to disturb his health belief system, anymore than his politics or religion.

Health as an Extra-Clinical Value

I have explored the scope of social control within the doctor–patient relationship. Another way of testing the social control paradigm of the doctor–patient relationship is to examine the impact of health values at the societal level, outside the clinical encounter. If we look at the broader sociocultural context from which norms governing the doctor–patient relationship are derived and which legitimizes the patient's resort to the sick role, a number of significant considerations emerge.

First, the value-commitment of American society to health as adaptive capacity seems to be related to, but not the same as, the social control exerted by the doctor within the proximate context of treatment. Like other major values in the Parsonian scheme, health stands high in a hierarchy of societal control, being characterized by relatively low "push," a large degree of cognitive generality, and reference to diverse situations, constraints, and opportunities within the society [17].

The sources of personal and group commitment to health run far beyond the influence of the physician in a clinical relationship. The considerable degree of personal discretion which the individual has in regard to the health assets and risks in his lifestyle and his approach to professional health resources enhances the value-commitment by its very voluntariness. Although the doctor *within* the doctor–patient relationship has an asymmetrical preponderance of influence [18], the patient has the prior option of deciding whether to consult him at all; and the continuing option to terminate the relationship lies much more with the patient than with the doctor. It is not at all uncommon for patients to discharge themselves from hospitals against medical advice, to refuse strongly advised treatment, or to deviate substantially from prescribed regimens concerning medication, diet, and the like [19, 20].

This is the patient's "own business," and the doctor can do no more than shake his head.

There is no broadly defined public interest requiring citizens to seek or receive medical treatment, except for a few public health laws dealing with communicable diseases. The disparity between the slight amount of legal obligation concerning health and the large amount of public funds and public policy devoted to health is perhaps an index of the strength of health as a societal value-commitment in the United States. It is also suggestive that positive health emphasis in the form of collective physical fitness, mass calisthenics demonstrations and exhortatory propaganda has been more characteristic of totalitarian societies than of societies with a liberal democratic, individualistic tradition. In the instrumental achievement value context of the United States, health stands as an individual adaptive resource, a necessary precondition for individual achievement of societally approved goals.

Public emphasis upon health within this societal value context seeks to remove health obstacles to achievement rather than directly to promote health. Hence access to treatment becomes important. The societal emphasis is effective at an individual rather than a collective or group level; it is illness-oriented or clinical, rather than positive or preventive. There is a high degree of cognitive congruence between societal concern with the access of *ill individuals* to medical care, apart from their collectivity memberships, and the bioscientific conception of the patient as a "case" detached from his social and even his physical environment.

Through processes of legitimation, much responsibility for health matters which cannot be carried out in lay or private voluntary hands falls by default to professional groups, especially the medical profession. This civic responsibility is borne awkwardly by the professionals because it transcends their workplace ethic and guild mentality [21]. The American Medical Association cannot tell, and in many respects does not *want* to tell, the American people what is good for their health in the same sense that the Supreme Court enunciates the law of the land or the Pope speaks authoritatively to Roman Catholics in matters of faith and morals.

The lack of a collective or centralized focus for the articulation and promulgation of health values is congruent with an individualistic emphasis at the level of cultural pattern-consistency in other spheres such as economic activity, political authority, and religious belief. The weight of commitment is perhaps enhanced by its individualistic voluntariness because the centralized mechanisms of social control are not strong.

The concept of health service as a governmental responsibility and citizen's right achieved a degree of recognition with the enactment of the Medicare legislation in 1966. It is important to note that this legislation provides for payment of services and stops far short of the direct giving of services. The comprehensiveness of services paid for and population covered is very limited in comparison with almost all other advanced industrial societies. Although the American political trend is clearly in this direction, no one would claim that governmental provision for individual and family health has been a major feature of the society.

A structurally decentralized health care system and a value system which is implemented primarily at the level of individual concern and responsibility together create a type of health behavior which is similar to the individualistic orientation in the Protestant religious tradition. Although there is some social expectation that he will look after himself, especially if ill, what a person does about his health is largely up to him. He has a great range of autonomy in regard to life style and the kind and amount of health services used. An analogue to religious sectarianism and pluralism is also to be found in the diverse health doctrines, single-factor disease theories and proclaimed cures which continue to spring up and to receive cultural tolerance despite the general ascendance of scientific medicine. The originators of these doctrines have wide latitude to promulgate their revelations, as do their adherents to engage in the recommended health behavior.

In the generally open and permissive situation regarding health behavior, many individuals seek extreme solutions to health problems while others deny the need for any special efforts or precautions at all. Christian Science is a good example of a belief system, thoroughly indigenous to the American cultural–religious environment, which combines a strong explicit focus upon health with an equally pronounced rejection of modern medicine.

Many of the widely prevalent health problems discussed above express not a rejection of system-goals but rather a neglect or rejection of health as an adaptive resource. This can be illustrated by a brief consideration of contempory use of alcohol and medicines.

American patterns of alcohol use suggest that alcohol is frequently used to cope with tensions arising in job situations, child-rearing, household management, or from social participation in valued reference groups [22].

Subsequently it may develop into "problem drinking." This kind of alcohol pattern is different from the escapist drinking of individuals and groups whose identification with societal values is low.

The widespread reliance on medications for minor distress is a contemporary health phenomenon which has attracted notice and aroused some concern in the ranks of the medical profession and the public at large. The trend under discussion here is not the application of medicine to clearcut clinical entities such as diabetes or congestive heart failure but rather the treatment of patient complaints of anxiety, tenseness and fatigue which arise in reaction to the demands of social roles and situations. Tranquilizers, sedatives, antacids, analgesics, stimulants and other types of pharmaceutical products are used to meet these needs. Although many such medicines are available as "over the counter" drugs in pharmacies, it is particularly significant for our discussion that many are also prescribed, at more concentrated dosage levels, by physicians in the context of the doctor–patient relationship. It is also significant that prescription medicine, like alcoholic beverages, can become a means whereby many individuals withstand, often on a long-term basis, tensions associated with the accomplishment of valued goals.

An internal medicine specialist of our acquaintance observed wryly that patients at one time expected medicine only when it was absolutely essential but now they seek it for anxiety which is keyed to stressful situations such as examinations, interviews, and committee meetings, as well as major life events—marriage, divorce, pregnancy, bereavement. His negative stance toward the the prescribing tendencies of his medical brethren raises in a somewhat different form the issue discussed earlier when we questioned whether the physician is indeed in a strong position to make a critical evaluation of the patient's difficulties, particularly if he is in a primary-care type practice with a heavy case load. One might argue, as does the internist, that those physicians whose resort to prescription medicines is too easy may foster a needless drug dependency in their patients, expose them to hazards of prolonged drug use, and basically fail to assist them in attaining a more self-sufficient and resourceful posture. In this view, the physician who relies heavily upon drugs as a therapeutic modality may be more the agent of deviance than of social control.

For purposes of sociological analysis, it seems unnecessary to be drawn into judgments which are best left to medically-qualified authorities. In terms of the larger scheme of argument here, it suffices to note that many individuals use a variety of drugs as a supportive resource in the pursuit and attainment of socially-approved goals. Many such drugs are available without prescription. Many others are prescribed by physicians. The medical rationale may base itself upon traditional medical values such as providing relief of symptoms, giving medical reinforcement to the patient's capacity for coping with the stresses and demands of life, or simply "doing something" in the face of the patient's complaints.

Our focus here has been upon routine drug use as an adaptive resource in goal-attainment. It is possible to extend the argument to include more extreme forms of drug dependence, drug abuse, and extra-legal use. Of course, there may be a certain point beyond which drug use fails to provide adaptive flexibility. It then becomes an end in itself or it immobilizes the individual in his attachment to fixed goals and role-performances. Much of the current participation in non-medical, so-called mood-altering drugs is no doubt part of a hedonistic quest for personal fulfillment in the "here and now." Yet it would be a mistake to suppose that this participation is totally escapist and entirely detached from the conduct of important social responsibilities.

The behavior of physicians as drug users is an interesting case in point. The medical profession enjoys high occupational prestige and the public demand for physicians' services is practically unlimited. It is a less well-known fact that physicians have a high rate of drug addiction. This is usually attributed to their privileged access to drugs, especially narcotics [23].

Without discounting this factor, it may be further suggested that occupational stress plays an independent contributory role. The very high physician suicide rate—three times the national average—is relevant, because it could scarcely be maintained that physicians have any special access to suicide [24].

Suicide is another way, albeit directly lethal, of coping with stress.

We have discussed alcohol and drug use as a category of behavior which is problematic from a health standpoint and yet at the same time figures in a pattern of achievement orientation. We shall not attempt it here, but a similar interpretation can be made of a number of other common behavior patterns, such as smoking and driving. In general, health-risking behavior may serve and support a hypermobilized, goal-ridden orientation where adaptive capacity is grossly diminished. Adaptive capacity presupposes a basic, underlying commitment of the actor to a normatively-approved goal. In the extreme, where large risks are habitually assumed, it may be seen that a process of addiction has replaced active choice and commitment. Instead of a flexible adaptation of behavioral and other resources toward a chosen goal, a more concrete and inflexible binding together of the goal and its means of attainment occurs.

Summary

This paper has attempted to bring into critical focus a number of Parsons' central ideas concerning the doctor–patient relationship and the status of health as a societal value, both inside and outside the clinical relationship. This has led to an examination of health problems from the dual perspectives of deviance and lack of adaptation, both of which have been represented within the evolving framework of Parsonian theory. Chronic illness and lack of preventive health care are significant features of contemporary society which have been explored in the light of the theoretical framework, and as a test of its adequacy. Analysis of these issues has also identified a need for a more specific theoretical delineation of the social structure of the medical profession and of the differential elements of societal support for health.

References

1. Parsons T. *The Social System.* Free Press, Glencoe, IL, 1951.

2. Parsons T. and Smelser N. J. *Economy and Society.* Free Press, New York, 1956.

3. Parsons T. Definitions of health and illness in the light of American values and social structure. (Edited by Jaco E. G.) pp. 165–187. *Patients, Physicians and Illness.* Free Press, Glencoe, 1958.

4. Horobin G. Sick-role and patient-role. Medical Sociology Research Unit, University of Aberdeen, unpublished paper, 1969.

5. Gill D. The sick role—illness and pregnancy. *Soc. Sci. & Med.* **6**, 561, 1972.

6. Gordon G. *Role Theory and Illness.* College and University Press, New Haven, 1966.

7. Twaddle A. Illness and deviance. Paper presented at *3rd Int. Conf. Soc. Sci & Med.* Copenhagen, Denmark, 1972.

8. Freidson E. *The Profession of Medicine.* Dodd, Mead, New York, 1970.

9. Parsons T. and Fox R. Illness, therapy and the modern urban American family. *J. Soc. Issues* **8**, 38, 1952.

10. Bowlby J. *Maternal Care and Mental Health.* World Health Organization: Monograph Series No. 2, 1951.

11. Scheff T. *Being Mentally Ill.* Aldine, Chicago, 1966.

12. Phillips D. L. Rejection: a possible consequence of seeking help for mental disorders. *Am. sociol. Rev.* **28**, 963, 1963.

13. Parsons T. The mental hospital as a type of organization. In *The Patient and the Mental Hospital.* (Edited by Greenblatt M., Levinson D. J. and Williams R. H.), p.116, Free Press, Glencoe IL, 1957.

14. Lieberson S. Ethnic groups and the practice of medicine. *Am. sociol. Rev.* **23**, 542, 1958.

15. Freidson E. Client control and medical practice. In *Patients, Physicians and Illness* (2nd Edn.) (Edited by Jaco E. G.), Free Press, New York, 1972.

16. Straus R. Sociological determinants of health beliefs and behavior. *Am. J. publ. Hlth* **51**, 1547, 1961.

17. Parsons T. On the concept of value-commitments. *Sociol. Inquiry* **38**, 135, 1968.

18. Wilson R. *The Sociology of Health.* Random House, New York, 1970.

19. Davis M. Variations in patients' compliance with doctors' advice. *Am. J. publ. Hlth* **58**, 274, 1968.

20. Abram H. S., Moore G. L. and Westervelt F. B. Suicidal behavior in chronic hemodialysis patients. *Am. J. Psychiat.* **127**, 119, 1971.

21. Freidson, E. *Professional Dominance.* Atherton, New York, 1970.

22. Straus R. Alcohol and alcoholism. In *Contemporary Social Problems* (Chap. 5) (Edited by Merton R. K. and Nisbet R.), Harcourt, Brace Jovanovich, New York, 1971.

23. Barber, B. *Drugs and Society.* Russell Sage, New York, 1967.

24. Weiss J. A. M. Suicide. In *American Handbook of Psychiatry* (2nd Edn.), Vol. 3. (Edited by Arieti S. and Brody E. B.), p. 752. Basic Books, New York, 1974.

B. Caring for the Ill: The Patient-Role

As societal efforts to cope further with illness and injury develop, facilities and services evolve to diagnose and treat those afflicted. In the organization of these treatment settings a specific role is also defined for those persons who receive their services and efforts, which is the *patient role*.

The patient role should not be confused with the aforementioned sick role. The larger society defines the legitimate incapacitating criteria for sickness for its members and the corresponding legitimate entry into the sick role; whereas the treatment setting, as a significant component of the larger society, establishes the criteria of normative behavior and expectations of the recipients of its attention and healing efforts, and thus defines the role of "patient" in that social organization and system. The expectant mother in the delivery room of a hospital has a different set of expectations and norms of conduct from that of the person receiving surgery or a medical regimen for a gastric ulcer. Patients in a children's hospital have different roles from that of the terminal cancer patient in a chronic disease facility, as does the schizophrenic patient in a large public mental hospital, the patient with a toothache in the dentist's chair, and the convalescing stroke patient in a skilled nursing home. These individuals are labeled respectively as "maternity patients," "surgical patients," "medical patients," "pediatric patients," "terminal patients," "mental patients," "dental patients," "nursing home patients," and are given specific social roles and corresponding social statuses by the institutionalized setting and significant actors organized to provide such "care." All are legitimate incumbents of the sick role, but they are also additionally interacting in organized situations and systems as "patients" in the patient role, which may or may not be related to the sick role itself.

It is further suggested that much criticism of the sick-role formulation could be alleviated if a full recognition of the distinctions between it and the patient role were given, especially with regard to the role of healers having far more relevance to the patient role than to the sick role.

How patients view their roles is analyzed in a definitive study by Daisy Tagliacozzo and Hans Mauksch of a large American metropolitan hospital.

Some of the negative consequences of being labeled a problem patient by the staff in the surgical service of a large hospital are analyzed in the significant study by Judith Lorber, further reinforcing the organizational source of the patient role itself.

Behavioral scientists have devoted much attention to physical disability recently. Richard Smith analyzes the contributions by social networks to the recovery of the physically disabled patient and offers some useful avenues for further research.

Increased interest in the terminal patient has also occurred in recent years. Concluding this part, Barney Glaser studies the special care needed (but too often neglected) by the dying patient in today's highly technical and scientific medical facilities and settings.

DAISY L. TAGLIACOZZO
and
HANS O. MAUKSCH

10 The Patient's View of the Patient's Role

Every society grants to the sick person special privileges and every society also imposes on the sick person certain obligations.[1] An understanding of such general norms can provide an effective guide to the study of the behavior and attitudes of the sick in our society. However, general norms gain meaning in a specific social setting, or may be modified by intra-institutional expectations. The extent to which a sick person may feel free to seek satisfaction for his emotional needs and to assume the "rights and privileges of the sick role" may thus depend on the social context within which behavior unfolds. Even if general rules for behavior remain the same, the patient may be influenced by considerations which involve efforts to accommodate to real or imagined expectations of significant others.

The experience of being hospitalized adds another dimension to the experience of being ill. This dimension consists of the rights and obligations which are legitimated by organizational forces and which are based on the fact that admission to the hospital is tantamount to assuming an organizational position with all the implications for normative compliance and sanctions. This discussion is based on a study which sought to ascertain to what extent the attitudes and needs which are organized around these two experiences, being ill and being hospitalized, may differ or even come into conflict with each other. The attitudes and reactions of patients were viewed within the context of a system of roles and as a consequence of the patient's efforts to conform to perceived systems of expectations. The study concentrated on the implications of hospitalization with less concern for the illness role *per se*. It explored to what extent the role of the hospitalized patient may be lacking clear definitions of rights and easily definable criteria for legitimate claims. The question was raised whether the position and the attitudes of patients deprive them of genuine means to control others in the system and thus limit their readiness to express their claims and desires without fear of sanction.

Throughout the study the patient is shown to be aware of the degree to which he is dependent on those who care for him. This dependency is based largely on the power to heal and to cure. It is also based on the power ascribed to hospital functionaries to give or to withhold those daily services which, for the hospitalized patient, can embrace some basic survival needs. The single or double rooms and the rapid patient turnover in the modern hospital do not foster an effective patient community which could serve as interpreter and modifier of hospital

[1]Parsons, T., "Definitions of Health and Illness in the Light of American Values and Social Structure," in E. G. Jaco (ed.), *Patients, Physicians and Illness*, New York: Free Press, 1958, pp. 165–187 (chap. 7 in this volume).

Based on a study conducted by the authors through the Department of Patient Care Research, Presbyterian-St. Luke's Hospital, Chicago, Ill. This study was supported by a grant from the Commonwealth Fund.

rules. The patient, therefore, is much more dependent on his previous learning, be it from direct or indirect experiences with the patient role. More importantly, the absence of adequate interpretations by the patient community makes the patient more dependent on hospital functionaries for clues about the appropriateness of his behavior, demands and expectations.

The fact that patients frequently remain strangers in the hospital community tends to add to the power of those who, as functionaries, are intimately familiar with the rules and expectations of the organization. The power which is vested in them can inhibit the patient to seek clarification and guidance. Also, those who are informed tend to become oblivious to the needs of their clients to be initiated into the "rules of the game."

The study was conducted in a metropolitan voluntary hospital with a capacity of 850 beds. The hospital is part of a large Midwest medical center. It is a teaching hospital for nurses and physicians. Patients occupy predominantly two-bed or private rooms.[2] This discussion rests on the analysis of 132 interviews which were administered to 86 patients. The sample was limited to patients who were admitted with cardio-vascular or gastro-intestinal diagnosis. All patients in the sample were Caucasian, American-born males or females between 40 and 60 years of age. All patients had been previously hospitalized and all were married. They paid for their hospitalization in part with private or industrial insurance. During the semi-structured interview, the patient was asked to express himself freely on present and previous hospital experiences. The interviews averaged one hour and were recorded and transcribed. The average day of interviewing was the fifth day of hospitalization. When possible, second interviews were conducted.

Physicians and Nurses: Their Significance

Physicians and nurses are among the significant others in the network of role relationships in which the hospitalized patient becomes involved. Their significance is derived from different sources. The physician represents authority and prestige. His orders legitimize the patient's demands on others and justify otherwise deviant aspects of illness behavior. The physician is not only the "court of appeal" for exemption from normal role responsibilities,[3] he also functions as the major legitimizing agent for the patient's demands during hospitalization. Yet his orders generally do not constitute guides to behavior in specific situations and they do not consider or modify the patient's understanding of the formal and informal expectations of nurses. Although the physician's authority ranks supreme in the eyes of most patients, they are also aware that he is only intermittently present and thus not in a position to evaluate the behavior of both patients and nurses and to sanction this behavior during the everyday procedures of hospital care.

The significance of the nurse stems not only from her authority in interpreting, applying and enforcing the orders of the physician but, in addition, from the fact that she can judge and react to the patient's behavior more continuously

[2]Thirty-two per cent of the patients in this sample occupied a private room; 61 per cent occupied a two-bed room and 7 per cent shared a room with two other patients.

[3]Parsons, T., *The Social System*, New York: Free Press, 1951, pp. 433–477.

than the physician. From the patient's point of view, he also depends upon the nurse as an intermediary in the provision of many other institutional services.

For most patients it is of greatest importance to feel that they adjust to the expectations of the nurse and of the physician. To accommodate themselves to what they feel is expected of them, patients must be able to perceive these expectations as congruent or they must cope with the strains involved in efforts to adjust to what may appear to them as conflicting demands. Conflict is thus likely to arise if the nurse executes a plan of care which, from the point of view of the patient, deviates in detail or emphasis from the patient's interpretation of the physician's orders.

Close adherence to the orders of the physician was not equally important for all patients and not all patients appear to be equally intense in their sensitivity to congruence in the plan of care and cure. Those patients who expressed concern for complete adherence to the physician's word and expected strictest observance and literal interpretation of medical orders typically expressed distrust in the reliability and efficiency of anyone except the physician. These patients frequently feared that even minor deviations may result in further physical harm. For some patients, close adherence to medical orders appeared congruent with their conceptions of themselves; as did some patients, who resisted following certain medical orders, they used this area of conformity to convey something essential about themselves.

Demands for rigid adherence to medical orders were associated with the desire for "reliable" nursing care and "efficiency." The eagerly co-operative patient not only emphasized that he followed all orders willingly, he also expected the nurse to "co-operate" with him in his efforts to carry out the orders of the physician as he understood them. The patient's concern typically expressed itself in close observations of hospital personnel, in emphasis on observance of punctuality and in worry whether "orders have been written" and "charts double-checked." Such efforts to "co-operate with the physician" by seeing that "things get done" may become a source of stress. The patient who is ready to act on behalf of medical orders may have to call for services from the nurse and impose demands on her time or ask her to alter behavior. Thus, if the patient hears from the physician that the "specimen should be warm," he may feel obligated to insist that a "cooling-off" delay be avoided. If the physician has told him that he may "stay in bed another day," the patient's interpretation may lead him to actively resist a nurse's urging that he do some things for himself: "My doctor said that I can stay in bed another day." Patients' insistence on rigid adherence to the orders of the physician were frequently defended in the light of one implication of the sick role—the obligation to make efforts towards the restoration of health. Thus, patients who were critical of deviations from the medical orders justified their criticisms by pointing out that they did not want to be "complainers" or "troublemakers"—but that they, after all, "want to get well."

When a patient's efforts to co-operate fully and to observe the details of medical orders expressed themselves in more frequent demands, he also reacted to the risks involved in violating his obligation not to be demanding of nurses. Those patients who reported that they had expressed their desire for compliance with medical orders in active demands or complaints also tended to be very observant of the reactions of members of the nursing staff. Praise and criticism of "good" and "bad" nurses revealed that these patients rejected the nurse who "grumbled" and that they praised enthusiastically the nurse who responded "willingly" and who "smiled" when she was asked to do things for the patient. Patients also praised the nurse who "helped the patient to co-operate" and who "did not mind" when she was reminded of an order.

Those patients for whom co-operation with a physician's order became the guiding principle during hospitalization tended to be very sensitized to the reactions of others. They appeared to be "on the alert" and reacted quickly to facial expression, a tone of voice and the general manner in which a request was received. If they felt that their demands were not well received, they frequently became angered and, when given an opportunity, expressed their antagonism in attacks on those members of the nursing staff who "do not treat you like a person," who "make you feel that you are at their mercy" and "who consider you just a case."

The conflict between the felt obligation to insist on precise implementation of medical orders and efforts not to appear demanding or inconsiderate *vis à vis* the nursing staff was often resolved in favor of striving for approval by nurses. The data indicate that many patients prefer not to risk appearing too demanding or too dependent. They accept what appears to them to be deviations from the physician's orders, and even violate what they believe is expected of them by the physician. They anxiously watch a medication being late, rather than object to the delay, and they watch the specimen get cold rather than pointing this out to a nurse. Frequently this endeavor to "please" the nurse may backfire. Patients who disobey the physician's orders and get up to do "small things" for themselves rather than call the nurse may find themselves reprimanded by her because she may view this as a lack of co-operation or even protest. She also may consider such behavior an incident which could incur the anger of the physician.

Thus, patients may pay for the security of "being liked" by nurses and of having them "know that I am not demanding" with concerns over arousing the physician's criticism or harming their own recovery. But even where the obligation to be co-operative with the physician is not immediately at stake, patients may somewhat reluctantly forego the privileges which they could claim as a result of being sick. As one patient expressed it:

> If it is a hotel you won't hesitate to pick up a phone or to complain; in a hospital you think twice about it—you figure maybe they are busy or shorthanded. . . . It's a much more human thing, the hospital . . . it's more personal.

Expectations and Constraints

When patients were asked what was expected of them by their physicians and by nurses, they responded with considerable consistency, indicating that several rules for "proper" conduct of patients were well defined and widely shared. The physician was seen as expecting "co-operation" and "trust and confidence." A large group of patients felt that the nurse, too, expected "co-operation." On the other hand, many patients were convinced that nurses expected them "not to be demanding," to be "respectful" and to be "considerate." Only very few patients listed these latter three categories for physicians.

Self-descriptions which patients introjected into the interviews followed a similar pattern. It was most important to patients that the interviewer saw them as having "trust and confidence" in those who took care of them. This was particularly true of those patients who also admitted to some negative reactions toward nurses or physicians. Many patients were eager to mention that they were not demanding, co-operative, not dependent and considerate. In spontaneous discussions of the obligations of the hospitalized patient, the pattern did not change significantly.

One of the factors underlying the patient's hesitation to impose demands on hospital personnel is his awareness of the presence of other, often sicker patients. Observation of other patients introduces restraints. Comparisons of "my illness" with the illness of the roommate appeared to intensify the moral obligation to "leave them free to take care of the seriously ill" and comparisons of one's own claims or criticisms with the behavior of a very ill person seemed to intensify restrained behavior: "After I observed him I felt kind of bad. I felt that I should be grateful and not ask for anything." It is well nigh impossible and a latent source of difficulty for the patient to judge his comparative status relative to patients in other rooms. The nurse summoned to give him a glass of water may have been called away from "a critical case." The isolation of the patient and the ensuing inability to establish relative claims serve as restraining forces on the expression of needs,[4] even though this concern is counterbalanced with an occasionally voiced concern about "getting one's share."

The patient's perceived entitlement for service is also linked to his definition of the severity of his illness. Patients apparently feel more secure in ascertaining their rights if their understanding of their condition permits them to rank themselves in the upper strata of a "hierarchy of illness." However, a secure assessment of "my case" may be difficult. Communications from the physician are general and understanding of the relative severity of the illness does not appear to be facilitated by his explanations. In many cases, a statement such as "I want you to stay in bed" does not legitimize the demand for a glass of water—the patient gets up to avoid being considered "too demanding."

Patients therefore seem to link the extent of their claims on service to readily perceived and objectively visible indices. Thus, being in traction, having tubes attached or being restrained by dressings are highly ranked legitimators for patients' demands. Fever also serves as a criterion for claims; the patient who asks the nurse what his temperature might be not only may inquire about the severity of his illness but indirectly may also ask: "To what services am I entitled today?" Hospital rules which prevent the nurse from giving such information may deny the patient guidelines for the rules applicable to his behavior.

Two-thirds of all patients in the sample indicated that they had refrained from expressing their needs and criticisms at least once. The observation that nurses are too busy, rushed and overworked was given as the most frequent reason for this reluctance. Beliefs about the conditions under which hospital personnel work serve thus as another limiting factor in the patient's expression of de-

---

[4]This phenomenon suggests a parallel to the concept of "relative deprivation" described by R. K. Merton and P. Lazarsfeld (eds.), *Continuities in Social Research*, New York: Free Press, 1950. Just as deprivation is experienced in relation to relative norms, legitimacy of claims rests on a relative basis. If this basis is not ascertainable, uncertainty functions as restraining force.

mands. One has to keep in mind the admiration for nurses and for "all those who do such difficult work" to understand why some patients may spend a night help-ing another patient when being told "that there is a shortage on the nightshift." Some patients did not engage in these activities without some conflict. They ad-mitted that they were concerned with the physician's reactions "if he finds out," and that they were fearful of the consequences of such activity for their health. Even though they never admitted it directly, many responses revealed indirectly their desire to take more advantage of the privileges of the sick.

Constraint in voicing demands was also reinforced by the patient's assess-ment of the power of hospital personnel and physicians relative to his own. Over one-fourth of those patients who admitted to restraint of their demands also ex-pressed their often resentful assessment of their own helplessness. Efforts to be "considerate" of the conditions which limit services may thus be convenient ra-tionalizations of the patient's fears of offending others and of endangering his good relationship with them. "Being on good terms" was seen by these patients not only as a convenient but as an essential factor for their welfare. They directly expressed their awareness of their inability to control those who are in charge of their care. Patients felt that they were subject to rewards and punishment and that essential services can be withheld unless they make themselves acceptable. Some of these patients were dependent upon intimate forms of physical assis-tance, and their points of view reflected their awareness of this dependence upon others.

Feelings of helplessness were directly expressed in observations that "one is at their mercy," that "trying to change things is futile" and "won't get you any-where" and that patients feel "helpless." The recognition of the power of others to withhold services also found expression in fears that one does not want to be considered a "complainer," or "trouble-maker" or a "demanding patient," and in such apprehensions as "they can refuse to answer your bell, you know," or "they can refuse to make your bed." The same fears were expressed in efforts "to save that button so they come when I really need them" or in enthusiastic re-actions to nurses who "come in to inquire why you never call for them" or who "do not mind if you ring once too often."

Patients very rarely expressed openly a concern that their physician may im-pose sanctions on inappropriate behavior. They tried to be intensely considerate toward him, since he, too, is considered "very busy" and "on his way" to other sick patients. Attempts to accommodate demands to these pressures on the physi-cian serve as a considerable restraint on the patient's willingness to ask questions.

The admiration for the physician was in most cases tied to a very personal and emotionally charged attachment to the man who is "so kind and understand-ing." Gratitude intensified efforts to "make things easy" for him. Although hos-tility or annoyances toward nurses was often directly expressed, patients actively resisted direct verbalization of any negative feelings toward "the physician." Typically, complaints were expressed reluctantly and in terms of "I wish he could" coupled with quick modifications such as "I know he can't—he is too busy."

Patients may also be concretely limited by the observation that the physician is "on the go." Thus, a patient may want to ask questions and feel that "taking his time" is legitimate, but may feel that the time is simply not made available:

> He'll say well, we'll talk about it next time. And next time he'll talk fast, he out-
> talks you—and rushes out of the room and then when he's out of the room you
> think, well, I was supposed to ask him what he's going to do about my medicine
> . . . you run in the hall and he has disappeared that fast.

A patient who was impressed with the fact that his physician was "overbur-
dened and rushed" tried to describe how the resulting pressure of his own tensions and anxiety prevented him from fully comprehending what he was told:

> All I know is that your mind sort of runs ahead. You sort of anticipate what
> they are going to say, and you finish what they are going to say in your mind. I
> guess it's because perhaps sometimes you have trouble following them or may-
> be you would want them to say certain things, and you are listening—well, I
> don't know . . . you try to think what they are going to say, because otherwise,
> you have difficulty understanding them, but then, when they are out of the
> room, you don't remember a thing about what they have said.

In view of the above, it is not surprising that patients who were asked directly
what they "considered their rights" had some difficulties responding. One-forth
of the respondents admitted that they did not know what their rights were; some
patients stated outright that they had no rights. The majority of respondents limited themselves to general answers such as "good care," followed by the modification that specific claims depended upon the "seriousness of the illness." The
belief that claims for service had to be justified in terms of immediate physical
needs over-shadowed any inclination to voice the rights of paying consumers.
Few patients justified their demands in relation to their monetary payment and
many of those who introduced the criteria of a paying consumer quickly added to
their demands other legitimizing factors, such as the nature of their illness or the
fact that they had been considerate in other respects. Conceptions of rights and
obligations provided guidelines for alternative actions. They are used and "fit-
ted" in accordance with the exigencies of situations and the developing meanings
which individuals and groups bring to bear upon them. The general patterns
which have been discussed should not conceal that differences in the characteristics of patients may contribute to significant variations in the more general
theme. The following observations will illustrate the importance of further research in this area.

Patients who do not experience active and well-defined symptoms and whose
activities are not visibly impaired may hesitate to present themselves to others as
seriously ill and may find "co-operation" at times more difficult. Patients with
cardio-vascular illness tended to focus more frequently on behavior involving co-
operation with physicians and nurses; particularly in relation to the physician,
this obligation appeared to preoccupy these patients. They were also more intent
on presenting themselves as co-operative to the interviewer. Some of these patients were severely ill from the medical point of view, requiring complete bed rest
and its concomitant extensive services. However, they seemed to have a difficult
time accepting this state without concern that they may be considered "too dependent" or overly "demanding." At times, these difficulties appeared enhanced
by social and economic pressures to leave the hospital, and by psychological
needs for denial which also seemed to find expression in the insistence that they

"really did not need any special attention" and that they were "not worried about their illness."

Some of the subtle difficulties of these patients are not easily verbalized. Only rarely can a patient formulate as forcefully the aftermath of a heart attack as did the patient quoted below. His statement sums up the allusions and hints dropped by other patients with a cardiac problem:

> Well, you know, a heart patient is a peculiar animal. That heart attack has done something to him, not only physically but mentally. I can tell you this because I have been through it. It brings up something which you don't want to let go of. If he tells you you must stay in bed, well, how come this sudden change? I don't want to stay in bed, and if he tells you that you cannot walk upstairs, he is telling you that you are weak, that you are no longer strong. He has taken something away from you—ah, your pride. You suddenly want to do what you are not supposed to do, what you have been doing all your life and that you have every right to do. Besides, a heart patient has an excitability built up in him.

Patients with cardio-vascular conditions verbalized criticisms less frequently than other patients. On the other hand, they stressed the importance of "dedication and interest" when discussing their ideal expectations of nurses and physicians.

One explanation for these tendencies may be found in some common fears which occur among patients who suffer from a type of illness in which the onset of a crisis can be sudden and unpredictable. For a patient with a cardio-vascular illness, as probably for all patients who fear a sudden turn for the worse, it is of utmost importance to know that someone will be there when the patient really needs help. The need for this type of security is revealed in the following responses of cardio-vascular patients:

> I think that there should be somebody out in front there all the time. I think the hospital would back me up on that. . . . If the patient was really ill, rang the buzzer and nobody was there to get it—no telling what would happen.

> Well, as I said, some patients may need more care because they have a more serious illness and when you have a heart disease then you need to be watched much more, also you are more frightened and it is important that somebody is around to watch your pulse.

Patients with non-specific gastro-intestinal conditions were more likely to be preoccupied with cancer. At times this was accompanied by the suspicion that the physician "really knows but will not tell me." Such apprehensions seemed to make it more difficult for the patient to sustain trust and confidence in personnel, particularly the physician.

Openly anxious and critical patients were found more frequently within the gastro-intestinal category. While patients with cardio-vascular conditions appeared to focus attention on concrete services which assured their safety, gastro-intestinal patients seemed more inclined to focus on the qualitative nature of their interactions with nurses and physicians. They were more easily threatened by the attitudes of others, more responsive to "personalized care" and more openly critical when these areas of expectations were not satisfied.

In each culture there is the recognition that it is legitimate to deviate from normal behavior under certain extreme conditions. For these conditions most societies develop differential standards for men and women. In our society men and women are generally not expected to respond in an identical fashion to pain nor are they expected to react identically to illness. We expect that expressive behavior (complaining or moaning) should be more controlled by men, and we frown less when women appear to exploit the illness role through passive and dependent behavior. All patients generally agreed that it was more difficult for men to be patients.

The data indicate that the sex of a patient may substantially affect orientations, needs and reactions to physicians and nurses. Evidence for such differences can be found in many areas. Women were considerably more critical of nursing care than were men, and more frequently expressed fear of negative sanctions from nurses. Women, more than men, emphasized personalized relationships when they discussed the needs of patients. Women were less concerned with problems of co-operation. On the other hand, they tended to focus on nurses' expectations for consideration and respect. When describing their expectations of nurses or when evaluating them, women focused more on personality attributes than men and also gave more emphasis to efficient and prompt care. Women were more critical when a quick response was not forthcoming and they were generally more concerned with efficiency. It is compatible with the male role to receive care and to have someone else maintain the physical surroundings. Women, however, are typically the managers of the home and the performers of major housekeeping tasks. They "know" from experience the standards of personal care and housekeeping, and thus tend to apply them to their judgment of the nursing team. The female patient's concern that the nurse may be critical of her may be indirectly an expression of her awareness that she tends to be demanding.

The more intense emphasis of women on "personality" and "personalized care" may also stem from a relationship which tends to be less personal and less informal than the relationship between nurses and male patients. Unlike his female counterpart, the male patient is probably not too critical of the technical aspect of those functions of the nurse which are reminiscent of the homemaker and mother. He may also derive satisfaction from his relationship to a member of the opposite sex. All this may not only contribute to tolerance of nursing care in general but may give the appearance of more "personalized" relationships. These conjectures may also help to explain the well-known preference nurses have for male patients.

Fears and Apprehensions

Apprehensions and fears are the frequent companions of illness. The nature of the patient's concern springs, on the one hand, from his intense preoccupations with himself, with *his* body and with *his* state of mind. His dependence on others, on the other hand, prompts simultaneous concern with the meaning and consequence of their activities. Once the patient enters the hospital his attention may shift back and forth from himself to others. He is sensitive to any physical changes and watchful of any new and unexplained symptoms. He wonders about the outcome of an examination and about the effectiveness of his treatment. He ponders the reliability of those who are responsible for the many procedures and activities which to the patient remain unknown or unknowable, albeit essential.

Patients are preoccupied with safety in the hospital. This is revealed in the preoccupation with protection from mistakes and neglect which prevails when patients talk about their own needs or the needs of other patients. It is expressed in the nature of their recall of past experiences. Not only do patients concentrate on negative experiences, but they select those occurrences which signify the dangers of neglect and lack of attention. Although patients generally deny that they, themselves, are fearful, they have a tendency to ascribe such feelings to other patients.

These apprehensions cannot be entirely alleviated by admiration for the professional groups who are responsible for his treatment, or by a very favorable relationship to the personal physician. Realistic awareness of the complexity of large organizations or simply the fact that among many competent and interested doctors and nurses there may always be a "few who are not competent" may at least put the patient on the alert. In the words of a male patient with gastro-intestinal illness this fear is expressed as follows:

> When you are really sick, you are at the mercy of the hospital staff. In my opinion, you've got to have luck on your side. You've got to be lucky enough to get key people in the hospital who are really alert and who wish to do a job; and have someone on the shift at the time you need them who want to give the service or you are just out of luck. I think you could die in one of these hospitals of a heart attack before anybody came in to help you.

Perceptions of the patient role make it unlikely that such fears will be openly expressed by many patients. It is one of the obligations of a patient to have "trust and confidence" in those who care for him. The expression of these concerns could thus be interpreted as a failure to conform to these obligations. Also a free expression of concerns is inhibited by the belief that the courageous, sick persons rather than "sissies" are valued and rewarded.

Apprehensions of certain "dangers" may be directly derived from previous experiences which were, to the patient, indicative of lack of competence, neglect, or lack of interest. They also may be derived indirectly from certain widely held conceptions about the nature of "some" doctors and nurses and the conditions under which they work. Thus, the belief that some nurses do not like "demanding patients" leads to the concern of many patients that asking for too much may result in a slow response to a call or in reduced attention to their needs. The belief that some nurses and some physicians may be prone to oversights because they are inevitably overworked and rushed may further contribute to insecurity. Some patients observed with concern that physicians occasionally are "too busy" to spend enough time to listen to their patients or that a nurse "under the pressure of work" may overlook a physician's order or fail to carry it out in time.

There is evidence in the data that both physicians and nurses, in effect, continuously have to prove themselves. Beliefs such as "some doctors are only interested in money," "some doctors are not interested in their patients," "some doctors are hard-hearted," appear as conceptions about "possibilities" which the patient is ready to have dispelled or confirmed upon first contact with a nurse or a physician in the hospital. Negative conceptions about physicians and nurses, therefore, are typically limited to specific individuals. Without this "specificity" in orientation, patients would find it difficult to sustain the trust and confidence which they consider so important.

The patient's search for safety and security in the hospital may also be indirectly expressed in expectations of good physicians and good nurses. Their behavior or attitudes are seen by the patient as being instrumental in recovery and recuperation. The attitudes of others in the hospital function as clues which are symbolic of good care. From the patient's point of view, the "dedicated nurse" or the nurse who gives "spontaneous and willing services" is a reliable nurse; the "kind" physician who visits the patient regularly is "trustworthy" and "thorough." Mistakes and neglect are more obviously avoided if the nurse responds promptly, if the physician "knows what is going on" and if the nurse is informed about the doctor's intent. A "prompt response" from a nurse appears as one of the most significant indices for establishing trust and confidence in nursing care.

Patient's perspectives are also shaped by the nature of the social process into which they have entered and by the nature of the interactions to which they are exposed. Those patients who were very responsive to the more impersonal phases of patient-care also tended to be among the more apprehensive. Such patients often felt that they were functioning in a situation in which they could not establish effective and meaningful relationships with others. Feelings of "unrelatedness" were expressed directly in the observation that other patients are often "lonely" and "fearful" or that one sometimes feels like "just a case":

> You're no more . . . no more a patient but just a number . . . you dare not ask a question; you know, they're too busy. And they come around, fine, that's it, "we'll see you next time" and that's it. . . .

The very isolation he fears may be aggravated by the patient himself. In his efforts to be "considerate" and "not demanding" he may intensify the consequences of the anonymity and segmentalization he observes in the modern hospital. Efforts to be a "good patient" may, therefore, trigger disappointments and criticisms of those who do not provide services "spontaneously." The demand for "spontaneous services" appears also to stem from the desire to obtain all necessary services and attentions without having to initiate action. Spontaneous services curtail those interactions in which the patient may be viewed as "too demanding" or "difficult."

The interviews suggest that conformity to the patient role may lead to discrepancies between the behavior and the emotional condition of a patient. The calm appearance of the "good patient" may often hide anxieties and tensions which may not come to the attention of physicians or nurses unless relationships develop which do not trigger fear of criticism or sanction. When patients fail to exercise the restraints on behavior which they think appropriate, guilt or fear may be the consequence. Deviation from the good patient model can be threatening to a patient, unless he is convinced that his behavior was, in the eyes of others, legitimate and/or justified by the condition of his illness:

> I know myself that I talked very rudely to my doctor on one occasion. Afterwards I was ashamed of myself. I was sick or I would never act that way. He is kind and understanding. When I apologized, he acted as if nothing happened. He didn't walk out of the room or tell me off or any of the things that I might do after someone talked to me that way. But I know they have to have a lot of patience with us.

Patients practice an economy of demands, based on their own "principles of exchange." They will indeed curtail their less urgent demands to assure for themselves a prompt response during times when they "really need it." Some patients appear to consider themselves entitled to a certain finite quantity of services which they use sparingly to draw upon during periods of crisis, and many patients seem to feel that their entitlement to service is more severely cut by a demand which does not meet the approval of doctors and nurses:

> I says, "I'm saving that button," I says, "When I push that thing you'll know I need help." She smiled . . . they kind of appreciate that. And from that day, all the times I've been in the hospital, I have never pushed the button unless it was something that I actually needed . . . not like some people that drive these nurses crazy; pushing it to raise the bed up; five minutes later push it again. "Oh, that's a little too high." To me it paid dividends, because every time I pushed that button I got service, every dog-gone time.

Discussion

The hospitalized patient is a "captive" who cannot leave the hospital without serious consequences to himself. These consequences do not apply to the patient's physical condition. Our society expects efforts of the sick to do everything in their power to get well as soon as possible. Open rebellion against the care by competent professional personnel is, therefore, subject to severe criticism. The obligation to be a "co-operative patient" is learned early in life and, as has been indicated, apparently taken very seriously by most patients. More aggressive interpretations of the patient role are not easily verbalized and, apparently, not often realistic alternatives for the patient. Prevalent images of the hospital as a crisis institution, the conception that rights and demands should be governed by the seriousness of the illness and consideration for other, possibly sicker patients, makes it extremely difficult to play the "consumer role" openly and without fear of criticism. Thus, self-assertion as a "client" is controlled by moral commitments to the hospital community as well as by considerations of practical and necessary self-interest.

The norms of our society permit the sick person conditionally passive withdrawal and dependence but, at the same time, emphasize the sick person's responsibility to co-operate in efforts to regain his health.[5] The prevailing image of the hospital increases the pressure to get well fast by enhancing the patient's awareness of the relative degree of the seriousness of his case. Many patients do not have to look far to find and hear about patients who seem more seriously ill. This pressure to get well also is intensified by the observation of "over-worked" and "rushed" nurses and physicians. The pattern of hospital relationships which, for the most part, prevents the development of those relationships which would reduce fears of being rejected or criticized, further discourages patients from exploiting the leniency to which illness *per se* may entitle them. A moral commitment to physicians and nurses is also strengthened by the gratitude and admiration of the sick for those who are "trying to help."

[5] Parsons, T., and R. Fox, "Illness, Therapy and the Modern Urban American Family," in E. G. Jaco (ed.), *Patients, Physicians and Illness*, New York: Free Press, 1st ed., 1958, p. 236.

Patterns of interaction are also affected by the controls which the participants can exert over each other and the understanding which they can have of the function of others. For a variety of reasons, the patient sees few areas in which he has control.

A prerequisite for controlling the actions of others is the capacity to feel competent to judge their achievements. Most patients feel quite helpless in evaluating the knowledge, skill and competence of nurses and physicians. This may be one reason for their intense emphasis on "personality." "Personality" is felt to be associated with, and an indicator of, those more technical qualities which patients do not feel qualified to judge.

Control does not only depend on the capacity to judge the competence or efficiency of others. It also involves the freedom to convey and impose judgments. Even if patients feel quite certain about their judgments, they may feel reluctant to express them if such action may portend a reduction in good patient care.

The institutional context affects the way the patients balance their perceived claims and obligations. They manage to communicate the conditional nature of their claims, the undesirability of their state and, therefore, the importance of their obligations. Their persistent verbal assertions that they should co-operate, that they must not be demanding, underscore their motivation to get well. The problem of patients does not stem from a rejection of major social values but rather from the dissonance created between the desire to broaden the boundaries of what seems a legitimate sphere of control and the tendency to adhere compulsively to behavior which reflects conformity to obligations.[6] The data confirm Parsons' contention that dependence is, in our society, a primary threat to the valued achievement capacity and that the sick, to this extent, are called upon to work for their own recovery.[7]

Efforts to adhere to obligations are accompanied by the complementary hope that others will meet their obligations in turn and thus will satisfy the patient's expectations. Recognition of the limitations under which hospital functionaries work does not prevent patients from forming "ideal" expectations which call for a model of care which the on-going work processes of the hospital do not readily approximate.[8] The restraint which is exercised by the hospitalized patient is partly an expression of his fears that he may be deprived of important service if he should deviate from acceptable behavior. However, while patients have some notions of the sanctions which can be applied should they violate standards for appropriate behavior, they appear much less certain what they could do if nurses or physicians do not meet their obligations. The feeling of helplessness

[6]At times the patient and his significant others among hospital functionaries may be less in disagreement over proper role relationships than significant others involved in their social network. Thus, in some cases patients were found to define their obligations in terms of all the previously discussed considerations. Their relatives, however, emphasized the rights of the paying consumer and expressed their opinion that the patient was "not asking for enough." For a discussion of the role of the third party see W. J. Goode, "A Theory of Role Strain," *American Sociological Review*, 25:483–496, August, 1960.

[7]Parsons, "Definitions of Health and Illness. . . .," *op. cit.*, p. 185.

[8]Reactions to experiences in the hospital assume, therefore, meaning not only in relation to "realistic" anticipations but also in relation to more subtly held "ideal" expectations. The relative discrepancy between "realistic" and "ideal" experiences is a significant variable in the patients' responses to actual experiences.

of patients is partly derived from an incapacity to judge adequately the competence of those who take care of them—in part, from the fact that their experiences do not provide easily defendable criteria for asserting their rights; and partly from their reluctance to use the controls which are available to them.

The interviews showed that patients always knew what they should not be like or what qualities or behavior would make them acceptable to others. Even much more difficult for them was to define what specific tasks they had a right to expect and what expectations could be transformed into active demands without deviating from general norms for behavior. A lack of familiarity with what constitutes proper care and cure procedures as well as the fact that a slight change in their condition could alter the legitimacy of demands appears to contribute to this difficulty. Rigid adherence to general rules of conduct appeared to be one way out of this dilemma.

Patients were also limited in the expression of their feelings by the fact that personalized and supportive care was not considered to lie within the sphere of the essential. They clearly felt that they had to subordinate such demands to their own or other patients' needs for physical care. The point of view of patients parallels the common distinction between the legitimacy of somatic and mental illness—a distinction which is accompanied by the notion that somatic illness legitimately entitles the ill to accept dependence as a result of manifestly impaired *physical* capacity for task performance. This dependence is narrowly defined in terms of permitting hospital functionaries to do things for the patient only as long as it is really *physically* necessary. Emotional dependence or other deviations from adult role performance are considered legitimate by most patients only in cases of extreme illness.[9]

The opportunities to obtain personalized care are limited and they are further restricted by patients who as "good patients" withdraw from those on whom they depend and with whom they wish to communicate but whom they do not wish "to bother." The control of the desire to obtain and demand more personal care tends to intensify alienation.[10] The expression of such emotional needs is checked not only by the various pressures to conform to the patient role, but also by the fact that those patient-care activities which direct themselves to the emotional needs of the patient are not institutionalized as role obligations of personnel in the general hospital. Personal concern, support or other emotionally therapeutic efforts tend to be from the patient's point of view pleasant (often

[9]Patients were not interviewed during the critical phases of their illness when, indeed, their claims may have been different. However, only a few patients in the sample considered themselves recovered. The majority of patients in the cardio-vascular category were recuperating from severe illness and were under orders for bedrest. The majority of the patients in the gastro-intestinal category were under treatment for ulcers or hospitalized for other chronic or acute gastro-intestinal conditions. In all of these cases the conditional nature of rights was bound to create some difficulties—either because of the absence of visible symptoms of illness or because the illness was not considered very serious. Case studies of the more seriously ill patients indicate that anxiety may cause them to "break through" the limits set by their role but that such a breakthrough often demands added efforts since claims, demands or irritations have to be justified. To reestablish an acceptable view of themselves seems to often constitute a major effort for these patients.

[10]Parsons, "Definitions of Health and Illness . . .," *op. cit.*, p. 186. The author points out that the supportive treatment of the sick person "undercuts the alienative component of the motivational structure of his illness."

unexpected) attributes of otherwise task-oriented personnel. Such activities are quickly praised and even "ideally" seen as the major attributes of the "good" nurse and of the "good" physician. But, since these do not really belong to the manifestly legitimate obligations, they are only reluctantly criticized when missing and rarely directly demanded.

Efforts to adhere to rules of conduct involve also the desire to project a specific image of self.[11] Being accepted is of more than passing importance to the hospitalized patient.[12] Self-consciousness about the norms to which one tries to conform may also suggest that the role is in certain respects alien to the performers and that they are not secure in essential social relationships. Efforts to reiterate conformity to general rules of conduct may thus, at least in part, stem from the patient's limited knowledge of the reality of the institutional setting and from fears that he may not be able to measure up to institutionalized expectations. Thus, uncertain about how far he can go before violating prescribed rules for behavior, patients may find their security in efforts to live up to the "letter of the law."[13]

The frequently expressed obligation to co-operate and the persistent attempt to seek approval is, within this frame of reference, not only a diplomatic effort to manipulate relationships to one's own advantage, but also an expression of the patient's perception of the degree of dependency associated with his status. The associated attitudes are thus not merely psychological consequences of the sick role but also reflect the patient's common sense assessments of the abrogation of independence and decision-making associated with his status in the hospital.[14] These deprivations are communicated to the patient beginning with the possessive gesture of the identification bracelet affixed during admission to the hospital, and they are continuously reinforced in daily experiences. The hospital preempts control and jurisdiction, ranging from the assumption of accountability of body functions to the withholding of information about medical procedures.[15]

The interviews reflect a degree of uncertainty whether physicians and nurses operate as effective teams in close communication or whether the patient ought to

[11]Goffman, E., "The Nature of Deference and Demeanor," *Amer. Anthropologist*, 58: 473–502, June, 1956; E. Goffman, *Encounters: Two Studies in the Sociology of Interaction*, Indianapolis, Ind.: Bobbs-Merrill, 1961, pp. 99–105.

[12]Efforts to give verbal evidence of conformity may aim at protection from criticism. Deviations tend to be viewed as forgivable as long as a person gives evidence of "good will." Goode emphasized that failure in role behavior tends to arouse less criticism than failure in emotional commitment to general norms. This principle may be particularly applicable to situations where it is also an obligation of alters to tolerate failures in role behavior. See W. J. Goode, "Norm Commitment and Conformity to Role Status Obligations," *Amer. J. Soc.*, 66: 246–258, November, 1960.

[13]See Merton's discussion of ritualism. Anxiety over the ability to live up to institutional expectations may contribute to compulsive adherence to institutional norms. R. K. Merton, *Social Theory and Social Structure*, New York: Free Press, Rev. Ed., 1957, pp. 184–187.

[14]Parsons and Fox stressed the need for a "well-timed, well-chosen, well-balanced exercise of supportive and the disciplinary components of the therapeutic process." Institutional factors as well as widely held social values may tend to shift the emphasis too much to the disciplinary components particularly in the setting of the general hospital which incorporate structurally as well as in terms of explicitly or implicitly held attitudes the distinction between the emotionally sick and the physically sick (Parsons and Fox, *op. cit.*, p. 244).

[15]Mauksch, H. O., "Patients View Their Roles," *Hospital Progress*, 43: 136–138, October, 1962.

function as interpreter and intermediary between these two all important functionaries. Sometimes patients wonder whether they are sources of conflict and competition between medicine and nursing. The physician is seen as supreme authority and patients repeatedly stress that "if something is really seriously wrong," they would turn to the physician. The physician, however, is for the most part not present to observe, respond or intervene. The nurse is continually present, or at least within reach of the call system. She is the physician's representative and interpreter, but she also is the one who has to bear the brunt of work resulting from the physician's orders. She represents hospital rules, and yet she is not infrequently seen by the patient as a potential spokesman for his needs and interests. These perceptions reflect remarkably well the organization of the hospital and the ambiguous position of the nurse at the crossroads of the care and cure structures.[16]

This study suggests that the patient role, like other comparable behavior syndromes organized around a status, are not adequately described by isolating attitudinal and normative responses to the role theme itself, i.e., illness. The full repertory of role behavior must be placed into the context of organizational processes if it is to encompass realistic orientations and behavior display.

The patient role described in this paper is specific to the hospital. The data support and amplify the implication of Merton's use of the role-set as an analytic concept.[17] The patient gropes for appropriate criteria and distinctions in defining his role with reference to a variety of significant relationships. The concept points to the importance of the difference in the power of the members of the role-set *vis-à-vis* the status occupant who has to manipulate between correspondents and to the significance of the support which the status occupant receives from others in like circumstances. However, the relatively isolated patient in the modern single or double hospital room is frequently left to his own devices in coping with differences in real or perceived expectations. This adds to the conditions favoring manifestations of withdrawal or dependence on the approval of others as realistic responses to institutionalized impotence.

The data also suggest a further elaboration of certain aspects of the theoretical model of role behavior. The concept of the role-set refines the differential system of expectations attached to a status from the point of view of the range of counter roles. The data reported in this paper suggest that an additional dimension of role expectation would be a useful addition to theory. Expectations which define a role are normally attributed to the social system surrounding a status.[18] It is suggested that a distinguishable difference exists between the pattern of expectations arising from the structural aspects of the status and those expectations which are attached to the function ascribed to the role. Thus, the role concomitants of being ill can be defined as the functional role segment of the patient role while the consequences of hospitalization, be they perceived or real, could be termed positional role segments.

[16]Mauksch, H. O., "The Organizational Context of Nursing Practice," in F. Davis (ed.), *The Nursing Profession*, New York: Wiley, 1966, pp. 109–137.

[17]Merton, R. K., "The Role Set," *British J. Sociology*, 8:106–120, June, 1957.

[18]*Ibid.*, pp. 113f.

Concern with the functional segment of the patient role has been evidenced in most previous treatments of the sick role in the literature.[19] The positional role segment in this study is specific to the hospital. Yet in other settings for patient behavior—be it the home, the clinic or the physician's office—these structural components of the patient role would also bear fruitful sociological investigation. This conceptual scheme aids in structuring the observations of potential strain and conflict between different aspects of the patient role.

This study suggests that a prevailing theme of successful role behavior is the ability of the status occupant to integrate into his own behavior and responses different components from the system of expectations surrounding him. In the case of the patient his efforts to be "a good patient," to meet the obligations as he perceives them and to strive to co-operate in recovery are handicapped by the inadequacy of the communications system within which he functions.[20] Were it more effective, it may permit the patient to cope with his role with greater certainty about rights and obligations, the controls at his disposal and the risks inherent in behavioral experimentation.

[19]Parsons, *The Social System, loc. cit.* Other writers, notably R. Coser, *Life in the Ward*, Lansing, Mich.: Michigan State Univ. Press, 1962, include positional considerations to a greater extent.

[20]Skipper, Jr., J. K., D. L. Tagliacozzo and H. O. Mauksch, "Some Possible Consequences of Limited Communication Between Patients and Hospital Functionaries," *J. Health and Human Behavior*, 5:34–39, Spring, 1964; J. K. Skipper, Jr., "Communication and the Hospitalized Patient", in J. K. Skipper and R. C. Leonard (eds.), *Social Interaction and Patient Care*, Philadelphia: Lippincott, 1965, pp. 61–82.

11 Good Patients and Problem Patients: Conformity and Deviance in a General Hospital

When a patient enters a hospital, he or she is an outsider in the health profes-sional's place of work. Like any other workers, doctors and nurses try to arrange for their work to be conveniently and easily performed (Freidson, 1970:302–331). Hospital rules and regulations are for their benefit, not for the convenience of patients. For the sake of the smooth and efficient running of the institution, pa-tients are categorized so they can be worked on with routines established as prop-er for their category. Freidson (1967) points out that rationalization, standardiza-tion, and depersonalization are felt to be "worth the price" when the results achieved clearly benefit the patient.

In order to ensure compliance even when the patient does not clearly perceive the benefits of a particular rule or regimen, doctors and nurses rely on procedures that reduce a sense of autonomy and encourage acceptance of routine treatment. A favored technique of diminishing the social status of the patient is treatment as a non-person. Goffman (1961:341–342) describes this technique as:

> . . . the wonderful brand of "non-person treatment" found in the medical world, whereby the patient is greeted with what passes as civility, and said farewell to in the same fashion, with everything in between going on as if the patient weren't there as a social person at all, but only as a possession someone has left behind.

Cartwright (1964:95), in her study of British hospital patients, found that hospital doctors did not even bother with ordinary civilities, such as introducing themselves to patients.

The ideal situation, Goffman (1961:340–342) points out, would be to have the patient's social self go home while the damaged physical container is left for repair. But patients do come to the hospital equipped with functioning eyes, ears, and mouths, and they are in an excellent position to notice and complain about real or imagined errors, failures, inattention, and other forms of sloppiness in work that can be kept out of sight, or "backstage," when the client sees only the front office. Since many sick people in hospitals have alert periods and ample time to spy out inequities, inefficiency, and malfeasance, their possible criticisms must be neutralized. The chief method for minimizing the potentiality of patients

This study was supported by U.S. Public Health Service Grant HS00013. For helpful criticisms on earlier drafts, I would like to thank Rose Coser, Arlene Daniels, Lynne Davidson, Eliot Freidson, Judith Gordon, Pamela Roby, and Gaye Tuchman.

An abridged version of this paper with the same title was read at the 1974 American Sociological Association Meetings, Montreal, Canada. Reprinted from *Journal of Health & Social Behavior*, 16:213–225, June, 1975, by permission of the author and Publisher.

to make trouble for doctors and nurses by criticizing their work is to withhold information, so the patient cannot argue from adequate knowledge.

The medical staff certainly does have superior knowledge and expertise for the task of treatment, and the patient can never be a true equal in this area (Freidson, 1967:497). Nevertheless, it has been argued that over and above what derives from professional expertise, doctors and nurses deliberately limit the communication of information to patients to prevent their work routines from constantly being interrupted with questions and to mask their shortcomings and failures from the scrutiny of clients who are living where they work (Brown, 1966:203; Roth, 1963a:30–59; Roth, 1963b; Skipper, 1965). In addition to shielding doctors and nurses from the criticisms of patients, limited communication protects the professional stance of detachment and concern (Davis, 1960; Quint, 1965). While the loss of personal identity seems to be the subject of vague complaints among hospital patients, explicit complaints about the difficulty of obtaining adequate information or satisfactory explanations are well-documented (Cartwright, 1964:75; Duff and Hollingshead, 1968:285–286; Lorber, 1971: Chapter VIII; Shiloh, 1965).

For the medical staff, the more like a helpless object the patient is, the easier they find it to do their job. But if the patient cannot be rendered insensate, or his or her views are ignored completely, the routinization of work is helped when the patient is objective, instrumental, emotionally neutral, completely trusting, and obedient. To Parsons' (1951:428–479), sick-role prescriptions of cooperation and motivation to get well, the hospital-patient role adds the obligations to submit to hospital routines without protest (King, 1962:355–358; Tagliacozzo and Mauksch, 1972). The result is a patient role that has the same dimensions as Parsons' (1951:428–479) professional role: it is universalistic, affectively neutral, functionally specific, and collectivity-oriented. The voluntary cooperativeness, one-to-one intimacy, and conditional permissiveness that constitutes the commonly used version of Parsons' patient role are applicable only to outpatient care by a private physician. Inpatient care imposes on patients a role characterized by submission to professional authority, enforced cooperation, and depersonalized status.

Hospitalized patients frequently resent the passivity and submission expected by doctors and nurses, yet they tend to conform. There is evidence that patients believe this is the proper way to act in a hospital; moreover, they are afraid that if they do not keep quiet and do as they are told, they may not get adequate care (Coser, 1962:80–95; Tagliacozzo and Mauksch, 1972; Skipper, 1964). Short-term patients have little recourse but conformity to what the hospital staff expects, for they are virtual loners in the hospital social system. Patients usually come into the hospital singly, without a supportive group of peers. As newcomers they are on their own in learning the informal rules of the organization (Rosengren and Lefton, 1969:147–148, 156–157). If they try to buck the rules, they find no one is exclusively on their side. Other patients feel that if any one patient makes excessive demands, less attention will be paid to their own needs. Restriction of family visits effectively limits outside support of patients' demands within the hospital. Where relatives are permitted unlimited visiting, as in terminal cases, they are likely to be co-opted by the doctors and nurses to keep the patient manageable (Glaser and Strauss, 1965:92).

Although most patients accept the general norms of the hospital-patient role, Coser (1956) and Shiloh (1965) found that patients differed in their degree of acceptance. The patients Coser described as "primary" in orientation toward medical care in the hospital and Shiloh called "hierarchal" completely accept passivity, trust, and docility as proper behavior for patients. The patients Coser described as "instrumentally" oriented and Shiloh called "equalitarian" tend to reject these norms and to feel a hospitalized patient should be autonomous, critical, and well-informed. Coser did not make a systematic analysis of the behavior of these two types of patients but, on the one hand, she felt that patients who were "instrumental" tended to cause disturbances in hospital routines because they refused to give up their "substantial rationality" and were critical of the care they received. On the other hand, while "primary" patients readily adapted to ward routines, their attitudes produced the dysfunctional consequence of making them very reluctant to leave the hospital (Coser, 1956: 11–17).

Coser (1956, 1962:99–128) found that older patients tended to feel a good patient was one who was submissive to hospital rules and regulations, and Cartwright (1964:80–81) presents data that suggest that younger patients and professional and non-manual workers are somewhat aggressive in seeking information while in the hospital. Skipper (1964) found that age was a better predictor of patients' attitudes than sex or education, with those over 45 seeing themselves as having more obligations towards doctors and nurses than those under 45.

This study of hospitalized patients was undertaken to determine the variations in patients' expectations of how they should act in the hospital, to see how they actually did act during a short-term hospitalization, and to get information on the doctors' and nurses' evaluations of their behavior. It was predicted that patients who felt a good patient was one who was cooperative, trusting, uncomplaining, and undemanding would conform to these norms during their own hospital stay, while patients who did not agree with these norms would be uncooperative, argumentative, complaining, and demanding—that is, deviant from the point of view of the staff.

Research Design

The study was done at a 600-bed hospital that is part of a medical center in a bedroom borough of New York City. Patients scheduled for elective surgery were chosen as subjects because, on entering the hospital, they could be interviewed about their attitudes toward how a hospital patient should behave, and their behavior could be studied after the operation. A quota sample was selected to represent a range of seriousness of surgical procedures of ordinary enough occurrence that the patients would not be singled out for special attention.

The operations were: *routine*—33 herniorrhaphies; *moderately serious*—26 cholecystectomies and 5 removals of polyps, masses, or benign tumors; *very serious*—35 gastric, colon, and abdominoperineal resections, 2 caval shunts, and 2 laparotomies with biopsy. Of those who had very serious surgery, 14 did not have cancer, and 25 did. The groupings into routine, moderately serious, and very serious surgery were corroborated by medical personnel who were asked to

rank seven typical procedures on extensiveness, and on amount of medical attention, nursing care, and reassurance they felt were needed by the patient.

The 103 patients on whom data were collected were fairly equally divided by
sex. By age, 16 percent were under 40, 17 percent were 41–50, 26 percent were
51–60, and 42 percent were over 60. (Percentages are rounded.) Their educational
attainment was low: 39 percent had not graduated from high school, 36 percent
were high school graduates and 25 percent had some college or were college
graduates. They were predominantly Jewish: 60 percent; 24 percent were
Catholic, 11 percent were Anglo-Saxon Protestant, 7 percent were other. Ethnic-
religious groups were based on the birthplace of self or father, where foreign-
born, of self and father where American-born, and own religion. Anglo-Saxon
Protestants included those whose own and/or father's birthplace was the United
States, England, Scotland, Scandinavia, or Canada.

In order to find out their attitudes about how a hospital patient should act,
on the day of admission or immediately after they were informed they would be
having surgery, patients were asked to agree, agree strongly, disagree, or disagree
strongly with six statements. In the following statements, agreement indicated
conforming attitudes.

> Doctors expect patients to obey them completely.
> The sicker a patient is, the more attention he or she can expect from the doctors
> and the nurses.
> The best thing to do in the hospital is to keep quiet and do what you're told.

In the following statements, disagreement indicated conforming attitudes:

> I cooperate best as a patient when I know the reason for what I have to do.
> When I'm sick I expect to be pampered and catered to.
> It would be nice to talk to my nurse about any family or personal problems I
> had.

In the final analysis, all the "agree" responses and all the "disagree"
responses were grouped in order to increase the size of the cell N's. The patients
were categorized as having very conforming, moderately conforming, and deviant attitudes according to the number of their conforming responses. The
number of conforming responses per group were: *very conforming*—6 (4 patients), 5 (29 patients); *moderately conforming*—4 (42 patients); *deviant*—3 (18
patients), 2 (8 patients), 1 (2 patients). The cutting points were set at what seemed
natural breaks to create groups of roughly equal size.

The responses to a self-administered questionnaire distributed to the doctors
and nurses who had cared for the patient supplied data on *their* evaluations of the
patients. The questionnaire was filled out at the end of the patient's stay in the
hospital, or shortly after the patient had been discharged.

Conforming and Deviant Attitudes

Between men and women, there was little difference in attitudes toward the
hospital-patient role. By ethnic-religious group, American-born Catholics tended
to have deviant attitudes, while Anglo-Saxon Protestants and Irish Catholics
tended to have very conforming attitudes. However, the ethnic-religious group-

ings were so skewed that these findings are merely suggestive. Age and education did have an effect on attitudes toward the hospital-patient role. The younger and better educated the patient, the less likely he or she was to express very conforming attitudes. The highest percentage of patients with very conforming attitudes was found among the elderly high school graduates. Very few of the poorly educated patients of any age expressed deviant attitudes. Among the college-educated, those under 60 tended to express deviant attitudes, and those over 60 to be moderately conforming in their attitudes.

It might be expected that the more serious the illness, the less likely the patient would be to express deviant attitudes, since the sicker patients would feel more dependent on doctors and nurses than those about to undergo routine procedures, or be too weak to be assertive. While the highest percentage of patients with very conforming attitudes was among those who had cancer, the next highest was among those who had routine hernia repairs, and the difference in percentages was very small. On the other hand, almost half the very serious surgery patients who did not have cancer had deviant attitudes, compared to about one-quarter of the patients having all the types of procedures. The herniorrhaphy patients, having been warned that the whole procedure was quite routinized, may have felt they had little to gain by insisting on their autonomy, while the cancer patients may have been scared by the ambiguities of the information they were given. (One woman, whose tumor really turned out to be benign, did not believe her surgeon was telling her the truth.) The very serious surgery patients who did not have cancer were among the best-informed patients, since they came to surgery usually after a long history of medically-treated illness. However, their extensive experience with medical settings had not overly socialized them into accepting the professional's model of the "good patient."

In this study, then, the best predictors of deviant or conforming attitudes toward the hospital-patient role were age and education. As the population gets better educated, and the social distance between lay people and professionals narrows, it is likely that patients will probably be asking more questions, demanding more explicit information about their cases, and insisting on more personalized attention.

Conforming and Deviant Behavior

A direct manifestation of acceptance or rejection of the norm of compliance is the extent to which a patient will argue about prescribed routines. In the interview given just before discharge, patients were asked if they had refused to follow a doctor's or nurse's order or questioned or complained about one. Of the 98 patients who answered the question about doctors, 24 percent said they had disagreed with doctors (mostly house staff and known as such to the patients). Of the 99 patients who answered the question about nurses, 18 percent said they had disagreed with nurses. The arguments were mostly over medication, tests, procedures, mechanical devices, and coughing (cf. Davis and Von der Lippe, 1968).

Patients with deviant attitudes, who did not subscribe to the norm of unquestioning obedience, had been expected to disagree more than patients with conforming attitudes. While only slightly more than one-third of the patients with deviant attitudes disagreed with either doctors or nurses, they did have the highest percentages of those disagreeing, as predicted. As Table 11-1 shows, patients with very conforming attitudes tended to disagree least, and patients with moderately conforming attitudes were midway between. In open confrontation, the association of attitudes with behavior was clearly in the predicted direction.

An ambiguous source of conflict between patients and medical staff is complaints of pain and discomfort. A certain amount of complaining is expected by doctors and nurses—the acceptable amount being determined by the extensiveness of the surgical procedure, the age and sex of the patient, and the ethnic group of doctor or nurse (Zborowski, 1969). Since the acceptable level varies so, complaints of physical discomfort can be used by hospital patients as subtle weapons of conflict and as a means of getting attention. Therefore, it was predicted that patients who accepted "good-patient" norms would be likely to complain less than patients whose attitudes were deviant.

In all the types of surgery studied, patients with deviant attitudes had the highest percentage of those who complained a great deal about minor discomforts, such as nausea, gas pains, insomnia, headache, and lassitude. In routine and moderately serious surgery, patients with very conforming attitudes had the lowest percentage of complainers, but in very serious surgery, patients with moderately conforming attitudes had the lowest percentage of complainers. In short, patients with very conforming attitudes tended to complain comparatively less and patients with deviant attitudes tended to complain comparatively more no matter how serious their illness, while patients with moderately conforming attitudes seemed to complain according to how much attention was paid them. In routine surgery, where they got little attention, they had almost as high a percentage of complainers as patients with deviant attitudes. In very serious surgery, where they got a great deal of attention, they had the lowest percentage of complainers.

According to these data, most hospital patients comply unquestioningly with doctors' and nurses' orders and limit their complaints , but patients with deviant views of their role tend to argue with the medical staff and to register frequent minor complaints. The question to be explored now is what the medical staff's reaction was to conforming and deviant patients.

Table 11-1   Disagreements with staff, by patients' attitudes

	Patients' Attitudes		
Disagreements with Doctors[a]:	% Very Conforming (N = 32)	% Moderately Conforming (N = 39)	% Deviant (N = 27)
Never Disagreed	88	74	63
Disagreed	13	26	37
Disagreements with Nurses[b]:	% Very Conforming (N = 32)	% Moderately Conforming (N = 39)	% Deviant (N = 28)
Never Disagreed	94	85	64
Disagreed	6	15	36

[a]Five patients did not answer this question.
[b]Four patients did not answer this question.

Good, Average, and Problem Patients

From nurses' description of patients, Duff and Hollingshead (1968:221–222, their emphasis) concluded that patients were divided into two categories—"problem" and "no problem." As they put it, "The definition of a *problem* is related to the degree to which the patient needed physical care or was unable to comply with orders." In other words, ". . . *problem* patients obstructed work and *no problem* patients facilitated work." In this study, the doctors' and nurses' choice of "good patient," "average patient," or "problem patient" on the self-administered questionnaire they were asked to fill out at the end of the patients' stay, plus their invited remarks on the questionnaire and in private conversation with the researcher, all bore out the relationship between the label of good or problem patient and the extent to which the patient made trouble for them. Patients who were considered cooperative, uncomplaining, and stoical by the doctors and nurses were generally labeled good patients, no matter what their procedure or postoperative complications.

For instance, the private-duty nurse who spent 36 nights caring for a young woman with extensive postoperative complications following a gallbladder removal wrote: ". . . A very good patient to my way of thinking because no matter how much pain, she was always pleasant and not disagreeable. She *tried at all times* [sic] to be cooperative even though the tension in her was great at all times." After 29 consecutive days of nursing a 55-year-old man who had a shunt operation for cirrhosis of the liver followed by almost fatal complications, the private-duty nurse said, "I really enjoyed taking care of him. He was never grouchy, always cooperative—even though he was sick." In talking of a 63-year-old woman who was vice-president of her local chapter of Cancer Care, and who had an extensive operation for cancer, her surgeon said to the researcher, "You sent me a questionnaire on the most cooperative patient I've seen in 35 years. . . . She had massive surgery—she had complications—but she never complains. She knows she had a malignancy, but she doesn't have to be reassured—she says, 'The axe had to fall sometime.' "

In contrast, patients whom the doctors and nurses felt were uncooperative, constantly complaining, overemotional, and dependent were frequently considered problem patients, whether they had routine or very serious surgery. For example, the resident and intern labeled a problem patient a 62-year-old man who had a hernia repair with no complications, but who had been extremely apprehensive about the operation. In the patient's medical record, the resident noted that he was "overreacting to his condition," and had "multiple complaints related to his personality." The intern simply called him "a *kvetch.*" A 74-year-old man who had a gallbladder removal with many postoperative complications, some psychosomatic, was labeled a problem patient by the surgeon, resident, intern, and day staff nurse. In the questionnaire, the resident said the patient's uncooperativeness made it difficult to perform routine procedures on him. The surgeon wrote that the patient was "lachrymose, combative, and generally impossible." To the researcher, the surgeon added that patient had called him names, lied, and generally carried on.

Another patient considered a problem patient by her surgeon, the day staff nurse, and a private-duty nurse (but a good patient by the intern) was a pretty, 30-year-old divorcee. She told everyone about her family problems and described herself as a "devout coward." She had an uncomplicated gallbladder removal, but cried a lot and was given tranquilizers. The day head nurse said of her, "This patient seemed to have been pampered very much. She barely cooperated and seemed to have been extremely dependent on her mother. She was much more of a baby than most people having the same surgery."

The doctors and nurses on a case frequently did not agree on the evaluation of the patient. The same patient could be labeled good, problem, and average, and no patient was labeled a problem by every doctor or nurse who returned a questionnaire on him or her. The doctor or nurse who bore the brunt of the difficulty was usually the one who considered the patient a problem patient, while the others labeled him or her good or average. This supports the original contention that problem patients were those who created trouble for the medical staff.

A case in point was a young, well-educated man with a wife and child who was discovered to have a fast-growing, inoperable, and extremely painful form of cancer. He was very agitated before and after surgery, and he was demanding after surgery. But only the resident, with whom he fought over the question of pain medication, labeled him a problem patient. The resident said of him, "Very argumentative about getting his own way." The patient needed little physical care, so the rest of the staff was able, in the words of the head nurse, to "humor him." The private-duty nurse on the case, a young woman, refused to fill out a questionnaire but told me, "I couldn't stand the man." She felt he was tyrannical and he thought her incompetent. With him for twelve hours a day, she would, of course, have borne the brunt of his troublesome behavior.

It was reported earlier that, while most patients were obedient and uncomplaining, patients with deviant attitudes toward the hospital-patient role were more argumentative and complained more than patients with conforming attitudes. Did the doctors and nurses more often label patients with deviant attitudes problem patients? Although the percentage differences were not large, they were in the expected direction: patients with deviant attitudes were most often labeled problem patients by the time they left the hospital, patients with moderately conforming attitudes less frequently, and patients with very conforming attitudes least of all. (See Table 11-2.)

Table 11-2 Medical staff evaluations, by patients' attitudes[a]

Staff Evaluations		% Very Conforming (N = 33)	% Moderately Conforming (N = 42)	% Deviant (N = 28)
Attending	Good	67	74	64
Physician	Problem	3	5	14
Resident	Good	36	41	46
	Problem	6	7	11
Intern	Good	46	52	36
	Problem	3	7	11
Day Staff	Good	33	38	39
Nurse	Problem	3	7	14

[a]Omits those labeled "average" and "no answer." Non-return of a questionnaire is an indication that the patient did not register one way or another; in general, the doctors and nurses were more inclined to fill out questionnaires for patients they either admired or found troublesome.

Note, however, that very conforming patients were not labeled *good* patients to any great degree. One consequence of their uncomplaining, passive behavior might have been that they did not ask for help when they really needed it, so the nurses had to take time to do frequent checks on their physical status. For instance, a nurse wrote in the questionnaire of a 62-year-old woman who had very extensive abdominal surgery and was herself a nurse, "This patient was far too considerate of the nurses . . . she 'didn't want to bother' us and often remained quiet when in pain and had to be frequently checked for comfort." The nurse's use of quotation marks around the phrase "didn't want to bother" highlights the point that by not asking for needed attention, the patient, who should have known better, disrupted the usual routine. In this way the too stoical or too passive patient can also cause trouble.

Routine Management and Extraordinary Trouble

The analysis of the doctors' and nurses' evaluations of patients suggested that ease of management was the basic criterion for a label of good patient, and that patients who took time and attention felt to be unwarranted by their illness tended to be labeled problem patients. Robert Emerson (1971) points out that those troublemakers who can be managed routinely by social control agents are treated relatively leniently; only those who do not let themselves be managed routinely—who need extraordinary solutions to their problems—are singled out for stronger sanctions.

In the hospital studied, the medical staff expected a certain amount of complaining from surgical patients, particularly about pain. The most frequently mentioned method of handling *any* complaint was the use of sedative or narcotic drugs. Sixty-nine percent of the 499 questionnaires returned by the doctors and nurses mentioned drugs as the method used to handle complaints. The next most popular method was mentioned in only 34 percent of the returned questionnaires; it was talking to patients—reassuring, encouraging, explaining, ordering, scolding, and so on. Physical methods, such as turning, positioning, walking around, examining, making comfortable, and so on, were mentioned in 22 percent of the returned questionnaires, and methods that used mechanical devices were listed in 14 percent. (Mentions were multiple.) All the less favored methods took more time than the administration of a shot or oral dose of pain reliever or sedative every four hours.

Negative evaluations of relatively high percentages of patients who took up more time and were talked to fit in with the medical staff's own designation of which were the usual and which the less common methods of managing complaints. When the reports of amount of time spent with patients were cross-tabulated with evaluations of the patients, it was found that the patients with whom more time was spent were much more likely to be labeled problem patients than those with whom average or less than average time was spent. The doctors labeled as problem patients from 25 to 36 percent of those they said took up more than the usual amount of time for that type of surgery. Between 80 and 91 percent of the patients the doctors said took up less than the average amount of time for their type of surgery were labeled good patients. In short, the less of the doctor's time the patient took, the better he or she was viewed.

Similarly, doctors and nurses were more likely to be label problem patients those they remembered having talked to, and less likely to label them good patients. Residents and day staff nurses, who had the responsibility for the daily management of the surgical wards, labeled as problem patients one-quarter of those they singled out as having been talked to. (See Table 11-3.)

The assumption that problem patients would be those who gave doctors and nurses the most trouble was borne out by other data, namely, the evaluations of patients having different types of procedures. Hernia-repair patients, who were so easy to care for they were virtually anonymous to the interns, residents, and nurses, were rarely labeled problem patients. Patients who had gallbladders removed, or other moderately serious surgery, were most often described as problem patients by attending surgeons, residents and interns. Though medically routine, the postoperative condition of these patients called for a lot of attention, most of which was the residents' responsibility. It is not surprising that residents labeled as good patients only 19 percent of the moderately serious surgery cases. (See Table 11-4.)

To summarize, there are two variables involved in whether a doctor or nurse in charge views the patient as manageable by routine methods or as needing extraordinary solutions taking more time and attention. Patients manageable by routine methods are average—they make ordinary, expected trouble. These patients have routine illnesses, no postoperative complications, are moderately cooperative, and only occasionally complain of pain or discomfort. (Some staff members labeled them good patients, especially if they couldn't remember them too well.) Patients who might be expected to cause extraordinary trouble because of the problematic nature of their illness, but who only cause ordinary trouble because of their extraordinary cooperativeness and cheerful stoicism, are frequently

Table 11-3   Medical staff evaluations of patients, by reports of talking to patients[a]

Staff Evaluations		Questionnaire Responses	
		% Reporting Talk	% Reporting No Talk
Attending		N = 20	N = 71
Physician	Good	60	83
	Problem	10	7
Resident		N = 29	N = 44
	Good	45	66
	Problem	24	2
Intern		N = 32	N = 45
	Good	41	76
	Problem	13	7
Day Staff		N = 25	N = 46
Nurse	Good	36	63
	Problem	24	4

[a] Omits those labeled "average" and "no answer."

Table 11-4   Medical staff evaluations of patients, by surgical procedure[a]

Staff Evaluations		% Routine (N = 33)	% Moderately Serious (N = 31)	% Very Serious No Cancer (N = 14)	% Very Serious Cancer (N = 25)
			Type of Procedure		
Attending Physician	Good	76	65	71	64
	Problem	3	10	7	8
Resident	Good	46	19	43	60
	Problem	6	13	0	8
Intern	Good	39	36	64	56
	Problem	3	16	7	0
Day Staff Nurse	Good	42	29	36	40
	Problem	0	13	14	8

[a] Omits those labeled "average" and "no answer."

rewarded with the accolade "good patient" by doctors and nurses who do not ordinarily use that label, and "great patient" by the rest.

As for those labeled problem patients, they are of two types. The first has an ordinary illness but takes up more time and attention than is warranted by the medical condition because he or she is uncooperative and/or complains and argues much of the time. Doctors and nurses consider such behavior unnecessary and therefore extraordinary trouble, and the patient is soundly condemned. The second type of problem patient has an extraordinary medical status, such as severe complications, poor prognosis, or difficult diagnosis. Troublesome behavior of the sort described above, while not approved of, is somewhat forgiven as understandable given the patient's medical condition. The first kind of problem patient seems to be considered deliberately deviant—willfully causing extraordinary trouble; the second kind of problem patient seems to be considered an accidental deviant—responding with troublesome behavior to an extraordinarily difficult situation beyond his or her control (cf. Lorber, 1967).

Possible Consequences of Being Labeled a Problem Patient

What do doctors and nurses do about those patients whose deviant behavior hinders their efficient routines? In the study reported here, patients whose behavior was troublesome and who did not respond to tranquilizers or sedation were sent home or recommended to a convalescent center where the nurses were trained to do psychotherapy. In one case, a staff psychiatrist was asked to see a troublesome dying patient who had been in psychiatric treatment before his illness. In short, deviant behavior on the part of these mostly middle-class, paying, short-term surgical patients was treated moderately permissively by the medical professionals who cared for them.

Indeed, the hospital tried various ways to meet the socio-emotional needs of its patients. A "patient-relations nurse coordinator" had been appointed for the general surgical wards for a short time before this research was done. This role was modeled after the "clinical nurse specialist" who worked closely with the open-heart surgeon. (See Bandman, Wolpin, and Rehm, 1964.) On the general surgery wards, where there were many more attending surgeons and their patients to contend with, this nurse-liaison did not work out. It was said in personal communication during preliminary fieldwork that the medical personnel felt she was spying on them, while the patients did not feel their complaints were taken care of adequately.

Another short-lived experiment that took place just after the fieldwork was done was to allow all patients on the surgical wards the same all-day visiting hours as the private-room patients. This attempt to give patients additional support lasted about two months. Given the fact that with regular visiting hours, more complaints by patients were reported on the staff questionnaires by the evening staff nurses than any other shift (evening visits were the most popular), it is probable that patient-staff conflict was exacerbated, not eased, by the constant presence of relatives.

Other studies have found that the troublesome patient tends to be somewhat neglected by the medical staff. Interns have admitted giving "superior care to the better liked, with minimum but adequate care to those not liked" (Daniels, 1960:263). Those not liked were patients who tended to be complaining and uncooperative and to ask a lot of questions. Responding to hypothetical situations, 40 nurses said they would do more for the non-compliant patient in the short run, but in the long run, predicted they would do more for the compliant patient (Keller, 1971). In their study of dying patients, Glaser and Strauss (1965) found that nurses scolded, reprimanded, and then avoided those patients who asked a lot of questions, created emotional scenes, or refused to cooperate with hospital routines. Roth and Eddy (1967:106–109), in their study of rehabilitation patients, noted that abusive and uncooperative patients were discharged from the ward, and thus denied retraining. However, young patients with a greater chance of successful rehabilitation than older ones were treated more leniently. Roth's (1963a:41) research on long-term tuberculosis patients showed that "noisy agitation" sometimes resulted in slightly earlier discharge, especially if the staff felt the patient might leave against medical advice. But he also found hospitals with locked wards for "recalcitrant" patients whose medical status was still poor (Roth, 1963a:25). The rare cooperative and cured patient who didn't want to leave the hospital left the staff in a complete quandary, and a psychiatrist was used as a last resort (Roth, 1963a:48).

Of all these responses to extraordinarily troublesome patients, the use of psychiatrists has the most potentially momentous consequences. Meyer and Mendelson (1961) studied 60 requests for psychiatric consultation with patients on medical and surgical wards, and found that a disruptive patient was first considered uncooperative or bad, but then defined as irrational and irresponsible, or "crazy," and a psychiatrist was called in. If a patient refuses to submit quietly to hospital routines and is referred to a psychiatrist because of disruptive behavior, he or she is labeled as someone with psychiatric problems. If the fact that he or she had seen a psychiatrist is entered into the medical records, the information becomes a permanent part of his or her future identity as a patient for all other professionals who have access to this set of records. His or her future behavior

will be interpreted in the light of the putative psychiatric problems, and any opposition to the way he or she is treated will never be taken seriously. Even if the
information is not officially recorded, ward scuttlebutt will certainly spread the
word around—problem patients are discussed *ad infinitum*. For the remainder of
the particular hospitalization, the patient will be treated as psychotic or neurotic,
and not as someone with possible legitimate complaints (cf. Phillips, 1963, and
Rosenhan, 1973).

Summary

On the basis of an attitude questionnaire administered to 103 surgical patients before their operations, this study found that most general-hospital patients enter the hospital feeling they should be obedient, cooperative, objective
about their illness, and expect attention only if they are very ill. As other researchers have found, the better educated and younger patients tended to have
more autonomous or deviant attitudes toward being a hospital patient. This study
found that patients with deviant attitudes tended to argue more with the
residents, interns, and nurses, and to complain more about minor discomforts as
a way of getting attention.

Although patients feel that doctors and nurses always approve of obedience,
cooperation, and undemandingness, a questionnaire administered to the medical
staff at the end of the patients' stay in the hospital revealed that the staff's
evaluations of the patients under their care depended on the amount of trouble
these patients gave them. In general, cooperative, uncomplaining, and stoical patients *were* considered good patients, but the staff expected patients to make them
aware of their needs; that is, to ask for attention when it was needed medically.
Patients whom the doctors and nurses felt were uncooperative, overemotional,
and who complained when it was not medically warranted were considered problem patients only by the staff member who had to bear the brunt of the trouble.
Patients who did not respond to sedation or tranquilizers—the chief methods of
handling complaints of pain and discomfort—but instead had to be reassured,
encouraged, given explanations or exhortations, and who therefore took up more
of the staff's time than they felt warranted by the extent of surgery, were also
considered problem patients to a greater degree than those who took up an
"average" amount of time and attention.

Patients who had the most routine surgery were usually labeled good patients, as were the very cooperative seriously ill patients. The patients who had
surgery that is major and painful by lay standards, but routine by medical standards, were labeled problem patients to the greatest degree, particularly by the
residents, who were primarily responsible for their care. (In this study, most of
these patients were, in the doctors' words, "well-nourished" middle-aged
women, which may have added to the impatience the residents, both male and
female, showed with them.)

In sum, doctors and nurses expect to carry out their work by well-established
routines, with a minimum of interruption from patients. Those patients who
make no trouble at all, who do not interrupt the smoothness of medical routines,
are likely to be considered *good* patients by the medical staff. In this study, good

patients usually had routine surgery and were out of the hospital within a week, or had uncomplicated major surgery and accepted whatever was done to them cheerfully and cooperatively. Doctors and nurses tend to consider *average* patients those whose complaints are medically warranted, who respond to established routines for handling such complaints, and who therefore take up the expected amount of time for their type of illness. In this study, most of the average patients had uncomplicated major surgery, complained a fair amount about pain and discomfort, but were satisfied when their requests for attention were answered with pain medication every four hours for two or three days.

Problem patients are of two kinds. Those who are seriously ill, and who complain a great deal, are very emotional, anxious, and need a lot of reassurance, encouragement, and attention from the staff are problematic, but "forgivable" because the situation is not of their own making. In this study, they were often given the time and attention they demanded, particularly if they were grateful for it. Nonetheless, the extraordinary amount of time and attention they took up made them "problem patients." (Conversely, seriously ill patients who were extraordinarily cheerful, cooperative, uncomplaining, and objective about their illness were considered *great* patients and talked about after discharge as "ideal.") Patients who are *not* seriously ill in the staff's eyes, but who nevertheless act as if they are by complaining, crying, and refusing to cooperate with medical routines, are the most soundly condemned by the staff. Such problem patients, in this study, were tranquilized, sometimes discharged early, and, in one case, referred to a psychiatrist—types of response to wilfully troublesome patients other researchers have also found.

Thus, the consequences of deliberate deviance in the general hospital can be medical neglect or a stigmatizing label, while conformity to good-patient norms is usually a return home with only a surgical scar.

References

Bandman, E., S. Wolpin and D. Rehm.
  1964 "The patient-relations nurse coordinator." American Journal of Nursing 64 (September): 133–135.

Brown, Esther Lucile.
  1966 "Nursing and patient care." Pp. 176–203 in Fred Davis (ed.) The Nursing Profession. New York: Wiley.

Cartwright, Ann.
  1964 Human Relations and Hospital Care. London: Routledge and Kegan Paul.

Coser, R.L.
  1956 "A home away from home." Social Problems 4 (July): 3–17.
  1962 Life in the Ward. East Lansing: Michigan State University Press.

Daniels, M.J.
  1960 "Affect and its control in the medical intern." American Journal of Sociology 61 (November): 259–267.

Davis F.
  1960 "Uncertainty in medical prognosis, clinical and functional." American Journal of Sociology 66 (July): 41–47.

Davis, M.S. and R.P. von der Lippe.
1968 "Discharge from hospital against medical advice: A study of reciprocity in the doctor-patient relationship." Social Science and Medicine 1: 336–342.

Duff, Raymond S. and August B. Hollingshead.
1968 Sickness and Society. New York: Harper and Row.

Emerson, Robert M.
1971 "Trouble and unmanageability: Working notes on social control and practical action." Unpublished manuscript.

Friedson, Eliot.
1966 "Disability as social deviance." Pp. 71–99 in Marvin B. Sussman (ed.), Sociology and Rehabilitation. Washington, D.C.: American Sociological Association.
1967 "Review essay: Health factories, the new industrial sociology." Social Problems 14 (Spring): 493–500.
1970 Profession of Medicine. New York: Dodd, Mead.

Glaser, Barner G. and Anselm L. Strauss.
1965 Awareness of Dying. Chicago: Aldine.

Goffman, Erving.
1961 Asylums. Garden City, New York: Doubleday Anchor.

Keller, N.S.
1971 "Compliance, previous access and provision of services by registered nurses." Journal of Health and Social Behavior 12 (December): 321–330.

King, Stanley H.
1962 Perceptions of Illness and Medical Practice. New York: Russell Sage Foundation.

Lorber, J.
1967 "Deviance as performance: The case of illness." Social Problems 14 (Winter): 302–310.
1971 Going Under the Knife: A Study of the Sick Role in the Hospital. Unpublished Ph.D. Thesis. New York: New York University.

Meyer, E. and M. Mendelson.
1961 "Psychiatric consultations with patients on medical and surgical wards: Patterns and processes." Psychiatry 24 (August): 197–220.

Parsons, Talcott.
1951 The Social System. Glencoe: Free Press.

Phillips, D.L.
1963 "Rejection: A possible consequence of seeking help for mental disorders." American Sociological Review 28 (December): 963–972.

Quint, J.C.
1965 "Institutionalized practices of information control." Psychiatry 28 (May): 119–132.

Rosengren, William R. and Mark Lefton.
1969 Hospitals and Patients. New York: Atherton.

Rosenhan, D.L.
1973 "On being sane in insane places." Science 179 (January 19): 250–258.

Roth, Julius A.
1963a Timetables: Structuring the Passage of Time in Hospital Treatment and Other Careers. Indianapolis: Bobbs-Merrill.
1963b "Information and the control of treatment in tuberculosis hospitals." Pp. 293–318 in Eliot Freidson (ed.), The Hospital in Modern Society. New York: Free Press.

Roth, Julius A. and Elizabeth M. Eddy.
1967 Rehabilitation for the Unwanted. New York: Atherton.

Shiloh, A.
  1965   "Equalitarian and hierarchal patients: An investigation among Hadassah Hospital patients." Medical Care 3 (April–June): 87–95.

Skipper, James K., Jr.
  1964   The Social Obligations of Hospitalized Patients: A System Analysis. Unpublished Ph.D. Thesis. Evanston: Northwestern University.
  1965   "Communication and the hospitalized patient." Pp. 61–82 in James K. Skipper, Jr., and Robert C. Leonard (eds.), Social Interaction and Patient Care. Philadelphia: J.B. Lippincott.

Tagliacozzo, Daisy L. and Hans O. Mauksch.
  1972   "The patient's view of the patient's role." Pp. 172–185 in E. Gartly Jaco (ed.), Patients, Physicians and Illness. Second Edition. New York: Free Press (chap. 10 in this volume).

Zborowski, Mark.
  1969   People in Pain. San Francisco: Jossey-Bass.

RICHARD T. SMITH

12 Disability and the Recovery Process: Role of Social Networks

The disability and rehabilitation process may be viewed as a sequence of events associated with the passage of an individual from the onset of illness to recovery. This general process involves three primary stages: illness behavior, treatment, and restoration. Each stage involves a transition in role behavior for the impaired individual, as well as changes in his primary social network, and at designated stages treatment and rehabilitation services function as agents of primary change (Rabinowitz and Spiro, 1964; Haber and Smith, 1971). The determination of factors that impede or facilitate rehabilitation constitutes an important facet of this process. Of particular concern is the role of social networks, both formal and informal, and their effect on subsequent rehabilitation and recovery.

Formal intervention systems providing supportive services for the disabled may be necessary but not sufficient elements in the recovery process. In addition to these formal networks, informal social supports may play an important role (McKinlay, 1972:130–131). As sources of support in time of crisis and during recovery, they may complement the formal intervention system. It is only under extreme conditions, when the informal network of support fails, that the individual must rely solely on the formal one (Susser and Watson, 1971:193–203).

Social support is described by Kaplan and his colleagues in terms of the availability of socially supportive networks, which include "the people one communicates with, and the links within these relationships" (1977:54). In examining the crisis of physical illness, Moos and Tsu point out that the social environment as a resource includes the relationships of patients and their families and the social supports in the wider community (such as friends and clergy) (1977:17).

Studies have shown that this informal social network, comprising family, friends, and neighbors, constitutes an important supportive resource for patients recovering from major health crises. In their study of heart patients, Croog and Levine (1977:256–272) found that patients reported extensive use of informal networks, as part of their "armory of services," in the process of recovery. The availability and utilization of kin and non-kin social networks may be a function of the level of social integration; "the better integrated the individual the higher the degree of assistance he receives" (Croog et al., 1972:39; see also Hyman, 1972). Other evidence presented by Croog and his colleagues suggests that except for immediate health care, limited reliance is placed on formal institutions and

The project upon which this report is based was performed pursuant to Contract No. SSA 72-2858 with the Social Security Administration, D.H.E.W. Analysis and interpretation of data represent the author's views only.
Revision of paper presented at the 72nd annual meeting of the American Sociological Association, Chicago, 1977. Used by permission of the author.

218

agencies by individuals recovering from severe illness (1972:39). A similar finding was noted by Finlayson and McEwen (1977:162) in their study of heart patients in Scotland.

Finlayson and McEwen also made similar observations about the supportive role of informal social networks. They noted that favorable recovery was associated with socially supportive networks, in terms of lay help and consultation, and a wider range of kin and non-kin sources tended to positively affect outcome (Finlayson, 1976:102; Finlayson and McEwen, 1977:157). New *et al.* (1968) and D'Afflitti and Weitz (1977) found that significant others, i.e., family and non-kin members, played a supportive role among heart and stroke patients undergoing recovery and rehabilitation. Litman (1966), on the other hand, did not find a significant relationship between family solidarity (i.e., level of social integration) and favorable rehabilitation in his study of orthopedically disabled patients. However, he did find evidence that the family played a supportive role in the patient's convalescence.

In general, similar observations about the supportive role of informal social networks have been made for other social situations, such as bereavement (Walker *et al.*, 1977), pregnancy (McKinlay, 1973), and preventive health behavior (Slesinger, 1976; Langlie, 1977).

With disabled adults currently numbering an estimated 15.6 million in the American population (Schechter, 1977), further investigation of the role of social networks in the recovery process, especially those outside the formal intervention system, seems appropriate. This study is both a replication and an extension of studies relating socially supportive networks to rehabilitation and recovery of the disabled in society. Results presented include an analysis of the extent to which social networks affect the recovery of disabled adults with chronic conditions, and in particular, the role of informal networks in this process. Other findings relate to the role of the formal intervention system, specifically vocational rehabilitation services, in improving outcome.

Data and Methods

The study population consisted of worker disability applicants processed through the Social Security Disability Determination Unit (DDU) in one metropolitan community during a one-year period (1971–72). A random sample of 950 subjects was selected from the total pool of disability applicants (3,033) who met the study requirements. New applicants with physical disabilities (excluding neoplasms and mental disorders), aged twenty-one or older, and resident in the area were eligible for inclusion. Data were derived from personal interviews* and from the records of disability and rehabilitation service agencies.

A comparison of the sampled study group with the target population reveals a high degree of equivalence (Table 12-1) in that most of the selected characteris-

---

*Of the 950 applicants initially in the sample, 770 (81.1 percent) were interviewed. Attrition was due to refusals (2.9 percent), death (8.8 percent), movement out of the area (5.8 percent), and lost to follow-up (1.4 percent).

Table 12-1   Comparison of sample with population distribution of disabled by selected characteristics (percentages)

Characteristic		Sample (N = 950)	Population (N = 3,033)
Primary Disabling Condition			
Cardiovascular (390–458)		37.9	39.6
Musculoskeletal (710–738)		12.9	13.3
Digestive (520–577)		5.7	6.2
Respiratory (460–519)		5.1	6.0
Nervous system (320–359)		4.7	3.7
Diabetes (250)		4.2	3.8
Visual impairments (360–389)		4.1	3.5
Genitourinary (580–629)		2.0	2.3
Accidents & injuries (800–999)		11.7	10.8
Other specified		6.9	6.0
Ill-defined & unspecified		4.8	4.8
Mobility			
Able to go outside w/o help		71.6	73.2
Able to go outside w/help		15.9	15.2
Restricted indoors		4.1	4.1
Institution		5.9	5.6
Unknown		2.5	1.9
Sex			
Male		67.2	67.5
Female		32.8	32.5
Race			
White		33.5	36.0
Black		27.3	26.4
Unknown		39.2	37.6
Education	Ave. (yrs.):	*8.3*	*8.3*
<6 years		16.0	15.2
6–8 years		34.4	37.5
9–11 years		26.1	24.6
12 years		16.8	15.3
>12 years		4.7	5.7
Unknown		2.0	1.7
Marital Status			
Married		73.5	72.7
Single		25.7	26.5
Unknown		0.8	0.8
Age at Alleged Onset			
* of Disability (AOD)*	Ave. age:	*50.8*	*51.1*
30		4.8	5.6
30–39		10.3	7.8
40–49		19.8	20.8
50–59		45.3	44.7
60–(64)		19.1	20.5
Unknown		0.7	0.6

Table 12-1 (Continued)

Year of A.O.D.		
≤1969	15.3	12.8
1970	16.6	15.0
1971	56.1	58.3
1972	11.3	13.3
Unknown	0.7	0.6
Disability Determination Status		
Allowed	61.3	61.1
Denied	38.7	38.9
Occupational Status		
Professional, technical, & managerial	7.7	7.8
Clerical & sales	13.5	12.9
Craftsmen, foremen, & kindred workers	18.8	17.8
Operatives & service workers	42.8	46.3
Laborers	15.0	12.5
Unknown	2.5	2.7

Variables used in this study include measures of outcome,* recovery (dependent variable), formal and informal social network as independent variables, and selected sociodemographic characteristics.

Recovery status is a composite index of outcome measures indicative of independence. Four measures are included: employment, limitations of mobility, source of income, and physician care. Current employment refers to work activity at the time of the follow-up interview. The variable, limitations of mobility, is defined in terms of current limitations of activity and restrictions in activities of daily living. Another outcome category includes a measure of current economic independence using the variable, present source of income (self, family, or formal agency). Finally, an indication of present health is reflected in being under a physician's care. In general, work activity, unrestricted mobility, self-derived income, and not being under a physician's care are indicative of greater independence and, hence, more favorable outcome in recovery.

Indicators of formal intervention, that is, agency assistance and agent support, include disability compensation, use of physician at time of disability evaluation, use of rehabilitation services, agency referrals, contact with the vocational rehabilitation (VR) agency, and formal agents (e.g., physician and social worker). Noninvolvement with formal intervention systems indicates the use of other social networks, including resources derived from one's informal support structure such as self or significant others.

Other measures relevant in this analysis are severity of disabling condition at the time of limitation, age at onset of disability, pre- or post-onset change in level tics examined show similarity. Overall, this tabulation suggests that the sample is similar to the original population from which it was drawn.

---

*An outcome may be defined as some measurable level of functional status comparable over time. This may range from complete independent social functioning, such as resumption of usual role activity, to limited functional improvement, such as reduction in physical limitations, to no change or to deterioration in functional status (Peterson, 1961).

of social activity, recent health, and basic sociodemographic characteristics (such as sex, education, occupation, and pre-onset income).

Data were analyzed by means of cross-tabulations and regression analysis. Multiple regression analysis was performed to assess the effect of each independent variable on the dependent variable, recovery status, with adjustments made for all other independent variables. This statistical technique describes the strength of the relationship, and the square of the multiple correlation coefficient (R^2) indicates the proportion of variation in the dependent variable as explained by the independent variables. In addition, through use of a "backward elimination" procedure, predictor (independent) variables can be removed from the regression equation that initially included all predictor variables, if such variables fail to augment the overall accuracy of the prediction (Nie, 1975:320–359).

Results

Discrete relationships between each independent variable and recovery are shown in Table 12-2. Not unexpectedly, those younger in age at onset, with less severity at the time of limitation, and who were denied disability compensation, showed greater recovery. Furthermore, the disabled who had received rehabilitation services and recently had improved in health were more likely to recover. These factors, in combination, may be reflected in the increased level of social activity of those recovering from their disability.

More interesting are the findings of association between recovery and primary support derived from one's informal social network, with the absence of formal agent support (physician) at the time of the disability evaluation. The

Table 12-2   Relationships between independent variables and high recovery status (Base N = 770)

Independent Variable	Relationship	N	x^2(df)	P<
Rehabilitation services	received	728	35.16(8)	.001
Age at alleged onset of disability	younger	720	53.56(16)	.001
Primary supportive agent	informal (self, other)	721	30.28(12)	.01
Severity of disability	lower	714	239.54(8)	.001
Recent health	improved	727	36.89(8)	.001
Social activity change index (pre-post)	more active than before	728	37.62(8)	.001
Disability determination	denied compensation	729	95.36(4)	.001
Sex	female	729	14.75(4)	.01
Education	higher	728	37.12(16)	.01
Income (pre-onset)	(none)	707	16.38(16)	NS
Lifetime occupation	(none)	729	37.77(32)	NS
Physician support (at disability evaluation)	absence of support	697	41.81(16)	.001
Referral source (to SS-DDU)*	(none)	703	5.78(8)	NS
VR referral by SS-DDU	(none)	729	4.68(4)	NS

*SS-DDU = Social Security Disability Determination Unit.

evidence suggests the importance of socially supportive networks beyond the formal intervention system.

A more systematic presentation of the relative influence of each of the independent variables on recovery is shown in the regression analysis (Table 12-3). A total of fourteen independent variables were included in the initial regression equation. Half were excluded in the final analysis, leaving seven variables which in combination explain 31.5 percent of the variation in the dependent variable. The primary source of explained variance can be attributed to severity of disability, age at alleged onset of disability (AOD), and disability determination (totaling 26.9 percent). It is interesting to note also that rehabilitation service has little, if any, influence on recovery. Other variables apparently having an influence include primary support agent, recent health, and index of change in social activity.

Favorable recovery, implying greater independence in work and economic status as well as in health and mobility, appears to be associated with lesser severity of the disabling condition, younger age at alleged onset of disability, denied determination status, recent improvement in health, primary support in dealing with disability derived from self and informal social network, and finally social activities that are not adversely affected by disability.

From the other perspective, individuals whose recovery is less than favorable exhibit characteristics suggesting dependence and reliance on formal systems for support and assistance. Such individuals can be characterized as older compensation cases with more severe disabling conditions, which have continued over time as reflected in poor health, who tend to rely on formal agencies for assistance and who have experienced a decrease in social activities following the onset of disability.

What is interesting in these findings is the fact that favorable recovery is associated with an individual's informal social network, implying that this factor is a viable source of support. Although the relationship is not strong, its presence as a determinant does suggest the importance of informal supportive agents in the process of disability and rehabilitation.

Finally, involvement with the vocational rehabilitation (VR) agency suggests support from formal intervention, which should increase the likelihood of recovery. For the adult, VR contact generally implies assistance to those with potential capacity to recover, that is, the younger and less severely disabled. Therefore, one

Table 12-3   Regression analysis for recovery status (Base N = 770)

Variable[a]	Multiple R	R^2	R^2 Change	Simple R	B
Rehabilitation services	.058	.003	.003	.058	0.159
Age at alleged onset of disability	.223	.050	.046	−.223	−0.017
Primary supportive agent	.254	.064	.015	−.133	−0.225
Severity of disability	.499	.249	.185	−.464	−1.112
Recent health	.517	.267	.018	.149	0.364
Social activity change index	.526	.276	.009	.136	0.246
Disability determination	.561	.315	.038	.363	0.825
(Constant) N = 713					7.607

[a]Excludes initial predictor variables of sex, education (pre-onset), income, lifetime occupation, physician support (at disability evaluation), referral source (to SS-DDU), and VR referral by SS-DDU; initial R^2 = .321.

would expect that contact with the VR agency, as a measure of formal intervention, would further increase recovery. Those without contact would be expected to show the reverse.

Data from this study on VR contact are presented in Table 12-4. The results are contrary to conventional expectations. Disabled adults without formal contact with the VR agency show a similar rate of recovery as those with contact (56 percent and 58 percent, respectively). Also, about twice as many disabled do not have contact with the VR agency, yet proportionately, the rate of recovery is about the same.

Conclusions

Rehabilitation services reportedly refer to all kinds regularly provided by agencies and individuals, including clinics, physicians, and such public agencies as state VR services (Treital, 1970:2; 1977:2, 9). One emphasis in this study has been on examining the role of formal agents, including those in VR systems. However, we have also observed the effects of other primary agents, particularly those from the informal social network, that lend support to the disabled worker during the process of rehabilitation and recovery. In general, the majority of disabled adults received rehabilitation services, of whatever kind, from sources other than the traditional formal intervention system of rehabilitation.

It is suggested that these support systems, informal and formal nonrehabilitation networks, constitute a viable community resource. Schematically, we can identify four general types of disabled groups in terms of outcome and the provision of rehabilitation services (Figure 12-1). Rather than using the formal rehabilitation system, as might be commonly expected, the majority of the disabled apparently use other sources of services and seemingly rely on other supportive networks in the community. These cases are identified as the nonintervention success in Figure 12-1.

There may be limited reliance placed on other formal systems of medical care in the community; a great deal of reliance may be placed on informal social networks, such as the family, associated kin, and friends, as well as on formal nonrehabilitation agencies and institutions, such as unions, employers, and fraternal and religious organizations. Another element may be self-reliance. These formal and informal networks seem to constitute the effective support system leading to successful rehabilitation and recovery of the disabled adult.

Table 12-4 Relationship between VR contact and recovery (Base N = 770)

VR Contact	Recovery				
	Low		High		
	No.	%	No.	%	Total
No contact	224	(44)	279	(56)	503
Contact	96	(42)	130	(58)	226
Total	320	(44)	409	(56)	729

$x^2 = 0.19$, NS.

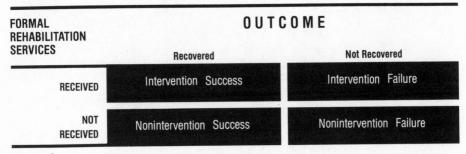

Figure 12-1.

In the recovery process, emphasis tends to be placed on medical care as the single most relevant source of support, to the exclusion of other relevant sources. However, family and non-kin appear to play a vital role, as reflected in the observation made by Croog and Levine in their study of heart patients: "Although it is commonly hypothesized that modern industrial institutions and organizations of the larger society are taking over many of the roles of the traditional kin groups, in this heart patient study population kin and quasi-kin played important supportive roles" (1977:262). The implication of this finding is evident. The formal intervention system is complemented by an "armory of services" that include links with informal social networks. In time of crisis and in coping with severe illness, these social networks constitute important supportive resources for the individual and appear to be effective in facilitating recovery.

Recognition and utilization of this extended resource base by providers of health care may be an effective supplemental tool of therapeutic intervention. As Kaplan and his colleagues suggest, "modern family medical practice should include a workup of one's 'personal networks' . . . and consider the possibility of providing or helping provide more functional social networks as an integral responsibility of the health care system" (1977:56).

References

Croog, Sydney H., and Sol Levine
    1977   *The Heart Patient Recovers.* N.Y.: Human Sciences Press.

Croog, S., A. Lipson, and S. Levine
    1972   Help Patterns in Severe Illness: The Roles of Kin Network, Non-Family Resources, and Institutions. *J. Marriage and the Family,* 34:32–41.

D'Afflitti, J. G., and G. W. Weitz
    1977   Rehabilitating the Stroke Patient Through Patient-Family Groups in R. H. Moos (ed.). *Coping with Physical Illness.* N.Y.: Plenum Medical Book Co.

Finlayson, Angela
    1976   Social Networks as Coping Resources. Lay Help and Consultation Patterns used by Women in Husbands' Post-Infarction Career. *Soc. Sci. & Med.,* 10:97–103.

Finlayson, Angela, and James McEwen
    1977   *Coronary Heart Disease and Patterns of Living.* N.Y.: Prodist.

Haber, Lawrence, and Richard Smith
    1971   Disability and Deviance: Normative Adaptation of Role Behavior. *American Sociological Review,* 36:87–97.

Hyman, M. D.
1972 Social Isolation and Performance in Rehabilitation. *J. Chron. Dis.,* 25:85–97.

Kaplan, B. H., J. C. Cassel, and S. Gore
1977 Social Support and Health. *Medical Care Supplement,* 15(5):47–58.

Langlie, Jean K.
1977 Social Networks, Health Beliefs, and Preventive Health Behavior. *J. Health & Soc. Behavior,* 18:244–260.

Litman, T. J.
1966 The Family and Physical Rehabilitation. *J. Chron. Dis.,* 19:211–217.

McKinlay, J. B.
1972 Some Approaches and Problems in the Study of the Use of Services—an Overview. *J. of Health and Social Behavior,* 13:115–152.

1973 Social Networks, Lay Consultation and Help-seeking Behavior. *Soc. Forces,* 51:275–292.

Moos, R. H., and V. D. Tsu
1977 The Crisis of Physical Illness. An Overview, in Rudolph H. Moos (ed.). *Coping with Physical Illness.* N.Y.: Plenum Medical Book Co.

New, P. K., *et al.,* Ruscio, A. T., Priest, R. P., Petritsi, D., and L. A. George
1968 The Support Structure of Heart and Stroke Patients. *Soc. Sci. and Med.,* 2:185–200.

Nie, N. H., Hull, C. H., Jenkins, J. G., Steinbrenner, K., and D. H. Bent
1975 *Statistical Package for the Social Sciences.* 2nd ed. N.Y.: McGraw-Hill Book Co.

Peterson, Warren A.
1961 *Service and Cost Analysis. Final Report* (Kansas City Community Studies, Inc.). Pub. No. 134.

Rabinowitz, Herbert, and Spiro Mitsos
1964 Rehabilitation as Planned Social Change: A Conceptual Framework. *Journal of Health and Human Behavior,* 5:2–14.

Schechter, E. S.
1977 Employment and Work Adjustments of the Disabled: 1972 Survey of Disabled and Non-Disabled Adults. *Soc. Sec. Bull.,* 40 (7):3–15.

Slesinger, D. P.
1976 The Utilization of Preventive Medical Services by Urban Black Mothers in David Mechanic: *The Growth of Bureaucratic Medicine.* N.Y.: John Wiley & Sons.

Susser, M. W., and W. Watson
1971 *Sociology in Medicine.* London: Oxford Press.

Treitel, Ralph
1970 *Rehabilitation of the Disabled.* 1966 Social Security Survey of the Disabled, Report No. 12.

1977 *Rehabilitation of Disabled Adults,* 1972. Social Security Disability Survey 1972: Disabled and Non-disabled Adults. Report No. 3.

Walker, K. N., A. MacBride, and M. L. S. Vachon
1977 Social Support Networks and the Crisis of Bereavement. *Soc. Sci. and Med.,* 11:35–41.

BARNEY G. GLASER

13 Disclosure of Terminal Illness

One of the most difficult of doctor's dilemmas is whether or not to tell a patient that he has a terminal illness. The ideal rule offered by doctors is that they should decide for each patient whether he really wants to know and can "take it." However, since, depending on the study, 69 to 90 per cent of doctors favor not telling their patients about terminal illness,[1] rather than making a separate decision for each patient, it appears that most doctors have a general standard from which the same decision flows for most patients—that he should not be told. This finding also indicates that the standard of "do not tell" receives very strong colleagueal support.

Many conditions reduce a doctor's inclination to make a separate decision for each case. Few doctors get to know each terminal patient well enough to judge his desire for disclosure or his capacity to withstand the shock of disclosure. Getting to know a patient well enough takes more time than doctors typically have. Furthermore, with the current increase of patient loads, doctors will have less and less time for each patient, which creates the paradox: with more patients dying in hospitals, more will not be told they are dying. Even when a doctor has had many contacts with a particular patient, class or educational differences or personality clashes may prevent effective communication. Some doctors simply feel unable to handle themselves well enough during disclosure to make a complicated illness understandable. If a doctor makes a mistake, he may be liable for malpractice. Some doctors will announce an impending death only when a clear-cut pathologist's report is available. Others do not tell because they do not want the patient to "lean" on them for emotional support, or because they simply wish to preserve peace on the ward by preventing a scene.

Similarly, a number of conditions encourage disclosure of impending death regardless of the individual patient's capacity to withstand it. Some doctors disclose to avoid losing the patient's confidence should he find out indirectly

[1]Feifel, H., "Death," in N. L. Farberow (ed.), *Taboo Topics*, New York: Atherton Press, 1963, p. 17.

This paper derives from an investigation of terminal care in hospitals supported by N.I.H. Grant NU 00047. I wish to thank Anselm Strauss for helpful comments and criticisms on an earlier draft. Other papers from this study are: A. Strauss, B. G. Glaser and J. Quint, "The Non-accountability of Terminal Care," *Hospitals*, 36:73–87, January 16, 1964; B. G. Glaser and A. Strauss, "The Social Loss of Dying Patients," *Amer. J. Nursing*, 64:119–121, June, 1964; B. G. Glaser and A. Strauss, "Awareness Contexts and Social Interaction," *Amer. Soc. Rev.*, 29:669–678, October, 1964; B. G. Glaser and A. L. Strauss, "Temporal Aspects of Dying as a Non-scheduled Status Passage," *Amer. J. Sociology*, July, 1965; B. G. Glaser and A. L. Strauss, "Discovery of Substantive Theory: A Basic Strategy Underlying Qualitative Research," *Amer. Behav. Scientist*, 8:5–12, February, 1965; J. C. Quint and A. Strauss, "Nursing Students, Assignments and Dying Patients," *Nursing Outlook*, Vol. 12, January, 1964; B. G. Glaser, "The Constant Comparative Method of Qualitative Analysis," *Social Problems* 12:436–445, Spring, 1965; two books, B. G. Glaser and A. Strauss, *Awareness of Dying*, Chicago: Aldine Press, 1966, and B. G. Glaser and A. Strauss, *Discovery of Grounded Theory*, Chicago: Aldine Press, 1970.

Reprinted from *Journal of Health & Human Behavior*, 7:83–91, Summer, 1966, by permission of the author and Publisher.

through other sources, such as changes in his physical condition, accidentally overhearing the staff discuss his case or comparing himself with other patients. Telling also justifies radical treatment or a clinical research offer; it also reduces the doctor's need to keep up a cheerful but false front. Some tell so that the patient can put his affairs in order, plan for his family's future or reduce his pace of living; others, because family members request it. Of course, if the chances for recovery or successful treatment are relatively good, a doctor is naturally more likely to disclose a possibly terminal illness; disclosing a skin cancer is easier than disclosing bone cancer.

The combined effect of these conditions—some of which may induce conflicting approaches to the same patient—is to make it much easier for doctors to apply to all patients a flat "no, he should not be told." For when people are in doubt about an action, especially when the doubt arises from inability to calculate the possible effects of many factors on which there is little information, it is almost always easier and safer to not act.[2]

Response to Disclosure

The intent of this paper is to formulate a descriptive, process model for understanding disclosure of terminal illness. This model combines *both* (1) the stages typically present in the response process stimulated by such disclosure *and* (2) the characteristic forms of interaction between the patient and staff attendant to each stage of the response process. Thus the focus in the following pages is just as much upon how hospital staff initiates, and attempts to guide and control the response process through interaction with the patient as upon the patient's responses per se.

First, the response process is stimulated by a doctor's *disclosure* to the patient. The patient's initial response is almost invariably *depression*, but after a period of depression he either *accepts* or *denies* the disclosure, and his ensuing behavior may be regarded as an affirmation of his stand on whether he will, in fact, die. Acceptance may lead to active preparation, to passive preparation or to fighting the illness. A particular patient's response may stop at any stage of the process, take any direction, or change directions. The outcome depends on the manner in which he is told, and then managed by staff, as well as his own inclinations. The response process is diagrammed in Figure 13-1, and the characteristic forms of staff–patient interaction that occur at each stage, often precipitating advance to the next stage, are discussed in the remaining pages.

Method and Research Site

This conception of the characteristic stages of a patient's response to disclosure of terminal illness is based largely on field observations and interviews with patients, doctors, nurses and social workers on the cancer wards of a Veter-

[2]For a conceptual analysis that applies to why there is less risk for doctors in not disclosing terminality, see T. J. Sheff, "Decision Rules, Types of Error, and Their Consequences in Medical Diagnosis," *Behavioral Science*, 8:97–107, April, 1963.

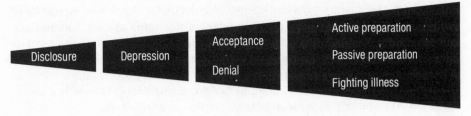

Figure 13-1. The response process.

ans' Administration Hospital in the San Francisco Bay Area. In this hospital the normal procedure is to disclose the nature of his illness to every patient; as a result, many patients are told of a fatal illness.[3]

By and large, the patients in these wards are in their middle or late years and in destitute circumstances. Since their care is free, they are captive patients—they have little or no control over their treatment, and if they do not cooperate, their care may be stopped. If a man goes "AWOL," the hospital is not obliged to re-admit him, or it can re-admit him but punish him by denying privileges. Because the patients lack financial resources, they typically have no alternative to their current "free" care, and their lower-class status accustoms them to accepting or to being intimidated into following orders from people of higher status. Since these captive lower-class patients are unable to threaten effectively the hospital or the doctors, disclosure of terminal illness occurs regardless of the patient's ex-pected reaction.

These patients seemed to exhibit a full *range* of responses to disclosure of im-pending death, which it is our only purpose to set forth here. (How differently, if at all, from higher socio-economic patients they might be distributed throughout the response process is unascertainable with the collected data.) So many cases of direct disclosure and the consequent variety of response patterns made this hos-pital a highly strategic research site for studying the problem. In other hospitals we found only a few cases of direct disclosure of terminal illness and the general aspects were the same as those of the VA cases.

Disclosing Terminal Illness

Disclosure of terminal illness to patients in this hospital has two major characteristics. First, the patient is told that he is certain to die, but not when he will die. Expectations of death have two dimensions: *certainty* and *time* of demise, and the first is the more readily determined in advance.[4] As one doctor put it: "In my opinion, however, no doctor should take it upon himself to say to a patient, 'You have ten weeks to live'—or three months, or two years or any time whatsoever." And another doctor said: "Doctors simply do not know when pa-tients are going to die." Stopping short of full disclosure tends to soften the blow to the patient and reduces chances of error for the doctor.

---

[3]This norm may be considered an aspect of "batch" treatment of captive inmates of a total in-stitution. It is also the procedure on the medical ward of the state penitentiary in California. See E. Goffman, "Characteristics of Total Institutions," in A. Etzioni (ed.), *Complex Organizations,* New York: Holt, Rinehart and Winston, 1961, pp. 312–340.

[4]See Glaser and Strauss, "Temporal Aspects . . .," *op. cit.,* for a full discussion of death expec-tations.

Second, the doctors typically do not give details of the illness, particularly mode of dying, and the type of patient under consideration usually does not ask for them. Primarily, this is a problem of communication: a doctor finds it hard to explain the illness to a working-class patient, while lack of familiarity with the technical terms, as well as a more general deference to the doctor, inhibits the patient's impulse to question him. In addition, not giving details is a tactic doctors use to cut down on talk with the patient and to leave him quickly.

In combination, these two characteristics of disclosure often result in *short, blunt announcements* of terminal illness to the patient. Even the nurses are often shocked by the doctor's bluntness. Nevertheless, they often feel that the patient is better off for being told because, as one nurse put it, he "becomes philosophical in a day or two."

A short, blunt announcement may be softened, however, in various ways. One way is to add a religious flavor: "You've had a full life now, and God will be calling you soon." This manner is perhaps most appropriate for older patients. Another is to muffle the language. To the patient's question, "Is is cancer, Doc?" the doctor responds, "We don't call it that . . ." and then gives it a technical name that the patient can understand only vaguely. The "suspicion" announcement also dulls the blow: "There is a high clinical suspicion that the tumor removed was cancer. However, we won't have a pathological report on it for ten days." The announcement that there is "nothing more to do" (to cure the patient) can be muffled with a hopeful lie such as by adding "but then who knows, next week, next month or maybe next year there may be a drug that will save you," or by suggesting to the patient that he join an experimental program that may help him, as well as mankind.[5] Finally, there is the important statement that softens any form of disclosure: "We can control the pain."

In some forms, the blunt announcement *sharpens* the blow of disclosure by forcing a *direct confrontation* of the truth with little or no preamble. The doctors are quite aware of, and favor the use of, this approach by colleagues. One doctor says, "With average patients, we tell them what they got." Another says, "I don't think the staff as a whole goes along with the hard-boiled approach, but me, I try to tell them the truth." The "hard-boiled" announcement is often linked with a report to the patient of the results of his surgery. In this hospital, patients are customarily told, two or three days after surgery for cancer, whether they will die. For example, one doctor walks into the patient's room, faces him says, "It's malignant" and walks out. To be sure, this tactic also eliminates having to answer the patient's questions. Another rather direct confrontation is, "We weren't able to get it [the malignant tumor] all out." Another form of sharp announcements is the *direct retort*: when a patient asks, "Doctor, do I have cancer?" the doctor replies, "Yes, you do." (One doctor commented, "If they ask directly, we answer as directly as possible.") Lastly, the *implied, but sharp, confrontation* of terminal illness is exemplified by the doctor who greeted a patient returning to the hospital with the order to sell her house and all her things, for she would not leave the hospital again.

---

[5] If the patient takes the experimental drug, he continually checks his condition by asking the doctor: "What next, Doc?" "What now?" "Am I better?" "Am I getting well?" When the experiment is over and the patient is still going to die, he must start through the response process again with a depressing "now what" feeling.

In this group of doctors who favor the short, blunt disclosure there is one who does not. He refuses to disclose in this fashion because he has had previous experience with errors due to changing pathology reports, and because he tries, through surgery, to make the patient's last weeks more comfortable. Other doctors tend to disagree that his "comfort surgery" is useful, but he continues because sometimes he actually saves the patient for years. This doctor continually maintains a cheerful and optimistic manner, never directly disclosing to the patient that he will die. What actually occurs when he offers the patient comfort surgery or participation in a clinical experiment is *silent disclosure*: both doctor and patient know of the latter's fatal illness, and both know the other knows, but they do not talk to each other about it.[6] The doctor reveals the patient's fatal illness by oblique references to it in proposing comfort surgery or experimental participation, the meaning of which the patient clearly understands. The patient thus begins his process of response-to-disclosure without the customary stimulus of direct disclosure.

Depression

The initial response of the patient to disclosure is depression. The large majority of patients come to terms with their depression sufficiently to go on to the next stage of the response process. A few do not. Their depression precipitates a *withdrawal* from contact with everyone, and they remain in a state of hopelessness. In this limiting sense they become non-interacting, non-cooperative patients; the nurses can not "reach" them. Depression is usually handled by staff with sedation until the patient starts relating to them again. In one case a nurse observed that a patient visibly shortened his life because of his period of anxiety and withdrawal.

Acceptance or Denial?

After the initial period of acute depression, the patient responds to the announcement by choosing either to accept or to deny the imminence of his death. In effect, he takes a stand on whether and how he will die, and this stand profoundly affects his relations with the staff from that time on.

In general, sharp, abrupt disclosure tends to produce denial, and dulled disclosure, acceptance.[7] When the disclosure is sharp, the depression is more immediate and profound, and denial starts right in as a mechanism to cope with the shock.[8] To predict an individual's response, however, one needs the kind of in-

---

[6]See Glaser and Straus, "Awareness Context . . .," *op. cit.,* for a discussion of the "mutual pretense awareness context" which silent disclosure institutes.

[7]These hypotheses complement the discussion by Feifel on the importance of "how telling is done" (*op. cit.*).

[8]For another discussion of denial of illness upon disclosure, see H. D. Lederer, "How the Sick View Their World," in E. Gartly Jaco (ed.), *Patients, Physicians and Illness,* New York: Free Press, 1958, pp. 247–250. Denial of dying is characteristic of our society as shown by R. Fulton's data: see "Death and the Self," *Journal of Religion and Health,* 3:359–368, July, 1964. See the analysis of denial of death in American Society by T. Parsons, "Death in American Society," *Amer. Behav. Scientist,* May, 1963, pp. 61–65.

timate knowledge of the patient that doctors would prefer to have. Without it, it is very difficult to say which path to death a patient will take, or for how long. In some cases, the patient's response changes; he cannot hold out against accumulating physical, social and temporal cues. The usual change is from denial to acceptance, though when patients improve briefly before growing worse or a new drug helps for a few days, acceptance may change, for a time, to denial. The direction an individual takes depends not only on how he is told, but also on a variety of social and psychological considerations impinging on the passage from life to death.

Acceptance—Patients may demonstrate acceptance of impending death by actively preparing for death, passively preparing, or fighting against it. *Active preparation* may take the form of becoming *philosophical* about dying, death and one's previous life; patients review and discuss how full their life has been with family, nurses, social workers and chaplain. They may pose the destiny question: "Why me?" and try to work through it with the philosphical help of others. This approach leads the patients to draw the nurses into the discussion which can be very difficult for them. Nurses are still only trained by and large to help motivate patients to live, not to die! If a nurse is to help a patient prepare himself she too must accept his impending death and refrain from chastising him for not fighting to live. Otherwise she is likely to consider the patient "morbid" and tends to avoid his invitations to help him face death squarely. She will usually try to transfer the burden to the social worker, sister or chaplain when they are available.

Some patients start immediately to prepare themselves for death through religion. For others it is an easy transition to slip from philosophical to religious terms, a transition often aided by the chaplain, who then helps the patient prepare himself.

Another form of active preparation for death is to *settle social* and *financial affairs*, perhaps linking this effort with philosophical or religious preparation. The typical helpers in settling affairs are family members and social workers. For example, upon learning that he was going to die, the patient turned to his wife and said, "Well, we've got to get everything lined up; I promised (so and so) my . . ." This immediate getting down to the provisions of a will was considered abnormal by one nurse who said, "I've never seen a reaction like that, it was almost morbid." Another patient began discussing with the social worker the various veteran's benefits they could obtain for his wife, and another tried to marry his wife, who was emotionally very dependent on him, to a hospital corpsman. One patient gave up his pain medication long enough to put his financial affairs in order with the aid of a social worker, for he knew that as soon as he was too drugged to operate effectively, his family would try to take over his estate.

To give the patient a chance to settle his affairs, to plan for the future of his family, is, of course, an important consideration when a doctor decides whether to disclose terminal illness. He can seldom be sure, however, that the patient's response will take this direction or advance so far. Moreover, some affairs to be settled are less important than social or financial ones, though they do allow patients to pick up loose ends or accomplish unfinished business. For example, before entering the hospital for cancer surgery one woman said, "I am going to do three things before I enter the hospital—things I've been meaning to do for a long time. I'm going to make some grape jelly. I've always dreamed of having a shelf full of jelly jars with my own label on them. Then I'm going to get up enough nerve to saddle and bridle my daughter's horse and take a ride. Then I'm going to apologize to my mother-in-law for what I said to her in 1949." Another patient with leukemia quit work and bought a sailboat. He planned to explore the delta region of the Sacramento and San Joaquin rivers until his last trip to the hospital.

Another form of active preparation is to attempt a *"full life"* before death.[9] This pattern is characteristic of younger patients (in contrast to older patients who review the fullness of their life) like the 22-year-old who, when told he had three months to three years to live, married a nurse. "If we have only two months," she said, "it will be worth it." The patient lived two years and had a son. Faced by certain death, he had achieved the most he could from life.

Auto-euthanasia (*suicide*) is another way of actively preparing for death.[10] It eliminates the sometimes very distressing last weeks or days of dying. One patient, who had no friends to visit him, felt that he was very alone and that no one in the hospital cared, so he tried to hasten his death by suicide. Some patients try to end their lives while they are physically presentable, not wanting their families to see their degeneration. Other stresses that encourage auto-euthanasia are unbearable pain and the discipline imposed by a clinical experiment to which one may be irrevocably committed. Others decide to end their life when they can no longer work.[11] Still others prefer auto-euthanasia as a way of controlling their dying as they controlled their living, thus wresting this control from the hands of the staff and the rigors imposed by hospital routine.[12]

Passive preparation for death, among patients who accept their terminal illness, also has some characteristic forms. One is to take the news in a *nonchalant* manner. Nurses sometimes find this response disturbing; one put it: "But some take it quite nonchalantly. We've had several very good patients—right to the end. One that upset me was here when I came. He was the hardest for me to see die—he was young and not only that—such a wonderful fellow. Even as sick as he was, he was always kind and courteous." Apart from the social loss factor—"young" and "wonderful"—which usually upsets nurses,[13] this nurse also found such a passive outlook on death rather disquieting.

Nurses, however, are grateful to patients who approach death with *calm resignation*. This response relieves them of the responsibility for cheering up the patient and improves their morale, too. Since it would not do for a nurse to be less calm or resigned than the patient, a patient who responds in this fashion raises and supports the nurse's morale. The *nonverbal* patient, who simply accepts his fate and does not talk about it, also relieves the nurse of possible stress

[9]This form of active preparation is appropriate in American society which stresses the value that death is unacceptable until one has had a full life; see: Parsons, *op. cit.*

[10]Shneidman feels a question deserving of research is "why so many cancer patients *do not* commit suicide." E. S. Schneidman, "Suicide," in Farberow, *op. cit.*

[11]For an account of a cancer patient who planned to commit auto-euthanasia after he could no longer work, see L. Wertenbaker, *Death of a Man,* New York: Random House, 1957.

[12]A growing problem that medical staff and hospitals must face is that people wish to control their own way of dying; they do not want it programmed for them by medical staff and hospital organization. To achieve this end, many patients also wish to die at home. (Fulton, *op. cit.,* pp. 363–364); see the analysis of this problem in J. Quint, "Some Organizational Barriers to Effective Patient Care in Hospitals," paper given at the American Medical Association convention, June 24, 1964.

[13]Glaser and Strauss, "The Social Loss . . .," *op. cit.*

in having to talk, as she often does with the more actively preparing patient. He makes few or no demands on nurses or social workers. A disquieting aspect of this response is the loss of contact with the patient: "It is very hard for us 'well people' to really grasp how they feel." One social worker bridges this gap by sitting with the patients for a time each day. She reports, "Sometimes it's a matter of just touching their hand—whatever is natural—to make them feel that you understand and care." Another version of the passive response is expressed by the patient who emerges from his depression only to turn his face to the wall, "the spirit drained out of him," and "passively wait to die."

Some patients accept their terminal illness but decide to *fight* it. Unlike denial behavior, this fight indicates an initial acceptance of one's impending death together with a positive desire to somehow change it. Three forms of fighting behavior are *intensive living, going to marginal doctors or quacks,* and *participating in an experiment.* One patient, for example, started going out on passes, and living it up, asserting, "I'll beat it," as if he could hold death off by living life to the full. He kept getting thinner and eventually died. This mode of fighting off death can be readily transformed into active preparation for death if it increases the patient's fullness of life before death.

Taking an outside chance with quacks or marginal doctors[14] gives some patients a feeling that they are actively combatting the disease. A regular physician usually permits his patient to go to a marginal doctor, since the visits keep the patient hopeful and busy and his permission allows the physician to see that the marginal treatments do not injure his patient. Denied this permission, a patient who wants to fight his disease in some way may break off relations with his physician, so that the physician loses control over both the patient and the marginal doctor. A rupture like this makes it difficult for the patient to return to the original doctor when, as is typical, the marginal treatment fails.[15]

The search for a way to fight the fatal illness can also lead a patient into a clinical experiment. If he does not win his own battle, he at least may help future patients with theirs. The chance to contribute to medical science does not, however, sustain the motivation of *all* research patients.[16] Some, when they see it is hopeless for themselves and find the experimental regime too rigorous to bear, try to extricate themselves from the experiment. If the doctors will not let them off, these patients sometimes interfere with the experiment by pulling tubes out, by not taking medicine or by taking an extra drink of water. Some attempt auto-euthanasia. Doctors may carry on the fight regardless of the patient's desire to give up. One nurse, at least, feeling that the lives of research patients are excessively prolonged, bitterly said: "They [doctors] keep them alive until the paper [the research report] is written."

Denial—Some patients deny they are approaching death and proceed to establish this stand in their interaction with staff members. Typical denying strategies are juggling time, testing for denial, comparing oneself to other pa-

[14]In this connection see B. Cobb, "Why Do People Detour to Quacks?" in Jaco, *op. cit.*

[15]For an illustration of how the doctor allowed, hence could control, a dying patient's submission to the rigorous treatment of a marginal doctor, see J. Gunther, *Death Be Not Proud,* New York: Harper Bros., 1949.

[16]Cf. R. Fox, *Experiment Perilous,* New York: Free Press, 1959. One gets the feeling that the patients in Fox's sample were all highly motivated to go on with the experiments to the bitter end.

tients, blocking communication, becoming intensely active, emphasizing a future orientation, and forcing reciprocal isolation. In the cancer ward, it is relatively easy to deny impending death by *juggling time*, for, as we have noted, disclosure implies certainty that death will occur, but no assurance as to *when* it will occur. Patients can therefore invent a time, and this becomes a way of denying that one is truly dying.[17] Some literally give themselves years. But even when a denying patient is given a time limit, he is still likely to start thinking, as one nurse said, "in terms of years, when it really is a matter of a month or two."

A patient can *test* the staff in various ways *to establish* his *denial*. A negative way is not to test, by failing to ask the questions called for. For example, the doctor who tells the patient he has a tumor adopts a grave manner, indicating that the tumor is malignant, and expects the patient to try to verify it. The patient never asks the doctor or anyone else. Other patients test the nurses, indirectly, by asking, "Why aren't I feeling better?" "Why aren't I gaining weight?" Since these patients can be assumed to know why, the nurse understands that they want these physical cues interpreted in such a way as to deny that they indicate impending death. Patients often ask nurses to manage temporal cues in the same way, by interpreting extended stays in the hospital or slow recuperation in ways that point away from death.

Another form of testing for denial is the *polarity game*. By questioning a nurse or social worker about the most extreme living or dying implications of his illness, the patient forces her to give a normalizing answer, which usually locates him a safe distance from death. For example, focusing on the dying implications, the patient asks, "Am I getting worse? The medicine isn't helping." The forced answer is, "Give yourself a chance—medicine takes a long time." Or focusing on the living implications, to a social worker trying to figure out his VA benefits for his family a patient replies, "Well, all right—but it won't be for long, will it?" Since the social worker cannot confront the patient with coming death if he "really doesn't know," she in effect denies it for him by classifying him with the living but disabled. "This is what welfare is for—to help the families of men who are disabled and can't work." Here, the social worker understood the patient's words as a request "for assurance that he wasn't going to die," and she responded appropriately.

Patients may deny their fate by using other patients as *comparative references*. Two common types of comparison are the exception and the favorable comparison. A patient using the first approach becomes very talkative about other patients with the same disease. He adopts a manner, or style, like that of staff members, that is, people who do not have the illness. In the end this borrowed objectivity and immunity leads him to conclude that he is an exceptional case, that somehow the illness that caused so many others to die will not kill him: he will be cured. The favorable comparison is a distorted effort to include one's illness in a non-fatal category: one patient said, "The doctor says I *only* have a (severe illness)." Another literally dying patient said, "Thank God, I am not as bad off as (another patient near death)."

[17]That in the case of dying, patients will tend to give themselves *more* time than they actually have, contrasts with studies of recovery which show that patients are likely to give themselves *less* time than it takes to recover. See F. Davis, *Passage Through Crisis*, Indianapolis: Bobbs-Merrill, 1963, and J. Roth, *Timetables*, Indianapolis: Bobbs-Merrill, 1963.

Some patients try to prove they are not terminal by *engaging in strenuous activities*. One patient, having been told he had a bad heart, left the hospital and started spading up his garden to prove the doctor wrong, that is, his denial correct. Another patient wouldn't stick to his diet. The death impending in the present can also be denied through *future-oriented talk* with the nurses. One patient began making plans to buy a chicken farm when he left the hospital—as soon as he learned he was going to die. *Communication blocks* of various sorts aid denial. Some patients simply don't hear the doctor, others refuse to admit it, others cannot use the word "cancer" in any verbal context, and still others avoid any discussion of the nature of their illness or the inevitability of death.

A denying patient can start an accumulating process of *reciprocal isolation* between himself and nurses, doctors, family members and social workers. After disclosure, others expect him to acknowledge his impending death, so they attempt to relate to him on this basis. Doctors speak to him and nurses give treatment on the understanding that his impending demise can be mentioned, or at least signaled. Family members and social workers may refer to plans for his burial and his finances. A patient who avoids the subject when he is not expected to avoid it forces others to avoid it, too, and thus renders them unable to help and prepare the patient. One social worker said, hopelessly, about a denying patient, "There was nothing I could do for him." At this first stage of the isolation process, the patient has forced an implicit agreement between himself and others that the topic of his illness will not be discussed.[18] In the next stage, some of these people may avoid all contact with the patient because he has frustrated their efforts to help him. Nurses, doctors and social workers tend to spend their time with patients they can help, to prevent the feeling of helplessness that often overcomes them while engaged in terminal care. As a result, the patient finds himself alone, apart from receiving the necessary technical care to insure painless comfort; thus his isolation is complete.

Avoidance of the denying patient occurs because he refuses to act as a dying patient, although it has been clearly pointed out to him that this is exactly what he is. In contrast, an unaware patient, who is not expected to act like a dying patient, will not be avoided on these grounds. Rather, he is likely to attract others who will gather around him in silent sympathy, wishing they could tell him and help him. In the end, both the denying patient and the unaware patient may die without preparation for death. But a denying patient had the chance to accept his impending death and prepare himself with the help of others, while the unaware patient's chances for preparation are mostly dependent on his doctor's decision not to disclose his terminal illness.

Implications for Disclosure

Many of the standard arguments given by doctors for and against disclosure anticipate a single, permanent impact on the patient.[19] The patient is expected to

---

[18]Thus, instituting a "mutual pretense awareness context" is part of this process: see Glaser and Strauss, "Awareness Contexts . . .," *op. cit.*

[19]For an illustration of this kind of argument, see the discussion between two doctors in "How Should Incurably Ill Patients Be Dealt with: Should They Be Told the Truth," *Parent's Magazine*, 71:196–206, January, 1963.

"be brave," "go to pieces," "commit suicide," "lose all hope," or to "plan for the future" and such. But the impact is not so simple. Since disclosing the truth sets off a response process through which the patient passes, to base the decision as to whether to disclose on a single probable impact is to focus on only one stage in the response process, neglecting the other stages and how each stage may be controlled through appropriate forms of interaction by hospital staff. For example, to predict that the patient will become too despondent is to neglect the possibility that he will overcome this despondency and with the aid of a nurse, chaplain, social worker or family member prepare adequately for his death and for his family's future. Or, to expect a patient simply to settle his affairs is to fail to evaluate his capacity for overcoming an initial depression, as well as the capacity of the staff to help him at this stage.

A doctor deciding whether to tell the patient therefore should consider not a single impact as a desiderata, but how, in what direction and with what consequences the patient's response is likely to go, and what types of staff are available and how will they handle the patient at each stage. A doctor who says "no" to disclosure because the patient will "lose hope" need not be in conflict with one who says "yes," to give the patient a chance to plan for his family. Each is merely referring to a different stage of the same process. For both, the concern should be to judge whether the patient can achieve the acceptance–active preparation stage.

Once again, the benefits and liabilities of unawareness (non-disclosure) as opposed to disclosure and the possibilities for acceptance or denial depend on the nature of the individual case. But on the whole, there is much to recommend giving more patients than are presently given an opportunity actively to manage their own dying and prepare for death. As a strong controlling factor, staff members in interaction with the patient could self-consciously soften the disclosure, handle the depression so as to encourage acceptance, and guide the patient into active preparations for death. They could also find interaction strategies that would convert a patient's denial to acceptance. Yet staff members may hesitate to tamper with a patient's choice of passage to death. For example, one social worker said of a denying patient, "I'm loathe to play God on this. Unless it could serve a useful purpose—would it really be helpful. Where a man shies away from something—maybe you should let him—why make him face this most terrible reality?"

The understanding that the descriptive model presented here affords will, we trust, give doctors as well as other parties to the dying situation, such as family members, nurses, social workers and chaplains, a perspective that is of use in deciding the advisability of disclosing terminal illness to a patient, and if advisable, how best it might be done, and how to guide the patient through the response process. Thus perhaps this understanding will reduce some of the current reluctance of medical staff to disclose and to tamper with patients' responses to disclosure. This model also provides sociologists with a beginning basis both for entering into, as consultants, the discussion on whether or not to disclose and for the needed social psychological research on the problem. For instance, further research could specify what types of terminal patients follow what kinds of patterns of movement through the response process under what conditions of patient-staff interaction—a problem only hinted at in this paper.

C. Healers and Healing Behavior

All societies have sickness and thus are in need of healers to treat and care for those afflicted. Consequently, another means of coping with disease and injury by society, when they cannot be prevented, is to devise specific social roles for their healers who may then legitimately perform their ministrations to the recipients of such efforts, labeled "patients." Healing behavior is the activity of healers as they go about their work. Depending upon the societal value of healing behavior and the forms it may take, a corresponding high or low status is assigned to the healer's role. Thus, societies that value scientific medicine will grant far higher social status or rank to scientific healers, like the medical doctor or physician, whereas societies or subcultures in a pluralistic society assigning more value to "folk" or "primitive" medicine may give a relatively high status to folk healers and witchdoctors and seek their aid more readily than that of physicians.

Healing behavior in the form of the practice of medicine has become a subject of increasing interest to social and behavioral scientists. Medicine is a distinct social system and institution in Western society, with its own established norms, roles, value systems, structured activities, and institutionalized relationships, and it has established a high degree of autonomy in the control of its own affairs. Societies also support organizations and settings to train healers and others caring for the sick.

Some of the consequences of urbanization and suburbanization of modern American medical practice are analyzed in the study by Alfred Miller. He cites three new types of medical practice: the teaching hospital-based physician, the suburban office-based physician, and the inner city office-based physician. Their implications for the future of medical practice are discussed.

Parsons and others have frequently discussed the superordinate-subordinate relationship between the physician and patient. An intensive microlevel analysis of the "encounters" held by patients with their personal physicians is presented by Timothy Anderson and David Helm.

The social role of the nurse and her important healing functions in caring for the sick has been a subject of much study by behavioral scientists. The article by the late Sam Schulman which appeared in the previous edition is again presented with some interesting commentary on some significant changes in the social role of the nurse in American society.

The emergence of new health occupations and the aspiring new "healers" in the United States is attracting increasing attention, and may portend significant innovations among the array of healers and healing behavior in contemporary American society. Specific roles of "physicians assistants," nurse practitioners, and community health workers have emerged in recent years. Henry Perry focuses on physicians assistants, their emerging role, and some problems they may face in the future.

ALFRED E. MILLER

14 The Changing Structure of the Medical Profession in Urban and Suburban Settings

In spite of the rapid growth of medical sociology, there has not been a major sociological analysis of the structure of the medical profession on a metropolitan areawide basis since the study of Providence, R.I. by Oswald Hall 30 years ago [1]. During the intervening period the organization of medical practice and of the profession has undergone a number of important changes that have major significance for health care delivery, policy, and planning, as well as for our understanding of the dynamics of professional behavior and social organization.

There has always been stratification within the medical profession. Hall's study of the structure of the profession and of medical practice in the early 1940s documented this and defined the mechanisms by which the differentiation within the profession came about and was maintained. However, the basis of the stratification was rather different then than it is today. At that time, the groupings within the profession corresponded closely to those of the patients they treated, and were based primarily on cultural and social class identity. The rich were cared for by Park Avenue type specialists, the poor by (usually co-ethnic) general practitioners or by the outpatient departments of voluntary and local government operated hospitals. However, this was accompanied by a system of referrals and consultations between parts of the profession and by hospital staff appointments at different ranks in the hierarchy, so that communication between groups of different status was possible and probably frequent. The resulting system of stratification was to some extent a continuous spectrum from the dominant "inner fraternity" downward [2].

The segment of the profession that Hall dubbed the "inner fraternity" was a small group of office based specialists practicing in a few medical-arts buildings in the high prestige East Side residential district of Providence (not unlike the Park Avenue area of New York City), which was also within easy access of the business district and downtown hospitals. There was a great deal of in-group solidarity between members of this group created by cross referral and consultation patterns as well as by joint membership on hospital staffs, committees, shared office space, etc. On a part-time, so-called "visiting" basis, these same men were chiefs of services at the major Providence voluntary hospitals, or held high ranking staff appointments there. By means of an informal sponsorship [3] system, the inner fraternity in effect controlled the flow of new physicians into the medical care system and the rate of their advancement on the hospital staffs. This in

I wish to express my thanks to Professor Rose Laub Coser for her encouragement in this undertaking and for the many valuable suggestions that I have tried to incorporate.
Reprinted from *Social Science & Medicine*, 11:233–243, March, 1977, by permission of the author and Publisher.

turn determined their prestige, potential for receiving referral patients, and hence the type of practice they could expect to establish, e.g. whether they could gradually limit their practices to single specialties. Separate but interlocking systems of hospital staff appointments and sponsorship existed at the Catholic hospitals, but the "inner fraternity", which was almost exclusively white, Anglo-Saxon and Protestant, clearly dominated the total system. Those who failed to obtain an effective sponsor to promote their advancement within the hospital staff system stayed at the bottom of the hierarchical spectrum and were forced to remain general practitioners [4] who depended on a clientele in the neighborhoods where they practiced. This exclusion of the ethnic neighborhood practitioners from the hospital system led to important differences in the quality as well as availability of medical care that various segments of the population received.

Today, the differences in status and type of practice (as well as level of health care provided) are based much more on the organization of care and the differing relation of physicians to the core technology of their profession, in particular to hospitals, than on the personal system of stratification noted by Hall. The changing technology of health care has led to major modifications in the structure of practice, with consequent changes in the role of physicians, their relations to patients, hospitals, and other health professionals. There appear to be three dominant underlying trends or causal factors that make it possible to interpret and at least partially explain this complex restructuring of the profession:

(1) Because of the growing complexity of medical technology and the enlarging corpus of scientific knowledge and skills required for practice, as well as the increasing financial and prestige incentives, there has been a tremendous movement toward specialization. In 1930, less than 20% of the active practitioners in the country listed themselves as specialists. In 1949, 37% of M.D.s in direct patient care were so listed, and in 1973, it was 82%. There is no sign of significant reversal in the trend. In spite of incentives to entice students toward family practice, well over 90% of each new graduating class of medical students today are entering specialty training [5-7]. Previously, specialty status was achieved by first building a general practice and developing a good reputation through obtaining prestigious hospital staff appointments which led to increasing numbers of referrals in the physician's area of special interest and competence. Then the practice was gradually limited to that specialty [8]. Today the road to specialty practice is by way of formal residency training in a teaching hospital leading to certification by the specialty examination board and immediate entry into the limited practice of that specialty.

(2) Because of the increasing importance of surgery, of complex diagnostic techniques requiring expensive equipment, and of intensive specialized care facilities for seriously ill patients, the hospital has come to play an ever more central role in medical practice. Today it is not only the physician's workshop, where care is conveniently provided for sicker patients, but a positive force in its own right, around which the organization of care is structured. When complicated cases are referred to a major medical center, the hospital as a whole, with its full time medical staff, takes the responsibility for care. Even for ambulatory care the hospital outpatient department rather than the individual office based practitioner has become "the physician" to large segments of the population. Instead

of the hospital being an adjunct to the physician's practice, today the physician is more and more becoming a cog in the organization of hospital practice (particularly in large urban teaching hospitals where medical research and training of new specialists take place). In 1930, fewer than 5% of (non-government) practicing M.D.s were hospital based. In 1974, the proportion reached 30%, and in New York City, 40%, as is presumably true for most major urban centers [9]. In New York City, another 10% of the physicians were engaged in teaching, research, or administration, leaving less than 50% in office based practice. Even in the suburban counties, the percentage of hospital based physicians increased from 8% in 1959 to 15% in 1973 (see Table 14-1).

(3) Thirty years ago, most physicians practicing in metropolitan areas were located in offices near the center of the city and therefore accessible to the largest number of potential patients. Other physicians served primarily urban residential neighborhoods, but with decreasing density as one travelled further from the business center. Manhattan, the traditional center for medical services for the city, with less than 25% of the population, was the location of almost half of the office based physicians in 1959. Over half of these in turn were specialists with offices in a small area along the upper East Side of the island, the so-called "Park Avenue", high prestige practice area. Partly as a result of the general socio-demographic shift of the middle class out of the central city, and partly as a result of increasing exclusion from privileges at the large urban teaching hospitals [10], office based physicians have relocated away from the urban center, or at least fewer new physicians are locating there.

Between 1959 and 1974 the number of office based physicians in New York City declined by 25% from 13,935 to 10,453, while the number of office based practitioners in the five suburban counties increased by 52%, from 4166 to 6317 (see Table 14-2). During this period the population of the New York central city remained essentially constant so that the density of office physicians also declined by 25%. During the same period, the population of the suburbs increased by approx 35%, so that much of the influx of physicians was simply parallel to the growth of population. Nevertheless, new physicians located in the suburbs at a rate exceeding the general influx of population, with the result that even the ratio of office based physicians per 100,000 population was 13% higher in 1974 than in 1959. In this last year for which data are available, the density of office physicians in the suburbs actually came to exceed that of the central city. Because of the uneven distribution of physicians within the central city, the 25% decrease in office practitioners still underestimates the effective loss of neighborhood primary care physicians from the poorer areas. Some indication is given by the differential changes in Manhattan and the rest of the city. Although Manhattan lost more office physicians than the remainder of the city combined, percentwise there was a much greater decline in the other boroughs, which do not have such high concentration areas of office specialists, like Park Avenue. These so-called "outer boroughs" are more representative of the neighborhood physician situation. The outer boroughs had, on the average, a 30% decline in their office based physician densities during the 15 years, and ended with only 83 per 100,000 scarcely 60% that of the adjacent suburbs. Brooklyn lost 38.4% of its office physicians. The Bronx, starting with a lower density, ended with only 68 office physi-

Table 14-1   Census of physicians by type of practice and geographic location—New York Metropolitan Area

	1959	1963	1966	1971	1973	Average annual % growth rate		
						1959-66	1966-73	1959-73
Manhattan								
total	9176	10354	11180	11359	10334	2.9	-0.8	1.0
office-based	6441 (70.2%)	6480 (62.6%)	6379 (57.1%)	5635 (49.7%)	5169 (50.0%)	-0.1	-2.9	-1.6
hospital-based	2304 (25.1%)	2846 (27.5%)	3588 (32.1%)	3934 (34.7%)	3641 (35.2%)	6.5	0.5	3.6
other	431 (4.7%)	1028 (9.9%)	1213 (10.8%)	1790 (15.8%)	1524 (14.7%)	16.4	4.2	9.2
Outer Boroughs (1)								
total	9296	10398	11316	11989	11313	2.9	0.2	1.5
office-based	7494 (80.6%)	7159 (68.6%)	6896 (60.9%)	5999 (50.0%)	5375 (47.5%)	-1.2	-3.4	-2.3
hospital-based	1582 (17.0%)	2853 (27.4%)	3926 (34.7%)	5000 (41.7%)	5113 (45.2%)	14.0	4.1	8.5
other	220 (2.4%)	386 (3.9%)	494 (4.4%)	990 (8.3%)	825 (7.3%)	12.4	9.0	10.8
New York City Total								
total	18472	20752	22496	23348	21647	2.9	-0.3	1.3
office-based	13935 (74.4%)	13639 (65.7%)	13275 (59.0%)	11634 (49.8%)	10544 (48.8%)	-0.7	-3.1	-2.0
hospital-based	3886 (21.0%)	5699 (27.5%)	7514 (33.4%)	8934 (38.3%)	8754 (40.4%)	9.9	2.5	6.0
other	651 (3.5%)	1414 (6.8%)	1707 (7.6%)	2780 (11.9%)	2349 (10.8%)	15.1	5.7	9.7
Suburban (2)								
total	5472	6822	7742	9203	9633	5.1	3.2	4.1
office-based	4882 (89.2%)	5628 (82.5%)	6092 (78.7%)	6310 (68.6%)	6422 (66.7%)	3.2	0.8	1.9
hospital-based	467 (8.5%)	984 (14.4%)	1377 (17.8%)	2171 (23.6%)	2412 (25.0%)	16.9	8.6	12.1
other	123 (2.2%)	210 (3.1%)	273 (3.5%)	722 (7.8%)	799 (8.3%)	12.2	17.5	15.0

Sources: Refs. [55]–[58].
(1) Bronx, Brooklyn, Queens and Staten Island.
(2) Nassau and Westchester counties in New York, Bergen and Union counties in New Jersey, Fairfield county in Connecticut.

Table 14-2 Density of physicians (per 100,000 population) by type of practice and geographic location—New York Metropolitan Area

	1959	1963	1966	1971	1973	Absolute change 1959-73	Total % change 1959-73	Average annual % growth rate		
								1959-66	1966-73	1959-73
Manhattan										
total	544	609	656	742	696	+152	+27.9%	2.7	1.2	2.0
office-based	380	381	374	368	348	-32	-8.4%	-0.2	-0.9	-0.5
hospital-based	137	167	211	257	245	+108	+78.8%	6.3	2.5	4.6
other	26	60	71	117	103	+77	+296.1%	15.8	6.4	10.2
Outer Boroughs (1)										
total	153	171	180	188	177	+24	+15.7%	2.4	-0.1	1.1
office-based	123	119	109	94	84	-39	-31.7%	-1.7	-3.5	-2.7
hospital-based	26	47	62	79	80	+54	+207.7%	13.4	3.9	8.1
other	4	6	8	16	13	+9	+225.0%	10.4	8.6	10.0
New York City										
Total										
total	237	267	281	296	274	+37	+75.6%	2.5	-0.1	1.2
office-based	179	175	166	147	134	-45	-25.1%	-1.0	-2.9	-2.0
hospital-based	50	73	94	113	111	+61	+122.0%	9.5	2.7	5.9
other	8	18	21	35	30	+22	+275.0%	15.2	6.3	9.9
Suburban (2)										
total	135	169	173	201	209	+74	+55.6%	3.7	2.8	3.0
office-based	121	139	136	138	139	+18	+14.9%	-1.8	0.3	0.8
hospital-based	12	24	31	47	52	+40	+333.3%	14.8	7.9	10.6
other	3	5	6	16	18	+15	+500.0%	10.6	17.9	14.3

(1), (2) See Table 14-1.

Note: No attempt has been made to adjust 1959, 1963 and 1966 data for the AMA reclassification of physicians which took place in 1968. The only category where this had a major influence was "other activities," which is not important for our conclusions. For detailed discussion of possible adjustment methods, see Leveson and Stevenson [59].

Sources: Same as Table 14-1.

cians per 100,000 population, just half the density of the suburbs—in spite of the fact that some more affluent parts of the Bronx, such as Riverdale, still have a rather high physician density. Spot checks of certain large known poverty areas have shown that there were fewer than 15 office physicians per 100,000 population in several neighborhoods, each with over 200,000 residents [11].

Most previous attempts at studies of these trends have been inconclusive [12], because most regularly collected physician data are on a county-wide basis, and in most cases this fails to distinguish between inner city and suburban practice. However, a recent study by Dewey [13] of the Chicago area, based on geographic units smaller than the county level, confirms the New York findings. Analysis by Rushing [14] of longitudinal data collected by the Association of American Medical Colleges on a sample of medical school graduates from the class of 1960 also suggests that recent graduates are predominantly locating their practice in the suburbs. The simultaneous trend toward hospital based practice in the city masks the loss of office based physicians in the same inner city areas, unless a careful distinction between the two types of practice is maintained in physician studies. Preliminary results from work currently under way indicate that if this distinction is observed, the trend can be found in many large older stable metropolitan areas. The distinction is important for medical care because hospital based physicians are much less available than office based physicians for primary care to the local residents, who see them only in inconvenient, overcrowded outpatient departments.

These trends in the distribution of physicians and the shifts in the mode of practice seem to be the result of several concomitant factors: (1) Certainly the general socio-demographic changes toward suburbanization of the middle class and deterioration of the inner city have had a major impact on the location of medical practices. (2) However, the role of the hospital in organizing practice and in attracting physicians to an area has been equally important. The massive development of specialty training in hospital based residency programs has led to a very different manner of channeling new physicians into practice than existed in Hall's time [3]. This new mode of entry into specialty practice has been accompanied by a major change in the professional power structure and social organization of physician practice within the metropolitan area.

As a result of these trends the numbers of physicians in three new types of practice have grown rapidly in the past two decades. Although these groups played a very minor role in the overall makeup of the profession in the United States 30 years ago, today physicians in these practice types seem well on the way to comprising the largest segments of the profession. These three new prominent groups have very different levels of prestige and competence, and quite differently structured professional organizational systems. In many ways the new groupings seem to represent the basis of an emerging new system of professional stratification replacing the old one described by Hall. However, unlike the old system, the new groups of physicians have very little interchange of personnel, knowledge, information, or direct patient referrals. Therefore, the emerging differentiation of the profession appears to be a division into three mutually isolated sections, rather than a continuous stratification in accord with patient class prestige, as was formerly the case. This situation could have important implications for the quality of care, availability of services to different parts of the population, continuing education of practicing professionals, and the effective use of services.

In the present article, the three emerging types of professional practice organization will be described and analyzed and some of the implications explored. These types are:

1. The full time, teaching hospital based physicians and medical school faculty;
2. The suburban, office based physicians loosely affiliated with community hospitals; and
3. The inner city, Medicaid clinic based physicians (usually foreign trained and without hospital affiliations), serving the new urban poor.

Of course, the transition to the new "stratification system" is nowhere near complete. Some of the old social class and ethnically determined differentiation of the profession continues to exist. In particular, the old high prestige medical practice areas have retained a considerable concentration of physicians wherever the adjoining business or residential districts have remained of high status. However, in cities that have medical schools or hospitals with prestigious residency programs, this group is progressively being excluded from the teaching hospitals where they once had private patient care privileges and teaching responsibilities [15]. As a result, younger physicians are locating in this type of practice much less rapidly than previously, and even the "Park Avenue" physicians seem destined to be only partially replaced in larger cities in the next generation.

Other interesting and important types of practice have been omitted from consideration in the present paper because they represent a small or declining segment of medical practice. For example, the residuals of the types described by Hall, such as the ethnic neighborhood practitioners, are rapidly disappearing, and the much discussed health maintenance organizations (HMOs) or prepaid group practice structure of physician services comprises less than 5% of the physicians in the metropolitan area.

The data for the present description are derived from a number of diverse sources. In part, the analysis is based on well documented statistics collected by public and private agencies, and on administrative studies of the profession. In part it is based on several excellent sociological studies by other investigators of particular aspects of professional practice and socialization. However, to a large extent it is derived from extensive, albeit unsystematic, participant observation during my own experience in teaching hospital and community hospital settings, as a member of a medical school faculty, as an urban public health officer, and as a health planner responsible for the city-wide investigation and planning of personal health services in New York City. Because of the fragmentary nature of the data on which they are based, the description and the conclusions drawn about the present structure and dynamics of the profession must be taken as preliminary and suggestive. Because of the importance of the analysis for policy reasons, and the need for comparison with the situation in other geographic areas, the preliminary results are being presented in the hope that interest will be awakened leading other investigators to examine the structure of medical practice in their own communities in reference to the framework suggested here.

The Teaching Hospital* Physician

Of the roughly 295,000 physicians engaged in direct care of patients in 1974, approx 93,000 were full time members of hospital staffs caring for inpatients within the hospital or caring for (ambulatory) outpatients in offices or clinics on the hospital premises [16]. Of these 93,000 physicians 58,000 were interns and residents, and 80% of these physicians in postgraduate training were working in university affiliated hospitals or large Federal teaching hospitals [17]. Another 6000 physicians are full-time faculty devoting more time to teaching than to patient care, and, on the basis of extrapolation of New York data, it seems likely that at least half of the 35,000 hospital based staff physicians who devote the majority of their time to patient care are located in teaching hospitals.

These physicians depend directly on the hospitals for at least part of their income and virtually all of their patients, since patients are referred to the hospital as a whole or to particular physicians because of their position at the hospital. Teaching hospital physicians, whether residents or staff, present a marked contrast to the solo office based practitioner who provided the traditional stereotype of the physician. Practice in this setting takes place on a team basis, which results in great interdependence among physicians and close identification with the organization in which they practice and on which they depend. Consequently

---

*For understanding the discussions to follow it will perhaps be helpful to non-American readers to describe briefly the various types of hospitals that exist here. General hospitals in New York City (and in the U.S. generally) can be classified according to sponsorship or financial auspices as voluntary, proprietary or government owned. Voluntary hospitals are privately owned non-profit institutions, which in most cases were sponsored originally by religious or public service groups but have come to be controlled by their self-perpetuating boards of trustees in combination with their medical staff organizations. Previously they were supported to a large extent by philanthropy and voluntary contributions of physicians' and laymen's efforts. Today, however, contributions make up only a tiny percentage of the total budget, the lion's share now coming from patient service charges paid by health insurance plans or government programs like Medicaid and Medicare. For the purpose of this paper, voluntary hospitals can be divided into two sub-types, teaching hospitals and community hospitals. The former are large (500–2000 beds) prestigious institutions with residency programs for intensive training of physicians in many different specialties and often with medical school affiliations as well. They are considered as referral medical centers by physicians with problem cases throughout the region. These hospitals tend to be located in the middle of large cities. Community hospitals, on the other hand, are usually much smaller, serving mostly patients in the immediate area and also staffed by local physicians who are largely office based practitioners. They have admitting privileges for their private patients, but little other responsibility to the hospital as an organization. In large metropolitan areas, like New York, they are found both in inner-city neighborhoods and in the suburbs, although new construction of such hospitals is almost entirely in the suburbs and many small inner-city community voluntaries are being forced to close.

Proprietary hospitals are privately owned (often by groups of physicians), operated for profit and tend to be very small. They provide a small percentage of the total hospital beds and do not really concern us in the present discussion. Local government general hospitals are tax supported (municipal or county in most cases, the States most often being the supporters of mental hospitals and other kinds of special institutions). They are usually large institutions providing care to the poor and tend to be looked on as less desirable by patients and staff alike. Local government hospitals may also be used for teaching and research by medical schools, but today their residency programs seldom have the high prestige enjoyed by the voluntary hospitals that are more directly affiliated with medical school teaching. So much government hospital effort is consumed in providing care on limited budgets to large numbers of patients that little opportunity remains for intensive teaching or research.

there is much more emphasis on the technical aspects and scientific quality of care than on the responsiveness to the patients involved.

Advancement in salary and status within the teaching hospital hierarchy, and hence in the profession, depends on technical virtuosity, astuteness in diagnosis and analysis of difficult cases, and perhaps most of all on national recognition within the chosen subspecialty group by means of research and publication [18]. Since income is largely determined by reputation and status, the chief motivating objective is to attain prestige within the subspecialty group. This is further influenced by the amount of geographic mobility which takes place between teaching hospitals by members of the faculty, similar to that found in other university faculties. Consequently, the subculture of the teaching hospital physicians is cosmopolitian, prestige-motivated, and colleague-oriented [19, 20]. The corresponding norms emphasize technical competence and team work, which can only be realized if the physicians focus their major attention on the technical elements of the disease process rather than on the patient as a person.

The dependency of the staff physician on the hospital produces a strong vested interest in the system of intensive specialty care, which is largely hospital based. This, together with the growing dependency of teaching hospitals on government funding for research and faculty support, leads to a further attitude that could come to be of great importance in regard to health-policy formulation and planning in the future. Unlike the traditional ideology of physicians in private practice, the teaching hospital physician more and more accepts a strong government role in the financing and even organizing of health services, as long as professionals maintain control of the technical aspects of care and research [21]. Many academic physicians would not even be averse to the creation of a national health service such as that in England—after all, their dominant position in the system is assured no matter what form of financing and organization of care exists.

The socialization of the teaching hospital physician transmits a direct line of tradition from one generation of medical school faculty to the next. This is the least problematic and least ambivalent professional socialization process as long as the physicians remain within the university hospital system. However, it may ill-prepare them attitudinally and socially if they later leave the teaching hospital to take up practice in the community office based health care system. Medical school itself is part of the direct line of socialization for teaching hospital physicians. Besides providing the student with the basic knowledge, skills, norms, and values of the profession as a whole, the setting of much of undergraduate medical education within the teaching hospital situation shapes attitudes, identification, and norms that are much more in accord with the role of the academic physician than of the physician in community office practice. If the new physician takes up practice outside the teaching hospital, other influences such as the altered structure of practice and changed vested interests have to undo or reshape the socialization of medical school. The process of professional socialization in medical school has been extensively studied from many points of view and the details need not be reviewed here since we are primarily interested in the results of that socialization in relation to other factors in the control of professional behavior.

During the 4 years leading to the M.D. degree, students are measured by and taught to think in terms of the standards of scientific medicine which can only be realistically maintained in the teaching hospital setting. They are constantly made aware of the prestige and financial advantages of specialty residency training in a university affiliated hospital and experience only the role model of the able, super-specialized faculty members and specialty residents in training. Even if their original intention was to go into general practice, which was still the case for the majority until very recently, by the end of medical school almost every student intends to pursue residency training and go into specialty practice, a key attitude necessary for teaching hospital practice.

Graduation from medical school today marks only the halfway point in medical education and professional socialization for those who will become teaching hospital physicians. A year of internship before licensure is required of all who wish to practice. Two to five years more of residency lie ahead for those wishing to qualify for their specialty and subspecialty board examinations. Beginning the internship marks a branching point in the process of socialization. Mumford [22] has carefully documented the important influences that this type of internship has on further professional socialization. The interns, who will eventually become and remain teaching hospital staff physicians, find themselves in a major teaching hospital with a graded residency program, research and medical student teaching, and the kind of highly specialized and prestigious superiors as role models that they were used to in medical school. Here the transition is not very abrupt. They move gradually up the hierarchy, learning from those above and teaching those below with the certainty that they will qualify for their specialty boards in due time and take their assured position among the professional elite [23]. Identification from here on is clearly with their hospital based colleagues, and especially with the leaders of their chosen specialty group, wherever they practice and teach. In Merton's [24] sense, they becomes cosmopolitans [25,26]. For professional advancement they must seek national recognition based on scientific publication and membership in nationwide societies. For recognition of technical excellence, the interactive structure of the teaching hospital situation affords frequent opportunity for display of brilliance in diagnosis and of knowledge of the latest literature during ward rounds, as well as in the constant informal consultation.

The increasing dependency of physicians on hospitals and the corresponding encroachment of hospitals on physicians' independence have effects that are of long range importance for health care policy and planning and for medical education. The greater involvement in hospital based patient care is probably having the effect of making physicians more closely knit and allied as a group but less dependent on patients' attitudes and pressures. As Freidson [27, 28] has pointed out in reference to group versus solo practice, physicians working in a setting where there is a high degree of professional interaction tend to be much more sensitive to opinions of colleagues about their medical judgments and professional standards. At the same time, however, they are less sensitive to the feelings of patients and less ready to meet their demands and expectations for personal consideration. This interactive influence on professional behavior must be even stronger in the case of hospital practice where there is not only interaction but also formal and informal surveillance of each other's work and increased opportunity to learn more directly about the latest standards and advances in clinical care from a technological point of view. An indirect effect of the increased role of hospitals in medical practice is therefore probably an improvement in the technical quality of care provided by physicians in these settings but a decreasing closeness of the physician–patient relationship and less responsiveness to the non-technical needs of patients in illness situations.

During residency, patients are seen almost exclusively in the hospital setting, usually as inpatients, and contact between the resident or intern and patients, families, or communities consists mostly of brief encounters on the wards under stressful conditions. Patients are considered as "teaching material", and though they usually receive excellent technical care, the resident has little chance to relate to them as people. Because of the system of incentives and dependencies, the primary sense of responsibility is to the professional colleague group in reference to the standards of care. This is accentuated by the pressure of the work load and the close identification of interests with the hospital as the specialists' work domain and the source of professional security, prestige, and income. These hospital dependent forces make for independence from patient pressures.

Thus the socialization process of teaching hospital residents prepares them very effectively for continuing practice in a teaching-hospital setting. However, it may ill prepare the resident who goes the same route and then leaves the teaching hospital for private office based practice. Therefore, it is not only the socialization but also the congruence between socialization and the continuing incentive and organizational system that is important for the perpetuation of a smoothly functioning professional sub-culture. The team-practice organization of care and the graded hierarchy of responsibility in the teaching hospital assure the continued orientation toward technical excellence and prestige. This, together with the dependency on the hospital for income and patients as well as for prestige rewards, assures the persistence of a research and disease orientation rather than a patient-orientation. In the university hospital, where referred patients present complex diagnostic and therapeutic problems, these attitudes serve well. In other settings the result is often less satisfactory.

The Suburban Office Based Physician

Unfortunately, the statistics available for the number of physicians engaged in community office based practice and their distribution are much poorer than those for hospital based practice. The difficulty is that most physician statistics are collected on a county basis which seldom distinguishes between central city and suburban locations of physicians. Nevertheless, the data on New York City and its surrounding suburban counties (see Table 14-1) suggests strongly that office based suburban practice is rapidly growing, although it is not known what percentage of the national total this group makes up.

Suburban office practice has many of the characteristics of the inner city office based practice described by Hall [29] 30 years ago, with the exception that it is less highly integrated professionally because it is geographically more diffuse and lacks the hierarchical structure of hospital appointments and consultation pattern found formerly. Suburban office based physicians nearly all have admitting privileges at the local community hospital, but cases are usually quite routine and uncomplicated, requiring comparatively little time from the physician for supervision. Since they also are not obligated to contribute time for teaching or working in the clinics, physicians do not spend much time interacting with colleagues in the hospital setting. Even if they are board-certified specialists, community physicians can seldom limit their practice entirely to a single subspecialty because the more scattered pattern of practice provides less opportunity for referral work. This decreases any identification they might have had with the national subspecialty peer group, and tends to evoke a solidarity with local colleagues of all specialties, more on a "guild" or political basis than on that of technical interdependency.

The community physician's income is nearly always on a fee-for-service basis, and as Freidson [30] and Roemer [31] have noted, this leads to much greater patient-dependence on the part of the physician. In order to develop a stable clientele, physicians in solo fee-for-service practice must conform to patients' expectations and pressures, often at the expense of the technical quality of care. Physicians in this setting tend to prescribe more freely ("to give the patient a feeling he is getting something for his visit"), to recommend more frequent return visits (which are usually shorter), and to postpone or avoid more complex diagnostic testing, as well as routine preventive care. As a result of the financial incentives and constraints embodied in the usual health care insurance schemes, as well as of the patient dependent pressure, solo fee-for-service leads to more frequent hospitalization and to more frequent surgery, especially for conditions where the decision is a subjective one (based on other than direct pathological evidence) such as tonsillectomy and much gynecological surgery [32].

Community physicians may be well trained and desirous of maintaining high technical standards of care, but they neither receive the constant new information and stimulation given the teaching hospital physician, nor do they have an incentive system that motivates them to keep abreast of the latest medical knowledge. Their livelihood and professional advancement depend not on research and teaching prestige, but on the good will of their fellow physicians and of their patients. They receive patients not by referral based on their position in the hospital and its prestige within the medical profession, but because of personal reputation within the community. Among patients this reputation derives from the physician's responsiveness, concern, professional image, and, more and more today, from sheer availability. Among fellow physicians this reputation is based to some extent on technical competence, at least to a minimum acceptable level for the group, but more importantly on following the norms of the local professional group, including reciprocity in referral and return of patients, solidarity in relation to the lay public, etc.

Thus the community physicians' incentive and sanction system plays down the learned profession element of their role and emphasizes the guild element. As Freidson [33] has pointed out, the sanction and incentive system of the self-regulating local guild structure tends to decrease opportunity for upgrading technical competence through interaction because doctors tend to establish referral and interactive networks with others who have about the same level and standards of competence [34]. If some physicians violate the ethical or technical standards of others, the only sanction usually available is simply to stop referring patients to them and to stop interacting with them. Such ostracized physicians then have to find groups of associates who come closer to their standards—or remain completely isolated professionally, something that is not difficult today, given the demand for physicians and the solo fee-for-service structure of practice. Thus a stratified division of the physician interaction system tends to build up in the community, with the result that little chance occurs for the less competent physicians to learn from the better trained.

The subculture of the community office based physician is predominantly "local" (parochial in Merton's sense), motivated by general social rewards and patient-oriented. The norms emphasize the practical concerns of the day-to-day practice of medicine, especially patient care and professional autonomy. The dependency of the physician on the patient, immediate community, and local colleague group leads to an ideology that strongly opposes any government initiative or power in the financing and organizing of health care [35, 36]. This is mirrored in the county medical societies' and AMA House of Delegates' stand against Medicare, Professional Standards Review Organizations (PSROs), etc.

This subculture obviously requires quite a different socialization process from that of the teaching hospital physician. Yet, the four years of medical school are the same for all physicians, leading, as we have seen, directly toward socialization for the teaching hospital setting. Until quite recently the route to community practice was often by way of internship in the community hospital serving the area where the physician hoped to establish himself [37]. However, there is evidence that this pattern is changing rapidly today as hospital based practice in the suburbs begins to encompass a major segment of physicians in these areas (see Table 14-1), and as the direct route from a teaching hospital residency to suburban community practice is becoming more common (see below). Nevertheless, the professional socialization process in the community hospital internship, as it reached its peak about ten years ago, will be described first because it represents the route that many of those physicians took who are now actively practicing in the suburbs.

The community hospital internship provided an opportunity for resocialization in a setting that both contained a continuation of the identity from the student role and a preparation for the solo-practice role of the community physician. Community hospital interns were more immediately on their own than those in teaching hospital settings where most decisions are part of a team effort. On the other hand, there was much less need and opportunity to develop sophisticated diagnostic and therapeutic skills, since cases were less complicated and attending physicians were more apt to make decisions unilaterally [38]. Thus, assumption of independent physician status was abrupt, but more limited in the long run in technical expertise. The orientation was toward competence in patient relations and service rather than teaching, research and complex diagnosis, or techniques of scientific management of diseases. This led to a shift in professional norms, values, and roles, accompanied by a change of reference group and incentive structure. Their reference group was no longer the highly specialized, cosmopolitan faculty with its prestige and incentive system, but the local community based physician group whom they served as interns, and on whom they would be dependent for referrals and cooperation when practicing in the community. This socialization fit them for solo practice, but made them less capable of working later in a group practice or in any structured professional hierarchical setting. It likewise led to the traditional ideology of physician autonomy. Thus, as with teaching hospital physicians, the socialization of community office based physicians was congruent with the social organization of their practice and the system of incentives and sanctions which motivated their actions. Consequently, all the influences that governed their professional behavior supported each other and were in turn supported by an ideology commensurate with the dependencies and vested interests generated by the technology and environment of their practice setting.

In recent years, however, the pattern of community hospital internship leading to office based practice in the same community has been rapidly disappearing. Partly as a result of conscious policy to bring residency training under more academic control, partly as a result of funding mechanisms, and partly because of preference on the part of residents for the prestige of university hospitals, the growth of training programs has been more rapid in university affiliated hospitals. By 1970, almost 90% of specialty residents were to be found in these hospitals [39]. Thus the vast majority of American Medical School graduates today receive their internship and specialty training in teaching hospitals.

At the same time, over 10,000 residents per year are now completing their training, and this is far more than can possibly be absorbed into permanent staff positions in teaching hospitals and on university faculties. Many of these graduates are finding new hospital based positions in non-academic settings—as indicated by the rapid growth in the percentage of physicians practicing primarily in hospital settings even in the suburbs. Many teaching hospital trained residents, who are attracted by the higher incomes and less stressful life of the suburban physician, also take up community office based practice. This influx of well trained physicians into the community system is important for maintaining and upgrading the average level of care. However, it leads to role ambivalence and resocialization problems that are not without serious consequences for the health care system. After eight to ten years of training in medical school and teaching hospital settings with emphasis on high technical standards of care, research, and teaching geared to the values, prestige, and incentive system surrounding esoteric and technically difficult cases, the physician who then elects to take up office practice in a suburban community finds himself facing a very different situation than he has been training for. The structure of community practice, as described above, is much more individualistic in organization, more concerned with routine kinds of cases and has less call for sophisticated technology or diagnostic virtuosity. Consequently, the physician is required to be less disease-oriented and more patient-oriented.

Unlike those who previously had community hospital internships, these new physicians do not have the opportunity for resocialization in the transitional local hospital setting. It is difficult to say precisely what the long-range effect will be of this new route to suburban office based practice. Many seem to be seeking out others of similar age and training in the community and establishing loose group practices with shared laboratory and office assistants. These multi-specialty, fee-for-service group "clinics" are becoming common in suburban areas. They have the advantage of allowing physicians to cover emergency calls for each other on a regular schedule and to consult fairly easily with each other, thereby improving the chance of maintaining a higher quality of care. They have the disadvantage of tending to preserve the hospital attitudes of disease-orientation rather than patient-orientation, thereby adding to the growing patient dissatisfaction with specialists. They also have the disadvantage of isolating the new, well trained physicians even more from older practitioners in the area, thus decreasing the probability that there will be diffusion of skills and knowledge.

Those who do not find such a group practice setting probably have a much harder time both in keeping up their technical competence and in fitting into community practice. Many try valiantly to do so. Some travel many miles several times weekly in order to keep some kind of teaching hospital affiliation. Others eventually move into full-time hospital positions. Some, perhaps especially those who take over a father's practice or otherwise have strong community ties, manage to make the transition completely to the community physician's attitude of responsiveness to the patients, but unfortunately there is then probably less chance that they will be able to maintain the technical quality of their care. In any case, this problem of fitting new hospital trained specialists into the present community system of medical care appears to be one of growing importance and needs to be better understood. They are being turned out in ever larger numbers with little planning for their integration into the existing health care system.

The Inner City Office Based Physician

The extremes of the professional stratification system are found not in suburban communities but in the central city. In the suburbs, where nearly all physicians have and use hospital staff privileges, there is at least this degree of interaction and mutual scrutiny between physicians with different levels of status and competence. In the central city, the physician population is rapidly moving toward complete division into two distinct groups. The teaching hospital group discussed above was traditionally extended by a part-time attending ("visiting") group of physicians having admitting privileges on the hospital's private services in exchange for contributing their time to teach medical students and often to provide services in the hospital's outpatient department. However, as the residency system continues to strengthen and the number of full-time salaried positions in the hospital grows, there is increasing restriction of hospital privileges for such part-time attending physicians, who are usually older and less research-oriented [40]. This is markedly increasing the isolation of the hospital based from the office based physicians in the inner city, even from the once prestigious but now shrinking group of "Park Avenue" physicians. Almost completely isolated from the teaching hospital physicians, however, is a newly growing group of physicians, the so-called "Medicaid physicians".

Side by side geographically with the hospital medical staff, but in no contact professionally, another group of physicians practice in the deteriorating neighborhoods in which the university affiliated hospitals are increasingly coming to find themselves. These inner city physicians often have no hospital privileges at all or have them only at one of the small, outmoded voluntary or proprietary hospitals which were left behind in the middle-class flight to the suburbs. Until 1965 they were mostly older men who had practiced all their lives in these areas, usually serving a particular ethnic group living in that neighborhood. As medicine moved on technically and the more upwardly mobile patients and physicians moved to the suburbs, these physicians remained behind both geographically and professionally in the quality of their care and in their associations. If present trends continue, this group will not be replaced in the next generation.

More recently, as Medicaid has again made private medical care financially feasible in these areas, these older physicians are being joined by increasing numbers of foreign trained physicians whose chances for a successful practice in the suburbs are not so good*, and by some entrepreneurial opportunists who are making handsome incomes in so-called "Medicaid centers" [42]. These physicians establish part-time offices in poor areas, usually in groups including dentists, podiatrists, pharmacists, and their own commercial laboratory facilities. By cross referral (so called "ping-ponging") excessive use of laboratory and prescription services, and seeing patients at a rapid rate, they are able to build up large charges even at the low rates paid by Medicaid fee schedules. Any patient who has a complicated problem or seems time-consuming is immediately referred to the nearest hospital outpatient department, which is the only specialty referral possibility open in these areas. It should be added that these Medicaid centers do perform an important service in the eyes of the local community members who use them. Patients in these areas usually have little other source of medical care except the hospital outpatient departments with their long waits and fragmented, impersonal health care. In the Medicaid clinics they can get prompt care and find out whether it is necessary to undertake the outpatient department ordeal.

Little information is available about the number of office based physicians practicing in these poverty areas or about their subculture, professional organization, and incentive systems. Consequently, the description and analysis presented here are based on very limited personal observation and on unsystematic reports from other sources. It must, therefore, be considered as tentative and suggestive until a more careful study is completed. What is obvious from the age distribution and density of physicians who have their primary offices in poverty areas is that the older ethnic neighborhood physician described by Hall [43] is a vanishing breed even in urban working-class ethnic communities [44]. The number of new (Medicaid) physicians is difficult to determine from regular physician censuses because they often have several offices, working in each only part of the time and giving the best neighborhood as their official address. Nevertheless, if one can judge from the high density of storefront Medicaid centers along the main streets of poverty communities, the number of physicians practicing in this way is considerable.

In spite of the fact that the Medicaid centers or clinics have the appearance of group practices and often list a half dozen M.D.s on their gaudy advertising sign boards, the professional organization of practice is essentially solo and fee-for-service. There is usually only one physician on the premises at a time—the other space being occupied by dentists, chiropodists, and other health practitioners. The part-time basis on which they practice in each location implies that they have no regular panel of patients, but only a shifting clientele available because of the restricted choice open to residents of such communities. Thus these physicians have neither the cosmopolitanism, colleague orientation, and prestige motivation of teaching hospital physicians, nor the localism, guild-like

*One recent sample of 100 new members consecutively admitted to the Queens County Medical Society revealed that 96 were foreign medical graduates [41].

professional solidarity, patient dependence, and community orientation of the suburban office based physician or the older urban ethnic community physician. They are excluded from the technology of the hospitals essential for the practice of high quality medicine and from the colleague solidarity or community ties necessary to develop a patient responsive practice. In a sense, the only incentive left open to them is the financial one, and therefore the only remaining possible organizational principle for professional activity is commercial!

Interestingly, the professional "socialization" of this group of physicians seems to be just as well matched to their final form of practice, subculture, and organizational and incentive systems as were those for the older groups described. Since they are largely foreign medical graduates, they are socialized essentially by exclusion. In part they are U.S.-born students who could not gain admission into American medical schools, but most are foreign nationals who come here with the original intent of getting better training and then returning home. Yet, once here and attracted by the high earnings and standard of living enjoyed by American physicians, they attempt to gain U.S. licensure and to become citizens. Generally considered poorly qualified by American physicians and patients they are systematically excluded from the more prestigious teaching hospital internships and residencies. They are forced to intern in large, rundown inner-city municipal hospitals serving the poor, or in smaller community hospitals, neither of which can otherwise fill their internships today because of the growth of the residency programs in the professionally more attractive teaching hospitals. Over fifty per cent of the interns in such hospitals are now foreign medical graduates. Community hospital and municipal hospital interns often receive very little supervision and have little opportunity to improve their knowledge or skills, and are essentially exploited as cheap professional labor in the face of the growing demand for M.D.s available on a full-time basis in such hospitals. They remain in such hospital positions until they can pass their state licensure examinations (which often requires several years and repeated attempts).

It quickly becomes clear to those foreign trained physicians who intern in suburban community hospitals that there is little chance of establishing viable practices in the surrounding community—at least for the foreign nationals, most of whom are from the Philippines, India, or South America [45] and are hardly welcomed in these white middle class enclaves. Thus, there are only a limited number of options open to them: (1) They can seek employment at local government (city, county, or state) hospitals serving the poor—or they may even find employment in a staff capacity in community hospitals in certain limited positions, such as in the emergency rooms. (2) They can perhaps gain admission to a residency program in one of the less visible specialties, such as anesthesiology or pathology. (3) They can set up general practice in Medicaid clinics in poverty communities, as described above, as soon as they pass their licensure examination. This final route, which is financially the most attractive and certainly the quickest way to establish themselves, appears to be an increasingly frequent choice. For those who take this route, the professionally controlled socialization is at an end. Further behavioral influences will come from the commercial setting in which they practice and to some limited extent from patient pressures.

In summary, the shifting demography of metropolitan areas and the changing technology of medicine, with the increase in specialization and in hospital based practice, appear to be leading to the development of a new structure for the medical profession. The old professional stratification, which was dominated by an office based elite who controlled both the hospitals and the status system of other office based physicians, is gradually disappearing by attrition. In its place a new system of differentiation is emerging based on three predominantly growing patterns of practice, with little interaction between them. Each of these types of practice is structurally stabilized, and growing as a result of the congruence between its socialization process that feeds new physicians into practice, its incentive system that continues to motivate professional behavior, and its organizational structure that determines interaction and vested interests—though the new route of socialization for suburban office practice seems less congruent and more problematic than previously.

The development of these new dominant patterns of practice as professional structures has important practical and theoretical implications which call for further study. From the perspective of the planning and delivery of health services, the shift of large numbers of physicians into hospital settings and suburban office practice threatens to worsen seriously the maldistribution of physician service available to different parts of the population and to perpetuate, or even to intensify, the two-class system of medical care already in existence. Due to the declining number of urban office based physicians, the poor in the inner city are forced either to use hospital outpatient departments and emergency rooms with their long waits, unpleasant settings, and impersonal care, or to risk the low technical quality of care in Medicaid clinics. Suburbanites, on the other hand, are apt to suffer the potential dangers of an overabundance of physicians, leading to the increasing tendency toward over-hospitalization and unnecessary surgery.

From the perspective of the sociologist concerned with the theory of professions, these findings pose interesting questions of a different kind. In regard to the medical profession, sociological theory until now has dealt largely with the problems of differences between professional and non-professional occupations [46–50] and to a limited degree with the different physician-patient relationships in solo and group practice settings. [51, 52]. With the exception of Hall's long outdated study [53], little consideration has been given to the differentiation within the profession—nor to the influences of changing technology and demography on its organization. To encompass these factors in a theory of professional dynamics seems to call for a much more inclusive theory of the relationship between professional behavior, social structure, and organization of practice around technology than has heretofore been available. The shifting structure of the medical profession in recent years provides a natural experiment from which to develop such a theory.

References

1. Hall O. The informal organization of medical practice in an American City. Unpublished Ph.D. dissertation, University of Chicago, 1944.
2. Hall O. The informal organization of the medical profession. *Can. J. Econ. polit. Sci.* **12**, 30, 1946.
3. Hall O. Stages in a medical career. *Am. J. Sociol.* **53**, 327, 1948.

4. Hall O. Types of medical careers. *Am. J. Sociol.* **55**, 243, 1949.

5. Stevens R. *American medicine and the Public Interest.* Yale University Press, New Haven, 1971.

6. Kendall P. Medical specialization: trends and contributing factors. In *Psychological Aspects of Medical Training* (Edited by Coombs R. and Vincent C.), C. C. Thomas, Springfield, Ill. 1971.

7. American Medical Association, *Reference Data on the Profile of Medical Practice,* Chicago, 1974.

8. Hall O. Stages in a medical career. *Am. J. Sociol.* **53**, 327, 1948.

9. American Medical Association, *Distribution of Physicians in the United States,* Chicago, 1973.

10. Kendall P. *The Relationship between Medical Educators and Medical Practitioners: Sources of Strain and Occasions for Cooperation,* Ass. Am. Med. Colleges, Evanston, Ill. 1965.

11. Miller A. The distribution and utilization of health services in NYC. New York Comprehensive Health Planning Agency, Mimeo., 1972.

12. Navarro V. A critique of the present and proposed strategies for redistributing resources in the health sector and a discussion of alternatives. *Med. C.* **12**, 721, 1974.

13. Dewey D. Where the physicians have gone. Chicago, Illinois, Illinois Regional Medical Program, Chicago Regional Hospital Study, 1973.

14. Rushing W. *Community, Physicians and Inequality,* D. C. Heath, Lexington, Mass. 1975.

15. Kendall P. *op. cit.*

16. American Medical Association, *op. cit.* 1974.

17. Stevens R. *op. cit.*

18. Mumford E. *Interns: From Students to Physicians.* Harvard University Press, Cambridge, 1970.

19. *Ibid.*

20. Miller S. *Prescription for Leadership: Training for the Medical Elite.* Aldine, Chicago, 1970.

21. Colombotos J., Kirchner C. and Millman M. Physicians view national health insurance: a national study, *Med. C.* **13**, 369, 1975.

22. Mumford E. *op. cit.*

23. Miller S. *op. cit.*

24. Merton R. K. Patterns of influence: local and cosmopolitan influentials. In *Social Theory and Social Structure* (Edited by Merton R. K.). Free Press, New York, 1968.

25. Kendall P. *op. cit.*

26. Mumford E. *op. cit.*

27. Freidson E. *Patients' Views of Medical Practice,* Russell Sage Foundation, New York, 1961.

28. Freidson E. *Profession of Medicine.* Dodd Mead, New York, 1970.

29. Hall O. *op. cit.* 1944.

30. Freidson E. *op. cit.*

31. Mumford E. *op. cit.*

32. Perrot *Federal Employees' Health Benefit Study,* Department of Health, Education, and Welfare, United States Government Printing Office, 1972.

33. Freidson E. *op. cit.*

34. Mumford E. *op cit.*

35. Strickland S. *U.S. Health Care: What's Wrong and What's Right.* Universe Books, New York, 1972.

36. Colombotos J., Kirchner C. and Millman M. *op. cit.*

37. Mumford E. *op. cit.*

38. *Ibid.*

39. Stevens R. *op. cit.*

40. Kendall P. *op. cit.*

41. Tuchman L. (personal communication), Queens County Medical Society, 1972.

42. *New York Times,* Nov. 15, 1976.

43. Hall O. *op. cit.* 1944.

44. Reibstein R. and Stevenson G. A study of physician mobility in New York City, 1960–1970. New York City Health Services Administration, Mimeographed, 1974.

45. American Medical Association, *Reference Data on the Profile of Medical Practice,* Chicago, 1974.

46. Parsons T. Professions. In *International Encyclopedia of the Social Sciences.* Macmillan, New York, 1963.

47. Goode W. Community within a community: the professions. *Am. sociol. Rev.* **22,** 194, 1957.

48. Barber B. Some Problems in the Sociology of the Professions. In *The Professions in America* (Edited by Lynn K. and Editors of *Daedalus*). Beacon Press, Boston, 1965.

49. Hughes E. *Men and their Work.* The Free Press, Glencoe, Ill. 1958.

50. Greenwood E. Attributes of a Profession. *Soc. Work* **2,** 45, 1957.

51. Freidson E. *op. cit.,* 1970.

52. Freidson E. *Professional Dominance.* Atherton, New York, 1970.

53. Hall O. *op. cit.*

W. TIMOTHY ANDERSON
and
DAVID T. HELM

15   The Physician-Patient Encounter: A Process of Reality Negotiation

The aim of this chapter is to discuss the socially constituted influences of place, structure, manifest and latent status, class, race, sex, and language on the physician–patient encounter. It is proposed that these factors, working individually and in combination, give the physician a disproportional advantage in the process of negotiation which occurs within this encounter.

The physician–patient encounter (often loosely referred to as the doctor–patient relationship) has been examined, analyzed, and widely debated since the early 1950s. L. J. Henderson first introduced systems theory as a mode of analysis of social relationships, and from this functionalist perspective reviewed the physician–patient encounter. Henderson (1956) cautioned physicians that they could do as much harm to the patient with the slip of a word as with a slip of the knife. Although he first introduced systems analysis, it was Talcott Parsons who initiated the broad interest in this social situation. Parsons (1951) argued that the physician was affectively neutral, collectively oriented, and universalistic in his application of a high degree of skill and knowledge. Further, he averred that the physician–patient encounter was harmonious and that both participants had similar goals and expectations.

In an updated analysis, Parsons (1975) argues that the encounter involves an "asymmetrical structure of the role relationship" (p. 264), which is "confined to a hierarchical component of authority, power and prestige." Thus Parsons refers to expertise (credentialed or licensed) or competency to deal with health-related issues; but he does not take into account the day-to-day features—the inanimate and tangible features—of the encounter, which have a profound effect upon it. Further, Parsons supports a notion that the expert should have an asymmetrical power-advantage over the patient in order to most effectively socialize the patient into adhering to the physician's regimen. We are not concerned, in this analysis, with what should or should not be, but rather with an explication of why the physician has this power-advantage in the typical encounter. What are the features of the encounter that foster or promote this type of relationship?

Although we agree with Parsons that the physician's credentialed expertise is the reason the patient seeks out his or her advice to begin with, there are many other features of the encounter besides symptomology and medicinal prescriptions that result in power differences. Such features as aspects of sex roles, orga-

The authors wish to thank John B. McKinlay, Irving K. Zola, Sol Levine, and Jeff Coulter for reading and commenting upon drafts of this chapter. We owe special thanks to Linda Finguerra and Teri Anderson for their continued support and assistance.

nizational ethos, language, type-1 or -2 errors, typifications, place, and functional uncertainty all play important parts in the overall picture—most of which has been ignored by Parsons and his disciples. Parsons' image of this encounter remained the dominant one until Eliot Freidson's analysis emerged some years later.

Freidson, working with a conflict, constructionist perspective, analyzed the relationship as one potentially and inherently conflictual because of the differing perspectives each participant brings to the encounter. Further, because Freidson concentrates his analysis on the sociology of work and professionalism, its major thrust deals with routinization of work, professional authority, and professional prestige (1970a, b). Although he acknowledges that medicine is practiced in "an organized framework which influences the behavior of doctors and patients" (1970a:91) he does not evaluate and analyze the situational, concrete, and nonbehavioral aspects of the encounter. That is, he does not emphasize sufficiently the mundane, taken-for-granted interactional components which have a profound impact on the interaction and outcome of the encounter. All students of the physician–patient encounter are indebted to Freidson for the powerful insight and lucidity he brings to the consideration of it as a social process, wherein he begins to "turn away from an uncritical optimism about the role of specialized knowledge in ordering human affairs" (1970a:xi).

Although Parsons and Freidson have presented the dominant views, there are a number of other important perspectives. For instance, Szasz and Hollander (1956), using a psychoanalytical perspective, divide the physician–patient encounter into three distinct categories: (1) activity/passivity, (2) guidance/cooperation, and (3) mutual participation. Thus, the critically ill emergency case involves an active physician and a passive patient. The chronically ill patient ideally falls into the third category, mutual participation, although the relationship often remains in the guidance/cooperation stage. Szasz and Hollander psychologize these categories as being similar to parent/infant, parent/child, and adult/adult types of relationships, respectively.

Wilson and Bloom (1972) view the physician–patient encounter as a social system. They stress that each participant enters into the relationship with expectations and an understanding of the procedure resulting from particularized reference groups all within a similar sociocultural matrix. It is argued that the encounter is actually a meshing of viewpoints and activities. Michael Balint's (1957:216) analysis carries this one point further when he refers to the apostolic function of the physician:

> Apostolic function means that every doctor has a vague, but unshakeably firm idea of how a patient ought to behave when ill. It is as if the doctor had the knowledge of what was right and wrong for the patient to expect and to endure, and further, as if he had the . . . duty to convert to his faith all the ignorant and unbelieving among his patients."

Quest for Dominance

These analysts have all implied, in varying degrees of explicitness, that the encounter involves a vying for, or a process of persuasion for, dominance by each participant. Waitzkin and Stoeckle (1976) have viewed it as a micropolitical system in which the physician uses control of information, at least in part, to maintain patterns of dominance and subordination. Again, the implication is that what is actually going on in the encounter is a process of reality negotiation between two (or more) participants with competing conceptualizations. It is the perceived scientific, "objective" nature of this encounter that has resulted in a mystification of the physician's dominance and position. By demystifying the encounter and examining it as a process, we hope to de-reify each participant's role and thereby further knowledge of the medical system.

Reality is socially constructed. This powerful concept, as developed by Berger and Luchmann (1967), increasingly informs much of the current investigation and analysis of society. The social reality that man knows, man has created. Perceived reality is intersubjective in nature, influenced by prevailing ideologies, environment, social context, and numerous other factors. Given the diverse nature of man and the myriad of social contexts extant in the world, there are many possible definitions of reality. In many social situations differing perceptions or definitions of them are held by the actors involved. The process of reaching some accord about the "true" nature of this reality is a process of reality negotiation—which rarely starts from a position of parity. That is, in some situations certain individuals have or obtain a mandate to impose their definition, especially for those situations entailing explanation. As Louch (1966) notes:

> . . . when we offer explanations of human behavior, we are seeing that behavior as justified by the circumstances in which it occurs. *Explanation of human action is moral explanation.* In appealing to reasons for acting, motives, purposes, intentions, desires, and their cognates, which occur in both ordinary and technical discussions of human doings, we exhibit an action in the light of the circumstances that are taken to entitle or warrant a person to act as he does. [Emphasis added]

Claims of objectivity or empirical warrant to the contrary, explanation of action must involve evaluation, and evaluation is necessarily affected by various subjective factors.

Awareness of the subjective nature of what has heretofore been regarded as objective, physical occurrences has salient implications for the study of events in medicine, for as Freidson (1970a:205) notes, "Medicine is involved in the creation of illness as a social state which a human being may assume." This is an ongoing process in which medical practitioners and institutions create and maintain the definitions of what is "health" and what is "illness." These categories established by and through the medical system constitute a social reality distinct from any physical reality. Within this model even a seemingly objective, physiological state such as pregnancy can be viewed as "a social construction which may be independent of 'objective' reality" (Miller, 1975:6). As Freidson (1970a:208) puts it so well: "Human, and therefore social, evaluation of what is normal, proper, or desirable is as inherent in the notion of illness as it is in the notions of morality."

The Encounter As Reality Negotiation

Given this perspective, the physician–patient encounter must be seen as a process of reality negotiation between frequently competing definitions of the situation. A new orientation is called for, one that focuses on the nature of these differing definitions and the ways in which they are typically resolved.

How then is the physician–patient encounter typically constituted for its participants? It is first and foremost a social situation, one that is an encounter, which occurs in a place and in which, typically, evaluation and explanation occur.

Place carries with it its own meaning and its own appropriate behavior (Gubrium, 1975). In America the usual context and structure of the physician–patient encounter, and therefore its perceived meaning, is in a process of transition. At the turn of the century most encounters occurred in the patient's home, on his "turf," at his convenience and request. As physicians gained status the site of the typical encounter shifted to the physician's office, where the physician's reality is reinforced by the context: the accouterments of the office, machines, nurses, etc. The patient was now coming *to* the physician, to his space, on his terms. The contemporary encounter between the physician and the patient increasingly occurs within an institution such as a clinic or hospital. Here the prevailing ideology is that of the institution, and the influence of place is even more compelling. The typical patient now goes not to see *the* doctor, but *a* doctor.

The physician–patient encounter often involves the presentation of accounts (Scott and Lyman, 1968). In order to diagnose, the physician asks for an account of "the problem" (i.e., a description of symptoms). The intersubjective nature of the account promotes the negotiative quality of the encounter. Accounts also arise *after* some consensus has been reached within the encounter, resulting in the social construction of evidence (Conrad, 1976), the reinterpretation of events in the patient's past in light of the present diagnosis. In the case of the child labeled hyperactive, for example, it means that behavior previously seen as "bad" or malicious is reevaluated in terms of the perceived "disease."

A factor that the intersubjective nature of accounts contributes to, and which is characteristic of the doctor–patient encounter, is uncertainty. Indeed, "uncertainty is often a factor in medical diagnosis in particular" (Conrad, 1976:52). Physicians have developed strategies to deal with uncertainty, including preferred error types (Scheff, 1963b), typification of symptoms and diseases (Scheff, 1973), batteries of protective tests, and conferences with peers or appeals to higher authority. Uncertainty is not always problematic for all parties. In fact, physicians can use uncertainty as a tool for dealing with patients (Davis, 1960), and in this vein, Davis distinguishes between clinical and functional uncertainty. The former is "real" uncertainty which is present in many aspects of medical diagnosis and prognosis; the latter is the uses, real or pretended, which the physician makes of uncertainty. That is, the physician may invoke uncertainty in order to foster hope in the patient and/or family, avoid scenes and make both patient and family more manageable, and abet the patient and his family in making the best of the illness.

Within any social situation the participating members are engaged in impression management (Goffman, 1959), which is dependent on others "not knowing." Thus in the physician–patient encounter, patients would be vulnerable to being discredited or discreditable (Goffman, 1963). The discredited are those with obvious stigmatizing traits; for example, they are blind, too fat, too short, or old. The discreditable have characteristics, diseases, or past experiences that could discredit them; for example, they may be homosexual, ex-convicts, ex-mental patients, hypertensive, or cancerous. Also, in most social situations the individual has controlled management techniques at his or her disposal, has the freedom to terminate the encounter, and is in a position to evaluate the social performance of the other. The physician, however, determines the length of the encounter, the where and when of it, and because of professionalism and medical mystique, is not usually subject to client evaluation (Freidson, 1970b).

Attempts at Conversion

Differing appraisals of the encounter may result in attempts at conversion, conceptualized by Balint as the "apostolic function" of the physician. This conversion is seen as necessary for the "succesful" encounter or the patient is likely to reject the physician's definition of the situation (i.e., as "illness") and not enter into or continue with what the physician feels is the appropriate treatment (Freidson, 1962). McIntosh (1974) cites the physician's awareness of this problem in regard to patients who have cancer. Miller (1975) notes further evidence in her examination of the process whereby women acquire the identity of pregnancy as medical as opposed to an essentially nonmedical natural identity; and medical literature is replete with examples of the poor compliance of patients diagnosed as hypertensive.

The differing appraisals of this encounter which necessitate the apostolic function both arise from and are present in many aspects of it. The presence of competing definitions of reality are structurally unavoidable in the professional–lay relationship. Whereas the patient is confronted with an immediate, personal, subjective experience of his or her symptoms or problems, often as a perceived crisis, the physician sees the patient as a case of, and frequently as a normal or typical case of, something or other. Thus the encounter is a routine one for the physician, whereas it is exceptional, often expensive, and frequently a cause of some apprehension for the patient. Stereotypical diagnoses thus serve to exacerbate the differing definitions of the situation held by patient and physician. Scheff (1963b) noted the categorization of illnesses at a rehabilitation agency; that is, physicians and staff classified illnesses and symptoms, often not taking the time or energy to thoroughly eliminate competing diagnoses, thereby facilitating a quicker diagnosis and thus increasing productivity. Freidson (1962) also notes that as patient's complaints are perceived to fall within an "ordinary" range, a mundane atmosphere may prevail, which serves to further reinforce, as opposed to the lay conceptualization of the situation, a separate world of experience and reference inherent to professional practice (Freidson, 1970b).

The impact of routinization on this separate world is vividly depicted by Sudnow (1967:101) in his discussion of physician reactions to a DOA (dead on arrival):

> It happened on numerous occasions, especially during the midnight-to-eight shift, that a physician was interrupted during a coffee break to pronounce a DOA and returned to his colleagues in the canteen with, as an account of his absence, some version of "Oh, it was nothing but a DOA."

Even death loses some of its compelling quality when it has been routinized— which of course may well help the physician cope with it on a recurrent basis. But it is still difficult to envision one's own death or that of those close to one as "nothing but a DOA."

Patients' expectations for and knowledge of the health-care system influence directly the course of the encounter. Those with too little knowledge are apt to try to evade the physician altogether, fail to carry out treatment, or fail to conform appropriately to the patient role. Those with "too much knowledge" are apt to be demanding, critical, or try to influence the physician in his course of treatment. "Only certain types of ideologies can be tolerated and implemented within the limits set by institutional necessities and the particular organization of treatment" (McIntosh, 1974:171).

The education, ideology, and ability of the patient to "play the game well" is frequently a function of ethnicity or social class. The patients' stock of knowledge will influence the degree to which they perceive the encounter as common or mysterious, scientific or magical, positive or negative. Indeed, Zola (1966) found that some ethnic groups tended to report their symptoms differently and even complained of different symptoms for the same illness. A frequent occurrence, especially in some of the more tenuous areas as mental illness or hyperactivity, is that after the diagnosis is made, the physician and the patient collaborate in the social construction of evidence. The ability of the patient and physician to "speak the same language" is important if consensus is to be reached.

McKinlay (1975) has demonstrated that working-class patients know a good deal more about medicine and medical terminology than physicians give them credit for. Yet,

> it has been observed that the amount of information a doctor gives to a patient
> is influenced by his perception of his socioeconomic status, or with attributes
> which he associates with it. . . . The higher the patient's status the more likely
> the doctor is to attribute to him a capacity to comprehend medical explanations.
> [McIntosh, 1974:172]

Thus, the physician is often in a position of talking down to his patients, as they are perceived as not having an equivalent stock of knowledge. Upper-class patients can be more demanding of physicians because they tend to view them as middle class (Hollingshead and Redlich, 1958).

Another aspect of the physician–patient encounter that promotes differing definitions of it is that for the patient it often represents, as well as a physical or psychological crisis, a severe monetary drain. When third-party payments are involved, this cost may be spread out over a long period, but it exists nonetheless. For those unable to pay, the encounter may thus be doubly threatening or embarrassing. In contrast, the encounter is one of financial gain for the physician. Although the profit motive has been emphasized in differing degrees by various analysts, it must be seen to have a significant impact on the physician's perception of the encounter, at least in fee-for-service medicine.

Recognizing that the encounter and the "problem" is differentially perceived by physician and patient, we can begin to see how the nature of the encounter provides for its process of reality negotiation, which most analysts allude to, at least implicitly. There are social, structural, and political features that tend to make the relative acceptance of their definition of the situation differ between patient and physician.

"The doctor's authority is in part based upon the esoteric nature of his knowledge" (McIntosh, 1974:168). Thus the physician's pronouncements are shrouded in a mystique based upon a stock of knowledge perceived to be inaccessible to the layman. This attitude is exemplified by the trepidation many medical professionals (both doctors and nurses) feel toward treating or being treated by a fellow professional ("When I found out he was a doctor, I nearly died").

The use of typification in diagnosis serves to anonymize or normalize the patient, thus making it easier to see him or her as an object and reinforcing the physician's authority. Typification can also lead to the assumption of illness, as noted by Scheff (1966) in his reports on sanity hearings in the midwest, where the interviewing psychiatrist assumed illness.

Type-1 and Type-2 Errors

Scheff (1966) also constructed a "preferred rule" for medical decision making. Basically there are two types of error: Type 1 rejects a hypothesis that is true; type 2 accepts a false hypothesis. In the courts the error to avoid is type 2, the conviction of an innocent man. In medicine, however, the one to avoid is type 1, dismissing a patient who is actually ill. Besides the personal or professional embarrassment for the physician or clinic, there is also the threat of malpractice lawsuits. Thus, patients are often given unnecessary, expensive, and sometimes potentially harmful tests in order to "cover" the doctor.

Along with the potential for legal and personal repercussions for the physician there is also the underlying assumption that unnecessary treatment or incorrect labeling is not as harmful as unattended disease or illness. Clearly this is not always the case. There are added costs to the patient, and often added gain for the physician. There may also be personal embarrassment, humiliation, or other unintended consequences for the patient. These added psychic and social costs are exemplified in the case of misdiagnosed mental illness. By avoiding a type-1 error in favor of the preferred type 2, the patient can be severely stigmatized. Interestingly, in the military psychiatric interview, the reverse is true (Daniels, 1973). Thus adherence to organizational criteria with a corresponding avoidance of the mental illness diagnosis permits the military psychiatrist to avoid the type-2 error.

Another feature fostering the physician's reality is his or her latent status and corresponding ability to intimidate the patient. Latent status is the professional's prestige within the community. "The established professions have obtained both the political power requisite for controlling the socio-legal framework of practice, and the social prestige for controlling the client in consultation" (Freidson, 1962:219). Szasz (1970) notes that the physician "legitimizes and illegitimizes the social aspirations and roles of others." The latent status or expertise ascribed to the physician results in an unequal balance of power for determining the resultant definition of the situation. The physician is well schooled and self-confident, whereas the lower-class patient is typically untutored, anxious, and uncertain about social roles; the middle-class patient is enamored with professionalism and the mystique of knowledge; and even the upper-class patient is increasingly un-questioning of the medical model and system. This attitude is exemplified by the weight attached to the pronouncements of physicians on matters far removed from the practice of medicine.

Setting also promotes inequality in the physician–patient encounter. Usually the examination is in the physician's office, a clinic, or a hospital. Clearly the physician is more familiar with, more comfortable with, and less mystified by these, his normal working surroundings, than is the patient. Emerson has pointed out that

> the definition of reality is validated by apparently trivial features of the social scene, such as details of the setting, person's appearance, demeanor, and in-consequential talk—thus reality is solidified by a process of intervalidation of supposedly independent events. [Emerson, 1970:75]

Further, the patient must be available at the physician's convenience, is often kept waiting, and has little control over when the encounter will be terminated. In those increasingly rare house calls, this advantage is neutralized or reversed. In clinics and hospitals the normal white attire of staff members and the institu-tional look of those places serve to further reinforce the feeling that the patient is an outsider, even an intruder.

In the encounter there are a number of other factors that increase the physi-cian's advantage in the negotiating sequence. Often the patient is at least partially disrobed, whereas the physician is fully dressed. This is an obvious strategic ad-vantage for the physician. Also the physician is frequently in a physically elevated position relative to the patient's. Whereas the patient is typically alone, the physi-cian is often assisted by a nurse, thus further legitimizing the physician's man-date. Indeed, in this vein, it is important to distinguish between technical and ceremonial acts, roles, and words in the physician's performance (Szasz, 1977).

Use of Language

Another major advantage those in the medical profession have in controlling and directing the reality negotiation is in their use of language. Physicians have available to them a highly complex, technical vocabulary which is not intelligible to the average lay person. The everyday language and talk of physicians can be even more inaccessible, as it is composed of abbreviations and shared (among physicians) tacit understandings. Language is often used to mystify, to desex-ualize, to confuse and intimidate the patient, as well as to reaffirm expertise. Emerson has noted that the gynecologist will refer to "the vagina" instead of "your vagina" when talking to a patient, again controlling the situation and the reality perception by role-distancing and desexualization.

It is through language that social realities are constructed, and through the expression of language that realities can be negotiated. The physician gains in power through his or her access to and control over the "legitimate" language of health and illness. Thus patients are urged in their presentation of symptoms and problems to recast their accounts in the appropriate nomenclature—which rein-forces the physician's mandate to determine *the* reality. Much of a physician's estimation of a patient's social status and expertise in medical matters comes through his or her evaluation of the patient's talk. Thus physicians' talk to patients reflects their assigned status and knowledge. McKinlay (1975) discusses the language physicians use while believing their patients to be ignorant of the meanings. In sum, language is an important tool for both achieving and maintaining power and authority in the physician–patient encounter.

The strategy of the interviewer plays an important part in the negotiation process (Scheff, 1963a). If the interviewer asks short, direct, concise questions that call for a similar response, the interviewer has an advantage. Similarly, the participant who refuses the first offer and proposes counteroffers also has a strategic advantage. The physician usually is in the advantageous position. The client has advantages if he or she knows that they, the participants, are negotiating. These two aspects are more readily seen in the legal rather than medical negotiation of reality. The patient's advantage is realized if he or she does all the responding and can propose counteroffers rather than initial offerings. Typically it is the physician who gathers control over the client in defining the resultant, shared definition of the situation. Daniels (1973) notes the phenomenon whereby most military patients are outranked by the military physician, and thus precluded from initiating interview strategy.

In organizational settings the interests, rules, and concerns of the organization often set the tone for the encounter in favor of the physician (Daniels, 1972, 1973). For instance, the army requires a ready and able fighting force; thus military medical personnel tend toward health rather than illness, especially psychiatric health. The soldier must first convince the nonmedical technician that he really has a problem, and then, if the lay technician is convinced, the soldier must renegotiate to try to convince the psychiatrist or physician. The psychiatrist presents an additional problem for the soldier during a war. If the patient is diagnosed as mentally ill or mentally incapacitated he is no longer available to fight, and in addition, may receive life-long disability payments from the government. The organizational criteria can effectively set an underlying assumption of health or illness that tends to focus the negotiation in favor of the physician who adheres to organizational goals and guidelines.

When the goals of the organization and the patient do not coincide, the question arises as to whose side the physician is on. This question is especially true of the employee physician who is the paid agent of a social organization rather than of an individual patient. Szasz articulates this problem in his article on "The Psychiatrist as Double Agent" (1973). The perception of the physician's allegiance, by both participants in the encounter, can have a pronounced effect upon its course. Consider some of the constraints that the hospital, as an organization with which physicians are frequently aligned, can exert upon the physician–patient encounter. One such constraint is patient load. Obviously the physician who is responsible for fifty or more seriously ill patients cannot give the same attention to bedside manner, patient counseling, etc. as the physician who is responsible for fewer patients. Similarly, the clinic physician who must see ten or more patients per hour is in a different position from the private physician who schedules two to four patients an hour. Organizational needs of the hospital can further shape the physician–patient encounter. Nanry and Nanry (1973) demonstrate how, in a teaching hospital, decisions regarding admission, treatment, and even discharge are in a large measure dependent upon organizational needs (i.e., which cases are good teaching cases) rather than the patient's needs.

As the current trend toward the physician as employee continues, organizational requirements, interests, and criteria will increasingly affect the physician–patient encounter. Professional concerns will more easily be co-opted by corporate interests and concerns, and the physician's pronouncements will be backed by the weight of the organization. McKinlay's article on "The Proletarianization of Physicians" (1978) clearly delineates this trend, as does the available data on the "company" doctor (Page and O'Brien, 1973).

Community Stature of the Hospital

Another way in which the organizational setting can affect the physician–patient encounter is through the general community stature of the hospital. Hospitals are increasingly being seen as "heavies" on the urban scene, engulfing and dispersing neighborhoods, underservicing and even abusing local lower-class and minority patients. This attitude may result in a group of patients treating the individual physician in that hospital with anger, resentment, or fear. The vast majority of physicians still come from middle- and upper-middle-class backgrounds, and are not always prepared or inclined to understand, appreciate, and effectively communicate with lower-class minority patients whose illnesses often reflect their lifestyles and living conditions.

Traditional sex roles also foster physician domination. The vast majority of American physicians today are male, and thus have recourse to that whole cluster of beliefs surrounding sex-appropriate behavior when dealing with female patients. "Medicine helps perpetuate the 'illness' role of women by giving the stamp of scientific approval to ideological myths" (Levinson, 1976:430). Indeed, sexism affects male patients as well, "for it is still considered 'unmasculine' to exhibit emotional or physical discomfort, complain, or submit to dependence on a medical practitioner" (Levinson, 1976:427).

We do not want to suggest that the patient has no recourse in the face of a domineering physician. He or she can evoke the defense of evasiveness, ignoring the physician's orders, avoiding further appointments, or playing "dumb" to effectively neutralize the physician's asymmetrical power-differences. Patients can also be too modest, too immodest, or ask "improper" questions. Since the patient rarely has higher community status or credentialed expertise in medical problems, his or her limited understanding of the pervasiveness of uncertainty in diagnosis can be beneficial. In other words, the patient can seek additional medical opinions and therefore does not need to rely on one physician's reality. (It should be noted that this behavior is deemed a violation of the "good patient" role in many settings today.)

It is recognized by the authors that in the preceding analysis the discussion of the superior status and power of the physician will be viewed by many as an implied, if not overt, criticism of the physician. Our intent was not, however, to be necessarily critical or judgmental. Rather it was to present a programmatic understanding of the social process of the physician–patient encounter as it occurs *in situ*, with an examination of the way in which various socially constituted social factors impinge upon it. However, in contemporary American society, the ascription of power carries with it a negative connotation. Despite this, power is a constitutive feature of many (if not all) everyday encounters, and as such must be recognized and its impact considered. This need is especially true where the encounters entail inherently differing or competing definitions of the situation, such as the physician–patient encounter.

It should be remembered that from the physician's perspective these differences in power and status are understandable and perhaps even essential. After all, one would not go to "healers" of any type unless he or she was deferring to their perceived expertise, knowledge, skill, and the like. For the physicians, their role, by definition, carries with it differences in authority and prestige. Furthermore, the way physicians are expected to behave—stereotypically cool, objective, and learned in the face of human suffering, sadness, and individual catastrophe—may facilitate distance, control, and self-preservation and enable them the psychic energy necessary to face the varied problems of the typical workday. Thus the social distance maintained by many physicians may help them cope with potentially stressful, emotional, and often negative interactions with patients and their families. Sudnow (1967) ably depicts the role of such social distancing in his discussion of the way medical personnel deal with death.

The features of the physician–patient encounter that have been discussed and analyzed work in varied combination. That is, the construction of the mutual reality is an asymmetrical process with the physician having the advantage in the typical encounter. Relating the structural and social features of the encounter to each participant's conception and expectation multiplies the physician's control. Usually an individual is the one who "knows" himself better than anyone else, but in an encounter with a physician the patient is potentially discreditable. The physician is the one who is in the position to tell the patient something new, something previously unknown to the patient. The physician has the power to illegitimize the patient's role; for example, he can diagnose schizophrenia, cervical cancer, venereal disease, or a variety of other discrediting traits.

The patient is often required to "play along" with conflicting realities. For instance, in a gynecological exam the physician has access to a woman's genitals, a potentially sexual, highly charged encounter. The patient is asked to accept this as a mundane, technical occurrence, that is, the physician's reality.

Conclusion

In conclusion, the social construction of reality in the patient–physician encounter is structured in an asymmetrical direction favoring the physician's reality. The patient's perception of reality can be negated or ignored by the physician. In the negotiating process the physician has the setting, language, latent status, stereotypical categorization of illness, tendency toward type-2 error, and organizational clout—all supporting his or her definition of reality over the patient's. The patient can ignore the physician's orders, fail to see the physician, directly challenge the doctor's reality, and in general be "irresponsible" in an effort to dominate the physician's reality. The patient can also try to change physicians or seek additional opinions. As the trend continues whereby the patient increasingly sees *a* doctor rather than *the* doctor, the physician's ability to control the negotiation will also increase. The physician–patient encounter is in a process of transition, but remains complex, inherently conflictual, and socially constituted.

References

Balint, Michael
1957 *The Doctor, His Patient and the Illness.* N.Y.: International Universities Press.
Berger, Peter, and Thomas Luchmann
1967 *The Social Construction of Reality.* N.Y.: Anchor Books.
Conrad, Pter
1976 *Identifying Hyperactive Children.* Lexington, Mass.: Lexington Books.
Daniels, Arlene
1972 "Military Psychiatry: The Emergence of a Subspecialty." In Eliot Freidson and Judith Lorber (eds.) *Medical Men and Their Work.* Chicago: Aldine Atherton Inc. Pp. 145–62.
1973 "The Philosophy of Combat Psychiatry." In Earl Rubington and Martin S. Weinberg (eds.) *Deviance: The Interactionist Perspective.* N.Y.: Macmillan Co. Pp. 132–140.
Davis, Fred
1960 "Uncertainty in Medical Prognosis, Clinical and Functional." *American Journal of Sociology.* 66. Pp. 41–47.
Emerson, Joan
1970 "Behavior in Private Places: Sustaining Definitions of Reality in Gynecological Examinations." *Recent Sociology.* No. 2. Pp. 73–100.
Freidson, Eliot
1962 "Dilemmas in the Doctor-Patient Relationship." In Arnold M. Rose (ed.) *Human Behavior and Social Processes.* Boston, Mass.: Houghton Mifflin.
1970a *Profession of Medicine.* N.Y.: Harper & Row.
1970b *Professional Dominance.* Chicago: Aldine.
Goffman, Erving
1959 *The Presentation of Self in Everyday Life.* N.Y.: Anchor.
1961 *Asylums.* N.Y.: Anchor.
1963 *Stigma.* Englewood Cliffs, N.J.: Prentice-Hall.
Gubrium, Jaber F.
1975 *Living and Dying at Murray Manor.* N.Y.: St. Martin's Press Inc.
Henderson, L. J.
1956 "Physician and Patient as a Social System." *New England Journal of Medicine.* Vol. 212. No. 18.
Hollingshead, A. B., and F. C. Redlich
1958 *Social Class and Mental Illness.* N.Y.: John Wiley & Sons.
Levinson, Richard
1976 "Sexism in Medicine." *American Journal of Nursing.* Vol. 76. No. 3.
Louch, A. R.
1966 *Explanation and Human Action.* Berkeley, Cal.: UCLA Press.
McIntosh, Jim
1974 "Processes of Communication, Information Seeking and Control Associated with Cancer." *Social Science & Medicine.* Vol. 8. No. 4.

McKinlay, John B.
1975 "Who Is Really Ignorant—Physician or Patient?" *Journal of Health and Social Behavior.* Vol. 16. No. 1. Pp. 3–11.
1978 "Towards the Proletarianization of Physicians." *Parts I & II International Journal of Health Services.* Vol. 8 (forthcoming).

Miller, Rita
1975 "The Social Construction and Reconstruction of Physiological Events: Acquiring the Pregnancy Identity." Presented at Midwest Sociological Society. April.

Nanry, Charles, and Jacqueline Nanry
1973 "Professionalization and Poverty in a Community Hospital." In Anselm L. Strauss (ed.) Second Ed. *Where Medicine Fails.* New Brunswick, N.J.: Transaction Books. Pp. 95–117.

Page, Joseph, A., and Mary-Win O'Brien
1973 *Bitter Wages.* N.Y.: Grossman Publishers.

Parsons, Talcott
1951 *The Social System.* N.Y.: The Free Press.
1975 "The Sick Role and the Role of the Physician Reconsidered." *Health and Society.* Summer. Pp. 257–278.

Scheff, Thomas J.
1963a "Negotiating Reality: Notes on Power in the Assessment of Responsibility." *Social Problems.* Vol. 16. Pp. 3–17.
1963b "Decision Rules and Types of Error, and Their Consequences in Medical Diagnosis." *Behavioral Science.* 8. Pp. 97–107.
1966 *Being Mentally Ill: A Sociological Theory.* Chicago: Aldine.
1973 "Typifications in Rehabilitation Agencies." In Rubington and Weinberg (eds.) *Deviance: The Interactionist Perspective.* N.Y.: Macmillan Co. Pp. 128–131.

Scott, Marvin B., and Stanford M. Lyman
1968 "Accounts." *American Sociological Review.* 33. Feb. Pp. 46–61.

Sudnow, David
1965 "Normal Crimes: Sociological Features of the Penal Code in a Public Defenders Office." *Social Problems.* No. 12.
1967 *Passing On: The Social Organization of Dying.* Englewood Cliffs, N.J.: Prentice-Hall.

Szasz, Thomas
1970 *Ideology and Insanity.* N.Y.: Anchor.
1973 "The Psychiatrist as Double Agent." In Anselm L. Strauss (ed.) Second Ed. *Where Medicine Fails.* New Brunswick, N.J.: Transaction Books. Pp. 225–242.
1977 *The Theology of Medicine: The Political-Philosophical Foundations of Medical Ethics.* N.Y.: Harper & Row.

Szasz, Thomas, and Marc Hollander
1956 "Contributions to the Philosophy of Medicine: Basic Models of Doctor-Patient Relationships." *Archives of Internal Medicine.* Vol. 97.

Waitzkin, Howard, and John D. Stoeckle
1976 "Information and Control and the Micro-Politics of Health Care." *Social Science and Medicine.* Vol. 6. June. Pp. 263–276.

Wilson, Robert, and Samuel Bloom
1972 "Patient-Practitioner Relationship." In Freeman, Levine, and Reeder (eds.) *Handbook of Medical Sociology.* Englewood Cliffs, N.J.: Prentice-Hall.

Zola, Irving K.
1966 "Culture and Symptoms—An Analysis of Patients' Presenting Complaints." *American Sociological Review.* 33. Pp. 615–630.

16 Mother Surrogate—After a Decade

Twenty years ago the writer terminated his article on "basic functional roles in nursing" with the statement that "nursing, with which the role of mother surrogate is so completely associated, will still be nursing [in the future], but it will be carried on by persons of other occupational affiliations, not the professional nurse."[1] Responses and comments to this statement came from many sources, chiefly from practicing nurses, nurse–educators and students in schools and colleges of nursing. Some were overtly hostile, others incredulous, others in agreement. Now a decade has passed and there is no longer any doubt that professional nursing has left the patient's bedside and that a majority of professional nurses have resolved the mother surrogate–healer role conflict by abandoning, circumventing or sublimating the mothering functions of the nurse's role. Although such a resolution is lamented by leaders in professional nursing,[2] it is difficult, if not impossible, to deny. The sociologist Rushing states that ". . . the conditions of social reality that sustain an image of the nurse as mother surrogate no longer exist."[3]

The obvious question which must then be raised is "Why?" What has happened to nursing and in nursing that has forced this resolution? This writer proposes that pressures from without as well as from within the discipline have molded, and are molding, the "new nurse," and that they have forced mother surrogate functions into the background if not into antiquity. There is no single factor which will explain the change: it is multi-causal with some factors immediate and apparent, others diffuse and evasive.

External Factors

Perhaps the most evasive factor which has affected the nurse's predominantly non-affective performance today is rooted in the American family. The mother surrogate role may be said to develop out of the multi-faceted functions of the traditional mother-parent. Long before the decade of change we are considering, the American mother–parent role had begun to change. As if in a geometric progression, the initial changes in this role were few, slow to reach fruition and epi-

[1]Schulman, S., "Basic Functional Roles in Nursing: Mother Surrogate and Healer," in E. G. Jaco (ed.), *Patients, Physicians and Illness,* New York: Free Press, 1958, chap. 54, p. 537.

[2]Reiter, F., "The Nurse–Clinician," *Amer. J. Nursing,* 66:278, February, 1966; F. Flores, "Role of the Graduate Nurse Today," *New England J. Med.,* 267:488, September 6, 1962; B. G. Schutt, "Conflicts in Medicine Raise Questions for Nursing," *Amer. J. Nursing,* 66:2419, November, 1966.

[3]Rushing, W. A., "The Hospital Nurse As Mother Surrogate and Bedside Psychologist: A Sociological Approach," *Mental Hygiene,* 50:74, January, 1966.

sodic; latter changes have been many, rapid and virtually constant. The American family and its constituent norms have come quickly to modernity. Familial affect has not been lost; in fact, as Parsons and Fox have noted, it has been intensified and has become strain-producing.[4] It does not depend, however, on the constant and multi-form emotional and physical presence of a mothering figure. The mothering figure, for an ever-growing number of middle-class American families, is a spasmodic one. Part-time or full-time jobs, community participation, Leagues of Women Voters, as well as the many time-saving devices which have "liberated" women from "children, kitchen, and church"—all have served to reduce home contacts of children with mother once infancy has been conquered. Both boys and girls are affected by this lack of contact with a traditional mothering figure. Girls, who later become young women and, hence, constitute the "manpower" pool available to professional nursing, are of primary interest to us.

In essence, a great many—if not most—of the young women who are recruited into the ranks of professional nursing have lacked an adequate model of a mother–parent. However highly motivated they may be (as the writer's earlier presentation had indicated) to enact the role of mother surrogate, they have seldom been sufficiently exposed to an immediate and intimate example to whom they may refer. To many young women the mother surrogate role, however commendable and desired it may be, is an alien role.

Dean Dorothy Smith of the College of Nursing of the University of Florida has specifically blended into the four-year curriculum of her students self-perceptive psychological group work at each stage of their nursing education. All her teaching staff, in addition, are prompted to allow their students the fullest possible expression of "self" even as they are subjected to the demanding discipline of their clinical experiences. Although there are, indeed, psychotherapeutic benefits garnered from such an approach in the preparation of professional nurses, a basic goal is that of permitting young women the opportunity of voicing their inabilities as "mother surrogates." Bringing these inadequacies into the open and examining them under sympathetic and competent guidance helps these young women achieve an affective potential which otherwise they might not have.

But Dean Smith's educational philosophy is not yet found in many schools and colleges of nursing. It is assumed, where such assumption is made at all, that nursing students will absorb the mother surrogate functions somehow—and most do not. In the analyses of nurses' roles where the lack of these functions is indicated there is a failure to comprehend that large numbers of professional nurses began their careers without them and do not possess them now.

Two-thirds of all professional nurses work in hospitals.[5] Prior to and during the past decade the hospital as a working environment has changed. It would be extraordinary, as Florence Flores states, that with momentous changes in the hospital that nursing would emerge today "unscathed and undisturbed."[6] The modern hospital must share in the responsibility of changes in nursing: it, too, is a

[4]Parsons, T., and R. Fox, "Illness, Therapy, and the Modern Urban American Family," *J. Social Issues,* 8:2–3, 31–44, 1952; reprinted in E. G. Jaco (ed.), *Patients, Physicians, and Illness,* New York: Free Press, 1958, chap. 25.

[5]Rushing, *op. cit.,* p. 74.

[6]Flores, *op. cit.,* p. 489.

causative agent in the move away from the mother surrogate role. Hospitals to-day are "big business" and, with the extension of hospital care through growing public and private medical programs, can only grow "bigger." The pragmatic ne-cessities of business force the hospital to utilize its personnel, professional and non-professional, to its most economical. With the relative scarcity of nurses, the major professional group in the therapeutic process over which the hospital exer-cises immediate control, and with the increasing utilization of non-professional nursing help, hospital administration has been forced to remove the nurse from the bedside. As seen by hospital administrators, nurses are more economically used in managerial and supervisory positions than in bedside nursing. Tasks in-volved in patient care run from the simple to the sophisticated, and hospital ad-ministration prefers, where it can, to use less-skilled and less expensive, but com-petent, personnel in simple tasks. Many of the jobs which relate directly to the immediate "custodial care" of hospitalized patients are classified as simple and, hence, are assigned to auxiliary nursing personnel. In 1963 the Surgeon General's office reported that 70 per cent of all bedside contacts with patients by all nursing personnel were made by auxiliaries. "I would suggest," states Rushing, "that the persons most suited for the mother surrogate role are nursing auxiliaries."[7]

It must be borne in mind that a great many hospital administrators are not ignorant of the fact that professional nurses, in large part, are better equipped to give bedside nursing care than are ancillary nursing personnel and that some—certainly not all—professional nurses regret their paucity of patient contacts. The director of a large southern medical center remarked to the writer, "It is a sorry affair, I know, to run a hospital like a machine tool plant. But when we can get our books to balance, and that isn't easy, we have to try to do so. And part of this is pushing the graduate nurse off the floor and behind a desk." The hospital, then, finds it necessary to optimize the services of professional nurses by substituting much of their patient-centered functions by managerial functions and by reducing their few actual patient contacts to those which demand greater skill and responsibility.[8] The professional nurse today is prevented from per-sonally giving total care to her patients. States Rushing:

> There are certain constraints placed on the nurse's hospital role that deter her from giving comprehensive nursing care. Furthermore, the types of nurse–pa-tient interaction that are becoming increasingly frequent deter the development and reinforcement of the sentiments and attitudes that are at the heart of pro-grams designed to encourage interaction with patients as "whole" persons [i.e., as persons with psychologic, interpersonal and social, as well as medical, needs].[9]

In the therapeutic process there are three essential role complexes which are systematically interrelated: those of patients, physicians and nurses. These con-stitute a fairly classic triadic relationship.[10] It is inevitable that any change in role performance of a member of the triad will affect the role performance of the other members. In this light, it might be said that changes in the behavior and at-

[7]Rushing, op. cit., p. 76.

[8]See M. Jahoda, "A Social Psychologist Views Nursing As a Profession," Amer. J. Nursing, 61:54–55, July, 1961.

[9]Rushing, op. cit., p. 71.

[10]Johnson, M. M., and H. W. Martin, "A Sociological Analysis of the Nursing Role," Amer. J. Nursing, 58:373–374, March, 1958.

titudes of patients and physicians will produce change in the behavior and attitudes of nurses. This writer thus feels that it is justified to find some of the causal factors for changes in nursing in the medical profession and in the patient population.

Within the context of the hospital milieu the physician typically cannot be present to perform personally nursing functions for his patients. He must depend on the hospital's nursing service to see that his patients are afforded the correct care associated with a therapeutic regimen which he designs. The physician sees professional nursing as the keystone of effective hospital care. It is quite probable that he would prefer that all care tasks performed for his patients were done by a professional nurse, for he respects her preparation, knowledge and abilities. In this regard, Flores relates the following anecdote:

> Some years ago I was a member of a group of doctors, hospital administrators and nurses (all appointed by their respective professional organizations) who were attempting to define the unique functions of the nurse. There was general agreement regarding matters of personal hygiene, nutrition and the like. When it was suggested that the nurse must meet some of the patient's emotional and psychologic needs, the physicians not only disagreed with the rest of the group but also disagreed with each other. Strangely enough, there was agreement that if the doctor didn't meet these needs, the nurse must.[11]

Physicians, however, recognize that total patient care given by professional nurses is not within the realm of possibility in modern hospitals. They, too, must abide the extension of care tasks to non-professional personnel. It is a "necessary evil." If, however, the care regimen is entrusted to a host of variously titled nursing personnel, the physician wants the leader of the team to be a professional nurse. If this means that the "leader" sits at a desk and manipulates others who are "hands and feet," then he directly supports the diminution of face-to-face nursing–patient contacts.

Medicine itself has for years been many medicines and is exaggeratedly so today. The family doctor of yore in medicine has gone the way of the mother surrogate in nursing. Medical specialties have grown in both number and diversity. The needs of medical specialists have demanded complementary professional nursing specialists. The cardiac surgeon, as an example, cannot accept whatever help may be assigned to him: he must have a nurse co-worker who has special interest, abilities and experience in working with cardiac patients and a highly profound knowledge of the intricate machines, techniques and medications involved in the treatment of heart conditions. When a medical specialist states that a particular nurse "is worth her weight in gold," he indicates that she can be trusted to execute the intricacies of the procedures within "their" specialty with ability and dispatch. There are probably few things as disturbing to a medical specialist than to find an unfamiliar and untried replacement for a nurse in whom he has confidence. With the possible exceptions of psychiatrists[12] and pediatricians, medical specialists are more "procedure-oriented" than "patient-oriented," and they prefer to work with professional nurses who have developed expertness in procedures. The pressure applied by the medical profession has not only supported

[11]Flores, *op. cit.,* p. 490.

[12]Olson, B. J., and J. E. Lubach, "Innovations in the Nursing Role in a Psychiatric Research Program," *Amer. J. Nursing,* 66:317–318, February, 1966.

the elevation of professional nurses to administrative and supervisory positions, but has also forced these nurses more-and-more into patient contacts mediated by gauges, tubes and electronic devices.

Patients, too, have been instrumental in helping nurses dissociate themselves from mother surrogate functions. Like physicians, patients would undoubtedly prefer to have the most capable of nursing personnel, i.e., professional nurses, minister to their needs. Distinct from physicians, however, they do not usually distinguish "one kind of nurse from another" among the squadrons of women in white who enter and leave their hospital rooms. Their needs are many and it is their right to call upon nursing service to satisfy these needs. Researchers have shown that patients have difficulty in communicating the depth of their needs, especially those who ask for emotional support.[13] Those patients who do vocalize their requirements ask for such things as bedpans, a more comfortable body position, the alleviation of pain, medications to induce sleep—simple things to ease their discomfiture. They do not overtly request emotional comfort. The simple things are supplied, in general, by non-professional personnel. Except in rare cases, since patients do not well express their insecurities and fears, their worries over their jobs or their homes, few members of nursing personnel, professional and non-professional alike, attempt to alleviate them. Hospitals are not warm nests where patients are coddled; they are efficient centers for the purpose of curing or ameliorating ailments, or they try to be so. Nurses of all rank and description fall prey to this ethos and help to maintain it. "Mother-surrogateness" is seldom encountered: in large measure, it is not asked for by patients nor is it given by nurses.

Patients, who are the clients of the big business of hospitals, want to achieve maximum benefit and return for their payments. Even though they cannot easily distinguish among the many women in white, their emphasis on optimal service for their money does so distinguish. The best possible service to patients parallels the physician's desire for the best possible internal organization for this service: physicians directly, and patients indirectly, demand the professional nurse head the team of non-professionals. In this sense, patients are supportive of the removal of professional nurses from patients'—their own—bedsides.

It bears mention that patients are parts of a greater collective, the lay public; they are that part of the lay public who are temporarily out of the usual run-of-things and in the hospital. Whereas inside hospital walls few patients would easily recognize the professional nurse, there is little doubt that the lay public, as a whole, has an altered image of the professional nurse today than yesterday. Professional nurses are no longer seen as "just anyone" who assumes the white uniform. The neighbor's daughter who is a university graduate must be a higher order of nurse. At one time most nurses were recruited from among lower- and lower-middle-class rural and small-town families who "worked" their way through three arduous years of hospital "training." Today, ever increasing numbers of young women from well-situated middle-class families of large urban centers earn their caps and pins after four or five years of "education" at highly respected and accredited universities. It is inevitable that the changes in origin and background of newer recruits into professional nursing as well as the changes

[13]Elder, R. G., "What Is the Patient Saying?," *Nursing Forum*, 2:25–37, 1963.

in nursing education programs will have had some impact on the public image of the professional nurse. This new nurse should be a leader, an authority, and well removed from menial tasks—these same simple tasks which have for many decades been associated with mother surrogate functions.

Internal Factors

Since the termination of World War II there has been a movement of great consequence to all nursing that can be best described as a "drive towards professionalization." The National League for Nursing, a younger organization dominated by the leading figures in nursing education, and the American Nurses Association, an older organization more dedicated to the rights and duties of nurses, have been prime movers in this direction. The League, specifically, has been able to challenge old ideas and sponsor new ideas in the professional preparation of nurses. The basic premises involved in the professionalization movement might be said to be: (1) in the past, the potential for nurses to do more responsible, involved and demanding tasks had not been realized; (2) decisions regarding the manner, magnitude and intensity of patient care could best be made by competent well-educated nurses; and (3) competent, well-educated nurses were not, in general, the products of weak and sometimes haphazard programs in schools of nursing in many hospitals where, at best, "training" was a three-year apprenticeship in simply hard work. Professionalization, then, has been approached from two major avenues: the upgrading of nursing education and, hence, of hospital nursing service; and a striving for more appropriate recognition and higher status within the health-associated disciplines in the hospital community.

Even prior to this drive towards professionalization a few universities (beginning with the University of Minnesota as early as 1909) recognized the need to offer more than hospital training as the proper preparation for better nurses. The program at these universities combined both hospital training and a baccalaureate program without sacrificing the specific merits of either. Their students "worked" alongside diploma students for a complete hospital experience and "studied" at the university. It was the exceptional early university nursing student who completed her dual curriculum in less than five or six years.

In the late 1940s and early 1950s many other universities, most of these with medical schools or colleges, joined the effort. They cut back on the work experience and magnified the study program, usually limiting the total curriculum to four years. The stress was, and still is, on a full and enriching university-level education. Following the pattern of medical colleges, nursing colleges may be associated primarily with a single medical center (such as that of the University of Texas) or may eclectically choose clinical affiliations from several cooperating institutions (such as that of Boston University).

Although there is no complete unanimity in educational philosophy or practice in university programs, the National League for Nursing, the national accrediting agency, demands a rigid minimum in clinical facilities, well-prepared teaching staffs and true university instruction. All university nursing programs, however, share an emphasis on the fact that their graduates are, indeed, well-prepared and capable professionals.

The elevation of nursing into the realm of a higher educational discipline has had its effects elsewhere in the education of nurses. Many of the once-proliferating weak hospital schools have disappeared, and those that remain have been upgraded and modernized. Sub-baccalaureate programs at junior colleges, usually of two-year duration, have emerged as an intermediary type, producing "graduate" nurses (those who may be licensed within a state and who may affix the "R.N." to their names, as do hospital and university graduates) who are not afforded the same status within the discipline as are their better-educated associates. Even the programs for "practical" nurses have been made "courses of study" rather than short and over-simplified periods of on-the-job training. On the other hand, the move upward has prompted university graduates of special talent or ambition to pursue even higher academic recognition through achieving graduate degrees.

Professionalization has brought a greater dignity to nursing, it is true. Even in the decade under consideration one senses the change that 10 graduate classes of modern professional nurses (and the subsequent retirement of 10-years-worth of nurses of the older tradition) have wrought. Esther Brown has described situations where professionally responsible nurses have challenged, and even admonished and corrected, medical authority when physicians have made incongruous or erroneous decisions.[14] At the University of Colorado Medical Center there has been initiated an experimental program of specialized education for a limited number of nurses where, under medical supervision and with medical approval, nurses are assuming certain physicians' functions in public health. A few years ago the writer proposed a program for the preparation of nurse–obstetricians (not nurse–midwives) who would replace and assist obstetrical specialists in hospitals, and the proposition was well-received by both physicians and nurses. Frances Reiter speaks of a "master practitioner" in nursing of great experience, special abilities and advanced education (the "nurse–clinician") who, in the not-too-distant future, would provide even more outstanding guidelines for patient care and who would be members of an Academy of Nursing.[15] The professional nurse is far from being a "hand-maiden," and her days as a drudge are in the remote past. She insists that she cannot be taken for granted as just a "professional employee" in the hospital. She has achieved, and is still achieving, a new status-role of greater authority and respect than she has ever had. And, even when the admission of this new status-role is only grudgingly made, she strives for this recognition.

Professional nurses have fought for, and received, acknowledgment in some difficult battles with other groups. The Fairview "incident," where a well-integrated sub-professional group set up barriers against them and where nurses tore them down, is a case in point.[16] In 1966, the status striving of nurses overcame their "ethical convictions" when they "struck" against the hospitals of a major American city—San Francisco—demanding greater monetary compensation in keeping with their professional status. Ten years earlier the San Francisco "strike" would have been unthinkable.

[14]Brown, E. L., *Newer Dimensions of Patient Care,* New York: Russell Sage Foundation, 1962, part 2, pp. 61–64.

[15]Reiter, *op. cit.,* p. 280.

[16]Lewis, E. P., "The Fairview Story," *Amer. J. Nursing,* 66:64–70, January, 1966.

The drive towards professionalization has, almost inadvertently, assisted in diminishing mother surrogate functions of professional nurses. Many of these functions seem to be "dirty work" and beyond the pale of professionals. As a nurse mentioned to the writer, "A girl doesn't go through four years of college to do *scut* work. There are other people who can do that." Rushing states that "professionals" must have exclusivity of functions, and, hence, professional nurses cannot "adopt the mother surrogate core of skills, for it is clearly an ability that requires no special expertise."[17]

An interesting study using the technique of factor analysis by Raskin and his associates has illustrated the intense concern of professional nurses with their person-to-person interactions. It is striking, however, that their desires for interaction are not primarily with patients, but are oriented towards acting as leaders, interacting with others by ordering them about.[18] A British physician involved in a one-year period of special study in the United States found American nurses to be rigid and disciplined, fond of their desks at nurses' stations and of the paraphernalia and norms of these stations. The visitor, W. Bryan Jennett, notes that American nurses do not "waste time" on patients: nor, for that matter, do they "waste time" on physicians.[19] He rather cynically notes:

> The convention of escorting doctors round the wards has long since lapsed. . . . Indeed, I was there for a long time before I ever saw a doctor and a nurse speaking to each other. A large notice reminded all comers that verbal orders were on no account to be accepted. The doctor wrote orders for the nurses, who in turn wrote reports for the doctors, and each stood around reading each other's writing with never a word exchanged.[20]

It is evident that nurses themselves have contributed to the diminishing, if not the disappearance, of the mother surrogate role: it no longer fits the profession's own image of itself. It is either archaic or inoperable.

Conclusion

Twenty years ago this writer noted that there was a conflict in nursing, and within nurses, between two sets of role expectations, those of the mother surrogate and of the healer. He further suggested that mother surrogate functions were rapidly decreasing among professional nurses and were becoming the proper functions of nursing non-professionals. However lamentable this may be—and it is, indeed, a moot question that it *is* lamentable—the past 20 years have strengthened and corroborated this opinion. It is his further opinion that this change was impossible to avoid, for there have been pressures from without nursing and from within nursing that could neither be abated nor negated. It might

[17]Rushing, *op. cit.*, p. 77.

[18]Raskin, A., J. K. Boruchow and R. Golob, "Concept of Task Versus Person Orientation in Nursing," *J. Applied Psychol.*, 49:182–187, June, 1965. It is also of interest to note that another major configuration in the factor analysis showed that there was a definite inclination for the nurses tested to exhibit a profile of characteristics attributed to the very rigid, politically conservative, "authoritarian personality"!

[19]Jennett, W. B., "Taking the Nursing out of Nursing: Trans-Atlantic Trends," *Lancet,* 2:95, July 8, 1961.

[20]Jennett, W. B., *Ibid.*

well be said that mother surrogate functions in professional nursing are dying or, to be stringent, that they are dead. It has been the purpose of these paragraphs to explain their demise.

It may very well be that as a *functional* role the mother surrogate has withered away within the realm of professional nursing. This does not imply that it does not have importance in another sense: that the *novice* nurse—even the pre-novitiate—does not have the ministering mothering image in mind as an ideal when she imagines what she shall be like when she wears white.[21] Like the novice lawyer who dreams of rescuing the defenseless from injustice, the novice clergyman who dreams of lifting hardened hearts to salvation, the novice physician who dreams of conquering all affliction, the novice sociologist who dreams of using the scientific method to make societies sound, the novice nurse still has her dream of tenderly ministering to those who are ill and in pain. In this sense, there shall always be a mother surrogate shadow that falls upon the nurse-to-be.

[21]Mauksch, H. O., "Becoming a Nurse: A Selective View," *Annals Amer. Acad. Pol. and Soc. Sciences,* 346:88–98, March, 1963, as reprinted in J. K. Skipper, Jr., and R. C. Leonard, *Social Interaction and Patient Care,* Philadelphia: J. B. Lippincott, 1965, pp. 335–336.

17 Physician Assistants: An Overview of an Emerging Health Profession

A decade has now elapsed since the establishment of the first physician assistant program at Duke University in 1965. Within this short period of time, over 50 programs have been established to train physician assistants, and the total annual number of graduates has increased rapidly to its present level of greater than 1,000.[11] The concept of physician delegation of patient care responsibilities to mid-level health professionals such as physician assistants is now generally considered to be appropriate and consistent with the provision of high quality medical care.

A number of studies concerned with physician assistants have been conducted during the past decade. A variety of issues, including their role acceptance,[8, 10, 16, 18] performance,[6] and geographic and specialty distributions[5, 7, 9, 20] have been examined. Most of the research published to date, however, is based upon small samples of physician assistants (PAs). As a result, one recent evaluation of the existing policy-related research concerned with physician assistants concluded that comprehensive studies of large samples of these new health professionals in a variety of practice settings should be undertaken.[4]

In response to this need, an extensive survey of the physician assistant profession has been undertaken.[17] In this paper, some findings from this research regarding the background characteristics, the work environments, and the job characteristics of physician assistants throughout the United States will be described.

Data Collection Procedure

During late 1974 and early 1975, 1,282 physician assistants were surveyed by means of mailed questionnaires. These physician assistants constitute virtually the entire physician assistant profession as it existed at that time. Completed questionnaires were obtained from 939 physician assistants, representing a response rate of 73 per cent. A comparison of selected characteristics of Duke and MEDEX respondents with those reported for their respective populations (*i.e.*, the total populations of Duke and MEDEX graduates)[12, 14] has failed to disclose any discernible response biases,[17] thereby increasing our confidence that the study sample is indeed representative of the physician assistant profession as it existed

The research reported here was supported by Grant No. 91-24-75-08 from the Manpower Administration of the United States Department of Labor. Appreciation is expressed to the Association of Physician Assistant Programs for their cooperation. The author bears full responsibility for the findings and conclusions contained in this report, however.

Reprinted from *Medical Care*, XV:982–990, December, 1977, by permission of the author and Publisher.

in late 1974 and early 1975. Approximately one-half of the study participants graduated in 1974 and an additional one-third graduated in 1973 (see Table 17-1).

Background Characteristics

Eighty-four per cent of the physician assistants in our study are men. The percentage of women among the 1974 graduates has not increased significantly over the earlier graduates. The educational backgrounds of physician assistants are shown in Table 17-2. Approximately one-third report four or more years of post-high school education before entering a physician assistant program. The average number of years of education at the time of admission has increased from 2.2 among those who graduated in 1972 or before to 2.8 among 1974 graduates.

The previous medical occupational backgrounds of physician assistants can be seen in Table 17-3. Only 22.4 per cent report no prior medical experience. Slightly over one-half had been medical corpsmen, and one-fifth had been medical technologists or technicians. Less than 5 per cent had been nurses. The typical physician assistant has worked 5.2 years in another medical field before becoming a physician assistant. Medical corpsmen constituted 66.8 per cent of the graduates before 1973 compared with 49.8 per cent of the 1974 graduates. Those with backgrounds in other medical fields (principally, non-nursing allied health occupations) are becoming more predominant, constituting 29.3 per cent of the 1974 graduates in contrast to only 11.5 per cent of the graduates before 1973.

Table 17-1   Year of graduation of physician assistants included in present study

Year of Graduation	Number	Percentage
1967	1	0.1
1968	8	0.9
1969	11	1.2
1970	17	1.8
1971	36	3.8
1972	136	14.5
1973	271	28.9
1974	442	47.0
Not known	17	1.8
Totals	939	100.0

Table 17-2   Post-high school education and training prior to beginning physician assistant training

Total Number of Years	Percentage (N = 932)
Less than 1	15.3
1	13.4
2	24.0
3	15.2
4	18.3
More than 4	13.8
Total	100.0
Mean	2.58 yrs

Table 17-3   Occupational background and number of years of medical experience prior to beginning physician assistant training

	Percentage* (N = 939)	Average Number Years Experience
Medical corpsman	54.6	6.0
Medical technologist or technician	21.6	5.2
Medical aide	8.3	2.3
Registered nurse	3.7	5.2
Licensed practical nurse	1.5	3.6
Physical or occupational therapist	0.7	5.3
Social worker	0.3	3.3
Other medical occupation	3.2	3.2
No previous medical occupation	22.4	0
Average number years experience for total study sample	—	5.2

*Since 16.3 per cent of the respondents listed more than one previous medical occupation, the sum of the percentages exceeds 100 per cent.

Work Environment Characteristics

Table 17-4 describes the specialties of the study participants.* Three-quarters of the study participants were working in primary care fields. General primary care fields (family and general practice) employed 43.6 per cent of physician assistants and specialty primary care fields (general internal medicine, general pediatrics, obstetrics and gynecology, and emergency medicine) employed an additional 29.3 per cent. Only 18.7 per cent were employed in surgical specialties and 8.4 per cent were working in other fields (primarily medical subspecialties). There has been no significant change in the specialty distribution of recent compared to earlier graduates.

Classification of physicians in the United States in a similar manner (Table 17-5) reveals that the percentage of physicians involved in specialty primary care and surgery is similar to that for physician assistants. Physician assistants, however, are considerably more likely than physicians to be working in general primary care fields. These statistics indicate that 72.9 per cent of physician assistants compared with 47.4 per cent of physicians are working in primary care specialties.

The practice settings of physician assistants are shown in Table 17-6. Exactly half the members of the profession were employed in private practice settings while the other half were working in health institutions. Those employed by institutional providers of health care are working in outpatient clinics, emergency rooms, and hospital inpatient units. Although precisely comparable data for physicians are not available, it is known that 73 per cent of nonfederal physicians involved in patient care are working in office-based practices while 27 per cent are engaged in hospital-based practices.[2] It appears, therefore, that physician assistants are more likely than physicians to be employed by health institutions.

* These data were obtained by asking the respondent to list the specialty of his supervising physician.

Table 17-4 Specialty of physician assistants

	N	Percentage (N = 902)
General primary care		
Family practice	262	29.1
General practice	130	14.5
Subtotal	392	43.6
Specialty primary care		
General internal medicine	166	18.6
General pediatrics	43	4.8
Obstetrics and gynecology	16	1.8
Emergency medicine	12	1.3
Multispecialty primary care	25	2.8
Subtotal	262	29.3
Surgery		
General surgery	107	11.9
Orthopedic surgery	13	1.4
Urologic surgery	13	1.4
Plastic surgery	3	0.3
Vascular surgery	2	0.2
Neurosurgery	7	0.8
Cardiothoracic surgery	20	2.2
Surgical oncology	1	0.1
Otolaryngology	4	0.4
Subtotal	170	18.7
Other specialties		
Cardiology	12	1.3
Nephrology	4	0.4
Endocrinology	4	0.4
Dermatology	4	0.4
Hematology-oncology	5	0.6
Gastroenterology	1	0.1
Neurology	1	0.1
Industrial and occupational medicine	16	1.8
Rehabilitation medicine	1	0.1
Pulmonary medicine	2	0.2
Multi-subspecialty medicine	8	0.9
Aerospace medicine	1	0.1
Radiology	4	0.4
Pathology	1	0.1
Psychiatry	10	1.1
Ophthalmology	3	0.3
Public health	1	0.1
Subtotal	78	8.4
Total	902	100.0

The geographic location of physician assistants as assessed by the size of the community in which they work is shown in Table 17-7.* Over half of the civilian respondents were located in communities with fewer than 50,000 persons. The available evidence for physicians, on the other hand, indicates that 28.0 per cent

* Of the study respondents 12.8 per cent were employed by the military. These persons have been excluded from Table 17-7.

Table 17-5   Specialty distribution of physician assistants in comparison with that of physicians in the United States

	Physician Assistants (N = 902)	Physicians* (N = 324, 367)†
General primary care	43.6%	16.6%
Specialty primary care	29.3	31.8
Surgery	18.7	21.9
Other specialties	8.4	29.7
Totals	100.0	100.0

*Source: American Medical Association.[1]
†Includes federal as well as nonfederal physicians involved in patient care.

Table 17-6   Practice settings of physician assistants

	Percentage of PAs (N = 870)
Private Practice	
Private solo practice	21.2%
Private group practice	28.6
Subtotal	49.8
Institutional practice	
Community or hospital clinic	21.7
Hospital emergency room or inpatient unit	11.3
Both clinic *and* other hospital settings	17.2
Subtotal	50.2
Total	100.0

are located in communities of this size.[13] These data suggest that physician assistants are almost twice as likely as physicians to be working in communities of 50,000 persons or less.

Job Characteristics

The wide variety of job responsibilities reported by physician assistants is shown in Table 17-8. By far, the most frequently mentioned responsibility is the diagnosis and treatment of common medical problems of ambulatory patients. History taking and physician examinations, emergency room care, and assisting in surgery constitute the other more frequently mentioned job responsibilities.

Table 17-9 describes the physician assistants' estimation of time devoted to particular activities. Approximately 80 per cent of their time was spent in the provision of patient care, the majority of which was provided with the supervising physician not actually present.

Turning to the physician assistants' description of their level of responsibility for patient care, one can see in Table 17-10 that 77.1 per cent of the respondents reported a "very great" or a "considerable" amount of responsibility for patient care. Fifty-one per cent considered themselves to have "a lot of influence" on the way their patients are cared for, and 66.2 per cent feel that they are allowed to

Table 17-7 Geographic distribution of civilian physician assistants, physicians, and U. S. population

Community Population	Civilian PAs* (N = 801)	Physicians† (N = 310,000)	U.S. Population† (N = 216,000,000)
Under 10,000	27.4%	11.0%	19.8%
10,000 to 49,999	25.3	17.0	17.1
50,000 or more	47.3	72.0	63.1
Totals	100.0	100.0	100.0

*These data are based upon self-reports of the population of the community where the physician assistant is employed.
†Source: Moore.[13]

Table 17-8 Job responsibilities listed by physician assistants

	Percentage (N = 939)
Primary care (diagnosis and treatment of common medical problems of ambulatory patients)	68.5
History taking and physical examination of ambulatory patients	29.3
Emergency room care	22.9
History taking and physical examination of hospitalized patients	16.3
Assisting in surgery	16.1
Making rounds on hospitalized patients	13.6
Suturing of minor wounds	12.8
Follow-up care	11.2
Nursing home visits	7.3
Initial screening and evaluation	7.3
Care of hospitalized patients	6.6
Writing hospital discharge summaries	6.6
Taking call during evening and weekend hours	6.1
Writing progress notes for hospitalized patients	5.4
Routine preoperative and postoperative care	5.2
Lab work	5.0
Casting	5.0
Arranging and ordering lab studies	4.5
Home visits	3.4
Counseling and psychotherapy	3.4
Reading electrocardiograms	2.0

make decisions about those aspects of patient care for which they have been appropriately trained. The level of responsibility reported by earlier graduates is only slightly greater than that of recent graduates. Furthermore, 55.4 per cent expressed a desire for more responsibility for patient care.[17] Even though physician assistants generally possessed a significant amount of patient care responsibility, most would have preferred still more.

Assessment of the supervisory support provided by the physician with whom physician assistants work are shown in Table 17-11. For all but one of the aspects of supervision shown in this table, 84 per cent or more of the respondents considered their supervision to be adequate. Only 56 per cent of the study participants felt that supervising physicians provide adequate help in improving their clinical skills, however.

The physician assistants' perception of their role acceptance by the physicians and nurses with whom they work is described in Table 17-12. Approximate-

Table 17-9   Time allocation among various types of activities for physician assistants

	Percentage of Time at Work Devoted to Particular Activity (N = 939)
Patient care with supervising physician present	31.6
Patient care with supervising physician absent	48.9
Technical or laboratory work	4.6
Clerical or secretarial work	4.3
Teaching other health professionals	5.5
Administration	2.1
Other activities	1.6

Table 17-10   Level of responsibility for patient care reported by physician assistants

	Percentage (N = 939)
I have a great or a considerable amount of responsibility for patient care	77.1
I have a lot of influence on the way patients are cared for	51.2
I have the authority to make decisions about those aspects of patient care for which I have received appropriate training	66.2

Table 17-11   Adequacy of support provided by supervising physicians

	Percentage of PAs Who Feel Particular Aspect of Supervisory Support Is Adequate (N = 939)
Personal interest in the physician assistant	86.2
Adequate consideration of questions	90.6
Adequate opportunity to present problems, complaints, or suggestions	86.2
Interest in ideas and suggestions	86.6
Recognition for work well done	84.1
Help in improving clinical skills	56.1
Interest in discussing problems of patient management	86.6

ly one-fifth of the respondents encountered problems in each of the various aspects of role acceptance shown in this table. Those who did encounter role acceptance problems classified them as either "minor" or "major" in nature. For each aspect of role acceptance, less than 5 percent of the problems encountered by respondents were considered to be major ones. Similar levels of role acceptance of physician assistants appear to exist among both nurses and physicians.

The incomes of physician assistants (expressed in 1974 dollars) are shown in Table 17–13.* The average income of respondents is $14,285. The income of earlier graduates is somewhat greater, although not substantially so. The average income of those graduating in 1972 or before is $15,629 compared to $14,748 and

---

* These findings refer, of course, only to the income derived from one's activity as a physician assistant. Income obtained from other sources is not included here.

Table 17-12   Role acceptance of physician assistants by physicians and nurses

	Percentage of PAs Who Encountered Problems with Physicians (N = 939)	Percentage of PAs Who Encountered Problems with Nurses (N = 939)
Obtaining assistance when needed	24.4	20.6
Following instructions given by PA	—	24.9
Developing warm working relationships	18.1	21.1
Acceptance of the PA's role	18.1	27.9

Table 17-13   Incomes of physician assistants

	Percentage (N = 939)
Less than $10,000	4.7
$10,000 to $12,499	26.5
$12,500 to $14,999	30.6
$15,000 to $17,499	25.7
$17,500 to $19,999	6.0
$20,000 and over	6.5
Total	100.0
Mean income	$14,285

$13,387 for 1973 and 1974 graduates, respectively. The incomes of physician assistants exceed those reported for nurse practitioners and hospital staff registered nurses. Only 8.2 per cent of the former earned $14,500 or more in 1974 while the mean starting salary for the latter was $9,096 at that time.[3, 5]

The final job characteristics of physician assistants to be considered are job opportunities and career plans. Table 17-14 describes the respondents' perception of their ability to obtain a different job. Only 16.1 per cent felt that they would have had any difficulty in locating another position, and 43.2 per cent already know of other available jobs. The job market for physician assistants appeared to be favorable at the time these data were collected.

Career opportunities are another matter, however. As Table 17-15 shows, 59.7 per cent of the respondents considered the career opportunities in their present jobs to be either limited or nonexistent. It is not surprising, then, that 22.7 per cent of the respondents indicate a strong interest in entering medical school and many others intend to obtain other types of additional education or training (see Table 17-16). The rather limited career opportunities perceived by the study participants may in large part account for the findings shown in Table 17-17: One-third have considered entering another occupational field and another third indicate that they might do so in the future.

Discussion

Our findings concerning the background characteristics of physician assistants suggest that persons with greater previous educational attainments and those with prior experience in nonnursing civilian health fields (principally as

Table 17-14   Job opportunities for physician assistants

	Percentage (N = 913)
I already know of one or more positions available to me	43.2
I could locate one with very little effort	11.7
I could find one without too much difficulty	29.0
It would be quite difficult to locate another job, but I could probably locate one eventually	14.8
It would be almost impossible to locate another job	1.3
Total	100.0

Table 17-15   Career opportunities for physician assistants in present job

	Percentage (N = 929)
Unlimited	7.3
Quite numerous	15.7
Fairly numerous	17.3
Limited	50.0
Non-existent	9.7
Total	100.0

Table 17-16   Educational plans of physician assistants

	Percentage (N = 928)
Obtain a baccalaureate degree	20.1
Obtain a master's degree	21.7
Obtain a Ph.D. degree	6.1
Enter a medical school	22.7

Table 17-17   Physician assistants' occupational plans

	Percentage (N = 939)
I have seriously considered entering a different field	11.0
I have considered entering a different field, but not seriously	20.7
I have not yet considered entering a different field, but I might in the future	38.8
I would never consider entering a different field	29.5
Total	100.0

medical technologists or technicians) are becoming more predominant in the profession. The tradition of recruiting principally men appears to be rather steadfast over the years covered by this research, although at the present time the percentage of women among students in many physician assistant programs is significantly greater than the 16 per cent level observed here. In fact, data reported by Fisher[7] indicate that 30 per cent of the graduates of physician assistant programs in 1975 and 1976 were women.

The present analysis of the work environments of physician assistants suggests that, if current patterns continue, this emerging health profession will make an important contribution toward increasing the availability of primary care, particularly in smaller communities. Although the present size of the physician assistant profession is still too small to make a significant national impact on the delivery of health services, with the continued growth of this profession and a continuation of the present pattern of choice of work environments, improvements in the specialty and geographic distribution of medical manpower are likely to result. The concerns raised by Sadler, Sadler, and Bliss in 1972 regarding the "likely co-option of the newly minted physician's assistant by subspecialty medicine"[19] now appear to be unwarranted.

This assessment of the job characteristics of physician assistants indicates that these new health professionals are engaged principally in the provision of direct patient care rather than in the performance of ancillary services. Physician assistants possess a substantial amount of responsibility for patient care, but most would like still more. Although the starting salaries of physician assistants are relatively attractive ($14,285), the salary increments received on the basis of increasing professional experience are rather modest. Physician assistants work an average of 50.4 hours per week, including 9.5 hours during evenings and weekends. The longer work week of physician assistants compared with that for nurse practitioners and hospital staff nurses may account, at least in part, for the greater incomes reported by physician assistants.

Physician assistants have established favorable professional relationships with supervising physicians and nurses. Physicians are generally viewed as adequate supervisors, although many physician assistants would like more assistance from them in expanding their clinical skills. Problems in role acceptance by physicians and nurses are not totally absent, but only in rare cases are they of major significance.

Job opportunities appear to be abundant, but the respondents possess a rather pessimistic view of their opportunities for career advancement within the physician assistant profession. Although we have no direct measure of the level of career aspirations of the study participants, indirect evidence suggests that it is relatively high. One-fifth of the respondents have "plans" to enter medical school and one-fifth have plans to obtain either a master's or a Ph.D. degree.

Whether physician assistants will be able to realize their career ambitions within this emerging health profession remains to be seen. For the time period covered by these data, increments in income and level of responsibility for patient care have been rather modest. Additional increments in income and responsibility as one's experience increases appear to be feasible.

According to one recent report,[14] for instance, the profitability of employing a physician assistant ranges between $8,000 and $14,000 per year.* In many practice settings, physician assistants are generating revenues in considerable excess of their salaries and overhead expenses. In these settings, at least, the incomes of physician assistants could be easily augmented as they become more experienced and more efficient. Level of responsibility could in many cases be expanded as well, as one becomes more experienced. These changes would make the career opportunities of physician assistants considerably more attractive.

Future research efforts will be important in assessing the extent to which the physician assistant profession has been successful in providing a rewarding career

---

* Profitability, as determined by these investigators, refers to the difference between the revenues generated by physician assistants and the cost of their employment (salary and overhead).

for its new members. Hopefully, disillusionment and entry into other fields will not become major problems. A more favorable structure of career advancement opportunities may become necessary, however, if these problems are to be avoided altogether.

References

1. American Medical Association: Distribution of Physicians in the U.S, 1973. Chicago, 1974, p. 39.

2. American Medical Association: Profile of Medical Practice '74. Chicago, 1974, p. 14.

3. American Nurses' Association: Facts About Nursing 75-76. Kansas City, 1976.

4. Cohen, E. D.: An Evaluation of Policy Related Research on New and Expanded Roles of Health Workers. Office of Regional Activities and Continuing Education, Yale University School of Medicine. New Haven, 1974.

5. Comptroller General of the United States: Report to the Congress: Progress and Problems in Training and Use of Assistants to Primary Care Physicians. 1975.

6. Crovitz, E., Huse, M. M., and Lewis, D. E.: Field Ratings of Physician's Assisants (Associates). Physician's Associate. January 19, 1973.

7. Fisher, D. W.: Physician Assistant: A Profile of the Profession, in D. L. Hiestand and M. Ostow, eds., Health Manpower Information for Policy Guidance, Ballinger Publishing Company, Cambridge, MA 1976.

8. Lairson, P D., Record, J. C., and James, J. C.: Physician assistants at Kaiser: Distinctive patterns of practice. Inquiry **11**:207, 1974.

9. Lawrence, D., Wilson, W. M., and Castle, H.: Employment of MEDEX graduates and trainees: Five-year progress report for the United States. JAMA **234**:174, 1975.

10. Laws, H. L., and Elliott, R. L.: Experience with a surgeon's assistant in a community practice. Ann. Surg. **38**:214, 1972.

11. Lewis, D. D.: The training of new health manpower. J. Med. Educ. **50**:75, 1975.

12. Lewis, D. E.: The Physician's Assistant Concept. Unpublished doctoral dissertation. Durham, Duke University Graduate Department of Education, 1975.

13. Moore, F. D.: Manpower goals in American surgery. Ann. Surg. **184**:125, 1976.

14. The National Council of MEDEX Programs in the United States, 1974.

15. Nelson, E. C., Jacobs, A. R., and Cordner, K.: Financial impact of physician assistants on medical practice. N. Engl. J. Med. **293**:527, 1975.

16. Nelson, E. C., Jacobs, A. R., and Johnson, K. G.: Patient's acceptance of physician's assistants. JAMA **228**:63, 1974.

17. Perry, H. B.: Physician Assistants: An Empirical Analysis of Their General Characteristics, Job Performance, and Job Satisfaction. Unpublished doctoral dissertation. Baltimore, The Johns Hopkins University, Department of Social Relations, 1976.

18. Record, J. C., and Greenlick, M. R.: New health professional and the physician role: An hypothesis from the Kaiser experience. Public Health Rep. **90**:241, 1975.

19. Sadler, A. M., Sadler, B. L., and Bliss, A. R.: The Physician's Assistant: Today and Tomorrow. New Haven, Yale University School of Medicine, 1972, p. 28.

20. Scheffler, R. M., and Stinson, O. D.: Characteristics of physician's assistants: A focus on specialty. Med. Care **12**:1019, 1974.

Society
and the
Organization
of Health
Services Systems

By now the reader should be aware of the societal processes by which the differential existence of disease and injury and its components lead to efforts to cope with their threats and misery. Roles and statuses are defined and assigned to those afflicted and also to those trained to treat and ameliorate such conditions and to the treatment settings in which they perform their healing behaviors. As these facilities and services become organized and institutionalized to detect, comprehend, treat, care for, and cope with disease and disability, the need to maintain them becomes increasingly demanding for the community and total society. The often unrelated, independent, and divergently developed health-care programs, facilities and services, as they have survived and expanded through time, have tended to develop cooperative and interdependent relationships that end in some form of health-care "system."

These so-called health-care or health-services systems are organized and coordinated efforts to stabilize and maintain existing facilities, services, and related programs of health care, and they attempt to legitimize previously established ways and means of producing, distributing, and consuming health services into a socially sanctioned health-care "establishment." Since each society differs in the existence of disease and disability for its members and inhabitants of its territory, in its ways and means of coping with such disease and injury, and in its social evolution of health services and facilities—that is, differs in the entire social process of perceiving and coping with illness and injury and thus in the development of its healing institutions and health subcultures—different societies have therefore evolved divergent systems in the maintenance and delivery of health and medical care to their constituents.

In many Western societies, especially the United States, many voluntary associations, groups, organizations, and religious sects have developed, organized, and maintained a wide array of health-care services and facilities, such as hospitals, clinics, sanitaria, medical and nursing schools, medical research organizations and units, etc. (comprising the so-called "private health sector"). These voluntary facilities augment similar services and facilities provided by governmental and public agencies, such as federal hospitals (including the military and veterans hospitals); state, county, city, and district hospitals; and clinics for curative services, as well as public health agencies and programs aimed at prevention and control of disease in the community (the so-called "public sector").

This section will analyze the development of health-service systems at two major levels: the microlevel of the health institution or facility, and the macrolevel of the community, regional, and national perspectives.

A. Microlevel

The modern acute (short-term) general hospital has increasingly become the centrally most important setting for the provision of medical care in American and other Western societies. Hospitals and other types of health-care facilities evolve and establish their own kinds of social organizations and systems of roles, statuses, and norms that define the various functions and skills of its role incumbents. The so-called "typical" hospital has been organized primarily to care for the acute and critically ill, with an average length of patient stay of a few days. Thus the "medical model" of patient care has dominated the social structure of the modern acute hospital, with an emphasis upon technical and physical care, permeated by a rather authoritarian caste-like social structure of staff dominance and patient subservience.

The social organization of the hospital is analyzed in the first chapter of this section by Basil Georgopoulos and Floyd Mann, reprinted from the previous edition.

Related to the foregoing are the effects of organizational socialization of hospital employees as studied by Daniel Feldman. His work suggests three specific stages of hospital socialization and four factors as possible outcomes of this entire process.

The potential effects of the physical layout of a hospital's nursing unit upon nursing and patient care are presented in the chapter by E. Gartly Jaco.

Herbert Shore advances the severe limitations of the medical model on nursing homes and long-term care and the need to replace it with a psychosocial model.

One important change in the governing of voluntary hospitals in recent years has been an increase in the voice of local consumers. Some of the problems and conflicts involved in this development are analyzed in an original chapter by Elianne Riska and James Taylor.

BASIL S. GEORGOPOULOS
and
FLOYD C. MANN

18   The Hospital as an Organization

The community general hospital is an organization that mobilizes the skills and efforts of a number of widely divergent groups of professional, semi-professional, and nonprofessional personnel to provide a highly personalized service to individual patients. Like other large-scale organizations, it is established and designed to pursue certain objectives through collaborative activity. The chief objective of the hospital is, of course, to provide adequate care and treatment to its patients (within the limits of present-day technical-medical knowledge, and knowledge of organizing human activity effectively, as well as within limits that may be imposed by the relative scarcity of appropriate organizational resources or by extraorganizational forces). Its principal product is medical, surgical, and nursing service to the patient, and its central concern is the life and health of the patient. A hospital may, of course, have additional objectives, including its own maintenance and survival, organizational stability and growth, financial solvency, medical and nursing education and research, and various employee-related objectives. But, all these are subsidiary to the key objective of service to the patient, which constitutes the basic organizing principle that underlies all activities in the community general hospital.

There is little ambiguity, if any, about the main organizational objective of the community general hospital. Unlike many organizations, the hospital is able to make the role it performs in the larger community psychologically meaningful to its members. And most of its members try to give unstintingly of their energies to perform the tasks assigned to them. Many doctors and nurses look upon their profession as a sacred calling. Others find working in the hospital deeply satisfying of needs that they cannot easily express in words. They see the hospital as a nonprofit institution dedicated to works of mercy, and they sense that their mission in life is to give of themselves in order to help others. Immediate personal comfort and satisfactions, and even material rewards, are defined by most members as less important than giving good care to the patient and meeting a higher order of obligation to mankind. Serious conflicts regarding material rewards, such as those found in organizations where profit is the chief motive, are virtually nonexistent in the hospital. For all these reasons, motivating organizational members toward the objectives of the organization is much less of a problem for the hospital in comparison to other large-scale organizations. The goals of individual members and the objectives of the organization are considerably more congruent in the case of the hospital.

Reprinted from *The Community General Hospital*, New York: Macmillan, 1962, pp. 5–15, by permission of the authors and Publisher.

To do its work, the hospital relies upon an extensive division of labor among its members, upon a complex organizational structure which encompasses many different departments, staffs, offices, and positions, and upon an elaborate system of coordination of tasks, functions, and social interaction.

Work in the hospital is greatly differentiated and specialized, and of a highly interactional character. It is carried out by a large number of cooperating people whose backgrounds, education, training, skills, and functions are as diverse and heterogeneous as can be found in any of the most complex organizations in existence. And much of the work is not only specialized but also performed by highly trained professionals—the doctors—who require the collaboration, assistance, and services of many other professional and nonprofessional personnel. In addition to the medical staff, which is highly specialized and departmentalized, there is the nursing staff, which includes graduate professional nurses in various supervisory and nonsupervisory positions, practical nurses, and untrained nurse's aids. In addition to the nursing staff and the medical staff, which are the two largest groups in the community general hospital, there are the hospital administrator and a number of administrative–supervisory personnel who head various departments or services (e.g., nursing, dietary, admissions, maintenance, pharmacy, medical records, housekeeping, laundry) and are in charge of the employees in these departments. There are also a number of medical technologists and technicians who work in the laboratory and x-ray departments of the hospital, as well as a number of miscellaneous clerical and secretarial personnel. And apart from all these staffs and professional–occupational groups, there is a board of trustees which has the overall formal responsibility for the organization, and which consists of a number of prominent people from the outside community. The trustees offer their services to the hospital without remuneration and are not employees of the organization. In short, professionalization and specialization are two of the hallmarks of the hospital.

Because of this extensive division of labor and accompanying specialization of work, practically every person working in the hospital depends upon some other person or persons for the performance of his own organizational role. Specialists and professionals can perform their functions only when a considerable array of supportive personnel and auxiliary services is put at their disposal at all times. Doctors, nurses, and others in the hospital do not, and cannot, function separately or independently of one another. Their work is mutually supplementary, interlocking, and interdependent. In turn, such a high interdependence requires that the various specialized functions and activities of the many departments, groups, and individual members of the organization be sufficiently coordinated, if the organization is to function effectively and attain its objectives. Consequently, the hospital has developed a rather intricate and elaborate system of internal coordination. Without coordination, concerted effort on the part of its different members and continuity in organizational operations could not be ensured.

It is also interesting and important to note here that, unlike industrial and other large-scale organizations, the hospital relies very heavily on the skills, motivations, and behaviors of its members for the attainment and maintenance of adequate coordination. The flow of work is too variable and irregular to permit coordination through mechanical standardization. And the product of the organization—patient care—is itself individualized rather than uniform or invariant. Because the work is neither mechanized nor uniform or standardized, and because it cannot be planned in advance with the automatic precision of an assembly line, the organization must depend a good deal upon its various members to make the day-to-day adjustments which the situation may demand, but which cannot possibly be completely detailed or prescribed by formal organizational rules and regulations. This is all the more essential, moreover, if one takes into account the fact that the patient, who is the center of all activity in the hospital, is a transient rather than a stable element in the system—in the short-stay hospital, he comes and goes very rapidly.

Fundamentally, then, the hospital is a human rather than a machine system. And even though it may possess elaborate and impressive-looking equipment, or a great variety of physical and material facilities, it has no integrated mechanical-physical systems for the handling and processing of its work. The patient is not a chunk of raw material that passively goes through an ordered progression of machines and assembly-line operators. At every stage of his short stay in the hospital, he is mainly dependent upon his interaction with the people who are entrusted with his care, and upon the skills, actions, and interactions of these different people. All of these factors necessitate heavy reliance upon the members of the organization to coordinate their activities on a voluntary, informal, and expedient basis.

Paradoxical as it may seem, however, the hospital is also a highly formal, quasi-bureaucratic organization which, like all task-oriented organizations, relies a great deal upon formal policies, formal written rules and regulations, and formal authority for controlling much of the behavior and work relationships of its members. The emphasis on formal organizational mechanisms and procedures and on directive rather than "democratic" controls, along with a number of other factors, gives the hospital its much talked about "authoritarian" character, which manifests itself in relatively sharp patterns of superordination–subordination, in expectations of strict discipline and obedience, and in distinct status differences among organizational members.

The authoritarian character of the hospital is partly the result of historical forces having their origins at a time when professionalization and specialization were at a primordial stage, and when nursing, medicine, and the hospital were all closely associated with the work of religious orders and military institutions. The absence of substantial professionalization and specialization characteristic of hospital personnel at those times, along with the emphasis of religious and military institutions on social arrangements in which the occupant of every position in the organization presumably knew "his place," and kept to his place by strictly adhering to specified rights, duties, and obligations, had much to do with the hospital's adopting a strict hierarchical and authoritarian system of work arrangements. But, the advent of professionalization and specialization, the gradual independence of hospitals from religious and military institutions, and the impact of an increasingly secular culture have greatly reduced the authoritarian character of the hospital. As Lentz[1] suggests, within the last 50 years the hospital

---

[1]Lentz, E. M., "The American Voluntary Hospital As an Example of Institutional Change," doctoral dissertation, Cornell University, 1956.

has undergone marked changes, dropping some of its authoritarian and paternalistic characteristics and taking on those of a bureaucratic, functionally rational organization.

Today's community general hospital, however, still has some of its traditional authoritarian characteristics along with its emphasis on rational organization. Moreover, it is unlikely that it will rid itself of all authoritarianism in the near future. There are several major counterforces at work in this connection. First, there is the fact that the hospital constantly deals with critical matters of life and death—matters which place a heavy burden of both secular and moral responsibility on the organization and its members. When human life is at stake, there is little tolerance for error or negligence. And, if error and negligence can be prevented by adherence to strict formal rules and quasi-authoritarian discipline, such rules are important to have and obedience cannot very well be questioned (although blind obedience is mitigated because the hospital increasingly relies on the expertness, judgment, and ethics of professionals who, while abhorring regimentation, are presumably capable of a good deal of self-discipline). Second, there is the great concern of the hospital for maximum efficiency and predictability of performance. In the absence of mechanically regulated workflows, this concern virtually forces the organization to use many quasi-authoritarian means of control (including rigid rules and procedures, directive supervision, rigorous discipline, etc.), in the hope of: (1) attaining some uniformity in the behavior of its members, (2) regulating their interaction and checking deviance within known limits of accountability, and (3) appraising their performance. Third, there is the temptation to adhere to traditional, familiar ways of doing things which, coupled with the lack of apparently equivalent or superior alternatives that could be employed to ensure clarity of responsibility and efficiency and predictability of performance, also serves to perpetuate organizational reliance upon customary directive means of control.[2]

In brief, while historical forces might account for the origins of the authoritarian characteristics of the hospital, it is not likely that some of these characteristics would continue to persist (especially within the context of a highly secular culture) unless they were more functional than not. And this clearly appears to be the case. In the first place, as in any organization designed to mobilize resources quickly in order to meet crises and emergencies successfully, a good deal of regimented behavior is required in the hospital. Lines of authority and responsibility have to be clearly drawn, basic acceptance of authority has to be assured, and discipline has to be maintained. In the second place, the hospital is expected to be able to provide adequate care to its patients at all times, with the precision of a machine system and with minimum error, even though it is a human rather than a machine system. It is expected to perform well continuously and to produce a machinelike response toward the patient, regardless of such things as turnover, absenteeism, and feelings of friendship or hostility among its personnel, or other organizational problems that it may be experiencing. It is also expected to be responsive to the health-related needs and demands of its community, and to

[2]Incidentally, the apparent unavailability of equivalent or superior organizational alternatives is partly the result of our inadequate knowledge about how best to organize and manage human activity in a situation such as that of the community general hospital, and partly the result of the inability of hospitals to utilize the findings of modern research to best advantage.

meet a variety of medicolegal requirements. Because of these expectations, the hospital places high premium on being able to count upon and predict the outcome of the performances of its members. And predictability of performance can be partly attained through directive, quasi-authoritarian controls which, in the absence of apparently superior alternatives, are rather tempting to the organization.

Coupled with this great concern for predictability of performance, moreover, there is an increasing concern that the hospital operate as efficiently and economically as possible. As the hospital has become a resource for all members of the community, and not just the indigent and the impoverished, the public has come to expect of it the best medical and nursing services that can be offered. These services, however, are quite costly, as are the facilities, equipment, supplies, and medicines that are required. And while the public may be willing (though not necessarily able to afford) to pay for these essential costs of hospital care, it also expects the best care possible at reasonable cost or even at least cost. At the same time, it is neither willing to tolerate nor prepared to pay any costs that may result from inefficient operations, poor administration, duplication of services, waste, negligence, and the like. It expects its hospitals to reduce to a minimum or eliminate altogether costs of this latter type and to operate with maximum economy. The hospitals themselves are quite aware of these and other pressures for efficiency, and have come to place very high emphasis on greater efficiency. Great emphasis on economic efficiency, however, is not entirely compatible with the hospital's traditional humanitarian orientation and objective of best service to the patient; the "best" service is not always or necessarily the most economical. Furthermore, this concern for efficiency results both in progressive rationalization of hospital operations and in the institution of more rigid controls within the organization. Such controls, incidentally, serve to maintain the remaining authoritarian characteristics of the community general hospital.

But, efficiency of operations and predictability of performance in the hospital could not possibly be attained only through quasi-authoritarian and directive controls. In fact, if carried to extremes, such controls would in the long run be inimical both to efficiency and to predictability. Efficiency and predictability of performance are also, and perhaps primarily, attained through a number of other factors, which are essential to effective organizational functioning. Probably the most prominent of these factors in the case of the community general hospital are organizational coordination and professionalization.

Because of the high degrees of specialization and functional interdependence found in the hospital, coordination of skills, tasks, and activities is indispensable to effective organizational performance and its predictability. The different specialized, but interacting and interdependent, parts of the organization must fit well together; they must not work at cross purposes or in their own separate directions. If the organization is to attain its objectives, its different parts and members must function according to each other's needs and the needs and expectations of the total organization. In short, they must be well coordinated. But, as we have already pointed out, the hospital is dependent very greatly upon the motivations and voluntary, informal adjustments of its members for the attainment and maintenance of good coordination. Formal organizational plans, rules, regulations, and controls may ensure some minimum coordination but of themselves are incapable of producing adequate coordination, for only a fraction of all the coordinative activities required in this organization can be programed in advance.

The other relevant factor that we wish to consider here, in addition to coordination, is that of professionalization—professionalization being one of the major distinctive features of the community general hospital. The majority of those who hold the principal therapeutic and nontherapeutic positions in the hospital are trained as professionals. The doctors, through their training, have been schooled in certain professional obligations, ethics, and standards of appropriate behavior and have acquired a number of common attitudes, shared values, and mutual understandings about their work and work relations with others. The same is true about the registered nurses. Other groups in the organization are also on the road to professionalization: the administrators, the medical librarians, the medical technologists, the dietitians, and others in paramedical positions.

This high degree of professionalization among those entrusted with the care of the patient has developed along lines of rational, functional specialization, and has had the effect of inculcating many complementary expectations and common norms and values in the members of the principal groups of the hospital—values, expectations, and norms that are essential to the integration of the organization. These include the norms of giving good care, devotion to duty, loyalty, selflessness and altruism, discipline, and hard work. This normative structure underpins the formal rational structure of the organization, and enables the hospital to attain a level of coordination and integration that could never be accomplished through administrative edict, through hierarchical directives, or through explicitly formulated and carefully specified organizational plans and impersonal rules, regulations, and procedures. However, increased professionalization and specialization have also had the effect of sharpening some of the status differences among the people working in the hospital—and sharp status distinctions bespeak of some authoritarianism.

Among other things, increased professionalization in the hospital has helped guarantee that certain minimum levels of competence and skill will exist in the organization, thus having a direct impact upon performance and organizational effectiveness. Similarly, professionalization and specialization have contributed to greater public confidence in the hospital, and to a wider acceptance of the hospital as a resource for the health needs of all people, for high professionalization and specialization imply expertness and knowledge. Increased professionalization has undoubtedly resulted in improved patient care and, in so doing, it has also raised the expectations of the public for both high-quality care and high efficiency in hospital operations. More and more of us go to the hospital for our various health needs nowadays, but, because of improved service, we stay there for a shorter and shorter period of time. In the last 30 years, the average length of stay for adult patients in general hospitals has decreased by about a third, from 12.6 to 8.6 days[3]—making it increasingly appropriate to refer to the community general hospital as the short-stay hospital.

Another of the distinctive characteristics of the community general hospital, closely related to professionalization and specialization, is the absence of a single line of authority in the organization. This feature has already been the subject of

[3]Health Insurance Institute, *Source Book of Health Insurance Data,* New York: Health Insurance Institute, 1959.

considerable discussion by Smith[4] and others, but is important enough to warrant some brief observations here. Essentially, authority in the hospital is shared (not equally) by the board of trustees, the doctors, and the administrator—the three centers of power in the organization—and, to some extent, also by the director of nursing. In the hospital, authority does not emanate from a single source and does not flow along a single line of command as it does in most formal organizations.

A formal organizational chart of the hospital shows the board of trustees as having ultimate authority and overall responsibility for the institution. The board delegates the day-to-day management of the organization to the hospital administrator. In turn, the administrator delegates authority to the heads of the various nonmedical departments (including the director of nursing, who also wields a different kind of authority that originates in her professional expertness). The heads of these departments, in turn, have varying degrees of authority over the affairs of their respective departments and personnel. In the formal organizational chart, the medical staff, its officers, and its members are not shown as having any direct-line responsibility; they are outside of the lay–administrative line of authority. Yet, as is well known both within and outside the hospital, the doctors exercise substantial influence throughout the hospital structure at nearly all organizational levels, enjoy very high autonomy in their work, and have a good deal of professional authority over others in the organization. Over the nursing staff and over the patients, their professional authority is dominant. And although the board of trustees is in theory shown as the ultimate source of authority, the board actually has very limited *de facto* authority over the medical staff. Partly because the doctors are not employees of the hospital (they are "guests" who are granted practice privileges), partly because they enjoy high status and great prestige, partly because they have almost supreme authority in professional-medical matters, and partly for other reasons, they are subject to very little lay–organizational authority.

Professionals in staff capacities in business corporations—lawyers, doctors, accountants, and others—have little or no authority to be involved in the activities of the line; they mainly serve as consultants and advisors. But this is not so in the case of the hospital. The absence of a single line of authority in the hospital, of course, creates various administrative and operational problems, as well as psychological problems having to do with the relative power and influence on organizational functioning on the part of doctors, trustees, administrators, and others. For one thing, it makes formal organizational coordination rather difficult. For another thing, it allows for instances in which it is not clear where authority, responsibility, and accountability reside. Similarly, it allows for a situation wherein a large number of organizational members, particularly members of the nursing staff, must be responsible to and take orders not only from their supervisors but also from the doctors. The lay authority and the professional authority to which nurses are subject, of course, are not always consistent. The absence of a single line of authority also makes for difficulties in communication, difficulties in the area of discipline, and difficulties in resolving problems

[4]Smith, H. L., "Two Lines of Authority: The Hospital's Dilemma," *Modern Hospital,* 84:59-64, March, 1955.

that must be resolved through cooperative efforts on the part of both the lay-administrative and the medical–professional sides. Frequently, the administrator, feeling that the responsibility for the overall management of the organization is his, and feeling that doctors through their power and pressure interfere in the discharge of his responsibilities, is motivated or actively attempts to circumvent the medical staff on various matters, and this too is apt to lead to problems. (The doctors, in turn, are likely to try to circumvent the administrator.) For the same reasons, the administrator is likely to be prone toward more and more bureaucratization in the hospital. And increased bureaucratization of organizational operations is likely to be fought and resented by the doctors, for it eventually means a reduction in their influence.

In general, multiple lines of authority require the maintenance of a very delicate balance of power in the organization—a balance of power that is rather precarious. On the positive side, multiple lines of authority may serve as a system of "checks and balances," which may prevent other kinds of possible problems, such as organizational inflexibility and authoritarianism, or may serve to lighten the burden of responsibility in situations where responsibility may be too great for any single group or individual to shoulder. Regardless of the advantages and disadvantages of a system of multiple lines of authority, such a system is an integral part of the community general hospital. Not only is it an integral part, moreover, but also a part that is virtually inevitable for an organization such as this. This is because much of the work in the hospital is performed by influential professionals and not by low-status workers, and because of the high degrees of both professionalization and specialization characteristic of the organization. As Parsons has aptly observed, "The multiplication of technical fields, and their differentiation from each other . . . leads to an essential element of decentralization in the organizations which must employ them."[5] For this reason, he goes on to explain that, unlike business and military organizations, "A university cannot be organized mainly on a 'line' principle. . . ."[6] In this respect, the community general hospital is very similar to a university. (Hospitals and universities have a number of other interesting characteristics in common, but here we are only interested in hospitals.)

Summary

In summary, the community general hospital is an extremely complex social organization that differs from business and other large-scale organizations in a number of important characteristics. Among its main distinguishing characteristics, the following are worth re-emphasizing:

1. The main objective of the organization is to render personalized service—care and treatment—to individual patients, rather than the manufacture of some uniform material object. And the economic value of the organization's products and objectives is secondary to their social and humanitarian value.

[5]Parsons, T., "Suggestions for a Sociological Approach to the Theory of Organizations: II," *Admin. Science Quart.*, 1:225–239, September, 1956 (especially p. 236).
[6]*Ibid.*

2. By comparison to industrial organizations, the hospital is much more directly dependent upon, and responsive to, its surrounding community, and its work is much more closely integrated with the needs and demands of its consumers and potential customers. To the hospital and its members, the patient's needs are always of supreme and paramount importance. Moreover, there is high agreement about the principal objective of the hospital among the members of the organization, and the personal needs and goals of the different members conflict little with the objectives of the organization.

3. The demands of much of the work at the hospital are of an emergency nature and nondeferrable. They place a heavy burden of both moral and secular-functional responsibility upon the organization and its members. Correspondingly, the organization shows great concern for clarity of responsibility and accountability among its different members and very little tolerance for either ambiguity or error.

4. The nature and volume of work are variable and diverse, and subject to relatively little standardization. The hospital cannot lend itself to mass production techniques, to assembly-line operations, or to automated functioning. It is a human rather than a machine system, with all the attributes this entails. Both the raw materials and end products of the organization are human. And, being human, they participate actively in the production process, thus having a good deal of control over it.

5. The principal workers in the hospital—doctors and nurses—are professionals, and this entails various administrative and operational problems for the organization.

6. By comparison to industrial organizations, the hospital has relatively little control over its workload and over many of its key members. In particular, it has little direct control over the doctors and over the patients—two of its most essential components. In the short-stay hospital, the patients are not only a very heterogeneous and very transient group, but are also, mainly and ultimately, in the hands of their doctors, who are not employees of the organization.

7. The administrator has much less authority, power, and discretion than his managerial counterparts in industry, because the hospital is not and cannot very well be organized on the basis of a single line of authority. The simultaneous presence of lay, professional, and mixed lay–professional lines of authority in the hospital creates a number of administrative and other problems, which business organizations are largely spared.

8. The hospital is a formal, quasi-bureaucratic, and quasi-authoritarian organization which, like most organizations of this kind, relies greatly on conventional hierarchical work arrangements and on rather rigid impersonal rules, regulations and procedures. But, more importantly, it is a highly departmentalized, highly professionalized, and highly specialized organization that could not possibly function effectively without relying heavily for its internal coordination on the motivations, actions, self-discipline, and voluntary, informal adjustments of its many members. Coordination of efforts and activities in the hospital is indispensable to organizational functioning, because the work is of a highly interactional character—the activities of organizational members are highly interlocking and interdependent, and the various members can perform their role only by working in close association with each other.

9. The hospital shows a very great concern for efficiency and predictability of performance among its members and for overall organizational effectiveness.

10. Finally, the community general hospital is an organization which is important to us all, and which is becoming increasingly important. Several basic social trends tend to ensure this: the accelerating accumulation of new medical knowledge, new medical, surgical, and nursing procedures, and new drugs and medicines; rising levels of family income in the nation; increased use of the general hospital for numerous different diseases and health needs; and a growing demand by the general public for the best possible quality of medical–surgical and nursing care.

19 Organizational Socialization of Hospital Employees: A Comparative View of Occupational Groups

What is it about the ways in which employees are recruited into and developed within hospital settings that make some new recruits feel competent and others helpless, makes some feel accepted as good organization members and others feel isolated and rejected, makes some workers passive, and others creative contributors to organizational success? These are the basic questions in the study of organizational socialization, the study of the ways employees are transformed from total outsiders of organizations to participating and effective members of them. The success of the socialization process is critical for hospital employees, for how their careers are managed by hospitals influences both the quality of their work life and the quality of their outside lives. As the delivery of good medical care becomes increasingly dependent on the commitment of employees rather than on traditional control systems, the questions posed here about organizational socialization become increasingly important to hospitals as well.

When we look at what we know about how employees are socialized into hospitals, we find that there is little research which deals with this topic directly.

While there is an extensive research on the professionalization of health care workers and the relationship of professionalization to organizational effectiveness,[5, 6, 11, 12] we know very little about the ways either professional workers or other occupational groups adjust to particular health care organizations. The author recently conducted a large-scale study of the socialization process at a community hospital, and this article discusses the highlights of this research. In particular, the research addresses four sets of questions:

1. What happens to employees as they enter hospitals and adjust to new work assignments? What are the indicators of good socialization experiences?

2. What are the differences between the socialization experiences of various occupational groups in hospitals? What accounts for these differences?

3. What are the results, or consequences, of socialization programs? What are the differences in outcomes between the socialization experiences of separate and distinct occupational groups?

The author wishes to thank J. Richard Hackman for helpful comments on this article. J. Richard Hackman, Clayton Alderfer, and Gerrit Wolf provided valuable assistance during the conduct of the research.
Reprinted from *Medical Care*, XV:779–813, October, 1977, by permission of the author and Publisher.

4. What are the implications of this research for the design of hospital socialization programs?

Each of these sets of questions is considered separately.

What Happens to Employees as They Enter Hospitals and Adjust to New Work Assignments? What Are the Indicators of Good Socialization Experiences?

The research proposes that there are three distinct and successive stages of the socialization process, each with its own set of activities. Associated with each stage in the process are a set of indicators which suggest how smoothly the process is going for individuals. The more positive the indicators, the more smoothly the socialization process is going for individuals; also, the more positive the indicators of one stage are, the more likely the individual will be to progress through the later stages of socialization.

Anticipatory Socialization

This first stage of the socialization process encompasses all the learning which occurs before the recruit enters the organization.[2, 4, 14] The stage has alternatively been labeled as "pre-arrival" by Porter, Lawler, and Hackman.[13] The main activities which the individual engages in at this stage [are] forming expectations about jobs (transmitting, receiving, and evaluating information with prospective employers) and making decisions about employment.

At anticipatory socialization, there are two indicators of progress through socialization:

- *Realism*, the extent to which the individual has a full and accurate picture of what life in the organization is really like, indicates how successfully the individual has completed the information sharing and information evaluation part of his recruitment.
- *Congruence*, the extent to which the organization's resources and individual needs and skills are mutually satisfying, indicates how successful the individual has been in making a decision about employment.

Accommodation

Accommodation, the second stage of the socialization process, is that period in which the individual sees what the organization is actually like and attempts to become a participating member of it. This phase encompasses the "encounter" stage of Porter, Lawler, and Hackman[13] and Van Maanen,[14] and parts of their "change and acquisition" and "metamorphosis" stages. There are four main activities which new employees engage in at the accommodation stage: learning new tasks; establishing new interpersonal relationships with co-workers; clarifying their roles in the organization; and evaluating their progress within the organization.

At accommodation, there are four indicators of progress through socialization:

- *Initiation to the task*, the extent to which the employee feels competent and accepted as a full work partner, indicates how successfully the employee has learned new tasks at work.
- *Initiation to the group*, the extent to which an employee feels accepted and trusted by co-workers, indicates how successful the employee has been in establishing new interpersonal relationships.
- *Role definition*, an implicit or explicit agreement with the work group on what tasks one is to perform and what the priorities and time allocation among those tasks is to be, indicates the extent to which the employee has fully clarified his role.
- *Congruence of evaluation*, the extent to which an employee and a supervisor similarly evaluate the employee's progress within the organization, indicates the degree of agreement between employee and supervisor about the employee's overall progress in the organization and about his particular strengths and weaknesses.

Role Management

In the third stage of socialization, the recruit has already come to some tentative resolution of problems in his own work group, and now needs to mediate the conflicts between his work in his own group and other groups which may place demands on him. There are two types of conflicts in particular which are crucial to manage at this point: conflicts between work life and home life (*e.g.*, over schedules, demands on the employee's family, effect of the job on the quality of home life) and conflicts between his work group and other groups in the organization (*e.g.*, over the inclusion or exclusion of certain tasks in the sets, over priorities assigned certain tasks, and so forth).

At role management, two indicators are important:

- *Resolution of outside life conflicts* indicates the extent to which an employee has come to be less upset by home life, work life conflicts and the extent to which he has come to some decision rules for dealing with these conflicts.
- *Resolution of conflicting demands* indicates the extent to which an employee has come to be less upset by conflicts among groups at work and the extent to which he has come to some decision rules for dealing with these conflicts.

The three stages of socialization and the indicators associated with each stage are diagrammed in Figure 19-1.

Methodology

Before examining the differences between the socialization experiences of various occupational groups, a few words on the methodology of this research are in order.

Sample. The site of data collection was a 350-bed community hospital in a medium-sized industrial city in New England. One hundred eighteen employees

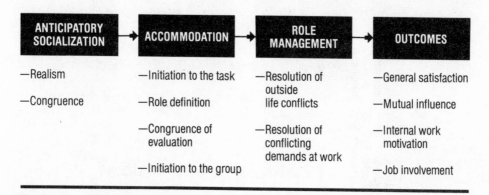

Figure 19-1. Process and outcome variables of socialization.

of the hospital participated in the study, roughly one-eighth of the total hospital employee population (excluding doctors), 28 engineers (licensed tradesmen, such as electricians and plumbers), 25 accounting clerks, 19 radiology technologists, 22 registered nurses, and 24 nursing technicians (orderlies, nurse's aides). Eighty per cent of the engineers, accounting clerks, and radiology technologists participated, with only those employees who were on sick leave or vacation leave not participating; the sample of nurses and nursing technicians represents 33 per cent of the Nursing Service population and were selected randomly. There were 79 female subjects, and 39 male subjects (almost all of whom were engineers); their average age was 33.

Procedure. Interviews and questionnaires were used to obtain ratings for each employee on the eight process variables and the four outcome variables. Each employee was interviewed individually for 45 minutes about his or her socialization experience, during which time the researcher rated the employee on each of the variables. At the end of the interview, the employee was given a questionnaire of 47 Likert items to complete, which went over much of the material in the interview. All data collection activities were conducted by the researcher during a six-week period.

Scales. Interview ratings and questionnaire items were combined in the formulation of the final scales; the interview rating was treated as an additional questionnaire item, and was averaged with the other questionnaire items in a scale. Interview–questionnaire correlations were sufficiently high to make this a reasonable strategy (67 per cent of the interview ratings correlated with their respective questionnaire items at the .001 level, and 88 per cent of the interview ratings correlated with their respective questionnaire items at the .05 level). The descriptive statistics for the scales are presented in Table 19-1. The scales have moderate internal consistency and are independent; the average Spearman–Brown reliability, corrected for attenuation, is .65 and the average correlation of scale items with items not in the same scale is .13.

Data Analysis. Partial correlations were used to determine the relationships between variables. The assumptions about the time order of variables outlined above imply that there are sets of "intervening variables" which are intermediate in the causal sequence between stages in the socialization process and the set of outcomes.[1] Partial correlations allow the researcher to look at the linear relation-

Table 19-1   Scale score statistics

Scale	Mean	Standard Deviation	Mean within Scale Correlation	Mean outside Scale Correlation	Spearman-Brown Reliability
Anticipatory Socialization					
Realism	4.523	1.253	.414	.126	.739
Congruence	4.932	1.301	.502	.157	.751
Accommodation					
Initiation to task	5.036	0.846	.201	.113	.501
Role definition	4.962	1.235	.463	.206	.775
Congruence of evaluation	4.212	1.387	.491	.180	.743
Initiation to group	5.079	1.026	.345	.122	.612
Role Management					
Resolution of conflicting demands	4.715	1.130	.333	.127	.667
Resolution of outside life conflicts	4.766	1.015	.181	.094	.400
Outcomes					
General satisfaction	5.214	1.143	.501	.108	.801
Mutual influence	3.404	1.339	.450	.110	.711
Internal work motivation	5.625	0.729	.214	.099	.521
Job involvement	3.461	0.924	.190	.095	.539

Note: Means on all scales range from 1 (very low) to 7 (very high).

ship between two variables *after* the linear effect of the "control variables" has been removed from both the independent and dependent variables, and make possible the identification of spurious and suppressed relationships. The following rules were used in calculating the partial correlations:

Between Variables in Two Different Stages. Between two variables in two successive stages (between indicator variables of anticipatory socialization and accommodation, between indicator variables of accommodation and role management, between indicator variables of role management and outcomes), all the other variables in these two stages were controlled. This was done because it might be possible for variables at one stage to be generally correlated with each other, and it was necessary to identify whether specific two-variable correlations were spurious.

Between two variables from stages which were not successive (between indicator variables of anticipatory socialization and role management, between indicator variables of anticipatory socialization and outcomes, and between indicator variables of accommodation and outcomes), the other variables in those two stages, as well as all variables from the intervening stages, were controlled. Here it was important to identify not only if correlations were spurious, but also if variables intervened in ways consistent with the model's assumptions about time.

Between Two Variables in the Same Stage (within anticipatory socialization, within accommodation, within role management, between outcomes).

At anticipatory socialization, a simple Pearson correlation between realism and congruence was calculated. No prior causes to these two variables were assumed nor were there other variables at this stage which might cause the relationship between congruence and realism to be spurious or suppressed.

Between any two variables in accommodation, the other two variables in accommodation as well as realism and congruence were held constant. It is assumed that only the variables from the immediately prior stage or the same stage could be the source of spurious relationships.

Between resolution of conflicting demands and resolution of outside life conflicts, the four variables of the most prior stage, accommodation, were controlled to eliminate a spurious or identify a suppressed relationship. It is assumed that only the variables from the immediately prior stage could be the source of these correlations.

Between any two outcome variables, the other two outcome variables as well as resolution of conflicting demands and resolution of outside life conflicts were held constant. Once again, it is assumed that only the variables from the immediately prior stage or same stage could contribute to spurious or suppressed correlations.

Table 19-2 presents the zero-order correlation between every two variables in the study and the partial correlation between every two variables, calculated according to the decision rules listed above. The statistically significant partial correlations are displayed in diagram form in Figure 19-2 [p. 314].

Analysis was also done to consider the effects of time on-the-job on respondents' answers since not all employees had started work at the same time. Time-on-the-job was not significantly related to any of the process variables, nor did it significantly moderate any of the relationships presented in Figure 19-2.

Table 19-2   Zero-Order and Higher-Order Correlations among Scale Scores

Variables	Zero-Order Correlation	Partial Correlation
Congruence with		
Realism	.283***	—
Initiation to task	.226**	.063
Initiation to group	.306***	.232**
Congruence of evaluation	.351***	.158*
Role definition	.377***	.214*
Res. conflicting demands	.124	− .065
Res. outside life conflicts	.094	− .013
General satisfaction	.694***	.605***
Mutual influence	.134	− .095
Work motivation	.117	.104
Job involvement	.034	− .081
Realism with		
Initiation to task	.152*	.061
Initiation to group	.076	− .029
Congruence of evaluation	.227**	.033
Role definition	.380***	.272**
Res. conflicting demands	.119	− .004
Res. outside life conflicts	.021	− .060
General satisfaction	.336***	.112
Mutual influence	.202*	.124
Work motivation	− .094	− .124
Job involvement	.053	.048
Initiation to task with		
Initiation to group	.294***	.229**
Congruence of evaluation	.294***	.124
Role definition	.191*	.052
Res. conflicting demands	.220**	.141
Res. outside life conflicts	.031	− .094
General satisfaction	.152*	− .014
Mutual influence	.273***	.159*
Work motivation	.016	.020
Job involvement	.105	.077
Initiation to group with		
Congruence of evaluation	.228**	.114
Role definition	.107	− .064
Res. conflicting demands	.112	− .027
Res. outside life conflicts	.164*	.137
General satisfaction	.206*	.101
Mutual influence	.219**	.079
Work motivation	.082	.095
Job involvement	.064	.015
Congruence of evaluation with		
Role definition	.434***	.317***
Res. conflicting demands	.356***	.210*
Res. outside life conflicts	.213*	.081
General satisfaction	.422***	.114
Mutual influence	.452***	.347***
Work motivation	− .003	− .053
Job involvement	.078	.059

Table 19-2 (Continued)

Variables	Zero-Order Correlation	Partial Correlation
Role definition with		
Res. conflicting demands	.307***	.148
Res. outside life conflicts	.191*	.085
General satisfaction	.472***	.237**
Mutual influence	.173*	.150
Work motivation	−.036	−.130
Job involvement	−.068	−.002
Res. conflicting demands with		
Res. outside life conflicts	.267**	.201*
General satisfaction	.217**	.155*
Mutual influence	.209*	.144
Work motivation	−.211*	−.189*
Job involvement	.040	−.026
Res. outside life conflicts with		
General satisfaction	.236**	.189*
Mutual influence	.175*	.108
Work motivation	−.141	−.092
Job involvement	−.117	−.132
General satisfaction with		
Mutual influence	.213**	.143
Work motivation	.026	.085
Job involvement	.085	.095
Mutual influence with		
Work motivation	−.045	−.014
Job involvement	.093	−.104
Work motivation with		
Job involvement	.116	.091

***$p \leq .001$.
**$p \leq .01$.
*$p \leq .05$.

What Are the Differences between Various Occupational Groups in Hospitals?

The main focus of this next section is on the *differences* between the socialization experiences of separate and distinct occupational groups in hospitals, and what accounts for these differences. Before an examination of the differences between experiences, however, a brief description of a typical hospital socialization program might illuminate these findings.

Generally, job applicants come to the hospital to apply for jobs on the advice of friends who already work in the hospital or on the advice of peers in the same line of employment. A personnel employee gives out a standardized biographical data sheet, and describes job duties to the applicant. After references are checked out and line supervisors are consulted by the personnel office, new employees are hired, often to start the next week.

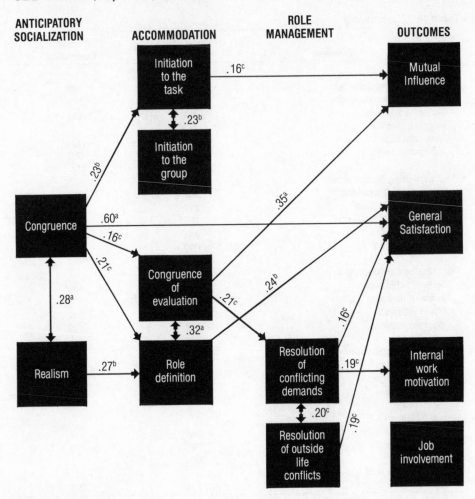

Figure 19-2. Significant correlations between process and outcome variables (a = p ≤ .001; b = p ≤ .01; c = p ≤ .05).

The formal socialization program is usually short. It begins with a one-day orientation to benefits, working conditions, hospital regulations, and physical plant by the personnel office. Then, depending on the department, new employees receive on-the-job training from a senior employee (not a supervisor) for anywhere from three days to three weeks. During this period, employees also begin to learn their co-workers, their counterparts in other departments, and so on. If any event were to be cited as the formal end of the initial socialization period, it would be the three-month evaluation, which signifies either the end of probation period or termination of employment. During the next nine months, employees are still more closely scrutinized than more senior workers; new employees do begin to take on some additional duties sometimes including temporary supervisor functions, and often go to additional in-service classes. The anniversary evaluation is generally seen as the end of the socialization program.

Table 19-3 presents the means of the total sample on all the indicator variables discussed above, as well as the means of the separate job categories on these indicators. A few differences between job categories stand out.

Table 19-3 Scale scores by job category

Scale	Total Sample	Accounting	Nursing Tech.	Engineers	Radiology Tech.	Nurses
Anticipatory socialization						
Realism*	4.52	4.20	4.44	4.39	5.36	4.40
Congruence	4.93	4.78	4.48	5.33	5.03	4.98
Accommodation						
Initiation to task	5.03	4.68	4.92	5.17	5.05	5.36
Initiation to group	5.07	4.84	4.97	5.08	4.87	5.63
Congruence of evaluation	4.21	4.08	4.44	4.28	4.52	3.74
Role definition	4.96	5.03	4.84	5.07	5.32	4.55
Role management						
Resolution of conflicting demands	4.71	4.59	4.94	5.02	4.55	4.35
Resolution of outside life conflicts	4.76	5.04	4.65	4.90	4.93	4.25
Outcomes						
General satisfaction*	5.21	5.25	5.03	5.63	5.39	4.68
Mutual influence	3.40	3.12	3.04	3.44	4.12	3.45
Job involvement*	3.46	2.87	3.49	3.77	3.61	3.57
Internal work motivation*	5.62	5.53	5.46	5.42	5.76	6.03

* F-test significant at .05 level.

In General, Unskilled Labor in Entry-Level Jobs Have the Most Difficult Time in Anticipatory Socialization. All nurses, radiology technologists, and engineers had to have occupational training before they were hired, so these employees generally knew by the end of their occupational training whether at least their occupational duties would be suited to them. Accounting and nursing technicians' jobs were entry-level jobs, and were most frequently held by people who had never worked before at all; their congruence scores were the lowest. The positiveness of the radiology realism score is due to the fact that the hospital had its own school of radiology technology, and regularly recruited its graduates to work as radiology technologists.

Professional Nurses Have the Highest Scores on Both Initiation to the Group and Initiation to the Task; Unskilled Entry-Level Labor Have the Lowest Scores. Members of nursing professional associations reported that their peers had extended themselves to make them feel welcome when they started to work at the hospital, and that they had likewise gone out of their way to help new employees. Moreover, the hospital provided little formal training or orientation for new employees; for those people who had professional colleagues there was a resource to turn to for work guidance and social support. Entry-level unskilled labor did not have professional groups for either social support or technical advice; paraprofessional and technical employees had some social support and work guidance, but not as much as the professional nurses.

Professional Nurses Have the Most Difficult Time in Defining Suitable Roles for Themselves and in Coming to Some Agreement with Supervisors Over Work Evaluations. Three-year diploma nurses tended to feel the mark of a good nurse is the ability to keep on schedule, to handle all patients quickly and efficiently, and to be solicitous of the attending physician's demands. In contrast, four-year degree nurses tended to feel that the mark of quality nursing care is emphasis on the total individual patient (both his physical and psychological needs) and that the nurse should share more fully in the diagnosis and treatment decisions made on the floor. These two views of nursing entail desires for very different types of tasks to perform and very different priorities among these tasks, and head nurses vary in how they want their staff nurses to perform. Given that nurses vary so greatly in the extent to which they want to define their jobs, both in terms of duties and in priorities, it is not surprising that nurses have the lowest scores. Nursing technicians ("to do transporting work and all other related duties") similarly experience difficulties in determining what they are expected to do. In contrast, engineers and accounting clerks have very prescribed duties, and do not have as much difficulty in clarifying their roles.

The whole issue of work evaluation was important at the hospital. The general feeling among supervisors was that "goodness is its own reward" and that positive feedback is demotivating. Employees interpreted this widespread lack of feedback as a sign they were not appreciated by their supervisors, and thus their congruence of evaluation is lowered; it is particularly low for nurses because staff nurses resented being evaluated by nurse administrators who rarely saw their work, and because the criteria for effective nursing performance are somewhat subjective.

Nurses Have the Severest Role Conflicts to Manage, Both at Work and at Home. Hospitals are generally seen as having two hierarchies: a medical hierarchy—from the chief of staff down to orderlies—which is responsible for medical care, and an administrative hierarchy—from the chief administrator down to first-line supervisors—which is responsible for the operation of the entire hospital facility. These two lines of authority are often seen as being in conflict with each other, and this bifurcated organization of hospitals is frequently cited as a major source of inefficiency and ineffectiveness in the delivery of health care.

The nurse's role is overloaded with responsibilities to both hierarchies. Although not part of management, staff nurses are the small group administrators of all lower levels of auxiliary medical personnel (*e.g.*, student nurses, licensed practical nurses, nurse's aides, technicians). They are responsible for their day-to-day work, their training, the scheduling of their hours, their patient load, and their performance evaluation. Staff nurses are responsible for requesting and accounting for all supplies, and for coordinating nursing floors with all ancillary medical services (*e.g.*, laboratory, x-ray, pharmacy).

The nurse also plays a major role in administering medical care. She is the main link between the head nurse and all other nursing service personnel, the main link between the doctor and the patient, and the main link between the doctor and the patient's family. She is the only employee who is allowed to give certain medical treatments and use certain medical equipment, and she is ultimately responsible for the medical services provided by all the staff under her. Thus, nurses are faced with many conflicting demands at work, and they expectedly have the lowest score on this variable.

Nurses also have the lowest score on resolution of outside life conflicts. The outside life conflicts nurses face revolve around two issues. The first is scheduling. All nurses must work every other weekend, and must take two nonconsecutive days off every other week (and these days off are different each week). There is limited vacation time and sick time available for nurses, and requesting either often involves a great deal of trouble. The number of time constraints on nurses' schedules, as well as the unpredictability of their occurrence, creates problems for nurses with heavy demands of family and friends on them. The second issue concerns the impact of work life on time spent outside the hospital. Nurses occasionally get very involved in their patients' lives, and worry about them at home; moreover, sometimes their families and friends resent hearing somber stories about work or providing support for hospital-related problems which result from concern with patients. In contrast, engineers, for example, have very little to do with the medical hierarchy at all, and can fairly well go about their business without being bothered; most rarely, if ever, have to work nights or weekends.

What Are the Results, or Consequences, of Socialization Programs? What Are the Differences in Outcomes between the Experiences of the Various Occupational Groups?

There has been little systematic research on which variables are the most appropriate to study as outcomes of the socialization process. In this research, we examine four possible outcomes of socialization: general satisfaction, mutual influence, internal work motivation, and job involvement. These outcomes are diagrammed in Figure 19-1; the means of the total sample and the job categories on these outcomes appear in Table 19-3.

1. General Satisfaction. General satisfaction is defined as "an overall measure of the degree to which the employee is satisfied and happy in his or her work."[9] Two types of outcomes have been most frequently associated with general satisfaction. The first of these outcomes are absenteeism and turnover. The research is convincing that the more satisfied a worker is, the longer he will stay on his job and the lower his absenteeism will be. The second of these outcomes is job performance. The evidence on this suggests that general satisfaction may be related to some moderate increase in job performance.

It is interesting to note that nurses are the lowest on general satisfaction, while engineers are the highest on this outcome (see Table 19-3). The reason for the differences become clearer when we look at the indicator variables positively correlated with general satisfaction—congruence, role definition, resolution of conflicting demands, and resolution of outside life conflicts. It is not surprising to find that congruence is most strongly correlated with general satisfaction, and accounts for over one-third of its variance; the better the fit between an individual and his job, the more happy and satisfied he will be with his job situation. The other three variables correlated with general satisfaction have to do with defining roles and managing role conflicts. Individuals who could largely determine what tasks they would do and how they could allocate their time among those tasks expressed more positive attitudes about the nature of their work and their relationships with other members of the work group. Role conflict, either at work or at home, serves as a constant irritant to hospital employees, making the overall quality of the work experience less positive; those employees who come to be less upset by role conflicts, and have come up with some decision rules for how to handle those role conflicts, are happier in their work situations.

Nurses are lowest on three of the four variables related to general satisfaction, and are lowest on general satisfaction, too. While nurses and engineers both have jobs which suit their skills and abilities, nurses have a good deal of difficulty in defining their jobs because they have many different tasks to do and disagreements about the priorities these tasks should claim; moreover, as was discussed above, nurses have the severest role conflicts to handle, managing the conflicting demands of medical and administrative duties at work and managing unusual scheduling problems and the effects of patients' problems at home.

2. Mutual Influence. Mutual influence refers to the extent to which an individual feels some control or power over the way work is carried out in his or her department. While an individual must generally accept the legitimacy of influence attempts of the organization as a condition of employment, if an individual can establish the legitimacy of influence on his part, he is likely to be a much more creative and participative member of his group.

Two variables at the accommodation stage are significantly related to mutual influence, initiation to the task and congruence of evaluation. Employees believe that until such time as they feel on top of their jobs, they would look foolish trying to suggest changes about work-related activities to co-workers or supervisors; people felt they needed to earn the right to make suggestions, and the way to do this was to demonstrate competence. The relationship between congruence of evaluation and mutual influence revolves around the probabilities employees assign to the receptiveness of supervisors to their suggestions. Where employees feel they themselves are not appreciated or evaluated fairly, they doubt their supervisors will appreciate and evaluate their suggestions favorably either. Supervisors are the people who will ultimately decide which suggestions to implement; when employees feel they are not valued by their supervisors, they have little reason to believe supervisors will heed their advice. In contrast, where employees feel they are evaluated fairly, they feel they have a good chance of getting at least an open hearing from a superior on some suggestions.

3. Internal Work Motivation and Job Involvement. Internal work motivation is "the degree to which an employee is self-motivated to perform effectively on the job."[8] At least in the management literature, internal work motivation is cited as a likely outcome of training and development programs. Besides the finding that internal work motivation is strongly related to individual satisfaction with opportunities to grow and develop at work, the organizational outcome most frequently related to internal work motivation has been job performance—*i.e.*, the greater the work motivation, the higher the quality of a person's work.

Job involvement refers to the degree to which an employee is personally committed and involved in his work; it is the degree to which the total work situation is an important part of an employee's life.[10] It is often cited as a necessary condition if the individual is to fully accept the demands placed upon him by members of an organization. Besides being an indicator of the degree to which employees feel they are active participants in their work organization, job involvement has also been found to be directly related to internal work motivation and general satisfaction.

It is important to note that *no* variable in this research is significantly and positively related to either internal work motivation or job involvement.* While no specific hypotheses are made about the relationships between socialization variables and outcome variables, it is more likely that the *nature of the work itself* rather than the way one is recruited or trained at work that makes a difference in increasing the levels of internal work motivation and job involvement.

Hackman and his colleagues[7, 8] show there are strong relationships between jobs with high "motivating potential scores" and internal work motivation and job involvement. Five job characteristics contribute to the motivating potential of jobs:

- *Skill Variety.* The degree to which a job requires a variety of different activities in carrying out the work, which involve the use of a number of different skills and talents of the employee.
- *Task Identity.* The degree to which the job requires completion of a "whole" and identifiable piece of work—*i.e.*, doing a job from beginning to end with a visible outcome.
- *Task Significance.* The degree to which the job has a substantial impact on the lives or work of other people—whether in the immediate organization or in the external environment.

---

* There is a significant negative correlation between resolution of conflicting demands and internal work motivation ($r = -.19$, $p \leq .05$). This result is more likely an artifact of this particular sample than it is a theoretical finding. Highly motivated people, those who are most concerned with doing their jobs effectively, are the most frustrated in dealing with the many conflicts at work, and are the least satisfied with the ways these conflicts are being handled.

- *Autonomy*. The degree to which the job provides substantial freedom, independence, and discretion of the employee in scheduling the work and in determining the procedures to be used in carrying it out.
- *Feedback from the Job Itself*. The degree to which carrying out the work activities required by the job results in the employee obtaining direct and clear information about the effectiveness of his or her performance.

When we examine the significant department differences on these two variables, we see that the three jobs which would have the highest motivating potential—nurse, radiology technologist, and engineer—also have the three highest scores on these two outcomes. All three jobs have high skill variety, task identity, and feedback from the job itself. These jobs involve the use of several different skills; workers do identifiable pieces of work; employees can tell right away—from patients, from films, or from equipment—whether they have performed effectively. In addition, nurses have high task significance and a moderate amount of autonomy in being team leaders or charge nurses.

In other jobs where the motivating potential would be lower—such as accounting clerk and nursing technician—employees experience lower internal work motivation and job involvement, too. Their jobs require fewer skills, allow less autonomy, and are much less significant than the other jobs studied. Accounting clerks do not even have high task identity, because each clerk only does a small piece of work involved in billing a patient or collecting payments.

There is additional evidence to support the idea that general satisfaction and mutual influence, rather than internal work motivation and job involvement, are outcomes of socialization. It is expected that the further along in the socialization process an individual is (*i.e.*, the more successful his socialization), the higher will be his outcome levels. To test this hypothesis, the researcher determined to what stage in the socialization process each employee's socialization had progressed. If an employee averaged 5.33 or higher (out of a possible 7) on the indicators of a stage, the person was judged to have completed that stage in socialization (C); if the average of the indicators of a stage was at least 4.0 and lower than 5.33, that person was judged to be making moderate progress in completing that stage (M); if the average of the indicators of a stage was lower than 4.0, that person was judged to have made little progress at that stage (L). There was thus a coding of C, M, or L for each employee on each of the three stages of socialization.

Table 19-4 compares the means of five groups which have made differing amounts of progress in the socialization process. These five groups were chosen because they represented the five most frequent points employees were at in their socialization process (44 per cent of the sample fell at these five points).

On general satisfaction, there is a perfect steady increase in group means from those who have not completed anticipatory socialization to those who have completed all three stages. A one-way analysis of variance indicates the differences between these five groups is significant at the .001 level. On mutual influence, with one exception, there is also a steady increase in group means corresponding to degree of progress through socialization; the one-way analysis of variance is significant at the .05 level. In contrast, on the two outcomes which were not significantly correlated with any indicators—internal work motivation and job involvement—the differences between groups are small in magnitude and are not statistically significant.

Table 19-4　Outcome levels by stage in socialization process

Progress Point	General Satisfaction***	Mutual Influence*	Internal Work Motivation	Job Involvement
1. LLL (N = 9)	4.11	1.96	5.88	3.28
2. CLL (N = 8)	5.46	3.17	5.78	3.07
3. CMM (N = 9)	5.47	3.29	5.61	3.42
4. CCM (N = 12)	5.77	4.05	5.64	3.64
5. CCC(N = 13)	6.17	3.59	5.59	3.67

Note: *Group 1*, LLL, represents those people who have made little progress at any stage in the socialization process; *Group 2*, CLL, represents those people who have completed anticipatory socialization, but have yet to make progress at the later two stages; *Group 3*, CMM, represents those people who have completed anticipatory socialization, and have made moderate progress at the later two stages; *Group 4*, CCM, includes those people who have completed anticipatory socialization and accommodation, but have not completed role management; and *Group 5*, CCC, represents those who have "completed" socialization, having completed successfully all three stages of the process.

***F-test significant at .001 level.
*F-test significant at .05 level.

What Are the Implications of These Findings for the Design of Hospital Socialization Programs?

1. *One of the Major Implications of This Research for Hospital Socialization Is That Socialization Programs Are Not Appropriate for Achieving Some of the Results Most Frequently Expected from Them.* When the supervisors at the hospital were asked what they hoped to accomplish with their socialization programs, most responded with "communicate," "motivate," and "indoctrinate." Supervisors expected that socialization programs would increase the motivation of employees, and would help employees better communicate with their co-workers and their supervisors.

If the results of this research are generalizable, then managers may have inappropriate expectations of what socialization can accomplish. None of the variables which have commonly been associated with the socialization process are significantly correlated with either internal work motivation or job involvement. Managers may need to look more to the design of individual jobs and work groups to increase the motivation and job involvement of employees, and to special training interventions to improve communication.

What socialization programs *do* affect are the general satisfaction of workers and the feelings of autonomy and personal influence workers have. This is important, because general satisfaction consistently relates to decreased turnover and absenteeism, and because mutual influence may increase the number and quality of creative suggestions which are made by workers. Employers need to consider more carefully just what they want to accomplish in the development of individuals, and tailor their programs more carefully to these ends. Socialization cannot do everything alone.

2. *The Hospital's Efforts in the Socialization Process Must Be Continuous.* The research identified three stages in the socialization process. It was found that the further along the individual was in the socialization process, the higher were his general satisfaction and mutual influence. If hospitals want to maximize the outcomes for individuals and themselves, their efforts must begin with the attraction and selection of applicants, and continue not only through the training and

development of individuals but also through helping employees deal with work and home-related role conflicts.

Different organizations and different levels of organizations tend to focus on one phase of socialization as particularly important, and underemphasize the other two phases. The two most common emphases in socialization programs are:

a. *Concentration on the Attraction and Recruitment of Workers.* This is most frequent in organizations which are heavily staffed with professional workers, such as hospitals, universities, and law and accounting firms. The levels at which this strategy is most frequently used are the higher levels of the organization, where the cost of hiring the wrong applicant or the implications of choosing the wrong candidate are greatest.

b. *Concentration on the Training and Development of Workers.* This is most often found in organizations which are heavily staffed with unskilled or low-skilled labor, such as production and manufacturing companies. This emphasis in socialization is also more common at the lowest levels in the organization (*e.g.*, nonsupervisory personnel). The rationale behind this strategy is that since the jobs are unskilled, only minimal effect should be put into recruitment, and much more effort should be put into training and developing new employees.

Where the quality of performance of the applicants is critical, hospitals are indeed wise to pay particular attention to their recruitment. However, the result of this type of concentration can be the recruitment of highly skilled and qualified workers who may take longer to adjust to their jobs and work groups than need be the case and who may become dissatisfied and leave the organization if the definition of their jobs and their role conflicts cause problems which are not attended to. Conversely, where there is a large pool of applicants and the skills needed for jobs are lower, hospitals can spend less energy on recruitment than they do on recruiting skilled labor, but lack of attention to recruitment has its drawbacks, too. Workers who know if their needs, as well as the hospital's, can be met will be more satisfied. Furthermore, the training and development of employees will be easier if employees are matched to jobs for which they are better suited.

There probably are not, and should not be, socialization programs which focus on the resolution of role conflicts to the exclusion of the earlier stages. Such programs would increase the chances of employees being hired for jobs for which they are not suited, pay little attention to their training and development, and then try to help employees adjust to their own jobs and work groups and to resolve role conflicts they might only slightly understand. Even in cases where a special emphasis on the resolution of role conflict might be appropriate (as in the case of nurses at this hospital, for example), to most effectively socialize new employees, hospitals must consider all *three* phases of the socialization process.

3. *Hospitals Are Depending on Occupational Socialization Too Heavily in Planning Their Own Socialization Programs.* The hospital provided virtually no formal socialization activities for new employees. For those groups which have had previous training (nurses, technologists, engineers), this lack of organizational socialization has less impact on their eventual feelings of competence (see Table 19-3). In contrast, for the two groups without this background—mainly accounting clerks and nursing service technicians—this lack of socialization is a more serious problem, and they come to feel less competent than their more highly trained counterparts.

However, even for professional and technical employees, there is a need for further socialization beyond that provided for in professional or technical school. As was noted above, these workers need to know and to learn how their particular job is practiced in a particular setting. They need to know whether their professional goals and personal needs can be met by this particular hospital; they need to know what particular procedures and tools are used in this particular hospital, what skills will be most utilized, and what activities will be required most frequently. They need to know what will be expected of them in terms of dealing with their co-workers, in terms of dealing with other groups in the organization, and the impact of this particular job on their outside lives. Hospitals need to pay more attention to the variance in behavior of professional and technical workers which may be attributable to socialization practices of *particular organizations* rather than occupations.

References

1. Blalock, H. M., Jr.: Causal Inferences in Nonexperimental Research, New York, W. W. Norton and Company, 1964.

2. Brim, O. E., and Wheeler, S., Eds.: Socialization after Childhood. New York, John Wiley and Sons, 1966.

3. Coe, R. M.: Sociology of Medicine. New York, McGraw-Hill, 1970.

4. Clausen, J. A., Ed.: Socialization and Society. Boston, Little, Brown, and Company, 1968.

5. Freidson, E., and Lorber, J.: Medical Men and Their Work. Chicago, Aldine-Atherton, 1972.

6. Georgopoulos, B. S., and Mann, F. C.: The Community General Hospital. New York, Macmillan Company, 1962.

7. Hackman, J. R., and Lawler, E. E.: Employee reactions to job characteristics. J. Appl. Psychol. Monographs **55**:259, 1971.

8. Hackman, J. R., and Oldham, G. R.: Development of the Job Diagnostic Survey. J. Appl. Psychol. **60**:159, 1975.

9. ———: Motivation through the design of work: Test of a theory. Organizational Behavior and Human Performance (in press).

10. Lodahl, T. M., and Kejner, M.: The definition and measurement of job involvement. J. Appl. Psychol. **49**:24, 1965.

11. Lynn, K. S., Ed.: The Professions in America. Boston, Houghton-Mifflin, 1965.

12. Mechanic, D.: Medical Sociology. New York, Free Press, 1968.

13. Porter, L. W., Lawler, E. E., and Hackman, J. R.: Behavior in Organizations. New York, McGraw-Hill, 1975.

14. Van Maanen, Jr.: Breaking in: A consideration of organizational socialization. Massachusetts Institute of Technology Technical Report (#644-73). Cambridge, Massachusetts, 1972.

E. GARTLY JACO

20 Ecological Aspects of Hospital Patient Care: An Experimental Study

Introduction

Man's use of space has long been a topic of scientific interest and particularly in the social and behavioral sciences (Simmel, Sorokin, Hawley, Quinn). These and more recent studies and conceptualizations have provided a theoretical and conceptual foundation upon which further and more sophisticated research on the potential linkages between human behavior and physical settings can be developed (Hall, Sommer, Barker, Osmond). Conceptualizations of *macrospace* concern the larger physical environment with such terms as "territory," "community," "locality," "natural area," "ecological area," and have traditionally been essential aspects of the fields of human and social ecology. Behavioral scientists have also been interested in human utilization of *microspace*, including perceptions of and reactions by individuals to their smaller and more immediate surroundings, offering such concepts as Hall's (1968) "proxemics," Osmond's (1957) "sociopetal space" and "sociofugal space," and Barker's "undermanned" and "overmanned" behavioral settings.

Nearly all of the above studies encompass a variety of phenomena other than the hospital and health care areas. Only recently have studies been conducted on certain aspects of the work environment in hospitals, particularly dealing with the impact of physical design and spatial arrangements on patient care and on the activities of hospital personnel such as nursing and medical staff. Furthermore, the few studies that have been undertaken did not seemingly benefit from the theoretical and conceptual formulations of the preceding ecological perspectives in other fields. Most have attempted to assess what impact, if any, the physical setting of the hospital might have on reactions, utilization, activity, or the satisfaction of patients, nursing, and medical staffs.

Investigations of the effects of physical environment on patient care are still remarkably sparse, nevertheless, since the bulk of patient studies have concentrated more on interpersonal relationships between hospital staff and patients. Only a very few investigations have focused on the physical setting and its shape in relation to patient care, leading Sommer and Dewar (1963, pp. 319f.) to comment: "Most research dealing with hospital patients has stressed the patient's relations with other people, especially nurses, doctors, other patients, and

Adapted from E. G. Jaco, "Ecological Aspects of Patient Care and Hospital Organization," in B. S. Georgopoulos, ed., *Organization Research on Health Institutions* (Ann Arbor, Michigan: Institute for Social Research, University of Michigan, 1972), Chap. 10. Reprinted by permission of the Publisher.

Acknowledgments are due the Hill Family Foundation for grant support of this project and to Roger R. Starn, administrator of the study-hospital, and his hospital staff for their cooperation and aid throughout the study.

visitors. Much less has been written about his reactions to the physical environment. This field has been regarded as almost exclusively the province of the architect and the interior designer."

This dearth of research possibly reflects the lack of similar studies of social organization from the ecological or morphological perspective in the social and behavioral sciences in recent years (Duncan and Schnore, 1959). Robinson's (1950) methodological criticism of "ecological correlations" also has cast some doubt on the general validity and utility of analyzing and predicting behavior in terms of areas and spatial dimensions. Nevertheless, the notion still persists that the environment, physical or otherwise, has some valid significance for the behavior and responses of human beings. While the old saw about igloos never being constructed in the Sahara desert nor refrigerators being found among the Eskimos is rarely heard today, Winston Churchill could still make the observation that "we shape our buildings and then they shape us" in urging that the House of Commons be rebuilt in its original form after being destroyed in World War II, holding that changing the building might alter the character of Parliament (Cf. Hall, 1963b).

One of the more recent studies in this area was conducted by Rosengren and DeVault (1963). It was concerned with the effects of the physical layout of an obstetrical service in a large general hospital. Such factors as the spatial distribution of activities in the delivery service of patients, the segregation of behaviors in which persons of differing status would perform differently in varying places, and the rhythm, tempo, and sequences of behavior in this service were studied. The researchers concluded that much of the activity in the OB service was at least partially a function of the kinds of spatial, symbolic, and physical segregation that set each area of the unit apart from each other. Furthermore, the degree of spatial segregation was related to the value put upon those activities in the area involving the basic objectives of the service. Physical segregation was related to status differences among hospital staff members. Symbolic forms of segregation between areas were related mostly to the communication of organizationally appropriate attitudes and values. That is, many of the normative components of the physician-nurse and physician-patient relationship were modified by the physical location in which such interaction occurred in this service, particularly in the interstitial areas of the unit. Moreover, "both the spatial and the temporal organization of the service seemed to be geared to cast the incoming patient into a role and mood that would allow the personnel of the service to behave in ways which they had learned to expect that they should. The staff members themselves— residents, interns, and so on—seemed to be subject to the same proscriptions that stemmed from the morphology of the hospital" (Rosengren and DeVault, p. 290).

Some insights into the effects of hospital furnishings upon patients are presented by Sommer and Dewar (1963). They stress the importance of such concepts as "personal space" and "territory" of patients, and suggest that patient complaints about lack of privacy may reflect intrusions into the patient's personal space, while comments about the impersonality or coldness of a hospital may indicate the patient's inability to acquire a territory within the institution. Finally, they point out the dearth of research on how the physical setting of the hospital affects the condition of patients.

While the researches of Sommer and Dewar and Rosengren and DeVault are valuable contributions to many facets of the impact of physical surroundings upon patient behavior, their results are derived more from selected observations and impressions than systematic statistical findings, and without related research controls that are truly needed in order to arrive at valid and reliable generalizations. Impressions and observations of patient and hospital staff behavior are subject to innumerable biases, distortions, and transitory illusions. Patient activity and the atmosphere of hospital units change markedly during the 24-hour day, day of the week, and season of the year. Nursing activities differ on the day shift from that of the relief and night periods of duty, as does patient behavior. Surgical units vary from medical, obstetrical, pediatric, and psychiatric services by virtue of having different needs of patients to attend as well as divergencies in the demographic, socioeconomic, and personality characteristics of patients placed in these areas of the hospital. Therefore, unless appropriate steps are taken to sample these parameters of patients and staff "worlds," the risk of inaccurate recording of such activities remains high. Needless to add, adequate replication of research findings in different settings, an urgent need, is further reduced when systematic and controlled observations are lacking.

The major purpose of this paper is to report the major aspects of a large-scale experiment to assess the effects on patient care provided by nursing staff in two divergent shaped hospital units, radial and angular designs, while also replicating many aspects of a previous study at another facility.

Some of the most elaborate experimental studies on the potential effects of hospital unit design on patient care were conducted at Rochester (Minnesota) Methodist Hospital by Sturdavant, Trites, and their associates. One type of design, the radial-shaped unit, arranges patient rooms in a circle around the nurses' station located in the center of the area. This allows constant observation of patients by the nursing staff without having to enter the patient rooms, and also reduces the travel distance needed to visit the rooms from the station, in contrast to the traditional single-corridor unit.

Some hypothesized effects of a radial design, in theory at least, were that the reduction in travel time made possible by it would: reduce fatigue of the nursing staff by reducing the amount of walking to attend patients; reduce tension and anxiety by permitting continual direct observation of the patients from the nurses' station at a minimum of effort; and bring about more direct bedside care of patients by nurses freed from the usual physical demands of the traditional angular-shaped layout. The patients supposedly would also benefit from the nursing tasks being made easier, and would feel more secure in having any critical needs attended to by the nursing staff who could readily observe them at all times with a minimum of effort.

The use of a circular shape was clearly based upon the premise that hospital physical design could be altered deliberately to improve performance of nursing tasks and functions (and be more functionally efficient) which, in turn, would enhance favorable responses on the part of patients benefiting from improved nursing service. The circular design was thought to be of more value to caring for the critically ill patients and was thus initially employed for intensive care units.

The first Rochester study (Sturdavant, 1960; Sturdavant *et al.*, 1960) was an effort to test some of these hypotheses for surgical patients needing intensive care. A radial unit was compared to a rectangular unit for such factors as types of nursing care, use of the unit by the nursing personnel, and reactions to both units by patients hospitalized therein and by nursing and medical staff. Although some of the results were ambiguous, the researchers concluded that the radial unit was superior to the rectangular unit in more effective use of nursing time, and greater satisfaction of patients, their relatives, nurses, and surgeons in the service. They credited the shape of the radial unit, which brought about less travel distance and high visual contact between patients and nursing personnel, for the results. The investigators also appropriately qualified their results as pertaining only to intensive care, small-sized units, and units containing only private rooms. Regardless of the relative merits of the circular- over the rectangular-shaped hospital units, this study clearly substantiated the assumption that the shape and arrangement of the unit had an impact on the behavior and responses of staff and patients.

The study stimulated sufficient interest and support to construct an entirely new hospital facility in which reasonably comparable units of different designs were built into the new structure. Three basic physical designs were constructed in the new hospital: the radial, double corridor, and single corridor. This permitted a unique opportunity to evaluate such designs under more reasonably comparable physical conditions than in the initial study, and to compare differently shaped units, although the radial units were smaller in area than were the other two designs in that hospital.

Trites and his associates (1969a, 1969b) report the results of this research. The initial statistical analysis indicated that the single-corridor unit was the least desirable, both with respect to nursing performance and use of the unit, and that there was no distinct difference between the radial and double-corridor units. But differences between the latter two types of units were found for measures related to location and activity variables, respectively. The researchers felt that such differences might be partially due to including travel necessary for such activities in each activity measurement. Recalculations of the measurements to eliminate travel yielded results which favored the radial unit. Another statistical analysis between the three daily shifts of the nursing staff indicated that the circular unit was superior to the single-corridor design 85 percent of the time, and to the double-corridor unit 60 percent of the time, while the double-corridor design surpassed the single-corridor unit 65 percent of the time. The investigators concluded that the radial design was best, followed by the double- and then the single-corridor designs, in terms of nursing activities and the location in the units where such activities occurred.

The overall results of these studies indicate that nursing personnel on the radial unit spent significantly more time with their patients and less time in travel than did the nurses on the single- and double-corridor units. The researchers further state that, despite these more favorable factors for the radial design, nursing staff on the radial units also were observed more often in the nurses' station and to have more nonproductive time on the day and evening shifts, in contrast to nurses on the other two designs.

The Experiment: Patient Care in Radial and Angular Units

Between the first Rochester study by Sturdavant and the later studies by Trites and associates, another research endeavor of a similar nature was conducted by this author and his associates in St. Paul, Minnesota, between 1963 and

1967 (Jaco, 1967, 1973). The major purpose was to evaluate the effectiveness of the radial unit compared to the traditional single-corridor angular unit for intermediate as well as for intensive and minimal levels of patient care in terms of: type, level, and amount of nursing care; nurses' utilization of the unit; patient welfare; satisfaction and reactions to the units by patients, nurses, and physicians; length of patient stay; and care costs for general medical and surgical patients. A second purpose was to appraise the potential intervening influences of such factors as nurse staffing patterns and occupancy levels, and a third was to replicate, as much as feasible and appropriate, Sturdavant's study, and to examine other variables potentially involved with and related to patient care of divergent levels in the radial type of physical design.

Research Design

For intermediate (nonintensive) general medical and surgical patients hospitalized in the same unit, twelve "study situations" were carried out on reasonably comparable radial and angular nursing units in which occupancy level and nurse staffing patterns were deliberately altered. Occupancy levels were altered from high (90 percent filled or more) to low (50 percent filled or less), and the nursing personnel was varied quantitatively at high, average, and low levels, and qualitatively by the ratios of registered nurses, licensed practical nurses, and nurse aides to total staff. Each of the study units contained twenty-two beds composed of two private, six semiprivate (double bedrooms), and two four-bed wards.

Each study situation was maintained for four consecutive weeks. Observations of the nursing staff and patients were made by trained observers using work-sampling methods for a five-day week, twenty-four hours per day (all three shifts). A one-week "resettling period" was held between each study situation to blur any potential "halo" effects. An effort was made to control for differences that might occur in the patient populations admitted to the units during the project by randomizing the assignment of patients to these units by the hospital admitting office. Similarly, an effort was made to use identical nursing personnel in both types of units during the study so that each nurse would be her own control for individual differences among the nursing staff, although this was not always feasible due to turnover of staff.

Nursing staff was interviewed privately at the end of each study situation, and physicians who had admitted patients to the study units were interviewed privately at the midpoint and end of the study. Nursing staff completed certain research forms daily in the unit. Patients were privately interviewed just prior to their discharge. A recording clerk, located in the nurses' station on the radial unit, recorded trips by nurses to the patient rooms and other areas to supplement the observations of the observing staff. Observations were made about five times per hour of every member of the nursing staff in ten randomly assigned sampling areas in the units. Appropriate probability statistical tests were computed for significant differences in the variables between the two physical designs.

Intensive level of care was studied only in the radial-shaped unit, due to the many obstacles and potential hazards involved in trying to convert the angular unit into such a service. The existing minimal care (self-care) unit in the study hospital was a single-corridor unit which was observed for a one-month period, after which the nursing staff was transferred to a radial unit similarly arranged in accommodations to provide a comparative study of minimal care on both designs. Since three major levels of patient care—intensive, intermediate, and minimal—were studied on circular units, and the latter two levels also on angular-shaped designs, the unusual opportunity arose to examine some of the different factors involved in progressive patient care for both physical designs.

Results for Intermediate Care

The results for intermediate-level care were mixed and often surprising. The type of nursing care differed significantly between the radial and angular designs. From more than 200,000 observations over a two-year period, approximately the same nursing staff gave on the radial unit *more* indirect care and general assistance and took more time out, but gave *less* direct bedside care, showed less standby, and traveled less than when on the angular-shaped unit. This paralleled somewhat the results of Sturdavant, who also found less direct care on the radial than the rectangular unit for a more severely ill patient population. However, the ratio of patient-involved care (direct care combined with indirect care and general assistance) to nonpatient-involved activity (standby and time out) was somewhat higher on the circular than on the angular unit. More physical and less social types of direct care were given on the radial than on the angular unit, and no difference in direct medical care between the two designs was found (Table 20-1).

The head and charge nurses on the circular unit provided more indirect care and general assistance, and took more time out with less standby and travel, than when on the angular unit. They gave about the same amount of direct care on both units. The registered nurses showed a somewhat different pattern than the head nurses, giving on the circle *more* indirect care and general assistance and *less* direct care than on the single-corridor unit. They also traveled less, and there was no difference in standby and time out. The licensed practical nurses differed from the RNs in providing on the circular unit *more* direct and indirect care and general assistance; they also took more time out than on the angular unit, while standby and travel were the same on both units. The nurse aides also diverged in their pattern of activity, giving *more* indirect and *less* direct care on the radial than on the angular unit; they showed more time out and travel, and no difference in general assistance and standby.

From these findings it can be seen that the different nursing personnel performed different functions and activities on the two units. On the premise that care provided by the more professionally trained nursing staff, such as head

Table 20-1 Medical, physical, and social types of direct care, by number of observations and percentages, total study, by shape of unit

Type of care	Total		Radial		Angular	
	Number	*Percent*	*Number*	*Percent*	*Number*	*Percent*
Medical	23,057	38	11,199	38	11,858	38
Physical	29,631	48	15,135	51	14,496	46
Social	8,650	14	3,446	11	5,204	16
Total	61,338	100	29,780	100	31,558	100

nurses and RNs, is of a higher level than that provided by LPNs and NAs, the ratio of care provided by the former compared to the latter types of personnel should be an indicator of higher level of patient care. It was found that a slightly higher level of care was provided on the radial than on the angular unit, particularly when the measure included indirect care and general assistance.

The amount of nursing care was measured by the number of staff trips to the patient rooms, classified as nurse-initiated or patient-initiated trips. Trips made in the patient's absence, as well as those involving patients, and staff-to-staff room visits were considered. The results were somewhat surprising in that the nursing staff on the radial unit made far *more* nurse-initiated trips and *fewer* visits when the patients were absent from the room, but about the same patient-initiated and staff-to-staff trips, on the two units. The nursing staff on the circle also exhibited a higher ratio of nurse-initiated to patient-initiated trips, and a somewhat higher ratio of nurse-initiated trips to trips when the patient was out of the room. These ratios suggest that patients on the circular unit received a higher amount of nursing care than those on the angular unit during this study (Table 20-2).

A more direct index of impact of the physical design involved those factors indicating the nursing staff's utilization of various areas within the units during their activities (Table 20-3). An efficiency index comprised of three measures was developed: a ratio of times nursing staff was observed in patient rooms when the patient was present to times when the patient was absent; a ratio of times observed in the corridors of the unit to other areas within the unit; and a ratio of times the staff was observed performing professional services in patient rooms to those times they were using unoccupied patient rooms for personal reasons. Other indicators were the proportions of time nursing staff was observed in patient rooms compared to other areas of the unit, and the proportion of times staff was in the unit but out of patient rooms.

The results suggest that the nursing staff on the radial unit spent slightly less time in the corridors than on the angular unit, but there was no difference in ratios of time spent in patient rooms when the patient was present or absent. More striking was the finding that the radial-unit staff used unoccupied patient rooms for personal rather than professional reasons more than on the angular unit during periods of low unit occupancy. Also the staff on the circular unit spent a greater proportion of their time off the unit entirely than when on the angular unit, indicating that nursing usage of areas and facilities off the unit itself does play a part in the utilization of nursing time which is independent of the

Table 20-2   Types of trips to patients' rooms by nursing staff in radial and angular units by number of observations and percentages

Types of trips	Total		Radial unit		Angular unit	
	Number	Percent	Number	Percent	Number	Percent
Nurse initiated	118,444	79	60,772	82	57,672	76
Patient initiated	4,235	3	2,100	3	2,135	3
Trips—pt. absent	11,843	8	5,619	7	6,224	8
Trips—no pts. involved	13,121	9	4,495	6	8,626	11
Staff to staff	2,409	1	1,251	2	1,158	2
Total	150,052	100	74,237	100	75,815	100

Table 20-3   Utilization of nursing unit by total nursing staff in radial and angular units, by number of observations and percentages

Unit subarea	Total		Radial		Angular	
	Number	Percent	Number	Percent	Number	Percent
Nurses' station	73,399	34	39,985	37	33,414	31
Medication area	9,313	4	4,850	4	4,463	4
Corridor in unit	17,634	8	8,393	8	9,241	9
Patients' rooms	46,608	22	22,002	21	24,606	23
Utility room	2,750	1	815	1	1,935	2
Tub and shower room	1,064	*	657	1	407	*
Nurses' conference room	34,574	16	14,010	13	20,564	19
Off units	24,380	11	13,068	12	11,312	10
Other areas in unit	5,377	3	3,009	3	2,368	2
Total	215,099	100	106,789	100	108,310	100

*Less than 1 percent.

shape or design of the nursing unit itself. Thus while the radial unit was only slightly more efficient in use of corridor space than was the angular unit, this did not result in bringing staff into the patient rooms any more, or in preventing fewer unnecessary trips to the patient rooms when the patients were absent.

Patient welfare was measured with three scales developed by Aydelotte and her associates (1960)—mental attitude, physical independence, and mobility—based on daily ratings of patient status by the nursing staff in their charge. The results showed no difference for any of the three scales for patients hospitalized during the study in the two units. The average length of stay of patients also did not differ significantly between the two units during the project.

Patient reactions. An attempt was made to replicate certain types of questions asked of hospitalized patients prior to their discharge that were also used in Sturdavant's Rochester study. Other questions were added to the interview schedule to examine factors that might reveal how the patients felt about the nursing service and the various physical and nonphysical features of the units and their rooms. One of the more significant questions asked of patients was if there were anything about the unit that they particularly liked. Most of the items spontaneously mentioned by the patients were items in their *rooms* rather than in the *unit*, such as their electric beds, handy bathroom, lavatory, air conditioning, television, telephone, call button, windows, lighting, furnishings, and the like. Responses to this question revealed that patients on the circular unit reported more features of their rooms *and* unit than patients on the angular type, the former averaging two items per patient and the latter 1.7 items per patient. This difference occurred despite the fact that both units and rooms in the two units were quite similar in decor, newness, air conditioning, etc.

This question was further analyzed by measuring the ratio of items mentioned that pertained strictly to the patients' rooms and those related to aspects outside their rooms, such as the windows, the sundeck, and lounge. The results showed that patients on the circular unit reported twice as many "particularly liked" items related to the *external* environment out of their rooms than did patients on the angular unit. It seems obvious that the high visual contact in the radial unit plus the large picture windows on the external wall in this unit may have affected the patients' reactions to their external milieu more on the circular than on the angular unit where such visibility was much lower.

This is further supported by the patients' responses to a question asking them how they compared their unit with others in which they had been previously hospitalized. The results were as follows:

Patients on Circular Unit		Patients on Angular Unit	
Positive toward the Circle	37%	Positive toward Angle	14%
Negative toward the Circle	2%	Negative toward Angle	9%
Neutral	61%	Neutral	77%
(Based on 401 patient interviews)		(Based on 395 patient interviews)	

When the patients were requested to rate the nursing service in terms of poor, fair, good, very good, and excellent, the results were surprising in view of the reported preference for the circular unit. A small but somewhat higher percentage of patients gave a "poor" rating to the nursing service they received on the circular unit contrasted to that on the angular unit, although a higher overall percentage gave a positive rating to their nursing service on the circular unit. A much higher percentage of patients on the angular unit, however, either refused to comment or said they "didn't know" in responding to this question, and this could imply that at least a certain portion of this group had negative feelings they did not want to express. Also the negative comments on the circle were confined to only a few study situations. Certainly, visual contact on the radial unit permits far greater observation than on the traditional angular unit, and perhaps it is easier for patients to be critical of what is often observed. Nevertheless, a higher percentage on the radial unit than on the angular one also expressed positive ratings about their nursing service, but the percentage from the angular unit could easily change if the interviewer had persisted in obtaining an evaluation from a higher proportion of patients. This renders interpretation of the responses to this question somewhat ambiguous and uncertain.

When asked if they were bothered by activity outside their room, significantly more patients on the angular unit reported being bothered by outside activity than those on the circle. Only 3 percent of the patients interviewed on the circular unit reported being bothered, while 14 percent did report this on the angular unit. Thus visual contact on the circular unit apparently was not a cause of concern to the patients. When asked about the amount of privacy on their units, however, significantly more patients indicated dissatisfaction with the amount of privacy on the circular than angular unit. Dissatisfaction with privacy was reported by 11 percent on the circle while only 5 percent did the same on the angular unit. This was not entirely surprising since lack of privacy on the radial unit was a frequent complaint by patients in the series of interviews conducted.

The patients were also asked to rate their satisfaction or dissatisfaction with eleven specific items: cleanliness, view from the window, room size, toilet facilities, privacy, bath and shower, room type, amount of noise, air freshness, storage space, and window space. Their responses were scored, and a total satisfaction score was computed for each patient and compared for the two units. Results showed only a slightly higher average score for the circular unit than the angular unit, indicating that *total satisfaction* with the two units was quite similar, and quite good, for the patients in them. Similarly, no difference was found in effect of the two units on the morale of patients, although a slightly higher percentage of patients on the circular unit felt that the unit had improved their morale (80 percent) compared to those on the angular unit (78 percent).

When asked to evaluate the charges for their rooms (which were identical for both units), no significant differences were found, although a slightly higher percentage of patients on the circular unit felt their room rates were too high than those on the angular unit (38 percent on the circle, 33 percent on the angle). Again, however, there was a higher percentage of "don't know" responses on the angular than the circular unit that could alter the total results if complete responses had been elicited in the interviews. These differences could have been due to chance alone.

In summary, the results concerning patient satisfaction indicate mixed reactions to both types of units. More positive features of the room and the unit were reported by the patients on the circular units. These patients had a more positive awareness of their environment, were less bothered by activity outside their rooms, gave more positive but also more negative evaluations of their nursing service, and mentioned more complaints about lack of privacy and about room charges. But generally, there was not much difference in overall satisfaction between the two units. The patients from the circular unit were somewhat more free to express their negative as well as positive reactions than were those on the angular unit, a factor which may have been influenced by having been on that kind of unit in itself. Thus we find some mixed reactions to the circular unit among the patients interviewed, although in general this unit was more positively favored for its physical features, especially features outside the rooms, than the angular unit, despite the fact that the two settings were quite similar in newness, decor, and related aspects.

Nursing staff attitudes. Private interviews were also conducted with the nursing staff. The interviews were held prior to initiating the study and periodically after each study situation during the course of the investigation on both units, to determine any possible shifts in opinions about the units by the staff. The more salient responses to the questions are reported here.

At the onset of the project, the participating nursing staff overwhelmingly favored the radial over the angular unit. Of the nursing personnel initially interviewed, 75 percent preferred the circular to the angular unit, 11 percent the angular to the circular, and 14 percent did not favor one over the other. It is of interest to note, however, that preference for the circular unit was related to status position within the nursing personnel. Specifically, at the time of their first interview, 100 percent of the head nurses, 74 percent of the RNs, 67 percent of the LPNs, 77 percent of the NAs, and 100 percent of the ward clerks favored the circular unit, reflecting a relationship between nursing staff status and unit preference.

During the two and a half year course of this project, only 5 percent of the nurses revealed that their preference had been altered, and in divergent ways. Of the five reporting a change of opinion, two were RNs, two LPNs, and one an NA. One of the RNs would not reveal in which direction her preference had shifted, while the other RN first changed her preference from negative to positive toward the angular unit, then later from positive to negative. The two LPNs and one NA changed from negative to positive regarding the angular type of unit. The lower staff levels thus still continued to show proportionately more positive feelings toward the angular type of unit than the higher level RNs. The total nursing personnel nevertheless largely and persistently favored the circular over the angular unit.

When asked what specific features they liked about the circular unit, by far the majority of the nursing staff mentioned attributes more related to their own convenience in performing their work than attributes favoring the care of patients. Features related to convenience of the nursing staff alone were mentioned by 41 percent while only 3 percent mentioned features involving direct benefit to patients alone. When asked to compare specifically the radial to the angular type of unit, the nursing staff similarly gave a more favorable evaluation to the circular unit, in varying degrees, as follows:

1. *Efficiency of the unit:* 86 percent of the total nursing staff preferred the circular to the angular type of unit, 1 percent the angular unit, and 13 percent felt no real difference.

2. *Convenience of the unit:* 82 percent favored the circular type, 2 percent the angular type, and 16 percent neither.

3. *Patient care:* 73 percent preferred the circular type of unit, 2 percent the angular, and 24 percent felt there was no difference.

4. *Relations to fellow nursing staff:* 34 percent favored the circular type of unit, 2 percent the angular type, and 63 percent felt there was no difference.

5. *Relations to patients:* 53 percent preferred the circular type of unit, 2 percent the angular type, and 44 percent felt there was no real difference for this factor.

Thus, according to these responses regarding specific attributes of the two units, the percentage favoring the circular to the angular unit was highest when efficiency and convenience for staff were concerned, but declining and shifting toward no difference as the factors of interpersonal relationships and patient care were involved. Nevertheless, the total nursing personnel working on these two types of units during the course of the project generally preferred the radial to the angular unit when a choice was involved.

Physician Attitudes. A sample of physicians who had attended patients on both types of units was interviewed during the time periods when the project staff was conducting their observations. All physicians were privately interviewed and their responses recorded by the same interviewer who interviewed the patients and the nursing staff. In general the physicians tended to prefer the radial unit for the majority of their patients, although some interesting mixed reactions and preferences also occurred.

Asked if patient care was better in the circular or the angular unit, 48 percent of physicians having patients on the circle reported better care on the circular unit while 52 percent felt there was no difference; none reported that care was worse on the circle. Of the physicians having patients on the angular unit during this part of the study, 66 percent reported that the circular unit gave better care than did the angular unit. In both instances there was no difference between the general practitioners and the specialists among the physicians interviewed. When asked for specific reasons why they believed their patients obtained better care on the radial than the angular, the doctors most frequently mentioned such factors as closer observation of patients, efficiency, and convenience for both nursing and medical staff.

When specifically queried about particular attributes of the two units, the physicians reported as follows:

1. *Patient progress:* The radial unit was favored over the angular for this factor, but not to the same extent as for the other factors explored. The general practitioners tended to favor the circular unit somewhat more than the specialists for this factor.

2. *Patient attitude or morale:* The specialists favored the circular unit more than did the general practitioners for this factor, but both tended to heavily favor the circle.

3. *Nursing care:* Both specialists and general practitioners favored the circle for this factor, with the former being somewhat more favorable in their responses.

4. *Convenience of the medical staff:* The physicians generally were overwhelmingly in favor of the circular unit for this factor, with the general practitioners somewhat more so than the specialists.

Although preference for the circular unit varied for the above factors, the preference was quite consistent for all for the radial over the angular unit. When asked if the circular unit had any specific drawbacks, the physicians mentioned lack of privacy together with lack of private rooms, which existed in these units at the time this study was initiated, as the major disadvantages of the present radial unit. Distance from nurses' station to patient rooms and lack of visibility were mentioned as drawbacks for the angular unit. Consequently, similar physical features were criticized for their presence or absence in both types of units by different physicians. Also of interest was the finding that the circular unit was reported as having "no drawbacks at all" by more physicians than was the angular unit.

This factor was perhaps related to the next question which inquired if the physicians had had any patients they would prefer not to admit to the circular unit. They were unanimous in having had patients they would not admit to the circle, with the general practitioners reporting this more than the specialists. Reasons mentioned for not admitting patients to the circular unit were: patient *wanted* a private room; patient *needed* a private room; patient was emotionally disturbed or under psychiatric care; patient was senile or disoriented; patient was an intolerant complainer; and patient was terminal. Moreover, all the physicians reported having patients who did not want to be admitted to the radial unit. The wish for privacy and for a private room were the major reasons given.

All of the doctors reported having had patients requesting transfer from the circular to the angular unit, and vice versa. The general practitioners had more patients wanting to transfer from the angular to the circular, while the specialists had the same percentage (60 percent) wanting to transfer to and from both units. By far the most frequent reason for wanting such a transfer from the circular unit was to obtain a private room. Whether such a wish for a private room included the desire for privacy off the circle was not clarified in their responses. When asked if they had a preference in admitting a patient to the two types of units, eight out of ten preferred the circular to the angular unit, one of ten preferred the angular unit, and one of ten had no real preference. Convenience of the nurses and physicians and high visibility were the reasons the physicians gave for preferring the circular unit, despite the previous reporting of lack of privacy as the major drawback of this type of unit.

In summary, the physicians by and large preferred the radial unit to the angular, recognized its virtues as well as drawbacks, indicated that they had patients not liking the circle and wanting to be transferred out of the circle, and even indicated some patients they treated would not be admitted to this kind of nursing unit under their care. Thus, as in the case of the nursing staff, there were some mixed reactions to the radial unit by the physicians interviewed, indicating that this type of unit, while more popular with the doctors than the angular unit, still is not universally or categorically preferred by the entire medical staff of the study hospital. It is thus very likely that if the hospital had only circular nursing units, even with private rooms, there would still be a loss of some patients who would prefer, or perhaps even need, the more traditional angular unit.

Summary. The results concerning intermediate care of general medical and surgical patients without regard to occupancy levels and nurse staffing patterns show that differences were found between the radial and angular units for type of nursing care; level of nursing care; amount of nursing care; utilization of the unit by the nursing staff; patient satisfaction with the unit; nursing staff satisfactions with the unit; physician satisfactions with the unit; and per bed per diem costs to the study hospital for a four-month period. No significant differences were found between the two types of units for patient welfare and average length of stay of patients as measured herein. In all but one of the factors found to differ between the two types of nursing units, such differences tended to favor the radial over the angular unit, the sole exception being utilization of nursing time on the unit, which slightly favored the angular unit. In many instances these results are similar to some of those found by the Rochester studies, but in other instances our results differ. We can thus conclude that the physical shape of the unit was related to the differences in the factors studied and that generally, with some notable exceptions, the radial type of unit was favored over the angular type of unit for this category of acute patients and level of patient care.

When twelve "study situations" were examined for the same intermediate level of care for general medical and surgical patients with occupancy levels and staffing patterns varied, the results provided some surprises. In general, the efficiency of the circular nursing unit was demonstrated in only a few of the twelve study situations. This occurred most significantly when the nursing staff was cut to a minimum and the unit was highly occupied. Under such pressing patient care conditions, the amount of direct bedside care was significantly greater on the radial unit than on the angular, and the level, amount, and patient-involved care were the highest of any of the study situations, when contrasted to the angular unit, under similar stressful conditions for the nursing staff. Indeed, when the nursing staff, comprising the customary components of RNs, LPNs, and NAs, was reduced in quantity for all of these components while conditions of high occupancy prevailed, the circular unit was at its best for intermediate medical and surgical patients.

But when the staff was drastically altered qualitatively, as in the situations of high LPN and high NA, and when the occupancy of the unit was drastically reduced, the features of the circular unit that contributed to high-level patient care in the foregoing situations now became disadvantageous to the nursing staff, and particularly to the head and charge nurses. In contrast to the angular unit having little visual contact between the patients in their rooms and the nursing staff going about their functions around the nurses' station, we found even "misuse" of certain areas of the circular unit, especially by the lesser trained staff such as NAs, particularly for personal activities in the empty patient rooms. The smaller corridor space and visibility of the nursing staff by the patients from their rooms are particular features that disturb the more professionally trained nursing personnel when they become extremely sensitive to patients witnessing anything bordering on substandard nursing performance. In the angular unit, where these features of visibility especially are lacking, the professionally trained nursing staff permit the lesser trained staff to perform many more functions, or are less critical of the performance of such staff, and the entire nursing operation seems to function more harmoniously for all concerned than when on a radial unit.

The major activities observed on the radial unit, contrasted to the angular unit, during these twelve study situations were as follows:

- more indirect care than direct care;
- more patient-involved than nonpatient-involved care;
- more time out and off the unit;
- higher level of nursing care, provided by higher trained staff;
- usually but not always more efficient use of the unit;
- more general assistance;
- less direct patient care;
- less verbal communication with patients (social direct care);
- less use of corridors;
- more personal use of unoccupied patient rooms, especially at times of low unit occupancy;
- less use of the nurses' conference room;
- usually but not always less nonpatient-involved travel;
- less use of lesser trained nursing personnel, such as LPNs and NAs, at varying time periods, occupancy conditions, and other conditions in the unit;
- perhaps more appropriate performance of nursing care functions, meeting patient needs when necessary and engaging in other activities when patient care is less needed;
- perhaps more flexibility in adapting to changing demands of the patient populations in the unit.

While there are possibly other features related to the radial unit than those delineated by this study, the above seem to be the most obvious.

Results Concerning Different Levels of Care

Since the study hospital maintained a progressive patient care program with intensive, intermediate, and minimal or self-care levels provided, it was feasible to study these levels of care in relation to the physical design of the radial and angular shapes. All three of these levels of progressive care were studied in the radial unit; the intermediate and minimal levels were observed in the single-corridor angular units. A summary of the main results is presented below.

On the radial unit the amount of indirect patient care increased as level of care decreased, i.e., going from intensive to minimal levels of care. An inverse relationship also was found for general assistance, which increased as level of care declined in intensity. Standby was positively related to level of care, decreasing as level of care decreased. The categories of direct care, time out, and travel were not found to be related to level of care on the circular unit. Travel and standby were inversely related to intensive and intermediate care, but positively associated with minimal level of care. The intensive care level was associated with more standby and less indirect care, general assistance, and travel than were the lesser care levels. The intermediate level involved more direct care, general assistance, and travel, and less standby, than the other levels of nursing care. The minimal or self-care level was associated with more indirect care and general assistance, less direct care, and also less standby, time out, and travel for nursing staff giving services on these three radially shaped nursing units in the study hospital.

Thus nursing care tended to vary considerably in terms of levels of progressive patient care for the same physical design, supporting the idea that these levels of patient care definitely comprise distinct and separate universes of hospital patient care. Utilization of the same circular nursing unit by the nursing personnel for these three levels of progressive patient care also was remarkably divergent, despite the fact that nursing care was provided in similar physically designed units, as follows:

Intensive care: When compared to the other two levels of care, the nursing staff was observed *more* in patient rooms with the patient present, utility room, nurses' conference room, miscellaneous areas, and in unassigned patient rooms (professional activity); less in the nurses' station, medication area, corridors, tub and shower room, and in unassigned patient rooms (personal activity); and neither more nor less in patient rooms with the patient absent and off the unit.

Intermediate care: When contrasted to the other two levels of care, nurses were found *more* in the medication area, corridors, tub and shower rooms, nurses' conference room, and off the unit; *less* in the nurses' station, utility room, miscellaneous areas, and in unassigned patient rooms (professional activity); and the *same* in patient rooms with the patient present, and absent, and in unassigned patient rooms (personal activity).

Self-care: When contrasted to the other two levels of care, nurses were found to be *more* in the nurses' station, medication area, corridors, patient rooms with patient absent, and in unassigned patient rooms (both personal and professional activity); *less* in patient rooms with patient present, utility room, conference room, miscellaneous areas, and out of the unit; and neither more nor less in the tub and shower room.

When self-care and intermediate care were analyzed for the angular units, some interesting differences were found, contrasted to the radial units. Significantly *more* direct care, standby, and time out occurred for the intermediate care angular unit, under similar staffing and occupancy conditions, and *less* indirect care, general assistance, and travel, while just the direct opposite occurred for the self-care patients on the angular unit. That is, that type of care which was given less for intermediate care patients was given more to self-care patients on the angular unit. The results also show that indirect care increased as level of care decreased, general assistance increased as level of care decreased. Direct care, time out, and travel, however, differed between radial and angular units. Thus surprisingly, the shape of the unit affects major aspects of nursing care to some extent at all levels of progressive patient care.

The physicians who attended patients during the course of the entire project tended to favor the radial unit increasingly as the need for intensive care correspondingly increased. But radial units came into disfavor as the level of care decreased from intensive to self-care, even to the point where some of the physicians had negative opinions about the radial self-care unit. This could indicate either that the physicians were genuinely accepting the radial unit more for intensive or seriously ill patients than self-care patients, or that they were not sufficiently familiar with the nursing activity observed by the research staff on the circular self-care unit (which indicated more direct care by the NAs on the radial than on the angular self-care units). Another possibility is that the doctors preferred that their patients be provided care by the more professionally trained nursing personnel, especially direct bedside care, rather than by the lesser trained personnel, even when their patients needed only a minimal level of care.

Conclusions and Interpretation

The major conclusions of this study may be stated as follows:

1.   Radial types of nursing units have distinctive advantages and also disadvantages for overall patient care in terms of prevailing utilization and traditional nurse staffing patterns.

2.   At times when demand for patient care on a hospital is heavy, and when nursing staff is scarce, the radial unit has many advantages in the provision of total patient care over the more traditional angular unit.

3.   Although perhaps more inflexible from an architectural standpoint than other shaped units, the radial unit shows promise for much functional flexibility in the provision of various types and levels of nursing and patient care.

4.   Provision of patient care is by *people*, and nursing care provided in a radial unit places different demands on the nursing staff, and to some extent on patients, from those in angular units.

5.   The radial unit is designed more for nursing and medical staff convenience than for patient convenience, with the patients assumed also to benefit in turn if the nursing and medical staff are benefited. This is a questionable assumption, since reducing the demands of patient care on the nursing staff in the radial unit was detrimental to the morale of the nursing staff contrasted to those on the angular unit.

6. Less professionally trained nursing personnel, such as LPNs and NAs, are less favorable toward the circular unit than are the professionally trained RNs, because they feel less able or permitted to perform higher level nursing functions on the circle due to the high visibility of patients and more supervision of their activities by the professional nurses.

7. Some types of patients are not suited to the radial unit, but no such "contraindications" were found for the angular unit. A general hospital having only circular units may thus lose a segment of the patient population to other hospitals in the area having more traditional angular units.

8. Occupancy levels affect the efficient utilization of the radial and angular units in opposite ways. Low occupancy level disrupts the efficient operation of the circular unit at typical nurse staffing patterns, while it improves the operation of the angular unit. High occupancy, with similar nursing staff, improves the efficiency of the radial unit but not always the efficiency of the angular unit when nursing staff are held equal.

9. Nurse staffing patterns affect the efficient use of the radial unit as much, if not more, as the use of the angular type of unit, especially for the lesser trained nursing personnel, such as LPNs and NAs.

10. The radial type of unit has unexplored possibilities for self-care utilization in the acute hospital. To regard the circle as primarily suitable for intensive care patients is contradicted by the results of this study, as all levels of care were benefited.

11. If the circular type of unit is expected to improve inevitably the quality of patient care and upgrade the efficiency of nursing service, then such expectations are unrealistic and disputed consistently by the findings of this study. Many intervening factors prevent the *automatic* improvement of nursing and patient care by physical design and related physical features. Rather, *how* those physical features and design are mobilized, utilized, and managed may enhance or diminish the potential effects of the shape and physical features of a nursing unit. . . .

Thus our study replicated many of the findings of the Rochester studies, but qualification of other results was also indicated. Freeing nurses from the demands of other duties does not necessarily lead to more time spent with patients. On the other hand, caring for patients in units of different designs raises some questions about what is regarded as "care." We noticed considerable "nonverbal" communication between patients and nurses in the radial unit, such as waving, smiling at each other from the nurses' station and the patient rooms, which may be regarded as "care" in a different sense from that of conversing with patients at the bedside by the nursing staff.

We also observed that a strong bond quickly developed between patients and nurses, more so in the radial than in the angular unit, since the patients could readily observe when nurses were busy, concerned, fatigued, or relaxed, and could better appreciate the work of nurses than when unable to see such activity in the angular unit. Patients in the circular unit could identify the different status symbols of the nursing staff, such as the caps and uniforms of RNs, LPNs, and NAs, which were related to their activities on the unit, but which could not be done by patients on the angular unit.

It should be also noted that high visual contact seemed more significant in staff-patient relations, and in the care of patients, on the radial unit than any increased physical efficiency from reduced travel time for the nursing staff giving such care. Such visibility provided by the radial unit's shape allowed the nursing staff more options in attending patients than when such visibility was lacking in the angular unit. In the circular units we found less verbal communication with patients by nursing staff (who can easily observe patients from the nurses' station) and more time in standby. This permits the staff more choices in the performance of their roles on the unit, if the nurse so chooses to utilize her time in a particular way.*

In short, our study confirmed a connection between physical design and patient care, and between unit design and the activities and responses of nursing staff, medical staff, and patients. But the results also indicated that the relationship was not of a mechanical, one-to-one nature vis-à-vis physical setting or shape. Rather, it appears that the physical setting may provide, on the positive side, certain alternatives or flexible options to human behavior, and negatively certain obstacles or hindrances to such activity within certain ranges or limits. We believe, for instance, that the radial unit provides more *potential* flexibility in nurse staffing patterns to care for the same level and number of patients than does the angular-shaped unit. The high visual contact in the radial unit allows the nurse to elect many more options in giving patient care than do units whose shape curtails or prevents such visibility.

But high visibility may have certain disadvantages in reducing personal privacy for patients in their rooms, which may eliminate the advantage of visual contact. And the more sensitive nursing staff member may dislike the "onstage" effect of being constantly watched by patients from their rooms. Consequently, hospital physical design can affect nursing staff and patient behavior for better or for worse. We do not yet know enough about the connection between hospital settings and staff and patient behavior to predict precisely how and what the effects will be. But we can conclude from our study that hospital design at least partially affects staff behavior and patient conduct, and this seems to depend largely upon how such units, once designed physically, are utilized socially, psychologically, medically, and administratively. Physical design alone is insufficient to account for such outcomes.

Conclusions

We have presented some theoretical considerations of man's use of physical space, and dealt with the problem of the effects of different work settings on his behavior and responses. Several studies of the effects of physical design or ecology of the hospital upon staff and patients were reported. These suggest that the hospital spatial environment has some impact upon staff behavior and attitudes and patient care. Despite the elaborate studies described, however, it is our assessment that only a small beginning has been made toward the development of secure knowledge about the intricate and complex relationships between physical design and hospital care. The need to conduct a vast array of research on this topic is still very great.

*It should be pointed out also that high visual contact between patients and staff can be provided by physical designs other than radial. A square unit, or one octagonal, spherical, and so on, can also provide high visibility so long as the nurses' station and the patient rooms are visible to each other in the unit layout.

The following are some suggested areas in need of research attention:

1. It seems important that we introduce more theoretical and conceptual aspects of human ecology, "ecological psychology," and "proxemics" into research on hospital physical design, so that more systematic and fruitful approaches may be developed and help guide such research. Osmond's concepts of "sociopetal" and "sociofugal" arrangements of the physical environment, for example, hold much promise in further conceptualizing spatial arrangements which pull people together or keep them apart. The radial-designed nursing unit would be an example of the "sociopetal" arrangement while the single-corridor angular-shaped unit would exemplify the "sociofugal" arrangement, the former tending to bring individuals more together and the latter separating them. The concepts of "personal space" and "territory" also have much potential for use in future studies.

2. The factor of arrangement of spaces and furnishings may be of equal, or even greater, signficance to the activities and organizational relationships of persons using such items as the physical layout or shape of patient units. For instance, arranging hospital beds so that patients can face each other might enhance interaction and communication between patients in double rooms and wards should this be desired. Locating such functional areas as the utility room, supply and storage area, and nurses' conference room adjacent to the patient bedrooms could well affect staff use of the unit differently than when these are placed off the unit or in areas away from patient rooms. Location of the nurses' station within the unit is a critical matter in traditional hospital physical design, although there is some question about the universal utility, or even need, for such a space in tomorrow's hospital. The arrangement of different room accommodations within the unit may also affect how such rooms are utilized by patients and staff.

3. Progressive patient care programs whereby different physical spaces in the hospital are set up for different levels of patient care, ranging from intensive to minimal levels, need to be more thoroughly examined for corresponding variances in spatial design as well as unit arrangement. The unexpected finding that the radial unit in our study provided more positive aspects of patient care than the single-corridor angular unit for minimal or self-care patients suggests that the physical setting is as important for this level of care as for the more seriously ill categories.

4. As the more modern and larger short-term hospitals develop more segregated spaces for specialized categories of patient care, the need to study optimum kinds of spatial arrangements and settings for these services becomes increasingly important. Our study hospital also had radial units for obstetrical patients and an adjacent nursery for the newborn infants which permitted considerable visual contact between mothers and their babies while occupying these separate spaces. Our impression is that this helped to sustain a high morale for the new mothers who could observe their babies in their cribs while lying in their own beds. Possibly other spatial arrangements are indicated for other categories of patients, such as pediatric, orthopedic, cardiac, and psychiatric.

Other functional uses of hospital space may also need reexamination for such functions as those related to pathology, the laboratories, radiologic services, postoperative and recovery rooms, surgical suites, and examining rooms. In particular, the emergency room and out-patient department of short-term hospitals require reevaluation of their spatial arrangements and settings. Similarly, spaces for the service functions, such as hospital laundry, kitchen, power plant, maintenance and repair, and storage can stand hard scrutiny as to efficient layout, arrangement, and location within the total hospital environment. Even the physical layout and location of administrative offices, physician lounges, meeting rooms, and visitor lounges may need examination. Any physical space utilized by people needs study as to its optimum provisions for human use.

5.   People tend to develop an identification with various components of space and the physical environment in which they work, live, and play. Anyone familiar with hospital life is aware of the strong identification that nursing staff members, for example, soon acquire for their stations, regarding their units as "homes," as we have heard it expressed by nursing personnel. How this identification develops and what elements enter into the acquisition of such "territory" by hospital staff needs further study. Such identification is perhaps a major reason why nurses dislike "floating" between different nursing units or dislike shifting their assigned areas within units, even though such resistance may be rationalized, e.g., by claims that floating prevents continuity of patient care by the nurses.

6.   While our discussion has focused almost entirely on short-term or acute care facilities, there is an even greater need to study spatial design and arrangements appropriate to extended care facilities and services for the chronically ill and convalescing categories of patients. When patients are hospitalized for long periods of time in the same facility or unit, the physical environment becomes even more important to their overall care than it is for the patient hospitalized for the typical short stay in today's acute general hospital. The need to cope with "hospitalitis" and other pathologic effects of institutionalization is well known, but the specific effects of physical design, arrangement, and furnishings are still largely unknown for the long-term patient populations. What may be an appropriate or optimum environment for the acutely ill short-term patient, of course, may not be optimal for the chronically ill long-term patient.

There is no longer any need to inquire "if" there is any relationship between the hospital physical environment and the activities and functioning of personnel and patients. Rather, the question is *how specifically* certain aspects of the physical setting, its composition, geometry, arrangement, layout, furnishings, and decor affect behavior and the responses of individuals interacting in such spaces. Furthermore, the impact of the physical environment on groups, organizational behavior, and social structures of the heatlh care facility is perhaps an even greater area for significant research than is the impact on individual behavior.

The need to improve the methodology of future ecological studies of hospitals is definitely indicated. Many previous studies have relied heavily on impressions, observations, and logical inferences. Others, particularly "efficiency" studies, have used highly quantitative data and mathematical models but have lacked comprehension of the "human" element. Some have used work-sampling methods, which usually generate more gross kinds of measurements that lack a desired degree of precision. There is also a question about the reliability and validity of such measures of the true parameters of staff and patient behavior in the hospital. To some extent, these shortcomings are related to the overall embryonic scientific development of the ecological and social sciences. Nevertheless, the need for so-called pure or basic methodological studies to devise more and better measurements and research instruments is evident, and should stimulate important research activity in this area.

Finally, we do not wish to exaggerate the relative importance of the physical environment in hospital organizational research. While the physical setting and its arrangements are indeed significant, and have been a neglected realm of hospital research, they are only one among many aspects and dimensions of health care facilities and systems related to the organization, structure, role, and functioning of such facilities and services. When our knowledge of the full effects of the physical environment on hospital care becomes better and more explicitly developed, then we shall be in a strategic position to evaluate how significant and important the physical setting is in relation to other factors involving hospital organization and functioning. It is likely that physical space and its arrangements may have more impact on some aspects of hospital care than on others, in a manner and degree similar to other factors of hospital organization and behavior. The need to conduct research into every phase of hospital operation is immense. We strongly suggest that the phase of physical design and ecology should be included in any sophisticated research program of hospitals and related health care facilities and services.

References

Aydelotte, M. K., *et al. An investigation of the relation between nursing activity and patient welfare.* Iowa City: State University of Iowa, 1960.

Barker, R. G. *Ecological psychology concepts and methods for studying the environment of human behavior.* Stanford: Stanford University Press, 1968.

Duncan, O. D., and Schnore, L. Cultural, behavioral, and ecological perspectives in the study of social organization. *American Journal of Sociology,* 1959, *65,* 132–146.

Hall, E. T. Proxemics. *Current Anthropology,* 1968, *9,* 83–108.

Hall, E. T. Proxemics: the study of man's spatial relations. In I. Galdston (Ed.) *Man's image in medicine and anthropology.* New York: International Universities Press, 1963 (a).

Hall, E. T. Quality in architecture: an anthropological view. *Journal of the American Institute of Architects,* 1963 (b), *40,* 44–48.

Hall, E. T. *The Hidden Dimension.* New York: Doubleday & Co., 1969.

Hawley, A. H. *Human Ecology.* New York: Ronald, 1950.

Jaco, E. G. Final report on research project titled: Evaluation of nursing and patient care in a circular and rectangular hospital unit, 1967 (dittoed, available from author).

Jaco, E. G. "Nursing Staffing Patterns and Hospital Unit Design: An Experimental Analysis," in *Proceedings of the Invitational Conference on Research on Nurse Staffing in Hospitals.* Washington, D.C.: Div. of Nursing, Bureau of Health Manpower Education, National Institutes of Health, 1973, pp. 59–76.

Osmond, H. Function as the basis of psychiatric ward design. *Mental Hospitals,* 1957, *8,* No. 4, 23–29.

Osmond, H. The historical and sociological: The relationship between architect and psychiatrist, and Development of mental hospitals. In C. Goshen (Ed.) *Psychiatric architecture.* Washington: American Psychiatric Association, 1959.

Quinn, J. A. *Human ecology.* Englewood Cliffs, N.J.: Prentice-Hall, 1950.

Robinson, W. S. Ecological correlations and the behavior of individuals. *American Sociological Review,* 1950, *15,* 351–357.

Rosengren, W. R., and DeVault, S. The sociology of time and space in an obstetrical hospital. In E. Freidson (Ed.) *The hospital in modern society.* New York: The Free Press, 1963.

Simmel, G. Social interaction as the definition of the group in time and space (translated from Georg Simmel, *Soziologie,* by Albion W. Small). In R. E. Park and E. W. Burgess (Eds.) *Introduction to the science of sociology.* Chicago: University of Chicago Press, 1921.

Sommer, R. Studies in personal space. *Sociometry,* 1959, *22,* 247–260.

Sommer, R. Man's proximate environment. *Journal of Social Issues,* 1966, *22,* 59–70.

Sommer, R. Classroom ecology. *Journal of Applied Behavioral Science,* 1967 (a), *3,* 489–503.

Sommer, R. Sociofugal space. *American Journal of Sociology,* 1967 (b), *72,* 654–660.

Sommer, R., and Dewar, R. The physical environment of the ward. In E. Freidson (Ed.) *The hospital in modern society.* New York: Free Press, 1963.

Sommer, R., and Ross, H. Social interaction on a geriatric ward. *International Journal of Social Psychiatry,* 1958, *4,* 128–133.

Sorokin, P. A. *Sociocultural causality, space, time.* Durham: Duke University Press, 1943.

Sturdavant, M. Intensive nursing service in circular and rectangular units compared. *Hospitals,* 1960, *34,* No. 14, 46–48.

Sturdavant, M., *et al. Comparisons of intensive nursing service in a circular and a rectangular unit.* Chicago: American Hospital Association, Hospital Monograph Series No. 8, 1960.

Trites, D. K., Galbraith, F. D., Jr., Sturdavant, M., and Leckwart, J. F. Final report of research project titled: *Influence of nursing unit design on the activities and subjective feelings of nursing personnel.* Rochester, Minnesota, Research Office, Rochester Methodist Hospital, 1969 (a).

Trites, D. K., Galbraith, F. D., Jr., Sturdavant, M., and Leckward, J. F. Radial nursing units prove best in controlled study. *Modern Hospital,* 1969 (b), *109,* 94–99.

21 The Psychosocial Model and Long-Term Care

Introduction

The present system of financing long-term care for the ill aged is inappropriately based on the medical model, borrowed from the acute, short-term care hospital. This modeling was based on expediency, even though it does not accurately reflect the needs of the population it was created to serve.

The Medical Model

The traditional medical model has been used to describe the disease-oriented, acute, short-term hospital care system. In the medical model, illness and subsequent cure are emphasized.

Wolfensberger has defined the medical model as one which generally implies the perception of the consumer of a human service as a "sick" "patient," who, after "diagnosis," is given "treatment" for his "disease" in a "clinic" or "hospital" by "doctors" who carry primary administrative and human management responsibility, assisted by a hierarchy of "paramedical" personnel, and "therapists," all this hopefully leading to a "cure." This objective of cure must not be overlooked or understated. It is central to a part of the problem. Medical care has been keeping people alive longer, but cure, not long-term care, is medicine's stock in trade. Thus we can begin to establish the conflict of the medical model on the one hand with "chronicity" on the other, and chronicity is the key factor for Wolfensberger[1] to call forth the need for the psychosocial health model.

The medical (disease) hospital model maintains the centrality of the physician and the supposition that benefits follow the care provided in the hospital, or in the post-hospital extended care facility, when ordered or directed by a physician. It is essentially and fundamentally conceived of as acute care and/or short term or convalescent stay. Thus long-term care, the major characteristic of which is chronicity, is inappropriately modeled on short-term care, the major characteristic being its acuteness.

Among the reasons long-term care was patterned on the acute hospital medical model appears to be the economics of long-term care. Society is immobilized by the lack of a public policy which defines what an older person is worth in our society. Being utilitarian, we invest in things that have a productive

---

[1]Wolfensberger, Wolf, *Normalization: The Principles of Normalization in Human Services*. National Institute on Mental Retardation, 1972, Chap. 1, p. 8.

future. Sick old people are consumers—no longer producers. What are they worth? How long do we support them? How open-ended is it? The dilemma is that as we extend life and conquer disease; as we invent pacemakers and pressure breathing machines, we increase the cost of support. If we use the hospital model we can arbitrarily limit benefit days and thus theoretically dispense with our obligations.

The Psychosocial Health Model

The medical model implies that all points in nursing homes are alike, that all have the same needs, and that nursing care is the way to care for all. But patients come for different reasons, although a health crisis usually precipitates the need for care. The average nursing time given to patients in nursing homes is 2½ hours per 24-hour day. Patients need psychosocial services, such as sensory awareness, educational, creative, and religious activities. These strengthen the patients' self-image so that they will believe they are a vital, significant part of society, not an unwanted burden. These programs often determine whether a long-term care patient will recover, or will regress into a hopeless, inevitable slide toward death. Psychosocial services are provided by social workers, activity directors, chaplaincy personnel, community volunteer workers, and others. Paradoxically, these are the services that are most important to the well-being of the patient, yet least recognized by the medical model.

The Evolution of the Modern Home for the Aged

The psychosocial model had its origin in the traditional Home for the Aged, usually under religious or public auspices. Homes for the Aged were a collective, communal response to meeting the needs of the homeless (the nameless, faceless) "inmate" of the past. If anything characterized the Home for the Aged during its first one hundred years of existence, it was "indigency"—facilities created to care for the impoverished. The early settlers and immigrant groups brought with them their hopes, aspirations, skills, tools, customs, values, religion, and love. The Elizabethan poor laws provided the rationale for the almshouse and asylum for the poor, maimed, and elderly. Since the aged were few in number the homes were sufficient to care for them.

Homes, as we know them today, evolved from certain forces which changed their direction and focus, and have been in existence less than forty years, more nearly the past twenty-five years. The initiation of Social Security and its categorical assistance programs (from Old Age Assistance, through Vendor/Medical, through Medicare/Medical and Supplemental Security Income) practically eliminated the primary function of the home serving the indigent. At the same time the findings of the social and behavioral sciences shifted the focus from the indigent "inmate" to meeting the needs of the individual person—the "resident."

Prior to World War II, the discovery of the broad spectrum of antibiotics (sulfa, penicillin, and the mycins) had a significant impact on the virtual elimination of pneumonia, urinary tract and post-surgical infections. The war itself contributed to vast advances in physical medicine and rehabilitation, restoration, and therapy (particularly with regard to orthopedics) as new surgical techniques and hardware made possible repair and replacement of broken hips and bones. Following the war the revolution in psychopharmacology and the fantastic contributions of the psychoactive and mood-altering drugs made possible the management of psychiatric disorders in the elderly. Those previously cared for in mental hospitals could now be helped in and out of institutions.

These advances contributed to larger numbers of sicker, older people, seeking help. Waiting lists burgeoned and the voluntary homes alone were unable to meet the demands.

Simultaneously with the growth of proprietary care facilities and government interest in the health, education, and welfare of its citizens, there came licensure of facilities, standards governing the physical plants (with the phasing out of the converted home) and great concern over fire and safety. There also arose increased programs for manpower training, new mechanisms of financing payments of care, and licensure of the administrator. The underlying concept seemed to be that if the government, through its various programs, was to pay for care, then government wanted to assure that such care would be good care. But in the absence of proven measures, the basis for such judgments of good care was to borrow the only existing model—that of the acute hospital and its medical model as the grid against which all other programs and services could be measured.

The differences between the hospital (acute medical model) and nursing home (long-term model) are not the only differences. Differences exist also between the nursing home as it is generally conceived and the geriatric health care facility (the psychosocial health model) which is not understood. The differences exist in philosophy, in thrust, and in organization, and they are just as real and compelling.

The "nursing home" refers to itself as an industry, the psychosocial health care facility as a field of service.

The following definition by Dr. Sol Geld differentiates between the nursing home and the Home for the Aged:

> In the current constellation of interests, services and communal care of the aged, a home for the aged is a voluntary, permanent, usually sectarian community of predominantly elderly men and women, sponsored, planned and supervised by either governmental and/or fraternal and/or religious bodies. It is acknowledged as a nonprofit social enterprise, and designed especially, but not exclusively, as a protective environment within a circumscribed single or multiple physical setting for that segment of our population whose declining years, accompanied frequently by physical, mental, economic and social deprivations, postulates an adequate philanthropic service subsidy, the size, variety and quality of which range from a minimum of food and shelter, plus personal services and social programs given exclusively to those within its walls, to the widest network of professional social and medical services given in cooperation with related health and welfare agencies to both its resident population and tangentially, in various degrees, to the aged population of its surrounding community.[2]

[2] Geld, Solomon, Toward a Definition of the Modern Home, *in* Leeds, Morton and Shore, Herbert, eds., *Geriatric Institutional Management*. G.P. Putnam's Sons, New York, 1964, p. 59.

There are several elements in this definition which require explanation. For example, "permanency of residence" is mentioned to draw a dividing line between a voluntary home, and a nursing home, with their generally transitory type of residents. The whole battery of services in facilities and programs in a home revolve around this principle of permanency, which is the outstanding feature of a home for the aged.

The phrase "community of the aged" implies a continuous process of social interaction; a home for the aged with anonymity or isolation of residents is functionally a contradiction in terms.

Most important, the (sectarian) community for the aged is a planned community. Planning with the client and his family prior to placement is another demarcation line separating the voluntary home from commercial nursing homes, where placement can be effected by means of a single contact between the client and his physician and the admitting office or proprietor.

Confusion of Governmental Officials

State and governmental officials and services approach both as if they are the same; they are not. Constance Beaumont points out that "the very terms 'skilled nursing facility' and 'intermediate care facility' are so awkward, so unfamiliar to most people and so deficient with respect to conjuring up any kind of image, that the public, the press and even members of Congress avoid these terms . . . and simply label everything a nursing home."[3]

The traditional nursing home attempts to follow the medical-hospital model, while the geriatric health center follows the psychosocial health, total person-care model.

The difference between the nursing home and the home derived as a social service agency must also be established. Some nursing homes provide social services and some homes provide nursing services. The difference is in concept. The home basically is conceived as the individual's long-term residence, the base from which all services are provided for his living, while the nursing home is for the more transient patients. The traditional home that evolved to today's nursing home offers a balance in the social and health components. The nursing home, as conceptualized by government, is a posthospital nursing care facility where social services are considered to be unimportant and usually unnecessary.

Our problems are compounded because government and institutions visualize a delivery system from different vantage points. Institutional care providers see the government's approaches as rigid, arbitrary, and indifferent to the needs of the individual, while the government sees the institution as inefficient, wasteful, and inappropriate. The government believes that it is acceptable to pay for medical care but questionable to support social care. The government does not understand long-term care, yet it controls the regulatory and payment mechanisms. We must redirect and redefine long-term care along the lines of the psychosocial model.

[3] Beaumont, Constance, Important Questions in Long-Term Care. *Congressional Record*, July 24, 1975, 17482.

Table 21-1 compares several characteristics of the three major types of facilities and is aimed at highlighting the significant differences between the nursing home and the geriatric psychosocial health facility.

Table 21-1 Characteristics of the hospital, nursing home, and psychosocial health facility

Characteristic	Facility		
	Hospital	Nursing Home	Psychosocial Health Facility
Type of Care:	Acute	Chronic	Rehabilitation, restoration
Model:	Medical	Nursing (medical)	Psychosocial health
Orientation:	Disease	Disability	Capability
Stay:	Short term	Extended	Long term
Stay:	Temporary	Temporary/Permanent	Permanent
Stay:	7–14 days	18 months	3 years
Designation:	Patient	Patient	Resident
Led by:	M.D.	R.N.	Team (Adm., Soc. Serv., M.D., R.N., etc.)
Admission:	M.D.	M.D./Family	Self/Family/Clergy/M.D.
Aim:	Discharge	Warehouse	Rehabilitate
Entry:	Crisis	Last resort	Congregate substitute home
Mix:	Age integrated	Age integrated	Age segregated
Image:	Efficient	Profit-making	Tender loving care (TLC)
Environ:	Sterile	Sterile	Home
Drug:	Drug therapy	Drug control	Therapy/Control
Staff:	Uniforms	Uniforms	Mix
Role:	Dependency	Dependency	Independence/Dep.

The more disabled the resident (patient) the more intense are the medical services. Figure 21-1 shows the relationship between the functioning of the individual and the program and the service emphasis of the facility. The ideal arrangement would meet the health needs of the patients and the social needs of the residents.

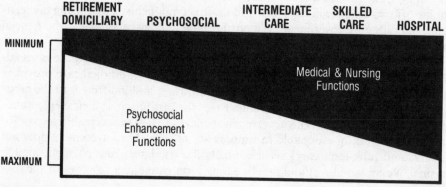

Figure 21.1[4]

[4] Miller, E. J., and Gwynne, G. V., A Life Apart: The Tasks and Functions of Residential Institutes. Lippincott, Philadelphia, 1972.

Two points emerge from this analysis: First, the geriatric total (psychosocial) health facility as it exists is substantially different from the nursing home (unfortunately it follows that if we have no public policy for nursing homes we certainly do not have one for psychosocial health); and second, the characteristic of psychosocial health is chronic illness—be it physical or mental or both.

Gerson and Strauss state:

> In the mid 1970's three major problems in the health field are beginning to merge into a larger and more complex series of problems for public policy. These are: (1) the increasingly chronic character of the illness load suffered by the total population; (2) the increasing emphasis, both within the medical profession and in general public discussion, on problems of quality of life; and (3) the increasing attention being given to the organization of health care focusing both on reducing costs and on improving the quality of care. . . .[5]

One of the interesting illustrations of the fiscal bankruptcy of current policy is the recognition that *Medicare essentially ends when long-term helplessness and surveillance begins*. The purpose of this legislation was to provide assistance with the cost of acute care episodes. To that end Medicare has been most helpful to older people, but it has misled them in their understanding and in their needs for long-term financing of chronic care.

Having selected an inappropriate and costly model, series of actions followed that have continued to confuse and to cost. And we have a circuitous problem of ever-increasing enforcement of rules and regulations and monitoring that won't and can't work because the model won't and can't work. Jerome Kaplan summed it up when he pointed out, "The aged-serving institution is to become a national mold of an imperfect model."[6]

If the hospital/medical/acute/disease model were replaced, than a host of other inappropriate and costly consequences of the model would change. These include *the rethinking of the medical chart as the regulatory document*, rethinking the use of medical directors (when paraprofessionals, health assistants, geriatric nurse practitioners, etc. would do as well at far less cost), and certainly rethinking the regulatory, inspection, enforcement process.

Present American health care is an intricate "non-system" (it has been characterized as an "illness system") of various disconnected categorical health delivery programs. The faulty functioning of any one program affects the actual workings of all the other partial health delivery efforts.

Obviously the goals of health care are related to the sources of financing for health care. Robbins says:

> . . . The administration and the costs of hospitals are determined by physicians and especially by surgeons. Somehow this condition must be changed and hospitals forced to operate with reasonable efficiency for the convenience of the community and in ways that will reduce the enormous drain on national resources and personal income now being devoted to health care—without a sacrifice of quality. Can it be done? We must start with a NEW PUBLIC POLICY OBJECTIVE: TO PROVIDE HIGHER QUALITY HEALTH CARE AT SIGNIFICANTLY LOWER COST.[7]

[5] Gerson, E. M., and Strauss, A. L., Time for Dying: Problems in Chronic Illness Care, *Social Policy*, November/December 1975, pp. 12–18.

[6] Kaplan, Jerome, The Hospital Model: Curse or Blessing for Homes Serving the Aged? *Gerontologist*, August 1974, p. 275.

[7] Robbins, J. D., Health Costs: A One Way Street, *Wall Street Journal*, May 1975.

We have the perpetual demands for unlimited services, high quality, and low cost—it can't be done. Why do we have infinite expectations with finite resources and commitments?

Rashi Fein further debunks some myths:

The basis of the myths about health care is the fallacy that the health industry is like other industries and that the health care market is governed by the same economic principles of supply and demand.

It is that view—that we are really dealing with a market that we have met before in other areas of economic life—that leads to explanations of behavior that are incorrect, insufficient and inappropriate—that, in a word, are myths.[8]

The Patient Population

Residents in long-term care facilities are generally viewed as having many of the same characteristics: poor adjustment, lack of self-confidence, social withdrawal, depression and unhappiness, intellectual ineffectiveness due to rigidity and lack of energy, negative self-concept, feelings of personal insignificance, and impotency and difficulties in interpersonal relationships. They are viewed as being dependent, docile, and submissive; as having few interests and activities; and as living in the past rather than in the future. They are powerless.

Abraham Kostick identifies another aspect that contributes to the problem: the institution in its role as caretaker fosters helplessness:

One of the key administrative problems in an institution for the aged relates to the structure and orientation of the institution and the consequences for the patient, or resident, dependency. The institution and staff are organized to take over and serve its clientele. The institutional structure is related to service and the availability of staff to serve its clientele. Two ingredients, that of the willingness of the institution to serve and the client's demand for service, intensify the symbiotic relationship that satisfies both. The problem in the institution often relates to the amount and the quality of service rather than the patient's selection of what service he desires and requires. The institution provides a package of services for each of its clients and urges them to use the services. In essence, the relationship encourages a mutual dependency. The institution and its staff create a cyclical bond of dependency to their mutual satisfaction.

The type of person who applies for institutional care is generally a person who is dependent and looking forward to "being taken care of." Sometimes this has a reality base. A person may be ill, may be disabled, may not be able to function on his own. At other times, the reality of everyday life overwhelms the applicant and he seeks refuge. He does not require the package of service, but rather protective care. Of course, these are polarities and they do not apply to each individual situation. However, the general tendency on the part of the institutional applicants is to seek security and support.

The general tendency of institutional staff is to offer services and help. The patterns of staffing enhances this dependency relationship. At times, professional institutions will develop programs to motivate its clientele to be self-assertive and independent, only to find that the basic staff wants to take care of people and thus undercut the tremendous investment of some staff to enhance the patient's attempts at some form of independence or self-assertiveness. The roles

---

[8] Fein, Rashi, Economist Seeks to Debunk Myths about Health Care, *Group Health and Welfare News*, December 1975, p. 7.

of staff, as defined by institutional administrators and the staffing patterns, gives the patient one message—"We want to take care of you. That is why you are here." On the other hand, the residents are told to maximize their independence and efforts are made to stimulate use of self. Given the basic dependency needs of most of the residents of institutions, they will follow the line of least resistance and accept a dependent relationship.

One cannot fault institutions for this type of approach. They are gearing themselves to service the sick and disabled, the emotionally dependent. The staff is oriented to taking care of people. For many of the residents of these institutions, this approach is what the residents require and it is helpful. The basic difficulty of the administrator is to find that fine line between dependency and independency, to be able to distinguish what are the real needs of his clientele, how much potential do the clients have for independence within their limitations and to what degree can you stimulate them to function at the optimum of their capacity to be independent.[9]

The problem, however, is that regardless of how the resident is viewed, the system leads to homogenization of all patients, both the physically and the mentally impaired.

Patients Differ

There are several different types of patients in homes. The so-called "well aged patients" function because they are in a protective environment. For this group of patients, with their chronic impairments, the medical model does not fit. A different social support system of care is necessary.

Another group is those patients with chronic, physically disabling illnesses. This group requires nursing care, as well as nurturing, and rehabilitative services.

Perhaps the most underserved and neglected but the most challenging are the patients with mental disabilities. In the medical model, if complex nursing procedures are not used, the patient is not thought to require skilled care. Thus the ambulatory, confused, impaired resident is not linked to the payment mechanism, although he requires additional therapeutic, skilled care.

Because the rationale imposed by government for nursing homes is to reimburse for physical illness and disability, another self-defeating cycle is assured. The negative incentive pays to keep the patient in bed and dependent, instead of stimulating functional improvement.

Although many federal studies report an alarming overtranquilization of patients, it was the psychopharmaceutical revolution that made possible the wholesale dumping of confused, elderly patients from state hospitals to nursing homes. These patients require a vast array of treatment modalities, including resocialization and remotivation. Because those who seek the specialized care of a home do so because they need treatment, the home should be an organization of treatment centers where specialized care will be provided according to the patient's needs.

Misunderstanding the social aspects of care compounds the problem. For example, the trauma of the Nursing Home Fire is well known. No one wants to see

⁹ Kostick, Abraham, address to the 27th Annual Scientific Meeting of the Gerontological Society, October 1974, Portland, Ore.

any life lost, for any reason. But how far can we go, at which point do we have "Congressional intent"; at which point can we tolerate risk and safety? Why is a ninety-year-old permitted an electric blanket if she lives in the community, but not permitted the same option if she lives in a nursing home?

I agree with the assertion that "more people die from poor quality of care than from fire." And we will be addressing ourselves to the issue of quality; however, I feel that poor quality of care arises from the demand that homes homogenize their patient-populations.

Long-term chronic illness is catastrophic, be it physical or mental. However, in the present inappropriate model and its inadequate payment system, residents with mental impairment, especially organic brain disease, are not thought to have an "illness" and therefore are not eligible for payment under skilled nursing criteria, as neurosis or psychosis as a primary diagnosis is not recognized as a disease. This lack gives even more credence to the need for not just a medical diagnosis but also a psychosocial one.

Care of the senile must be taken out of present financing systems and paid for as the catastrophic illness it is. Instead of dumping grounds for the former state hospital patients, homes and services must be recognized as specialized treatment centers. There should be massive infusions of money to encourage new treatment approaches and therapeutic modalities. Our present "system" has led us to homogenize our populations and to perpetuate their physical disabilities. Not all residents are alike; not all their needs are alike. The rules and regulations as promulgated recognize the skilled patient, the intermediate, and the custodial! The custodial patient functions in our homes because of the superb support he receives in personal, social, and therapeutic care. Take away these supports (the bathing, feeding, dressing, medicating, surveillance, and activity programming) and he cannot function.

In the homes I am familiar with there are few custodial patients. There are patients who are physically ill, who require vast amounts of good health care; there are psychiatric patients who require psychiatric supervision; there are confused and disturbed and disturbing patients. I look at the populations of the geriatric treatment centers I visit and I see vast pathologies.

It is my contention that as we make it possible for payments to be made for individuals in long-term care facilities on a basis other than their disease diagnosis we can begin to move toward total function models, which may be less costly and more efficient.

Having selected an inappropriate and costly model, we have been committed to a series of sequences that have been equally costly and inadequate. The result is circuitous frustration and distrust. Homes are expected to be mini-hospitals; they must give superior care, but must not be costly. You can by legislative manipulation create a situation in which you downgrade the facility, the patient classification system, and thus the payment mechanism. The lack of public policy or "failure" in public policy is nothing more than our failure to select the appropriate models and pay appropriately. We have been so myopically preoccupied with costs, which is irrelevant for much of modern decision making, that we have lost sight of what it is we want to buy and pay for. What does the inappropriate model truly cost society in lack of satisfaction for the provider and consumer, in policing and enforcement costs, in waste of professional talent?

Surely one of the questions we must confront is what is the cost of securing the data and information we are required to collect and store? Perhaps the cost is prohibitive and its use not justifiable.

The time has come to accept psychosocial care for what it is—total geriatric health care—and in so doing accept the appropriateness of paying for it. Once we are willing to recognize that for some older people congregate care is the appropriate treatment of choice, once we recognize the chronic nature of their conditions, we can develop innovative models and establish standards that are realistic and appropriate. Then we can go about the business of meeting the needs of the aged in a partnership of family, facility, and government.

ELIANNE RISKA
and
JAMES A. TAYLOR

22 Consumer and Provider Views on Health Policy and Health Legislation

Contemporary literature on the nation's health-care system virtually unanimously agrees that American health care is facing a crisis. One can distinguish four different current interpretations of this crisis. Some researchers view it as an economic problem and argue that it is a function of an imbalance in supply and demand. According to this view, costs have increased because of increased demands on an essentially static supply of health services.[1] Others postulate that the crisis is a result of an "overmedicalization" of our lives and suggest as a remedy increased self-reliance by the consumers of their health needs.[2] Yet others again view the crisis from an organizational perspective and argue that fragmentation and specialization of programs and services have resulted in a costly and inefficient health-care system.[3] Finally, there are those who suggest that the present crisis in the health sector is political in nature and that it is but a reflection of inequalities in ownership and control in American society at large;[4] improvement of the health-care system would require steps toward the elimination of capitalism. These differences in perspective have led to suggestions for policy alternatives that span a wide economic and politician spectrum.

Aside from the conventional wisdom that people are concerned about the quality and cost of medical care, little research has examined consumer perceptions of problems and appropriate reforms or their level of knowledge about recent health legislation. Even rarer is research comparing positions advocated by health policy makers with those held by consumers. This chapter is intended to improve the situation in this regard by presenting the results of a study of the attitudes toward and knowledge about health policy and programs among hospital board members and a sample of consumers in a midwestern urban community.

[1] Victor R. Fuchs, *Who Shall Live?* (New York: Basic Books, 1974).

[2] Ivan Illich, *Medical Nemesis: The Expropriation of Health* (New York: Pantheon Books, 1976).

[3] Ruth Roemer, Charles Kramer, and Jeanne A. Frink, *Planning Urban Health Services: From Jungle to System* (New York: Springer Publishing Company, 1975).

[4] Vincente Navarro, *Medicine Under Capitalism* (New York: Prodist, 1976).

Revision of paper presented at the 72nd annual meeting of the American Sociological Association, Chicago, September, 1977. Supported by a General Research Support Grant (RR05656–08) from the General Research Support Branch Division of Research Facilities and Resources, NIH; and by an All University Grant from the College of Social Sciences, Michigan State University.

356

Local Health Policy Making and Consumers

American health-care delivery is characterized by its voluntary hospital system. Community voluntary hospitals dominate in-patient health care; in fact, less than one-fourth of the community hospital beds are in state and local government hospitals.[5] Some view this pluralistic system as the result of dominant structural interest groups, such as hospitals, health insurance companies, and the medical profession, which all have vested interests in resisting social change and therefore defend the *status quo*.[6] Others have interpreted the voluntary nature of the American system as being based on a broadly shared value system that prefers to have services and programs provided by private groups and agencies rather than by the government.[7] The reluctance to ask the government to take responsibility for solving community problems has been manifested in a tradition of privatism.[8] This tradition is most clearly expressed in the leadership of the economic elites on the boards of community welfare agencies, for example, community fund-raising agencies and hospital boards of directors. The preferences for the private initiative in responding to social problems in the community has given legitimacy to private powerholders or "private elites" to make and implement local health policies as opposed to the prevalence of public elites so characteristic of health-care systems in other countries.

This tradition of voluntarism and privatism is maintained by the boards of directors of community hospitals, which are typically composed of selected volunteers from the economic and professional elites in the community.[9] A number of studies have shown that this elite representation often has contributed to the adoption of rather narrow hospital policies.[10] Hospital boards of directors have

[5] Dorothy P. Rice and Douglas Wilson, "The American Medical Economy: Problems and Perspectives," *Journal of Health Politics, Policy and Law*, 1 (Summer 1976), 151–172.

[6] See for example the argument advanced by Robert R. Alford, *Health Care Politics: Ideological and Interest Group Barriers to Reform* (Chicago: University of Chicago Press, 1975).

[7] For a review of this value system, see Harold L. Wilensky and Charles N. Lebeaux, *Industrial Society and Social Welfare* (New York: Free Press, 1965).

[8] Timothy K. Barnekow and Daniel Rich, "Privatism and Urban Development: An Analysis of the Organized Influence of Local Business Elites," *Urban Affairs Quarterly*, 12 (June 1977), 431–460; Grant McConnell, *Private Power and American Democracy* (New York: Alfred A. Knopf, 1966).

[9] Most of these studies have been done in northeastern cities: Robert G. Holloway, Jay Artis, and Walter E. Freeman, "The Participation Patterns of Economic Influentials and Their Control of a Hospital Board Trustee," *Journal of Health and Human Behavior*, 4 (Summer 1963), 88–99; Ray Elling and Ollie J. Lee, "Formal Connections of Community Leadership to the Health System," *Milbank Memorial Fund Quarterly*, 44 (July 1966), 294–306; Theodore Goldberg and Ronald Hemmelgarn, "Who Governs Hospitals?" *Hospitals*, 45 (August 1971), 72–79; Ian Berger and Robert Earsy, "Occupations of Boston Hospital Board Members," *Inquiry*, 10 (March 1973), 42–46; Jeffrey Pfeffer, "Size, Composition and Function of Hospital Boards of Directors: A Study of Organization–Environment Linkage," *Administrative Science Quarterly*, 18 (September 1973), 349–364; Anthony R. Kovner, "Hospital Board Members as Policy Makers: Roles, Priorities and Qualifications," *Medical Care*, 12 (December 1974), 971–982.

[10] L. Vaugh Blankenship and Ray H. Elling, "Organizational Support and Community Power Structure: The Hospital," *Journal of Health and Human Behavior*, 3 (Winter 1962), 257–269; Ray H. Elling, "The Hospital-Support Game in Urban Center," *The Hospital in Modern Society*, ed. Eliot Freidson (New York: Free Press, 1963), pp. 73–111; Charles Perrow, "Goals and Power Structures: A

both the legal responsibility for the quality of care offered by the hospital and the ultimate decision-making power on policies for hospital affairs. In the latter capacity, the hospital trustees can in principle strongly influence, not only the character of hospital policy, but also the nature of the local health-care system.

Maybe an even more important consequence of this elite representation has been the documented lack of interest of and involvement by community residents in hospital affairs. For example, in his study of *Health in Regionville*, Koos concluded: "As long as only Class I members constitute the governing board, as was the case in Regionville, the other social classes are likely to view the hospital as Class I vested interest and to view their relation to it negatively."[11]

But an opportunity for community residents to participate in the determination of the nature and the priorities among community health needs has been institutionalized in recent federal health legislation. Although the war on poverty legislation in the 1960s initiated the efforts to integrate community residents in health policy making, the concept of consumer participation came to gain a broader meaning only in subsequent health legislation. The Comprehensive Health Planning Act of 1966 (P.L. 89-749, Section 314) called for participation of "consumers of health services" on regional health-planning boards. The subsequent National Health Planning and Resources Development Act of 1974 (P.L. 93-614, Section 1512) asked for participation of "consumers of health care" and "major purchasers of health care" on the boards of health systems agencies. Legislation concerning health maintenance organizations has also stipulated the participation of representatives of enrolled consumers in the governing body. The operational definition of the term consumer has been presented as "a person who does not make a living in the health-service industry,"[12] and as a "person living in the service area who meets all eligibility criteria to use services and is therefore a potential user."[13]

Despite federal stipulations on the quota for "consumer" participation on local health-planning boards, community residents have had little influence on local health policy making. Some observers relate the consumers' powerlessness to the lack of an explicit definition of their role on these boards.[14] Others argue that consumers in general have been coopted or are tokens of a democratic process in health planning.[15]

Historical Case Study," *The Hospital in Modern Society*, pp. 112–145; Stan Ingman, "Health Planning in Appalachia: Conflict Resolution in a Community Hospital," *Social Science and Medicine*, 8 (1974), 135–142.

[11]Earl L. Koos, *Health in Regionville* (New York: Columbia University Press, 1954), p. 85.

[12]Benjamin B. Wells, "Role of the Consumer in Regional Medical Programs," *American Journal of Public Health*, 60 (November 1970), 2134.

[13]John Campbell, "Working Relationships Between Providers and Consumers in a Neighborhood Health Center," *American Journal of Public Health*, 61 (January 1971), 98.

[14]G. M. Hochbaum, "Consumer Participation in Health Planning: Toward Conceptual Clarification," *American Journal of Public Health*, 59 (September 1969), 1698–1705; Dale B. Christensen and Albert J. Wertheimer, "Consumer Action in Health Care," *Public Health Reports*, 91 (September–October 1976), 406–411; Paul Starr, "The Undelivered Health System," *The Public Interest*, 42 (Winter 1976), 83.

[15]Hans B. C. Spiegel, "Citizen Participation in Federal Programs: A Review," *Journal of Voluntary Action Research*, 1 (1971), 4–31; Eliot A. Krause, "Health Planning as a Managerial Ideology," *International Journal of Health Services*, 3 (Summer 1973), 445–463; Nancy Milio, "Di-

The institutions most directly affected by recent health legislation—community general hospitals—are still governed by a self-nominated elite of boards of directors. One purpose of this study is to determine whether or not the attitudes toward health policy and programs held by hospital board members reflect prevailing opinion within the community they presumably represent. In this respect, we are guided by Verba and Nie, who define *concurrence* as the degree to which leaders and citizens agree on the most important problems facing their community.[16] As far as health policy issues are concerned, the studies by Kunitz *et. al.*, Stratman *et. al.*, and Weaver are among the few that have examined consumers' attitudes toward issues of control, cost, and financing of health services.[17] These studies show that attitudes toward public involvement in health care vary significantly with social class and ethnic group.

This chapter will address three aspects of the issue of leaders' responsiveness to the concerns of consumers. First, if the members of hospital boards are elite members of the community, one would expect them to be substantially different in income, age, education, and occupation—the principal characteristics that distinguish elites from the general population. Second, if the members of hospital boards are by virtue of their dominant social positions defending specific interests, particularly interests mitigating against substantive change, then one would expect a difference between the positions adopted by the board and those of the community at large. Third, if the consumers' views on the desired direction of health policy differ significantly from those of the hospital board, there might occur a "mobilization bias" in the decision-making process, i.e., some issues are organized into hospital policy and others are organized out.[18] In this regard, hospital policy would reflect "nondecision making" because *status-quo* oriented individuals or groups limit the scope of the actual decision making to relatively noncontroversial matters.[19]

Methods

A number of community leaders (N = 20) were interviewed about key issues in local health policy. These interviews provided the basis for generating the items that subsequently appeared on our survey questionnaires.

---

mensions of Consumer Participation and National Health Legislation," *American Journal of Public Health,* 64 (April 1974), 357–363; Sherry R. Arnstein, "A Ladder of Citizen Participation," *Journal of The American Institute of Planners*, 35 (July 1969), 216–224.

[16]Sidney Verba and Norman H. Nie, *Participation in America: Political Democracy and Social Equality* (New York: Harper and Row, 1972), pp. 301–302.

[17]Stephen J. Kunitz, Andrew A. Sorensen, and Suzanne B. Cashman, "Changing Health Care Opinions in Regionville, 1946–1973," *Medical Care*, 13 (July 1975), 549–561; William C. Stratman, James A. Block, Stephen P. Brown, and Marshall V. Rozzi, "A Study of Consumer Attitudes About Health Care: The Control, Cost and Financing of Health Services," *Medical Care*, 13 (August 1975), 659–668; Jerry L. Weaver, *National Health Policy and the Underserved: Ethnic Minorities, Women and the Elderly* (Saint Louis: C. V. Mosby Company, 1976), pp.122–132.

[18]For a more detailed discussion of this concept concerning latent power, see Peter Bachrach and Morton S. Baratz, "Two Faces of Power," *American Political Science Review*, 56 (December 1962), 947–952; "Decisions and Nondecisions: An Analytical Framework," *American Political Science Review*, 57 (September 1963), 632–642.

[19]*Ibid.*

Two groups are compared in this study: members of local hospital boards and a sample of community residents. In January 1976, a questionnaire was mailed to the hospital trustees and chief administrative officers (N = 73) of six hospitals in a midwestern urban area.[20] All hospital administrators and fifty-one of the hospital board members responded; the remainder refused to participate or could not be located.

A second questionnaire, prepared for the community at large, was administered to a sample of individuals drawn randomly from the local telephone book (N = 117). The telephone interviewing took place during July and August of 1976. This method was preferable to a mail survey because it minimized the problems of cost and timeliness.[21]

Eleven variables were measured using a common format for both groups: level of education, income, residency in the community, birthplace, employment status, employment type, age, and three policy attitude scales. In addition, respondents to both questionnaires were asked to indicate what they thought was the most important problem facing the local health-care system.

In his review of the social values underlying approaches to medical-care policy, Donabedian distinguishes between two major viewpoints—the libertarian and the egalitarian.[22] The libertarian view corresponds to the nineteenth-century liberal ideology defending individual freedom against government intervention, whereas the egalitarian viewpoint is more clearly an expression of a welfare-state ideology indicating a more positive view of government involvement in securing social rights. Donabedian's differentiation between these two major perspectives guided our construction of a scale on attitudes toward health policy. The items address the following issues: (1) the role of the federal government, (2) the desirability of a free market of health care, and (3) the acceptability of increased consumer participation in local policy making. For example, subjects were presented with statements of the general form: "Increased federal involvement could prevent medical expenses from going higher." They were then asked to indicate their opinion on this issue on a five-point scale, ranging from strongly agree (1) to strongly disagree (5). The consumer sample was also asked to indicate its perception of the importance of national health insurance as an issue in the forthcoming presidential election and their confidence in the ability of the health-care system to provide good health care.

Finally, consumers were asked about their knowledge of (1) national health insurance ("Have you heard or read about any plans about national health insurance?"), (2) prepaid health programs ("Have you heard or read about prepaid

---

[20]The data in this research were collected during 1975–76 in a midwestern standard metropolitan statistical area of approximately 250,000 people.

[21]A methodological problem must be acknowledged. The administration procedure differed for the two groups being studied, and we did not test experimentally the degrees to which differences in data methods affected the obtained results. However, a comparison of the interitem correlations indicates that the magnitudes and direction of the Pearson r's remained stable within and between both groups. Second, the standard errors for each variable is relatively low, usually falling in the range between 0.03 and 0.15, and consistently the standard errors are the same for both the consumers and the hospital board members for each variable.

[22]A summary of the arguments is reported in Avedis Donabedian, *Aspects of Medical Care Administration: Specifying Requirements for Health Care* (Boston: Harvard University Press, 1973), pp. 1–28.

health programs?" and "Have you heard or read about health maintenance organizations?"), and (3) regional health-planning agencies ("Have you heard about regional health-planning agencies; for example, the past Comprehensive Health Planning Agency and the present Health Systems Agency?"). Responses on these items were coded into categories of "yes," "no," and "don't know."

Findings

We have indicated that if the members of the hospital boards constitute an elite, they should be statistically different from the sample of consumers. Table 22-1 gives T-test results using separate variance estimates and a two-tailed significance test. It can be readily seen that striking differences exist between the two groups. In summary, the board members earn an average of $17,000 more per year, they have lived in the community somewhat longer, have considerably more education, and are on the average thirteen years older than consumers. A more detailed examination shows that 64 percent of the hospital trustees have an income over $35,000 as compared to only 3 percent of the consumers. In addition, whereas a majority of the hospital trustees have some graduate-school education or an advance graduate degree (59 percent), only a few of the consumers (11 percent) have achieved this level of education.

There are stong differences in occupation as one might expect. Two-thirds of the hospital board are executives of large businesses. Well over a third of the board members are corporate presidents, whereas the average consumer works either in local or state government administration or in local factories as a lower-level manager and an assembly-line worker.

The social profile of the two groups—the hospital boards and the consumers —suggests that the hospital trustees represent rather narrow interests in the community. They are recruited, as other studies also have documented, from local business and professional elites. But their narrow base has a long tradition in this community as in so many other American communities. As the hospital administrator of the largest hospital in the community notes:

Table 22-1 Comparison of social characteristics of consumers and hospital board members

	Means				
	Consumers (N = 117)	Hospital Boards (N = 57)	T-Value	D.F.	Significance
Income[a]	$14,420	$31,950	− 7.45	155	.0001
Residency[b]	3.03	3.52	− 3.14	147	.002
Education[b]	2.92	4.84	− 9.78	119	.0001
Age	42	55	− 5.92	158	.0001

[a]T-Value derived from categories of $5,000 for each level.
[b]The values are means of the following categories used:
   Residency = (1) Under five years, (2) five–ten years, (3) 11–20 years, (4) 21 years or more.
   Education = (1) Less than 12 years of school, (2) high school diploma or equivalent, (3) 1–3 years of college, (4) bachelor's degree, (5) some graduate school, (6) an advanced graduate degree.

He [the founder of the hospital] said there should be eighteen male trustees; none of them should be in the medical profession. All men and no doctors is what he said in effect. So, these guys who were appointed to the original board were prominent citizens in the community just as our board is now. I think it is still fair to say that assignment to the board in this hospital is the most prestigious voluntary board assignment that a male can get in this community.

A relevant question is, however, what difference does it make who governs hospital boards? One answer may be that if those who govern have significantly different attitudes toward and knowledge about health policy and programs than community residents, then this difference will have an impact on the biases used in making and implementing health policy.

Attitudes Toward Control, Financing, and Quality of Health Care

Table 22-2 provides the T-test for differences between the hospital board and the consumer groups on the following health-policy issues: (1) government's involvement in health care, (2) increased consumer involvement in health policies, (3) free market of health-care delivery. The results indicate a strong level of disagreement between the two groups.

The consumers agreed that increased governmental involvement would probably prevent medical expenses from rising. Their favorable attitude contrasts to the negative attitude held by members of the boards of directors in the same community (means = 2.93 and 4.34). Almost all the hospital board members (82 percent) disagreed with the statement that increased federal involvement was a vehicle to control rising medical costs, whereas only a third of the resident sample disagreed. In short, the hospital board members are hostile to public intervention in regulating medical costs, whereas consumers tend to favor regulation.

These differences in political views between the two groups could be related to social class. This interpretation is supported by analyzing correlations of responses within our sample of the community population (Table 22-3). A favorable attitude toward the federal government's capacity to regulate rising medical cost is inversely related to income ($r = .23$, $p < .01$) and education ($r = .22$, $p < .01$).[23]

Support for increased federal intervention was related to two other attitudinal variables among the consumers. Persons supporting federal regulation of medical costs view support for a presidential candidate who favors a national health insurance as important ($r = .51$, $p < .001$). Furthermore, those favoring federal intervention in controlling medical costs tend to favor giving consumers more voice in decision making and in planning the priorities in health care ($r = .31$, $p < .001$).

There was a significant difference between means of the two groups in the second issue (T – value = 4.51, $p < .001$)—consumer participation in health planning. Consumers support an increased voice in health planning as compared to a more conservative position held by hospital board members. This finding is

[23]Positive correlations result from scalar inversions, but still reflect inverse relationships; i.e., a response of 1 indicates strong agreement and an income of 1 is the lowest income group.

Table 22-2 Comparison of attitudes on health issues between hospital board members and consumers

	Means[a]				
	Consumers (N = 117)	Hospital Boards (N = 57)	T-Value[b]	D.F.	Significance
Government involvement	2.93	4.34	−7.45	150	.0001
Consumer involvement	2.13	3.09	−4.51	124	.0001
Free market	2.18	1.85	1.96	154	.05

Note: [a]1 = Strongly Agree and 5 = Strongly Disagree
[b]Two-tailed.

interesting since the literature on participation of citizens in politics in general has indicated that a low level of participation is an indicator of general satisfaction with existing policies.[24] Data above clearly suggest differences in the views between health-care providers and consumers, but also a desire by the latter group to become more involved in health politics. It is not surprising that hospital trustees oppose increased consumer participation in policy making since they represent community elites rather than organized consumers.

The first health-policy item summarizes respondents' attitudes toward the preferred behavior of government in health care, but the third item operationalizes the underlying political ideology that justifies federal involvement. There is an interesting difference between the two groups in their perception of the role of

Table 22-3 Consumers: Intercorrelations* of health-policy attitudes and social characteristics

	(1)	(2)	(3)	(4)	(5)	(6)	(7)	(8)	(9)
(1) Government involvement									
(2) Consumer involvement	.31[b]								
(3) Free market	−.15	−.12							
(4) President choice									
Preference	.51[b]	.12	−.12						
(5) Confidence	−.04	−.18	.06	−.09					
(6) Length of residence	.02	.04	−.11	−.06	−.18				
(7) Education	.22[a]	.03	.09	.30[b]	−.09	−.39[b]			
(8) Income	.23[a]	.10	.02	.31[b]	−.06	−.04	.21		
(9) Age	.13	.08	−.09	.01	−.08	.48[b]	−.24[a]	−.16	

*Pearson Correlations.
[a]$p < .01$.
[b]$p < .001$.

[24]For a review of this literature, see Robert R. Alford and Roger Friedland, "Political Participation and Public Policy," *Annual Review of Sociology*, ed. Alex Inkeles, James Coleman, and Neil Smelser (Palo Alto, Cal.: Annual Reviews Inc., 1975), I: 429–479.

government. When considering the extent of federal involvement, the two groups differ widely; however, both groups, on the average, believe that the private and voluntary character of the health industry is a strength, although board members feel more strongly about this than consumers ($\overline{X}$ board = 1.85, $\overline{X}$ cons = 2.18, T = 1.96, p < .05). It is not surprising that the group providing health care endorsed the voluntary nature of the American system (77%); after all, they constitute the core group supporting the ideology of privatism in their capacity as hospital trustees of a voluntary hospital system in the community. In addition, the hospital board also expressed considerable optimism concerning the efficiency of voluntary coordination in the community, viewing its level as being higher (44 percent) if not the same (33 percent) as in other communities. This confidence in voluntary coordination of health resources is another way for the hospital trustees to express trust in localism, that is, a self-sufficiency in solving community problems.[25]

The consumers' positive response to the item on the voluntary nature of the American system is more interesting. Their answers may indicate that although consumers want more decision-making authority over health-policy issues, such a desire does not extend to completely removing the health-care system from the free-market economy. Furthermore, participation of the federal government in industry is nothing new, and may be seen by consumers as an intervention that would not destroy the "private and voluntary" character of the system. Finally, respondents may have emphasized more the transaction between private physicians and their patients than the economic dimension of this item.

The fourth policy item measured the importance of public access to health care. Respondents were asked: "In the presidential election in the fall, do you think it is important to support a candidate who favors national health insurance?" The aggregate data show that 54 percent of the consumers reported that it was important to support such a candidate. As other studies have shown, support for national health insurance (NHI) has been related to socio-economic criteria.[26] This relationship was also confirmed in our study: as income and education decrease, support for a candidate favoring NHI increases (r = .32, p < .001, r = .29, p < .001, respectively).[27] In fact, 76 percent of those with a family income below $15,000 indicated that this was an important issue as compared to 36 percent of those with income over $15,000.

We also found that support of a national health insurance was significantly related to other attitudinal variables. First, respondents supporting NHI are more likely to mention that they do not feel that existing health-insurance plans meet their needs (X^2 = 8.26, p < .08). Second, as mentioned previously, those supporting a presidential candidate favoring NHI are more likely to agree that increased federal involvement could prevent medical expense from going higher

[25]It is interesting to note, however, that the hospital board elite is concerned about threats to the self-regulation of the local health-care system. When asked about the most important problem (see Table 25-4), the hospital board ranked "lack of coordination among providers" as a problem. This selection might mean that although they think that the present level of coordination is higher among health providers than in other communities, they are concerned that this level is not high enough to encounter public involvement in the affairs of health providers.

[26]Kunitz *et al.*, *op. cit.*; William C. Stratman *et al.*, *op. cit.*

[27]See note 23.

(r = .51, p <.001). Finally, and not surprisingly, those who gave support to NHI as an election issue were also more likely to have heard of such plans ($X^2 = 9.17$, p <.05).

The final scale measured confidence in the present health-care system. In response to the statement, "If I become seriously ill, I'm confident that I would receive good care," 77 percent of the consumers agreed. This response suggests an interesting point. Although the respondents previously indicated a need for governmental involvement to control and cover rising medical expenses, they still trust the institution of medicine. This point becomes even clearer as one reviews the results of all attitude scales on health policy. The results indicate a paradox in the residents' views because the ideological indicators of public involvement appear inconsistent. The respondents in our sample support the private and voluntary nature of health care and have confidence in its efficiency in responding to their needs. Nevertheless, they also think that federal involvement in controlling and covering rising medical bills is desirable.

Problems in Local Health Care Delivery

Verba and Nie define concurrence as the degree to which leaders and citizens agree on the most important problems facing their community.[28] Although a high concurrence may indicate leaders' responsiveness to concerns of citizens, it may also reflect the penetration of the ideology and interests of the elite into community residents. A low consensus would indicate little responsiveness of leaders to the concerns of citizens.

Both the group of hospital trustees and our sample of consumers were asked to identify the most important problem in local health care. The hospital board and the consumers, with the exception of "rising costs," offer strikingly different answers. Table 22-4 gives the five most frequently indicated responses for each group.

An examination of the two lists in Table 22-4 provides an interesting opportunity to speculate on the source of the differences between the hospital board members and the consumer representatives. The findings suggest different perceptions about the consequences of recent changes in the market model of health care.

The hospital board tends to emphasize shifts in "demand" as the principal source of problems. The elite's list (no individual was allowed to provide more than one response) includes legal problems concomitant with recent increases in demand for health services, rising costs for the hospital, administrative difficulties arising from third-party relationships, and a lack of primary-care providers making the hospital emergency room a substitute for the general practitioner.

The consumers look at the problems as a "supply" dysfunction, especially the problem of rising costs. The perceived problems are lack of sufficient numbers of health providers, poor doctor-patient relations, inadequate health insurance programs, and deficient health care for the elderly.

These data point to a fundamental dichotomy in the perception of consumers and those who control the organizations providing health services. Neither

[28]Verba and Nie, *op.cit.*

Table 22-4   Rank order of most important problems in local health delivery

Rank	Consumers	Hospital Board Members
1.	Rising costs	Malpractice suits
2.	Shortage of providers	Rising costs
3.	Deterioration of physician–patient relationship	Reimbursement by third-party payers
4.	Inadequate insurance plans	Lack of primary care
5.	Poor treatment of aged	Lack of coordination among providers

viewpoint can be claimed to represent a "correct" position on the issue. The perception by the hospital trustees suggests that they are more influenced by the hospital administrative staff and physicians than by consumers. For example, about a third of the trustees reported that the hospital administrative staff, other board members, and physicians had been "very influential" in shaping their ideas about community health needs. One-fourth reported that consumer groups have had "no influence at all" in this respect.

It seems evident that there is little communication between the hospital trustees and consumers concerning key issues in local health policy. The power of the hospital board lies in its ability to restrict the scope of policy making in the hospital. The result of the hospital board's narrow view on community problems in health care may be a "mobilization bias" in the issues that come up for overt decision making. Consequently, some issues, although considered important by large segments of the community, might in this way never be acknowledged or considered by the decision makers. If such decision making occurs, the resulting hospital policy can be characterized as "nondecision making."[29]

Knowledge About Recent Health Legislation and Programs

Scientific medicine has generated an increasing specialization and complexity in medical care. This development of medicine creates, not only a dependency on professional expertise to define health needs, but also a lack of a sense of power to influence the decision making on health policy among laypersons.[30] How much do consumers even know about existing alternative health programs and avenues for them to influence policy making? This question was addressed by examining the level of knowledge that the residents had about some alternatives to present health care. Our data suggest that consumers have only a meager knowledge about health legislation that would lead to a more consumer-oriented system.

In response to the question, "Have you heard or read of any plans about a national health insurance?" 56 percent of the sample answered positively. Data show that the level of information on this matter is significantly higher among males than among females ($X^2 = 6.27$, $p < .01$): 45 percent of the females knew of such plans as compared to 69 percent of the males. Furthermore, it was also

[29]See Bachrach and Baratz, "Decisions and Nondecisions."

[30]Illich, *op. cit.*, pp. 39–124, argues that technological development in medicine has created an addictive dependency of the population to the organization of medicine. Illich views the increasing "medicalization" of society as being counterproductive to health, a phenomenon that he calls the social iatrogenesis of medicine.

found that those who know about any plans for a NHI are more likely to enroll in a prepaid health program if it were established in the area ($X^2 = 8.57$, $p < .01$). This finding suggests that there is a group of people who are attracted to alternative forms of health-care delivery.

When these data were gathered, the community had no prepaid health program although some efforts have been made since then to establish a health maintenance organization (HMO). At the time, however, only 50 percent of our sample had heard or read about prepaid health programs. This finding is rather surprising in the light of the publicity surrounding federal and state initiatives in this area. An even higher proportion (70 percent) were unaware of HMO's. Moreover, only 37 percent of our sample indicated that they would join a prepaid program if given the opportunity. The respondents attracted to these programs represent approximately 60 percent of the group who were aware of prepaid programs—which further suggests that there is an untapped market for these programs in the community.

The establishment of prepaid health programs is a product of the mobilization of community resources, and thereby, ultimately the action of local elites. It is also the result of the orientation of hospital board members who will not only support or oppose such programs, but who will also decide if their hospital should provide facilities for them. Only 7 percent of the hospital board members were strongly opposed to having their hospital be the center for a prepaid health program. Most others were neutral, and 37 percent supported the idea. One explanation for why consumers are ignorant of prepaid programs becomes apparent. Since the hospital board does not express very much interest in the idea, it is not surprising that the question has been a "nonissue" in the community. The inaction on prepaid programs in this community is an example of an important policy issue that has neither arisen nor been formulated as hospital policy. The hospital board has acted as "nondecision makers" with the power to neglect this issue.[31]

The community population is almost unaware of the existence of the structural avenues—the past Comprehensive Health Planning (CHP) and present Health Systems Agency (HSA)—through which they could influence formulation of local health needs as well as the priorities and direction of local health policies. Our data show that only 15 percent of our sample shows awareness of the existence of any regional health-planning agencies, although federal guidelines have secured the representation of consumers on these agencies. In contrast, the hospital board was found to be well aware of the regional health-planning agency and its influence; in fact, the members oppose extending its power. This attitude is consistent with its opposition to giving consumers more voice in decision making and planning the priorities in local health care.

Conclusion

The findings of this study point to three constraints that affect the decision-making process and policies of hospitals: (1) hospital board members have social

---

[31]Bachrach and Baratz, "Decisions and Nondecisions."

characteristics that are substantially different from those of consumers of health services; (2) hospital board members adopt positions on health policy that are significantly different from those held by consumers; and (3) policies of hospitals might reflect "nondecision making," a process that unilaterally excludes information and choices from consideration.

We found that hospital board members are significantly different in their sociodemographic composition from the consumer sample. In addition, the occupational distribution of hospital board members gave further evidence that they were more representative of local elites than of the aggregate of consumers. The impact of this elite representation becomes evident in the substantial differences found between the attitudes to health policy issues of the consumers and those of the hospital board members.

In our study of attitudes to health policy, we were guided by Donabedian's proposition that social values influence choices of action in the administration of medical care. He also argues that the libertarian viewpoint more frequently is prevalent among the elite segments in the population, whereas the egalitarian viewpoint appears to be more salient to the underprivileged.[32] This argument was confirmed in our findings in the viewpoints held by the hospital board and the consumer sample. For example, the hospital board rejects government intervention as a viable method of reducing the rate of cost increases in the health sector. Furthermore, it opposes consumer involvement and ardently supports the notion that the voluntary character of the American health-care system is the source of its strength. In short, the hospital board elite's viewpoints on policy seem to fit Donabedian's description of the libertarian ideology.

Yet this viewpoint of the hospital board elite is hardly surprising in light of the fact that the board is composed of persons with economic influence in the local business community. In this respect, one could interpret the views on health-policy issues among board members as an extension of their general interest in the strength of the free-enterprise system in the community. But it also was apparent that the hospital trustees had been influenced by the medical staff's and hospital management's views on economic and political issues. The hospital trustees perceived the most important problems in local health care as demand dysfunctions within the framework of a market model of health-care delivery, a view that reflected a provider bias.

The consumer sample, however, seems to reflect the egalitarian viewpoint described by Donabedian. The consumers would like to see increased government intervention in the health-care industry and they indicate a preference for a presidential candidate who supports national health insurance. They are also much less supportive than the hospital board elite of the voluntary, free-market nature of the American system. In addition, a majority of the consumers supported an expansion of consumer participation in policy making. As such would threaten the traditional structure of decision making, it was found to be viewed negatively by the hospital board, which constitutes the present decision makers on hospital affairs. Finally, it was shown that the consumer sample emphasized the consequences of inadequate supply of health care as the major problem.

[32]Donabedian, *op. cit.*, p. 10.

In short, we found that the hospital board elite perceives issues as well as problems in local health care in very different terms than the consumers. If values are important in arriving at decisions and the decision makers hold values different from those of the rest of the population, one can anticipate a "mobilization bias" to occur in hospital policies. The hospital board may defend its positions by failing to respond to demands for change and only adopting such innovations that affirm the *status quo*. In this respect, "nondecision making" implied that consumer demands for changes in policies will be obstructed or neglected by the decision makers on hospital boards. In general, the hospital trustees may be more interested in limiting the decision making to relatively "safe" issues than in addressing the more controversial issues relevant to consumers.

Although the consumers expressed both different ideological preferences than the hospital board and were well aware of the most important problems in local health care delivery, they were not well informed about alternatives that would enable a more consumer-oriented system. Thus, little information seems to flow to consumers about alternative ways of organizing health care delivery. This lack of information is partly related to the absence of a debate on health policy in most communities. Since social inequality in health is not as visible as other inequities, health is still interpreted by consumers in individual rather than sociopolitical terms despite the attention the issue has received at the national level.

It has increasingly become the federal government's responsibility to protect the interests of consumers, as hospital management and trustees of community hospitals have failed to respond to demands for change. The federal efforts to expand consumer participation have had as one objective the limitation of the professional and bureaucratic power of health providers. One example of such an effort constitutes the neighborhood health centers established as part of the war on poverty in the 1960s. The purpose of these community programs was not only to decentralize service delivery, but to give consumers a more active role in making health policy as well. Subsequent health legislation has secured consumer involvement on the boards of health maintenance organizations and regional health-planning agencies such as the Health Systems Agencies.

The results of this study, however, show that until consumers become more aware of these avenues for influencing local health policy, hospital management and trustees will probably remain the primary policy makers. Their priorities and definitions of community health needs and problems will to a large extent determine the character of health care that community residents will receive. A hospital board consisting of individuals who represent diverse community interests could bring up a wider range of concerns for decision making. A wider representation on hospital boards may also eliminate the notion of health-care facilities as the vested interests of local elites.

B.   Macrolevel

An increasing interest in the comparative study of the health systems of different nations around the world has brought into focus some of the hazards and difficulties in making this comparison. The chapter by Jesús De Miguel offers a conceptual framework for the sociological study of national health systems.

The congruence between some contemporary issues in organization theory and operational and policy issues confronted by health-care delivery organizations such as the hospital is suggested in the study by Stephen Shortell.

To conclude this section, David Mechanic offers an insightful analysis of the varying impact of increasing medical technology and bureaucracy on the provision of medical care, giving particular attention to the various modes of rationing health care and their consequences.

23 A Framework for the Study of National Health Systems

This paper presents a framework for the study of national health systems using a sociological approach. It attempts to make a contribution to the understanding of health systems and their relationship to the processes of change in societies. The model is heavily influenced by Elling's paper on "Case Studies of Contrasting Approaches to Organizing for Health: An Introduction to a Framework."[1] I will develop his scheme further by defining a causal model for health systems. To support this analysis I will also review the comparative health literature from the 1930s to the present. The contribution of the late E. Richard Weinerman on "Research on Comparative Health Service Systems"[2] is the starting point of the analysis. The brief review of the literature includes most of the relevant "within-nation" and "between-nations" research, as well as changes in the level of analysis (micro-, macro- and micro-macro-) in comparative health studies.

The concept of "health systems" is central to the topic of research, although there is no agreement about its exact meaning. It is a fact that health services alone do not determine human health; there are many other social factors that affect the health status of populations. Sociologists often help define, measure and influence policy-making about health status in relation to these factors. This model offers different possibilities for such an analysis, as it divides health systems into subsystems, articulating them into "open-linked systems" theory as Caudill[3] suggested. In summary, my purpose is to define a general analytic framework for health systems, applicable to diverse cases and constructed by cross-national and systems analysis approaches.

Cross-National Research

In their beginning the social sciences stressed comparative studies, something that was underemphasized during the long fight for the institutionalization of

[1]Elling, R. H. "Case Studies of Contrasting Approaches to Organizing for Health: An Introduction to a Framework," *Social Science and Medicine* 8:263–270 (1974).

[2]Weinerman, E. R. "Research on Comparative Health Service Systems," *Medical Care* 9:272–290 (May–June 1971).

[3]Caudill, William. *Effects of Social and Cultural Systems in Reactions to Stress,* Pamphlet No. 14 (New York: Social Science Research Council, 1958).

The author is deeply grateful for the critical comments of Ray H. Elling, August B. Hollingshead, Juan J. Linz and Jerome K. Myers; for the numerous suggestions made by Brian E. Carter and Benjamin Oltra; and for the technical assistance of Antonio Benitez and Joan P. Cianciolo. This paper is part of a longer study entitled "Health in the Mediterranean Region: A Comparative Analysis of the Health Systems of Portugal, Spain, Italy, and Yugoslavia," supported by grants from the Social Science Research Council and Juan March Foundation. The opinions stated here are those of the author and do not necessarily reflect those of the above institutions.

these disciplines in academia. In some sense there has been a new revival of comparative studies in almost all fields of social sciences.[4] In the opinion of Wendell Bell,[5] "the comparison of different cultures and societies is essential for any proper and adequate study of man and his institutions—a truism much neglected by sociologists for well over two decades beginning about 1930." As created by the founding fathers (Comte, Marx, Weber, Durkheim), sociology was very much a comparative field, but after a while it began to use a noncomparative approach. The explanations for this behavior have been varied: 1) the reformist, action-oriented focus of sociology from the 1930s to the 1950s;[6] 2) the lack of comparative data in the time during which sociology fought to be institutionalized; and 3) the lack of an effective international scientific community, except for a few scholars at a very high level.

Comparative health systems—as a field or discipline—includes the analysis of health organizations, health factors and health processes, both within and between nations. Only by taking into account many different cases is it possible to establish an unbiased theory. Consequently, such an approach may give us the opportunity of constructing a broader, more complete theory about health. The underlying question of any comparative study of health systems is the existence of a health system "superior" to all others "that can be copied, adapted, and reinforced to match local and national patterns."[7] However, very few cross-national studies of health matters have dealt directly with the difficult goal of appraising or measuring the efficiency and/or effectiveness of the medical planning and organization of a health system. Thus the main question of comparative health systems remains unanswered.

There has been a hesitancy about deciding which systems work better than others and why. The ideology is that, generally speaking, all health systems are valuable; thus cross-national studies on health care systems have carefully avoided concluding that one system is better than another. It has been thought that this is primarily because of the approach to the topic and/or the value-free scientific method, but it may also be due to ideological premises.

The methodology of international health comparisons uses the operative definition of micro- and macro-analyses of health systems.[8] Micro-analyses tend to stress studies of the health behavior of individual patients, populations and small groups; analyses of family attitudes; reactions to health troubles; studies of roles and the medical profession; and many other relationships between single variables. Macro-analyses focus on the interrelationships among socioeconomic

[4]This point is rather well developed by: Rokkan, Stein. "Comparative Cross-National Research: The Context of Current Efforts," in: Merritt, R. L. and Rokkan, S. (eds.) *Comparing Nations, The Use of Quantitative Data in Cross-National Research* (New Haven: Yale University Press, 1966) pp. 3–9.

[5]Bell, Wendell. "Comparative Studies: A Commentary," in: Riggs, F. W. (ed.) *International Studies: Present Status and Future Prospects* (Philadelphia: The American Academy of Political and Social Science, 1971) pp. 57–58.

[6]Hopkins, Terence K. and Wallerstein, Immanuel. "The Comparative Study of National Societies," *Social Science Information* 6:35 (1967).

[7]Fry, John. *Medicine in Three Societies: A Comparison of Medical Care in the U.S.S.R., U.S.A. and U.K.* (London: MTP, 1969) p. vii.

[8]Rabin, David L. (ed.) "International Comparisons of Medical Care," *Milbank Memorial Fund Quarterly* 50:1–99 (July 1972) part 2.

factors related to health; studies of structures and processes in the social system; the importance of health economics and planning in the development of society; the relationships of medical associations and institutions to the whole community; and so on.[9] Table 23-1 summarizes the important studies of comparative health systems,[10] differentiated by level of analysis (micro-, macro- and micro-macro-) and the scope or units of observation (within-nation and between-nations). Each study is placed according to its date of publication from 1930 to 1975 (in a logarithmic scale for reasons of clarity). This table may pigeonhole the studies too neatly and, consequently, not very exactly. Nevertheless, it is only a tentative classification, and changes can be made easily. I am conscious of the fact that some of the studies are on the borderline of two types, and that others may even include two or three different perspectives.

According to this table, "within-nation" studies, especially those with a sociological perspective, started earlier than "between-nations" studies. Also, "within" studies have a tendency to be "macro," and "between" studies "micro." The most sophisticated "micro-macro-between" type of works did not appear until recently. Taking this fact into account one cannot expect a higher level of theoretical and/or methodological construction from this type of research. And it seems fairly clear from the table that this latter type of investigation is becoming the most popular one, while other types are decreasing, especially "micro-within" comparative analysis.

[9]Rokkan, Stein, *et al. Citizens, Elections, Parties: Approaches to the Comparative Study of the Processes of Development* (New York: David McKay, 1970).

[10]Abel-Smith, Brian, "The Major Patterns of Financing and Organization of Medical Services That Have Emerged in Other Countries," *Medical Care* 3:33–40 (1965); Abel-Smith, Brian. *An International Study of Health Expenditures and Its Relevance for Health Planning,* Public Health Paper No. 32 (Geneva: WHO, 1967); Aiken, M. and Hage, J. "Organizational Interdependence and Intra-organizational Structure," *American Sociological Review* 33:912–930 (1968); Altenstetter, Christa. "Planning for Health Facilities in the United States and in West Germany," *Milbank Memorial Fund Quarterly* 51:41–47 (1973); Altman, I. "Medical Care Research in Israel," *Medical Care* 6:424–429 (1968); American College of Hospital Administrators. *The Swedish Health Services System,* lectures from the ACHA's Twenty-Second Fellows Seminar, Stockholm, 1969 (Chicago: ACHA, 1971); The American Foundation. *American Medicine: Expert Testimony Out of Court* (New York: The American Foundation, 1937); Andersen, Ronald; Smedby, Bjorn; and Anderson, Odin W. *Medical Care Use in Sweden and the United States: A Comparative Analysis of Systems and Behavior,* Research Series No. 27 (Chicago: Center for Health Administration Studies, University of Chicago, 1970); Anderson, Odin W. "Toward a Framework for Analyzing Health Services Systems," *Social and Economic Administration* 1:16 (1967); Anderson, Odin W. *Health Care: Can There Be Equity? The United States, Sweden, and England.* (New York: John Wiley & Sons, 1972); Anderson, Odin W. and Kravits, Joanna. *Health Services in the Chicago Area. A Framework for Use of Data,* Research Series No. 26 (Chicago: Center for Health Administration Studies, University of Chicago, 1968); Anderson, T. R. and Warkov, S. "Organizational Size and Functional Complexity: A Study of Administration in Hospitals," *American Sociological Review* 26:23–28 (1961); Babson, John H. *Health Care Delivery Systems: A Multinational Survey* (Bath, England: Pitman Medical, 1972); Badgley, Robin F. "Social Science and Health Planning: Culture, Disease and Health Services in Colombia," *Milbank Memorial Fund Quarterly* 46:1–352 (1968) part 2; Badgley, Robin F., *et al.* "International Studies of Health Manpower: A Sociological Perspective," *Medical Care* 9:235–252 (1971); Baker, Timothy D. and Perlman, Mark. *Health Manpower in a Developing Economy: Taiwan, A Case Study in Planning* (Baltimore: The Johns Hopkins Press, 1967); Becker, Howard S., *et al. Boys in White: Student Culture in Medical School* (Chicago: The University of Chicago Press, 1961); Ben-David, Joseph. "Scientific Productivity and Academic Organization in Nineteenth Century Medicine," *American Sociological Review* 25:828–843 (1960); Bice, T. W. and Kalimo, E. "Comparisons

of Health Related Attitudes: A Cross-National, Factor Analytic Study," *Social Science and Medicine* 5:283-318 (1971); Bierman, Pearl, *et al.* "Health Services Research in Great Britain," *Milbank Memorial Fund Quarterly* 46:9-102 (1968); Biörck, Gunnar. "Trends in the Development of Medical Care in Sweden," *Medical Care* 2:156-161 (July-September 1964); Blum, Richard and Blum, Eva. *Health and Healing in Rural Greece* (Stanford: Stanford University Press, 1965); Brand, Jeanne L. *Doctors and the State: The British Medical Profession and Government Action in Public Health, 1870-1912* (Baltimore: The Johns Hopkins Press, 1965); Bravo, A. L. "Development of Medical Care Services in Latin America," *American Journal of Public Health* 48:434-447 (1958); Brewster, A. W. and Seldowitz, E. "Trends in the National Health Service in England and Wales, 1949-1960," *Public Health Reports* 77:735-744 (1962); Bryant, John. *Health and the Developing World* (Ithaca, N.Y.: Cornell University Press, 1969); Btesh, B. "International Research in the Organization of Medical Care," *Medical Care* 3:41-46 (1965); Butterfield, W. J. H. *Priorities in Medicine* (London: Nuffield Provincial Hospital Trust, 1968); Caudill, William. *The Psychiatric Hospital as a Small Society* (Cambridge; Harvard University Press, 1958); Chen, W. Y. "Medicine and Public Health in China Today," *Public Health Reports* 76:699-711 (1961); Cochrane, A. L. *Effectiveness and Efficiency: Random Reflections on Health Services* (London: Nuffield Provincial Hospital Trust, 1972); Collings, Joseph S. "General Medical Care in New Zealand and Great Britain," *Journal of the National Medical Association* 42:65-72 (1950); Coser, R. L. "Authority and Decision-making in a Hospital: A Comparative Analysis," *American Sociological Review* 23:56-63 (1958); De Miguel, Jesús M. "Health in the Mediterranean Region: The Case of Spain," *Revista International de Sociología* (1975); Dewhurst, J. Frederich, *et al. Europe's Needs and Resources* (New York: Twentieth Century Fund, 1961); Duff, Raymond S. and Hollingshead, August B. *Sickness and Society* (New York: Harper and Row, 1968); Eckstein, Harry. *The English Health Service* (Cambridge: Harvard University Press, 1958); Eckstein, Harry. *Pressure Group Politics: The Case of the British Medical Association* (Stanford: Stanford University Press, 1960); Ehrenreich, Barbara and Ehrenreich, John. *The American Health Empire: Power, Profits, and Politics* (New York: Random House, 1970); Elling, R. H. "Health Planning In International Perspective," *Medical Care* 9:214-234 (1971); Elling, R. H. "Case Studies," *op. cit.;* Elling, R. H. and Lee, Ollie J. "Formal Connections of Community Leadership to the Health System," in: Jaco, E. G. (ed.) *Patients, Physicians, and Illness,* 2nd ed. (New York: The Free Press, 1972) pp. 296-303; Emery, G. M. "New Zealand Medical Care," *Medical Care* 4:159-170 (1966); Evang, K. "Medical Care in Europe," *American Journal of Public Health* 48:427-433 (1958); Evang, K.; Murray, D. S.; and Lear, W. J. *Medical Care and Family Security— Norway, England, U.S.A.* (Englewood Cliffs, N.J.: Prentice Hall, 1963); Falk, I. S. *Security Against Sickness: A Study of Health Insurance* (New York: Doubleday, Doran, 1936); Falk, I. S. "Medical Care in Two Areas of Southeast Asia: Malaya and Singapore," *American Journal of Public Health* 48:448-453 (1958); Faris, Robert E. L. and Dunham, H. Warren. *Mental Disorders in Urban Areas: An Ecological Study of Schizophrenia and Other Psychoses* (Chicago: The University of Chicago Press, 1939); Fendall, N. R. E. "Planning Health Services in Developing Countries: Kenya's Experience," *Public Health Reports* 78:977-988 (1963); Field, Mark G. *Doctor and Patient in Soviet Russia* (Cambridge: Harvard University Press, 1957); Field, Mark G. *Soviet Socialized Medicine* (New York: The Free Press, 1967); Field, Mark G. "The Concept of the 'Health System' at the Macrosociological Level," *Social Science and Medicine* 7:763-785 (1973); FOESSA, Fundación. *Estudio sociológico sobre la situación social de España 1970* (Madrid: Euramérica, 1970); Forsyth, Gordon. *Doctors and State Medicine: A Study of the British Health Service* (London: Pitman Medical Publishing, 1966); Fry, *Medicine in Three Societies, op. cit.;* Gemmill, Paul F. *Britain's Search for Health* (Philadelphia: University of Pennsylvania Press, 1960); Ginzberg, Eli and Ostow, Miriam. *Men, Money, and Medicine* (New York: Columbia University Press, 1969); Glaser, William A. "The Problems of the Hospital Administrator: Some American and Foreign Comparisons," *Hospital Administration* 9:6-22 (1964); Glaser, William A. *Paying the Doctor: Systems of Remuneration and Their Effects* (Baltimore: The Johns Hopkins Press, 1970); Glaser, William A. *Social Settings and Medical Organization: A Cross-National Study of the Hospital* (New York: Atherton Press, 1970); Goldmann, Franz. "Foreign Programs of Medical Care and Their Lessons," *New England Journal of Medicine* 234:156-160 (1946); Goldmann, Franz. "Public Medical Care in Great Britain and the Scandinavian Countries," *New England Journal of Medicine* 243:362 (1950); Grant, John B. "International Trends in Health Care," *American Journal of Public Health* 38:381-397 (1948); Gurin, Gerald; Veroff, Joseph; and Feld, Sheila. *Americans View Their Mental Health* (New York: Basic Books, 1960); Haber, Lawrence D. "Some Parameters for Social Policy in Disability: A Cross-National Comparison," *Milbank Memorial Fund Quarterly* 51:319-340 (1973); Halevi, M. S. "Health Services in Israel: Their Organization, Utilization and Financing," *Medical Care* 2:231-242 (1964); Hall, Thomas L. *Health Manpower in Peru. A Case Study in Planning* (Baltimore: The Johns Hopkins Press, 1969); Health Insurance Plan of Greater New York (Committee for the Special Research Project). *Health and Medical Care in New York* (Cambridge: Harvard University Press, 1957); Hilleboe, Herman E.; Barkhuus, Arne; and Thomas, William C. *Approaches to National Health Planning,* Public Health Paper No. 46 (Geneva: WHO, 1972); Hollingshead, August B. and Redlich, Frederick C. *Social Class and Mental Illness: A Community Study* (New York: John Wiley & Sons, 1958); International Labour Office. "Medical Care Protection Under Social Security Schemes—A Statistical Study of Selected Countries," *International Labour Review* 89:570-593 (1964); Kadushin, Charles. *Why People Go To Psychiatrists* (New York: Atherton Press, 1969); King, Maurice (ed.) *Medical Care in Developing Countries: A Primer on the Medicine of Poverty and a Symposium from Makerere* (London: Oxford University Press, 1966); Last, J. M. "The Organization and Economics of Medical Care in Australia," *New England Journal of Medicine* 272:293-297 (1965); Leighton, Alexander H., *et al. My Name is Legion* (New York: Basic Books, 1959); Lewis, Oscar. "Medicine and Politics in a Mexican Village," in: Paul, B. D. and Miller, W. B. (eds.) *Health, Culture and Community* (New York: Russell Sage Foundation, 1955) pp. 403-434; Lindsey, Almont. *Socialized Medicine in England and Wales* (Chapel Hill: University of North Carolina Press, 1962); Litman, T. J. and Robins, L. "Comparative Analysis of Health Care Systems. A Sociopolitical Approach," *Social Science and Medicine* 5:573-581 (1971); Logan, R. F. L. "Assessment of Sickness and Health in the Community: Needs and Methods," *Medical Care* 2:173-190 and 218-225 (1964); Lovell-Smith, J. B. *The New Zealand Doctor and the Welfare State* (Auckland: Blackwood & Janet Paul, 1966); Lynch, L. Riddick. *The Cross-Cultural Approach to Health Behavior* (Rutherford, N.J.: Fairleigh Dickinson University Press, 1969); Lynch, Matthew J. and Raphael, Stanley S. *Medicine and the State* (Springfield, Ill.: Charles C Thomas, 1963); Mabry, John H., *et al.* "The Natural History of an International Collaborative Study of Medical Care Utilization," *Social Sciences Information sur les Sciences Sociales* 5:37-55 (1966); Mechanic, David. *Medical Sociology: A Selective View* (New York: The Free Press, 1968); Mechanic, David. *Public Expectations and Health Care* (New York: John Wiley & Sons, 1972); Mechanic, David. *Politics, Medicine, and Social Science* (New York: John Wiley & Sons, 1974); Merton, Robert K.; Reader, George G.; and Kendall, Patricia L. (eds.) *The Student-Physician: Introductory Studies in the Sociology of Medical Education* (Cambridge: Harvard University Press, 1957); Mott, Frederick D. and Roemer, Milton I. *Rural Health and Medical Care* (New York: McGraw-Hill, 1948); Mountain, J. W. and Perrott, G. St. J. "Health Insurance Programs and Plans of Western Europe," *Public Health Reports* 62:369-399 (1947); Myers, Jerome K. and Bean, Lee L. *A Decade Later: A Follow-Up of Social Class and Mental Illness* (New York: John Wiley & Sons, 1968); Myers, Jerome K. and Roberts, Bertram H. *Family and Class Dynamics in Mental Illness* (New York: John Wiley & Sons, 1959); Myrdal, Gunnar. *Asian Drama: An Inquiry Into the Poverty of Nations* (New York: Pantheon, 1968) volume 3, pp. 1553-1619; National Medical Association. "Emergent Africa," *Journal of the National Medical Association* 59:227-264 (1967); Navarro, Vicente. "Methodology on Regional Planning of Personal Health Services. A Case Study: Sweden," *Medical Care* 8:386-394 (1970); Newman, George. *The Building of a Nation's Health* (London: Macmillan, 1939); Newsholme, Arthur. *International Studies on the Relation Between the Private and Official Practice of Medicine with Special Reference to the Prevention of Disease* (London: George Allen & Unwin Ltd., 1931) 3 volumes; Newsholme, Arthur and Kinsbury, John A. *Red Medicine: Socialized Health in Soviet Russia* (New York: Doubleday, Doran, 1933); Peterson, Osler L., *et al.* "What is Value for Money in Medical Care? Experiences in England and Wales, Sweden, and the U.S.A.," *The Lancet* (April 8, 1967) pp. 771-776; Political and Economic Planning (PEP). *Report on the British Health Services* (London: PEP, 1937); Popov, G. A. *Principles of Health Planning in the U.S.S.R.,* Public Health Paper No. 43 (Geneva: WHO, 1971); Querido, A. *The Development of Socio-Medical Care in the Netherlands* (London: Routledge and Kegan Paul, 1968); Rabin, *op. cit.;* Roemer, Milton I. "Rural Health Programs in Different Nations," *Milbank Memorial Fund Quarterly* 26:58-89 (1948); Roemer, Milton I. "Health Service Organization in Western Europe," *Milbank Memorial Fund Quarterly* 29:139-164 (1951); Roemer, Milton I. "Health Departments and Medical Care — A World Scanning," *American Journal of Public Health* 50:154-160 (1960); Roemer, Milton I. "General Hospitals in Europe," in: Owen, J. K. (ed.) *Modern Concepts of Hospital Administration* (Philadelphia: W. B. Saunders, 1962) pp. 17-37; Roemer, Milton I. "Workmen's Compensation and National Health Insurance Programs Abroad," *American Journal of Public Health* 55:209-214

The Health System Concept

Health can be considered both a source of energy and a basic resource.[11] The
health system is several things at the same time (the expression "health industry"

(1965); Roemer, Milton I. *The Organization of Medical Care under Social Security* (Geneva: International Labour Office, 1969); Roemer, Milton I. and Elling, R. H. "Sociological Research on Medical Care," *Journal of Health and Human Behavior* 4:49–68 (1963); Sand, René. *The Advance to Social Medicine* (London: Scandinavian Study Group); "Health Services Research in Scandinavia," *Milbank Memorial Fund Quarterly* 44:227–261 (1966); Schoeck, Helmut (ed.) *Financing Medical Care: An Appraisal of Foreign Programs* (Caldwell, Idaho: The Caxton Printers, 1962); Seham, Max. "An American Doctor Looks at Eleven Foreign Health Systems," *Social Science and Medicine* 3:65–81 (1969); Sigerist, Henry E. *American Medicine* (New York: Norton, 1934); Sigerist, Henry E. "From Bismarck to Beveridge: Developments and Trends in Social Security Legislation," *Bulletin of the History of Medicine* 8:365–388 (1943); Sigerist, Henry E. *Medicine and Health in the Soviet Union* (New York: Citadel Press, 1947); Somers, Herman M. and Somers, Anne R. *Doctors, Patients, and Health Insurance* (Washington, D.C.: The Brookings Institution, 1961); Srole, Leo, *et al. Mental Health in the Metropolis: The Midtown Manhattan Study* (New York: McGraw-Hill, 1962); Stern, Bernhard J. *American Medical Practice in the Perspectives of a Century* (New York: The Commonwealth Fund, 1945); Stevens, Rosemary. *Medical Practice in Modern England* (New Haven: Yale University Press, 1966); Stevens, Rosemary. *American Medicine and the Public Interest* (New Haven: Yale University Press, 1971); Stritesky, Jan. "Some Observations on the Czechoslovak Health Services," *Medical Care* 5:78–84 (1967); Sydenstricker, Edgar. *Health and Environment* (New York: McGraw-Hill, 1933); Taylor, Carl E., *et al. Health Manpower Planning in Turkey* (Baltimore: The Johns Hopkins Press, 1968); Tollefson, E. A. *Bitter Medicine. The Saskatchewan Medical Feud* (Saskatoon, Saskatchewan: Modern Press, 1963); Torrey, E. F. "Health Services in Ethiopia," *Milbank Memorial Fund Quarterly* 45:275–285 (1967); Ugalde, Antonio. *A Study of Decision Making in the Health Sector of Iran*, Consultantship report (Geneva: WHO, 1972); Ugalde, Antonio. *Consideraciones teóricas sobre el proceso de toma de decisiones en el sector salud* (Medellín, Colombia: Escuela Nacional de Salud Pública, 1972); U. S. Department of Health, Education and Welfare. *Social Security Programs Throughout the World* (Washington, D.C.: GPO, 1969); United States Public Health Service. *The Chicago-Cook County Health Survey* (Washington, D.C.: GPO, 1939); Wegman, Myron; Lin, Tsung-Yi; and Purcell, Elizabeth F. (eds.) *Public Health in the People's Republic of China* (New York: Josiah Macy, Jr. Foundation, 1973); von Hofsten, Erland. "The Effects of Social Change and Population Growth on the Health Status of the Nations; Their Implications for Medicine and Allied Professions," *Journal of Medical Education* 43:169–175 (1968); Weinerman, E. R. "Research into the Organization of Medical Practice," *Milbank Memorial Fund Quarterly* 44:104–145 (1966) part 2; Weinerman, E. R. "The Organization of Health Services in Eastern Europe," *Medical Care* 6:267–279 (1968); Weinerman, E. R. *Social Medicine in Eastern Europe: The Organization of Health Services and the Education of Medical Personnel in Czechoslovakia, Hungary and Poland* (Cambridge: Harvard University Press, 1968); Weinerman, "Research on Comparative Health Service Systems," *op. cit.*; White, Kerr L., *et al.* "International Comparisons of Health Service Systems," *Milbank Memorial Fund Quarterly* 46:117–125 (1968) part 2; White, Kerr L., *et al.* "International Comparisons of Medical-Care Utilization," *New England Journal of Medicine* 277:516–522 (1967); Willcocks, Arthur J. *The Creation of the National Health Service. A Study of Pressure Groups and a Major Social Policy Decision* (London: Routledge and Kegan Paul, 1967); World Health Organization. *First Report on the World Health Situation 1954–1956*, No. 94 (Geneva: Official Records of the WHO, 1959); World Health Organization. *Second Report on the World Health Situation 1957–1960*, No. 122 (Geneva: Official Records of the WHO, 1963); World Health Organization. *National Health Planning in Developing Countries*, Technical Report Series, No. 350 (Geneva: WHO, 1967); World Health Organization. *Third Report on the World Health Situation 1961–1964*, No. 155 (Geneva: Official Records of the WHO, 1967); World Health Organization. *Fourth Report on the World Health Situation 1965–1968*, No. 192 (Geneva: Official Records of the WHO, 1971); and World Health Organization, Regional Office for Europe. *Health Services in Europe* (Copenhagen: WHO, 1965).

[11]See, for example: Field, *Soviet Socialized Medicine, op. cit.,* p. ix; and Falk, *Security, op. cit.,* p. 3.

is often used as a synonym): a system of power relationships,[12] a matter of pressure group politics,[13] a system of social control,[14] a scientific biomedical setting, and a problem of allocation of resources. All these concepts are included, at different levels, in the general picture of the "health system," and they all have in common the human being—he is part of the input, the object of the transforming processes and the goal of the output. Finally, human beings are both patients and doctors.

Until now, we have used the term "health system" without specifying its content. It is possible to summarize the most important notions of "health system" from the most narrow to the most broad, thus obtaining an accurate "imagery" of it, to employ Lazarsfeld's terminology.[15] Several studies identify "health system" with "health services" or "health services system," phrases that are used interchangeably. The way the term is used here, the health system is something more than merely health services; it includes the medical profession, planning and implementation of health policies, payment system, preventive medicine, medical teaching and research, health education of the population, health bureaucracies, health ideologies and so on.

A common definition of this broader notion can be found in Bice and White:[16] "personnel and facilities which are organized in order that specialized knowledge and skills can be applied to individuals, collectivities of individuals, or their environment for purposes of promoting, protecting, or restoring their health."

The workshop proceedings on International Studies of Medical Care[17] defined the national health services system as:[18]

> . . . the organization, distribution and lay use of socially or legally sanctioned personnel, facilities and equipment which are employed in preventive actions for, and the rehabilitation and treatment of, persons who have departed from physical, emotional or social well-being, or who are at risk of doing so.

The definition of health system recently used by Mark G. Field is still a broader one:[19] "that societal mechanism which transforms generalized resources or inputs (mandate, knowledge, personnel and resources) into specialized outputs in the form of health services aimed at the health problems of the society." This includes all kinds of institutions, activities and efforts of a society related to the health of its people. This concept is very close to that of "health services systems" as it was usually employed by Weinerman:[20] "all of the activities of a

---

[12]Anderson and Kravits, *op. cit.*

[13]Eckstein, *Pressure Group Politics, op. cit.*

[14]Twaddle, Andrew C. "The Concept of Health Status," *Social Science and Medicine* 8:30 (1974).

[15]Lazarsfeld, Paul and Rosenberg, M. (eds.) *The Language of Social Research* (Glencoe, Ill.: The Free Press, 1955).

[16]Bice, Thomas W. and White, Kerr L. "Cross-National Comparative Research on the Utilization of Medical Services." *Medical Care* 9:253–271 (1971).

[17]The workshop was held in Asilomar, California, August, 1969.

[18]Cited in: Mabry, John H. "International Studies of Health Care," *Medical Care* 9:193–202 (1971).

[19]Field, "The Concept," *op. cit.,* p. 772.

[20]Weinerman, "Research on Comparative Health Service Systems," *op. cit.,* p. 272.

Table 23-1 A typology of comparative health systems research

Level of Analysis	Units of Observation	Years* (Logarithmic scale: 1930 · 1940 · 1950 · 1960 · 1970 · 1975)
Micro	Within	Faris and Dunham (1939) · Lewis (1955) · Field (1957) · Coser (1958) · Hollingshead and Redlich (1958) · Myers and Roberts (1959) · Gurin et al. (1960) · Anderson (1961) · Brewster and Seldowitz (1962) · Fendall (1963) · Bjorck (1964) · Last (1965) · Blum and Blum (1965) · Emery (1966) · Torry (1967) · Taylor (1968) · Aiken and Hage (1968) · Myers and Bean (1968) · Kadushin (1969) · Elling and Lee (1972)
Macro	Within	Newsholme and Kingsbury (1933) · PEP (1937) · Newman (1939) · USPHS (1939) · Sigerist (1943) · Caudill (1958) · Eckstein (1958) · Chen (1961) · Somers and Somers (1961) · Lindsey (1962) · Tollefson (1963) · Halevi (1964) · Brand (1965) · Lovell-Smith (1966) · Willcocks (1967) · Stritesky (1967) · Altman (1968) · Querido (1968) · Butterfield (1968) · Bierman et al. (1968) · Anderson and Kravits (1968) · Hall (1969) · Navarro (1970) · Ehrenreich and Ehrenreich (1970) · Popov (1971) · ACHA (1971) · Ugalde (1972) · Cochrane (1972)
Micro-Macro-	Within	Sydenstricker (1933) · Sigerist (1934) · The American Foundation (1937) · Stern (1945) · Sigerist (1947) · Mott and Roemer (1948) · Merton et al. (1957) · Health Insurance Plan (1957) · Leighton (1959) · Gemmill (1960) · Becker et al. (1961) · Srole et al. (1962) · Roemer and Elling (1963) · Forsyth (1966) · Stevens (1966) · Field (1967) · Baker and Perlman (1967) · Badgley (1968) · Duff and Hollingshead (1968) · Ginzberg and Ostow (1969) · Stevens (1971) · Elling et al. (1971) · Wegman et al. (1973)
Micro	Between	Falk (1936) · Goldmann (1946) · Mountain and Perrot (1947) · Grant (1948) · Roemer (1948) · Collings (1950) · Goldmann (1950) · Evang (1958) · Bravo (1958) · Boemer (1960) · Eckstein (1960) · Ben-David (1960a) · Logan (1964) · ILO (1964) · Glaser (1964) · Blesh (1965) · Roemer (1965) · Abel-Smith (1965) · King (1966) · White et al. (1967) · Peterson et al. (1967) · Lynch (1969) · DHEW (1969) · Foessa (1970) · Badgley (1971) · Bice and Kalimo (1971) · Haber (1973)
Macro	Between	Newsholme (1931) · Roemer (1951) · Sand (1952) · Falk (1958) · WHO (1959) · Dewhurst et al. (1961) · Roemer (1962) · Schoeck (1962) · WHO (1963) · Anderson (1963) · Evang et al. (1963) · WHO Europe (1965) · Scandinavian Study Group (1966) · WHO (1967a) · WHO (1967b) · Abel-Smith (1967) · Myrdal (1968) · Hofsten (1968) · Mechanic (1968) · Weinerman (1968) · Seham (1969) · Bryant (1969) · WHO (1971) · Hilleboe et al. (1972) · Field (1973)
Micro-Macro-	Between	Lynch and Raphael (1963) · Weinerman (1966) · Mabry et al. (1966) · Anderson (1967) · NMA (1967) · White (1968) · Fry (1969) · Roemer (1969) · Weinerman (1969) · Glaser (1970a) · Glaser (1970b) · Anderson et al. (1970) · Weinerman (1971) · Litman and Robins (1971) · Rabin (1972) · Babson (1972) · Mechanic (1972) · Anderson (1972a) · Altenstetter (1973) · Elling (1974) · Mechanic (1974) · De Miguel (1974)

*Logarithmic scale.
Sources: See Reference #10 for complete citations.

society which are designed to protect or restore health, whether directed to the individual, the community, or the environment."

My own definition of health system is closer to the notion of society as it relates to health, already developed by Elling.[21] *A health system is the set of relationships among institutions, social groups and individuals that is directed toward maintaining and improving the health status of a certain human population.*[22] This includes, needless to say, not only factual but ideological relationships.

"System" in my definition should be considered in the traditional systems analysis or systems sense.[23] According to Mervyn Susser, a system is a "set or assembly of factors connected with each other in some form of coherent relationships. A system is an abstraction."[24] The health system (as a social system) can be considered both a structure and a process. The main function of the health system is to transform inputs into outputs. Inputs are scarce, and we want certain outputs and not others.[25] Feedback in a systems approach is considered as the effect that processes and/or outputs may have on future inputs.

The definition of a system includes the delimitation of inside factors and of those that are operatively considered as external forces. Then the latter group is excluded from the analysis, although its existence is often reconsidered. In this sense a system is an operative definition of a sphere of relationships, trying to minimize external inputs and outputs. Consequently, a systems approach stresses the relationships of structures and the interdependence among factors. The goal of systems analysis, in any field, is to build a model and then to measure its closeness of fit to the real system.

Health Systems as Open Systems

The problems of conceptualization and measurement of health systems are greater than those of physical systems.[26] The health organization works as an open system in which the output, the health status of the population, reactivates the system, being in itself part of the new input.[27] This is shown in Figure 23-1 where I have adapted Weinerman's model of the relationships in the development of health services systems.[28]

[21]Elling, R. H. "The Shifting Power Structure in Health," *Milbank Memorial Fund Quarterly* 46:119–143 (1968).

[22]White, *op. cit.,* p. 119.

[23]An appropriate description of the system approach to any kind of organization is: Katz, Daniel and Kahn, Robert L. *The Social Psychology of Organizations* (New York: John Wiley & Sons, 1966) pp. 14–29; see especially chapter 2, "Organizations and the Systems Concept." A systems analysis model applied to health services can be found in: PAHO Advisory Committee on Medical Research. *Systems Analysis Applied to Health Services* (Washington, D.C.: PAHO, 1972).

[24]Susser, Mervyn. *Causal Thinking in the Health Sciences. Concepts and Strategies of Epidemiology* (New York: Oxford University Press, 1973) p. 48.

[25]Easton, David. "An Approach to the Analysis of Political Systems," *World Politics* 9:385 (1957).

[26]Anderson, *Health Care, op. cit.,* p. 12.

[27]Studies about the relationships between inputs and outputs can be found in: Cochrane, *Effectiveness and Efficiency, op. cit.;* and May, J. Joel. *Health Planning: Its Past and Potential* (Chicago: Center for Health Administration Studies, University of Chicago, 1967).

[28]Weinerman, "Research on Comparative Health Service Systems," *op. cit.,* p. 275.

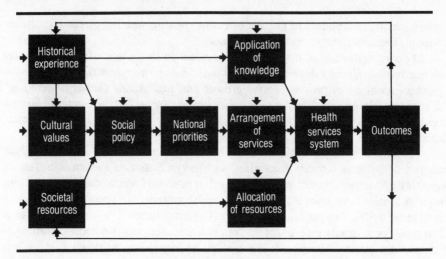

Source: Weinerman, E.R. "Research on Comparative Health Service Systems," *Medical Care* 9:272–290 (May–June 1971).

Figure 23-1. Relationships in the development of health service systems.

The scheme of an ideal comparative study of health systems could be summarized as follows:

1. INPUTS: These are the determinants of the system, including the study of different health care organizations, use of resources, planning, implementation, decision making mechanisms,[29] controls, etc.

2. PROCESSES: These are interactions between the different factors of the system, including relationships between health services and the health status of the population and the distribution of health delivery systems. They can be approached by analyzing within-unit differences of variables such as region, sex, social class, income, education, age, occupation, ethnicity-race, and so on.

3. OUTPUTS: These are consequences of the system, and include the health status of the population from a biological, medical and sociological point of view; and the medical ideologies, knowledge, attitudes and practices of the population related to health matters as outcomes of the given structure and of the medical profession.

4. EVALUATION: A summary would include the assessment of the effectiveness, efficiency and adequacy of health services systems in terms of their explicit goals, such as the attainment of the equality principle; the analysis of relationships between the health care system and the health status of the population; and the study of alternatives and priorities in the health system.

The organizational object of a health system is "to provide the highest level of health care to the greatest number of people at the least possible cost."[30] This

---

[29]A decision-making process model applied to a division of health environment can be found in: Ugalde, *Consideraciones, op. cit.;* and in: Ugalde, Antonio. "A Decision Model for the Study of Public Bureaucracies," *Policy Sciences* 4:75–84 (1973).

[30]Wagner, C. J. and Spring, S. "Program Packaging. A Process of Health Program Planning and Implementation," *Archives of Environmental Health* 12:660–669 (1966).

means maximizing the quantity of health care and number of people served, improving the conditions of life and quality of care, and minimizing cost. The goal of a health system has been stated as *one open system providing equal access to the highest quality of health care for all citizens in a given area or nation,* or even better, for all residents in an area.[31] A very efficient health delivery system can make irrelevant characteristics such as where the patients live, their race or income, or how educated they are. What such a system will not avoid is having relatively more cases from lower-income groups, the less educated population, rural and slum dwellings, etc. Equality, as far as the functioning of a national health care system is concerned, is only an "illusory sun" (to use the Marxian expression) if the rest of the society is not based on the same principle.[32] Relative inequality seems to be part of every type of existent health organization, whether it be a pluralistic, health insurance, health service, or even socialized system.[33]

The idea of control (as it has been stated already by Boguslaw)[34] suggests that the results of a system should be consistent with the expected values. The measures of outputs of health systems can be various. One may look at, among other things: effects (results of some special actions); and effectiveness or efficacy (the system is able to bring about the result intended); and efficiency (state or quality of being able to perform duties well). In sum, a health system model is a model for manipulation.

For the measurement of the functioning of a health system, one should look at least at the following features: 1) the ability of the system to produce the results planned and/or intended; 2) the ability of the system to perform its duties well, and with a relative maximum of quality; 3) the possibility of introducing the "equality principle" into all the different aspects and/or stages of health care; 4) the transformation of increases of inputs into proportional increases of outputs; and 5) the level to which the system controls itself or depends on external factors or decisions.

A Causal Model for Health Systems

A model is a mechanism that "simulates" reality. Skepticism about a whole-systems approach is partially based on the difficulties in dealing with its study and application to reality.[35] Backett has pointed out that medical research has suffered from a notable absence of models.[36]

---

[31]Bryant, *op. cit.,* p. 311.

[32]The main conclusion of a study done by the Research for Policy Committee of the Committee for Economic Development (never accused of leftism), in April 1973, referring to the United States, was: "Faulty allocation of resources is a major cause of inadequacies and inequalities in U.S. health services that result today in poor or substandard care for large segments of the population." Committee for Economic Development. *Building a National Health-Care System* (New York: CED, 1973).

[33]Rabin, *op. cit.,* p. 83; and Mechanic, *Politics, op. cit.,* p. 279.

[34]Boguslaw, Robert. *The New Utopians: A Study of System Design and Social Change* (Englewood Cliffs, N.J.: Prentice Hall, 1965) p. 31.

[35]LaPalombara, Joseph. "Macrotheories and Microapplications in Comparative Politics: A Widening Chasm," *Comparative Politics* 1:52–78 (1968).

[36]Backett, E. Maurice. "Local and Intermediate Health Service Administration in Britain, A Personal Note on Problems," WHO/CHS/INF, Geneva, 1971 (reproduced).

The main goal—or expected output—of a health system is to improve the health status of the human population in some defined area. But "health status of the population" is a vague term. In order to measure outputs in relation to the inputs introduced into the system, it is necessary to make clear detailed objectives. There is a tendency to see the health status of a population as a fatalistic outcome of some external (and difficult to control) factors such as the social, economic and political environments, and on this point the policies between (and even within) countries may change.[37] In general, the intended output has been to improve the level of and equality of distribution of the health status of a given population in a defined area. This principle was defined in 1944 by Sigerist in the following terms: "All the people should have medical care, irrespective of race, creed, sex, or economic status, and irrespective of whether they live in town or country."[38] Thus the concept of health status includes both level and distribution of health.

Among the classic functions of a health system have been: prevention, prognosis, diagnosis, treatment, custody and rehabilitation of a given population. In addition to these, we can include the education of health professionals and the health education of the population.

Other authors have divided health systems into factors within only one level of analysis,[39] but I am going to take into account different subsystems. The advantage of doing so is that all ranges of variables and data can be included, from the most internal to the most external factors, in order to explain the whole health system. These subsystems are considered "open-linked systems" in Caudill's terminology.[40] Subsystem A represents individual variables; subsystem B, variables related to institutions or similar human groups; subsystem C, variables that refer to the global society; and subsystem D, variables that depend on larger systems. Within each subsystem I have included several factors (or sets of indicators):

Subsystems	Factors	
Individual	A1	Health status
	A2	Biomedical factors
	A3	Psychological factors
Institutions	B1	Health services
	B2	Health organization
	B3	Health planning
Society	C1	Sociocultural patterns
	C2	Political structure
	C3	Economic development
	C4	Demographic structure
Larger systems	D1	Environment

[37]Messing, Simon D. "Discounting Health: The Issue of Subsistence and Care in an Underdeveloped Country," *Social Science and Medicine* 7:911–916 (1973).

[38]Sigerist, Henry. "Medical Care for All the People," *Canadian Journal of Public Health* 35:253–267 (1944).

[39]Bice and White, *op. cit.,* p. 253; and Andersen, Smedby, and Anderson, *op. cit.*

[40]Caudill, *Effects of Social and Cultural Systems, op. cit.*

The Individual Subsystem

Health status (A1) is the dependent variable (or the output) of the health system. It can be measured by such indicators as mortality rates, morbidity, analysis of causes of death, positive mental health, etc.[41] The quoted definition of the World Health Organization (WHO)[42] embraces a triple state of mental, social and physical well-being: "health status has to be looked at from the community as well as from the personal point of view. Social well-being might therefore be regarded as a state of predisposing conditions of health." There are no limits to the health status of a population. The term "health status" may also fall within the labelling theory, and then "status" is understood in its sociological sense, as "a kind of social label which can be attached to an individual and which defines to some extent how he is expected to behave and how others should behave towards him."[43] This approach is rarely used in the comparative literature.

The biomedical factors (A2) are mainly related to the incidence of illness, while social factors are more related to the "prevalence" of illness. Biomedical factors include race, weight, height, biological inheritance, impairment, etc. They are linked to various deviations from the normal functioning of the body, influencing the present and/or future health status of an individual. One of the important facts of health systems research (sometimes forgotten) is that morbidity and mortality cannot always be modified simply by a better health care organization. In fact, the fantastic decline of mortality rates in this century has not reduced illness, and some experts think that morbidity rates have probably increased.[44] The outputs are often inconsistent with the inputs and/or the explicit national goals of the planning procedures.

Psychological factors (A3) grow more important each day, due to their influence on the mental health status of the populations of developed (and undeveloped) countries. There is an abundant bibliography on stress (or social stress) that supports this statement.[45] Social-psychological measures of health, as opposed to purely biomedical measures, include the ability to perform a social role,[46] and such behavioral expressions as sickness, quality of life, positive mental health,

[41]Patrick, D. L.; Bush, J. W.; and Chen, M. M. "Toward an Operational Definition of Health," *Journal of Health and Social Behavior* 14:6–23 (1973).

[42]World Health Organization. *Measurement of Levels of Health,* Technical Report Series, No. 137 (Geneva: WHO, 1957) p. 8.

[43]Twaddle, *op. cit.*

[44]Somers and Somers, *op. cit.*

[45]Grinker, Roy R. and Spiegel, John P. *Men Under Stress* (Philadelphia: Blakiston, 1945); Selye, Hans. *The Stress of Life* (New York: McGraw-Hill, 1956); Janis, Irving L. *Psychological Stress: Psychoanalytic and Behavioral Studies of Surgical Patients* (New York: John Wiley & Sons, 1958); Caudill, *Effects of Social and Cultural Systems, op. cit.*; Langner, Thomas S. and Michael, Stanley T. *Life Stress and Mental Health* (New York: The Free Press, 1963); Dohrenwend, Bruce P. and Dohrenwend, Barbara S. *Social Status and Psychological Disorders: A Causal Inquiry* (New York: Wiley-Interscience, 1969); and Levine, Sol and Scotch, Norman A. (eds.) *Social Stress* (Chicago: Aldine, 1970).

[46]See: Elinson, J. "Toward Socio-medical Health Indicators," paper presented at the International Conference of Medical Sociology, Jablonna, Poland, August 20–25, 1973, pp. 5ff; and Parsons, Talcott. *The Social System* (New York: The Free Press, 1951).

happiness and satisfaction, unmet needs for health care, and so on. Satisfaction with care includes analyses of expectations, costs, treatment procedures, racial or religious segregation, etc. These analyses can be made at different levels and samples, such as the whole population, the politicians, planners, providers, the medical profession, and patients. Sociological studies of health systems apparently have not paid enough attention to these biomedical and psychological factors. Psychological variables have a strong influence on modern life, and we are living, according to some authors, in a sick society.

The Institutions Subsystem

Popov has defined health services (B1) as "all those personal and community services, including medical care, directed toward the protection and promotion of the health of the community."[47] Health services are the institutionalized media for maintaining and restoring people's health. Health services are, consequently, institutions structured and designed to cure people; hospitals are no longer places where one is sent to die. Health services also include assessment of the quantity and quality of health equipment and health manpower, distribution of services, resources and supplies, accessibility of services, etc. The demand for health services depends largely on 1) technical and scientific levels of society; 2) social and cultural values, and our awareness of them; and 3) the accessibility of resources. Therefore, the existence of health services is different from the use of health services. The barriers can be, among others, geographical, cultural, economic, educational or those of appropriate coordination of efforts. We may consider that "within very wide ranges there is no such entity as an adequate health service."[48]

Sociological research about regional and rural-urban differences in health services is scarce.[49] An accurate model for health systems should differentiate between *health services resources* and *health services utilization* because both factors have different relations to other variables. It is crucial to remark that health status depends on the utilization of health services and not on the availability of health services, a topic sometimes neglected in the literature. Paradoxically, some studies have demonstrated that health services have nothing to do with the health status of the population, and that socioeconomic level and other conditions of life are more crucial.

A similar health status of the population can be obtained through a different health organization (B2). This is the "equifinality principle," which is to say that a system can obtain the same objectives from different initial conditions and by different paths.[50] The present literature in the comparative health systems field has recognized that there are several ways of producing a similar output.[51] In general, "there is a growing convergence in medical care organization in modern

[47]Popov, *op. cit.,* p. 11.

[48]Anderson, "Toward a Framework," *op. cit.,* p. 30.

[49]Krapio, Leo A. "The Future of Health and Social Services: Europe," paper presented at the International Conference on Medical Sociology, Jablonna, Poland, August 20–25, 1973, p. 9.

[50]Katz and Kahn, *op. cit.,* pp. 25–26.

[51]For example: "Low death rates are compatible with quite different levels of medical care provision and utilization." See: Peterson, *op. cit.,* p. 744.

nations," a statement that has been repeated by many authors.[52] Nevertheless, we are witnesses of a certain "cultural lag" between health technology advances and health organizations, a lag found in almost all countries.

The health organization factor may include such indicators as: centralization and structure of the decision-making processes, levels of control of the health organization, institutional competition, fragmentation of services, regionalization of services, coordination of tasks, coverage of the population, private practitioners, group practice and other forms of medical practice, channels of information and public understanding about health organization, health education, and, among the most important ones, prepayment and/or insurance systems.

There are probably more books about health planning (B3) than there are actual health plans. In most countries health planning is simply nonexistent.[53] Even if it exists, the important aspect is the degree to which a given health plan is really implemented; and even if it is implemented, its efficacy and/or efficiency can be minimal. In the latter case, the effects of health planning on health status can be zero or even negative if such planning means unequal distribution of resources.

Among the problems that should be taken into account in health planning, sociologists are more interested in: 1) the analysis of health needs and problems; 2) the inclusion in planning of basic general guidelines, and the coordination of planning with other sectors;[54] 3) the allocation of resources;[55] 4) the power to implement the plan, whether by suggestion or compulsion; 5) the presentation of alternatives and/or strategies; 6) the definition of priorities; 7) the methods for evaluating outputs; 8) the development of preventive and public health measures; and 9) the rigidity of planning. The first principle of health planning is to relate all factors of the health system to each other. This is illustrated by Sigerist's example:[56]

> . . . building hospitals in the Soviet Union is not primarily a question of money, as it is in capitalistic countries. It is also a question of the amount of labor and bricks available.

According to these ideas, health planning is not merely allocation of resources and/or control, but the integration of health planning in other subsystems. Many times the term "health planning" is used for ex post facto policies, based not on expert advice or planning but simply politically dictated. Hilleboe et al.[57] have pointed out that "there has been a tendency in some less developed countries to start planning partly because it is fashionable and partly as a way of attracting

[52]Mechanic, *Politics, op. cit.,* p. 37.

[53]Planning is in essence "an organized, conscious and continual attempt to select the best available alternatives to achieve specific goals." See: Waterston, Albert. *Development Planning: Lessons of Experience* (Baltimore: The Johns Hopkins Press, 1965) p. 26.

[54]Elling has specified it as "the extent to which planning in this sphere [planning for health] takes into account plans in other sectors and the extent to which general economic and social planning takes into account planning for health." Elling, "Case Studies," *op. cit.*

[55]For example, a Markovian model for planning personal health services is presented by: Navarro, Vicente. "Planning Personal Health Services: A Markovian Model," *Medical Care* 7:242–249 (1969).

[56]Sigerist, Henry. *Socialized Medicine in the Soviet Union* (New York: Norton, 1937) p. 14.

[57]Hillboe, Barkhuus and Thomas, *op. cit.,* p. 18.

foreign grants and loans.'' Many of these plans have had little if any effect on the health status of the population.

The Society Subsystem

Sociocultural patterns (C1) should not be neglected since they explain some of the variance in the health of a population that is not determined by purely economic or political factors. Mechanic[58] has suggested studying both the relationships between cultural content and cultural lifestyles and between definitions of health and responses to illness. On the other hand, Twaddle[59] thinks that much of the variation in the appraisal of health status categories can be attributed to differences in how illness is defined by societies or even smaller groups. From a cultural point of view the relativity of the concept of disease is more important. Caudill has affirmed that it is possible "at a certain point in society's history to die of a disease without ever being sanctioned as sick by the society itself."[60]

Cultural patterns are important in the way in which people perceive, react and respond to symptoms and/or illnesses. Among these sociocultural patterns, it is worthwhile to study values,[61] attitudes, level of education, personal hygiene, nutrition and sanitation patterns, religion, ideologies of the medical and paramedical professions, traditions, folk medicine, ethical considerations,[62] social mobility and social isolation, and so on. Last but not least, social stratification is one of the most important variables in the determination of the health status of a population. The general principle is that "the social class system of a society results in a different distribution of rewards, including health and health care."[63] The implicit hypothesis may be stated as: the availability of health services varies inversely with the need for it in a certain area and population.[64]

It is also a fact that health systems greatly depend upon the political structure (C2) of the society[65] and the power relationships between groups and institutions.[66] Other variables that should be observed are: regime structure, concentration of authority and power, channels of power, decision-making processes, mass media structure, legal considerations of the political subsystem, role of elites and intelligentsia and local leadership structure.[67] Generally speaking, health status

[58]Mechanic, *Medical Sociology, op. cit.,* p. 52.

[59]Twaddle, *op. cit.*

[60]Caudill, William, "Applied Anthropology in Medicine," in: Kroeber, A. L. (ed.) *Anthropology Today* (Chicago: The University of Chicago Press, 1953) p. 780.

[61]A classic example of this group is "water boiling" in Peru: Wellin, Edward. "Water Boiling in a Peruvian Town," in: Paul and Miller, *op. cit.,* pp. 71–103; or "voodoo death," see: Cannon, Walter B. "Voodoo Death," *American Anthropologist* 44:169–181 (1942).

[62]See, for example: Grundy, F. and Reinke, W. A. *Health Practice Research and Formalized Managerial Methods,* Public Health Paper No. 51 (Geneva: WHO, 1973) p. 22.

[63]Elling, R. H. (ed.) *National Health Care* (Chicago: Aldine, 1971) p. 65.

[64]See also: Hart, J. T. "The Inverse Care Law," *The Lancet* (1971) p. 405.

[65]Field, "The Concept," *op. cit.*

[66]Elling, R. H. "The Shifting Power Structure in Health," *Milbank Memorial Fund Quarterly* 46:119–143 (January 1968) part 2; Eckstein, *The English Health Service, op. cit.;* Ugalde, *A Study of Decision Making, op. cit.;* Ugalde, *Consideraciones, op. cit.;* and Ugalde, "A Decision Model," *op. cit.*

[67]See: Lewis, Oscar, *op. cit.* The influence of community leaders in the decision-making processes of the health systems is described in: Elling and Lee, *op. cit.*

depends on the political structure through health organization, payment systems, regional imbalances, etc.

It is almost automatic to link health status to economic development (C3).[68] But we should be aware that this relationship is not always positive—for example, in such cases as venereal diseases, congenital malformations, lung cancer, poliomyelitis and cirrhosis of the liver. Nevertheless, it is still true that in the world "the chief cause of disease is poverty."[69] In studies of health systems of developing and underdeveloped countries we discover that in some areas of the world hospitals are still places where people go to die, that there are more doctors than nurses, that some health authorities stress native and quack medicine, that cholera (among other illnesses) is endemic and that most of the population is not served by modern medicine. Economic development is usually measured by global indicators of goods and services produced, capital resources, investment, etc., with limited attention to their distribution among members of the society and their consequences for the quality of life (food, clothing, housing, etc.). Other indicators to take into account are, obviously: economic resources, socioeconomic circumstances, financial structure, level and distribution of income and occupational structure.

The demographic structure (C4) has been traditionally linked to the health status of a population as both its cause and effect. Nonetheless there have been cases in which both the mortality rate and health status have decreased.[70] Among demographic factors, it is possible to distinguish between the demographic characteristics of the units of observation (generally speaking, nations, regions, areas, cities), such as size, density, urbanization, etc.; and personal variables, such as rates of divorce, age, sex, marital status, migration, illegitimacy, and so on. Except for extreme cases, the latter group has a stronger influence on health status.

Larger Systems as a Subsystem

The influence of environment (D1) on health status seems less important in post-industrial societies than in underdeveloped or developing countries. If we distinguish between social and physical environments, then we can recognize that social environment plays an important role in the mental health status of a population.[71] In addition, such factors as geographical structure, physical environment, climatic factors, etc. clearly affect physical health. Indicators such as housing conditions, water supply, sewage disposal, water and atmosphere pollution, control and hygiene of food and disposal of rubbish and excreta are part of the public health structure of a given area.

Linked Open Systems

All of the factors just mentioned are the most important ones related to health status within an operative definition of health system. Figure 23-2 presents

---

[68]Bryant, *op. cit.,* p. 312.

[69]Sigerist, Henry. "Socialized Medicine," *The Yale Review* 463–481 (Spring 1938).

[70]Moya, Gonzalo, *et al.* "Las enfermedades neurologicas enfermedades sociales," *Revista de Sanidad Pública e Higiene* (1964).

[71]Coe, Rodney M. *Sociology of Medicine* (New York: McGraw-Hill, 1970) p. 15.

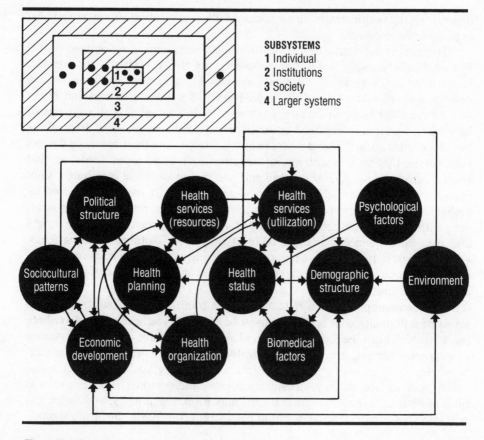

SUBSYSTEMS
1 Individual
2 Institutions
3 Society
4 Larger systems

Figure 23-2. Causal model for health systems.

a tentative scheme of a causal model for health systems, showing graphically the causal relationships between these factors, and, in the upper right hand corner, their clustering by subsystems. Health services resources and health services utilization have been separated as I have already suggested.

The purpose of a causal model is both to represent reality and to give a scheme for predicting effects. The present causal model for the analysis of health systems does not exhaust either the complex problem of defining *all* the factors that produce changes in the health status of a population or all their possible relationships. I have chosen only those factors and relationships that have a strong influence (direct or indirect) on the health status of the population in order to study them, not in an isolated way, but as interacting variables with multiple, mutual relationships. Up to a certain level most of the relationships of the causal model (Figure 23–2) are reciprocal and multiple; however, there are several feedback processes in the model. To illustrate, the bettering of the health status of a population can be reflected in a substantial reduction of the mortality rate (and vice versa); and if there is no change in birth rates, it may contribute to appreciable changes in economic growth per capita. The arrows indicate a supposed causal direction of influence where the effects are more clear and/or important. We have eliminated the error arrows (using "path analysis" terminology) for reasons of clarity. There are as many models of actual health systems as there are countries; the present one is only a general model that can and should be varied in each study.

The causal model of health systems allows us to concentrate resources and efforts on any of the independent variables. Sometimes changes in subsystems 3 and 4 (see Figure 23-2), such as demographic structure or sociocultural patterns, can have a greater impact than changes in subsystem 2 (health services, health planning or health organization). One school of thought, for example that of Miller Guerra in Portugal,[72] or Giovanni Berlinguer in Italy,[73] considers that a real change in subsystem 2 cannot be accomplished without previous changes in subsystem 3. Putting it another way, reform of health services and organization can only begin by a change of the whole political structure of a country, especially in authoritarian regimes. This is not an original idea, and the modern discussion may include all subsystems of society. In the case of health, this is dubious because an authoritarian regime may socialize medicine even more easily than a pluralistic society. Juan Campos has called attention to these paradoxes in his recent article, "Medicine: Socialization for What?",[74] referring to one such authoritarian regime, Spain.

Conclusion

In some sense, the health system is a "black box"—we still do not know how it functions, and for the most part, present day research is still exploratory. The links of economic, political and cultural factors to the health status of the population have not been systematically analyzed in the literature.[75] Empirical research in health systems is rather new and, consequently, current theories and data are minimal. But we should not fall into the trap of believing that lack of data is the most important problem. Even more pressing is *who* uses the data and *how*. Knowledge alone in the health field is meaningless without analysis of the political use and implementation of that knowledge. This is especially important in nondemocratic countries, which are still the majority today. For this reason it is not surprising to find that those countries needing information the most are also those that do not have the information.

[72]Guerra, J. P. Miller. *Medicina e sociedade* (Lisbon: Morais, 1961); Guerra, J. P. Miller, "Tradicão e modernidade nas facultades de Medicina," *Análise social* 6:639–681 (1968); Guerra, J. P. Miller. *As universidades tradicionais e a sociedade moderna* (Lisbon: Moraes, 1970); Guerra, J. P. Miller. *Progresso na liberdade,* 2nd ed. (Lisbon: Moraes, 1973); and Guerra, J. P. Miller and Tome, F. "A profissão medica e os problemas de saúde e da assistencia," *Análise Social* 2:623–651 (1964).

[73]Berlinguer, G. *La sanità pubblica nella programmazione economica (1964–1968)* (Rome: Leonardo Edizioni Scientifiche, 1964); Berlinguer, G. *Sicurezza e insicurezza sociale* (Rome: Leonardo Edizioni Scientifiche, 1968); Berlinguer, G. *Psichiatria e potere* (Rome: Editori Riuniti, 1969); Berlinguer, G. *Medicina e politica* (Bari: De Donato, 1973); Berlinguer, G., *et al. Enti locali è politica sanitaria* (Rome: Editori Riuniti, 1966); Berlinguer, G. and Delogu, S. *La medicina é malata* (Bari: Editori Laterza, 1959); and Berlinguer, G. and Terranova, F. *La strage degli innocenti. Indagine sulla mortalità infantile in Italia* (Florence: La Nuova Italia, 1972).

[74]Campos, Juan. "Medicine: Socialization for What?" *Social Science and Medicine* 7:959–966 (1973).

[75]Peterson, *op. cit.,* p. 771.

24 Organization Theory and Health Services Delivery

Delivery of health services to the American people has increasingly become an organizational, as opposed to an individual, process. The changing character of health care delivery patterns over the last 10 years reflects this trend. Greater percentages of physicians and related health professionals are employed by organizations; many more consumers are looking to organizations rather than individual practitioners for receipt of health services; and there has been a tremendous growth in hospital emergency room utilization. Furthermore, individual delivery organizations, such as hospitals, clinics, nursing homes, and health departments, are finding themselves enveloped in larger organizational relationships in which they must not only contend with each other, but with a growing number of outside agencies as well (for example, the Social Security Administration, planning agencies, state rate review bodies, Professional Standards Review Organizations).

The increasing involvement of the Federal government as both a purchaser and a deliverer of services, developments in medical technology, and changes in social norms and legal definitions of illness (for example, alcoholism and drug addiction) have been major forces in reshaping the delivery of health services. As a result, the individual delivery organization has found itself operating in an environment that appears day by day to become more complex and diverse, to be subject to rapid change and to increased difficulty in predicting both the occurrence and content of change. Currently, there appears to be a general demand for greater organizational responsiveness and accountability, but little recognition that these demands frequently come from different groups with varying notions of accountability, often placing the organization in the position of having to reconcile incompatible objectives. For the Federal government, accountability is often defined in terms of cost control and rapid adjustment to programs designed to bring costs under control, while for local consumer groups accountability is often defined in terms of added facilities and services and greater consumer participation in decision-making. For health services administrators, physicians, and other health care professionals, major organizational issues are raised involving the ability to adapt to such divergent demands, to adopt innovations and implement changes, to manage external dependencies, and to restructure internal relationships. In brief, health care professionals with an expanded knowledge of their specialized fields are also being called upon to have an increased understanding of

This paper was supported in part by a general research grant from the National Institute of Health of the School of Public Health and Community Medicine, University of Washington. The author wishes to especially acknowledge the assistance of Kathy Green in the preparation of this paper.

how organizations work as well as the organization's potential for growth and change.

To a considerable extent, developments in the field of organization theory and behavior parallel the ferment occurring in the delivery of health services. Basic disciplinary differences in the approach to the study of organizations, the state of current theory and measurement, and varying priorities for further research characterize much of the existing literature. Reviews by Pugh,[1] Lichtman and Hunt,[2] Argyris,[3] and Sofer[4] summarize some of these issues—in particular, the disciplinary differences in terms of the psychologists' interests in the effects of the organization on individual behavior and job satisfaction, the social psychologist's concern with group problem-solving and group dynamics, and the sociologist's concern with the effects of size and related variables such as the division of labor. The literature pertaining solely to health services delivery organizations—in particular, hospitals[5, 6]—also reflects these differences. Given this state of affairs, the issue that this paper addresses is the extent to which organization theory can provide any guidelines to health care professionals charged with the daily management of hospitals, clinics, and related delivery organizations. Specifically, this paper will discuss issues of policy and administrative importance and relate these to developments in organization theory; examine the limitations of present research; suggest a framework to remedy such shortcomings; and explore the implications of this framework for further understanding of health services delivery organizations.

Policy/Administrative and Disciplinary Issues

Table 24-1 outlines some of the major policy/administrative issues facing health services delivery organizations, along with the associated disciplinary issues relevant to the further development of organization theory. Major policy/administrative issues are concerned with the efficiency and quality of services delivered, the influence of environmental forces and the impact of new medical technology on such services, the causes and effects of organizational change, and the internal structuring and accommodation to such change by health professionals. In operational terms, the concern is with the organizational impact of reimbursement policies, unionization efforts, certificate-of-need legislation, rate review boards, Professional Standards Review Organizations (PSROs), regionalization versus decentralization of new technology and services (for example,

[1]Pugh, D. S. "Modern Organization Theory: A Psychological and Sociological Study," *Psychological Bulletin* 66:235 (1966).

[2]Lichtman, C. M. and Hunt, R. G. "Personality and Organization Theory: A Review of Some Conceptual Literature," *Psychological Bulletin* 76:271 (1971).

[3]Argyris, C. *The Applicability of Organizational Sociology* (Cambridge, England: Cambridge University Press, 1972).

[4]Sofer, C. *Organizations in Theory and Practice* (New York: Basic Books, 1972).

[5]Georgopoulos, B. S. *Organization Research on Health Institutions* (Ann Arbor: Institute for Social Research, The University of Michigan, 1972).

[6]Georgopoulos, B. S. *Hospital Organization Research: Review and Sourcebook* (Philadelphia: W. B. Saunders, 1975).

cancer treatment and kidney dialysis treatment),[7] and demands for greater consumer involvement and public accountability. Major organization theory issues concern the ability to build more comprehensive theories of organizations;[8] to develop a greater understanding of interorganizational relationships and the impact of the external environment on organizational behavior; to develop a fuller understanding of the consequences of technological change; and to examine in greater detail the management and implementation of change in organizations, particularly in regard to the coordination and integration of new work activities with old ones and the rearrangements of power and role relationships among those affected.

New Medical Technology

One issue that cuts across all of these concerns is the introduction of new medical technology. It represents a change in the external environment which frequently involves increased interorganizational relationships and often affects the internal structuring of hospital departments and role relationships. Furthermore, the introduction of new medical technology frequently interacts with changes in "software" relationships—that is, with changes in peoples' knowledge, values and attitudes toward the delivery of health services (for example, health care as a right) that have given rise to behavioral changes in the form of new legislation, new agencies, and new programs. These changes are complicated by the secondary consequences of earlier technological change, such as the relative value of coronary care units and their geographic distribution[9] and the ethical resource allocation problems posed by the introduction and refinement of renal dialysis and related lifesaving technology. Thus, the impact of technology on health care delivery organizations is primarily through its interaction with basic changes in software relationships and in the management of the secondary consequences of prior technological change.

As Scott[10] has noted, these issues particularly come to the forefront in terms of the different perceptions that different groups of professionals have regarding technology. Physicians, for example, see technology as being very problematic and requiring the exercise of a great deal of individual judgment. Physicians build their professional careers by being able to exercise discretion in the use of technology. Administrators, on the other hand, view technology as something to be routinized if possible, to be made predictable and controllable. Administrators build their professional careers by structuring and rationalizing the technological core of their organizations.

---

[7]For an excellent description and analysis of the issues surrounding new medical technology (in particular, transplantation and kidney dialysis), see: Fox, R. L. and Swazey, J. P. *The Courage to Fail: A Social View of Organ Transplants and Dialysis* (Chicago: University of Chicago Press, 1974).

[8]Hage, J. "The State of Organizational Theory," paper presented at the annual conference of the American Sociological Association, Montreal, Canada, August 1974.

[9]Bloom, B. S. and Peterson, O. L. "Patient Care Needs and Medical Care Planning: The Coronary Care Unit as a Model," *New England Journal of Medicine* 290:1171 (May 1974).

[10]Scott, W. R. "Professionals in Hospitals: Technology and the Organization of Work," in: Georgopoulos, *Organization Research*, pp. 139–158.

Table 24-1.   Key policy/administrative and disciplinary issues

Public policy/administrative issues	Disciplinary issues
1 How can health services delivery organizations be organized to achieve greater efficiency and effectiveness in terms of costs, technical quality of care, patient satisfaction, and meeting community needs? What are the managerial implications of the fact that these broad objectives may be incompatible with each other?	1 Is enough known to begin to build a more comprehensive theory of organizations? For example, can a theory be developed that would systematically link environmental, structural and process variables not only with each other but with organizational outcomes as well? In brief, is it possible to move beyond existing "middle-range" theories?
2 In what specific ways does the environment influence the efficiency and effectiveness of health services delivery organizations? Particular issues concern the effects of health planning organizations, third-party reimbursement strategies, and various state and national groups (e.g., PSROs). How are health services organizations adapting to these forces? Are some strategies better than others?	2 In what ways does an organization's environment affect its internal structuring of activities and the outcomes (efficiency, effectiveness, etc.) that it experiences? In what ways can an organization affect other organizations with which it interacts?
3 What is the effect of introducing new medical technology? Are some strategies of introducing technological change better than others, and under what circumstances?	3 A literature on the innovation process in organizations is beginning to accumulate. There exists a need to refine current theories, particularly in regard to the impact of technological innovations on organizational effectiveness. A sub-issue in the study of health care organizations is the fact that technological innovation increasingly raises moral and ethical issues involving questions of who should live and who should die. This situation places additional stress on physicians, nurses and other health professionals working in hospitals and represents a key factor to be considered in the study of technological change in these organizations.
4 What will be the effects of increased vertical and horizontal integration of health services organizations, e.g., multifacility systems, mergers, shared services, growth in ambulatory care functions such as health maintenance organization affiliations?	4 In what ways (if any) is the initiation and implementation of change in largely nonprofit organizations different from proprietary organizations? What is the relationship between an organization's goal structure, internal structuring of activities, outcomes, and change? What modes of coordination are used to integrate new and often different work activities?
5 What are the causes and effects of changes in relationships between community groups, board members, health services administrators, physicians, and allied health professionals? A major issue concerns the increased demand for accountability. A related development appears to be a push toward greater integration of clinical and administrative decision-making. What effects are likely to result?	5 In what ways are power and influence in organizations affected by key participants' abilities to manipulate external forces? What strategies do key participants use to mold changes in their own self-image and self-conception of their work, and what effect does this have on organization efficiency and effectiveness?

Practical Contributions

The main purpose of Table 24–1 is to juxtapose the two sets of issues and suggest that many of the operational concerns of health care policy-makers, administrators, and providers are of direct interest to social scientists interested in the study of organizations.

Furthermore, organization theory as a field appears to offer two inherent advantages in its potential ability to contribute to the "world of practice."[11] First, by its very nature organization theory is a multidisciplinary field involving contributions by sociologists, psychologists, economists, political scientists, and others trained in multidisciplinary-oriented behavioral science centers. There exists a general consensus that the study of organizations requires such an approach and, perhaps more importantly, that a greater degree of interdisciplinary work is required in which the different perspectives are brought together within single study teams to focus on related issues of importance. In particular, this would appear to be true for those interested in obtaining a more comprehensive understanding of health care delivery organizations and in developing a more comprehensive theory of organizational behavior.

Second, there is a recognized subdivision of organization theorists who work primarily in the applied area; namely, those engaged in organizational consultation and development. While communications and linkages between the theorists and empiricists and the organizational development investigators have not yet fulfilled their potential, the possibility exists for a greater merging of theory and practice than is perhaps true in many other fields.

The following section examines the relative failure of organization researchers to contribute to further understanding of the organizational issues surrounding the delivery of health services and to fulfill the potential suggested by these observations.

Limitations of Organizational Research

Five limitations of organizational research on health services delivery institutions will be discussed. These include: 1) the lack of an integrative framework for the comprehensive study of health services delivery organizations; 2) the lack of a systematic approach for building cumulative knowledge; 3) the relative neglect of the impact of the external environment on internal structure and performance; 4) difficulties involved in obtaining reliable and valid measures of performance; and 5) the relative inability to conceptualize and operationalize variables in a way that would enable findings to be relevant to health care policy-makers, health services administrators, and related health professionals. Each of these limitations will be discussed in turn.

Integrative Framework

Table 24–2 summarizes 19 major comparative empirical studies of hospitals 12–30 according to a relatively comprehensive but basic set of organizational var-

---

[11]For a discussion of the inherent tensions between discipline-based and policy-based research and the need for disciplinarians to collaborate with practitioners in defining problems relevant to the world of practice, see: Coleman, J. *Policy Research in the Social Sciences* (Morristown, N.J.: General Learning Press, 1972).

Table 24-2 Classification of major organizational variables and 19 comparative empirical studies of hospitals*

Authors	Number of hospitals studied	Environment	Goals	Task technology	Decision-making structure	Reward system	Modes of coordination	Performance outcomes (efficiency and/or effectiveness)
1 Anderson and Warkov,[12] 1961	49 V.A. hospitals			X**	X		X	
2 Elling and Halebsy,[13] 1961	36 short-term general hospitals	X	X					X
3 Levine and White,[14] 1961	5 hospitals (17 health agencies)	X	X					
4 Georgopoulos and Mann,[15] 1962	10			X	X	X	X	X
5 Belknap and Steinle,[16] 1963	3	X						
6 Revans,[17] 1964	15 British hospitals			X	X			X
7 Rosengren,[18] 1967	80 psychiatric hospitals 52 short-term general		X	X	X		X	X
8 Glaser,[19] 1970	Approximately 100 hospitals in 16 different countries	X	X	X	X	X	X	X
9 Goss, 1970[20]	Summary of studies dealing with relationship between hospital goals and quality of care		X					X

Table 24-2   (continued)

	Sample								
10 Starkweather,[21] 1970	704 U.S. hospitals			X		X	X	X	X
11 Roemer and Friedman, 1971[22]	10 California hospitals			X		X	X	X	X
12 Neuhauser,[23] 1971	30 short-term general hospitals in Chicago		X	X	X	X			X
13 James, 1972[24]	91 short-term general hospitals in Kentucky and Tennessee					X			
14 Heydebrand,[25] 1973	6,825 U.S. hospitals	X		X		X	X	X	X
15 Pfeffer, 1973[26]	57 short-term general hospitals in Illinois	X		X		X	X	X	X
16 Starkweather,[27] 1973	6 religiously-affiliated community hospitals	X						X	
17 Roos, et al.,[28] 1974	1,490 U.S hospitals	X			X	X			X
18 Morse, et al.,[29] 1974	388 government hospitals	X		X		X		X	X
19 Rushing,[30] 1974	91 hospitals; 69 voluntary and 22 proprietary	X	X	X		X	X	X	X
Total studies in each category		10	10	13	3	13	10	9	15

* Criteria for selection included: 1) the organization itself had to be the primary unit of analysis; 2) the study had to be empirical; 3) the study had to compare two or more hospitals; and 4) the relationship between at least two of the major organizational variables had to be examined. In addition, the list is limited to explicitly "organizational" studies of hospitals and does not include, for example, econometric studies of hospital costs. Finally, the list does not include several ongoing studies, partial results of which are reported for the first time in this volume. See articles by Shortell et al., Money et al., and Scott et al.

** X indicates the primary concern of each study.

iables. As can be seen, only Glaser's[31] comparative study of hospitals in 16 different countries attempts to examine all of the variables, but it is only a broad-brush description of differences country-by-country rather than an analysis at the hospital-by-hospital organizational level. Table 24-2 reveals the gaps in the existing literature, the most noticeable being that only three of the 19 studies say anything about reward systems. Furthermore, although most of the studies are of a hypothesis-testing nature, many are not firmly grounded in theory in terms of testing an interrelated set of propositions logically deduced from explicit premises or assumptions.

Criticism might be made that the 19 studies selected are not representative of the better work in the field. But a recent review by Georgopoulos[32] of all hospital

[12]Anderson, T. and Warkov, S. "Organizational Size and Functional Complexity," *American Sociological Review* 26:25 (February 1961).

[13]Elling, R. and Halebsy, S. "Organizational Differentiation and Support," *Administrative Science Quarterly* 6:185 (September 1961).

[14]Levine, S. and White, P. "Exchange as a Conceptual Framework for the Study of Interorganizational Relationships," *Administrative Science Quarterly* 5:583 (March 1961).

[15]Georgopoulos, B. S. and Mann, F. C. *The Community General Hospital* (New York: Macmillan, 1962).

[16]Belknap, I. and Steinle, J. *The Community and Its Hospitals* (Syracuse, N.Y.: Syracuse University Press, 1963).

[17]Revans, R. W. *Standards for Morale: Cause and Effect in Hospitals* (London: Oxford University Press, 1964).

[18]Rosengren, W. R. "Structure, Policy and Style: Strategies of Organization Control," *Administrative Science Quarterly* 12:140 (June 1967).

[19]Glaser, W. A. *Social Settings and Medical Organization: A Cross-National Study of the Hospital* (New York: Atherton Press, 1970).

[20]Goss, M. E. W. "Organizational Goals and the Quality of Medical Care," *Journal of Health and Social Behavior* 11:255 (December 1970).

[21]Starkweather, D. "Hospital Size, Complexity and Formalization," *Health Services Research* 5:330 (Winter 1970).

[22]Roemer, M. and Friedman, J. *Doctors in Hospitals* (Baltimore: John Hopkins University Press, 1971).

[23]Neuhauser, D. *The Relationship Between Administrative Activities and Hospital Performance,* Research Series No. 28 (Chicago: Center for Health Administration Studies, University of Chicago, 1971). Also see: Becker, S. and Neuhauser, D. *Organization Efficiency* (New York: Elsevier Press, 1975).

[24]James, T. F. "The Administrative Component in Complex Organizations," *Sociological Quarterly* 13:533 (Fall 1972).

[25]Heydebrand, W. *Hospital Bureaucracy: A Comparative Study of Organizations* (New York: Dunellen Press, 1973).

[26]Pfeffer, J. "Size, Composition and Function of Hospital Boards of Directors: A Study of Organization-Environment Linkage," *Administrative Science Quarterly* 18:349 (September 1973).

[27]Starkweather, D. "Hospital Organizational Performance and Size," *Inquiry* 10:10-18 (September 1973).

[28]Roos, N. P.; Schermerhorn, J. R.; and Roos, L. L., Jr. "Hospital Performance: Analyzing Power and Goals," *Journal of Health and Social Behavior* 15:78 (June 1974).

[29]Morse, E. V., *et al.* "Hospital Costs and Quality of Care: An Organizational Perspective," *Milbank Memorial Fund Quarterly* 52:315-345 (Summer 1974).

[30]Rushing, W. "Differences in Profit and Non-Profit Organizations: A Study of Effectiveness and Efficiency in General Short-Stay Hospitals," *Administrative Science Quarterly* 19:473-484 (December 1974).

[31]Glaser, "Social Settings."

[32]Georgopoulos, *Hospital Organization Research.*

organizational research in the 1960s reveals that this is not the case. Using Georgopoulos' criteria[33] most of the 19 studies are among the best work in the field. Thus, even the better work has not begun to address hospital organizational behavior in a comprehensive fashion. It can be argued that the existing literature should not be criticized for this failure in that the approach of much of science and other knowledge-building activity is to start small. After two-variable and three-variable relationships are well understood, it then becomes possible to build more elaborate models. The existing literature can, however, be criticized for failing to suggest the implications and possible relationships of the two-variable and three-variable findings for other aspects of hospital operations, particularly for purposes of building a more complete and comprehensive understanding of hospitals as organizations. For example, studies of the relationship between hospital size and administrative/employee ratios are important in their own right, but their significance is enhanced if the impact of these variables on hospital goal-setting or decision-making processes could be examined. And, of course, the ultimate question is what does it all mean in terms of the efficiency and quality of care provided?

Systematic Approach

Related to the lack of a comprehensive framework for study is the relative lack of a systematic approach for building cumulative knowledge. The literature has not tended to be cumulative in terms of later studies systematically building upon earlier studies. Unlike the Aston group research,[34] secondary analysis and replication have been nonexistent. In part, the problem of unsystematic and noncumulative research may be related to the fact that many of those working in theoretical areas are doing very little empirical research, while, at the same time, the empiricists are doing little theorizing. The result is that theory goes untested while individual empirical findings remain unorganized. The net consequence is the lack of an organized body of knowledge.

External Environment

A third limitation concerns the relative neglect of the effect of the external environment on internal structure and performance. This is particularly unfortunate in view of the many external changes faced by hospitals and other health services delivery organizations. For example, what are the organizational and

---

[33]The evaluative criteria used by Georgopoulos included: substantive relevance to the field, theoretical interest and usefulness, probable substantive theoretical significance, estimated methodological adequacy, and overall quality. The overall quality index was derived by summing and averaging each study's scores on the other four measures and converting the product into a three-point scale. See pp. 22–23 of Georgopoulos, *Hospital Organization Research, ibid.*

[34]See, for example: Aldrich, H. "Technology and Organization Structure: A Re-examination of the Findings of the Aston Group," *Administrative Science Quarterly* 17:26–43 (March 1972); Hickson, D. J., *et al.* "Operations Technology and Organizational Structure: An Empirical Reappraisal," *Administrative Science Quarterly* 14:378–398 (September 1969); Child, J. "Organizational Structure and Strategies of Control: A Replication of the Aston Study," *Administrative Science Quarterly* 17:163–177 (June 1972).

managerial implications of certificate of need, prospective reimbursement, rate review boards, and PSROs? How does the health services administrator manipulate the organization's work procedures, decision-making structures, coordination mechanisms, and information-processing system to better meet the demands of these forces? What types of strategies and configurations might result in better performance than others? While answers to these questions may never be available in any precise sense, the existing literature offers little guidelines. Examination of the impact of the external environment on the internal structure and performance of health services delivery organizations remains a fertile area for investigation.

Measures of Performance

A fourth limitation has been the difficulty involved in determining valid and reliable measures of performance, particularly in regard to the quality of care delivered. Reliance has been placed primarily on employees' or medical staff members' perceptions of quality, or reputational evaluations made by expert judges. Unlike cost and productivity data, which can usually be obtained from existing data sources, objective measures of quality must usually be collected first-hand by the researcher in each organization. This, of course, raises problems of gaining access to medical records, which contributes to the more general problem of obtaining the participation of hospitals and other health services delivery organizations in the proposed research. Despite these difficulties, greater attention needs to be paid to developing more reliable and valid measures of performance.

Conceptualization

A final limitation has been the relative inability to conceptualize health services delivery organizations in realistic terms; that is, in terms understandable to health services administrators. As a result, there have also been problems in constructing realistic operational indicators of particular variables. Simply put, the practicing administrator seldom has the opportunity to consider simple two-way or even three-way relationships. Rather, he or she must be concerned with the entire organization and its subcomponents and, further, consider both short-run and long-run implications of particular decisions which might affect an entire array of variables. This is related to the first point mentioned earlier; namely, the need to consider a broader set of organizational variables and to build more comprehensive models of organizational behavior that realistically reflect the complexity of hospitals and other delivery organizations. In constructing such models, the input of practicing administrators and other health professionals is essential, both in developing more realistic models of how health care organizations really function and in constructing more specific and sensitive operational measures of the variables felt to be important.

Given these limitations, how might the future study of health care delivery organizations proceed? This paper suggests that an organization design approach to theory-building represents an alternative that has the potential of overcoming many of the limitations noted.

A Proposed Framework

The limitations that have been discussed give rise to the need to study the relationships among a large number of organizational variables with particular emphasis on analyzing the impact of the external environment on internal structure and performance. Existing literature[35,36] suggests the following set of variables are relevant to developing a more comprehensive approach to organizational analysis: environment, goals, technology, size, work specification activities, decision-making structure, reward systems, coordination and control systems, and performance.

A key to making existing theory and research more meaningful is to group these variables into clusters according to the degree to which they are under the manager's control. It is suggested that environment, goals, technology, and size be treated as *context variables* essentially not under the manager's control, at least usually not in the short run. Operationally, they may be viewed as exogenous variables. Work specification procedures, decision-making structure, reward systems, and coordination and control mechanisms are to be viewed as *organization design variables* essentially under the manager's control. Operationally, they may be viewed as endogenous variables. For health services delivery organizations, performance variables include efficiency and quality of care delivered and will be called *outcome variables*. Growth might also be considered an outcome variable, as well as employee job satisfaction, although the latter might best be viewed as an "intermediate outcome" variable with the ultimate interest being the relationship between employee job satisfaction and efficiency and quality of care. Efficiency or quality of care then becomes the ultimate dependent variable to be explained by the other variables under study.

By studying this particular set of variables and grouping them in this fashion, it becomes possible to address some of the important operational issues facing hospitals and other health services delivery organizations, as well as to build a knowledge base that may be drawn upon in the future. Specifically, it is possible to develop models and propositions regarding the relationships between the context, organization design, and outcome variables. In operational terms, what is the relationship between hospital medical staff organizational structure, PSRO implementation, and quality of medical care? In others words, are some medical staff organization structures more conducive to implementing PSRO requirements than others? Does the level at which decisions are made within the medical staff make a difference? Do the mechanisms used to coordinate the work of the various medical departments make a difference? Does the way in which information is processed and fed back to physicians make a difference? A series of such questions related to other types of external environmental changes, such as new medical technology, new planning and regulatory laws, and new reimbursement mechanisms can be asked and addressed.

Models

An example of a specific model that can be tested using this framework is Thompson's notion of coalignment between organization design and the external

[35]Heydebrand, W. *Comparative Organizations: The Results of Empirical Research* (Englewood Cliffs, N.J.: Prentice-Hall, 1973).

[36]Georgopoulos, *Hospital Organization Research.*

environment.[37] The basic thesis of this model is that the efficiency or quality of care that a hospital or related delivery organization attains depends on the extent to which its organization design is appropriately matched with the nature of its environment. The thesis to be tested is that hospitals operating in environments characterized by a high degree of complexity, diversity, instability, and uncertainty will show different internal organizational design configurations than those hospitals functioning in environments of less complexity, diversity, instability, and uncertainty.[38]

Table 24–3 suggests some possible relationships, with the basic assumption being that there is a greater need for internal flexibility when the organization is operating in a highly complex, diverse, unstable, and uncertain environment than when it is not operating in such an environment. Table 24–3 indicates that hospitals faced with a highly intense environment are likely to experience greater efficiency and effectiveness with a relatively lower degree of work specification, more decentralized/participative decision-making, a more differentiated reward system, and more nonprogrammed coordination and control mechanisms. In contrast, in an environment of lower intensity, a higher degree of work specification, more centralized/nonparticipative decision-making, a more standardized (i.e., undifferentiated) reward system, and more programmed (i.e., rules and regulations) coordination and control mechanisms are likely to result in greater efficiency and effectiveness. These, of course, are ideal-type relationships.

Examples of propositions that could be tested include:

1. The greater the degree of congruence between hospital organizational design and the extent of environmental intensity (composite of the complexity, diversity, instability, and uncertainty dimensions), the greater the efficiency and quality of care delivered.

2. The greater the degree of congruence between hospital organizational design and the extent of environmental intensity, the greater the adoption of innovations.

Operationally these types of propositions might be tested by specifying the following functional form:

$$E = a_1 + b_2 (WS - b_1 E) + \ldots n + e_1$$

where E represents the dependent variable whether it be efficiency, quality of care or innovation adoption ratios; a_1 represents the intercept term; b_2 represents the coefficient for the constructed variable $WS - b_1 E$; $WS - b_1 E$ is the constructed variable representing the extent to which the organization's actual work specification procedures (WS) deviate from that expected, given the nature of the hospital's environment ($b_1 E$); b_1 represents the coefficient obtained by regressing the work specification scores of the entire group of study hospitals or delivery organizations operating in generally similar environments on the individual environmental dimensions (E) to arrive at an expected work specification score; and e_1 equals the error term.

[37]Thompson, J. *Organizations in Action* (New York: McGraw-Hill, 1967).
[38]Shortell, S. M. "The Role of Environment in a Configurational Theory of Organizations," *Human Relations,* in press, 1976.

Table 24-3   Ideal-type relationships suggested by coalignment model variables*

Context	Internal design	
Environment	Low work specification ←———————→ High work specification	
	Decentralized/participative ←———————→ Centralized/nonparticipative decision-making	decision-making
	Differentiated reward system ←———————→ Undifferentiated reward system	
	Nonprogrammed coordination ←———————→ Programmed coordination	
	Nonprogrammed control ←———————→ Programmed control	
High intensity**	High efficiency/effectiveness	Low efficiency/effectiveness
↑		
Low intensity	Low efficiency/effectivenss	High efficiency/effectiveness

* The arrows indicate that these variables lie on a continuum.
** The term intensity is used to include the dimensions of complexity, diversity, instability, and uncertainty.

It is also possible to develop causal models of organizational behavior in which, as implied earlier, the context variables are treated as exogenous, and the organization design and outcome variables as endogenous, with the outcome variables serving as the ultimate dependent variables to be explained. With longitudinal designs, nonrecursive (two-way causation) models can be developed and tested to better capture the dynamics of organizational behavior.[39]

Different models and propositions could be developed, but the important point to note is that the framework appears to address many of the limitations discussed earlier. The interrelationships among a large number of variables are considered and organized into a coherent framework from which systematic and cumulative testing might proceed; explicit consideration is given to the influence of the environment; and a distinction is made between variables that can be more easily changed by administrators from those that are less changeable, thus providing a framework for analyzing the effects of changes in public policy and other types of changes on management decision-making. Related advantages include the possibility of being able to explain more of the variance in efficiency and quality of care than currently exists, obtain a better understanding of the impact of change and innovation on organizational performance as mediated by organization design variables, and learn more about which particular design variables are important for different types of policy and related changes, so that intervention strategies may be developed.

Research Implications

The proposed framework suggests the need for larger sample sizes, greater use of longitudinal study designs, further development and testing of multivariate models, continuing attention to issues of measurement reliability and validity, and selection of relatively comparable health care organizations for purposes of making inferences regarding organizational effectiveness. While several of these observations have been noted by others,[40] it is useful to elaborate their significance within the context of the current proposal.

[39]Blalock, H. M. *Causal Models in the Social Sciences* (Chicago: Aldine, 1971).
[40]Georgopoulos, *Hospital Organization Research.*

Perhaps the most obvious implication is the need to study larger numbers of health care organizations. Models involving larger numbers of variables require larger sample sizes in order to increase the stability and robustness of statistical tests and the validity of inferences that can be drawn. The need for larger sample sizes often conflicts with the reality of gaining the participation of health care organizations in the research. The alternative is to rely on secondary precollected data sources that may not offer measures of sufficient reliability and validity or may not offer any measures of some important variables. A useful compromise strategy employed by several of the studies reported in this volume is to make use of whatever precollected data can be obtained on the full sample of organizations to be studied and then randomly select a sub-sample for more intensive on-site data collection on variables that cannot be measured using secondary data sources.

Implicit in the grouping of the context, organization design, and outcome variables is the determination of possible causal relationships among these variables. Since the problems of drawing causal inferences from cross-sectional data are well known, there is a need for a greater number of both longitudinal and experimental or quasi-experimental studies of health care delivery organizations. This is particularly true for analyzing the effects of new medical technology or managerial or programmatic innovations. For example, a cross-sectional study of the effect of PSROs on hospitals will say something about the effects of initial implementation, but little about the long-run implications for the organization in terms of eventual changes in task technology, decision-making structures, methods of coordinating work, and performance.

It can be argued that even inferences regarding initial effects are unwarranted because they could have been produced by a number of factors other than PSRO implementation itself. Longitudinal, experimental and quasi-experimental designs are, of course, costly and difficult to implement, but are the price to be paid if one is really serious about analyzing the impact of policy and legal changes on the organizations responsible for delivering services to clients and patients.

A third implication suggested by the proposed framework is the need for additional multivariate analysis involving the analysis of *several dependent variables*. Most of the existing research is characterized by an interest in a single dependent variable, such as the administrative component, complexity of service, employee job satisfaction, average length of stay, or costs. These are important issues in and of themselves, but if knowledge is to be advanced, future research must begin examining the relationships among these variables, even if the research designs are only of a cross-sectional nature. Operationally, several dependent variables can be examined within a cross-sectional study by making certain assumptions regarding the time order of events and constructing systems of structural equations.[41] For example, an investigator might be interested first in explaining differences in technology, which in turn might be used, along with other variables, to explain differences in decision-making structures, and so on, until the reduced form equation explains differences in organizational outcomes. Such strategies reinforce the need for an interdisciplinary approach involving

[41]Duncan, O. D. *Introduction to Structural Equation Models* (New York: Academic Press, 1975).

econometricians, as well as sociologists, psychologists, and other types of social scientists.

The proposed framework implies that considerable work is needed in developing reliable and valid measures of the external environment. The perceptions of key organizational members are important, as well as the development of unobtrusive measures. Discussions with practicing administrators and policy-makers can be useful in constructing such measures. The need to develop better measures of efficiency and quality of care has been discussed. In attempting to measure hospital efficiency, for example, greater attention needs to be paid to controlling for differences in patient case-mix and the quality of care delivered. In regard to quality, more direct process and outcome measures are needed along the lines of Brook,[42] Payne and Lyons,[43] and the approach described by Scott.[44]

Finally, since the proposed framework places emphasis on explaining differences in organizational outcomes, it is important that the organizations studied be generally similar in their goals and orientations. This is particularly true for purposes of drawing inferences for the development of public policy. For example, it makes little sense to compare a 150-bed community general hospital with a 700-bed medical center, or a 10-person rural health department with a 300-person city health department. This is not to say that any particular model cannot be tested across such different types of organizations in order to assess the model's ability to explain more of the variance in performance in one type of organization than another, or to assess the differential importance of predictors across different types of organizations. But to say that a particular organization is more or less effective than another organization without taking into account possible differences in environment or goal structures is of dubious value.

Summary

This paper has suggested that a strong congruence exists between contemporary issues in organization theory and operational and policy issues faced by health care delivery organizations. It has also identified several limitations of existing health services organizational research, suggested a framework for overcoming some of these limitations, and outlined the research implications of the proposed framework. Perhaps the most important implication is the need for greater collaboration between organizational researchers and health services administrators and policy-makers. The researcher needs to go out more to the world of practice and gather the input of practitioners and policy-makers in defining problems, as well as constructing and measuring variables. Administrators and policy-makers, on the other hand, must recognize data collection requirements and the extent of cooperation that is essential to successfully address the issues that have been raised.

[42]Brook, R. H. "Quality of Care Assessment: Comparison of Five Methods of Peer Review," DHEW Publication No. HRA-74-3100 (1973).

[43]Payne, B. C. and Lyons, T. F. *Methods of Evaluating and Improving Personal Medical Care: Episode of Illness Study* (Ann Arbor: University of Michigan Press, 1972).

[44]Scott, W. R. "Professionals in Hospitals: Technology and the Organization of Work," *in* B. S. Georgopoulos, ed., *Organization Research in Health Institutions* (Ann Arbor: Institute for Social Research, Univ. of Michigan, 1972), Chap. 6.

25 The Growth of Medical Technology and Bureaucracy: Implications for Medical Care

Despite significant differences in ideology, values, and social organization, most Western developed countries—and probably most countries in the world—face common problems of financing, organizing, and providing health care services. As populations increasingly demand medical care, there is growing concern among the governments of most nations to provide a minimal level of service to all and to decrease obvious inequalities in care. To use available technology and knowledge efficiently and effectively, certain organizational options are most desirable. Thus, there is a general tendency throughout the world to link existing services to defined population groups, to develop new and more economic ways to provide primary services to the population without too great an emphasis on technological efforts, to integrate services increasingly fragmented by specialization or a more elaborate division of labor, and to seek ways to improve the output of the delivery system with fixed inputs. Although all of these concerns to some extent characterize national planning in underdeveloped countries, they particularly describe tendencies among developed countries as they attempt to control the enormous costs of available technologies. Throughout the world there is increasing movement away from medicine as a solitary entrepreneurial activity and more emphasis on the effective development of health delivery systems.

Having discussed these trends elsewhere in detail (Mechanic, 1974, 1976), what I will do here is examine how changing technology and organization affect not only the provision of medical care, but also the underlying assumptions of practitioners and patients. My thesis is that medical care constitutes a complex psychological system of assumptions and meanings that is significantly affected by the bureaucratization of medical tasks and the growing specification of the technical aspects. Public policies everywhere in the world increasingly play a role in the financing and organization of care, but when such public policies violate the psychological assumptions and social expectations of health practitioners and patients, they may have consequences very different from those intended.

Modes of Rationing Health Services

Medicine has in recent decades undergone an enormous development in specialized knowledge and in technology. While these advances have brought con-

Prepared for the Colloque International de Sociologie Medicale, Paris, July 1976. Supported in part by a grant from the Robert Wood Johnson Foundation.

Reprinted from *Health and Society, Milbank Memorial Fund Quarterly*, 55:61–78, Winter, 1977, by permission of the author and Publisher.

siderable progress in treating some diseases, most of the major diseases affecting mortality and morbidity—from heart disease and the cancers to the psychoses and substance abuse—are only poorly understood, and existing efforts, while they ameliorate suffering and sometimes extend life, are not able to cure or prevent the incidence of most of these conditions. The technologies that do exist are often extraordinarily expensive, require intensive professional manpower, and must be applied repeatedly to a patient during the long course of a chronic condition. Take an example where success has been quite impressive, such as in hemodialysis and transplantation in end-stage kidney disease: intensive and expensive efforts must be made over a long period to sustain life and functioning, which on a per capita basis consume a very high level of expenditure (Fox and Swazey, 1974). As these halfway technologies have developed—intensive care units, radiation therapy for cancers, coronary bypass surgery—the aggregate costs of medical care have continued to move upward, with medical services consuming a larger proportion of national income. In the United States, for example, where in 1940 the cost of health care was $4 billion and 4 percent of the gross national product, 1976 costs were almost $140 billion and 8.6 percent of the gross national product. While the proportional increase is not as large in nations having a centralized prospective budgeting process, as in England, the trend, nevertheless, is the same and a source of concern among all thoughtful people.

Since the prevalence of illness and "dis-ease" is extremely high in community populations, as has been repeatedly demonstrated by morbidity surveys (White et al., 1961), there is almost unlimited possibility for the continued escalation of medical demand and increased medical expenditures. As people have learned to have higher and more unrealistic expectations of medicine, demands for care for a wide variety of conditions, both major and minor, have accelerated. No nation that follows a sane public policy would facilitate the fulfillment of all perceptions of need that a demanding public might be willing to make. As in every other area of life, resources must be rationed. The uncontrolled escalation of costs in developed countries results in part because techniques of rationing are in a process of transition, and most countries have yet to reach a reasonable end point in this transitional process. The process is one of movement from *rationing by fee* through a stage of *implicit rationing* through resource allocation to a final stage of *explicit rationing*. In this process the role of physician shifts from entrepreneur to bureaucratic official, and medical practice from a market-oriented system to a rationalized bureaucracy. These shifts, in turn, have an important bearing on the psychological meaning of the doctor-patient relationship, on the uses of medical excuses for various social purposes, and on the flexibility of medicine as an institution to meet patient expectations and to relieve tensions in the community at large. The remainder of this paper will explicate each of these points.

Types of Rationing

In the traditional practice of medicine, and in much of the world still today, the availability of medical care has been dependent on the ability to purchase it. Those with means could obtain whatever level of medical care was available, while those without means were dependent on whatever services were made available by government, philanthropists, the church, or by physicians themselves.

Since affluence was limited, and medical technology and knowledge in any case offered only modest gains, the marketplace was a natural device for rationing services. Indeed, it worked so well that physicians were often supporters of government intervention and direct payments for care since such support increased their opportunities for remuneration.

Fee-for-service as an effective system of rationing broke down due to a variety of factors. First, medical technology and knowledge expanded rapidly, greatly increasing the costs of a serious medical episode, and imposed on the ill a financial burden that was large and unpredictable. Associated with this was a growing demand on the part of the public for means of sharing such risks through benevolent societies and insurance plans and, as costs mounted, for government to assume a growing proportion of these expenditures. Because of the traditions of medical practice, however, and the political monopoly that physicians had gained over the marketplace, the rise of third-party payment was not associated with careful controls over the work of the physician and how he generated costs. While third-party payment increased access to services, the orientations of increasingly scientific and technologically inclined physicians resulted in a large acceleration in the use of diagnostic and treatment techniques. The consequence has been the escalation of costs which we now almost view as inevitable. Physicians have been trained to pursue the "technological imperative"—that is, the tendency to use any intervention possible regardless of cost if there is any possibility of gain (Fuchs, 1968). This contrasts with a cost-benefit calculation in which there is consideration of the relative costs and benefits of pursuing a particular course of action. The "technological imperative," when carried to its extreme, incurs fantastic expense for relatively small and, at times, counterproductive outcomes.

In a provocative analysis, Victor Fuchs (1976) asks why almost all the developed countries in the world pursue national health insurance when such a policy is "irrational" from an economic point of view in that it encourages the overconsumption of services relative to other needs. Moreover, he argues, it often results in the purchase of the wrong and, perhaps, less useful types of care. He comes up with the intriguing suggestion that the thrust toward national health insurance may have relatively little to do with health.

> Externalities, egalitarianism, the decline of the family and traditional religion, the need for national symbols—these all play a part. In democratic countries with homogeneous populations, people seem to want to take care of one another through programs such as national health insurance, as members of the same family do, although not to the same degree. In autocratic countries with heterogeneous populations, national health insurance is often imposed from above, partly as a device for strengthening national unity. The relative importance of different factors undoubtedly varies from country to country and time to time, but the fact that national health insurance can be viewed as serving so many diverse interests and needs is probably the best answer to why Bismarck and Woodcock are not such strange bed-fellows after all.

Many developed nations shifted quite early away from fee-for-service rationing to what I have referred to as *implicit rationing*. Under health insurance plans in various European countries, rationing was imposed either by the centralized prospective budgeting procedures of the government, as in England, or through the limited resources available to "sickness societies" that contracted with physicians and hospitals for services for their members. For example, in England under the

National Health Insurance Act of 1911, and later through the enactment of the National Health Service in 1946, the central government budgeted fixed amounts for providing community medical services on a capitation basis, and hospital services as of 1948 on a global budget. Similarly, sickness societies in other countries had to make contractual agreements with physicians within the means available, thus limiting the extent of services that could be rendered.

In European countries that adopted national health insurance through an indirect method, such as mandated employer-employee contributions, governments increasingly assumed a larger proportion of the costs of physician services and institutional care. Since government had little control over how costs were generated by physicians and hospitals, there was continuing pressure for increased expenditures by both patients and physicians. Governments took on the obligation in making up deficits between costs generated by health professionals and the funds available from employer-employee contributions. They did so either by raising the social security tax rates or by making larger contributions each year from general revenues. In England, where the government had direct budgetary control, costs were more successfully contained, but there were constant pressures from health professionals for increased expenditure, nevertheless. Despite direct control, the proportion of national income allocated to health care escalated, but at a lesser rate than in many other countries that had more open-ended budgeting systems.

Implicit rationing depends on the queue. Limited resources, facilities, and manpower are made available, and the health care system adapts to demand by establishing noneconomic barriers (Mechanic, 1976:87–97). Health professionals, having their own styles of work and professional norms, accommodate as many patients as they can, making judgments as to priorities and need. Access to services may be limited by long appointment or referral waiting periods, by limited sites of care (and therefore greater barriers of distance and inconvenience), longer waiting times, bureaucratic barriers, and the like. Rationing also may occur through the control exercised over the extent of elaboration of services: the laboratory tests ordered, the diagnostic techniques used, the rate of hospitalization, the number of surgical interventions, and the time devoted to each patient. Capitation or salary as a form of professional payment tends to limit the extent of these modalities; fee-for-service increases the rate of discrete technical services for which a fee is paid (Glaser, 1970; Roemer, 1962).

Implicit rationing has the effect of limiting expenditures, but not necessarily in a rational way. Such rationing is based on the assumption that the professional is sufficiently programmed by his socialization as a health practitioner to make scientifically valid judgments as to what constitutes need, what treatment modalities are most likely to be effective, and which cases deserve priority. It is supposed that the exercise of clinical judgment will result in rational decision making. But as Eliot Freidson (1976:136–137) has noted, evaluation of medical judgment by professional peers is so permissive that only "blatant acts of ignorance or inattention" are clearly recognized as mistakes. Moreover, it is the more knowledgeable, more aggressive, and more demanding individuals who get more service; and these patients are usually more educated, more sophisticated, but less needy (Hetherington et al., 1975). In short, under implicit rationing the assumption is that physicians exercise agreed-upon standards for care and that services are equitably provided in light of these standards. The fact is that these standards are very murky, if they exist at all, and even the most obvious ones have little relationship to any existing knowledge on the implications of varying patterns of care for patient outcome. Under these conditions, the most effective and vocal consumers may get more than their share of whatever care is available. Moreover, given the ambiguities of practice, physicians and other health professionals may play out their own personal agendas, cultural preferences, and professional biases. Being remunerated on salary, they may work at a comfortable and leisurely pace; and they may choose to emphasize work they find most interesting, neglecting important needs of patients, such as needs for empathy and support, which may be perceived as professionally less fulfilling functions.

There is considerable evidence that systems of implicit rationing provide care at lower cost because of the limited budget available and the containment in provision of resources and manpower, but there is little evidence to support the contention that the result is a fairer allocation of social resources. Under implicit rationing, large disparities continue in the availability of facilities, in allocation of manpower and resources per capita (and in relation to known rates of morbidity in the population), and in access to services (Cooper, 1975; Logan, 1971; Hetherington et al., 1975). Affluent areas tend to retain more facilities, manpower, and other resources, and relatively little redistribution takes place. There are very large variations from area to area and institution to institution in the procedures performed, work load, ancillary assistance available, and the level of technology.

Increasingly, governments are seeking means to move from implicit to explicit forms of rationing. The idea of explicit rationing is not only to set limits on total expenditures for care, but also to develop mechanisms to arrive at more rational decisions as to relative investments in different areas of care, varying types of facilities and manpower, new technological initiatives, and the establishment of certain minimal uniform standards. The difficulty with establishing such priorities and standards is the overall lack of definitive evidence as to which health care practices really make a difference in illness outcomes. While standards for processes of care are readily formulated, it is difficult to demonstrate for most facets of care that such process norms have any clear relationship to outcomes that really matter. Indeed, health services random trials tend to show that such expensive innovations as coronary intensive care or longer hospitalizations for a variety of diseases seem to make little difference in measurable outcomes for populations where they are routinely used (Cochrane, 1972).

The difficulty of imposing explicit rationing, however, is more political than scientific. While there is always danger in establishing general guidelines that the overall formulation will not fit a specific case, there are many instances in medical practice where intelligent restrictions on practices of physicians are likely to lead to both improved and more economical practice. The fact is, however, that physicians resist such guidelines as intrusions on their professional judgment and autonomy, and tend to do whatever they can to subvert them. Even with a certain amount of slack, intelligent guidelines—sensitive to the realities of medical practice and human behavior—can be an important contribution toward more effective rationing than usually exists under the implicit system.

There are a variety of techniques that are used under many insurance systems to restrict the options of health practitioners (Glaser, 1970), and these are becoming more commonly adopted. The most straightforward is the simple exclusion or restriction of certain types of services that may involve large costs but dubious benefits—for example, psychoanalysis, orthodontia, rest cures, plastic surgery for cosmetic purposes, etc. In the case of essential components of treatment, the program may set maximal numbers of procedures that will be paid for or establish required time intervals between procedures that can be repeated and remain eligible for coverage. These limitations have the function of restricting the physician's discretion although to a modest degree. In theory, however, they can be very much extended. Another technique is to limit the cost of a treatment by requiring the physician to provide justification if he wishes to exercise a more expensive option. Since physicians tend to dislike additional required paperwork, if the guidelines are reasonable they are likely to be effective.

In the United States emphasis is now being given to mandatory peer review, a process whereby utilization practices and, in the future, the quality of care as well will be evaluated. Moreover, justification under federal programs must be provided if certain established norms are to be exceeded. While these requirements are still very weak, and frequently insufficiently responsive to contingencies at the service level, and involve a great deal of unnecessary administrative effort, in theory they can be quite valuable if the review process is an intelligent one and if control over the review mechanism is not captured by physicians who wish to maintain on-going practices. The necessity of any guideline or standard should be evaluated in terms of its costs and benefits. When the costs exceed the benefits, the rule is obviously pointless.

Some countries require pre-review for specified expensive procedures. If pre-review is used too extensively it becomes a costly and inefficient technique but, if used sparingly to control expensive work of dubious effectiveness and possibly dangerous as well, it can have effects both as a deterrent and as a means of controlling irresponsible practitioners. Particularly in the area of surgical intervention and perhaps also in the use of dangerous classes of drugs, pre-review functions both to reduce costs and to encourage a higher quality of care. In short, both government itself and nongovernmental insurance programs are becoming more bold in intruding on areas that physicians regard as within their discretion. We have every reason to anticipate that this trend will continue.

Rationing and Primary Medical Care

The most salient aspect of medical organization in modern countries is the enormous growth of specialization and subspecialization that has occurred. While much of this development is due to the growth of biomedical science and technology, specialization is also a political process bringing economic advantages and greater control over one's work and responsibilities (Stevens, 1971). Specialization, moreover, allows physicians to dominate a specified domain and to restrict competition. While the traditional concept of the specialist was as a consultant physician who assisted the generalist with puzzling problems or those of greater complexity, existing specialties are organized around varying population groups such as pediatrics or geriatrics, types of technology such as radiology, organ systems such as nephrology, etiologies such as infectious disease, and disease categories such as pulmonary disease. The most recent distortion of the concept of the consulting physician was the development of a specialty in family practice, which in effect defines the generalist as another type of specialist.

While there are many issues relevant to the manner in which specialization has emerged, the distinction with the greatest importance for rationing is the one between physicians who engage in primary care and those who provide specialty care or more complex hospital services. Everywhere in the world, nations are seeking to define the appropriate functions and responsibilities for each of the levels of care and their most efficient balance. Most discussions of primary care, particularly in countries that retain the provision of services at least in part within the private marketplace, suffer from confusions among the organizational, service, and manpower dimensions of the situation.

The most typical view of primary care is that it is the care given by certain types of practitioners who work as generalists: general practitioners, family practitioners, nurse practitioners, and so on. It is assumed that the training received by such practitioners prepares them adequately to provide first-contact care and to take continuing responsibilities for overall needs of the patient. While convenient, this definition includes as primary care highly complex medical and surgical procedures that are more adequately performed by physicians who are highly conversant with the field and who perform these procedures sufficiently frequently to do them expertly. While a considerable amount of major surgery is performed by general practitioners in the United States and elsewhere, major surgery is not appropriately included as primary care. Similarly, many specialists insist that they devote significant amounts of their time to primary care, and thus the shortage of primary care physicians is exaggerated. It should be clear then that this approach to understanding the appropriate role of primary care is not particularly helpful.

It is frequently suggested that one way of resolving the issue of primary care is to divide arbitrarily medical functions into primary, secondary, and tertiary. Such an approach, however, misses the major point which is that the practice of medicine is a conceptual and intellectual endeavor in which physicians with diverse training perceive, evaluate, classify, and manage comparable patients differently. The evaluation of a patient in good medical practice comes from listening to the patient, getting to know the person, and developing a clinical context in which the patient is willing to reveal himself or herself. How physicians will come to view a patient's problem depends on their orientations and how accessible the patient is to them psychologically as well as physically. The key point is that differences between primary and specialist practitioners are not simply a matter of what they do, but also a matter of how they do it. An essential aspect of primary care is the physician's attitude, assumptions and storage of information about the particular patient, and the way the practitioner goes about evaluating the patient's complaint. Many patients first contacting a physician are in a stage in which their symptoms are unorganized and fluid (Balint, 1957). What the physician defines as important, what he inquires about, and how he evaluates the patient's symptoms and illness behavior are molded by his knowledge of the patient as well as his training and orientations. In understanding how varying types of general and subspecialty training affect medical practice, it is necessary to have a good appreciation of how patients with comparable presenting complaints are evaluated and managed differently.

Still another way of viewing primary care is as part of an organizational system. Here the emphasis is less on a particular type of practitioner and how he is trained, and more on how different levels of care are organized and how they relate to one another. For example, in most organized medical care systems there are designated primary care physicians who have responsibility for first-contact care, for assuming continued responsibility for an enrolled population, and for dealing with the more common and less complicated problems of their patients. These systems are often established so that patients are required to seek more specialized services through the referral of their primary doctor. Similarly, secondary and tertiary care facilities are organized in relation to the system as a whole, and attempts are made to specify the conditions for coordination among varying levels of care. Although the particular type of practitioner used at varying levels of care is not an unimportant issue, the major focus shifts to defining responsibilities for care functions at each level of care. Primary care services, however they are defined by the system, may be organized in a variety of ways with alternative types of personnel as long as the necessary functions are performed. In this context, primary care is a level of service, not a particular type of practitioner.

The formulation of a planned system of primary, secondary, and tertiary functions has important implications for rationing. When the primary practitioner is the source of entry into the care system and a gatekeeper to access to more specialized practitioners and technologies, the rate of use of specialized technologies can be very much diminished. Systems of care that use primarily a sole source of entry through a primary physician make do with many fewer specialists and specialized facilities, and without any major loss in effective care. As Paul Beeson (1974:48), who has held responsible positions in both England and the United States, has noted:

> There are 22,000 in family practice in the United Kingdom and 70,000 in family practice in the United States. There are 8,000 in specialist practice in the United Kingdom and 280,000 in specialist practice in the United States. . . . The striking difference is economy in the use of specialists. To me this is the most obvious reason why America has a badly distributed, excessively costly system.

An effective system of care, moreover, allows an opportunity to organize manpower rationally relative to population groups, thus limiting the extent to which doctors generate marginal efforts due to their excessive concentration in any area. Also, by emphasizing functions and patterns of care, rather than types of medical specialties, it is much less difficult to develop functional substitutes to physicians in performing many primary care services. Because the emphasis is on a service, it is more possible to develop participation of health practitioners who are trained and willing to perform functions that physicians are unwilling to do, that they do poorly, or that they provide inefficiently—for example, health education, patient monitoring, medically related social services, and the like.

When primary care is defined as part of a system, problems still remain in coordination and motivation. The point at which referrals should take place from one level to another, for example, is left to the individual practitioner and is often affected by the implicit incentives built into the organization of health services or in how health personnel are remunerated. A common complaint in organized systems of care based on a capitation arrangement is that unnecessary referral is made to secondary services because of the lack of incentive for continued care at the primary level (Forsyth and Logan, 1968). These problems can be alleviated, if not avoided, by a good understanding of the epidemiology of help-seeking, with specification of standards for referral and with incentives promoting good care.

The Structure of Doctor-Patient Interaction under Varying Rationing Arrangements

Each of the types of rationing described tends to be associated with a particular mode of physician-patient interaction, although there is great variation within each type, dependent on the personalities of the actors involved, the work load and work flow, and the incentives operative in any particular situation. Eliot Freidson (1961, 1970, 1976) has written extensively on these types of relationships, and in this section I draw heavily on his work. Very simply, it is my contention that, as rationing varies from fee-for-service to implicit to explicit rationing, the types of influence shift from client control to colleague control to bureaucratic control. Similarly, the nuances in the physician's role shift from "entrepreneur" to "expert" to "official."

Freidson has convincingly illustrated how the shift from fee-for-service practice to prepaid group practice is accompanied by lesser flexibility and responsiveness of the physician. When the retention of the patient is no longer an economic issue for the physician, there is no need to "humor the patient" nor bend to the patient's wishes when they are contrary to the physician's best judgment. Freidson argues that in the prepaid situation colleagues are a more important reference group, and while the physician may be more inflexible he may practice a higher standard of medical care. The extent to which differences between fee-for-service and prepaid practice will exist depends greatly on the competition for patients existing in any practice area. As competition increases, physicians may be more willing to provide greater amenities to patients and to be flexible to their requests in order to retain their patronage. When the physician has more patients than he requires, there may be little client control even in the fee-for-service situation. As the physician becomes less dependent on the patient—either because he is only one of a large number of physicians servicing an enrolled population or because he is in a favorable competitive situation—he can more easily play the role of the neutral expert, one whose decisions are quite isolated from any personal financial stake he may have in his work.

In theory, implicit rationing encourages the physician to play the role of the expert, but in actuality the difficulty lies in the ambiguity of his expertise. Since the physician by the very nature of his work is required to come to many social decisions quite irrelevant to his technical expertise, and since physicians differ radically on these social judgments, there is no clear basis for these decisions. For example, consider the frequently occurring issue of whether a hospitalized mother should be sent home or retained for a few more days because the physician anticipates that her family will expect her to resume usual duties, or because she may be inclined to quickly reassume responsibilities. In theory, when the patient must incur part of the fee, such potential cost will influence the decision. However, when third parties assume the cost, neither the physician nor the patient has any incentive to choose the more parsimonious decision. If the physician acts as an expert, his bias is to use resources if he sees any potential benefit. Incentives to do otherwise come only when he is personally faced with a limitation of resources. A global budget without further guidelines, although it may restrict the physician's actions to some extent, does not insure rational decision making and may encourage highly preferential behavior depending on the physician's perceptions of and attitudes toward the patient.

Although the evidence is not fully clear, most existing prepaid group practices seem to conserve resources more by controlling inputs—numbers of primary care physicians, beds, and specialists—than by directly affecting the manner in which physicians make decisions in allocating resources. While it has been alleged that the incentives for physicians to avoid unnecessary work may be an important factor, there is no impressive evidence that such incentives substantially affect decision making itself (Mechanic, 1976). Most of the rationing that takes place seems to be at the administrative planning level, and then physicians seem to adjust to whatever resources are available. Thus, in most prepaid group practices or in health centers or polyclinics, physicians still very much retain the role of "expert."

As health care plan administrators or government officials attempt to tighten expenditures by moving toward a system of explicit rationing, physicians are pushed to a larger degree into the role of bureaucratic official. The case of the Soviet physicians, described by Field (1957), who were limited in the number of sickness certifications they could issue, provides an extreme example of how bureaucratic regulation can substantially limit the options available for physician decision making. While no explicit rationing system in the world has gone this far in any systematic way, there is a discernible tendency toward greater administrative control. In such circumstances the physician must explicitly determine which patients are more needy of a particular service, and he must develop ways to discourage or influence other patients who insist on such service. Increasingly, for example, the physician will require pre-review of certain decisions or have other decisions reviewed after the fact. The intrusion of such requirements or review, if seriously performed, can have a significant effect on decision making, particularly on the "technological imperative."

Everywhere in the world physicians have retained considerable autonomy; even in such highly bureaucratized contexts as military medicine, industrial medicine, and the health services of communist countries, physicians have persisted in their roles more as experts than as bureaucratic functionaries. The shift is more nuance than drama, and while such tendencies will grow throughout the world, rationing is more likely to be imposed on the total framework of services and less on the decisions of the individual physician treating a particular patient. In any case, the growing bureaucratization of medicine poses some serious dangers, and I conclude this paper with a brief consideration of these.

The Effects of Bureaucratization on
Medicine as a Social Institution

Medicine as a social institution has extremely broad functions. Not only does medicine deal with the prevention and treatment of pain, disease, disability, and impairment, but it also provides an acceptable excuse for relief from ordinary obligations and responsibilities, and may be used to justify behaviors and interventions not ordinarily tolerated by the social system without significant sanctions. The definition of illness may also be used as a mechanism of social control to contain deviance, to remove misfits from particular social roles, or to encourage continued social functioning and productive activity. Thus, the locus of control for medical decision making is a key variable in examining the implications of medical care for social life more generally.

In the case of fee-for-service medicine, the physician acts as the agent of the patient. Although his own personal economic interests may intrude in the relationship, his role is to defend the interests of the patient against any other competing interest. The increasing employment of physicians by health programs or complex organizations involves changes in the auspices of medical care that depart in significant ways from traditional concepts (Mechanic, 1976). As I have noted throughout this paper, and specifically in my discussion of rationing, bureaucratic medical settings involve multiple interests, thus putting the physician under pressure to sacrifice certain potential interests of an individual patient to satisfy organizational needs. In the case of such institutions as health maintenance organizations, for example, increased administrative directions for rationing, as well as financial incentives, are developed to encourage physicians to avoid providing unnecessary services. But since the concept of "necessary" is itself vague, the determination may reflect the balance of pressures on the physician.

The bureaucratization of medicine also has the effect of diluting the personal responsibility of the provider, making it more likely that interests other than those of the patient will prevail. By segmenting responsibility for patient care, the medical bureaucracy relieves the physician of direct continuing responsibility. If the patient cannot reach a physician at night or on weekends, obtain responsive care, have inquiries answered, or whatever, the problem is no longer focused on the failure of an individual physician, but on the failures of the organization. It is far easier for patients to locate and deal with individual failures where responsibility is clear than to confront a diffuse organizational structure where responsibility is often hazy and the buck is easily passed. To the extent the physician knows that a patient is his or her charge, the physician feels a certain responsibility to protect the patient's interests against organizational roadblocks and requests that may not be fully appropriate. But when responsibility is less clear it is easier to make decisions in the name of other interests such as research, teaching, demonstration, or the "public welfare," whatever that might be.

The growth of bureaucratic medicine is in many ways an effective response to the development and complexity of medical knowledge. But it also involves some significant threats to the concept of physician responsibility for the best interests of the individual patient and for the empathic and supportive relationships that are so vital to effective care of the whole person. It also involves a shifting in the balance of power in dealing with the broader problems for which patients use the medical system such as in alleviating anxieties and excusing failure. The physician's role as advocate of the patient derives from a close and continuing relationship and knowledge of the patient and a certain relational alignment to him. Bureaucratic structures tend to promote more segmented and detached relationships and ambiguities and conflicts in relational alignments. While in theory bureaucratic structures could be developed to promote empathy, continuity, and humane care, the tendency is for bureaucratic and technical functions to be given higher priority. Physicians are rewarded more for being good managers and researchers or for coping with a large work load than for providing interested and humane care. While physician care in bureaucracies is often humane, such behavior seems to occur despite bureaucratic structure rather than because of it.

Bureaucratization in medicine is inevitable. The challenge thus is to promote organizational arrangements that ration wisely and fairly, and that provide incentives for listening to the patient and caring for him. Humane medicine is an effective component of good patient care. Medical outcomes often depend on the understanding and cooperation of patients and their willingness to engage their problems in a serious and committed way. Medicine without caring, no matter how effective the technique, has a limited capacity to fulfill the broad potential of medicine as a sustaining institution for those who come to depend upon it. The development of bureaucratic incentives, thus, must be designed to enhance humane values while capitalizing on advances in knowledge and technology (Howard and Strauss, 1975). In my estimation this can be most effectively accomplished by upgrading the role and performance of the primary care sector and by regulating carefully through the planning process the availability and provision of the more expensive, complex, and dangerous technologies. Within broad guidelines, physician and patient must remain as free as possible to negotiate satisfactory solutions to the personal and social dilemmas that bring them together.

References

Balint, Michael.
  1957 *The Doctor, His Patient, and the Illness.* New York: International Universities Press.
Beeson, Paul.
  1974 "Some good features of the British National Health Service." *Journal of Medical Education* 49 (January):43–49.
Cochrane, A.L.
  1972 *Effectiveness and Efficiency: Random Reflections on Health Services.* London: Nuffield Provincial Hospitals Trust.
Cooper, Michael.
  1975 *Rationing Health Care.* New York: John Wiley (Halsted Press).
Field, Mark.
  1957 *Doctor and Patient in Soviet Russia.* Cambridge: Harvard University Press.
Forsyth, G., and Logan, R.
  1968 *Gateway or Dividing Line: A Study of Hospital Out-Patients in the 1960's.* New York: Oxford University Press.

Fox, Renee, and Swazey, Judith.
    1974   *The Courage to Fail: A Social View of Organ Transplants and Dialysis.* Chicago: University of Chicago Press.

Freidson, Eliot.
    1961   *Patients' Views of Medical Practice.* New York: Russell Sage Foundation.

    _____.
    1970   *Profession of Medicine: A Study of the Sociology of Applied Knowledge.* New York: Dodd-Mead.

    _____.
    1976   *Doctoring Together: A Study of Professional Social Control.* New York: Elsevier.

Fuchs, Victor.
    1968   "The growing demand for medical care." *New England Journal of Medicine* 279:190–195.

    _____.
    1976   "From Bismarck to Woodcock: The 'irrational' pursuit of national health insurance." Center for Economic Analysis of Human Behavior and Social Institutions, Working Paper No. 120. National Bureau of Economic Research.

Glaser, William A.
    1970   *Paying the Doctor: Systems of Remuneration and Their Effects.* Baltimore: Johns Hopkins Press.

Hetherington, Robert, et al.
    1975   *Health Insurance Plans: Promise and Performance.* New York: Wiley-Interscience.

Howard, Jan, and Strauss, Anselm, eds.
    1975   *Humanizing Health Care.* New York: Wiley-Interscience.

Logan, R.F.L.
    1971   "National health planning—An appraisal of the state of the art." *International Journal of Health Services* 1 (February):6–17.

Mechanic, David.
    1974   *Politics, Medicine, and Social Science.* New York: Wiley-Interscience.

    _____.
    1976   *The Growth of Bureaucratic Medicine: An Inquiry into the Dynamics of Patient Behavior and the Organization of Medical Care.* New York: Wiley-Interscience.

Roemer, Milton.
    1962   "On paying the doctor and the implications of different methods." *Journal of Health and Social Behavior* 3 (Spring): 4–14.

Stevens, Rosemary.
    1971   *American Medicine and the Public Interest.* New Haven: Yale University Press.

White, K.L., et al.
    1961   "The ecology of medical care." *New England Journal of Medicine* 265:885–892.

Epilogue The Future of Health Care in America: Some Ethical Considerations

Since the contents of this volume have demonstrated a close relationship between the character of a society and its health-care system, to predict the future of the latter would necessarily involve forecasting the future of the former, an enormously difficult if not impossible task. Certainly one major feature of the American health services system is, analogous to American society itself, its pluralistic nature, with a wide range of providers of health care from the "private," voluntary sector as much if not more than from the "public" sector. Clearly a major factor in American health care in recent years has been the increasing role of government, as a payer if not provider of health care, and the advent of some form of national or universal health insurance will further increase government's role as a "third party" in health care—which will probably be resisted in varying degrees of success by existing providers and their organizational representatives.

Underlying all this activity by societal, political, economic, professional, legal, and other interest groups to determine public policy is the premise that scientific medicine is good, although expensive, and is worth fighting for. Only in few quarters is the efficacy of medical care in this nation seriously questioned. The American public is "sold" on scientific medicine and is also optimistic about the wonders it will bring in the future.

Despite this widespread belief of biomedical progress, in medical and other circles there has been some recent reevaluation of its ethical and existential issues. Renée Fox suggests that a serious reexamination of some basic cultural assumptions underlying modern medicine is occurring and may have significant consequences for the future of medical care in the United States and other Western countries.

In the concluding chapter of this section and volume, Dan Beauchamp discusses the ethical bases of public health, which may be out of step with the prevailing "market-justice" of American society and may need to develop a new public health ethic and policy that would render its practices far more effective than under existing premises.

These final chapters, comprising the epilogue of this volume, point out the ethical, cultural, and value-premises of the medical- and health-care enterprise. Such premises change, however, and are possibly undergoing subtle but perceptible alteration today. Any changes in the ethical foundations of medicine and medical care would have profound changes in the structure, practice, and delivery of medical care to the American people in the future.

This change should be an important topic of study of the social and behavioral sciences as another contribution to our better understanding of human health and life.

RENÉE C. FOX

26   Ethical and Existential Developments in Contemporaneous American Medicine: Their Implications for Culture and Society

Contemporaneous Western medicine is often depicted as a vast body of scientific knowledge, technical skills, medicaments, and machinery wielded by physician-led teams of hospital-based professionals and paraprofessionals, garbed in uniforms of starched white, surgical green, and auxiliary pink or blue. Underlying this image is the conception that medicine is shaped primarily by scientific and technological advances, and that its major impetus derives from a highly organized collective effort vigorously to preserve life, by attaining a progressive mastery over illness and preventable death.

However commonplace and accurate this notion of modern medicine may be in some regards, it is distorted and obsolete in others. It does not take into account a new and important set of developments in present-day medicine that seems to be gaining momentum. Over the course of the past fifteen years, in a number of European and American societies, concerned interest in ethical and existential issues related to biomedical progress and to the delivery of medical care has become both more manifest and legitimate in medical circles and in other professional and organized lay groups as well. This is a phenomenon that merits sociological attention for it suggests that a serious re-examination of certain basic cultural assumptions on which modern medicine is premised may be taking place.

This paper will identify some of the forms in which these moral and metaphysical problems are currently being raised in the medical sector of American (U.S.A.) society. It will also essay an interpretive analysis of the broader sociocultural implications of the more general re-evaluative process that I believe is occurring in this fashion.

> Recent advances in biology and medicine make it increasingly clear that we are rapidly acquiring greater powers to modify and perhaps control the capacities and activities of men by direct intervention into and manipulation of their bodies and minds. Certain means are already in use or at hand—for example, organ transplantation, prenatal diagnosis of genetic defects, and electrical stimulation of the brain. Others await the solution of relatively minor technical problems . . . still others depend upon further basic research. . . .

Prepared for presentation at the Conference on Medical Sociology, sponsored by the Polish Academy of Sciences and endorsed by the Research Committee on the Sociology of Medicine of the International Sociological Association. Warsaw (Jablonna), Poland, August 20–August 25, 1973. The article is a somewhat altered version of the original paper. It has been changed primarily to report certain bioethical developments which have occurred since 1973.

Reprinted from *Health and Society, Milbank Memorial Fund Quarterly*, 52: 445–483, Fall, 1974, by permission of the author and Publisher.

While holding forth the promise of continued improvement in medicine's abilities to cure disease and alleviate suffering, these developments also pose profound questions and troublesome problems. There are questions about who shall benefit from and who shall pay for the use of new technologies. . . . There will be questions about our duties to future generations and about the limits on what we can and cannot do to the unborn. . . . We shall face questions concerning the desirable limits of the voluntary manipulation of our own bodies and minds. . . . We shall face questions about the impact of biomedical technology on our social institutions. . . . We shall face serious questions of law and legal institutions . . . [and] problems of public policy. . . .

. . . as serious and vexing as these practical problems may be, there is yet another matter more profound. The biomedical technologies work directly on man's biological nature, including those aspects long regarded [as] most distinctively human. . . . The impact on our ideas of free will, birth, and death, and the good life is likely to be even more staggering than any actual manipulation performed with the new technologies. These are matters of great moment and we urgently need to take counsel from some of our best minds. . . .

The statement quoted above was not made by a physician, a scientist, or a philosopher. It was delivered by the Honorable Walter F. Mondale of Minnesota, a member of the United States Senate. He made these remarks from the floor of the Senate in 1971, as he introduced a bill to establish a National Advisory Commission on Health Science and Society. The measure was intended to provide for "study and evaluation of the ethical, social and legal implications of advances in biomedical research and technology." What is particularly significant about the Mondale proposal is that it demonstrates that involvement with the issues it cites is not confined to medical and academic milieux. Rather, these matters have entered political and public domains in American society.

The specific advances in biology and medicine to which Mondale alludes are those most generally invoked in the various contexts where such ethical, existential, and social questions are pondered. Actual and anticipated developments in genetic engineering and counseling, life support systems, birth technology, population control, the implantation of human, animal, and artificial organs, as well as in the modification and control of human thought and behavior are principal foci of concern. Within this framework, special attention is concentrated on the implications of amniocentesis (a procedure for detecting certain genetic disorders *in utero*),[1] *in vitro* fertilization, the prospect of cloning (the asexual reproduction of an unlimited number of genetically identical individuals from a single parent), organ transplantation, the use of the artificial kidney machine, the development of an artificial heart, the modalities of the intensive care unit, the practice of psychosurgery, and the introduction of psychotropic drugs. Cross-cutting the consideration being given to these general and concrete areas of biomedical development, there is marked preoccupation with the ethicality of human experimentation under various conditions, with the proper definition of death and the human treatment of the dying, and with the presumed right of every individual and group to health and adequate health care. Certain moral and metaphysical themes recur in the discussions of all these aspects of the so-called new biology and medicine. Problems of uncertainty, meaning, of the quality of

---

[1]This technique involves the insertion of a hollow needle through the abdominal and uterine walls of a pregnant woman into the amniotic sac, and withdrawing fluid and cells shed by the fetus.

life and death, of scarcity, equity and distributive justice, of freedom and coercion, dignity and degradation, solidarity and societal community, and of the vigor with which one ought to intervene in the human condition are repeatedly mentioned.

The media and agencies through which these concerns are expressed are manifold. Articles and editorials on these topics not only appear frequently in medical and scientific journals,[2] but also in popular magazines and daily newspapers. In the course of the week of July 8 to July 15, 1973,[3] for example, the New York *Times* published the following relevant items: two bulletin-type articles on the performance of two new heart transplants; two articles on recent cases of "euthanasia" or "mercy killing" that raise questions about the "right to die" and "death with dignity"; a long article reporting and analyzing a decision rendered by the Wayne County Circuit Court in Michigan that experimental psychosurgery may not be performed on persons confined against their will in state institutions, even when such a person's consent for this surgery is formally obtained; two feature articles with photographs, and an editorial on the ethical and legal implications of a case under investigation by three federal agencies and a Senate subcommittee, in which it is alleged that two mentally retarded black girls, ages 12 and 14, were sterilized by a federally funded family planning clinic in Montgomery, Alabama, without either their informed consent or that of their parents; another article with byline, announcing that based on comparable cases, the American Civil Liberties Union was filing a suit in federal district court, seeking to void as unconstitutional a North Carolina law allowing sterilization of "mentally defective" persons; a substantial article summarizing a report published in a journal of biomedical ethics concerning five experiments on human beings funded by grants from divisions of the Public Health Service that raise "disturbing ethical questions"; an article by one of the paper's medical writers on the "complex and not always obvious issues of medical research ethics" that have surfaced in a "recent spate" of stories of "abuse, real or potential," evoking "newly critical looks at medical ethics [by] Government and private citizens and new proposals for more effective controls"; and, finally, an article by the same writer on the redesigning of a national blood policy that is now under way in the United States with the goal of achieving an all-volunteer donor system in the next two years.

The numbers of books that have been published on such subjects and themes in the past ten years is impressive.[4] Leading the list, in saliency and frequency, is a group of books on death and dying. [For a more recent and extensive review of the burgeoning literature, see Fox, 1976.] The most famous of these, written by a

---

[2]In *Research on Human Subjects,* Barber et al. (1973: 2) comment that "the recent increase of concern in the biomedical research community . . . [about] the possible or actual abuse of the subjects of medical experimentation and medical innovation . . . can be seen perhaps most clearly in the dramatic rise of medical journal articles devoted to facets of this problem." Barber et al. (1973: 2-3) report that in a survey they made of articles listed in *Index Medicus* over the period 1950 to 1969, those that dealt with the ethics of biomedical research on human subjects increased "in both the absolute number and the proportion of articles in this area. . . . The figure begins to get large in 1966."

[3]This is the week when I happened to be writing this section of my paper. In that sense, it was chosen randomly.

[4]For an excellent review-essay of the scope and content of the burgeoning literature on ethical and existential aspects of medicine published during the decade 1960-1970, see J.R. Elkinton (1970).

psychiatrist, Dr. Elizabeth Kubler-Ross, and published in 1969, had sold over 100,000 copies in the paperback edition alone by the end of 1972. Presenting firsthand case materials based on her intensive work with incurably ill and dying patients, Dr. Kubler-Ross delineates what she considers to be the five psychological stages through which a dying person characteristically evolves. She both explicitly and implicitly affirms that persons passing through these "final stages of life" can be our "teacher(s)," helping medical professionals, and all of us, not to "shy away from the 'hopelessly' sick," as she feels we are inclined to do in American society. Those who "get closer" to the dying, she asserts, will not only "help them during their final hours . . . they will learn much about the functioning of the human mind, the unique human aspects of our existence, and will emerge from the experience enriched . . . perhaps with fewer anxieties about their own finality."[5] Less directly, Dr. Kubler-Ross's book also evokes questions about the rationality and humanity of our medical and cultural propensity to do everything possible to "save" and prolong life. If there is a phenomenon akin to a "death and dying movement" occurring in the United States, as we believe there may be, then Elizabeth Kubler-Ross is one of its charismatic leaders.[6]

Another important collection of books that has appeared in the last few years is devoted to the ethics and legal aspects of biomedical research on human subjects. . . . In all these books, the problem of the rights and adequate protection of subjects looms large, as does the question of how best to establish surveillance and social control over the activities of investigators, without unduly impeding research. A great deal of consideration is given to the necessity and difficulties of obtaining truly informed and voluntary consent from subjects. Special attention is focused on candidates for research who are already subject to particular kinds of dependence, disability, or constraint, such as children, persons who are mentally retarded or mentally ill, prisoners, the poor, and the minimally educated. The question of what constitutes the most just allocation of limited and costly experimental therapies is debated in these works, along with the issue of when a society may expose some of its members to risk or harm, in order to seek benefits for them, for others, or for the society as a whole. Each of these volumes cites and examines problematic instances of human experimentation that are known to have taken place.

Two other types of relevant books are being published in significant numbers: those dealing with ethical and existential aspects of specific biomedical developments, and those that treat a broad range of such moral and metaphysical issues as they apply to numerous medical phenomena. . . .

A number of social patterns applicable to this flow of articles and books are worthy of note. To begin with, the authors of these works come from a broad spectrum of fields, including journalism, politics, the law, the clergy, philosophy, ethics, theology, social science, social work, nursing, and psychiatry, as well as medicine and biology. Secondly, a considerable amount of the research and reflection on which these writings are based has been sponsored or supported by

---

[5]Elizabeth Kubler-Ross (1969: Preface, no page given).

[6]Professor Diana Crane (who is also a member of the Department of Sociology of the University of Pennsylvania) and I are planning a paper on this phenomenon, tentatively entitled, "The Death and Dying Movement: A New Kind of Social Movement?"

established private foundations like the Ford, Robert Wood Johnson, Joseph P. Kennedy, Jr., Rockefeller, and Russell Sage Foundations, by scholarly bodies, such as the American Academy of Arts and Sciences, the New York Academy of Sciences, the United States National Academy of Sciences, and by some government agencies, notably, several branches of the National Institutes of Health and the National Endowment for the Humanities.

What is perhaps more striking is the fact that the interest and work that these publications reflect have brought into being a network of new organizations whose principal *raison d'être* is to deal with these matters. Among the most prominent in the United States are the Institute of Society, Ethics and the Life Sciences in Hastings-on-the-Hudson, New York; the Society for Health and Human Values in Philadelphia; the Foundation of Thanatology in New York City; the Euthanasia Society of America and the Euthanasia Educational Fund, both in New York City; the Committee on the Life Sciences and Social Policy of the National Research Council, a division of the National Academy of Sciences of Washington, D.C.; and the Joseph and Rose Kennedy Institute for the Study of Human Reproduction and Bioethics, located at Georgetown University in Washington. With the exception of the two euthanasia societies, these groups, and others like them, have all been founded since 1969.[7]

Mention has been made of the National Advisory Commission on Health Science and Society proposed by Senator Walter Mondale. In addition, the health subcommittees both of the Senate and the House of Representatives have been transformed by their respective chairmen, Senator Edward M. Kennedy of Massachusetts and Representative Paul G. Rogers of Florida, into groups that are actively engaged in conducting investigations and hearings on medical issues of social, ethical, and existential import, in raising public consciousness about these matters, and in proposing legislation and other control mechanisms bearing upon them. It is of some consequence to observe that the medico-moral concerns to which Mondale, Kennedy, and Rogers are addressing themselves have sufficient public resonance to enhance the political following and prestige of these men in the eyes of their local and national constituencies. The most important piece of legislation that has thus far resulted from their activities is the National Research Act (H.R. 7724) which was passed by both houses of Congress, and signed into law by President Nixon on July 12, 1974. Title II of this act established a temporary two-year National Commission for the Protection of Human Subjects of Biomedical and Behavioral Research. The commission, an advisory body to the Department of Health, Education, and Welfare (HEW), is composed of eleven members who were named by HEW Secretary Caspar Weinberger on September 10, 1974. Their task is to study a number of ethical issues set forth in

[7]In the international sphere, there are some comparable developments. For example, the Council for International Organizations of Medical Science (CIOMS), a nongovernmental agency created in 1949 by the World Health Organization and UNESCO to re-establish scientific communications after World War II, has now turned its primary attention to interdisciplinary conferences and publications on topics such as the "protection of human rights in the light of scientific and technological progress in biology and medicine" (Round Table Conference scheduled to be held in Geneva, November 14–16, 1973). Furthermore, the CIOMS has recommended that a new international entity be established to explore the "moral and social issues" raised by new and forthcoming developments in biomedicine.

the law. These include fetal research, the problem of obtaining informed voluntary consent for investigations in which children, prisoners, or persons who are mentally ill or retarded are asked to participate as subjects, and the ethics of psychosurgery. When the two-year life span of the commission is ended, a permanent council to deal with these matters will come into being.[8]

Their growing numbers and diverse backgrounds notwithstanding, the scholars, scientists, medical and legal practitioners, authors, foundation officials, organization members, and legislators seriously involved in considering ethical and existential aspects of biomedicine can be said to constitute a closely knit "social circle." Not only do they belong to overlapping groups and read each other's work attentively, but they participate in many of the same formal meetings, meet informally, communicate with one another through correspondence and by telephone, call upon one another as consultants, and recommend each other for relevant assignments and honors.[9]

The new institutional forms that are being summoned forth by these developments in contemporaneous medicine extend beyond the establishment of pertinent contemplative and action-oriented groups. Another kind of emergent phenomenon is the gradual formation of "bioethics," an incipient new discipline. Its contours are still not clear. In the words of Daniel Callahan (1973: 68), "Most of its practitioners have wandered into the field from somewhere else, more or less inventing it as they go. Its vague and problematic status in philosophy and theology is matched by its even more shaky standing in the life sciences." Callahan (1973: 73) goes on to advocate that if bioethics is to develop into a full and accepted field, it should be interdisciplinary and problem- and case-focused in the following regard:

> . . . so designed, and its practitioners so trained that it will directly—at whatever cost to disciplinary elegance—serve those physicians and biologists whose position demands that they make practical decisions. This requires, ideally, a number of ingredients as part of the training . . . of the bioethicist: sociological understanding of the medical and biological communities; psychological understanding of the kinds of needs felt by researchers and clinicians, patients and physicians, and the varieties of pressures to which they are subject; historical understanding of the sources of regnant value theories and common practices; requisite scientific training; awareness of and facility with the usual methods of ethical analysis as understood in the philosophical and theological communities . . . and personal exposure to the kinds of ethical problems which arise in medicine and biology.

Although bioethics is still a tentative field, and its definition and legitimacy are under discussion, a comprehensive *Encyclopedia of Bioethics* already is in preparation. Its editor (Warren T. Reich, a former theology professor at Catholic University) and his staff are based at the Kennedy Institute of Georgetown University. Their advisory editors are drawn from multiple university, foundation, and government milieux. And the project is financed by the Kennedy Foun-

[8]For a competent and critical account of the history of the National Research Act, its development and its provisions, see Culliton (1974a).

[9]A systematic study of the sociometry of this circle, its patterns of communication, and their consequences for intellectual growth and policy formation in this area, such as Diana Crane carried out in two scientific communities, would be illuminating. See Crane (1972).

dation and the National Endowment for the Humanities.[10] [*Editor's note:* The *Encyclopedia of Bioethics* was ready for publication in late 1978; the project was also financed by other foundations and endowments.]

Quite apart from the prognosis for bioethics as a discipline, a new conception of medical ethics seems to be unfolding in the medical profession. Increasingly, medical ethics is being viewed less exclusively as a code of professional etiquette. It is coming to be regarded as a component virtually of all medical decision making and to including the questions of how such decisions should be made and who should participate in them, as well as what ideally ought to be done in given cases. Even the conservative American Medical Association has expanded its ethical program to encompass these broader considerations, along with the dilemmas posed by recent biomedical advances.

But it is in medical schools that one sees the most significant activity in this regard. In 1970, for example, under the aegis of Drs. Robert M. Veatch and Willard Gaylin, both members of the Institute of Society, Ethics and the Life Sciences, the Columbia College of Physicians and Surgeons launched an experimental Medical Ethics Program (see Veatch and Gaylin, 1972). This Program included lectures, seminars, clinical case conferences, dinner-discussion meetings and intensive workshops for students in every stage of medical school training. An internship in medical ethics for several fourth-year students was also created; an interdisciplinary seminar on "the new biology and the law" that brought medical students together with students from Columbia Law School and the Union Theological Seminary was organized; and sessions on medical ethics for interested faculty and clinical staff were arranged. This Program has had wide repercussions. Its staff has made a survey of the teaching of medical ethics in medical schools throughout the country, has developed bibliographies and case studies that are available upon request, has acted as consultants to other medical schools, and, in June 1972, organized a National Conference on the Teaching of Medical Ethics. Although their survey revealed that in the curricula of most medical schools medical ethical issues are presented largely on an informal and somewhat *ad hoc* basis, institutional response to the Medical Ethics Program staff "suggests a rapidly developing interest in the [formal] teaching of medical ethics" (Veatch and Gaylin, 1972: 785). By October 1971, the program's staff already had been consulted by 29 American medical schools, in addition to faculty in biology, philosophy, religion, law, and social science departments; and about 150 representatives from medical school faculties attended the National Conference on the Teaching of Medical Ethics.

In my view, one of the most significant patterns that Veatch and Gaylin (1972: 783) report is that their whole undertaking was initiated by medical students:

> Early in 1970 a group of students, upon hearing a lecture pointing out the ethical implications of the judgments made in the practice of psychiatry, ap-

---

[10]An interesting history and sociology of science kind of question that might be posed here is whether there is any precedent or principle that would lead one to assume that the preparation of such an encyclopedia will help to establish a field that only potentially exists. For, normally, one would expect an encyclopedia to appear when a field is firmly rooted and recognized, with a sufficiently well-defined body of theory, methodology, and empirical data to be articulated.

proached the curriculum committee of the school and members of the Institute of Society, Ethics and the Life Sciences and asked that a full program be established, one which would make ethical and social perspectives an integral part of their medical education. . . .

This is consistent with what I believe to be a fundamental shift in the outlook of American medical students. It has been remarked that medical students of the late 1960s and early 1970s appear to be more socially concerned than their predecessors. They are especially outspoken about the inadequacies and inequities in the nation's system of health care delivery, about the responsibility that they feel the established medical profession bears for the existence of these deficiences and injustices, and about their own determination to play an active role as physicians in eliminating them. How deep these concerns and commitments of the "new" medical student go, and how enduring they will prove to be is a matter of some debate not only among medical educators, but also among students themselves (who are inclined to be self-critical in this, as well as in other matters). Whatever their long-term import, these medical student tendencies are sufficiently notable to have elicited continuing discussion about whether or not they will persist under the impact of students' medical educational experiences and the demands that their subsequent medical careers will make upon them.[11] Accompanying the ostensible social consciousness of present-day medical students, and integrally related to it, is their manifest interest in ethical and existential aspects of medicine. Along with their concern about a more just allocation of material and immaterial medical resources in American society, one of the areas in which students' moral and metaphysical interests are most apparent is that of "death and dying." Their orientation is distinctly different from the attitudes toward death and the ambiance surrounding it that predominated in American medical schools twenty years ago. In a recent article, I have portrayed the contrast as follows (Parsons et al., 1972: 367–415):

> . . . In the medical school climate of the 1950's . . . faculty virtually never raised questions with students like "what is death?" "why death?" or "in what deeper senses, if any, does death differ from life?" Even in situations conducive to such querying—notably, the anatomy laboratory, the autopsy, or in the face of students' early confrontation with terminally ill patients—instructors rarely initiated such discussions. And if a student made a timorous effort to do so, he was likely to be silenced by classmates and faculty alike with the quip, "that's too philosophical." Decoded, this meant "the matters of which you speak are

---

[11]Studies of the social backgrounds of men and women currently entering medical school, of the attitudes, values, sentiments and life experiences that led them to opt for medicine, and of the sociopsychological as well as cognitive learning that they undergo in the course of medical school, house officer training, and their early years of practice are very much needed. Whereas several such major studies of medical socialization were carried out in the 1950s, for reasons that merit investigation, no such studies that are comparable in depth and scope have been attempted more recently.

My own comments about medical student attitudes and interests set forth in this paper are based upon the data I gathered as chief field worker for a study of the education and socialization of medical students conducted in the mid-1950s by the Columbia University Bureau of Applied Social Research. *The Student Physician* (Merton et al., 1975) was a product of that investigation. My observations on medical students in the late 1960s and early 1970s are less extensive and systematic. They grow out of my role as a sociologist in the Departments of Psychiatry and Medicine of the University of Pennsylvania, and from the numerous opportunities that I have to visit other medical schools as a consequence of my continuing research and teaching in the sociology of medicine.

not sufficiently rational, objective, scientific or pragmatic to fall within the proper domain of medicine, or of truly professional behavior.'' It was also characteristic of this decade that [medical students and their teachers] were more inclined to speak euphemistically about the death of a patient—"he [she] expired," "passed on," or "was transferred to Ward X"—than straightfor-wardly to state that death had occurred. In sharp contrast to such medical at-titudes in the 1950's (at least in academic milieux where new physicians were be-ing trained and scientific research emphasized), the late 1960's and early 1970's appear very "philosophical." . . .

In addition to new organizations, new intellectual disciplines and new perspec-tives on the part of medical students and educators, certain spokesmen for medical practitioners, some legislators and sectors of the lay public, the ethical and existential refocusing of medicine has been accompanied by three other in-stitutional responses. These consist of new guidelines, or codes, several morato-ria, and a number of legal decisions and statutes.

Perhaps the most momentous guideline issued thus far is the new criterion for judging a person dead that was formulated and proposed by Harvard Medical School's Ad Hoc Committee to Examine the Definition of Brain Death (1968), chaired by Dr. Henry K. Beecher, and consisting of nine physicians, a lawyer, a historian of science, and a theologian. The Harvard report opened with the state-ment that the Committee's "primary purpose [was] to define irreversible coma as a new criterion for death," and that there were two reasons why there was "a need for a definition":

(1) Improvements in resuscitative and supportive measures have led to increased efforts to save those who are desperately injured. Sometimes these efforts have only partial success so that the result is an individual whose heart continues to beat but whose brain is irreversibly damaged. The burden is great on patients who suffer permanent loss of intellect, on their families, on the hospitals, and on those in need of hospital beds already occupied by these comatose patients.
(2) Obsolete criteria for the definition of death can lead to controversy in ob-taining organs for transplantation.

The report went on to identify and describe in detail the major characteristics of a state of irreversible coma, which indicates a *"permanently* [italicized in the report] nonfunctioning brain." These are: "unreceptivity and unresponsivity [to] externally applied stimuli and inner needs," "no spontaneous muscular move-ments or spontaneous respiration," and "the absence of elicitable responses." A flat or isoelectric electroencephalogram is held to be "of great confirmatory value." Furthermore, it is advocated that all the tests involved in these various determinations (which not only assess higher brain functions, but brain stem and spinal cord activity and spontaneous respiration, as well) should be "repeated at least 24 hours later with no change." In effect, the committee has recommended that the traditional method used by physicians for ascertaining and pronouncing death—the total cessation of all vital signs, that is, heart beat and respiration—be replaced by criteria for "cerebral death" or "brain death." Although this pro-posal has evoked a certain amount of commentary and some disquietude both in lay and professional circles, by and large, it has been well received, particularly in the medical community. "It is remarkable," Dr. David D. Rutstein of Harvard Medical School has observed with concern (1970: 386) that "a revolution in our cultural concept of death . . . this major ethical change . . . has occurred right before our eyes, and that this change is more and more widely accepted with little public discussion of its significance. This new definition . . . raises more questions than it answers.''

A second important set of guidelines that has been set forth is that ''relating to moral and ethical aspects of clinical investigation.'' A policy statement formulated in 1966 by the National Institutes of Health (NIH) and Public Health Service (PHS) (see Curran, 1970: 402–454) mandated that all clinical research involving human subjects supported by the NIH or PHS should be submitted to peer review by a committee of colleagues from the principal investigator's institution. That review should address itself to the rights and welfare of the human subjects involved, to the appropriateness of methods used to secure their informed consent, and to the risk-benefit ratio that the research entails. In 1971, these requirements were extended to all research on human subjects supported by any agency of the Department of Health, Education, and Welfare (HEW), the parent organization of the NIH and PHS. It is expected that over the next two years, the federal commission on ethics created by the National Research Act will supplement these general guidelines with more specific recommendations concerning psychosurgery, as well as clinical research on the fetus, the abortus, children, prisoners, and on the institutionalized mentally disabled. In principle, the commission has no regulatory authority, and its guidelines apply only to research funded by HEW. But its *de facto* influences on HEW and also on other agencies is expected to be considerable. For, the act requires that whenever the commission submits a recommendations to the Secretary of HEW, within 60 days, he must publish it in the *Federal Register* for comment. No more than 180 days later, the Secretary must act upon the recommendation, and if he decides to reject it, he must give his reasons for doing so, in writing. Although legally, the commission's deliberations are only relevant to research funded by HEW, many members of Congress are eager to have guidelines developed that are broadly applicable to other governmental organizations. And the commission has been asked to devise a mechanism to make the rules pertaining to human experimentation uniform.

A third type of policy statement has been set forth. This concerns a formal determination of where, on the experiment-therapy spectrum, a therapeutic innovation can be said to fall at a given phase in its development, and how and when, in the light of its status, it ought (or ought not) to be utilized. The best example of this sort of guideline is the statements on human cardiac transplantation issued by several different medical associations and government-affiliated medical groups. . . . The over-all judgment on heart transplants that emerges from these position papers is that ''the procedure of total cardiac replacement is so formidable, and uncertainties about the duration of life after replacement are so great, that physicians may be expected to be conservative about recommending it for an individual patient.'' Replacement cannot ''as yet be regarded as an accepted form of therapy, or even an heroic one. It must be clearly viewed for what it is, a scientific exploration of the unknown, only the very first step of which is the actual feat of transplanting an organ.'' For this reason, ''it may be reasonably assumed that imminent death will be the basic criterion for total cardiac replacement, at least in the near future.'' The ''primary justification'' for heart transplants at this time is deemed to be the ''new knowledge of benefit to others in our society'' that may come from it. In light of this view, and in recognition of the fact that ''theologians, lawyers and other public-spirited persons, as well as physicians are discussing with deep concern the many new questions raised by the transplantation of vital organs," specific recommendations are made about the proper treatment of donors and recipients, the types of medical center qualified to undertake the operation, and the appropriate reporting of a transplantation both in medical journals and the mass media.

This period of "deep concern" about the issues raised by human experimentation and by biomedical advances like the increasing ability to maintain certain signs of life artificially or to transplant human organs has also generated moratoria of several kinds. The first of these is what Judith P. Swazey and I have called clinical moratoria: the suspension of the use of a still experimental medical or surgical procedure on patients. This type of moratorium usually occurs in the stage of development of a new treatment when the uncertainties and risks associated with it are very high and become starkly apparent. Often, the patient mortality rate seems unbearable or unjustifiable. Pressure for such a moratorium can come from physician-investigators' own reactions to the situation and/or from "external" sources (from their colleagues, the institution in which they work, patients and their families, organizations sponsoring their research, and, less frequently, from the courts).

One important instance of such a moratorium (that we have personally had an opportunity to study) is the virtual cessation of human heart transplants (see Fox and Swazey, 1974: 122–148). As compared with 1968, for example, which was heralded by the mass media as the "Year of the Transplant," because 105 cardiac transplantations were performed throughout the world in that year alone, 1974 is a time when only an occasional heart transplant is done. The very high mortality rate of the persons who have undergone this procedure and their relatively short period of survival have been primary factors in the demise of the operation. The pressures that resulted in this moratorium came principally from within the medical profession itself, from prospective donors, recipients and their families, and from the mass media's continual publishing of heart transplant "box scores."

I have already identified another, more recent moratorium that was enacted into state law in July 1973 in a Michigan circuit court. Here, three judges renderd a unanimous opinion against the experimental performance of psychosurgery on persons involuntarily confined to state institutions. The judges based their opinion on the fact that brain surgery to attempt the correction of behavioral abnormalities like murderous aggression is "clearly experimental, poses substantial danger to research subjects, and carries substantial unknown risks," such as the blunting of emotions, the deadening of memory, the reduction of affect, and limitation of ability to generate new ideas. Furthermore, the judges reasoned, there is "no persuasive showing" that, in its present stage of development, this neurosurgical procedure would have its intended beneficial effects. In addition to the "unfavorable risk-benefit ratio" involved, it was concluded that the procedure ought not to be performed in the kind of case under consideration, because an involuntarily confined mental patient, living in an "inherently coercive atmosphere," has been intrinsically deprived of the basic conditions that are requisite to voluntary consent.[12]

[12]As already indicated, the ethics of psychosurgery is one of the major questions that the National Commission for the Protection of Human Subjects of Biomedical and Behavioral Research,

This ruling is related to another type of moratorium that is being considered: the halting of medical experimentation on certain categories of persons. In this case, what is being contemplated is calling a moratorium on research conducted on "captives" of the state—prisoners, as well as involuntarily committed mental patients—in order to provide optimal conditions for re-evaluating the circumstances, if any, under which such research might be justified. The major impetus for this moratorium has been coming from the Senate Health Subcommittee, while a serious review of research on prisoners, mentally ill and mentally retarded persons, and on children is under way at the National Institutes of Health as part of their general inquiry into ethical guidelines for clinical research.[13] The federal commission on ethics created by the National Research Act has also been asked to examine this question.

Two other moratoria which have developed are concerned with embryonic human life, in both the literal and figurative senses of the term. The first of these moratoria, a ban on fetal research, was officially declared by Title II of the National Research Act. The act charges the National Commission for the Protection of Human Subjects of Biomedical and Behavioral Research with the task of studying the nature, extent, and purposes of research involving living fetuses, as well as alternative ways of achieving these purposes. The commission has been given four months to complete this study, and to make recommendations to the Secretary of HEW. Until regulations are issued governing fetal research, HEW has decreed that its health agencies, grantees, and contractors "may not conduct or support research in the United States or abroad on a living human fetus, before or after the induced abortion of such fetus, unless such research is done for the purpose of assuring the survival of such a fetus."

This moratorium grows partly out of the fact that many more abortions are now being legally performed by reputable physicians, as a consequence of a recent United States Supreme Court decision (Roe v. Wade, 1973) in which it was stated that there exists "no compelling State interest" to warrant intervention in abortion decisions during the first two trimesters of pregnancy. The purpose of the moratorium is to give relevant experts the time and responsibility systematically to reflect on how to deal with the complex ethical and existential

---

created by the National Research Act, has been asked to study. Until their deliberations are completed, HEW is maintaining the position that psychosurgery is a highly experimental procedure, which should be done only under the most rigorously defined and controlled circumstances.

[13]Concern over the conditions under which serious medical procedures ought to be carried out on persons whose ability to give informed voluntary consent may be constrained by institutional pressures to which they are subject has spread beyond the realm of human experimentation. For example, this issue is being vigorously debated in connection with the controversy over the way in which sterilization has been carried out on girls and women in HEW-sponsored welfare programs. Earlier in this article, mention was made of the case of two mentally retarded, teenaged, black, Alabama girls whose family was on relief, and who were sterilized without their own or their parents' understanding of the procedure or its consequences. Since the disclosure of that case, numerous others like it have been revealed. The American Civil Liberties Union, Ralph Nader's Health Research Group, the Mental Health Law Project, and at least fourteen other women's and civil rights groups, as well as some state legislators and the Senate Health Committee have all entered this arena of dispute. In response to the growing argument, the HEW has been trying to draft a set of acceptable regulations that would permit federal funds to be used for nontherapeutic sterilization, without violating informed voluntary consent or other civil and client rights. A number of lawsuits involving sterilization are in process. For a useful summary of the sterilization controversy, see Coburn (1974).

questions that increasing opportunities to conduct experiments on, or manipulate human fetuses have begun to raise. When does life begin? When does a living human embryo acquire "protectable humanity" (Kass, 1972: 32)? Is there any morally viable way in which proper consent for experimentation on human fetuses can be obtained? From whom should such consent be sought: from the would-have-been mother and/or father, for example? To whom does the aborted fetus "belong," or, at least, to whom should it be entrusted?

Certain states and cities have taken local measures to enforce a moratorium on fetal research. A law passed in California in 1973 forbids scientific experiments on human fetuses. Cleveland, Ohio, now has an ordinance that prohibits research on products of aborted human conception, or the medical use of these products. And on April 11, 1974, in Boston, Massachusetts, four physicians at Boston City Hospital were indicted by a county grand jury who accused them of violating an 1814 Massachusetts grave-robbing law, because they had studied the effect of two antibiotics on aborted fetuses, as well as on the women who had been pregnant with them.[14]

There is a second moratorium associated with the issues raised by fetal research, which has been developing. This is an incipient moratorium, rather than one that has already been formally declared, and it applies to *in vitro* fertilization: the implantation into a woman's uterine cavity of human egg cells that have been fertilized by human sperm in the test tube.

Various biologists, physicians, theologians, and philosophers, as well as members of the right to life movement have actively worked to deter this line of biomedical research. The *Journal of the American Medical Association* has gone so far as to publish a statement advocating a complete "moratorium on experiments that would attempt to implant an in vitro-conceptus into a woman's womb." Such individuals and groups have asserted that a ban on embryo implants ought to be enacted in order to avert the social, moral, and metaphysical problems that they anticipate would ensue from the successful application of a "new method for making babies" (Kass, 1972: 19). Among the objections to *in*

[14]For a detailed account of the Boston "grave-robbing" case, see Culliton (1974b). Among the factors that brought it to the attention of the district attorney's office, the public, and the court were the political activities of a local branch of the National Right to Life Committee. This is an organized antiabortion movement, headed by the Reverend Warren A. Schaller, Jr., an Episcopal priest. The committee was incorporated as a nonprofit organization in 1973, after several years of formal affiliation with the United States Catholic Conference. The 1973 Supreme Court decision on abortion added momentum to the right to life movement. It has been particularly vigorous and influential in Boston, in political and Roman Catholic milieux.

Another medical area in which ethical and existential issues closely associated with some of those raised by experimentation with human fetuses has been surfacing concerns the decisions made in special-care nurseries about whether or not to treat infants born with severe genetic defects. In an article entitled "Moral and ethical dilemmas in the special-care nursery," which has attracted a great deal of professional and public attention, Dr. Raymond S. Duff and Dr. A.G.M. Campbell (1973) confront the question, "who decides for a child":

. . . It may be acceptable for a person to reject treatment and bring about his own death. But it is a quite different situation when others are doing this for him. We do not know how often families and their physicians will make just decisions for severely handicapped children. Clearly, this issue is central in evaluation of the process of decision making that we have described. But we also ask, if these parties cannot make such decisions justly, who can? . . .

vitro fertilization that have been raised, two are especially prominent. It has been contended that reproduction is human, personal, and moral only when conception results from so-called ordinary, heterosexual intercourse (preferably within the confines of marriage). It has also been argued that because it is an "artificial," "engineered" mode of reproduction, *in vitro* fertilization may be conducive to the development of fetal anomalies and aberrations that could be difficult to prevent, remedy, or eliminate.[15]

One other genre of moratorium on biomedical research that has recently been invoked is perhaps the rarest of them all. Unlike the other moratoria, it does not concern clinical research that is conducted on human subjects. Rather, it addresses itself to certain kinds of experiments that involve the genetic manipulation of living cells and viruses, which a group of distinguished molecular biologists feel could have unpredictably hazardous "bioconsequences" for man. These scientists form the Committee on Recombinant DNA Molecules of the Assembly of Life Sciences of the National Research Council, which is under the aegis of the National Academy of Sciences. They have asked "scientists throughout the world" to join them in "voluntarily deferring" research which would insert either new bacterial or viral genetic material into bacteria (such as *Escherichia coli*, which commonly resides in the human intestinal tract), that could infect human beings. Their appeal was issued in the form of a cosigned statement that was published in July, 1974, in *Science*, and also in *Nature* (Berg et al., 1974: 303). They have appealed to all investigators working in this area temporarily to halt these types of research "until attempts have been made to evaluate the hazards and some resolution of the outstanding questions has been achieved." They have also recommended that experiments that entail inserting animal genes

---

[15]Some writers, like Leon Kass, who take this point of view also believe that because a "test-tube" embryo is so willfully created and "wanted," it may be more immoral to resort to abortion to destroy such a fetus (if, for example, it is seriously defective), than it would be if the fetus were conceived through sexual intercourse.

It should be mentioned here that in July of this year, at the annual scientific meeting of the British Medical Association at Hull, in Yorkshire, Dr. Douglas Bevis, a professor of gynecology and obstetrics at Leeds University, handed out a press release in which he announced that human embryos conceived *in vitro* had been successfully implanted in the wombs of three women, who had given birth to normal babies. According to his report, the women had been infertile due to diseased, blocked, or missing Fallopian tubes. Eggs had been surgically removed from the women, fertilized in test tubes with their husbands' sperm, and subsequently reimplanted in the women's wombs. Dr. Bevis said that out of the thirty such attempts he had made, these were the only successful ones. The babies were said to range in age from twelve to eighteen months, and to be developing normally. By and large, medical scientists and physicians in Britain and abroad responded to this report with a mixture of skepticism and criticism. The fact that Dr. Bevis had worked in secret, had never published his findings in a medical scientific paper, and refused to reveal the identities or whereabouts of the infants and their parents, in the name of safeguarding their privacy, contributed to the disbelief and disapproval of the medical scientific community. The frustrated competitive ambitions of some clinical researchers who had aspired to be "first" in this area may also have been involved in the adverse reaction. But the apprehension that physicians and scientists expressed over the biological and moral consequences that might ensue from such an accomplishment, whenever it might occur, sounded genuine. In a later news report, Dr. Bevis was quoted as expressing chagrin over the reaction that his original press release had evoked. He affirmed that because of it, he was seriously considering calling a halt to this aspect of his work. If, in fact, he has now done so, his act can be thought of as a personally imposed moratorium, brought about by the disapproving attitudes of the medical profession, conveyed to Dr. Bevis largely through the media of mass communication.

into bacteria "should not be undertaken lightly." According to *Science*, this is "apparently the first time that biologists have publicly called attention to the possible public hazards of their own research" since 1969, and that they "have ever suggested that their own line of investigation should be halted" (Wade, 1974: 332).

A final indicator of the degree to which not only the American medical profession but the society at large has been deliberating ethical and existential issues associated with biomedicine is some of the legislation concerned with life and death matters that has been drafted in the last few years. The Kansas Death Statute, the Uniform Anatomical Gift Act and the United States Supreme Court decision on the Texas abortion case of Roe *v*. Wade represent three such major pieces of legislation.

In 1970, the state of Kansas (1970) adopted "An Act relating to and defining death," which was the first attempt legislatively to reformulate the standards for determining death. The Kansas statute sets forth and grants equal validity to two "alternative definitions of death": the traditional notion that a person is "medically and legally dead" if a physician determines "there is the absence of spontaneous respiratory and cardiac function and . . . attempts as resuscitation are considered hopeless"; and the new, irreversible coma criterion of death, which turns on the absence of spontaneous brain function if during "reasonable attempts" either to maintain or restore spontaneous circulatory or respiratory function, "it appears that further attempts at resuscitation or supportive maintenance will not succeed." The statute has received a great deal of attention. It has served as a model for similar legislation enacted in the state of Maryland in 1972, as well as for statutes now under consideration in a number of other jurisdictions. It has also been vigorously criticized for its dualistic approach to death, for the fact that it implies that a special definition of death, "brain death," has been developed to facilitate cadaveric organ transplantation, and because it mixes the question "When is the patient dead?" with "When may the doctor turn off the respirator?" and "When may a patient be allowed to die?" (see Capron and Kass, 1972: 104–111).

The Uniform Anatomical Gift Act is a statute designed to insure the provision of a more adequate supply of cadaver organs for transplantation than has been possible under traditional American law.[16] In this common law heritage, courts have ruled that in order for the next of kin adequately to discharge his (her) responsibility for proper burial of the deceased, that relative has the right to receive the body in the same condition as it was at the time that death occurred. Furthermore, in keeping with Judeo-Christian views on the sacredness of the body and respect for the dead, the body of a deceased person is not to be regarded as an item of commerce, to be bought, sold, or used to pay off debts. Courts expressed these premises by stating that there are no "property rights" in the body of the deceased. From this, there developed the ruling that a person could not direct the manner of his burial, because the body is not property and therefore not part of his estate.

[16]For the account of the legal background of the Uniform Anatomical Gift Act and its provisions that follows, I am indebted to the writings of Blair L. Sadler and Alfred M. Sadler, Jr., especially their co-authored article, "Providing cadaver organs: three legal alternatives," 1973.

In recent years, partly as a consequence of advances in the transplantation of corneal and other tissues, these views have come under increasing criticism. In the 1950s, donation statutes were enacted in several states which allowed an individual to determine what was to be done with his remains and to authorize donation for medical purposes. However, "most statutes failed to recognize the unique time requirements for organ and tissue removal and frequently viewed the act of donation as merely an extension of the testamentary disposition of property" (Sadler and Sadler, 1973: 16). The Uniform Anatomical Gift Act is the product of a three-year investigation into the matter of cadaver organ procurement that was conducted by a Special Committee of the National Conference of Commissioners on Uniform State Laws. The study was initiated in 1965. On July 30, 1968, the act was approved by the commission. It was endorsed by the American Bar Association on August 7 of the same year, and subsequently received support from virtually every relevant medical organization.

Blair and Alfred Sadler (1973: 25), who played a major role in drafting the Uniform Anatomical Gift Act, summarize its key provisions as follows:

> Under the Uniform Act, a person of sound mind and 18 years of age or more may give all or part of his body for any purpose later specified in the Act, the gift to take effect after death. In the absence of a contrary statement by the deceased before death, the next of kin (in a specified order of priority) are authorized to donate all or part of the body of the deceased. The individual's interests are paramount to the next of kin's. Consequently, if a physician obtains adequate consent from an individual via the card mechanism [a donor card], he need not consult the next of kin for this purpose. The consent mechanism is greatly simplified under the Act and includes any written instrument such as a card carried on the donor's person, signed by the donor, and witnessed by two people. Consent by the next of kin can be obtained by an unwitnessed document or by recorded telegraphic or telephonic message.

The act forms the basis of new laws that have now been adopted in 51 jurisdictions, including the District of Columbia. It has "enjoyed unprecedented success," for, "never in the 78-year history of the National Conference of Commissioners on Uniform State Laws has a uniform act been so widely adopted during the first three years of consideration by state legislatures" (Sadler and Sadler, 1973: 25). When one considers the existentially fundamental and sacrosanct nature of what this act has legislatively influenced or altered, the ease and rapidity with which it has been widely accepted is all the more remarkable. Like the Kansas statute, it represents a basic change in conceptions of death and of the human body. It also places the desires and commitments of the individual with respect to his body at death above those held by members of his family (including inhibiting traditional religious sentiments that his relatives may hold in this connection). The act not only makes it easily possible for many individuals to make a sacrificial gift of life-in-death, but it also implicitly encourages them to do so. And it legally sanctions a new and ultimate way of expressing the Judeo-Christian injunction to be "our brothers' [and our] strangers' keepers" (Titmuss, 1971).

The Supreme Court abortion decision handed down on January 22, 1973, has been called one of the most controversial decisions of this century. Its core rulings are as follows:

> 1. A state criminal abortion statute of the current Texas type, that excepts from criminality only a *life saving* [italics in text] procedure on behalf of the mother

without regard to pregnancy stage and without recognition of the other interests involved, is violative of the Due Process Clause of the Fourteenth Amendment.

(a) For the stage prior to approximately the end of the first trimester, the abortion decision and its effectuation must be left to the medical judgment of the pregnant woman's attending physician.

(b) For the stage subsequent to approximately the end of the first trimester, the State, in promoting its interest in the health of the mother, may, if it chooses, regulate the abortion procedure in ways that are reasonably related to maternal health.

(c) For the stage subsequent to viability the State, in promoting its interest in the potentiality of human life, may, if it chooses, regulate, and even proscribe, abortion except where it is necessary, in appropriate medical judgment, for the preservation of the life or health of the mother.

The full legal and moral implications of this decision are too complex to discuss here. But several aspects of the ruling should at least be singled out, because they bear so directly on the matters we are considering. To begin with, although ostensibly the Court's decision grants a woman what it deems a "right" to abortion, it not only regulates this right, but also equivocates about it. For, while affirming the right, throughout its exposition, the Court recurrently declares that abortion is "inherently and primarily, a medical decision" to be "left to the medical judgment of the pregnant woman's attending physician." Furthermore, after the first six months of pregnancy, the life of the fetus, termed here "the potentiality of human life," is given precedence over all other considerations short of "the preservation of the life or health of the mother" herself. In these ways, the Court has adhered to the conviction about the sanctity of life and the importance of safeguarding it, that is so strongly upheld in the traditional legal as well as value system of American society.

The definition of health developed by the Court is a broad one. It has been extended to include "the stigma of unwed motherhood," "the distress for all concerned associated with the unwanted child," and an unspecified complex of conditions referred to as "the full setting of the case." The fact that such psychological and social considerations have been incorporated into this legal conception of health can be expected to have influence that extends beyond the abortion situation.

From our perspective, the dimension of the Court's decision that is the most significant and debatable is its implicitly expressed point of view on when human life begins. In his majority opinion, Associate Justice Harry A. Blackmun disclaims that the Court has done so. "We need not resolve the difficult question of when life begins," he states. "When those trained in the respective disciplines of medicine, philosophy, and theology are unable to arrive at any consensus, the judiciary, at this point in the development of man's knowledge, is not in a position to speculate as to the answer." However, in fact, the Court's decision does more than speculate. It says by implication that life does not begin during the first two trimesters. And it suggests that it begins in "the stage subsequent to viability" when it mandates the state, "if it chooses," not only to regulate, but to "even proscribe" abortion thereafter. The Court's position on the point at which personhood comes into being is more blurred. It reaffirms that "the word 'person,'"as used in the Fourteenth Amendment, does not include "the unborn"; but it does not distinguish the commencement of human life from the inception of personhood.

What emerges from the overview sketched out in these pages is a picture of a contemporaneous system of medicine that has reached a stage of development characterized by diffuse ethical and existential self-consciousness. This state of awareness involves the searching out of ways in which certain moral principles and metaphysical assumptions on which American society is traditionally based have been imperfectly realized, or violated. It also entails a reaffirmation of these premises and the initiation of various forms of social action intended to modify the medical system, so that it will more fully actualize its stated ideals. Among the major values and beliefs that are being reasserted are the right of every individual to some modicum of integrity, dignity, autonomy, and fulfillment; the right of all men, women, and children, independently of their personal endowment or social status, to have equal access to conditions, like the alleviation of illness-induced suffering, that are indispensable to their personal and collective humanity; and the right freely to give of one's self to others in life-enhancing ways.

In other regards, this ethical and existential *prise de conscience* in American medicine is accompanied by what appear to be major shifts in fundamental conceptions about health and illness, life and death. Increasingly, health is being defined as a universal human right, rather than as a privilege, a sign of grace, or an aleatory consequence of good fortune. Both health and illness are coming to be viewed in a more societal and less individualistic framework. Along with the absence of adequate medical care, lack of good health and affliction with illness are now more frequently attributed to society-borne stresses, deprivations, and injustices than they were in the past. A discernible modification is also occurring in the absolute nature of the cultural commandment to preserve life. While the sacredness of human life and its preservation continue to be affirmed, the new operational definition of death, the assertion, however qualified, of the right to abortion and the mounting insistence both on "the right to die" and on "death with dignity" all suggest that medicine is moving from an ethic based on the unconditional "sanctity of life" to one premised on the "quality of life."[17] Furthermore, the reconceptualization of death as "brain death" and the Supreme Court decision on abortion are important crystallized expressions of the point that American society has now reached, in what seems to be a gradual movement toward revised definitions of viable life, personhood, and "humanness."

Finally, numerous of the phenomena that I have identified and discussed suggest that there is a peaking of doubt over the unconditional virtue of still another important value-component of American medicine. The debates over how much ought to be done to maintain the life of terminally ill or dying patients, for example, the proposed moratorium on experimentation with *in vitro* fertilization, the apprehension about what the consequences of prospective developments in genetic engineering and behavior control may prove to be, all constitute challenges to the energetic, often aggressive meliorism for which American medicine is known. This blend of activism and meliorism rests on the assumption

[17]This opinion was offered by the ethical scholar, Joseph Fletcher, in the course of a keynote address that he delivered at the National Conference on the Teaching of Medical Ethics, held at the Tarrytown Conference Center, Tarrytown, New York, on June 1-3, 1972. The conference was co-sponsored by the Institute of Society, Ethics and the Life Sciences and the Columbia University College of Physicians and Surgeons.

that out of unrestrictedly vigorous efforts to advance and apply biomedical knowledge and technique will come indisputable gains in human capacities, health and longevity, and in the alleviation of suffering. That conviction is now being thrown into question by many biologists and physicians, as well as by members of other professions, of government agencies, and of the general public. There is palpable skepticism about whether we have the "ultimate wisdom," to deal with the fact that "recent advances in biology and medicine suggest . . . we may be rapidly acquiring the power to modify and control the capacities and activities of men by direct intervention and manipulation of their bodies and minds" (Kass, 1971: 779, 786):

> If we can recognize that biomedical advances carry significant social costs, we may be willing to adopt a less permissive, more critical stance toward new developments. We need to reexamine our prejudice not only that all biomedical innovation is progress, but also that it is inevitable. Precedent certainly favors the view that what can be done will be done, but is this necessarily so? Ought we not to be suspicious when technologists speak of coming developments as automatic, not subject to human control? Is there not something contradictory in the notion that we have the power to control all the untoward consequences of a technology, but lack the power to determine whether it should be developed in the first place? . . .

Although the danger of excessively deterring medical progress is continuously reiterated, as the various moratoria cited suggest, the present trend is clearly in the direction of greater regulation of actual and incipient biomedical developments. The origins of this tendency are complex, but one of the important factors contributing to it is the growing belief that heroic medical scientific and technical efforts to improve "man's estate" are not unequivocally admirable or good, and that some of their consequences may be seriously harmful to collective as well as individual human existence.

The data presented suggest that modern American medicine is entering a new evolutionary stage. Organized concern about ethical and existential matters has become one of its salient features. The prominence and legitimacy of medicine's interest in these issues, and the involvement of many non-medical groups in them indicate that a new rapprochement is taking place in the profession and the society. The overweening emphasis on scientific and technological phenomena that has characterized modern medicine, and its insistence on separating these so-called objective considerations from more "subjective" and "philosophical" orientations toward health and illness, life and death, seem to be giving way to a closer integration between the two dimensions. Some of the ethical and existential issues under consideration in medicine entail reaffirmations of ultimate values in American culture and society. Others involve either a modulation or a broader generalization of such basic values. In two critical respects, the ethical and existential reorientation that is occurring implies a sharper break with cultural tradition, and seems to presage more radical socio-cultural change. We refer here to the major shifts away from some of the principles on which are founded the ethic of the sanctity of life and the ethic of progress.

It is tempting to assume that these value shifts and changes are predominantly, if not exclusively, caused by recent biomedical developments. And, indeed, this allegation is frequently made in the relevant literature. However, such an interpretation does not take note of the fact that in many other domains of American society, there is increasing preoccupation with the same questions of values, beliefs, and meaning that have been raised in the medical sector. Concern about the quality, dignity, and meaningfulness of life, about "assaults" on nature and the human condition, about distributive justice, equity, universalism, solidarity, community, and the "theme of the gift" (Mauss, 1954: 66) also have been prominent, for example, in the civil rights, peace, anti-poverty, ecology, and population control movements visible on the American scene.[18] From my perspective, these are but some of the phenomena which suggest that the ethical and existential developments in contemporaneous medicine examined in this paper may be part of a broader process of change that is carrying American society into a new stage of modernity.

References

Ad Hoc Committee of the Harvard Medical School to Examine the Definition of Brain Death
1968 "A definition of irreversible coma." Journal of the American Medical Association 205, No. 6 (August 25): 85–88.

Alsop, Stewart
1973 Stay of Execution. Philadelphia: J.B. Lippincott.

American College of Cardiology's Fifth Bethesda Conference
1968 "Cardiac and other organ transplantation in the setting of transplant science as a national effort." American Journal of Cardiology 22 (December): 896–912.

American Medical Association Judicial Council
1968 "Ethical guidelines for organ transplantation." Journal of the American Medical Association 205 (No. 6, August 5): 341–342.

Bailey, Herbert
1958 A Matter of Life and Death. New York: G.P. Putnam's Sons.

Barber, Bernard, et al.
1973 Research on Human Subjects. New York: Russell Sage Foundation.

Beecher, Henry K.
1970 Research and the Individual. Boston: Little, Brown and Company.

Berg, Paul, et al.
1974 "Letter to the editor—potential biohazards of recombinant DNA molecules." Science 185 (July 26): 303.

Brim, Orville G., Jr., et al. (eds.)
1970 The Dying Patient. New York: Russell Sage Foundation.

Cadbury, H.J., et al. (eds.)
1970 Who Shall Live? (for the American Friends' Service Committee). New York: Hill and Wang.

[18]Many of the participants in these social movements have been young people, relatively affluent and well-educated. Once again, this raises the question whether or not the "new" youth will prove to be effective agents of change. It also suggests the intriguing hypothesis that one of the prerequisites for widespread collective involvement in the kinds of moral and metaphysical issues dealt with here is a sufficient level of prosperity and fulfillment to free whole groups in a society from primordial anxieties about food, shelter, employment, and the like.

Callahan, Daniel
1970 Abortion. New York: The Macmillan Company.
1973 "Bioethics as a discipline." The Hastings Center Studies 1, No. 1: 66–73.

Capron, Alexander Morgan, and Leon R. Kass
1972 "A statutory definition of the standards for determining human death: an appraisal and a proposal." University of Pennsylvania Law Review 121, No. 1 (November): 87–118.

Coburn, Judith
1974 "Sterilization regulations: debate not quelled by HEW document." Science 183 (March 8): 935–939.

Cooper, I.S.
1973 The Victim Is Always the Same. New York: Harper and Row.

Crane, Diana
1972 Invisible Colleges. Chicago: University of Chicago Press.

Culliton, Barbara J.
1974a "National Research Act: restores training, bans fetal research." Science 185 (August 2): 426–427.
1974b "Grave-Robbing: the charge against four from Boston City Hospital." Science 186 (November 1): 420–423.

Curran, William J.
1970 "Governmental regulation of the use of human subjects in medical research." In Freund, Paul A. (ed.), Experimentation with Human Subjects. New York: George Braziller.

Cutler, Donald R. (ed.)
1968 Updating Life and Death. Boston: Beacon Press.

Delgado, José
1969 Physical Control of the Mind. New York: Harper and Row.

Dobzhansky, Theodosius
1962 Mankind Evolving. New Haven, Connecticut: Yale University Press.

Dubos, René
1972 A God Within. New York: Charles Scribner's Sons.

Duff, Raymond S., and A.G.M. Campbell
1973 "Moral and ethical dilemmas in the special-care nursery." The New England Journal of Medicine (October 25): 890–894.

Elkinton, J.R.
1970 "The literature of ethical problems in medicine" (Parts 1, 2, and 3). Annals of Internal Medicine 73: 3, 4, and 5 (November): 495–498, 662–666, 863–870.

Ehrenreich, Barbara, and John Ehrenreich
1970 The American Health Empire (a report from the Health Policy Advisory Center). New York: Random House.

Etzioni, Amitai
1973 Genetic Fix. New York: Macmillan Publishing Company, Inc.

Fletcher, Joseph
1967 Moral Responsibility. Philadelphia: The Westminster Press.
1974 The Ethics of Genetic Control: Ending Reproductive Roulette. Garden City, New York: Anchor Press/Doubleday.

Fox, Renée C.
1976 "Advanced medical technology—social and ethical implications," Annual Review of Sociology 2: 231–268.

Fox, Renee C., and Judith P. Swazey
1974 The Courage to Fail: A Social View of Organ Transplants and Dialysis. Chicago: The University of Chicago Press.

Freund, Paul A. (ed.)
1970   Experimentation with Human Subjects. New York: George Braziller.

Fulton, Robert (ed.)
1965   Death and Identity. New York: John Wiley and Sons, Inc.

Glaser, Barney G., and Anselm L. Strauss
1965   Awareness of Dying. Chicago: Aldine Publishing Company.
1968   Time for Dying. Chicago: Aldine Publishing Company.

Handler, Philip
1970   Biology and the Future of Man. New York: Oxford University Press.

Hendin, David
1973   Death as a Fact of Life. New York: W.W. Norton and Company, Inc.

Hinton, John
1967   Dying. Baltimore: Penguin Books.

Kansas
1970   Law of Mar. 17, 1970, ch. 378 [1970] Kan. Laws 994 (codified at KAN. STAT. ANN. § 77-202) (Supp. 1971).

Kass, Leon R.
1971   "The new biology: what price relieving man's estate?" Science 174, No. 4011 (November 19): 779–788.
1972   "Making babies—the new biology and the 'old' morality." The Public Interest 26 (Winter): 18–56.

Katz, Jay, with the assistance of Alexander M. Capron
1972   Experimentation with Human Beings. New York: Russell Sage Foundation.

Kennedy, Edward M.
1972   In Critical Condition. New York: Simon and Schuster.

Kubler-Ross, Elizabeth
1969   On Death and Dying. New York: The Macmillan Company.

Ladimer, Irving (ed.)
1970   New Dimensions in Legal and Ethical Concepts for Human Research. Annals of the New York Academy of Sciences 169.

Ladimer, Irving, and Roger W. Newman (eds.)
1963   Clinical Investigation in Medicine. Boston: Boston University Law-Medicine Research Institute.

Lasagna, Louis
1968   Life, Death and the Doctor. New York: Alfred A. Knopf.

Lepp, Ignace
1968   Death and its Mysteries. New York: The Macmillan Company.

London, Perry
1969   Behavior Control. New York: Harper and Row.

Mack, Arien (ed.)
1973   Death in American Experience. New York: Schocken Books.

Mannes, Marya
1973   Last Rights: A Call for the Good Death. New York: William Morrow and Company, Inc.

Mauss, Marcel
1954   The Gift. Translated by Ian Cunnison. Glencoe, Illinois: The Free Press.

Mendelsohn, Everett, Judith P. Swazey, and Irene Taviss (eds.)
1971   Human Aspects of Biomedical Innovation. Cambridge, Massachusetts: Harvard University Press.

Merton, Robert K., et al. (eds.)
1957   The Student Physician. Cambridge, Massachusetts: Harvard University Press.

Monod, Jacques
1971   Chance and Necessity. New York: Alfred A. Knopf.

Moore, Francis D.
1965   Give and Take. Garden City, New York: Doubleday Anchor Books.
1972   Transplant: The Give and Take of Tissue Transplantation (later edition of above title). New York: Simon and Schuster.

National Academy of Sciences
1968   "Cardiac transplantation in man: statement prepared by the Board of Medicine of the National Academy of Sciences." Journal of the American Medical Association 24 (No. 9, May 27): 805–806.

National Heart Institute
1969   Cardiac Replacement. A Report by the Ad Hoc Task Force, National Heart Institute. Washington, D.C.: U.S. Government Printing Office.

Noonan, John T., Jr.
1965   Contraception. Cambridge, Massachusetts: The Belknap Press of Harvard University.

Papworth, M.H.
1967   Human Guinea Pigs. London: Routledge and Kegan Paul; Boston: Beacon Press.

Parsons, Talcott, Renée C. Fox, and Victor M. Lidz
1972   "The 'gift of life' and its reciprocation." Social Research 39, No. 3 (Autumn): 367–415.

Pearson, Leonard (ed.)
1969   Death and Dying. Cleveland: The Press of Case Western Reserve University.

Peterson, Virginia
1961   A Matter of Life and Death. New York: Atheneum Press.

Ramsey, Paul
1970   Fabricated Man. New Haven, Connecticut: Yale University Press.
1970   The Patient as a Person. New Haven, Connecticut: Yale University Press.

Rutstein, David D.
1970   "The ethical design of human experiments." In Freund, Paul A. (ed.), Experimentation with Human Subjects. New York: George Braziller.

Sadler, Blair L., and Alfred M. Sadler
1973   "Providing cadaver organs: three legal alternatives." The Hastings Center Studies 1, No. 1: 14–26.

Schneidman, Edwin S. (ed.)
1967   Essays in Self-Destruction. New York: Science House.
1972   Death and the College Student. New York: Behavioral Publication.

Schoenberg, Bernard, et al.
1970   Loss and Grief: Psychological Management in Medical Practice. New York: Columbia University Press.

Sudnow, David
1967   Passing On. Englewood Cliffs, New Jersey: Prentice-Hall.

Supreme Court of the United States
1973   Roe et al. v. Wade. District Attorney of Dallas County, Appeal from the United States District Court for the Northern District of Texas, No. 70-18. Argued December 13, 1971; reargued October 11, 1972; decided January 22, 1973.

Swazey, Judith P., and Renée C. Fox
1970   "The clinical moratorium: a case study of mitral valve surgery." In Freund, Paul A. (ed.), Experimentation with Human Subjects. New York: George Braziller.

Taylor, Gordon
  1968   The Biological Time Bomb. Cleveland: World Publishing Co.

Titmuss, Richard M.
  1971   The Gift Relationship: From Human Blood to Social Policy. New York: Pantheon Books.

Torrey, E. Fuller (ed.)
  1968   Ethical Issues in Medicine. Boston: Little, Brown and Co.

Veatch, Robert M., and Willard Gaylin
  1972   "Teaching medical ethics: an experimental program." The Journal of Medical Education 47, No. 10 (October): 779–785.

Wade, Nicholas
  1974   "Genetic manipulation: temporary embargo proposed on research." Science 185 (July 26): 332–334.

Williams, Robert H. (ed.)
  1973   To Live and to Die. New York: Springer-Verlag.

Wolfenstein, Martha, and Gilbert Kliman (eds.)
  1965   Children and the Death of a President. New York: Doubleday and Company, Inc.

Wolstenholme, G.E.W., and M.O. Connor (eds.)
  1966   Ethics in Medical Progress. Boston: Little, Brown and Company.

DAN E. BEAUCHAMP

27 Public Health as Social Justice

Anthony Downs[1] has observed that our most intractable public problems have two significant characteristics. First, they occur to a relative minority of our population (even though that minority may number millions of people). Second, they result in significant part from arrangements that are providing substantial benefits or advantages to a majority or to a powerful minority of citizens. Thus solving or minimizing these problems requires painful losses, the restructuring of society and the acceptance of new burdens by the most powerful and the most numerous on behalf of the least powerful or the least numerous. As Downs notes, this bleak reality has resulted in recent years in cycles of public attention to such problems as poverty, racial discrimination, poor housing, unemployment or the abandonment of the aged; however, this attention and interest rapidly wane when it becomes clear that solving these problems requires painful costs that the dominant interests in society are unwilling to pay. Our public ethics do not seem to fit our public problems.

It is not sufficiently appreciated that these same bleak realities plague attempts to protect the public's health. Automobile-related injury and death; tobacco, alcohol and other drug damage; the perils of the workplace; environmental pollution; the inequitable and ineffective distribution of medical care services; the hazards of biomedicine—all of these threats inflict death and disability on a minority of our society at any given time. Further, minimizing or even significantly reducing the death and disability from these perils entails that the majority or powerful minorities accept new burdens or relinquish existing privileges that they presently enjoy. Typically, these new burdens or restrictions involve more stringent controls over these and other hazards of the world.

This somber reality suggests that our fundamental attention in public health policy and prevention should not be directed toward a search for new technology, but rather toward breaking existing ethical and political barriers to minimizing death and disability. This is not to say that technology will never again help avoid painful social and political adjustments.[2] Nonetheless, only the technological Pollyannas will ignore the mounting evidence that the critical barriers to protecting the public against death and disability are not the barriers to technological

[1]Downs, A. "The Issue-Attention Cycle and the Political Economy of Improving Our Environment," revised version of the Royer Lectures presented at the University of California at Berkeley, April 13-14, 1970.

[2]Etzioni, A. and Remp, R. "Technological 'Shortcuts' to Social Change," *Science* 175:31-38 (1972).

This paper is a slightly revised version of a paper presented at the annual meeting of the American Public Health Association in Chicago, November 18, 1975, entitled, "Health Policy and the Politics of Prevention: Breaking the Ethical and Political Barriers to Public Health."

progress—indeed the evidence is that it is often technology itself that is our own worst enemy. The critical barrier to dramatic reductions in death and disability is a social ethic that unfairly protects the most numerous or the most powerful from the burdens of prevention.

This is the issue of justice. In the broadest sense, justice means that each person in society ought to receive his due and that the burdens and benefits of society should be fairly and equitably distributed.[3] But what criteria should be followed in allocating burdens and benefits: Merit, equality or need?[4] What end or goal in life should receive our highest priority: Life, liberty or the pursuit of happiness? The answer to these questions can be found in our prevailing theories or models of justice. These models of justice, roughly speaking, form the foundation of our politics and public policy in general, and our health policy (including our prevention policy) specifically. Here I am speaking of politics not as partisan politics but rather the more ancient and venerable meaning of the political as the search for the common good and the just society.

These models of justice furnish a symbolic framework or blueprint with which to think about and react to the problems of the public, providing the basic rules to classify and categorize problems of society as to whether they necessitate public and collective protection, or whether individual responsibility should prevail. These models function as a sort of map or guide to the common world of members of society, making visible some conditions in society as public issues and concerns, and hiding, obscuring or concealing other conditions that might otherwise emerge as public issues or problems were a different map or model of justice in hand.

In the case of health, these models of justice form the basis for thinking about and reacting to the problems of disability and premature death in society. Thus, if public health policy requires that the majority or a powerful minority accept their fair share of the burdens of protecting a relative minority threatened with death or disability, we need to ask if our prevailing model of justice contemplates and legitimates such sacrifices.

Market-Justice

The dominant model of justice in the American experience has been market-justice.[5] Under the norms of market-justice people are entitled only to those

[3] Jonsen, A. R. and Hellegers, A. E. "Conceptual Foundations for an Ethics of Medical Care," in: Tancredi, L. R. (ed.) *Ethics of Health Care* (Washington, D.C.: National Academy of Sciences, 1974).

[4] Outka, E. "Social Justice and Equal Access to Health Care," *The Journal of Religious Ethics* 2:11-32 (1974).

[5] Some might object strenuously to the marriage of the two terms "market" and "justice." One theory of the market holds that it is a blind hand that rewards without regard to merit or individual effort. For this point of view, see: Friedman, M. *Capitalism and Freedom* (Chicago: University of Chicago Press, 1962); and Hayek, F. *The Constitution of Liberty* (Chicago: University of Chicago Press, 1960). But Irving Kristol, in his "When Virtue Loses All Her Loveliness" [*The Public Interest* 21:3-15 (1970)], argues that this is a minority view; most accept the marriage of the market ideal and the merits of individual effort and performance. I agree with this point of view—which is to say I see the dominant model of justice in America as a merger of the notions of meritarian and market norms.

valued ends such as status, income, happiness, etc., that they have acquired by fair rules of entitlement, e.g., by their own individual efforts, actions or abilities. Market-justice emphasizes individual responsibility, minimal collective action and freedom from collective obligations except to respect other persons' fundamental rights.

While we have as a society compromised pure market-justice in many ways to protect the public's health, we are far from recognizing the principle that death and disability are collective problems and that all persons are entitled to health protection. Society does not recognize a general obligation to protect the individual against disease and injury. While society does prohibit individuals from causing direct harm to others, and has in many instances regulated clear public health hazards, the norm of market-justice is still dominant and the primary duty to avert disease and injury still rests with the individual. The individual is ultimately alone in his or her struggle against death.

Barriers to Protection

This individual isolation creates a powerful barrier to the goal of protecting all human life by magnifying the power of death, granting to death an almost supernatural reality.[6] Death has throughout history presented a basic problem to humankind,[7] but even in an advanced society with enormous biomedical technology, the individualism of market-justice tends to retain and exaggerate pessimistic and fatalistic attitudes toward death and injury. This fatalism leads to a sense of powerlessness, to the acceptance of risk as an essential element of life, to resignation in the face of calamity, and to a weakening of collective impulses to confront the problems of premature death and disability.

Perhaps the most direct way in which market-justice undermines our resolve to preserve and protect human life lies in the primary freedom this ethic extends to all individuals and groups to act with minimal obligations to protect the common good.[8] Despite the fact that this rule of self-interest predictably fails to protect adequately the safety of our workplaces, our modes of transportation, the physical environment, the commodities we consume, or the equitable and effective distribution of medical care, these failures have resulted so far in only half-hearted attempts at regulation and control. This response is explained in large part by the powerful sway market-justice holds over our imagination, granting fundamental freedom to all individuals to be left alone—even if the "individuals" in question are giant producer groups with enormous capacities to create great public harm through sheer inadvertence. Efforts for truly effective controls over these perils must constantly struggle against a prevailing ethical paradigm that defines as threats to fundamental freedoms attempts to assure that all groups—even powerful producer groups—accept their fair share of the burdens of prevention.

[6]Marcuse, H. "The Ideology of Death," in: Feifel, H. *The Meaning of Death* (New York: McGraw-Hill, 1959).

[7]Illich, I. "The Political Uses of Natural Death," *Hastings Center Studies* 2:3–20 (1974).

[8]For excellent discussions of the notion of market "externalities," see: Hardin, G. *Exploring New Ethics for Survival* (Baltimore, Md.: Penguin Books, 1972); Mishan, E. *The Costs of Economic Growth* (New York: Praeger, 1967); and Kapp, W. *Social Costs of Business Enterprise,* 2d ed. (New York: Asia Publishing House, 1964).

Market-justice is also the source of another major barrier to public health measures to minimize death and disability—the category of voluntary behavior. Market-justice forces a basic distinction between the harm caused by a factory polluting the atmosphere and the harm caused by the cigarette or alcohol industries, because in the latter case those that are harmed are perceived as engaged in "voluntary" behavior.[9] It is the radical individualism inherent in the market model that encourages attention to the individual's behavior and inattention to the social preconditions of that behavior. In the case of smoking, these preconditions include a powerful cigarette industry and accompanying social and cultural forces encouraging the practice of smoking. These social forces include norms sanctioning smoking as well as all forms of media, advertising, literature, movies, folklore, etc. Since the smoker is free in some ultimate sense to not smoke, the norms of market-justice force the conclusion that the individual voluntarily "chooses" to smoke; and we are prevented from taking strong collective action against the powerful structures encouraging this so-called voluntary behavior.

Yet another way in which the market ethic obstructs the possibilities for minimizing death and disability, and alibis the need for structural change, is through explanations for death and disability that "blame the victim."[10] Victim-blaming misdefines structural and collective problems of the entire society as individual problems, seeing these problems as caused by the behavioral failures or deficiencies of the victims. These behavioral explanations for public problems tend to protect the larger society and powerful interests from the burdens of collective action, and instead encourage attempts to change the "faulty" behavior of victims.

Market-justice is perhaps the major cause for our over-investment and over-confidence in curative medical services. It is not obvious that the rise of medical science and the physician, taken alone, should become fundamental obstacles to collective action to prevent death and injury. But the prejudice found in market-justice against collective action perverts these scientific advances into an unrealistic hope for "technological shortcuts"[11] to painful social change. Moreover, the great emphasis placed on individual achievement in market-justice has further diverted attention and interest away from primary prevention and collective action by dramatizing the role of the solitary physician-scientist, picturing him as our primary weapon and first line of defense against the threat of death and injury.

The prestige of medical care encouraged by market-justice prevents large-scale research to determine whether, in fact, our medical care technology actually brings about the result desired—a significant reduction in the damage and losses suffered from disease and injury. The model conceals questions about our pervasive use of drugs, our intense specialization, and our seemingly boundless com-

---

[9]Brotman, R. and Suffet, F. "The Concept of Prevention and Its Limitations," *The Annals of the American Academy of Political and Social Science* 417:53–65 (1975).

[10]Ryan, W. *Blaming the Victim* (New York: Vintage Books, 1971). See Barry, P. "Individual Versus Community Orientation in the Prevention of Injuries," *Preventive Medicine* 4:45–56 (1975), for an excellent discussion of "victim-blaming" in the field of injury-control. Also, see Beauchamp, D. "Alcoholism As Blaming the Alcoholic," *The International Journal of Addictions* 11 (1) (1976); and "The Alcohol Alibi: Blaming Alcoholics," *Society* 12:12–17 (1975), for discussion of the process of victim-blaming in the area of alcoholism policy.

[11]Etzioni and Remp, *op. cit.*

mitment to biomedical technology. Instead, the market model of justice encourages us to see problems as due primarily to the failure of individual doctors and the quality of their care, rather than to recognize the possibility of failure from the structure of medical care itself.[12] Consequently, we seek to remedy problems by trying to change individual doctors through appeals to their ethical sensibilities, or by reshaping their education, or by creating new financial incentives.

Government Health Policy

The vast expansion of government in health policy over the past decades might seem to signal the demise of the market ethic for health. But it is important to remember that the preponderance of our public policy for health continues to define health care as a consumption good to be allocated primarily by private decisions and markets, and only interferes with this market with public policy to subsidize, supplement or extend the market system when private decisions result in sufficient imperfections or inequities to be of public concern. Medicare and Medicaid are examples. Other examples include subsidizing or stimulating the private sector through public support for research, education of professionals, limited areawide planning, and the construction of facilities. Even national health insurance is largely a public financing mechanism to subsidize private markets in the hope that curative health services will be more equitably distributed. None of these policies is likely to bring dramatic reductions in rates of death and disability.

Our current efforts to reform the so-called health system are little more than the use of public authority to perpetuate essentially private mechanisms for allocating curative health services. These reforms are paraded as evidence that the system is capable of functioning equitably. But, as Barthes[13] points out (in a different context), reform measures may merely serve to "inoculate" the larger society against the suspicion that it is the model itself (in our case, market-justice) that is at fault. In fact, the constant reform efforts designed to "save the system" may better be viewed as an attempt to expand the hegemony of the key actors in the present system—especially the medical care complex. As McKnight says, the medical care complex may need the hot air of reform if its ballooning empire is to continue to inflate.[14]

Public Health Measures

I have saved for last an important class of health policies—public health measures to protect the environment, the workplace, or the commodities we purchase and consume. Are these not signs that the American society is willing to accept collective action in the face of clear public health hazards?

I do not wish to minimize the importance of these advances to protect the public in many domains. But these separate reforms, taken alone, should be cautiously received. This is because each reform effort is perceived as an isolated exception to the norm of market-justice; the norm itself still stands. Consequent-

[12]Freidson, E. *Professional Dominance* (Chicago: Aldine, 1971).

[13]Barthes, R. *Mythologies* (New York: Hill and Wang, 1972).

[14]McKnight, J. "The Medicalization of Politics," *Christian Century* 92:785–787 (1975).

ly, the predictable career of such measures is to see enthusiasm for enforcement peak and wane. These public health measures are clear signs of hope. But as long as these actions are seen as merely minor exceptions to the rule of individual responsibility, the goals of public health will remain beyond our reach. What is required is for the public to see that protecting the public's health takes us beyond the norms of market-justice categorically, and necessitates a completely new health ethic.

I return to my original point: Market-justice is the primary roadblock to dramatic reductions in preventable injury and death. More than this, market-justice is a pervasive ideology protecting the most powerful or the most numerous from the burdens of collective action. If this be true, the central goal of public health should be ethical in nature: The challenging of market-justice as fatally deficient in protecting the health of the public. Further, public health should advocate a "counter-ethic" for protecting the public's health, one articulated in a different tradition of justice and one designed to give the highest priority to minimizing death and disability and to the protection of all human life against the hazards of this world.

Social Justice

The fundamental critique of market-justice found in the Western liberal tradition is social justice. Under social justice all persons are entitled equally to key ends such as health protection or minimum standards of income. Further, unless collective burdens are accepted, powerful forces of environment, heredity or social structure will preclude a fair distribution of these ends.[15-17] While many forces influenced the development of public health, the historic dream of public health that preventable death and disability ought to be minimized is a dream of social justice.[18] Yet these egalitarian and social justice implications of the public health vision are either still not widely recognized or are conveniently ignored.

[15]Tawney, R. *Equality* (London: G. Allen and Unwin, 1964).

[16]Hobhouse, L. T. *Liberalism* (New York: Oxford University Press, 1964).

[17]Rawls, J. *A Theory of Justice* (Cambridge: Harvard University Press, 1971).

[18]I am aware that I am passing too quickly over a very complex subject: The formative influences for public health. I am simply asserting that the dream of eliminating or minimizing preventable death and disability involves a radical commitment to the protection and preservation of human life and that this vision ultimately belongs to the tradition of social justice. Further, one can clearly find social justice influences in the classics of the public health literature. For example, see: Smith, S. *The City That Was* (Metuchen, N.J.: Scarecrow Reprint Corporation, 1973); and Winslow, C.-E.A. *The Life of Hermann Biggs, Physician and Statesman of the Public Health* (Philadelphia: Lea and Febiger, 1929).

There are several reasons why public health has seldom been treated as standing in the tradition of social justice. Public health usually entails public or collective goods (such as clean air and water supplies) where the question of distributive shares seems not important. However, for collective goods and in the case of death and disability, the key distributive questions are the *numbers* or *rates* of persons who suffer these fates, that no group or individual be unfairly or arbitrarily excluded from protection, and that the *burdens* of collective policies be fairly distributed. Writers in the tradition of social justice (such as Rawls) do not pay sufficient attention to the social justice implications of public or collective goods. This helps explain in part why many in the public health movement seldom saw themselves as involved in a drive for social justice—their work was defined as protection for the entire

Seeing the public health vision as ultimately rooted in an egalitarian tradition that conflicts directly with the norms of market-justice is often glossed over and obscured by referring to public health as a general strategy to control the "environment." For example, Canada's "New Perspectives on the Health of Canadians"[19] correctly notes that major reductions in death and disability cannot be expected from curative health services. Future progress will have to result from alterations in the "environment" and "lifestyle." But if we substitute the words "market-justice" for environment or lifestyle, "New Perspectives" becomes a very radical document indeed.

Ideally, then, the public health ethic[20] is not simply an alternative to the market ethic for health—it is a fundamental critique of that ethic as it unjustly protects powerful interests from the burdens of prevention and as that ethic serves to legitimate a mindless and extravagant faith in the efficacy of medical care. In other words, the public health ethic is a *counter-ethic* to market-justice and the ethics of individualism as these are applied to the health problems of the public.

This view of public health is admittedly not widely accepted. Indeed, in recent times the mission of public health has been viewed by many as limited to that minority of health problems that cannot be solved by the market provision of medical care services and that necessitate organized community action.[21] It is interesting to speculate why many in the public health profession have come to accept this narrow view of public health—a view that is obviously influenced and shaped by the market model as it attempts to limit the burdens placed on powerful groups.[22]

Nonetheless, the broader view of public health set out here is logically and ethically justified if one accepts the vision of public health as being the protection of all human life. The central task of public health, then, is to complete its un-

---

community (and often the entire community, rather than a minority, seems threatened in the age of acute infectious epidemics or in the drive for sanitary reform). Further, while there was opposition to even these reforms, the question of distributing the burdens of collective action did not arise so acutely as it does in the present period.

[19]Government of Canada. *A New Perspective on the Health of Canadians* (Ottawa, Ontario, Canada: Ministry of National Health and Welfare, 1974).

[20]By the "public health ethic" I mean several things: The assignment of the highest priority to the preservation of human life, the assurance that this protection is extended maximally (consistent with maintaining basic political liberties: See Rawls, *op. cit.,* and note 33), that no person or group should be arbitrarily excluded, and finally that all persons ought accept these burdens of preserving life as just.

[21]Two examples of this point: A standard text in health administration, John Hanlon's *Public Health Administration and Practice* (St. Louis, Missouri: C. V. Mosby, 1974), does reference very broad definitions of public health but quickly settles down to discussing public health in terms of those various programs designed to deal with market failures or inadequacies. Nowhere does Hanlon seem to view the concept of public health as an ethical concept standing as a fundamental critique of the existing measures to protect human life. Second, a recent proposed policy statement on prevention for adoption by the American Public Health Association (*The Nation's Health,* October 1975) does give a very high priority to prevention but contains within it a major concession to the norm of market-justice—the category of voluntary or self-imposed risks and the treatment of this category as distinctively different from other public health hazards.

[22]Beauchamp, D. "Public Health: Alien Ethic in a Strange Land?" *American Journal of Public Health* 65:1338–1339 (December 1975).

finished revolution: The elaboration of a health ethic adequate to protect and preserve all human life. This new ethic has several key implications which are referred to here as "principles"[23]: 1) Controlling the hazards of this world, 2) to prevent death and disability, 3) through organized collective action, 4) shared equally by all except where unequal burdens result in increased protection of everyone's health and especially potential victims of death and disability.

These ethical principles are not new to public health. To the contrary, making the ethical foundations of public health visible only serves to highlight the social justice influences at work behind pre-existing principles.

Controlling the Hazards

A key principle of the public health ethic is the focus on the identification and control of the hazards of this world rather than a focus on the behavioral defects of those individuals damaged by these hazards. Against this principle it is often argued that today the causes of death and disability are multiple and frequently behavioral in origin.[24] Further, since it is usually only a minority of the public that fails to protect itself against most known hazards, additional controls over these perilous sources would not seem to be effective or just. We should look instead for the behavioral origins of most public health problems,[25] asking why some people expose themselves to known hazards or perils, or act in an unsafe or careless manner.

Public health should—at least ideally—be suspicious of behavioral paradigms for viewing public health problems since they tend to "blame the victim" and unfairly protect majorities and powerful interests from the burdens of prevention.[26] It is clear that behavioral models of public health problems are rooted in the tradition of market-justice, where the emphasis is upon individual ability and capacity, and individual success and failure.

Public health, ideally, should not be concerned with explaining the successes and failures of differing individuals (dispositional explanations)[27] in controlling the hazards of this world. Rather these failures should be seen as signs of still weak and ineffective controls or limits over those conditions, commodities, services, products or practices that are either hazardous for the health and safety of members of the public, or that are vital to protect the public's health.

[23] I hasten to add that I am not arguing that there are exactly four principles of the public health ethic. Actually, the four offered here can be easily collapsed to two—controls over the hazards of this world and the fair sharing of the burdens of these controls. However, the reason for expanding these two key principles is to draw out the character of the public health ethic as a counter-ethic or counter-paradigm to the market model, and to demonstrate that the public health ethic focuses on different aspects of the world, asserts different priorities and imposes different obligations than the market ethic.

[24] Brotman and Suffet, *op. cit.*

[25] Sade, R. "Medical Care As A Right: A Refutation," *The New England Journal of Medicine* 285:1288–1292 (1971).

[26] Ryan, *op. cit.* See also: Terris, M. "A Social Policy for Health," *American Journal of Public Health* 58:5–12 (1968).

[27] See Brown, R. *Explanation in Social Science* (Chicago: Aldine, 1963) for an excellent discussion of the limitations of dispositional explanations in social science. Also, see Beauchamp, D. "Alcoholism as Blaming the Alcoholic," *op. cit.,* for a further discussion of the pitfalls of dispositional explanations in the specific area of alcohol policy.

Prevention

Like the other principles of public health, prevention is a logical consequence of the ethical goal of minimizing the numbers of persons suffering death and disability. The only known way to minimize these adverse events is to prevent the occurrence of damaging exchanges or exposures in the first place, or to seek to minimize damage when exposures cannot be controlled.

Prevention, then, is that set of priority rules for restructuring existing market rules in order to maximally protect the public. These rules seek to create policies and obligations to replace the norm of market-justice, where the latter permits specific conditions, commodities, services, products, activities or practices to pose a direct threat or hazard to the health and safety of members of the public, or where the market norm fails to allocate effectively and equitably those services (such as medical care) that are necessary to attend to disease at hand.

Thus, the familiar public health options:[28]

1. Creating rules to minimize exposure of the public to hazards (kinetic, chemical, ionizing, biological, etc.) so as to reduce the rates of hazardous exchanges.

2. Creating rules to strengthen the public against damage in the event damaging exchanges occur anyway, where such techniques (fluoridation, seat-belts, immunization) are feasible.

3. Creating rules to organize treatment resources in the community so as to minimize damage that does occur since we can rarely prevent all damage.

Collective Action

Another principle of the public health ethic is that the control of hazards cannot be achieved through voluntary mechanisms but must be undertaken by governmental or non-governmental agencies through planned, organized and collective action that is obligatory or non-voluntary in nature. This is for two reasons.

The first is because market or voluntary action is typically inadequate for providing what are called public goods.[29] Public goods are those public policies (national defense, police and fire protection, or the protection of all persons against preventable death and disability) that are universal in their impacts and effects, affecting everyone equally. These kinds of goods cannot easily be withheld from those individuals in the community who choose not to support these services (this is typically called the "free rider" problem). Also, individual holdouts might plausibly reason that their small contribution might not prevent the public good from being offered.

[28]For excellent discussions of the strategies of public health, see: Haddon, W., Jr. "Energy Damage and the Ten Countermeasure Strategies," *The Journal of Trauma* 13:321–331 (1973); Haddon, W., Jr. "The Changing Approach to the Epidemiology, Prevention, and Amelioration of Trauma," *American Journal of Public Health* 58:1431–1438 (1968); and Terris, M. "Breaking the Barriers to Prevention," paper presented to the Annual Health Conference, New York Academy of Medicine, April 26, 1974.

[29]Olson, M. *The Logic of Collective Action* (Cambridge: Harvard University Press, 1965).

The second reason why self-regarding individuals might refuse to voluntarily pay the costs of such public goods as public health policies is because these policies frequently require burdens that self-interest or self-protection might see as too stringent. For example, the minimization of rates of alcoholism in a community clearly seems to require norms or controls over the substance of alcohol that limit the use of this substance to levels that are far below what would be safe for individual drinkers.[30]

With these temptations for individual noncompliance, justice demands assurance that all persons share equally the costs of collective action through obligatory and sanctioned social and public policy.

Fair-Sharing of the Burdens

A final principle of the public health ethic is that all persons are equally responsible for sharing the burdens—as well as the benefits—of protection against death and disability, except where unequal burdens result in greater protection for every person and especially potential victims of death and disability.[31] In practice this means that policies to control the hazards of a given substance, service or commodity fall unequally (but still fairly) on those involved in the production, provision or consumption of the service, commodity or substance. The clear implication of this principle is that the automotive industry, the tobacco industry, the coal industry and the medical care industry—to mention only a few key groups—have an unequal responsibility to bear the costs of reducing death and disability since their actions have far greater impact than those of individual citizens.

Doing Justice: Building a New Public Health

I have attempted to show the broad implications of a public health commitment to protect and preserve human life, setting out tentatively the logical consequences of that commitment in the form of some general principles. We need, however, to go beyond these broad principles and ask more specifically: What implications does this model have for doing public health and the public health profession?

The central implication of the view set out here is that doing public health should not be narrowly conceived as an instrumental or technical activity. Public health should be a way of doing justice, a way of asserting the value and priority of all human life. The primary aim of all public health activity should be the elaboration and adoption of a new ethical model or paradigm for protecting the public's health. This new ethical paradigm will necessitate a heightened consciousness of the manifold forces threatening human life, and will require thinking about and reacting to the problems of disability and premature death as primarily collective problems of the entire society.

[30]Beauchamp, D. "Federal Alcohol Policy: Captive to an Industry and a Myth," *Christian Century* 92:788–791 (1975).

[31]This principle is similar to Rawls' "difference principle." See Rawls, *op. cit.*

Right-to-Health

What concrete steps can public health take to accomplish this dramatic shift? Perhaps the most important step that public health might take to overturn the application of market-justice to the category of health protection would be to centrally challenge the absence of a right to health. Historically, the way in which inequality in American society has been confronted is by asserting the need for additional rights beyond basic political freedoms. (By a right to health, I do not mean anything so limited as the current assertion of a right to payment for medical care services.) Public health should immediately lay plans for a national campaign for a new public entitlement—the right to full and equal protection for all persons against preventable disease and disability.

This new public commitment needs more than merely organizational and symbolic expression; ultimately, it needs fundamental statutory and perhaps even constitutional protection. I can think of nothing more helpful to the goal of challenging the application of market-justice to the domain of health than to see public health enter into a protracted and lengthy struggle to secure a Right-to-Health Amendment.[32] This campaign would in and of itself signal the failure of market-justice to protect the health of all the public. Once secured, this legislation could serve as the basic counterpoise to our numerous and countless policies sanctioning unreflecting growth, uncontrolled technology or unrelenting individualism. Such an amendment could enable public health in all of its activity to constantly, relentlessly, stubbornly, militantly confront and resist all efforts to dishonor the integrity of human life in the name of progress, convenience, security and prosperity, as well as assist public health in challenging the dubious stretching of the principle of personal freedom to protect every corner of social life.[33]

A second step on the path to a fundamental paradigm change is the work of constructing collective definitions of public health problems.[34] Creating and disseminating collective definitions of the problems of death and disability would clearly communicate that the origins of these fates plainly lie beyond merely individual factors (but, as always, some individual factors cannot be totally ig-

[32]I must confess a certain ambivalence about the term "right to health." This expression is not only confused with a right to payment for medical care services, it suffers the further limitation of not conveying the full intent of the public health ethic which, at least as I see it, is to give the highest priority to life and to assure collective rules and arrangements that embody and incarnate that priority. The term "right to health" could easily be construed as something far less ambitious than these goals.

[33]I am not unaware that I have not begun to clarify the issue of just how far a society can go in protecting life and limb without jeopardizing political liberty. I agree with Rawls, *op. cit.,* as to the priority of liberty. However, I tend to think of liberty in terms of specific constitutional guarantees (freedom of speech, religion, due process, etc.) rather than in the more extensive sense of a positive freedom to act as one chooses except where one's actions bring harm to others. Also, shedding light on this issue of the conflict between liberty and the protection of the public's health would help shed light on just what "minimizing" death and disability specifically entails. I am satisfied at this point however that the public health ethic would move us much further toward protecting all of the public's health, without relinquishing those basic liberties and freedoms that are the attributes of a just political community and without which the very notion of social justice itself would be in jeopardy.

[34]Friedmann, J. *Retracking America: A Theory of Transactive Planning* (Garden City, New York: Doubleday Anchor Books, 1973).

nored), and are to be found in structural features of the society such as the rules that govern exposure to the hazards of this world. These new collective descriptions, as they create more accurate explanations of public health problems, would in and of themselves expose the weakness of the norm of individual responsibility and point to the need for collective solutions.

These new definitions of public health problems are especially needed to challenge the ultimately arbitrary distinction between voluntary and involuntary hazards, especially since the former category (recently termed "lifestyle") looms so large in terms of death and disease.[35] Under the current definition of the situation, more stringent controls over involuntary risks are acceptable (if still strenuously resisted by producer groups), while controls over voluntary risks (smoking, alcohol, recreational risks) are viewed as infringements of basic personal rights and freedoms.

These new definitions would reveal the collective and structural aspects of what are termed voluntary risks, challenging attempts to narrowly and persuasively limit public attention to the behavior of the smoker or the drinker, and exposing pervasive myths that "blame the victim."[36] These collective definitions and descriptions would focus attention on the industry behind these activities, asking whether powerful producer groups and supporting cultural and social norms are not primary factors encouraging individuals to accept unreasonable risks to life and limb, and whether these groups or norms constitute aggressive collective structures threatening human life.

A case in point: Under the present definition of the situation, alcoholism is mostly defined in individual terms, mainly in terms of the attributes of those persons who are "unable" to control their drinking. But I have shown elsewhere that this argument is both conceptually and empirically erroneous. Alcohol problems are collective problems that require more adequate controls over this important hazard.[37]

This is not to say that there are no important issues of liberty and freedom in these areas. It is rather to say that viewing the use of, for example, alcohol or cigarettes by millions of American adults as "voluntary" behavior, and somehow fundamentally different from other public health hazards, impoverishes the public health approach, tending (as Terris has suggested)[38] to divorce the behavior of the individual from its social base.

In building these collective redefinitions of health problems, however, public health must take care to do more than merely shed light on specific public health problems. The central problems remain the injustice of a market ethic that unfairly protects majorities and powerful interests from their fair share of the burdens of prevention, and of convincing the public that the task of protecting

[35]See: *A New Perspective on the Health of Canadians, op. cit.*

[36]Destroying these "myths" could be a major task of public health activity. See Ryan, *op. cit.*, for the best discussion of "victim-blaming" myths. See Beauchamp, "The Alcohol Alibi," *op. cit.*, for a foray against the "myth" of alcoholism. I am using myth here in the specific sense: The confusion and false definitions that arise when we discuss a *public* problem in an individual idiom. For a good discussion of the concept of myths in general, see Ryle, G. *The Concept of Mind* (New York: Barnes and Noble, 1949).

[37]Beauchamp, "The Alcohol Alibi," *op. cit.*

[38]Terris, "A Social Policy for Health," *op. cit.*

the public's health lies categorically beyond the norms of market-justice. This means that the function of each different redefinition of a specific problem must be to raise the common and recurrent issue of justice by exposing the aggressive and powerful structures implicated in all instances of preventable death and disability, and further to point to the necessity for collective measures to confront and resist these structures.

Political Struggle

Doing public health involves more than merely elaborating a new social ethic; doing public health involves the political process and the challenging of some very important and powerful interests in society. The public health model involves at its very center the commitment to a very controversial ethic—the radical commitment to protect and preserve human life. To realize and make visible this commitment means challenging the embedded and structured values—as well as sheer political power—of dominant interests. These interests will not yield their influence without struggle.

This political struggle for a *truly* public health policy crucially involves bringing the medical care complex under the control of a new public health ethic. The medical care industry, like other powerful groups, must bear its fair share of the burdens of minimizing death and disability. Of all the perils presently confronting the public health community, there is none greater than that of gradually limiting and diminishing its mission to that of public medical care. I am deeply concerned that national health insurance—and here I have the Kennedy plan in mind—will become a vehicle to be used by what Alford has labelled the "corporate rationalizers"[39] to further finance, extend, solidify and entrench the power of the medical care complex. The nation's leading medical care issue is not to expand the medical care service market; the central issue is to control a powerful and expansionist medical care industry. Challenging medical dominance could go a long way toward reclaiming health as a public concern and an issue of social justice.

Challenging these centers of power in order to incarnate the priority of human life requires not only a new ethic but a supporting base of power. I believe that while professional prestige is an important attribute in the modern day public policy process, public health is ultimately better understood as a broad social movement. There is simply no way that we can hope to capture public health under a defining set of competences, skills and professional backgrounds. The political potential of public health goes beyond professionalism; at its very heart is advocacy of an explosive and radical ethic. Doing public health should be a ubiquitous, pervasive, common and routine activity accomplished in every public and private agency, at every level of government, among all peoples, and at every moment of our common history. Health policy is most decidedly not the sole preserve of physicians, schools of public health, health educators, consumer groups or any other special interest group; rather it is a fundamental concern of all human activity and a distinguishing sign of a just community. By stressing the

[39]Alford, R. "The Political Economy of Health Care: Dynamics Without Change," *Politics and Society* 2:127–164 (1972).

pervasive character of public health and the problems of death and disability, the foundation for a broad social movement can be established.

At the same time, public health should always hold in mind that this power struggle is meant to be not only instrumental but also dialectical, informative and symbolic. The point of the struggle is not merely to assure that producer interests accept their fair share of the costs of minimizing death and disability, but also—and once again—to reveal through the process of confrontation and challenge the structured and collective nature of the problems of death and disability and the urgency for more adequate structures to protect all human life.

I also believe that the realism inherent in the public health ethic dictates that the foundation of all public health policy should be primarily (but not exclusively) national in locus. I simply disagree with the current tendency, rooted in misguided pluralism and market metaphors, to build from the bottom up. This current drift will, in my opinion, simply provide the medical care industry and its acolytes (to cite only one powerful group) with the tools necessary to further elaborate and extend its hegemony. Confronting organizations, interests, ideologies and alliances that are national and even international in scope with such limited resources seems hopelessly sentimental. We must always remember that the forces opposed to full protection of the public's health are fundamental and powerful, deeply rooted in our national character. We are unlikely to successfully oppose these forces with appeals or strategies more appropriate for an earlier and more provincial time.

Finally, the public health movement must cease being defensive about the wisdom or the necessity of collective action. One of the most interesting aspects of market-justice—and particularly its ideological thrusts—is that it makes collective or governmental activity seem unwise if not dangerous. Such rhetoric predictably ignores the influence of private power over the health and safety of every individual. Public health need not be oblivious to the very real concerns about a proliferating bureaucracy in the emergent welfare state. In point of fact, however, the preventive thrust of public health transcends the notion of the welfare or service state and its most recent variant, the human services society. Much as the ideals of service and welfare are improvements over the simple working of market-justice, the service society frequently functions to spread the costs of public problems among the entire public while permitting the interests, industries, or professions who might remedy or prevent many of these problems to operate with expanding power and autonomy.

Conclusion

The central thesis of this paper is that public health is ultimately and essentially an ethical enterprise committed to the notion that all persons are entitled to protection against the hazards of this world and to the minimization of death and disability in society. I have tried to make the implications of this ethical vision manifest, especially as the public health ethic challenges and confronts the norms of market-justice.

I do not see these goals of public health as hopelessly unrealistic nor destructive of fundamental liberties. Public health may be an "alien ethic in a strange land.''[40] Yet, if anything, the public health ethic is more faithful to the traditions of Judeao-Christian ethics than is market-justice.

The image of public health that I have drawn here does raise legitimate questions about what it is to be a professional, and legitimate questions about reasonable limits to restrictions on human liberty. These questions must be addressed more thoroughly than I have done here. Nonetheless, we must never pass over the chaos of preventable disease and disability in our society by simply celebrating the benefits of our prosperity and abundance, or our technological advances. What are these benefits worth if they have been purchased at the price of human lives?

Nothing written here should be construed as a per se attack on the market system. I have, rather, surfaced the moral and ethical norms of that system and argued that, whatever other benefits might accrue from those norms, they are woefully inadequate to assure full and equal protection of all human life.

The adoption of a new public health ethic and a new public health policy must and should occur within the context of a democratic polity. I agree with Terris[41] that the central task of the public health movement is to persuade society to accept these measures.

Finally, it is a peculiarity of the word freedom that its meaning has become so distorted and stretched as to lend itself as a defense against nearly every attempt to extend equal health protection to all persons. This is the ultimate irony. The idea of liberty should mean, above all else, the liberation of society from the injustice of preventable disability and early death. Instead, the concept of freedom has become a defense and protection of powerful vested interests, and the central issue is viewed as a choice between freedom on the one hand, and health and safety on the other. I am confident that ultimately the public will come to see that extending life and health to all persons will require some diminution of personal choices, but that such restrictions are not only fair and do not constitute abridgement of fundamental liberties, they are a basic sign and imprint of a just society and a guarantee of that most basic of all freedom—protection against man's most ancient foe.

[40] Beauchamp, "Public Health: Alien Ethic in a Strange Land?" *op. cit.*
[41] Terris, "A Social Policy for Health," *op. cit.*

Name Index

D'Afflitti, J. G., 219
Daniels, A., 265, 267
Daniels, M. J., 213
Davis, F., 70, 85, 203, 262
Davis, M. S., 92, 206
De Miguel, J. M., 370-389
Dean, A., 96
Deutsch, C. P., 70, 97-98
Deutsch, J. A., 70, 97-98
DeVault, S., 325
Dewar, R., 324, 325-326
Dewey, D., 244
Dillon, P. B., 80-81
Donabedian, A., 58, 360, 368
Donnes, J., 75
Dow, T., 98
Downs, A., 443
Duff, R. S., 203, 208
Duncan, O. D., 325
Durkheim, E., 107, 133, 372

Eddy, E. M., 213
Eichhorne, R. C., 81
Elling, R. H., 86, 371, 379, 395
Emerson, J., 266
Emerson, R. M., 210
Erickson, E. H., 111

Farber, B., 70, 94, 101
Feichner, A., 85
Fein, R., 352
Feldman, D. C., 295, 306-323
Field, M. G., 54-55, 142, 377, 414
Finlayson, A., 219
Fisher, D. W., 289
Flores, F., 273, 275
Forsyth, G., 413
Fox, R. C., 61, 70, 83, 91-92, 93, 273, 406, 418-438
Freeman, H. E., 70
Freidson, E., 54-55, 78, 79, 170, 175, 202-203, 248, 250, 260-261, 263, 265, 408, 413
French, J. R. P., 107
Freud, S., 140
Fried, N., 106-107
Friedman, J., 396
Fuchs, V., 407

Gallagher, E. B., 119, 162-183
Gaylin, W., 425-426
Geld, S., 348-349
Georgopoulos, B. S., 295-306, 395, 397-398
Gerson, E. M., 351
Glaser, B. G., 203, 213, 227-237
Glaser, W. A., 395, 397, 408, 410
Gleicher, 106-107
Goffman, E., 202, 262-263
Gordon, G., 153-154
Gordon, N. B., 95
Gore, S., 102-112
Goss, M. E. W., 395
Graham, S., 58
Gray, R. M., 87
Gruenberg, C., 106-107
Gubrium, J. F., 262
Guerra, J. P. M., 389

Haber, L., 218
Hackman, J. R., 307, 319
Haggerty, R. J., 69-70, 73-74, 75-76, 77, 95
Halesby, S., 395
Hall, E. T., 324, 325
Hall, O., 239-240, 244, 249, 254, 256
Hassinger, E., 79
Hawley, A. H., 324
Hecht, 95
Helm, D. T., 238, 259-270
Henderson, L. J., 259
Henry, J. P., 104
Herman, M. W., 58
Hessler, R., 56
Hetherington, R., 408, 409
Heydebrand, W., 396
Hill, R. R., 74, 94
Hilleboe, H. E., 385-386
Hollander, M., 260
Hollingshead, A. B., 88, 203, 208, 264
Holmes, T., 104-105
Howard, J., 416
Hunt, R. G., 391
Hunter, D., 56
Hyman, M. D., 218

Ireland, G., 82

Jaco, E. G., 295, 324–344
Janes, T. F., 396
Jennett, W. B., 279

Kadushin, C., 58
Kaplan, B. H., 102–112, 218, 225
Kaplan, J., 351
Kasl, S., 54–55
Kasper, J. D., 81–82
Kass, L. R., 431–432, 433, 437
Keller, N. S., 213
Kennedy, E. M., 423
Khurana, R. C., 85
King, S. H., 203
Klein, 95
Klein, R., 94
Klein, S., 74
Knowles, J. H., 1–8
Knutson, A., 157
Koos, E. L., 58, 79, 88, 153, 358
Kosa, J., 61, 145–146
Kostick, A., 352–353
Krapp, D. A., 78
Kriesberg, L., 87
Kronick, J., 98
Kübler-Ross, E., 421–422
Kunitz, S. J., 359
Kutner, B., 95

Langlie, J. K., 219
Lawler, E. E., 307
Lawrence, P. S., 58, 69
Lazarsfeld, P., 377
Lefton, M., 203
Lei, T.-J., 76
Leighton, A., 106–107, 109
Lenski, G., 155
Lentz, E. M., 298–299
Leveson, I., 54–55
Levine, S., 218, 225, 395
Levinson, R., 268
Lewis, V., 85
Lichtman, C. M., 391
Liddel, H., 104
Litman, T. J., 29, 69–101, 219
Logan, R., 413

Logan, R. F. L., 409
Lorber, J., 184, 202–215
Louch, A. R., 261
Lowenthal, M. F., 111
Luchmann, T., 261
Lyman, S. M., 262
Lyons, T. F., 404

MacMahon, B., 30
Mann, F. C., 295–306, 395
Marbry, J. H., 77
Marx, K., 372
Matsumoto, Y. S., 109
Mauksch, H. O., 184–201, 203
Mauss, M., 438
McBroom, W. H., 58
McEwan, P. J. M., 82–83, 99
McEwen, J., 219
McIntosh, J., 263–264, 265
McKinlay, J. B., 1–2, 9–25, 53, 58, 218–219, 264, 267, 268
McKinlay, S. M., 58
McKnight, J., 447
McNamara, R. L., 79
Meadows, K. P., 95
Mechanic, D., 55–56, 60, 88, 154, 157, 158, 159, 370, 386, 405–416
Mendelson, M., 213–214
Merrill, M. H., 86–87
Merton, R. K., 139–140, 248
Metz, A. S., 87
Meyer, E., 213–214
Meyers, J., 70
Miller, A. E., 238–256
Miller, F. W., 76
Miller, M. H., 78
Miller, R., 261, 263
Mitchell, J. C., 109–111
Mohler, D., 92
Mondale, W. F., 419–420, 423
Monteiro, L. A., 63
Moody, P. M., 87
Moos, R. H., 218
Morse, E. V., 396
Mueller, A. D., 98
Mumford, E., 248
Murray, H., 106–107

Subject Index